The Official Scrabble® BRAND Word-Finder

ROBERT W. SCHACHNER

Wiley Publishing, Inc.

Official Scrabble® Brand Word-Finder

Copyright ©1988, 1998 by Orion Press, Inc. All rights reserved.
Published by Wiley Publishing, Inc., New York, NY

For general information on our other products and services or to obtain technical
support please contact our Customer Care Department within the U.S. at 800-762-
2974, outside the U.S. at 317-572-3993 or fax 317-572-4002.

Wiley also publishes its books in a variety of electronic formats. Some content
that appears in print may not be available in electronic books.

Word lists given in this book have been compiled from the vocabulary of The
Official Scrabble® Players Dictionary, used by permission of the publishers,
Merriam-Webster, Inc. of Springfield, Massachusetts. The Official Scrabble®
Players Dictionary is the dictionary of first reference for all official Scrabble®
Players Crossword game tournaments.

Scrabble® is a trademark of Hasbro in the United States and Canada. All
rights reserved. For more about the Scrabble game community, log onto
the National Scrabble® Association website, www.scrabble-assoc.com,
or call (613) 477-0033.

Library of Congress Cataloging-in-Publication Data:
ISBN 0-02-862132-8

Manufactured in the United States of America.
20 19 18 17 16 15 14 13

To Fritzy Schachner, 1907–1996

Acknowledgment is gratefully extended to:

John Whited, Ellie Gorinstein, Jerry Houle II, McGladrey, Hendrickson and Pullen, Kathy Zukowski, The Broward Community College Central Campus Library, and Mr. John Williams, president of the National Scrabble® Association, in the original edition, and

Carol Cole, whose dedication and hard work made this new edition possible.

Cheri and James Williamson, whose help and dedication have been invaluable.

Marcy J. Goldberg, for her detailed suggestions, and Victor Scudiery, who has always kept the faith.

CONTENTS

FOREWORD

We are the species that uses language, and that is enough to set us apart from all other creatures.

—JOHN CIARDI

Little did the inventor of Scrabble® know in 1931 that by the 1990s there would be 35 million leisure Scrabble® players enjoying the game in the United States and Canada. Or that 100 million sets would be sold worldwide since the popular word game was first developed and originally named Lexiko. Nor did the inventor know that his world game would become the most popular word game of all time, spawning world championships in twenty-two nations.

With the increase in popularity of the Scrabble® board game came the proliferation of dictionaries, word books, and word finders. And among those available, one of the most popular of all, is our own Official Scrabble® Word-Finder. This new edition, the first in ten years, has some important new features.

First and foremost, *The Official Scrabble® Word-Finder,* Second Edition, has been brought up to speed to match *The Official Scrabble® Players Dictionary*, Third Edition. This means that words that have been dropped or added (and fall into one of our categories) have been added or subtracted correspondingly in our Word-Finder. In addition, we have included a new section, "Ten Tips for a Better Game," and, for the first time, have listed all 955 three-letter words in a separate chapter. The Quick-Check Usage Guide has also been expanded to include technological words and sporting words.

If you are one of the tens of thousands of users of our *Official Scrabble® Word-Finder*, you will be pleased to have this updated edition. And, if you are a newcomer to this publication, I am sure you will find it beneficial to your knowledge of the game of Scrabble® and the enjoyment the world's most popular word game brings to your life.

—RWS

INTRODUCTION

---

*Respect for the word—to employ wit
with scrupulous care and heartfelt love of truth—
is essential . . . .*

—Dag Hammarskjöld
Markings

This book is the product of a loser—me—a frustrated Scrabble® player, who has been beaten game after game by a person with whom I dearly love to play. She always seems to beat the clock and find the unusual word and the highest-scoring combination of letters, leading to my almost certain defeat. This has been going on for years, and I suspect I'm not alone. Scrabble® has been the most popular word game since its invention by Alfred Butts, at the time an out-of-work architect, during the Great Depression. Mr. Butts counted the letters used on the front page of *The New York Times* and produced what was eventually released commercially as Criss-Cross Words. It became Scrabble® in 1948 and has since then sold more than 90 million copies worldwide.

Scrabble®'s fun to play, win or lose, but who wants to lose? Who enjoys watching the score mount against him as round by round the reservoir of unused letters is depleted? Who enjoys scrambling through a dictionary, trying to memorize esoteric words? No one except a masochist. So, if you want to be a winner, this book is for you.

I began by considering ways of rearranging the dictionary of acceptable Scrabble® words to suit my number one need as a player: constructing the highest-scoring word in the shortest possible time. The word lists in this book are the result of that effort.

Word-Finder (Chapter 1) is a powerful new tool providing quick access to thousands of high-scoring words. For each letter of the alphabet (except vowels) there are three lists:

1. Words beginning with that letter

2. Words ending with that letter

3. Words having that letter in approximately the middle of the word

In Chapter 2 you'll find a listing of all "legal" two-letter words (based on standard Scrabble® rules) for those tough situations that arise during play.

In Chapter 3, we provide an alphabetical listing of two-letter words that can be made into a new word with the addition of one letter. For quick recognition. the letter to be added stands apart from the original two-letter word.

Prefixes, suffixes, and plurals can be a boon to the Scrabble® player and in Chapter 4 we provide a review of the rules for their use. Again, for easy reference, the base word shown is detached from the new addition.

Everyone who has played Scrabble® has experienced an opponent who uses a word drawn from his or her special knowledge. Little-known legal, medical, military, and other specialized words are, if contested, time consuming to check, and, if not challenged, can be very successful for the player using them. In Chapter 5 we present a new kind of word list, a Quick-Check Usage Guide covering the various categories.

Now that you know how the *Official Scrabble® Word-Finder* works, you should be aware of some other aspects of the game and the word use that affects it.

Players of Scrabble® must, in the interests of their continued friendship and the nonviolent settlement of arguments, have a mutually agreeable dictionary at hand. Since dictionaries vary enormously from publisher to publisher and editor to editor, the agreement of the "standard" or dictionary of play must be made at the outset of any game. The *Word-Finder* is not such a dictionary and does not cover every "legal" word nor provide definitions of the words included, although it does contain approximately 60,000 words culled from the complete *Official Scrabble® Players Dictionary.*

There are also many acceptable variations of play. Only those actually playing the game can decide by which set of rules they wish to test their vocabulary strength against their opponents. There are also interpretations of rules, both official and those agreed upon by the players. One of the most controversial areas in interpretation of the rules in "designated foreign words." For instance, *oui* (yes) is not found in the

Oxford dictionaries, and the word *si* is shown as a musical note in the full *Oxford*. However, in *Funk & Wagnalls, si* is shown as meaning "yes" in Portuguese, Italian, and Spanish as well as an alternate for *ti* (musical note), and *oui* (yes in French) is permissible for "yes." You can see that with that degree of variation some discussion before the start of play is necessary to agree upon the interpretation of the rules. The *Word-Finder* does not provide a set of rules nor does it attempt to interpret the rules.

Another factor determining the acceptability of words is the particular set of rules chosen by the participants before play begins. The official rules may be used or the rules for any of the many games, such as "theme" Scrabble® , solitaire, clock-racing or timed play, foreign, or even "sex" Scrabble®. The game you choose to play will, of course, affect the "legality" or acceptability of words used in play, the *Word-Finder* may not always prove useful in these more unconventional games.

Now go forth, *Official Scrabble® Word-Finder* in hand, and with a new sense of confidence. I'm sure these word lists will prove as useful for you as they have been for me.

—RWS

P.S. While compiling this book I became fascinated with certain interesting facts and statistics about our language and its cataloging. For instance, there are eighty-two two-letter words in our general use language and seven hundred seventy-nine three-letter words. There are twenty-four kinds of antelope, twenty-eight words for types of carriages, one hundred thirty-seven listings of foreign, domestic, and ancient coins in the dictionary, and fourteen words meaning prostitute, including some that you would probably have never hear of regardless of your sexual proclivities. Whole dictionaries exist on the subject of underground language like *A Dictionary of Historical Slang* and *A Dictionary of the Underworld.* Words from the American West and words used in obsolete English are cataloged by the thousands in volumes of their own. There are dictionaries of usage, of style, of diplomacy, of dates—even of narcotics. And just in case you are feeling smug because you have a so-called unabridged, remember that *The Oxford English Dictionary,* in eleven volumes weighing one hundred thirty-two pounds, has 500,000 entries.

Increasing your word power will not just make you a better Scrabble® player, it will enrich your knowledge and understanding of the world in which we live. One method of vocabulary building is to play Scrabble® using the *Official Scrabble® Word-Finder* in combination with the *Official Scrabble® Players Dictionary*. The *Word-Finder* will guide your play and help you obtain the highest possible score, while the dictionary will teach you the meaning of a word that may be new to your vocabulary. Learning the idea behind unfamiliar words will facilitate adding those words to your vocabulary—permanently.

CHAPTER 1

Ten Tips for a Better Game

1. Memorize two-letter words to improve your game.

2. Learn the following twelve *q* words that do not have a *u* in them (*q* is worth ten points on its face):

    FAQIR
    QAID
    QAT
    QATS
    QOPH
    QAIDS
    QANAT
    QINDAR
    QINTAR
    QOPHS
    QWERTY
    TRANQ

3. Learn three-letter words. There are 955.

4. Move tiles around on your rack frequently.

5. Try not to duplicate letters on your rack unless it is an *e*.

6. Save better combinations of letters on your rack when possible.

7. Watch for *AID* and *AT*, which are helpful to opponents for dumping *O*s.

8. Once you find a good play, look for an even better one.

9. Always look at the board to see if your opponent's last move has changed your options.

10. Watch for words that can rid you of bad letters (low scoring and difficult).

CHAPTER 2

Word-Finder

Words listed in this section are arranged alphabetically and according to the number of letters they contain. High-scoring words are shown in boldface type (10–14 points), extra high-scoring words (15 points or more) are shown with an asterisk in addition to the boldface type. Words with the value of 3 points or less are not shown at all. The vowels have been omitted in Word-Finder as separate categories because most words contain them; their inclusion would make the book cumbersome and difficult to use. Also, having been assigned the most numerous allotment of letters in the game, vowels have the lowest point value (based on face value of the letter). With your highest point-value letters and Word-Finder to maximize your score, you will most certainly use the vowels you are holding.

Based on the standard Scrabble® rules, the following words will also not be contained in Word-Finder since their use is not "legal" in normal play:

  Capitalized words

  Hyphenated words

  Prefixes and suffixes (standing alone)

  Abbreviations

  Words requiring an apostrophe

The maximum length of words shown in Word-Finder is eight letters (the maximum letters held at any one time, plus one letter on the board). The skilled vocabularist and experienced player will, at times, construct longer words out of existing words already on the board, but *The Scrabble® Word-Finder* is designed to be a *quick* reference to locate as high a scoring word as possible in the shortest possible time.

Here's the most effective way to use the Word-Finder. First, turn to the list based on the letter you plan to build onto. You'll notice that the

list has three sections: words beginning with that letter, words ending with that letter, and words containing that letter in the middle. Thus, you have a variety of word suggestions built around your key letter. All you have to do is choose the highest-scoring word that fits the other letters on your rack.

B

BAAL	**BEAK**	BIRR	BONY	BRUT	**BADDY**
BAAS	**BEAM**	BISE	BOOB	BUBO	BADGE
BABA	**BEAN**	**BISK**	**BOOK**	BUCK	**BADLY**
BABE	**BEAR**	BITE	BOOM	**BUFF**	*BAFFY
BABU	**BEAT**	BITT	BOON	BUHL	BAGEL
BABY	**BEAU**	*BIZE	BOOR	BUHR	**BAGGY**
BACH	**BECK**	BLAB	BOOT	BULB	BAIRN
BACK	BEEF	BLAE	BORA	**BULK**	**BAITH**
BADE	BEEN	BLAH	BORE	BULL	*BAIZA
BAFF	BEEP	BLAM	BORN	**BUMF**	*BAIZE
BAHT	BEER	BLAT	BORT	**BUMP**	**BAKER**
BAIL	BEET	BLAW	**BOSK**	BUND	BALAS
BAIT	BELL	BLEB	BOSS	BUNG	**BALDY**
BAKE	BELT	BLET	BOTA	**BUNK**	BALER
BALD	BEMA	BLIN	BOTH	BUNT	**BALKY**
BALE	BEND	BLIP	BOTT	BUOY	**BALLY**
BALL	BENE	BLOB	BOUT	BURA	BALMY
BALM	BENT	BLOC	BOWL	BURD	BALSA
BAND	BERG	BLOT	*BOXY	BURG	BANAL
BANE	BERM	BLOW	BOYO	BURL	BANCO
BANG	BEST	BLUB	*BOZO	BURN	**BANDY**
BANI	BETA	BLUE	BRAD	BURP	**BANJO**
BANK	BETH	BLUR	BRAE	BURR	BANNS
BARB	**BEVY**	BOAR	BRAG	BURY	**BANTY**
BARD	BHUT	BOAT	BRAN	BUSH	BARBE
BARE	BIAS	**BOCK**	BRAT	**BUSK**	BARDE
BARF	BIBB	BODE	BRAW	BUSS	BARER
BARK	BICE	**BODY**	BRAY	BUST	BARGE
BARM	BIDE	**BOFF**	BRED	BUSY	BARIC
BARN	BIER	**BOGY**	BREE	BUTE	**BARKY**
BASE	**BIFF**	BOIL	BRIE	BUTT	**BARMY**
BASH	**BIKE**	BOLA	BRIG	*BUZZ	**BARNY**
BASK	BILE	BOLD	BRIM	BYRE	BARON
BASS	**BILK**	BOLE	BRIN	BYRL	BARRE
BAST	BILL	BOLL	BRIO	BYTE	**BARYE**
BATE	BIMA	BOLO	BRIT		BASAL
BATH	BIND	BOLT	BROO	BABEL	BASED
BATT	BINE	**BOMB**	BROS	**BABKA**	BASER
BAUD	BINT	BOND	BROW	BABOO	BASES
BAND	BIRD	BONE	BROS	BABUL	BASIC
BAWL	**BIRK**	BONG	BROW	**BACCA**	BASIL
BEAD	BIRL	**BONK**	BRRR	BACON	BASIN

3

BASIS	BENNE	BISON	**BOBBY**	**BOVID**	BROMO
BASSI	BENNI	**BITCH**	**BOCCE**	**BOWEL**	BRONC
BASSO	**BENNY**	BITER	**BOCCI**	**BOWER**	BROOD
BASSY	BERET	**BITSY**	**BOFFO**	**BOWSE**	**BROOK**
BASTE	BERME	**BITTY**	BOGAN	**BOXER**	BROOM
BATCH	**BERRY**	**BLACK**	**BOGEY**	**BOYAR**	BROSE
BATHE	**BERTH**	BLAIN	**BOGGY**	**BOYLA**	**BROSY**
BATIK	**BERYL**	BLAME	BOGIE	BRACE	**BROTH**
BATON	BESET	BLAND	BOGLE	**BRACH**	**BROWN**
BATTU	BESOM	**BLANK**	BOGUS	BRACT	**BRUGH**
BATTY	BESOT	BLARE	**BOHEA**	BRAID	BRUIN
BAULK	BETEL	BLASE	BOING	BRAIL	BRUIT
BAWDY	BETON	BLAST	BOITE	BRAIN	BRUME
BAWTY	BETTA	BLATE	BOLAR	**BRAKE**	BRUNT
BAYOU	**BEVEL**	*BLAZE	BOLAS	**BRAKY**	**BRUSH**
*BAZAR	BEVOR	**BLEAK**	BOLUS	BRAND	**BRUSK**
*BAZOO	BEWIG	BLEAR	**BOMBE**	**BRANK**	BRUTE
BEACH	*BEZEL	BLEAT	BONER	**BRASH**	BUBAL
BEADY	*BEZIL	BLEED	**BONEY**	BRASS	**BUCKO**
BEAKY	**BHANG**	BLEEP	BONGO	**BRAVA**	**BUDDY**
BEAMY	**BHOOT**	BLEND	BONNE	**BRAVE**	**BUDGE**
BEANO	BIALI	BLENT	**BONNY**	**BRAVI**	**BUFFI**
BEARD	BIALY	BLESS	BONUS	**BRAVO**	**BUFFO**
BEAST	BIBLE	BLEST	*BONZE	**BRAWL**	*BUFFY
BEAUT	**BIDDY**	**BLIMP**	**BOOBY**	**BRAWN**	**BUGGY**
BEAUX	BIDER	**BLIMY**	**BOOGY**	**BRAWS**	BUGLE
BEBOP	BIDET	BLIND	**BOOMY**	*BRAXY	BUILD
BECAP	BIELD	BLINI	BOOST	*BRAZA	BUILT
BEDEL	*BIFFY	**BLINK**	**BOOTH**	*BRAZE	BULGE
BEDEW	**BIFID**	BLISS	**BOOTY**	BREAD	BULGY
BEDIM	**BIGHT**	BLITE	*BOOZE	**BREAK**	BULKY
BEECH	**BIGLY**	*BLITZ	*BOOZY	BREAM	BULLA
BEEFY	**BIGOT**	BLOAT	BORAL	BREDE	**BULLY**
BEERY	**BIJOU**	**BLOCK**	**BORAX**	BREED	**BUMPH**
BEFIT	**BIKER**	**BLOKE**	BORED	BRENT	**BUMPY**
BEFOG	**BIKIE**	BLOND	BORER	**BREVE**	**BUNCH**
BEGAN	BILBO	BLOOD	BORIC	BRIAR	BUNCO
BEGET	BILGE	BLOOM	BORNE	BRIBE	BUNDT
BEGIN	**BILGY**	BLOOP	BORON	BRICK	**BUNKO**
BEGOT	**BILLY**	**BLOWN**	*BORTZ	BRIDE	**BUNNY**
BEGUM	**BIMAH**	**BLOWY**	**BOSKY**	**BRIEF**	**BUNYA**
BEGUN	BINAL	BLUED	BOSOM	BRIER	BURAN
BEIGE	BINDI	BLUER	BOSON	BRILL	BURBS
BEIGY	BINGE	BLUET	**BOSSY**	BRINE	BURET
BEING	BINGO	**BLUEY**	BOSUN	BRING	**BURGH**
BELAY	BINIT	**BLUFF**	**BOTCH**	**BRINK**	BURIN
BELCH	BIOME	BLUME	BOTEL	**BRINY**	**BURKE**
BELGA	BIONT	BLUNT	**BOTHY**	**BRISK**	**BURLY**
BELIE	BIOTA	BLURB	BOUGH	BRITT	BURNT
BELLE	**BIPED**	BLURT	BOULE	BROAD	BURRO
BELLY	**BIPOD**	**BLUSH**	BOUND	**BROCK**	**BURRY**
BELOW	**BIRCH**	**BLYPE**	BOURG	BROIL	BURSA
*BEMIX	BIRLE	BOARD	BOURN	**BROKE**	BURSE
BENCH	BIRSE	BOART	BOUSE	BROME	BURST
BENDY	**BIRTH**	BOAST	**BOUSY**	BROME	**BUSBY**

BUSHY	BANANA	BASHER	BEDLAM	BEMEAN	*BIAXAL
BUSTY	BANDER	BASIFY	BEDPAN	BEMIRE	BIBBED
BUTCH	BANDIT	BASING	BEDRID	BEMIST	BIBBER
BUTEO	BANDOG	BASION	BEDRUG	BEMOAN	BICARB
BUTLE	BANGER	BASKET	BEDSIT	*BEMOCK	BICEPS
BUTTE	BANGLE	*BASQUE	BEDUIN	BEMUSE	BICKER
BUTTY	BANIAN	BASSET	BEDUMB	BENAME	BICORN
BUTUT	BANING	BASSLY	BEEBEE	BENDAY	BICRON
BUTYL	BANISH	BASTER	*BEECHY	BENDEE	BIDDEN
*BUXOM	*BANJAX	BATBOY	BEEPER	BENDER	BIDDER
BUYER	BANKER	BATEAU	BEETLE	BENIGN	BIDING
BWANA	BANNED	BATHER	BEEVES	BENNET	BIFACE
BYLAW	BANNER	BATHOS	*BEEZER	BENUMB	BIFFIN
*BYWAY	BANNET	BATING	BEFALL	*BENZAL	*BIFLEX
	BANTAM	BATMAN	BEFLAG	*BENZIN	BIFOLD
BABBLE	BANTER	BATTED	BEFLEA	*BENZOL	BIFORM
BABIED	BANYAN	BATTEN	BEFOOL	*BENZYL	BIGAMY
BABIES	*BANZAI	BATTER	BEFORE	BERAKE	BIGEYE
BABOOL	BAOBAB	BATTIK	BEFOUL	BERAKE	BIGGER
BABOON	BARBAL	BATTLE	BEFRET	BERATE	BIGGIE
BACKER	BARBEL	BATTUE	BEGALL	BERIME	BIGGIN
*BACKUP	BARBER	BAUBEE	*BEGAZE	BERLIN	BIGWIG
BADDIE	BARBET	BAUBLE	BEGGAR	BERTHA	BIKING
BADGER	BARBUT	*BAULKY	BEGGED	BESEEM	BIKINI
BADMAN	BARDIC	BAWBEE	BEGIRD	BESIDE	BILBOA
BAFFLE	BAREGE	*BAWDRY	BEGLAD	BESMUT	BILKER
BAGASS	BARELY	BAWLER	BEGONE	BESNOW	BILLER
BAGFUL	BAREST	BAWTIE	BEGRIM	BESTIR	BILLET
BAGGED	BARFLY	BAYAMO	BEGULF	BESTOW	BILLIE
BAGGER	BARHOP	BAYARD	BEHALF	BESTUD	BILLON
BAGGIE	BARING	BAYMAN	BEHAVE	BETAKE	BILLOW
BAGMAN	BARITE	*BAZAAR	BEHEAD	BETHEL	BINARY
BAGNIO	BARIUM	*BEACHY	BEHELD	BETIDE	BINATE
BAGUET	BARKER	BEACON	BEHEST	BETIME	BINDER
BAGWIG	BARLEY	BEADLE	BEHIND	BETISE	BINDLE
BAILEE	BARLOW	BEAGLE	BEHOLD	BETONY	BINGER
BAILER	BARMAN	BEAKER	BEHOOF	BETOOK	BINNED
BAILEY	BARMIE	BEANIE	BEHOVE	BETRAY	BINOCS
BAILIE	BARONG	BEARER	BEHOWL	BETTED	BIOGAS
BAILOR	BARONY	BEATER	BEKISS	BETTER	BIOGEN
BAITER	*BARQUE	BEAUTY	BEKNOT	BETTOR	BIOPIC
*BAKERY	BARRED	BEAVER	BELADY	BEVIES	BIOPSY
BAKING	BARREL	BECALM	BELAUD	BEWAIL	BIOTIC
BALATA	BARREN	BECAME	BELDAM	BEWARE	BIOTIN
BALBOA	BARRET	BECKET	BELEAP	BEWEEP	*BIPACK
BALDLY	BARRIO	BECKON	BELFRY	BEWORM	BIRDER
BALEEN	BARROW	BECLOG	BELIEF	BEWRAP	BIRDIE
BALING	BARTER	BECOME	BELIER	BEWRAY	BIREME
BALKER	BARYON	BEDAMN	BELIKE	BEYLIC	BIRKIE
BALLAD	BARYTA	BEDAUB	BELIVE	*BEYLIK	BIRLER
BALLER	BARYTE	BEDBUG	BELLOW	BEYOND	BISECT
BALLET	BASALT	BEDDED	BELONG	*BEZANT	BISHOP
BALLON	BASELY	BEDDER	BELTER	*BEZOAR	*BISQUE
BALLOT	BASEST	*BEDECK	BELUGA	*BHAKTA	BISTER
BALSAM	BASHAW	BEDELL	BEMATA	*BHAKTI	BISTRE

BISTRO	**BODIED**	BORIDE	BRASIL	**BRUMAL**	BURGLE
*BITCHY	**BODIES**	BORING	**BRASSY**	*BRUMBY	BURGOO
BITING	**BODILY**	**BORROW**	**BRATTY**	**BRUNCH**	BURIAL
BITTED	**BODING**	**BORSCH**	**BRAVER**	BRUNET	BURIED
BITTEN	**BODKIN**	**BORSHT**	**BRAWLY**	**BRUSHY**	BURIER
BITTER	**BOFFIN**	*BORZOI	**BRAWNY**	BRUTAL	BURIES
*BIZONE	**BOGGED**	**BOSKER**	**BRAYER**	**BRYONY**	**BURKER**
*BLABBY	**BOGGLE**	**BOSKET**	*BRAZEN	**BUBALE**	**BURLAP**
BLAMER	BOGIES	**BOSOMY**	*BRAZER	**BUBBLE**	BURLER
BLANCH	*BOHUNK	*BOSQUE	*BRAZIL	*BUBBLY	**BURLEY**
BLASTY	BOILER	BOSTON	**BREACH**	**BUCCAL**	BURNER
*BLAZER	BOLERO	**BOTANY**	**BREADY**	**BUCKER**	BURNET
*BLAZON	BOLETE	*BOTCHY	BREAST	**BUCKET**	BURNIE
BLEACH	BOLIDE	**BOTFLY**	**BREATH**	**BUCKLE**	BURRED
BLEARY	*BOLLIX	BOTHER	**BREECH**	**BUDDER**	BURRER
BLENCH	*BOLLOX	BOTTLE	**BREEKS**	**BUDDLE**	**BURROW**
BLENDE	**BOLSHY**	**BOTTOM**	*BREEZE	**BUDGER**	BURSAR
BLENNY	BOLSON	BOUBOU	*BREEZY	**BUDGET**	BURTON
BLIMEY	BOLTER	**BOUCLE**	BREGMA	**BUDGIE**	BUSBOY
BLINIS	*BOMBAX	**BOUFFE**	BREVET	**BUFFER**	BUSHEL
*BLINTZ	**BOMBER**	**BOUGHT**	**BREWER**	**BUFFET**	**BUSHER**
BLITHE	*BOMBYX	BOUGIE	BREWIS	**BUGEYE**	**BUSHWA**
*BLOCKY	**BONACI**	BOULLE	BRIARD	**BUGGED**	BUSIED
BLONDE	**BONBON**	**BOUNCE**	**BRIBEE**	**BUGGER**	BUSIER
BLOODY	BONDER	**BOUNCY**	**BRIBER**	BUGLER	BUSIES
BLOOEY	**BONDUC**	**BOUNTY**	*BRICKY	**BUGSHA**	**BUSILY**
BLOOIE	BONIER	BOURNE	BRIDAL	**BULBEL**	BUSING
BLOOMY	BONING	**BOURSE**	**BRIDGE**	**BULBIL**	**BUSKER**
BLOTCH	BONITA	BOUTON	BRIDLE	**BULBUL**	**BUSKIN**
BLOTTO	BONITO	**BOVINE**	**BRIGHT**	BULGER	**BUSMAN**
BLOTTY	BONNET	**BOWERY**	BRINER	BULGUR	BUSSED
BLOUSE	BONNIE	**BOWFIN**	**BRIONY**	BULLET	BUSSES
BLOUSY	BONSAI	**BOWING**	**BROACH**	**BUMBLE**	BUSTER
*BLOWBY	*BONZER	**BOWLEG**	**BROCHE**	**BUMKIN**	BUSTIC
BLOWER	**BOOBOO**	**BOWLER**	BROGAN	**BUMMED**	BUSTLE
BLOWSY	**BOODLE**	**BOWMAN**	**BROGUE**	**BUMMER**	BUTANE
BLOWUP	**BOOGER**	**BOWPOT**	**BROKEN**	**BUMPER**	BUTENE
*BLOWZY	**BOOGEY**	*BOWWOW	**BROKER**	*BUNCHY	BUTLER
BLUELY	BOOGIE	**BOWYER**	**BROLLY**	**BUNDLE**	BUTTER
BLUEST	**BOOHOO**	*BOXCAR	**BROMAL**	**BUNGEE**	BUTTON
BLUESY	**BOOKER**	*BOXFUL	**BROMIC**	**BUNGLE**	BUYOUT
BLUING	**BOOKIE**	*BOXIER	**BROMID**	BUNION	*BUZUKI
BLUISH	**BOOMER**	*BOXING	**BROMIN**	**BUNKER**	*BUZZER
BLUNGE	BOOTEE	**BOYARD**	**BRONCO**	**BUNKUM**	BYELAW
BLURRY	BOOTIE	**BOYISH**	*BRONZE	BUNTER	**BYGONE**
BOATEL	*BOOZER	**BRACER**	*BRONZY	**BUPPIE**	**BYLINE**
BOATER	**BOPEEP**	**BRAGGY**	**BROOCH**	*BUQSHA	**BYNAME**
BOBBER	**BOPPER**	**BRAHMA**	**BROODY**	**BURBLE**	BYPASS
BOBBIN	BORAGE	**BRAINY**	**BROOMY**	**BURBLY**	BYPAST
BOBBLE	BORANE	BRAISE	**BROTHY**	**BURBOT**	*BYPATH
BOBCAT	BORATE	*BRAIZE	**BROWNY**	BURDEN	*BYPLAY
BOCCIA	BORDEL	**BRANCH**	**BROWSE**	BURDIE	**BYRNIE**
BOCCIE	BORDER	**BRANDY**	BRUCIN	BUREAU	**BYROAD**
BODEGA	BOREAL	**BRANNY**	BRUISE	**BURGEE**	**BYSSUS**
BODICE	BOREEN	**BRASHY**	BRULOT	BURGER	*BYTALK

*BYWORD	BANDANA	BASTING	BECRAWL	*BEJEWEL	BESTEAD
*BYWORK	*BANDBOX	BASTION	BECRIME	BELABOR	BESTIAL
*BYZANT	BANDEAU	BATCHER	*BECROWD	BELACED	BESTREW
	BANDIED	*BATFISH	BECRUST	BELATED	BESTROW
BAALISM	BANDIES	*BATFOWL	BECURSE	BELCHER	BESWARM
BABASSU	BANDORA	BATHING	BEDDING	BELDAME	BETAINE
BABBITT	BANDORE	BATHMAT	BEDEMAN	BELIEVE	*BETAXED
BABBLER	BANEFUL	BATHTUB	BEDEVIL	BELLBOY	*BETHANK
BABESIA	*BANGKOK	*BATHYAL	BEDFAST	BELLEEK	*BETHINK
*BABICHE	BANKING	BATISTE	BEDGOWN	BELLHOP	BETHORN
*BABYISH	BANKSIA	BATLIKE	BEDIGHT	BELLIED	*BETHUMP
BACALAO	BANNING	BATSMAN	BEDIRTY	BELLIES	BETIMES
BACCARA	*BANNOCK	BATTEAU	*BEDIZEN	BELLMAN	BETOKEN
BACCATE	*BANQUET	BATTERY	BEDLAMP	BELOVED	BETROTH
*BACCHIC	BANSHEE	BATTIER	BEDLESS	BELTING	BETTING
*BACKFIT	BANSHIE	BATTING	BEDLIKE	*BELTWAY	BETWEEN
*BACKHOE	BANTENG	BATTLER	BEDMATE	BELYING	*BETWIXT
*BACKING	BAPTISE	BATWING	BEDOUIN	BEMADAM	BEVELER
*BACKLIT	BAPTISM	BAUSOND	BEDPOST	BENCHER	BEVOMIT
*BACKLOG	BAPTIST	*BAUXITE	BEDRAIL	BENEATH	*BEWEARY
*BACKOUT	*BAPTIZE	*BAWCOCK	BEDRAPE	BENEFIC	*BEWITCH
*BACKSAW	BARBATE	BAWDIER	*BEDROCK	BENEFIT	*BEWORRY
*BACKSET	BARBELL	BAWDIES	BEDROLL	BENEMPT	*BEZIQUE
BADGING	BARBULE	*BAWDILY	BEDROOM	BENISON	*BEZZANT
BADLAND	BARCHAN	*BAWDRIC	BEDSIDE	BENOMYL	BHEESTY
BADNESS	BAREFIT	BAWSUNT	BEDSORE	BENTHAL	BHISTIE
*BAFFIES	BARGAIN	BAYONET	*BEDTICK	BENTHIC	*BIAXIAL
*BAFFLER	BARGING	*BAYWOOD	BEDTIME	BENTHOS	BIBASIC
BAGASSE	BARILLA	*BAZOOKA	BEDUNCE	*BENZENE	*BIBBERY
BAGGAGE	*BARKEEP	BEADIER	BEDWARD	*BENZINE	BIBBING
BAGGING	BARLESS	BEADILY	*BEDWARF	*BENZOIN	*BIBCOCK
BAGPIPE	BARMAID	BEADING	BEEFALO	*BENZOLE	BIBELOT
BAGSFUL	BARONET	BEADMAN	BEEFIER	*BENZOYL	BIBLESS
*BAGWORM	BARONNE	BEAMIER	*BEEFILY	BEPAINT	*BIBLIKE
BAHADUR	*BAROQUE	BEAMILY	*BEEHIVE	*BEQUEST	BIBLIST
*BAILIFF	*BARRACK	BEAMISH	BEELIKE	BEREAVE	BICOLOR
BAILOUT	BARRAGE	BEANBAG	BEELINE	BERETTA	BICORNE
BAIRNLY	BARRIER	BEANERY	*BEESWAX	BERGERE	*BICYCLE
*BAKLAVA	BARRING	BEARCAT	BEETLER	*BERHYME	BIDARKA
*BAKLAWA	BARROOM	BEARHUG	BEEYARD	BERLINE	BIDDING
BALANCE	BARTEND	BEARISH	*BEFLECK	BEROBED	BIFILAR
BALCONY	BARWARE	BEASTIE	BEGGARY	BERSEEM	BIFOCAL
BALDIES	BASCULE	BEASTLY	BEGGING	BERSERK	BIGFOOT
BALDISH	BASEMAN	*BEATIFY	BEGLOOM	BESCOUR	BIGGEST
BALDRIC	*BASENJI	BEATING	BEGONIA	BESEECH	BIGGETY
BALEFUL	*BASHFUL	BEATNIK	BEGORAH	BESHAME	BIGGING
BALLADE	*BASHLYK	BEBEERU	BEGORRA	BESHOUT	BIGGISH
BALLAST	BASILAR	BEBLOOD	BEGRIME	*BESHREW	BIGGITY
BALLIES	BASILIC	BECAUSE	BEGROAN	BESIDES	BIGHEAD
BALLOON	BASINET	*BECHALK	BEGUILE	BESIEGE	BIGHORN
BALLUTE	BASMATI	*BECHARM	BEGUINE	BESLIME	BIGNESS
BALNEAL	BASSIST	BECLASP	*BEHAVER	BESMEAR	BIGOTED
BALONEY	BASSOON	*BECLOAK	*BEHOOVE	BESMILE	BIGOTRY
BAMBINO	BASTARD	BECLOUD	BEIGNET	*BESMOKE	*BIKEWAY
BANDAGE	BASTILE	BECLOWN	*BEJESUS	*BESPEAK	BILAYER

BILIARY	BLABBER	BLUEISH	*BOOKFUL	*BOXFISH	BRICOLE
BILIOUS	*BLACKEN	*BLUEJAY	BOOKING	*BOXHAUL	BRIDLER
BILLBUG	*BLACKLY	*BLUFFER	*BOOKISH	*BOXIEST	BRIDOON
BILLIES	BLADDER	BLUNDER	BOOKLET	*BOXLIKE	BRIEFER
BILLING	BLAMING	BLUNGER	*BOOKMAN	*BOXWOOD	*BRIEFLY
BILLION	BLANKET	BLURTER	*BOOMBOX	*BOYCHIK	BRIGADE
*BILLOWY	*BLANKLY	BLUSHER	BOOMIER	BOYCOTT	BRIGAND
BILOBED	BLARNEY	BLUSTER	*BOOMKIN	*BOYHOOD	BRIMFUL
BILSTED	BLASTIE	BOARDER	BOOMLET	BRABBLE	BRIMMED
BILTONG	BLASTIE	BOARISH	BOONIES	BRACERO	BRIMMER
BIMETAL	BLATANT	BOASTER	BOORISH	BRACHET	BRINDED
BIMODAL	BLATHER	BOATFUL	BOOSTER	BRACING	BRINDLE
BINDERY	BLATTED	BOATING	BOOTERY	*BRACKEN	BRINGER
BINDING	BLATTER	BOATMAN	BOOTIES	*BRACKET	BRINIER
BINNING	*BLAUBOK	*BOBBERY	BOOTLEG	BRADAWL	BRINIES
BINOCLE	*BLEAKLY	BOBBIES	BORACES	BRADOON	BRINING
*BIOCHIP	BLEATER	BOBBING	BORACIC	BRAGGER	BRINISH
BIOCIDE	BLEEDER	*BOBECHE	BORDURE	BRAIDER	BRIOCHE
BIOGENY	BLELLUM	BOBSLED	BOREDOM	BRAILLE	*BRIQUET
BIOHERM	BLEMISH	BOBSTAY	BORNEOL	BRAKING	BRISKET
BIOLOGY	BLENDER	BOBTAIL	BORNITE	BRALESS	*BRISKLY
BIOMASS	*BLESBOK	BODHRAN	BOROUGH	BRAMBLE	BRISSES
BIONICS	BLESSED	*BOFFOLA	BORSCHT	*BRAMBLY	BRISTLE
BIONOMY	BLESSER	BOGBEAN	BORSTAL	*BRANCHY	BRISTLY
BIOPSIC	BLETHER	BOGGIER	BOSCAGE	BRANDER	BRISTOL
BIOPTIC	*BLIGHTY	BOGGING	BOSKAGE	BRANNED	BRITSKA
BIOTICS	BLINDER	BOGGISH	*BOSQUET	BRANNER	BRITTLE
BIOTITE	BLINDLY	BOGGLER	BOSSDOM	BRASIER	BRITTLY
BIOTOPE	BLINKER	*BOGYISM	BOSSIER	BRASSIE	*BRITZKA
BIOTRON	*BLINTZE	*BOGYMAN	BOSSIES	BRATTLE	*BROADAX
BIOTYPE	BLISTER	BOHEMIA	BOSSISM	BRAVADO	BROADEN
BIPARTY	BLITHER	*BOILOFF	BOTANIC	*BRAVERY	BROADLY
BIPLANE	BLOATER	BOLETUS	BOTCHER	BRAVEST	BROCADE
BIPOLAR	*BLOCKER	BOLIVAR	BOTONEE	BRAVING	*BROCKET
BIRCHEN	BLOOMER	BOLIVIA	BOTTLER	BRAVURA	BROCOLI
BIRDING	BLOOPER	BOLLARD	BOTULIN	BRAWLER	BROIDER
BIRDMAN	BLOSSOM	BOLOGNA	BOUCHEE	BRAWLIE	BROILER
BIRETTA	*BLOTCHY	BOLONEY	BOUDOIR	*BRAZIER	BROKAGE
BIRLING	BLOTTED	BOLSHIE	BOULDER	*BRAZING	BROKING
BISCUIT	BLOTTER	BOLSTER	BOUNCER	BREADTH	BROMATE
BISMUTH	BLOUSON	BOMBARD	BOUNDEN	BREAKER	BROMIDE
BISNAGA	*BLOWFLY	BOMBAST	BOUNDER	*BREAKUP	BROMINE
BISTATE	BLOWGUN	BOMBING	*BOUQUET	*BREATHY	BROMISM
BISTORT	BLOWIER	*BONANZA	BOURBON	BRECCIA	*BROMIZE
BITABLE	*BLOWOFF	BONDAGE	BOURDON	*BRECHAM	BRONCHI
BITTERN	BLOWOUT	BONDING	BOURREE	BRECHAN	BRONCHO
BITTIER	BLOWSED	BONDMAN	*BOWHEAD	BREEDER	*BRONZER
BITTING	*BLOWZED	BONESET	*BOWKNOT	BREVIER	BROODER
*BITTOCK	BLUBBER	BONFIRE	BOWLDER	*BREVITY	BROOKIE
BITUMEN	BLUCHER	BONIEST	BOWLESS	BREWAGE	BROTHEL
*BIVALVE	BLUDGER	BONKERS	*BOWLFUL	*BREWERY	BROTHER
*BIVINYL	BLUECAP	*BONNOCK	*BOWLIKE	BREWING	BROUGHT
BIVOUAC	BLUEFIN	BOOBISH	BOWLINE	BRIBERY	BROWNIE
*BIZARRE	BLUEGUM	BOODLER	BOWLING	BRIBING	BROWSER
*BIZNAGA	BLUEING	BOOKEND	*BOWSHOT	*BRICKLE	BRUCINE

BRUISER	BULLIES	BUSSING	*BACKRUSH	BANDITRY	BARRATRY
BRUITER	BULLION	BUSTARD	*BACKSEAT	BANDSMAN	BARRETOR
BRULYIE	BULLISH	BUSTIER	*BACKSIDE	BANGTAIL	BARRETRY
*BRULZIE	*BULLOCK	BUTANOL	*BACKSLAP	BANISHER	BARRETTE
BRUSHER	BULLOUS	BUTCHER	*BACKSLID	BANISTER	BARSTOOL
BRUSHUP	BULLPEN	BUTLERY	*BACKSPIN	*BANJOIST	BARTERER
*BRUSQUE	BULRUSH	BUTTALS	*BACKSTAY	*BANKBOOK	BARTISAN
BRUTELY	*BULWARK	BUTTERY	*BACKSTOP	*BANKCARD	*BARTIZAN
*BRUTIFY	BUMBLER	BUTTIES	*BACKWARD	BANKNOTE	BARYTONE
BRUTING	BUMBOAT	*BUTTOCK	*BACKWASH	BANKROLL	BASALTES
BRUTISH	BUMMEST	BUTTONY	*BACKWOOD	*BANKRUPT	BASEBALL
BRUTISM	BUMMING	BUTYRAL	*BACKWRAP	*BANKSIDE	BASEBORN
*BRUXISM	*BUMPKIN	BUTYRIC	*BACKYARD	BANNERET	BASELESS
BUBALIS	BUNDIST	BUTYRIN	BACTERIA	BANNEROL	BASELINE
BUBBLER	BUNDLER	*BUTYRYL	BACTERIN	BANTERER	BASENESS
BUBINGA	BUNGLER	*BUYBACK	BACULINE	BANTLING	BASEMENT
BUBONIC	BUNRAKU	*BUZZARD	*BADGERLY	BAPTISIA	*BASICITY
*BUCKEEN	BUNTING	*BUZZWIG	BADINAGE	*BAPTIZER	BASIDIUM
*BUCKEYE	BUOYAGE	BYLINER	*BADMOUTH	BARATHEA	BASIFIER
*BUCKISH	BUOYANT		BAGHOUSE	BARBARIC	BASILARY
*BUCKLER	BURBLER	*BAASKAAP	*BAGPIPER	BARBASCO	BASILICA
*BUCKRAM	*BURDOCK	*BABBLING	BAGUETTE	BARBECUE	BASILISK
*BUCKSAW	BURETTE	BABIRUSA	*BAIDARKA	*BARBEQUE	BASINFUL
BUCOLIC	BURGAGE	*BABUSHKA	BAILMENT	*BARBERRY	*BASKETRY
BUDDIED	BURGEON	*BABYHOOD	BAILSMAN	BARBETTE	*BASOPHIL
BUDDIES	BURGESS	BACCARAT	*BAKEMEAT	BARBICAN	BASSINET
BUDDING	BURGHER	*BACCATED	*BAKESHOP	BARBICEL	BASSNESS
BUDGING	BURGLAR	*BACCHANT	*BAKSHISH	BARBITAL	BASSWOOD
BUDLESS	BURGOUT	*BACCHIUS	BALANCER	BARBLESS	BASTARDY
BUDLIKE	BURKITE	*BACHELOR	*BALDHEAD	*BARBWIRE	BASTILLE
*BUDWORM	BURLESK	BACILIAR	BALDNESS	*BAREBACK	*BATHETIC
*BUFFALO	BURNING	BACILLUS	BALDPATE	BAREBOAT	BATHLESS
*BUFFIER	BURNISH	*BACKACHE	*BALDRICK	BAREFOOT	*BATHROBE
*BUFFOON	BURNOUS	*BACKBEAT	BALEFIRE	BAREHEAD	*BATHROOM
BUGABOO	BURNOUT	*BACKBEND	BALISAUR	BARENESS	BATTALIA
BUGBANE	BURRIER	*BACKBITE	BALKLINE	BARESARK	BATTENER
BUGBEAR	BURRING	*BACKBONE	BALLGAME	BARGELLO	BATTERIE
BUGGERY	BURRITO	*BACKCAST	*BALLHAWK	BARGEMAN	BATTIEST
BUGGING	BURSARY	*BACKCHAT	BALLISTA	BARGHEST	*BAUDEKIN
BUGLOSS	BURSATE	*BACKDATE	BALLONET	BARGUEST	BAUDRONS
BUGSEED	BURSEED	*BACKDOOR	BALLONNE	BARITONE	BAUHINIA
BUILDER	BURSERA	*BACKDROP	BALLOTER	BARKLESS	BAWDIEST
BUILDUP	BURSTER	*BACKFILL	*BALLPARK	BARLEDUC	BAYADEER
BUIRDLY	BURTHEN	*BACKFIRE	BALLROOM	BARNACLE	BAYADERE
BULBLET	BURWEED	*BACKFLOW	*BALLYHOO	BARNYARD	*BAYBERRY
BULBOUS	BUSHIDO	*BACKHAND	BALLYRAG	BAROGRAM	BDELLIUM
BULIMIA	BUSHIER	*BACKHAUL	BALMORAL	BARONAGE	*BEACHBOY
BULIMIC	*BUSHILY	*BACKLAND	BALSAMIC	BARONESS	BEADIEST
BULKAGE	BUSHING	*BACKLASH	BALUSTER	BARONIAL	*BEADLIKE
BULLACE	BUSHMAN	*BACKLESS	BANALITY	*BAROUCHE	BEADROLL
BULLATE	*BUSHPIG	*BACKLIST	*BANALIZE	BARRABLE	BEADSMAN
BULLBAT	BUSHTIT	*BACKMOST	BANAUSIC	BARRANCA	*BEADWORK
BULLDOG	*BUSHWAH	*BACKPACK	BANDAGER	BARRANCO	BEAMIEST
BULLIED	BUSIEST	*BACKREST	BANDANNA	BARRATER	BEAMLESS
BULLIER	BUSLOAD	*BACKROOM	BANDEROL	BARRATOR	*BEAMLIKE

BEANBALL	BEGETTER	BEROUGED	*BIFACIAL	BIRACIAL	*BLENCHER
BEANLIKE	*BEGGARLY	BERRETTA	*BIFIDITY	BIRADIAL	*BLESBUCK
BEANPOLE	BEGINNER	*BESCORCH	BIFORATE	BIRAMOSE	BLESSING
BEARLIKE	BEGIRDLE	BESCREEN	*BIFORKED	BIRAMOUS	BLINDAGE
BEARSKIN	BEGLAMOR	BESETTER	*BIFORMED	*BIRDBATH	*BLINKARD
*BEATIFIC	BEGORRAH	*BESHADOW	BIGAMIES	BIRDCAGE	BLISTERY
BEATLESS	BEGOTTEN	*BESHIVER	BIGAMIST	BIRDCALL	*BLIZZARD
BEAUCOUP	BEGRUDGE	BESHROUD	BIGAMOUS	*BIRDFARM	*BLOCKADE
*BEAUTIFY	BEGUILER	BESIEGER	BIGARADE	*BIRDLIKE	*BLOCKAGE
*BEBOPPER	*BEHAVIOR	BESLAVED	BIGAROON	BIRDLIME	*BLOCKISH
BECARPET	*BEHEMOTH	*BESMIRCH	*BIGEMINY	BIRDSEED	BLONDISH
*BECHAMEL	BEHOLDEN	*BESMOOTH	*BIGMOUTH	BIRDSEYE	BLOODFIN
*BECHANCE	BEHOLDER	BESMUDGE	BIGNONIA	BIRDSHOT	BLOODIED
*BECKONER	*BEJABERS	BESOOTHE	*BIHOURLY	BIRDSONG	BLOODIER
BECLAMOR	*BEJEEZUS	BESOUGHT	*BIJUGATE	BIRRETTA	BLOODIES
*BECLOTHE	*BEJUMBLE	BESPOUSE	*BIJUGOUS	*BIRTHDAY	BLOODILY
*BECOMING	*BEKNIGHT	BESPREAD	BILABIAL	BISECTOR	BLOODING
*BECOWARD	BELABOUR	BESPRENT	BILANDER	*BISEXUAL	BLOODRED
BECUDGEL	BELIEVER	BESTIARY	*BILBERRY	BISTOURY	*BLOOMERY
*BEDABBLE	*BELIQUOR	BESTOWAL	BILINEAR	*BITCHERY	*BLOSSOMY
*BEDARKEN	BELITTLE	BESTRIDE	BILLETER	BITEWING	BLOTLESS
*BEDAZZLE	BELLBIRD	BETATRON	*BILLFISH	BITINGLY	BLOTTIER
*BEDCHAIR	BELLOWER	BETATTER	BILLFOLD	*BITSTOCK	BLOTTING
*BEDCOVER	BELLPULL	BETELNUT	BILLHEAD	BITTIEST	BLOVIATE
BEDEAFEN	BELLWORT	BETHESDA	*BILLHOOK	*BIUNIQUE	*BLOWBACK
BEDESMAN	*BELLYFUL	BETRAYAL	BILLIARD	BIVALENT	*BLOWBALL
*BEDFRAME	BELTLESS	BETRAYER	*BILLYCAN	BIVALVED	*BLOWDOWN
BEDIAPER	BELTLINE	BEUNCLED	BILOBATE	*BIWEEKLY	*BLOWFISH
*BEDIMPLE	BEMADDEN	BEVATRON	BIMANOUS	*BIYEARLY	*BLOWHARD
*BEDMAKER	BEMINGLE	BEVELLER	BIMANUAL	*BLACKCAP	*BLOWHOLE
BEDOTTED	BEMUDDLE	BEVERAGE	BIMENSAL	*BLACKFIN	BLOWIEST
BEDPLATE	BEMURMUR	BEWAILER	BIMESTER	*BLACKFLY	*BLOWPIPE
*BEDQUILT	*BEMUZZLE	BEWILDER	*BIMETHYL	*BLACKGUM	*BLOWTUBE
*BEDRENCH	*BENDWAYS	*BEWINGED	BINAURAL	*BLACKING	*BLUBBERY
BEDRIVEL	BENDWISE	*BEWRAYER	*BINDWEED	*BLACKISH	BLUDGEON
BEDSHEET	*BENEDICK	BHEESTIE	BINNACLE	*BLACKLEG	BLUEBALL
BEDSONIA	BENEDICT	*BIACETYL	BINOMIAL	*BLACKOUT	BLUEBELL
BEDSTAND	*BENEFICE	BIANNUAL	BIOASSAY	*BLACKTOP	BLUEBILL
BEDSTEAD	*BENJAMIN	BIASNESS	BIOCLEAN	BLAMABLE	BLUEBIRD
BEDSTRAW	BENTWOOD	BIATHLON	*BIOCYCLE	*BLAMEFUL	*BLUEBOOK
*BEDWARDS	*BENZIDIN	BIBULOUS	*BIOETHIC	*BLANCHER	BLUECOAT
BEEBREAD	*BENZOATE	BICAUDAL	BIOGENIC	BLANDISH	*BLUEFISH
*BEECHNUT	*BEPIMPLE	*BICHROME	BIOLOGIC	BLASTEMA	BLUEGILL
*BEEFCAKE	*BEQUEATH	*BICKERER	BIOLYSIS	BLASTIER	BLUEHEAD
BEEFIEST	BERASCAL	BICOLOUR	*BIOMETRY	BLASTING	*BLUEJACK
BEEFLESS	BERBERIN	*BICONVEX	BIOPLASM	*BLASTOFF	BLUELINE
*BEEPWOOD	BERBERIS	*BICUSPID	BIOSCOPE	BLASTOMA	BLUENESS
BEESWING	BERCEUSE	*BICYCLER	*BIOSCOPY	BLASTULA	BLUENOSE
BEETROOT	*BERDACHE	*BICYCLIC	BIOTICAL	*BLATANCY	BLUESMAN
BEFINGER	BEREAVER	*BIDARKEE	*BIOTOXIN	BLATTING	BLUESTEM
*BEFLOWER	BERGAMOT	BIDDABLE	BIOVULAR	*BLAZONER	*BLUETICK
BEFOULER	BERIBERI	BIDENTAL	BIPAROUS	*BLAZONRY	BLUEWEED
BEFRIEND	BERINGED	BIENNALE	BIPARTED	*BLEACHER	BLUEWOOD
BEFRINGE	BERMUDAS	BIENNIAL	*BIPHASIC	*BLEAKISH	*BLUSHFUL
*BEFUDDLE	BERNICLE	BIENNIUM	*BIPHENYL	BLEEDING	BLUSTERY

BOARDING	BOOKREST	*BOYARISM	BRINIEST	BULLETIN	BUTYLENE
BOARDMAN	*BOOKSHOP	*BOYCHICK	BRISANCE	BULLFROG	BUTYRATE
*BOARFISH	*BOOKWORM	BRABBLER	BRISLING	BULLHEAD	BUTYROUS
BOASTFUL	BOOMIEST	BRACELET	*BRITCHES	BULLHORN	*BUZZWORD
BOATBILL	*BOOMTOWN	*BRACHIAL	*BRITZSKA	BULLIEST	BYSTREET
*BOATHOOK	*BOONDOCK	*BRACHIUM	*BROACHER	*BULLNECK	
BOATLIKE	*BOOTJACK	BRACIOLA	*BROADAXE	BULLNOSE	K B AR
BOATLOAD	BOOTLACE	BRACIOLE	BROADISH	BULLPOUT	M B IRA
BOATSMAN	BOOTLESS	*BRACKISH	BROCATEL	BULLRING	B I B B
BOATYARD	*BOOTLICK	BRACONID	BROCCOLI	BULLRUSH	CO B B
BOBBINET	BORACITE	BRACTLET	*BROCHURE	BULLSHOT	*JI B B
*BOBOLINK	*BORDEAUX	BRAGGART	*BROCKAGE	BULLWEED	KO B O
*BOBWHITE	BORDELLO	BRAGGEST	BROGUERY	*BULLWHIP	MA B E
*BOCACCIO	BORDERER	BRAGGING	BROGUISH	*BULLYBOY	SI B B
BODEMENT	BORECOLE	BRAIDING	BROIDERY	BULLYRAG	VI B E
BODILESS	BOREHOLE	BRAINIER	BROMELIN	*BUMBLING	CA B O B
*BODINGLY	BORESOME	BRAINILY	*BROMIDIC	*BUNCOMBE	KA B A B
BODYSUIT	BORINGLY	BRAINISH	*BRONCHIA	BUNDLING	KA B O B
*BODYSURF	BORROWER	BRAINPAN	*BRONCHUS	BUNGALOW	KI B B E
*BODYWORK	*BOSCHBOK	*BRAKEAGE	*BRONZING	BUNGHOLE	KI B B I
*BOEHMITE	*BOSHVARK	*BRAKEMAN	BROOKITE	BUNGLING	KI B EI
*BOGEYMAN	BOTANICA	*BRANCHIA	BROOKLET	*BUNKMATE	NA B O B
BOGGIEST	BOTANIES	BRANDISH	*BROUGHAM	BUNTLINE	NO B LE
*BOHEMIAN	BOTANISE	BRANNING	*BROUHAHA	*BUOYANCE	PI B AL
BOISERIE	BOTANIST	BRANTAIL	*BROWBAND	*BUOYANCY	RA B AT
*BOLDFACE	*BOTANIZE	BRASILIN	*BROWBEAT	BURDENER	RE B AR
BOLDNESS	*BOTCHERY	BRASSAGE	BROWLESS	BURGLARY	RE B UY
*BOLLOCKS	*BOTHRIUM	BRASSARD	BROWNIER	BURGONET	TA B UN
*BOLLWORM	BOTONNEE	BRASSART	*BROWNISH	BURGRAVE	YO B B O
BOLTHEAD	BOTRYOID	BRASSICA	BROWNOUT	*BURGUNDY	BA B B LE
BOLTHOLE	BOTRYOSE	BRASSISH	BRUCELLA	BURNABLE	BA B IED
BOLTONIA	BOTRYTIS	BRATTICE	BRUNETTE	BURNOOSE	BA B IES
BOLTROPE	BOTTOMER	BRAUNITE	*BRUNIZEM	BURRIEST	BA B OOL
BOMBESIN	*BOTTOMRY	*BRAZENLY	BRUSHIER	BURROWER	BA B OON
*BOMBLOAD	BOTULISM	*BRAZILIN	*BRUSHOFF	BURSITIS	BI B BED
*BOMBYCID	*BOUFFANT	*BREACHER	*BRYOLOGY	BURSTONE	BI B B ER
BONDMAID	*BOUGHPOT	*BREADBOX	*BRYOZOAN	*BUSHBUCK	BO B B ER
BONDSMAN	BOUGHTEN	BREADNUT	BUBALINE	BUSHELER	BO B B IN
*BONEFISH	BOUILLON	*BREAKAGE	*BUCKAROO	*BUSHFIRE	BO B B LE
BONEHEAD	BOUNDARY	*BREAKING	*BUCKAYRO	BUSHGOAT	BO B CAT
BONELESS	BOURGEON	BREAKOUT	*BUCKBEAN	BUSHIEST	BU B ALE
BONEMEAL	BOURTREE	BREATHER	*BUCKEROO	BUSHLAND	BU B B LE
BONEYARD	BOUSOUKI	BREEDING	*BUCKSHEE	BUSHLESS	*BU B B LY
BONGOIST	*BOUTIQUE	BRETHREN	*BUCKSHOT	*BUSHLIKE	CA B ALA
*BONHOMIE	*BOUZOUKI	*BREVETCY	*BUCKSKIN	BUSINESS	CA B ANA
*BONIFACE	*BOVINELY	*BREVIARY	*BUCKTAIL	BUSTLINE	CA B B IE
BONINESS	*BOVINITY	*BRICKBAT	BUDDLEIA	BUSULFAN	CA B LET
BONSPELL	*BOWFRONT	BRIDALLY	BUDGETER	*BUSYBODY	CA B MAN
BONSPIEL	*BOWINGLY	BRIDGING	*BUFFETER	BUSYNESS	CE B OID
*BONTEBOK	*BOWLLIKE	BRIEFING	*BUFFIEST	*BUSYWORK	CO B ALT
*BOOGYMAN	*BOWSPRIT	BRIGHTEN	BUGHOUSE	BUTANONE	CO B B ER
*BOOKCASE	*BOXBERRY	*BRIMFULL	*BUHLWORK	*BUTCHERY	CO B B LE
BOOKLORE	*BOXBOARD	BRIMLESS	BUILDING	BUTTONER	CO B NUT
*BOOKMARK	*BOXINESS	*BRIMMING	*BULKHEAD	BUTTRESS	*CO B WE B
*BOOKRACK	*BOXTHORN	BRINDLED	*BULLDOZE	BUTYLATE	CU B ISM

CU B IST	*HY B RID	RA B IES	SU B ITO	B OB STAY	GA B B LER
CU B OID	HY B RIS	RE B AIT	SU B LET	B OB TAIL	GA B ELLE
CY B ORG	*JA B B ER	RE B ATE	SU B LOT	B U B ALIS	GA B FEST
DA B B ER	*JA B IRU	RE B ATO	SU B MIT	B U B B IES	GI B B ING
DA B B LE	*JI B B ER	RE B ECK	SU B NET	B U B B LER	GI B B OSE
DE B ARK	*JO B B ER	RE B ILL	SU B ORN	B U B INGA	GI B B OUS
DE B ATE	*JU B B AH	RE B IND	SU B PAR	B U B ONIC	GO B B ING
DE B EAK	*JU B HAH	RE B ODY	SU B SEA	CA B ARET	GO B B LER
DE B ONE	*JU B ILE	RE B OIL	SU B SET	CA B B AGE	GO B IOID
DE B RIS	*KA B AKA	RE B OOK	SU B TLE	CA B B ALA	GO B ONEE
DE B TOR	KA B ALA	RE B OOT	SU B UR B	CA B B ING	HA B ITAN
DE B UNK	*KA B AYA	RE B ORE	SU B WAY	*CA B EZON	HA B ITAT
DI B B ER	*KA B IKI	RE B ORN	TA B ARD	CA B ILDO	HA B ITUE
DI B B LE	*KA B UKI	*RE B OZO	TA B B ED	CA B INET	HA B ITUS
*DI B B UK	KE B B IE	RE B UFF	TA B B IS	CA B LING	HE B ETIC
DO B B ER	*KE B LAH	RE B UKE	TA B LET	*CAB OMB A	*HI B ACHI
DO B B IN	*KI B B EH	RE B URY	TA B OUR	CA B OOSE	HO B B IES
DO B LON	KI B B LE	RI B ALD	TA B ULI	CI B OULE	HO B B LER
DU B B ER	*KI B ITZ	RI B AND	TU B ATE	CO B B IER	*HO B B NO B
DU B B IN	*KI B LAH	RI B B ED	TU B B ED	CO B B LER	*HO B LIKE
*DY B B UK	*KI B OSH	RI B B ER	TU B B ER	CU B B AGE	HO B NAIL
FA B LER	KO B OLD	RI B B ON	TU B FUL	CU B B ING	HO B OISM
FA B RIC	*KY B OSH	RI B IER	TU B IST	*CU B B ISH	*JA B B ING
FI B B ER	LA B IAL	RI B LET	TU B ULE	CU B ICAL	*JI B B ING
FI B RIL	LA B IUM	RI B OSE	VI B IST	CU B ICLE	*JI B B OOM
FI B RIN	LA B OUR	RO B ALO	VI B RIO	*CU B ICLY	*JO B B ERY
GA B B ED	LA B RET	RO B AND	WAB B LE	DA B B LER	*JO B B ING
GA B B ER	LA B RUM	RO B B ED	*WA B B LY	DA B STER	*JO B LESS
GA B B LE	LI B B ER	RO B B ER	*WE B FED	DE B ACLE	*JO B NAME
GA B B RO	LI B IDO	RO B B IN	WO B B LE	DE B ASER	*JU B ILEE
GA B IES	LI B LA B	RO B UST	*WO B B LY	DE B ATER	*KA B ALAH
GA B ION	LO B ATE	RU B ACE	YAB B ER	*DE B AUCH	*KE B B OCK
GA B OON	LO B B ED	RU B ATO	*ZE B ECK	DE B ONER	*KE B B UCK
GI B B ER	LO B B ER	RU B B ED	*ZI B ETH	*DE B OUCH	*KI B B ITZ
GI B B ET	LO B ULE	RU B B LE	BA B ASSU	DE B RIDE	*KI B B UTZ
GI B B ON	LU B B ER	RU B B LY	BAB B ITT	DE B RIEF	LA B ARUM
GI B LET	LU B RIC	RU B IED	BAB B LER	DI B ASIC	LA B ELER
GI B SON	MO B LED	RU B IER	BA B ESIA	DI B B ING	LA B IATE
GO B ANG	NE B ULA	RU B IES	*BA B ICHE	DI B B LER	LA B ORER
GO B B ED	NE B ULE	RU B IGO	*BA B YISH	DO B B IES	LA B ROID
GO B B ET	NE B ULY	RU B OFF	BE B EERU	DU B B ING	LI B ELEE
GO B B LE	NO B ODY	RU B OUT	BE B LOOD	DU B IETY	LI B ELER
GO B IES	NU B B IN	RU B RIC	BI B ASIC	DU B IOUS	LI B ERAL
GO B LET	NU B B LE	SAB B AT	*BI B B ERY	FA B LIAU	LI B ERTY
GO B LIN	NU B B LY	SA B B ED	BI B B ING	FA B LING	LI B RARY
GO B ONY	NU B ILE	SA B INE	*BI B COCK	FA B ULAR	LI B RATE
HA B ILE	PA B LUM	SO B B ER	BI B ELOT	FE B RILE	LO B ATED
HA B OO B	PE B B LE	SO B EIT	BI B LESS	FI B ROID	LO B B ING
HO B B IT	*PE B B LY	SO B FUL	*BI B LIKE	FI B ROIN	LO B B YER
HO B B LE	PU B LIC	SU B B ED	BI B LIST	FI B ROMA	LO B EFIN
HO B NO B	RA B ATO	SU B DEB	*BOB B ERY	FI B ROUS	LO B ELIA
*HU B B LY	RA B B ET	SU B DUE	BO B B IES	GA B B ARD	LO B STER
*HU B B UB	RA B B IN	*SU B FIX	BO B B ING	GA B B ART	LO B WORM
*HU B CAP	RA B B IT	SU B GUM	*B O B ECHE	GA B B IER	*MO B B ISH
HU B RIS	RA B B LE		BO B SLED	GA B B ING	

MO B ILIS	SA B B ING	SU B SIST	*BAB B LING	CRI B ROUS	GLO B ULAR
MO B OCRA	SE B ACIC	SU B SITE	B AR B ARIC	*CRI B WORK	GLO B ULIN
NE B B ISH	SE B ASIC	SU B SOIL	B AR B ASCO	CUM B ERER	GOM B ROON
NI B B ILE	SI B LING	SU B SUME	B AR B ECUE	CUM B ROUS	GOR B ELLY
NI B B LER	SO B ERLY	SU B TASK	*BAR B EQUE	*CUP B OARD	*GOR B LIMY
*NI B LICK	SU B ACID	SU B TEEN	*BAR B ERRY	CUR B SIDE	GRA B B IER
NI B LIKE	SU B ADAR	SU B TEND	B AR B ETTE	*CYMBALER	GRA B B ING
NO B B IER	SU B ALAR	SU B TEST	B AR B ICAN	*CYMBALOM	GRA B B LER
NO B B ILY	SU B AREA	*SU B TEXT	B AR B ICEL	*CYM B IDIA	*GRUBWORM
NO B B LER	SU B ARID	SU B TILE	B AR B ITAL	*CYM B LING	GUM B OTIL
NO B LEST	SU B ATOM	SU B TONE	B AR B LESS	DA B B LING	*HAG B ERRY
NU B B IER	SU B B ASE	SU B TYPE	*BAR B WIRE	*DAY B REAK	HAR B ORER
NU B B LES	SU B B ASS	SU B UNIT	B EE B READ	*DEW B ERRY	HER B ARIA
PA B ULUM	SU B B ING	SU B VENE	B ER B ERIN	DIA B ETES	HER B IEST
*PI B ROCH	SU B CELL	SU B VERT	B ER B ERIS	DIA B ETIC	HER B LESS
PU B ERTY	SU B CLAN	*SU B ZERO	*B IL B ERRY	DIA B LERY	*HER B LIKE
PU B LISH	SU B CODE	*SU B ZONE	*BLUB B ERY	DIA B OLIC	*HO B B YIST
RA B B ITY	SU B COOL	TA B ANID	B O B B INET	DIO B OLON	HOT B LOOD
RA B B LER	SU B CULT	TA B ARET	B OM B ESIN	DIS B OSOM	*HUM B LEST
RA B B ONI	SU B DEAN	TA B B IED	*BOMBLOAD	DIS B URSE	*HUM B LING
RE B ATER	SU B DUAL	TA B B IES	*BOM B YCID	*DOG B ERRY	*JA B B ERER
RE B EGIN	SU B DUCE	TA B B ING	*BOX B ERRY	DOU B LING	*JAM B OREE
RE B IRTH	SU B DUCT	TA B ETIC	*BOX B OARD	DOU B LOON	*JAW B ONER
RE B LEND	SU B DUER	TA B LEAU	B RA B B LER	DOU B LURE	*KAB B ALAH
RE B LOOM	SU B ECHO	TA B LING	*BUM B LING	DOU B TFUL	*KEY B OARD
RE B OANT	SU B EDIT	TA B LOID	*CAB B ALAH	DRA B NESS	KOL B ASSI
RE B OARD	SU B ERIC	TA B ORER	*CAM B OGIA	DRI B B LER	LAM B ASTE
RE B OUND	SU B ERIN	TA B ORET	*CAR B AMIC	DRI B B LET	*LAMB ENCY
RE B REED	SU B FILE	TA B ORIN	*CAR B AMYL	DRU B B ING	LAM B IEST
RE B UILD	SU B FUSC	TA B OULI	*CAR B ARYL	*DUMB B ELL	*LAMB KILL
RE B UKER	SU B GOAL	TA B ULAR	CAR B INOL	*DUMB CANE	*LAM B LIKE
RI B B AND	SU B HEAD	TO B ACCO	CAR B OLIC	*DUMB HEAD	*LAM B SKIN
RI B B IER	SU B IDEA	TU B AIST	*CAR B ONYL	DUM B NESS	LAP B OARD
RI B B ONY	SU B ITEM	TU B B ING	*CAR B OXYL	FAU B OURG	LAR B OARD
RI B LESS	*SU B JECT	TU B LIKE	CAR B URET	*FEE B LISH	LEE B OARD
RI B LIKE	*SU B JOIN	TU B ULAR	CAT B RIER	FLA B ELLA	LIM B LESS
RI B WORT	SU B LATE	TU B ULIN	*CHU B ASCO	*FOG B OUND	LIM B TEST
RO B B ERY	SU B LIME	VE B ROSE	*CIM B ALOM	FOR B IDAL	*LOB BYGOW
RO B B ING	SU B LINE	VI B RANT	CLU B A B LE	FOR B ORNE	*LOB B YISM
RO B OTRY	SU B MENU	VI B RATE	*CLUB B ING	*FRA B JOUS	*LO B B YIST
RO B USTA	SU B MISS	VI B RATO	*CLUB FOOT	FRI B B LER	LUM B ERER
RU B A B OO	SU B ORAL	VI B RION	*CLUB HAND	FUR B ELOW	*MOP B OARD
RU B ASSE	SU B OVAL	WA B B LER	*CLUB HAUL	GAL B ANUM	*MOR B IFIC
RU B B ERY	SU B PART	*WE B B ING	CLU B ROOT	GAM B ESON	*MUL B ERRY
RU B B ING	SU B PENA	*WE B FOOT	CO B B IEST	GAM B USIA	*MYO B LAST
RU B B ISH	SU B PLOT	WE B LESS	COM B ATER	*GAR B ANZO	NO B B IEST
RU B DOWN	SU B RACE	*WE B LIKE	COM B INER	GAR B LESS	NON B ASIC
RU B ELLA	SU B RENT	WE B STER	*COM B INGS	GAR B OARD	NON B EING
RU B EOLA	SU B RING	*WE B WORM	*COM B LIKE	GER B ILLE	*NON BLACK
RU B IEST	SU B RULE	*WE B WORM	*COW B ERRY	GI B B SITE	NON B RAND
RU B IOUS	SU B SALE	WO B B LER	CRA B MEAT	GLA B ELLA	NU B B IEST
SA B ATON	SU B SECT	*ZE B RASS	*CRA B WISE	GLA B RATE	NUM B ERER
SA B AYON	SU B SERE	*ZE B RINE	*CRIB B AGE	GLA B ROUS	*NUM B FISH
SA B B ATH	SU B SIDY	*ZE B ROID	*CRIB B ING	GLI B NESS	NUM B NESS
			*CRIB B LED	GLO B ATED	NUT B ROWN

PAN B ROIL	*SNO B BERY	TUR B INAL	GLO B	KEDA B	SU B DE B
PEG B OARD	SNO B B IER	TUR B OCAR	GRA B	KERO B	SU B UR B
PLE B EIAN	*SNO B B ILY	TUR B OFAN	GRU B	NA B O B	SUPER B
*POT B ELLY	*SNO B B ISH	*TUR B OJET	HER B	NAWA B	B ATHTU B
PRE B ASAL	SNO B B ISM	*VAM B RACE	*JAM B	PLUM B	CORNCO B
PRE B LESS	SNU B NESS	*VER B ALLY	*JI B B	REDU B	COULOM B
PRE B OUND	SOM B RERO	*VER B ATIM	KER B	REHA B	*COWHER B
PRO B AB LE	SOM B ROUS	VER B IAGE	KNO B	RHOM B	*COXCOM B
*PRO B ABLY	SOR B ITOL	VER B LESS	LAM B	RHUM B	DISTUR B
PUR B LIND	*SOW B ELLY	VER B OTEN	LIM B	SAHI B	*FLU B DU B
*QUI B BLER	SOW B READ	*WAX B ERRY	NUM B	SCRU B	*HO B B NO B
RA B B ITER	STA B LEST	*ZAI B ATSU	PLE B	SHRU B	MINICA B
*RAB B ITRY	STA B LING	*ZOM B IISM	SCA B	SLUR B	MINILA B
RAM B UTAN	STA B LISH		SI B B	*SQUA B	PEDICA B
RAW B ONED	STI B NITE	B AR B	SLA B	*SQUI B	PERTUR B
REA B SOR B	STU B B LER	B IB B	SLO B	THRO B	POTHER B
*RED B RICK	*STU B B ILY	B LA B	SLU B	THUM B	PROVER B
*REO B JECT	STU B B ING	B LE B	SNI B	*ZINE B	REPLUM B
REO B TAIN	STU B B ORN	B LO B	SNO B	BAO BA B	RHU B AR B
*RHA B DOME	SU B B REED	B LU B	SNU B	B EDAU B	SANDDA B
RI B B IEST	*SUN B AKED	B OM B	SOR B	B EDUM B	*SUCCUM B
RUB BABOO	SUN B ATHE	B OO B	STA B	B ICAR B	*TAXICA B
RUM B LING	*SUN B LOCK	B UL B	STO B	CHERU B	*WASHTU B
SA B B ATIC	SUN B URST	CHU B	STU B	*CO B WE B	*CATACOM B
SAW B ONES	*SYM B IONT	CLU B	SWA B	CONFA B	*CHORIAM B
*SCA B BARD	*SYM B IOTE	CO B B	SWO B	*CORYM B	CORNCRI B
SCA B IOSA	*SYM B OLIC	COM B	TOM B	DENUM B	*DIVE B OM B
SCA B IOUS	TAG B OARD	CRA B	VER B	DESOR B	*DOORJAM B
SCA B LAND	TAM B OURA	CRI B	WOM B	HA B OO B	*DOORKNO B
*SCA B LIKE	TAR B OOSH	CUR B	B LUR B	HO B NO B	*FIRE B OM B
SCA B ROUS	TEA B ERRY	DAR B	CA B O B	*HU B BU B	*FORELIM B
*SEA B EACH	TEA B OARD	DAU B	CARO B	LI B LA B	*HECATOM B
SEA B OARD	THE B AINE	DRA B	CELE B	MIDRI B	LANDGRA B
SEA B ORNE	TOL B OOTH	DRI B	CHIM B	MIHRA B	*MEMSAHI B
*SKY B ORNE	TOM B LESS	DRU B	CLIM B	MILNE B	REA B SOR B
*SLA B BERY	*TOM B LIKE	DUM B	CLOM B	PREFA B	SILLA B U B
SLA B B ING	TRA B EATE	FLA B	COOM B	RECOM B	SILLI B U B
SLA B LIKE	TRI B ASIC	FLU B	CRUM B	RESOR B	SPARERI B
*SLO B BERY	*TRI B RACH	FOR B	CURE B	REVER B	*SU B SHRU B
*SLO B BISH	TRI B UNAL	GAM B	DEMO B	SCARA B	*SYLLABUB
SLU B B ING	TU B BABLE	GAR B	KA B A B	SERDA B	*WELLCUR B
SLY B OOTS	TUM B LING	GLI B	KA B O B	SKI B O B	

C

CACA	CAIN	CALX	CARD	CASA	CAVY
CADE	CAKE	CAME	CARE	CASE	CEDE
CADI	CAKY	CAMP	CARK	CASH	CEDI
CAFE	CALF	CANE	CARL	CASK	CEIL
CAFF	CALK	CANT	CARN	CAST	CELL
CAGE	CALL	CAPE	CARP	CATE	CELT
CAGY	CALM	CAPH	CARR	CAUL	CENT
CAID	CALO	CAPO	CART	CAVE	CEPE

CERE	COAX	CRAB	CAIRD	CAULK	*CHEVY
CERO	COBB	CRAG	CAIRN	CAUSE	*CHEWY
CESS	COCA	CRAM	CAJON	CAVED	CHIAO
CETE	COCK	CRAP	CAKEY	CAVER	*CHICK
CHAD	COCO	CRAW	CALIF	CAVIE	CHICO
CHAM	CODA	CREW	CALIX	CAVIL	CHIDE
CHAO	CODE	CRIB	CALLA	CEASE	CHIEF
CHAP	COED	CRIS	CALVE	CEBID	CHIEL
CHAR	COFF	CROC	CAMAS	CECUM	CHILD
CHAT	COFT	CROP	CAMEL	CEDAR	CHILE
CHAW	COHO	CROW	CAMEO	CEDER	CHILI
CHAY	COIL	CRUD	CAMPI	CEIBA	CHILL
CHEF	COIN	CRUS	CAMPO	CELEB	CHIMB
CHEW	COIR	CRUX	CAMPY	CELLA	CHIME
*CHEZ	COKE	CUBE	CANAL	CELLO	CHIMP
CHIA	COLA	CUFF	CANDY	CELOM	CHINA
CHIC	COLD	CUIF	CANER	CENSE	CHINE
CHIC	COLE	CUKE	CANID	CENTO	CHINK
CHIN	COLT	CULL	CANNA	CEORL	CHINO
CHIP	COLY	CULM	CANNY	CERED	CHIRK
CHIT	COMA	CULT	CANOE	CERIA	CHIRM
CHON	COMB	CURB	CANON	CERIC	CHIRO
CHOP	COME	CURD	CANSO	CESTA	CHIRP
CHOW	COMP	CURE	CANST	CESTI	CHIRR
CHUB	CONE	CURF	CANTO	CHAFE	CHIVE
CHUG	CONI	CURL	CANTY	*CHAFF	*CHIVY
CHUM	CONK	CURN	CAPER	CHAIN	*CHOCK
CIAO	CONN	CURR	CAPON	CHAIR	CHOIR
CINE	CONY	CURT	CAPUT	CHALK	CHOKE
CION	COOF	CUSK	CARAT	CHAMP	*CHOKY
CIRE	COOK	CUSP	CARBO	CHANG	CHOLO
CIST	COOL	CUSS	CARER	CHANT	CHOMP
CITE	COON	CUTE	CARET	CHAOS	CHOOK
CITY	COOP	CYAN	CAREX	CHAPE	CHORD
CLAD	COOT	CYMA	CARGO	CHAPT	CHORE
CLAG	COPE	CYME	CARLE	CHARD	CHOSE
CLAM	COPY	CYST	CARNY	CHARE	CHOTT
CLAN	CORD	*CZAR	CAROB	CHARK	*CHUCK
CLAP	CORE	CABAL	CAROL	CHARM	CHUFA
CLAW	CORK	CABBY	CAROM	CHARR	*CHUFF
CLAY	CORM	CABER	CARPI	CHART	CHUMP
CLEF	CORN	CABIN	CARRY	CHARY	CHUNK
CLEW	CORY	CABLE	CARSE	CHASE	CHURL
CLIP	COSH	CABOB	CARTE	CHASM	CHURN
CLOD	COSS	CACAO	CARVE	CHEAP	CHURR
CLOG	COST	CACHE	CASED	CHEAT	CHUTE
CLON	COSY	CADDY	CASKY	CHEEK	CHYLE
CLOP	COTE	CADET	CASTE	CHEEP	*CHYME
CLOT	COUP	CADGE	CASUS	CHEER	CIBOL
CLOY	COVE	CADGY	CATCH	CHELA	CIDER
CLUB	COWL	CADRE	CATER	CHERT	CIGAR
CLUE	COWY	CAGER	CATTY	CHESS	CILIA
COAL	COXA	CAGEY	CAULD	CHEST	*CIMEX
COAT	*COZY	CAHOW		CHETH	CINCH

CIRCA	**CLOWN**	CONIC	CRAAL	**CRUMP**	CYDER
CIRRI	*CLOZE	CONIN	**CRACK**	CRUOR	*CYLIX
CISCO	**CLUCK**	**CONKY**	**CRAFT**	CRUSE	CYMAR
CISSY	**CLUMP**	CONTE	**CRAKE**	**CRUSH**	CYMOL
CITER	CLUNG	CONTO	**CRAMP**	CRUST	CYNIC
CIVET	**CLUNK**	CONUS	CRANE	**CRWTH**	CYTON
CIVIC	**COACH**	**COOCH**	**CRANK**	**CRYPT**	CABALA
CIVIE	COACT	COOEE	CRAPE	**CUBBY**	CABANA
CIVIL	COALA	COOER	**CRASH**	CUBEB	CABBIE
*CIVVY	**COALY**	**COOEY**	CRASS	CUBER	CABLET
CLACH	COAPT	**COOKY**	CRATE	**CUBIC**	CABMAN
CLACK	COAST	**COOLY**	**CRAVE**	CUBIT	CACHET
CLADE	COATI	**COOMB**	**CRAWL**	**CUDDY**	CACHOU
CLAIM	**COBBY**	COOPT	*CRAZE	CUING	CACKLE
CLAMP	COBIA	COPAL	*CRAZY	**CUISH**	CACTUS
CLANG	COBLE	COPEN	**CREAK**	**CULCH**	CADDIE
CLANK	COBRA	COPER	CREAM	CULET	CADDIS
CLARO	**COCCI**	COPRA	CREDO	**CULEX**	CADENT
CLARY	*COCKY	COPSE	CREED	**CULLY**	CADGER
CLASH	COCOA	CORAL	**CREEK**	CULPA	CAECUM
CLASP	**CODEC**	**CORBY**	CREEL	CULTI	CAEOMA
CLASS	CODED	CORER	CREEP	CUMIN	CAESAR
CLAST	CODEN	CORGI	CREME	CUPEL	CAFTAN
CLAVE	CODER	**CORKY**	CREPE	**CUPID**	CAGIER
CLAVI	*CODEX	CORNU	CREPT	**CUPPA**	CAGILY
CLEAN	CODON	**CORNY**	**CREPY**	**CUPPY**	CAGING
CLEAR	COGON	CORPS	CRESS	**CURCH**	CAHIER
CLEAT	**COHOG**	CORSE	CREST	**CURDY**	CAHOOT
CLEEK	COIGN	COSEC	**CRICK**	CURER	CAIMAN
CLEFT	COLIC	COSET	CRIED	CURET	*CAIQUE
CLEPE	COLIN	**COSEY**	CRIER	CURIA	*CAJOLE
CLERK	**COLLY**	COSIE	CRIES	CURIE	CALAMI
CLICK	COLOG	COSTA	CRIME	CURIO	CALASH
CLIFF	COLON	COTAN	**CRIMP**	**CURLY**	CALCAR
CLIFT	COLOR	COTTA	CRIPE	**CURRY**	CALCES
CLIMB	*COLZA	**COUCH**	CRISP	CURSE	CALCIC
CLIME	COMAL	COUDE	**CROAK**	CURST	CALESA
CLINE	**COMBE**	**COUGH**	CROCI	**CURVE**	CALICO
CLING	**COMBO**	COULD	**CROCK**	**CURVY**	CALIPH
CLINK	COMER	COUNT	**CROFT**	CUSEC	CALKER
	COMET	COUPE	CRONE	**CUSHY**	CALKIN
CLIPT	*COMFY	COURT	**CRONY**	CUSSO	CALLAN
CLOAK	**COMIC**	**COUTH**	**CROOK**	**CUTCH**	CALLER
CLOCK	*COMIX	**COVEN**	CROON	CUTES	CALLET
CLOMB	**COMMA**	**COVER**	CRORE	**CUTEY**	CALLOW
CLOMP	**COMMY**	**COVET**	CROSS	CUTIE	CALLUS
CLONE	**COMPO**	**COVEY**	CROUP	CUTIN	**CALORY**
CLONK	**COMPT**	COVIN	CROWD	CUTIS	CALPAC
CLOOT	COMTE	**COWER**	**CROWN**	**CUTTY**	*CALQUE
CLOSE	**CONCH**	**COWRY**	*CROZE	CUTUP	CALVES
CLOTH	CONDO	**COYLY**	**CRUCK**	**CYANO**	CAMAIL
CLOUD	**CONEY**	COYPU	CRUDE	**CYCAD**	CAMASS
CLOUR	CONGA	*COZEN	CRUEL	**CYCAS**	CAMBER
CLOUT	CONGE	*COZEY	CRUET	**CYCLE**	CAMBIA
CLOVE	CONGO	*COZIE	**CRUMB**	**CYCLO**	CAMERA

CAMION	CARBOY	CASUAL	CEREUS	*CHEEKY	CHORUS
CAMISA	CARCEL	CATALO	CERING	CHEERY	CHOSEN
CAMISE	CARDER	*CATCHY	CERIPH	CHEESE	*CHOUGH
CAMLET	CARDIA	CATENA	CERISE	CHEESY	CHOUSE
CAMPER	CAREEN	CATGUT	CERITE	CHEGOE	CHOUSH
CAMPUS	CAREER	CATION	CERIUM	*CHEMIC	CHOWSE
CANAPE	CARESS	CATKIN	CERMET	*CHEQUE	CHRISM
CANARD	CARFUL	CATLIN	CEROUS	CHERRY	CHROMA
CANARY	CARHOP	CATNAP	CERTES	CHERTY	CHROME
CANCAN	CARIBE	CATNIP	CERUSE	CHERUB	CHROMO
CANCEL	CARIES	CATSUP	CERVID	CHESTY	*CHUBBY
CANCER	CARINA	CATTED	*CERVIX	CHETAH	*CHUCKY
CANCHA	CARING	CATTIE	CESIUM	CHEVRE	*CHUFFY
CANDID	CARLIN	CATTLE	CESTOS	CHEWER	*CHUKAR
CANDLE	CARMAN	CAUCUS	CESTUS	CHIASM	*CHUKKA
CANDOR	CARNAL	CAUDAD	CESURA	CHIAUS	*CHUMMY
CANFUL	CARNET	CAUDAL	CETANE	*CHICHI	*CHUNKY
CANGUE	CARNEY	*CAUDEX	*CHABUK	CHICLE	*CHURCH
CANINE	CARNIE	CAUDLE	*CHACMA	*CHICLY	*CHYMIC
CANING	CAROCH	CAUGHT	CHADAR	CHIDER	CICADA
CANKER	CAROLI	CAULES	CHADOR	CHIELD	CICALA
CANNED	CARPAL	CAULIS	CHAETA	CHIGOE	CICELY
CANNEL	CARPEL	CAUSAL	CHAFER	CHILDE	CICERO
CANNER	CARPER	CAUSER	*CHAFFY	CHILLI	CILICE
CANNIE	CARPET	CAUSEY	CHAINE	CHILLY	CILIUM
CANNON	CARPUS	CAVEAT	CHAISE	CHIMAR	CINDER
CANNOT	CARREL	CAVERN	*CHAKRA	CHIMER	CINEMA
CANOLA	CARROM	CAVIAR	CHALAH	CHIMLA	CINEOL
CANOPY	CARROT	CAVIES	CHALEH	*CHINCH	*CINQUE
CANTER	CARTEL	CAVING	CHALET	*CHINKY	CIPHER
CANTIC	CARTER	CAVITY	*CHALKY	CHINTS	CIRCLE
CANTLE	CARTON	CAVORT	CHALLA	*CHINTZ	CIRCUS
CANTON	CARTOP	CAYMAN	CHALLY	*CHIPPY	*CIRQUE
CANTOR	CARVEL	CAYUSE	CHALOT	CHIRAL	CIRRUS
CANTUS	CARVEN	CEBOID	*CHAMMY	*CHIRPY	CISTUS
CANULA	CARVER	CEDING	*CHAMPY	CHIRRE	CITHER
CANVAS	CASABA	CEDULA	CHANCE	CHISEL	CITIED
CANYON	CASAVA	CEILER	*CHANCY	CHITAL	CITIES
CAPFUL	CASBAH	CELERY	CHANGE	CHITIN	CITIFY
CAPIAS	CASEFY	CELIAC	CHANTY	CHITON	CITING
CAPITA	CASEIN	CELLAR	CHAPEL	CHITTY	CITOLA
CAPLET	CASERN	CEMENT	CHARAS	*CHIVVY	CITOLE
CAPLIN	CASHAW	CENOTE	CHARGE	CHOANA	CITRAL
CAPOTE	CASHEW	CENSER	CHARRO	CHOICE	CITRIC
CAPPED	CASHOO	CENSOR	CHARRY	*CHOKER	CITRIN
CAPPER	CASING	CENSUS	CHASER	*CHOKEY	CITRON
CAPRIC	CASINO	CENTAL	CHASSE	CHOLER	CITRUS
CAPRIS	CASITA	CENTER	CHASTE	CHOLLA	CIVICS
CAPSID	CASKET	CENTRA	CHATTY	CHOOSE	CIVISM
CAPTAN	*CASQUE	CENTRE	CHAUNT	CHOOSY	*CLAMMY
CAPTOR	CASSIA	CENTUM	CHAWER	CHOPIN	CLAMOR
CARACK	CASSIS	CERATE	*CHAZAN	*CHOPPY	*CLAQUE
CARAFE	CASTER	CERCIS	CHEAPO	CHORAL	CLARET
CARATE	CASTLE	CERCUS	*CHEBEC	CHOREA	CLASSY
CARBON	CASTOR	CEREAL	CHEDER	CHORIC	CLAUSE

CLAVER	COBNUT	COLLOP	COOKIE	COSIES	*CRAPPY
CLAVUS	*COBWEB	COLONE	COOLER	COSIGN	CRASES
CLAWER	COCAIN	COLONI	COOLIE	COSILY	CRASIS
*CLAXON	COCCAL	COLONY	COOLLY	COSINE	CRATCH
CLAYEY	COCCIC	COLOUR	COOLTH	COSMIC	CRATER
CLEAVE	COCCID	COLTER	COOMBE	COSMOS	CRATON
CLENCH	COCCUS	COLUGO	COOPER	COSSET	CRAVAT
CLEOME	*COCCYX	COLURE	COOTER	COSTAR	CRAVEN
CLERGY	COCHIN	COMAKE	COOTIE	COSTER	CRAVER
CLERIC	COCKER	COMATE	*COPECK	COSTLY	CRAWLY
CLERID	COCKLE	COMBAT	COPALM	COTEAU	CRAYON
CLEVER	*COCKUP	COMBER	COPIED	COTING	*CREAKY
CLEVIS	COCOON	COMEDO	COPIER	COTTAR	CREAMY
CLICHE	CODDED	COMEDY	COPIES	COTTER	CREASE
CLIENT	CODDER	COMELY	COPING	COTTON	CREASY
*CLIFFY	CODDLE	COMETH	COPLOT	COTYPE	CREATE
*CLIMAX	CODEIA	COMFIT	COPPED	COUGAR	CRECHE
CLINAL	CODEIN	COMING	COPPER	COULEE	CREDAL
CLINCH	CODGER	COMITY	COPPRA	COUNTY	CREDIT
CLINGY	*CODIFY	COMMIE	COPRAH	COUPLE	CREEPY
CLINIC	CODING	COMMIT	COPTER	COUPON	CREESE
*CLIQUE	CODLIN	*COMMIX	COPULA	COURSE	CREESH
*CLIQUY	COELOM	COMMON	*COQUET	COUSIN	CRENEL
CLITIC	COEMPT	COMOSE	CORBAN	COUTER	CREOLE
CLIVIA	COERCE	COMOUS	CORBEL	COVERT	CREPEY
CLOACA	COEVAL	COMPEL	CORBIE	COVING	CREPON
CLOCHE	COFFEE	COMPLY	CORDER	COWAGE	CRESOL
CLODDY	COFFER	*COMPLY	CORDON	COWARD	CRESYL
CLOGGY	COFFIN	CONCHA	CORING	*COWBOY	CRETIC
CLONER	COFFLE	*CONCHY	CORIUM	COWIER	CRETIN
CLONIC	COGENT	CONCUR	CORKER	COWMAN	CREWEL
CLONUS	COGGED	CONDOM	CORMEL	COWPAT	*CRIKEY
*CLOQUE	COGITO	CONDOR	CORNEA	COWPEA	*CRIMPY
CLOSER	COGNAC	CONFAB	CORNEL	COWPIE	CRINGE
CLOSET	*COGWAY	CONFER	CORNER	*COWPOX	CRINUM
CLOTHE	COHEAD	CONFIT	CORNET	COWRIE	CRIPES
CLOTTY	COHEIR	CONGEE	CORNUS	COYDOG	CRISIS
CLOUDY	COHERE	CONGER	CORODY	COYISH	CRISPY
CLOUGH	COHORT	CONGOU	CORONA	COYOTE	CRISTA
CLOVEN	COHOSH	CONIES	CORPSE	COYPOU	CRITIC
CLOVER	COHOST	CONINE	CORPUS	*COZIED	*CROAKY
*CLUBBY	COHUNE	CONING	CORRAL	*COZIER	CROCUS
*CLUMPY	COIFFE	CONIUM	CORRIE	*COZIES	*CROJIK
CLUMSY	COIGNE	CONKER	CORSAC	*COZZES	CROSSE
*CLUNKY	COILER	CONNED	CORSET	*CRABBY	CROTCH
CLUTCH	COINER	CONNER	*CORTEX	*CRACKY	CROTON
COALER	COITUS	CONOID	CORTIN	CRADLE	CROUCH
COARSE	*COJOIN	CONSOL	CORVEE	CRAFTY	CROUPE
COATEE	COLDLY	CONSUL	CORVES	CRAGGY	CROUPY
COATER	COLEAD	CONTRA	CORVET	CRAMBE	CROUSE
*COAXAL	COLEUS	*CONVEX	*CORYMB	CRAMBO	*CROWDY
*COAXER	COLIES	CONVEY	*CORYZA	CRANCH	CROWER
COBALT	COLLAR	CONVOY	COSHER	CRANIA	CRUCES
COBBER	COLLET	COOKER	COSIED	*CRANKY	CRUDDY
COBBLE	COLLIE	*COOKEY	COSIER	CRANNY	CRUISE

*CRUMBY	CURLEW	CABOOSE	CALUMET	CAPELIN	CARNIES
*CRUMMY	CURRAN	*CACHEXY	CALUMNY	CAPERER	*CARNIFY
CRUNCH	CURRIE	*CACHING	*CALVARY	CAPITAL	CAROACH
CRURAL	CURSED	*CACIQUE	CALYCES	CAPITOL	CAROCHE
CRUSET	CURSER	*CACKLER	CALYCLE	CAPLESS	CAROLER
CRUSTY	CURSOR	*CACODYL	CALYPSO	CAPORAL	CAROLUS
CRUTCH	CURTAL	CADAVER	*CALZONE	*CAPOUCH	CAROTID
CRYPTO	CURTLY	CADDICE	CAMBIAL	CAPPING	CAROTIN
CUBAGE	CURTSY	CADDISH	*CAMBISM	CAPRICE	CAROUSE
CUBING	CURULE	CADELLE	CAMBIST	CAPRINE	CARPALE
CUBISM	CURVEY	CADENCE	*CAMBIUM	*CAPROCK	CARPING
CUBIST	CUSCUS	*CADENCY	*CAMBRIC	*CAPSIZE	CARPOOL
CUBOID	CUSHAT	*CADENZA	CAMELIA	CAPSTAN	CARPORT
CUCKOO	CUSHAW	CADMIUM	CAMISIA	CAPSULE	*CARRACK
CUDDIE	CUSPID	CAESIUM	CAMORRA	CAPTAIN	CARRELL
CUDDLE	CUSPIS	CAESTUS	*CAMPHOL	CAPTION	CARRIED
CUDDLY	CUSSER	CAESURA	*CAMPHOR	CAPTIVE	CARRIER
CUDGEL	CUSTOM	*CAFFEIN	CAMPIER	CAPTURE	CARRIES
CUESTA	CUSTOS	CAGEFUL	*CAMPILY	*CAPUCHE	CARRION
CUISSE	CUTEST	CAGIEST	CAMPING	CARABAO	CARROCH
CULLAY	CUTESY	CAISSON	CAMPION	CARABID	CARROTY
CULLER	CUTLAS	*CAITIFF	CAMPONG	CARABIN	CARRYON
CULLET	CUTLER	*CAJAPUT	CANAKIN	CARACAL	*CARSICK
CULLIS	CUTLET	*CAJOLER	CANASTA	CARACOL	CARTAGE
CULTCH	CUTOFF	*CAJUPUT	CANDELA	CARACUL	CARTOON
CULTIC	CUTOUT	CALAMUS	CANDENT	CARAMBA	CARVING
CULTUS	CUTTER	CALANDO	CANDIDA	CARAMEL	*CARWASH
CULVER	CUTTLE	*CALCIFY	CANDIED	*CARAPAX	CASCADE
CUMBER	CYANIC	CALCINE	CANDIES	CARAVAN	CASCARA
CUMMER	CYANID	CALCITE	CANDLER	CARAVEL	CASEASE
CUMMIN	CYANIN	CALCIUM	CANDOUR	*CARAWAY	CASEATE
CUNDUM	CYBORG	CALDERA	CANELLA	CARBARN	CASEOSE
CUNEAL	CYCLER	CALDRON	CANIKIN	CARBIDE	CASEOUS
CUNNER	*CYCLIC	CALECHE	CANNERY	CARBINE	CASERNE
CUPFUL	CYESIS	CALENDS	CANNIER	CARBORA	CASETTE
CUPOLA	CYGNET	CALIBER	CANNILY	CARCASE	*CASHBOX
CUPPED	*CYMBAL	CALIBRE	CANNING	CARCASS	CASHIER
CUPPER	CYMENE	CALICES	CANNOLI	CARDIAC	CASSABA
CUPRIC	CYMLIN	CALICHE	CANNULA	CARDING	CASSATA
CUPRUM	CYMOID	CALICLE	CANONRY	CARDOON	CASSAVA
CUPULA	CYMOSE	CALIPEE	CANSFUL	CAREFUL	CASSINO
CUPULE	CYMOUS	CALIPER	CANTALA	CARFARE	*CASSOCK
CURACY	*CYPHER	CALLANT	CANTATA	CARIBOU	CASTING
CURAGH	CYPRES	CALLBOY	CANTDOG	CARICES	*CASTOFF
CURARA	CYPRUS	CALLING	CANTEEN	CARIOCA	CASUIST
CURARE	CYSTIC	CALLOSE	*CANTHUS	CARIOLE	CATALOG
CURARI	CABARET	CALLOUS	CANTINA	CARIOUS	CATALPA
CURATE	CABBAGE	CALOMEL	CANTRAP	CARITAS	CATARRH
CURBER	CABBALA	CALORIC	CANTRIP	CARLESS	CATAWBA
CURDLE	CABBING	CALORIE	CANVASS	CARLINE	CATBIRD
CURFEW	*CABEZON	CALOTTE	*CANZONA	CARLING	CATBOAT
CURING	CABILDO	CALOYER	*CANZONE	CARLISH	CATCALL
CURITE	CABINET	*CALPACK	CAPABLE	CARLOAD	CATCHER
CURIUM	CABLING	CALTRAP	CAPELAN	CARMINE	*CATCHUP
CURLER	*CABOMBA	CALTROP	CAPELET	CARNAGE	CATCLAW

CATECHU	CENTNER	*CHAPMAN	CHETRUM	CHORALE	CITADEL
CATERAN	CENTRAL	*CHAPPED	*CHEVIED	CHORDAL	CITATOR
CATERER	CENTRIC	CHAPTER	*CHEVIES	CHORIAL	CITHARA
CATFACE	CENTRUM	CHARADE	*CHEVIOT	CHORINE	CITHERN
CATFALL	CENTURY	CHARGER	*CHEVRON	CHORING	CITHREN
*CATFISH	CERAMAL	CHARIER	*CHEWINK	CHORION	*CITIZEN
CATHEAD	CERAMIC	*CHARILY	CHIASMA	*CHORIZO	CITRATE
CATHECT	CERATED	CHARING	*CHIBOUK	CHOROID	CITRINE
CATHODE	CERATIN	CHARIOT	CHICANE	CHORTLE	CITROUS
CATLIKE	CEROTIC	CHARISM	CHICANO	CHOUSER	CITTERN
CATLING	CERTAIN	*CHARITY	*CHICKEE	*CHOWDER	*CIVILLY
CATMINT	*CERTIFY	*CHARKHA	*CHICKEN	CHRISOM	CLABBER
CATSPAW	CERUMEN	*CHARLEY	*CHICORY	*CHRISTY	CLACHAN
CATTAIL	CERVINE	CHARLIE	*CHIEFLY	*CHROMIC	*CLACKER
CATTALO	CESSION	CHARMER	*CHIFFON	*CHROMYL	CLADIST
CATTERY	CESSPIT	CHARNEL	CHIGGER	CHRONIC	CLADODE
CATTIER	CESTODE	CHARPAI	CHIGNON	CHRONON	CLAIMER
CATTILY	CESTOID	*CHARPOY	CHILIAD	*CHUCKLE	CLAMANT
CATTING	*CEVICHE	*CHARQUI	CHILLER	*CHUDDAH	CLAMBER
CATTISH	CHABLIS	CHARRED	CHILLUM	CHUDDAR	CLAMMED
*CATWALK	*CHABOUK	CHARTER	*CHIMBLY	CHUDDER	CLAMMER
CAUDATE	*CHAFFER	CHASING	CHIMERA	CHUGGER	CLAMOUR
CAULINE	*CHAFING	CHASSIS	CHIMERE	*CHUKKAR	CLAMPER
CAULKER	*CHAGRIN	CHASTEN	*CHIMING	CHUNTER	CLANGER
CAUSING	*CHALAZA	CHATEAU	*CHIMLEY	*CHURCHY	CLAPPER
CAUSTIC	*CHALCID	CHATTED	*CHIMNEY	CHURNER	*CLAQUER
CAUTERY	CHALICE	CHATTEL	*CHINCHY	CHUTIST	CLARIES
CAUTION	*CHALLAH	CHATTER	CHINNED	CHUTNEE	*CLARIFY
CAVALLA	CHALLIE	*CHAUFER	CHINONE	*CHUTNEY	CLARION
*CAVALLY	CHALLIS	*CHAYOTE	*CHINOOK	*CHUTZPA	CLARITY
*CAVALRY	CHALLOT	*CHAZZAN	*CHINTZY	*CHYMIST	CLARKIA
CAVEMAN	CHALONE	*CHAZZEN	*CHIPPED	*CHYMOUS	CLASHER
CAVETTO	*CHALOTH	CHEAPEN	*CHIPPER	CIBOULE	CLASPER
CAVIARE	*CHALUTZ	CHEAPIE	*CHIPPIE	*CICHLID	CLASSER
CAVILER	*CHAMADE	*CHEAPLY	CHIRPER	CICOREE	CLASSES
CAYENNE	*CHAMBER	CHEATER	CHIRRUP	CIGARET	CLASSIC
*CAZIQUE	*CHAMFER	*CHECKER	CHITLIN	CILIARY	CLASSIS
CEDILLA	CHAMISE	*CHECKUP	CHITTER	CLIATE	CLASTIC
CEILING	CHAMISO	CHEDDAR	*CHIVARI	CINDERY	CLATTER
CELADON	CHAMOIS	CHEDITE	*CHLAMYS	CINEAST	CLAUCHT
CELESTA	*CHAMPAC	CHEEPER	CHLORAL	CINEOLE	CLAUGHT
CELESTE	*CHAMPAK	CHEERER	CHLORIC	CINERIN	CLAVATE
CELLIST	*CHAMPER	CHEERIO	CHLORID	*CIPHONY	CLAVIER
CELLULE	CHANCEL	*CHEERLY	CHLORIN	CIPOLIN	*CLAYISH
CELOSIA	CHANCRE	*CHEETAH	*CHOKING	CIRCLER	CLAYPAN
CEMBALO	CHANGER	*CHEFDOM	CHOLATE	CIRCLET	CLEANER
CENACLE	CHANNEL	CHELATE	CHOLENT	CIRCUIT	CLEANLY
CENSUAL	CHANSON	CHELOID	CHOLERA	CIRRATE	CLEANSE
CENSURE	CHANTER	CHEMISE	CHOLINE	CIRROSE	CLEANUP
CENTARE	*CHANTEY	*CHEMISM	*CHOMPER	CIRROUS	CLEARER
CENTAUR	CHANTOR	CHEMIST	CHOOSER	CIRSOID	CLEARLY
CENTAVO	*CHANTRY	*CHEQUER	*CHOOSEY	CISSOID	CLEAVER
CENTILE	CHAPATI	*CHERISH	CHOPINE	CISTERN	CLEMENT
CENTIME	CHAPEAU	CHEROOT	*CHOPPED	CISTRON	CLERISY
CENTIMO	CHAPLET	*CHERVIL	*CHOPPER	CITABLE	*CLERKLY

*CLICKER	*COCKILY	COLLIES	CONCAVE	CONTENT	CORNUTE
CLIMATE	*COCKISH	COLLINS	CONCEAL	CONTEST	CORNUTO
CLIMBER	*COCKNEY	COLLOID	CONCEDE	*CONTEXT	COROLLA
CLINGER	*COCKPIT	COLLUDE	CONCEIT	CONTORT	CORONAL
CLINKER	*COCKSHY	COLOBUS	CONCENT	CONTOUR	CORONEL
CLIPPER	COCOMAT	COLOGNE	CONCEPT	CONTROL	CORONER
*CLIQUEY	COCONUT	COLONEL	CONCERN	CONTUSE	CORONET
CLIVERS	COCOTTE	COLONIC	CONCERT	CONVECT	CORPORA
CLOBBER	*COCOYAM	COLONUS	CONCHIE	CONVENE	CORRADE
*CLOCKER	CODABLE	COLORED	CONCISE	CONVENT	CORRECT
CLOGGER	CODDING	COLORER	CONCOCT	CONVERT	CORRIDA
CLONING	CODDLER	COLUMEL	CONCORD	CONVICT	CORRODE
CLONISM	CODEINA	*COMAKER	CONCUSS	*CONVOKE	CORRODY
CLOSEST	CODEINE	COMATIC	CONDEMN	*COOKERY	CORRUPT
CLOSING	*CODFISH	*COMATIK	CONDIGN	COOKIES	CORSAGE
CLOSURE	CODICES	COMBINE	CONDOLE	COOKING	CORSAIR
CLOTTED	CODICIL	COMBUST	CONDONE	COOKOUT	CORSLET
CLOTURE	CODLING	COMEDIC	CONDUCE	*COOKTOP	CORTEGE
CLOUTER	CODRIVE	COMETIC	CONDUCT	COOLANT	CORULER
CLOWDER	COELIAC	COMFIER	CONDUIT	COOLIES	CORVINA
CLUBBER	COELOME	COMFORT	CONDYLE	COOLISH	CORVINE
CLUBMAN	COENACT	*COMFREY	CONFECT	COONCAN	COSIEST
CLUMBER	COENURE	COMICAL	CONFESS	COONTIE	COSMISM
CLUNKER	*COEQUAL	COMITIA	CONFIDE	COOPERY	COSMIST
CLUPEID	COERCER	COMMAND	CONFINE	COPAIBA	*COSSACK
CLUSTER	COERECT	COMMATA	CONFIRM	COPEPOD	COSTARD
*CLUTCHY	COESITE	COMMEND	*CONFLUX	COPIHUE	COSTATE
CLUTTER	*COEXERT	COMMENT	CONFORM	COPILOT	COSTIVE
CLYPEUS	*COEXIST	COMMIES	CONFUSE	COPIOUS	COSTREL
CLYSTER	*COFFRET	COMMODE	CONFUTE	*COPPERY	COSTUME
COACHER	COFOUND	*COMMOVE	CONGEAL	*COPPICE	COTERIE
COACTOR	*COGENCY	COMMUNE	CONGEST	COPPING	COTHURN
COAEVAL	COGGING	COMMUTE	CONGIUS	*COPYBOY	COTIDAL
COAGENT	COGNATE	*COMPACT	CONICAL	*COPYCAT	COTTAGE
COALBIN	COGNISE	*COMPANY	CONIFER	COPYIST	COTTIER
*COALBOX	*COGNIZE	COMPARE	CONIINE	*COQUINA	COTTONY
COALIER	COHABIT	COMPART	*CONJOIN	*COQUITO	COUCHER
*COALIFY	COHERER	COMPASS	*CONJURE	CORACLE	COUGHER
COALPIT	COINAGE	COMPEER	CONNATE	CORANTO	COULDST
COAMING	COINFER	COMPEND	CONNECT	CORBEIL	COULOIR
*COANNEX	COINTER	COMPERE	CONNING	CORBINA	COULOMB
COARSEN	COITION	COMPETE	CONNIVE	CORDAGE	COULTER
COASTAL	COLDISH	COMPILE	CONNOTE	CORDATE	COUNCIL
COASTER	COLICIN	*COMPLEX	*CONQUER	CORDIAL	COUNSEL
COATING	*COLICKY	COMPLIN	CONSENT	CORDING	COUNTER
*COAXIAL	COLITIS	COMPLOT	CONSIGN	CORDOBA	COUNTRY
COBBIER	COLLAGE	COMPONE	CONSIST	COREIGN	COUPLER
COBBLER	COLLARD	*COMPONY	CONSOLE	CORKAGE	COUPLET
COCAINE	COLLATE	COMPORT	CONSORT	CORKIER	COURAGE
COCCOID	COLLECT	COMPOSE	CONSULT	CORNCOB	COURANT
COCHAIR	COLLEEN	COMPOST	CONSUME	CORNFED	COURIER
COCHLEA	COLLEGE	COMPOTE	CONTACT	CORNICE	COURLAN
*COCKADE	COLLIDE	COMPUTE	CONTAIN	CORNIER	*COURSEP
*COCKEYE	COLLIED	COMRADE	CONTEMN	CORNILY	COURTER
*COCKIER	COLLIER	CONATUS	CONTEND	CORNROW	COURTLY

COUTEAU	CRAWLER	CROWDER	CULTURE	CUTLERY	*CACHEPOT
COUTHIE	CREAMER	CROWDIE	CULVERT	CUTLINE	*CACHEXIA
COUTURE	CREASER	CROWNER	CUMARIN	CUTOVER	*CACHUCHA
COUVADE	CREATIN	CROWNET	*CUMQUAT	CUTTAGE	*CACOMIXL
COVERER	CREATOR	*CROZIER	*CUMSHAW	CUTTIES	CADASTER
COVERUP	CREDENT	CRUCIAL	CUMULUS	CUTTING	CADASTRE
COVETER	CREEPER	CRUCIAN	CUNEATE	*CUTWORK	CADUCEUS
COWBANE	CREEPIE	*CRUCIFY	CUNNING	CUTWORM	*CADUCITY
COWBELL	CREMATE	CRUDITY	*CUPCAKE	CUVETTE	CADUCOUS
*COWBIND	CRENATE	CRUELTY	CUPELER	CYANATE	*CAFFEINE
*COWBIRD	CREOSOL	CRUISER	*CUPLIKE	CYANIDE	CAGELING
*COWEDLY	CRESSET	CRULLER	CUPPING	CYANINE	CAGINESS
*COWFISH	CRESTAL	CRUMBER	CUPRITE	CYANITE	*CAJOLERY
*COWFLAP	CREVICE	CRUMBLE	CUPROUS	CYCASIN	*CAJOLING
*COWFLOP	CREWMAN	*CRUMBLY	CUPSFUL	CYCLASE	*CAKEWALK
COWGIRL	CRIBBER	*CRUMBUM	CUPULAR	*CYCLERY	*CALABASH
*COWHAGE	*CRICKET	CRUMMIE	CURABLE	*CYCLING	CALADIUM
*COWHAND	*CRICKEY	CRUMPET	CURACAO	CYCLIST	CALAMARI
*COWHERD	CRICOID	CRUMPLE	CURACOA	*CYCLIZE	*CALAMARY
*COWHIDE	CRIMMER	*CRUMPLY	CURATOR	*CYCLOID	CALAMINE
COWIEST	CRIMPER	*CRUNCHY	CURBING	CYCLONE	CALAMINT
*COWLICK	CRIMPLE	CRUNODE	CURCUMA	*CYCLOPS	CALAMITE
COWLING	CRIMSON	CRUPPER	CURDIER	*CYMLING	*CALAMITY
*COWPLOP	CRINGER	CRUSADE	CURDLER	CYNICAL	CALATHOS
*COWPOKE	CRINGLE	CRUSADO	CURETTE	CYPRESS	CALATHUS
COWRITE	CRINITE	CRUSHER	CURIOSA	CYPRIAN	CALCANEA
*COWSHED	CRINKLE	CRUSILY	CURIOUS	CYPSELA	CALCANEI
*COWSKIN	*CRINKLY	CRUSTAL	CURLING	CYSTEIN	CALCEATE
COWSLIP	CRINOID	*CRUZADO	CURRACH	CYSTINE	*CALCIFIC
*COXALGY	CRIOLLO	*CRYBABY	CURRAGH	CYSTOID	CALCSPAR
*COXCOMB	CRIPPLE	CRYOGEN	CURRANT	*CZARDAS	*CALCTUFA
COYNESS	CRISPEN	*CRYPTIC	CURRENT	*CZARDOM	*CALCTUFF
*COZENER	CRISPER	CRYSTAL	CURRIED	*CZARINA	CALCULUS
*COZIEST	CRISPLY	CTENOID	CURRIER	*CZARISM	CALDARIA
CRABBER	CRISSUM	*CUBBISH	CURRISH	*CZARIST	CALENDAL
*CRACKER	CRITTER	CUBICAL	CURSING	CABALISM	CALENDAR
*CRACKLE	CRITTUR	CUBICLE	CURSIVE	CABALIST	CALENDER
*CRACKLY	CROAKER	*CUBICLY	CURSORY	CABALLED	*CALFSKIN
*CRACKUP	CROCEIN	*CUCKOLD	CURTAIL	*CABBALAH	CALIFATE
CRADLER	CROCHET	CUDBEAR	CURTAIN	CABERNET	*CALIPASH
CRAMMED	CROCINE	CUDDIES	CURTATE	CABESTRO	CALISAYA
CRAMMER	*CROCKET	CUDDLER	CURTESY	*CABEZONE	CALLALOO
CRAMPIT	CROFTER	CUDWEED	CURVING	*CABLEWAY	*CALLBACK
CRAMPON	CROOKED	CUIRASS	CUSHIER	*CABOCHED	CALLIOPE
CRANIAL	CROONER	CUISINE	*CUSHILY	*CABOCHON	CALLIPEE
CRANING	CROPPED	CUITTLE	CUSHION	CABOODLE	CALLIPER
CRANIUM	CROPPER	CULICID	CUSTARD	*CABOSHED	CALMNESS
CRANKLE	CROPPIE	CULLIED	CUSTODY	CABOTAGE	*CALORIZE
*CRANKLY	*CROQUET	CULLIES	*CUTAWAY	CABRESTA	*CALOTYPE
CRANNOG	*CROQUIS	CULLION	*CUTBACK	CABRESTO	*CALTHROP
CRAPPIE	CROSIER	CULOTTE	*CUTBANK	CABRETTA	CALUTRON
CRASHER	CROSSER	CULPRIT	CUTDOWN	CABRILLA	CALVADOS
CRAUNCH	CROSSLY	CULTISH	CUTESIE	CABRIOLE	CALVARIA
CRAVING	CROUTON	CULTISM	CUTICLE	CABSTAND	*CALYCATE
CRAWDAD	CROWBAR	CULTIST	CUTLASS	*CACHALOT	*CALYCEAL

*CALYCINE	*CAPACITY	CARINATE	CATEGORY	CENTRIST	*CHARCOAL
*CALYCULI	*CAPESKIN	*CARMAKER	CATENARY	CENTROID	CHARIEST
*CALYPTER	*CAPEWORK	CARNAUBA	CATENATE	CENTUPLE	*CHARISMA
*CALYPTRA	CAPITATE	CARNIVAL	CATENOID	*CEPHALAD	*CHARLADY
*CAMBOGIA	CAPITULA	CAROLLED	CATERESS	*CEPHALIC	*CHARLOCK
CAMELEER	*CAPMAKER	CAROTENE	*CATFIGHT	*CEPHALIN	*CHARMING
CAMELLIA	CAPONATA	CAROUSAL	CATHEDRA	CERAMIST	CHARRIER
CAMISADE	CAPONIER	CAROUSEL	CATHETER	CERASTES	CHARRING
CAMISADO	*CAPONIZE	CAROUSER	*CATHEXIS	CERATOID	CHARTIST
CAMISOLE	*CAPRICCI	CARRIAGE	*CATHOLIC	CERCARIA	CHASSEUR
CAMOMILE	*CAPRIFIG	CARRIOLE	CATHOUSE	CEREBRAL	CHASTISE
*CAMPAGNA	CAPRIOLE	*CARRITCH	CATNAPER	CEREBRUM	*CHASTITY
*CAMPAIGN	CAPSICIN	CARROTIN	CATTIEST	CEREMENT	*CHASUBLE
*CAMPFIRE	*CAPSICUM	CARRYALL	CATTLEYA	*CEREMONY	*CHATCHKA
*CAMPHENE	CAPSOMER	CARRYOUT	CAUDATED	CERNUOUS	*CHATCHKE
*CAMPHINE	CAPSTONE	CARTLOAD	CAUDILLO	*CEROTYPE	CHATTING
CAMPIEST	CAPSULAR	CARTOONY	CAULDRON	CERULEAN	*CHAUFFER
CAMPOREE	CAPTIOUS	*CARTOUCH	CAULICLE	CERUSITE	CHAUNTER
CAMPSITE	CAPTURER	CARUNCLE	*CAULKING	CERVELAS	CHAUSSES
*CAMSHAFT	*CAPUCHIN	*CARYATIC	CAUSABLE	CERVELAT	*CHEAPISH
CANAILLE	*CAPYBARA	CARYATID	CAUSALLY	*CERVICAL	*CHECHAKO
CANALISE	CARABINE	CARYOTIN	CAUSERIE	CESAREAN	*CHECKOFF
*CANALIZE	CARACARA	CASCABEL	*CAUSEWAY	CESARIAN	*CHECKOUT
CANALLED	CARACOLE	CASCABLE	CAUTIOUS	CESSPOOL	*CHECKROW
CANALLER	CARAGANA	*CASEBOOK	CAVALERO	CETACEAN	*CHEDDITE
CANCELER	CARAGEEN	CASELOAD	CAVALIER	CETOLOGY	*CHEEKFUL
CANCROID	CARANGID	CASEMATE	CAVATINA	*CHACONNE	*CHEERFUL
*CANDIDLY	CARAPACE	CASEMENT	CAVEATOR	*CHADARIM	CHEERIER
*CANEPHOR	CARASSOW	*CASEWORK	CAVEFISH	*CHAINMAN	*CHEERILY
CANEWARE	*CARBAMIC	*CASEWORM	*CAVELIKE	*CHAINSAW	CHEERLED
CANFIELD	*CARBAMYL	*CASHBOOK	*CAVICORN	*CHAIRMAN	CHELATOR
CANINITY	*CARBARYL	CASHLESS	CAVILLER	*CHALAZIA	*CHELIPED
CANISTER	CARBINOL	*CASHMERE	*CAVITARY	CHALDRON	*CHEMICAL
CANITIES	CARBOLIC	CASIMERE	CAVITATE	CHALLIES	*CHEMURGY
CANNABIC	*CARBONYL	CASIMIRE	CAVORTER	*CHALLOTH	CHENILLE
CANNABIN	*CARBOXYL	CASSETTE	CEINTURE	*CHAMBRAY	*CHENOPOD
CANNABIS	CARBURET	CASTANET	CELERIAC	*CHAMFRON	*CHESSMAN
CANNELON	*CARCAJOU	*CASTAWAY	CELERITY	*CHAMPION	*CHESTFUL
CANNIBAL	CARCANET	CASTEISM	*CELIBACY	*CHANCERY	CHESTNUT
CANNIEST	*CARDAMOM	CASTRATE	CELIBATE	*CHANCIER	*CHEVALET
CANNIKIN	CARDAMON	CASTRATO	CELLARER	*CHANCILY	*CHEVERON
CANNONRY	*CARDAMUM	CASUALLY	CELLARET	CHANDLER	*CHIASMUS
CANOEIST	CARDCASE	CASUALTY	CELLMATE	*CHANFRON	*CHICANER
CANONESS	CARDIGAN	*CATACOMB	CELLULAR	CHANTAGE	*CHICCORY
CANONISE	CARDINAL	CATALASE	CEMENTER	CHANTIES	*CHICKORY
CANONIST	CARDIOID	CATALYST	CEMENTUM	*CHAPATTI	*CHICKPEA
*CANONIZE	CARDITIS	*CATALYZE	*CEMETERY	*CHAPBOOK	*CHICNESS
CANOODLE	CAREENER	CATAMITE	CENOBITE	*CHAPERON	*CHIEFDOM
CANOROUS	CAREERER	CATAPULT	*CENOTAPH	*CHAPITER	CHIGETAI
CANTICLE	CAREFREE	CATARACT	CENSURER	*CHAPLAIN	*CHILDBED
CANTONAL	CARELESS	CATBRIER	CENTAURY	*CHAPPATI	*CHILDING
CANTRAIP	CARESSER	*CATCHALL	CENTESIS	*CHAPPING	*CHILDISH
CANULATE	CARETAKE	*CATCHFLY	CENTIARE	*CHAQUETA	*CHILIASM
CANVASER	CAREWORN	*CATECHIN	CENTRING	*CHARACID	CHILIAST
*CANZONET	CARILLON	*CATECHOL	CENTRISM	*CHARACIN	*CHILIDOG

*CHILOPOD	*CHUCKLER	*CLASSIFY	*COACHMAN	*COEFFECT	COLLIDER
*CHIMAERA	*CHUGALUG	CLASSILY	COACTION	*COEMBODY	COLLIERY
*CHIMBLEY	*CHUMSHIP	CLASSISM	*COACTIVE	*COEMPLOY	COLLOGUE
*CHIMERIC	*CHURCHLY	CLASSIST	COADMIRE	COENAMOR	*COLLOQUY
*CHINBONE	CHURNING	CLATTERY	*COAGENCY	COENDURE	COLLUDER
CHINLESS	*CHUTZPAH	CLAUSTRA	COAGULUM	COENURUS	COLLUVIA
CHINNING	*CHYMOSIN	*CLAVICLE	COALESCE	*COENZYME	COLLYRIA
*CHIPMUCK	CIBORIUM	CLAWLESS	*COALFISH	*COEQUATE	COLOBOMA
*CHIPMUNK	*CICATRIX	*CLAWLIKE	COALHOLE	COERCION	COLOCATE
*CHIPPING	CICERONE	*CLAYBANK	COALIEST	*COERCIVE	COLONIAL
CHISELER	CICISBEO	*CLAYLIKE	COALLESS	*COEVALLY	COLONISE
*CHITCHAT	CILANTRO	*CLAYMORE	*COALSACK	*COEVOLVE	COLONIST
CHITLING	CILIATED	*CLAYWARE	COALSHED	*COEXTEND	COLONIZE
CHITOSAN	*CIMBALOM	CLEANSER	COALYARD	*COFACTOR	*COLOPHON
*CHIVALRY	*CINCHONA	CLEARING	*COANCHOR	COGITATE	COLORADO
*CHIVAREE	CINCTURE	CLEAVAGE	COAPPEAR	*COGNIZER	COLORANT
*CHLOASMA	CINEASTE	CLEIDOIC	COASSIST	COGNOMEN	COLORFUL
CHLORATE	CINERARY	CLEMATIS	COASSUME	COGNOVIT	COLORING
CHLORDAN	CINGULUM	*CLEMENCY	COASTING	*COGWHEEL	COLORISM
CHLORIDE	CINNABAR	*CLENCHER	COATLESS	COHERENT	COLORIST
CHLORINE	CINNAMON	CLERICAL	*COATRACK	COHERING	*COLORIZE
CHLORITE	*CINNAMYL	*CLERIHEW	COATROOM	COHESION	COLORMAN
CHLOROUS	*CINQUAIN	*CLERKDOM	COATTAIL	*COHOBATE	COLOSSAL
*CHOCKFUL	CIOPPINO	*CLERKISH	COATTEND	COHOLDER	COLOSSUS
*CHOIRBOY	CIRCLING	CLEVEITE	COATTEST	*COIFFEUR	*COLOTOMY
*CHOLERIC	*CIRCUITY	CLINALLY	COAUTHOR	*COIFFURE	COLOURER
CHOOSING	CIRCULAR	*CLINCHER	COBBIEST	COINCIDE	COLPITIS
*CHOPPING	CIRRIPED	*CLIPPING	*COBWEBBY	COINHERE	COLUBRID
CHORAGUS	CISLUNAR	*CLIQUISH	*COCCIDIA	COINMATE	*COLUMBIC
*CHORALLY	CISTERNA	CLITELLA	COCINERA	COINSURE	COMANAGE
CHORDATE	CITATION	CLITORIS	*COCKAPOO	COINVENT	COMATOSE
CHOREGUS	CITEABLE	*CLOCHARD	*COCKATOO	COISTREL	COMATULA
*CHOREMAN	CITREOUS	CLODPATE	*COCKBILL	COISTRIL	COMBATER
CHOREOID	*CITYFIED	CLODPOLE	*COCKBOAT	*COKEHEAD	COMBINER
*CHORIAMB	*CITYWARD	CLODPOLL	*COCKCROW	COLANDER	*COMBINGS
CHORIOID	*CITYWIDE	CLOISTER	*COCKEREL	*COLDCOCK	*COMBLIKE
CHORTLER	*CIVICISM	CLOSEOUT	*COCKIEST	COLDNESS	*COMEBACK
CHOUSING	CIVILIAN	CLOTHIER	*COCKLIKE	COLEADER	COMEDIAN
*CHOWCHOW	CIVILISE	CLOTHING	*COCKLOFT	COLESEED	COMEDIES
*CHOWTIME	*CIVILITY	CLOTTING	*COCKSHUT	COLESLAW	*COMEDOWN
CHRESARD	*CIVILIZE	CLOUDLET	*COCKSPUR	COLESSEE	*COMEMBER
*CHRISMON	CLADDING	*CLOWNERY	*COCKSURE	COLESSOR	*COMETHER
CHRISTEN	CLAIMANT	*CLOWNISH	*COCKTAIL	COLEWORT	*COMFIEST
CHRISTIE	*CLAMBAKE	CLUBABLE	COCOBOLO	COLICINE	COMINGLE
*CHROMATE	*CLAMMING	*CLUBBING	COCREATE	*COLIFORM	*COMMANDO
*CHROMIDE	CLAMORER	*CLUBBISH	*CODEBOOK	COLINEAR	*COMMENCE
*CHROMING	*CLAMWORM	*CLUBFOOT	CODEBTOR	COLINIES	*COMMERCE
*CHROMITE	CLANGOUR	*CLUBHAND	CODELESS	COLISEUM	COMMONER
*CHROMIUM	CLANNISH	*CLUBHAUL	CODERIVE	COLISTIN	*COMMONLY
*CHROMIZE	CLANSMAN	CLUBROOT	CODESIGN	COLLAGEN	COMMUNAL
*CHROMOUS	CLAPTRAP	CLUELESS	CODIFIER	COLLAPSE	COMMUTER
*CHRONAXY	CLARENCE	*CLUMPISH	CODIRECT	COLLARET	*COMPADRE
*CHTHONIC	CLARINET	CLUPEOID	*CODPIECE	COLLATOR	COMPARER
*CHUBASCO	CLASSICO	CLUSTERY	CODRIVER	COLLEGER	COMPILER
*CHUCKIES	CLASSIER	CLUTTERY	COEDITOR	COLLEGIA	COMPLAIN

COMPLEAT	*CONQUEST	*COPYHOLD	*COSTMARY	CRANKOUS	*CRONYISM
*COMPLECT	*CONQUIAN	*COPYREAD	COSTUMER	*CRANKPIN	*CROOKERY
COMPLETE	CONSERVE	*COQUETRY	*COSTUMEY	CRANNIED	CROPLAND
*COMPLICE	CONSIDER	*COQUETTE	COTENANT	CRANNIES	CROPLESS
*COMPLIED	CONSOLER	*COQUILLE	COTHURNI	CRANNOGE	*CROPPING
COMPLIER	CONSOMME	CORACOID	COTILLON	*CRAPPING	CROSSARM
COMPLIES	CONSPIRE	CORDELLE	*COTQUEAN	*CRAVENLY	CROSSBAR
COMPLINE	CONSTANT	CORDLESS	COTTAGER	*CRAWFISH	*CROSSBOW
COMPOSER	CONSTRUE	*CORDLIKE	COTYLOID	*CRAWLWAY	CROSSCUT
*COMPOUND	CONSUMER	CORDOVAN	*COUCHANT	*CRAYFISH	CROSSING
COMPRESS	CONTAGIA	CORDUROY	*COUCHING	*CREAMERY	CROSSLET
COMPRISE	CONTEMPT	CORDWAIN	COULDEST	CREATINE	CROSSTIE
*COMPRIZE	CONTINUA	*CORDWOOD	COULISSE	CREATION	*CROSSWAY
COMPUTER	CONTINUE	COREDEEM	COUMARIN	CREATIVE	*CROTCHET
CONATION	CONTINUO	CORELATE	COUMAROU	CREATURE	CROUPIER
CONCEDER	CONTRACT	CORELESS	COUNTESS	CREDENCE	CROUPOUS
*CONCEIVE	CONTRAIL	COREMIUM	COUNTIAN	CREDENDA	*CROWFOOT
CONCERTO	CONTRARY	CORKIEST	COUPLING	*CREDENZA	*CROWSTEP
*CONCHOID	CONTRAST	*CORKLIKE	COURANTE	CREDIBLE	CRUCIATE
*CONCLAVE	CONTRITE	*CORKWOOD	COURANTO	CREDITOR	CRUCIBLE
CONCLUDE	CONTRIVE	CORNBALL	COURSING	CREEPAGE	*CRUCIFER
CONCRETE	CONVENER	*CORNCAKE	COURTESY	CREMAINS	*CRUCIFIX
CONDENSE	CONVENOR	CORNCRIB	COURTIER	CREMATOR	CRUDITES
CONDOLER	CONVERGE	CORNEOUS	COUSCOUS	CRENATED	CRUISING
CONDONER	CONVERSE	*CORNETCY	COUSINRY	CRENELLE	CRUMBIER
CONDUCER	*CONVEXLY	*CORNHUSK	COVALENT	CREODONT	*CRUMHORN
CONELRAD	*CONVEYER	*CORNICHE	COVENANT	CREOLISE	*CRUNCHER
CONENOSE	*CONVEYOR	CORNICLE	COVERAGE	*CREOLIZE	CRUSADER
CONEPATE	*CONVINCE	CORNIEST	COVERALL	CREOSOTE	CRUSTOSE
CONEPATL	*CONVOKER	CORNMEAL	COVERING	CRESCENT	*CRUZEIRO
CONFEREE	*CONVOLVE	CORNPONE	COVERLET	*CRESCIVE	*CRYOGENY
*CONFERVA	CONVULSE	CORNUTED	COVERLID	CRESTING	CRYOLITE
CONFETTO	COOINGLY	*CORONACH	*COVERTLY	*CRESYLIC	*CRYONICS
CONFIDER	*COOKBOOK	CORONARY	COVETOUS	CRETONNE	CRYOSTAT
CONFINER	COOKLESS	CORONATE	*COWARDLY	CREVALLE	CRYOTRON
CONFLATE	*COOKSHOP	CORONOID	*COWBERRY	CREVASSE	CTENIDIA
*CONFLICT	*COOKWARE	COROTATE	COWINNER	CREWLESS	CUBATURE
*CONFOCAL	COOLDOWN	CORPORAL	*COWORKER	*CREWMATE	*CUBICITY
CONFOUND	COOLNESS	CORPSMAN	*COXALGIA	*CREWNECK	CUBICULA
CONFRERE	COONSKIN	CORRIDOR	*COXSWAIN	*CRIBBAGE	*CUBIFORM
CONFRONT	COOPTION	CORRIVAL	*COZENAGE	*CRIBBING	*CUCUMBER
CONFUTER	COPARENT	CORSELET	*COZINESS	*CRIBBLED	CUCURBIT
CONGENER	COPASTOR	CORSETRY	CRABMEAT	CRIBROUS	CUDGELER
CONGLOBE	COPATRON	CORTISOL	*CRABWISE	*CRIBWORK	*CUFFLESS
CONGRATS	COPEMATE	CORUNDUM	*CRACKING	CRICETID	CULICINE
CONGRESS	COPLANAR	CORVETTE	*CRACKNEL	CRIMINAL	CULINARY
*CONICITY	*COPPERAH	*CORYBANT	*CRACKPOT	CRIPPLER	CULPABLE
CONIDIUM	COPPERAS	*CORYPHEE	CRAGSMAN	CRISPATE	CULTIGEN
CONIOSIS	COPREMIA	COSCRIPT	*CRAMMING	CRISTATE	CULTIVAR
*CONJUGAL	COPRINCE	COSECANT	*CRAMOISY	CRITERIA	CULTRATE
*CONJUNCT	COPULATE	COSIGNER	CRAMPOON	*CRITIQUE	CULTURAL
*CONJURER	*COPURIFY	COSINESS	CRANIATE	CROCEINE	CULVERIN
*CONJUROR	*COPYBOOK	COSMETIC	CRANKIER	*CROCKERY	CUMBERER
CONNIVER	*COPYDESK	COSMICAL	*CRANKILY	CROCOITE	CUMBROUS
CONODONT	*COPYEDIT	COSTLESS	*CRANKISH	*CROMLECH	CUMULATE

CUNEATED	*CYMOGENE	S C OFF	BA CKER	DE CKER	*JI CAMA
CUNEATIC	*CYNICISM	S C OLD	*BA CKUP	DE CKLE	*JO CKEY
*CUNIFORM	CYNOSURE	S C ONE	BE CALM	DE COCT	*JO COSE
*CUPBOARD	*CYPRINID	S C OOP	BE CAME	DE CODE	*JO CUND
CUPELLER	CYSTEINE	S C OOT	BE CKET	DE CREE	*KE CKLE
*CUPIDITY	CYSTITIS	S C OPE	BE CKON	DE CURY	*KI CKER
CUPREOUS	CYTASTER	S C ORE	BE CLOG	DI CAST	*KI CKUP
CUPULATE	CYTIDINE	S C ORN	BE COME	DI CIER	*KU CHEN
CURARINE	*CYTOGENY	S C OUR	BI CARB	DI CING	LA CHES
*CURARIZE	*CYTOKINE	S C OUT	BI CEPS	DI CKER	LA CIER
CURASSOW	*CYTOLOGY	S C OWL	BI CKER	*DI CKEY	LA CILY
CURATIVE	CYTOSINE	S C RAG	BI CORN	DI CKIE	LA CING
CURBSIDE	*CZAREVNA	S C RAM	BI CRON	DI CTUM	LA CKER
CURCULIO	*CZARITZA	S C RAP	BO C CIA	DO CENT	*LA CKEY
CURDIEST		S C REE	BO C CIE	DO CILE	LA CTAM
CURELESS		S C REW	BU C CAL	DO CKER	LA CTIC
CURLICUE	S CAB	S C RIM	BU CKER	DO CKET	LA CUNA
*CURLYCUE	S CAD	S C RIP	BU CKET	DO CTOR	LA CUNE
*CURRENCY	S CAG	S C ROD	BU CKLE	DU CKER	LE CHER
CURRICLE	S CAM	S C RUB	BU CKRA	DU CKIE	LE CTIN
CURRIERY	S CAN	S C RUM	CA CHET	DU CTAL	LE CTOR
CURRYING	S CAR	S CUBA	CA CHOU	FA CADE	LI CHEE
*CURTALAX	S CAT	S CUDO	CA CKLE	FA CETE	LI CHEN
CURTNESS	S COP	S CUFF	CA CTUS	FA CEUP	LI CKER
CUSHIEST	S COT	S CULK	CI CADA	FA CIAL	LI CTOR
*CUSHIONY	S COW	S CULL	CI CALA	FA CIES	LO CALE
CUSPIDAL	S CUD	S CULP	CI CELY	FA CILE	LO CATE
CUSPIDOR	S CUM	S CURF	CI CERO	FA CING	LO CHAN
CUSSEDLY	S CUP	S CUTA	CO CAIN	FA CTOR	LO CHIA
CUSSWORD	S CUT	S CUTE	COC CAL	FA CULA	LO CKER
CUSTODES	S CALD	S CENIC	COC CIC	FE CIAL	LO CKET
CUSTOMER	S CALE	S CALDIC	COC CID	*FE CKLY	LO CKUP
CUSTUMAL	S CALL	S CEPTIC	COC CUS	FE CUND	LO CULE
*CUTCHERY	S CALP	S CIATIC	*CO C CYX	*FI CKLE	LO CUST
CUTENESS	S CALY	YE CH	CO CHIN	FU COID	LU CENT
CUTGRASS	S CAMP	YO CK	CO CKER	FU COSE	LU CERN
CUTICULA	S CANT	YU CA	CO CKLE	FU COUS	LU CKIE
CUTINISE	S CAPE	YU CH	*CO CKUP	*HA CKEE	LY CEUM
*CUTINIZE	S CARE	YU CK	CU CKOO	*HA CKER	LY CHEE
CUTPURSE	S CARF	DE CAF	CY CLER	*HA CKIE	*MI CKEY
CUTTABLE	S CARP	DI CTY	*CY CLIC	*HA CKLE	*MO CKUP
CUTWATER	S CART	FI CUS	DA CKER	*HA CKLY	MU CLUC
*CYANAMID	S CARY	*KI CKY	DA COIT	*HE CKLE	NA CHAS
CYANOGEN	S CATT	MA CON	DA CTYL	HE CTIC	NA CHES
CYANOSIS	S CAUP	MI CHE	DE CADE	HE CTOR	NE CKER
*CYCLAMEN	S CAUR	NA CHO	DE CAMP	*HI C CUP	NE CTAR
*CYCLECAR	S CENA	NI CAD	DE CANE	*HI CKEY	NI CETY
*CYCLICAL	S CEND	RE C CE	DE CANT	*HO CKER	NI CKEL
*CYCLITOL	S CENE	SI CKO	DE CARE	*HO CKEY	NI CKER
CYLINDER	S CENT	SO CKO	DE CEIT	*HO CKEY	NI CKLE
*CYMATIUM	S CHAV	WA CKO	DE CENT	*HU CKLE	NO CENT
*CYMBALER	S CHMO	*YE C CH	DE CERN	*JA CANA	NU CHAL
*CYMBALOM	S CHUL	*YE C HY	DE CIDE	*JA CKAL	NU CLEI
*CYMBIDIA	S CHWA	*YU C CH	DE CILE	*JA CKER	*PA CIFY
*CYMBLING	S CION	*YU CKY	DE CKEL	*JA CKET	PA CING

PA C KER	RE C TAL	TE C HIE	*BU C KLER	DE C LINE	*JA C INTH
PA C KET	RE C TOR	TE C TAL	*BU C KRAM	DE C ODER	*JA C KASS
*PA C KLY	RE C TUM	TE C TUM	*BU C KSAW	DE C OLOR	*JA C KDAW
PE C HAN	RE C TUS	TI C KER	BU C OLI C	DE C ORUM	*JA C KIES
PE C KER	RE C USE	TI C KET	*C A C HEXY	DE C OYER	*JA C KLEG
PE C TEN	RI C HEN	TI C TA C	*C A C HING	DE C REER	*JA C KPOT
PE C TIN	RI C HES	TI C TO C	*C A C IQUE	DE C RIAL	*JA C OBIN
PI CARA	RI C HLY	TI C KLE	*C A C KLER	DE C RIED	*JA C OBUS
PI CARO	RI C ING	TO C HER	*C A C ODYL	DE C RIER	*JA C ONET
*PI C KAX	*RI C KEY	TO C SIN	C I C OREE	DE C ROWN	*JO C ULAR
PI C KER	RI C RA C	TU C HUN	*C I C HLID	*DE C RYPT	*KA C HINA
PI C KET	RO C HET	TU C KER	C O C AINE	DE C UMAN	*KI C KIER
PI C KLE	RO C KER	TU C KET	C O C C OID	DE C UPLE	*KI C KOFF
*PI C KUP	RO C KET	TY C OON	C O C C OON	DE C URVE	LA C IEST
PI C NIC	RO C OCO	VA C ANT	C O C HAIR	DI C IEST	LA C ONI C
PI C RI C	RU C HED	VA C UUM	C O C HLEA	DI C KENS	*LA C QUER
PO C KET	RU C KLE	VE C TOR	*C O C KADE	DI C LINY	*LA C QUEY
PU C KER	RU C KUS	VI C ING	*C O C KEYE	DI C OTYL	LA C TARY
RA C EME	SA C BUT	VI C TIM	*C O C KIER	DI C TATE	LA C TASE
RA C HET	SA C HET	VI C TOR	*C O C KILY	DI C TIER	LA C TATE
RA C HIS	SA C KER	VI C UNA	*C O C KISH	DI C TION	LA C TEAL
RA C IAL	*SA C QUE	*WI C KER	*C O C KNEY	*DI C Y C LY	LA C TEAN
RA C IER	SA C RAL	*WI C KET	*C O C KPIT	DO C ETI C	LA C TONE
RA C ILY	SA C RED	*WI C OPY	*C O C KSHY	*DO C KAGE	LA C TOSE
RA C ING	SA C REM	*ZE C HIN	C O C OMAT	DU C HESS	LA C UNAR
RA C ISM	SA C RUM	BA CALAO	C O C ONUT	DU C KIER	*LE C HERY
RA C IST	SA C ULE	BA C CARA	C O C OTTE	DU C KIES	LE C TERN
RA C KER	SE C ANT	BA C CATE	*C O C OYAM	*DU C KPIN	LE C TION
RA C KET	SE C EDE	*BA C CHI C	*C U C KOLD	DU C TILE	LE C TURE
RA C KLE	SE C ERN	*BA C KFIT	C Y C ASIN	DU C TING	LI C EN C E
RA C OON	SE C OND	*BA C KHOE	C Y C LASE	DU C TULE	LI C ENTE
RE C ALL	SE C PAR	*BA C KING	*C Y C LERY	FA C IEND	LI C ENSE
RE C ANE	SE C RET	*BA C KLIT	*C Y C LING	FA C TION	*LI C HTLY
RE C ANT	SE C TOR	*BA C KLOG	C Y C LIST	FA C TOID	LI C KING
RE C AST	SE C UND	*BA C KOUT	*C Y C LIZE	*FA C TORY	LO C ALLY
RE C EDE	SE C URE	*BA C KSAW	C Y C LOID	FA C TUAL	LO C ATER
RE C ENT	SI C KEE	*BA C KSET	C Y C LONE	FA C TURE	LO C ATOR
RE C EPT	SI C KIE	BE C AUSE	*C Y C LOPS	*FA C ULTY	LO C KAGE
RE C ESS	SI C KLE	*BE C HALK	DA C OITY	FI C TILE	*LO C KBOX
RE C HEW	SI C KEN	*BE C HARM	DE C ALOG	FI C TION	LO C KNUT
RE C IPE	*SI C KLY	BE C LASP	DE C ANAL	*FI C TIVE	LO C KOUT
RE C ITE	SO C AGE	*BE C LOAK	DE C APOD	*FO C ALLY	*LO C KRAM
RE C KON	SO C C ER	BE C LOUD	DE C AYER	FO C USER	LO C OISM
RE C LAD	SO C IAL	*BE C LOWN	DE C EASE	*FU C HSIA	LO C ULAR
RE C OAL	SO C KET	BE C RAWL	DE C EIVE	*FU C HSIN	LO C ULUS
RE C OCK	SO C MAN	BE C RIME	*DE C EN C Y	*HA C HURE	LO C USTA
RE C ODE	SU C C AH	*BE C ROWD	DE C IARE	*HA C KBUT	LU C ARNE
RE C OIL	SU C C OR	BE C RUST	DE C IBEL	*HA C KLER	LU C EN C E
RE C OIN	SU C KER	BE C URSE	DE C IDER	*HA C KMAN	LU C ERNE
RE C OMB	SU C KLE	BI C OLOR	DE C IDUA	*HA C KNEY	LU C IFER
RE C OOK	TA C KER	BI C ORNE	DE C IMAL	*HA C KSAW	*LY C HNIS
RE C OPY	*TA C KEY	*BI C Y C LE	*DE C KING	HE C TARE	*MA C AQUE
RE C ORD	TA C KLE	*BU C KEEN	DE C LAIM	*HI C KORY	*MA C C HIA
RE C ORK	TA C TIC	*BU C KEYE	DE C LARE	*JA C AMAR	*MA C HZOR
RE C OUP	TE C HED	*BU C KISH	DE C LASS		

*MA C UMBA	PO C OSIN	SA C C ATE	TI C KING	*DU C KWALK	*ZE C C HINO
*MI C RIFY	PS C HENT	*SA C KBUT	TI C KLER	*DU C TWORK	*ZU C C HINI
*MI C ROHM	PU C C OON	*SA C KFUL	TO C C ATA	*FO CAC C IA	CRU C K
*MO C KERY	*PU C KERY	SA C KING	*VA C AN CY	*HI C COUGH	NAT C H
*MU C KIER	*PU C KISH	SA C LIKE	VA C C INA	*JA C KROLL	PIS C O
*MU C KILY	RA C C OON	SA C RING	VA C C INE	*JO C KETTE	RE C C E
*MY C OPOD	RA C EMIC	SA C RIST	*VA C UITY	*KI C KBALL	SPA C Y
NA C ELLE	*RA C EWAY	SE C EDER	VA C UOLE	*KI C KIEST	WRI C K
NE C KING	RA C IEST	SE C LUDE	VA C UOUS	*LE C YTHIS	*YE C C H
NE C KTIE	*RA C KETY	SE C ONDE	*VI C ARLY	*LO C KDOWN	*YUC C H
NE C ROSE	*RA C KFUL	SE C ONDO	*VI C EROY	MA C ARONI	BO C C IA
NE C TARY	*RA C QUET	SE C RECY	VI C INAL	MA C AROON	BO C C IE
NI C OTIN	RE C ARRY	SE C RETE	VI C IOUS	*MAC C ABAW	BU C C AL
NI C TATE	RE C EIPT	SE C TARY	VI C OMTE	*MAC CABOY	CAL C I C
NO C TUID	RE C EIVE	SE C TILE	*VI C TORY	*MAC COBOY	C OC C AL
NO C TULE	RE C ENCY	SE C TION	VI C TUAL	MA C ERATE	C OC C I C
NO C TURN	RE C HART	SE C ULAR	VI C UGNA	MA C RURAN	C OC C ID
NO C UOUS	RE C HEAT	SE C URER	VO C ABLE	MA C ULATE	C OC C US
NU C LEAL	*RE C HECK	*SI C KBAY	*VO C ABLY	*ME C HANIC	*C OC C YX
NU C LEAR	RE C ITAL	*SI C KBED	VO C ALIC	ME C ONIUM	FAL C ES
NU C LEIN	RE C ITER	*SI C KISH	*VO C ALLY	MI C ROBAR	FRA C TI
NU C LEON	RE C LAIM	SI C KOUT	VO C ODER	MI C ROBUS	GLU C AN
NU C LEUS	RE C LAME	SO C CAGE	*WI C KAPE	MI C RODOT	*HI C C UP
NU C LIDE	RE C LASP	SO C IETY	*WI C KING	MO C C ASIN	*KIM C HI
PA C HISI	RE C LEAN	*SO C KEYE	*WI C KIUP	*MUCHACHO	LOU C HE
*PA C HUCO	RE C LINE	*SO C KMAN	*WI C KYUP	MU C ILAGE	MUD C AT
*PA C IFIC	RE C LUSE	SU C C EED	YA C HTER	*NI C KELIC	PAS C AL
*PA C KAGE	RE C OLOR	SU C C ESS	*ZA C ATON	NU C LEOID	PRE C UT
*PA C KING	RE C OUNT	SU C C ORY	*ZE C C HIN	*PA C HALIC	REE C HY
*PA C KMAN	RE C OUPE	SU C C OTH	BA C C ARAT	*PA C HINKO	SIT C OM
*PA C KWAX	RE C OVER	SU C C OUR	*BA C C ATED	PE C CABLE	SO C C ER
PA C TION	RE C RATE	SU C C UBA	*BA C CHANT	*PEC CAN CY	SPA C EY
PE C CANT	RE C ROSS	*SU C C UMB	*BA C CHIUS	PE C ORINO	SU C C AH
*PE C CARY	RE C ROWN	SU C C USS	*BA C KBEAT	PI C IFORM	SU C C OR
*PE C CAVI	RE C RUIT	SU C KLER	*BA C KCAST	PI C OMOLE	*WHA C KO
*PE C KISH	*RE C TIFY	SU C RASE	*BA C KCHAT	*PY C NOSIS	*ZIN C I C
PE C TASE	RE C TORY	SU C ROSE	*BA C KDATE	*PY C NOTIC	BA C CARA
PE C TATE	RE C TRIX	SU C TION	*BA C KFLOW	RA C HILLA	BA C CATE
*PE C TIZE	RE C URVE	SY C OSIS	*BA C KHAUL	RE C AMIER	*BA C CHIC
*PI C ACHO	RE C USAL	TA C HISM	*BA C KLAND	*RE C YCLER	BAR C HAN
PI C ADOR	RE C YCLE	TA C HIST	*BA C KROOM	RO C AILLE	*BIO C HIP
PI C C OLO	RI C TUS	*TA C HYON	*BA C KRUSH	SA C CULAR	BOU C HEE
PI C EOUS	RI C INUS	TA C KIER	*BA C KWRAP	SA C C ULUS	*BOY C HIK
*PI C KAXE	RI C KETS	*TA C KIFY	BI C AUDAL	SE C ALOSE	C AT C LAW
*PI C KEER	*RI C KETY	*TA C KILY	*BI C YCLIC	SO C KLESS	C HI C ANO
*PI C KIER	RI C KSHA	TA C KLER	*C OC C IDIA	SU C C INCT	*C HI C KEE
*PI C KING	RI C OTTA	TA C NODE	*C OCKAPOO	SU C C INIC	C OA C TOR
*PI C KOFF	*RO C KABY	TA C TFUL	*DA C TYLIC	*SU C C INYL	C OC C OID
PI C OLIN	*RO C KERY	TA C TILE	DE C OUPLE	SU C C ORER	C OC C OON
PI C OTEE	RO C KIER	TA C TION	DE C URIES	SU C C UBUS	C ON C HIE
*PI C QUET	RO C KOON	TA C TUAL	*DI C HOTIC	*TA C HISME	*C RI C KEY
PI C RATE	RU C HING	TE C HNIC	*DI C HROIC	TE C TONIC	DEI C ING
PI C RITE	RU C TION	TE C TITE	DI C ROTIC	*TU C KSHOP	DEI C TIC
PI C TURE	SA C ATON	*TE C TRIX	DI C TIEST	*VA C CINEE	FRA C TAL
*PO C HARD	SA C C ADE		*DI C YCLIC	*VA C C INIA	FRA C TUS

KAT C INA	BER C EUSE	*CHA C ONNE	DIS C LAIM	GOL C ONDA	NAR C OSIS
*KEY C ARD	*BES C ORCH	*CHE C HAKO	*DIS C LIKE	GRA C EFUL	NAR C OTIC
*KIM C HEE	BES C REEN	*CHE C KOFF	DIS C LOSE	GRA C ILIS	NAS C ENCE
*MA C CHIA	BIA C ETYL	*CHE C KOUT	DIS C OLOR	GRA C IOSO	*NAS C ENCY
MAR C ATO	BIO C LEAN	*CHE C KROW	DIS C OUNT	GRA C IOUS	NES C IENT
*MAT C HUP	BIO C YCLE	*C HI C ANER	DIS C OVER	GUA C HARO	*NEW C OMER
MID C ULT	BIT C HERY	*CHI C CORY	DIS C REET	*HAT C HECK	NON C LING
MIS C ODE	*BLA C KCAP	*CHI C KORY	DIS C RETE	*HAT C HERY	NON C OLOR
NON C OLA	*BLA C KFIN	*CHI C KPEA	DIS C ROWN	*HAT C HING	NON C RIME
NUT C ASE	*BLA C KFLY	*C HI C NESS	DRA C AENA	*HAT C HWAY	*NUN C HAKU
PE C CANT	*BLA C KGUM	*CHO C KFUL	DRA C ONIC	*HEN C HMAN	PAN C ETTA
*PE C CARY	*BLA C KING	*C HU C KIES	DUE C ENTO	HER C ULES	PAN C REAS
*PE C CAVI	*BLA C KISH	*CHU C KLER	DUL C ETLY	*HIC C OUGH	PAR C ENER
PI C COLO	*BLA C KLEG	*C IN C HONA	DUL C IANA	*HOA C TZIN	*PAR C HESI
POR C INO	*BLA C KOUT	C IN C TURE	DUL C IMER	*HOT C HPOT	*PAR C HISI
PRA C TIC	*BLA C KTOP	C IR C LING	DUL C INEA	*HYA C INTH	*PAY C HECK
PRE C ODE	*BLO C KADE	*C IR C UITY	*DUT C HMAN	*JUN C TION	*PEA C EFUL
PRE C OUP	*BLO C KAGE	C IR C ULAR	FAL C ATED	*JUN C TURE	*PEA C ENIK
*PSY C HIC	*BLO C KISH	*C LO C HARD	*FAL C HION	KAT C HINA	*PEA C OCKY
PU C COON	*BOS C HBOK	*COA C HMAN	FAL C ONER	*KER C HIEF	*PE C CABLE
RA C COON	*BOT C HERY	C OA C TION	FAL C ONET	*KNA C KERY	*PEC C ANCY
RAN C HMA	*BOY C HICK	*C OA C TIVE	*FAL C ONRY	*KNI C KERS	*PEN C HANT
RI C CINO	BRA C ELET	C ON C EDER	FAN C IFUL	*KNO C KOFF	PEN C ILER
SA C CADE	*BRA C HIAL	*C ON C EIVE	*FAR C ICAL	*KNO C KOUT	*PER C EIVE
SA C CATE	*BRA C HIUM	C ON C ERTO	*FAS C ICLE	*KNU C KLER	PIA C ULAR
*SAL C HOW	BRA C IOLA	*C ON C HOID	*FEN C EROW	LAN C ELET	PIE C RUST
*SHI C KER	BRA C IOLE	*C ON C LAVE	FEN C IBLE	LAN C IERS	*PIL C HARD
SME C TIC	*BRA C KISH	C ON C LUDE	*FIS C ALLY	LAR C ENER	*PIN C HBUG
SO C CAGE	BRA C ONID	C ON C RETE	*FLA C KERY	*LAT C HKEY	PIS C ATOR
*SPA C KLE	BRA C TLET	C OS C RIPT	FLE C TION	LEA C HATE	*PIT C HIER
*STA C KUP	*BRI C KBAT	*C OU C HANT	*FLI C HTER	LEU C EMIA	*PIT C HILY
*STO C KMA	BRO C ATEL	*C OU C HING	*FLI C KERY	*LIN C HPIN	*PIT C HMAN
SUB C ODE	BRO C COLI	*C RA C KING	*FOR C EFUL	LUN C HEON	*PIT C HOUT
SUB C ULT	*BRO C HURE	*C RA C KNEL	*FOR C IBLE	LUS C IOUS	PLA C ABLE
SU C CEED	*BRO C KAGE	*C RA C KPOT	*FOR C IPES	*LYN C HING	PLA C ATER
SU C CESS	BRU C ELLA	C RI C ETID	FRA C TION	*LYN C HPIN	PLA C EMAN
SU C CORY	*BUN C OMBE	C RO C EINE	FRA C TURE	*MAC C ABOY	PLA C ENTA
SU C COTH	*BUT C HERY	*C RO C KERY	FRI C ANDO	*MAC C OBOY	PLE C TRON
SU C COUR	C AL C ANEA	C RO C OITE	FRI C TION	*MAR C HESA	PLE C TRUM
SU C CUBA	C AL C ANEI	C RU C IATE	*FRU C TIFY	*MAR C HESE	PLI C ATED
*SU C CUMB	*C AL C EATE	C RU C IBLE	FRU C TOSE	*MAT C HBOX	POA C EOUS
SU C CUSS	*C AL C IFIC	*C RU C IFER	FUN C TION	*MER C HANT	*POE C HORE
TO C CATA	C AL C SPAR	*C RU C IFIX	FUR C RAEA	*MER C IFUL	PRA C TICE
VA C CINA	*C AL C TUFA	C UR C ULIO	*FUR C ULUM	*MIS C ARRY	PRA C TISE
VA C CINE	*C AL C TUFF	*C UT C HERY	*GIM C RACK	*MIS C HIEF	*PRE C HECK
*ZE C CHIN	C AL C ULUS	*DAB C HICK	GLA C IATE	MO C CASIN	*PRE C HILL
*ZOE C IUM	C AN C ELER	DEA C ONRY	GLU C AGON	*MOS C HATE	*PRE C IEUX
BAC C ARAT	C AN C ROID	DES C RIBE	GLU C INUM	*MOU C HOIR	PRE C INCT
*BAC CATED	*C AR C AJOU	DES C RIER	GLY C ERIN	*MUN C HIES	PRE C IOUS
*BAC CHANT	C AR C ANET	DIA C ETYL	GLY C EROL	*MUN C HKIN	PRE C ITED
*BAC CHIUS	C AS C ABEL	DIA C ONAL	*GLY C ERYL	MUS C ADET	PRE C LEAN
*BEACHBOY	C AS C ABLE	DIE C IOUS	*GLY C OGEN	*MUT C HKIN	PRE C LEAR
*BED C HAIR	*C AT C HALL	DIO C ESAN	*GLY C ONIC	NAR C EINE	PRE C LUDE
*BED COVER	*C AT C HFLY	DIS C IPLE	*GLY C OSYL	NAR C ISSI	*PRE C RASH
*BEE C HNUT	C ER C ARIA		*GOD C HILD		PRI C IEST

*PRI C KIER	SPE C IATE	TIE C LASP	*WAT C HDOG	GAMI C	BROMI C
*PRI C KING	*SPE C IFIC	TIN C TURE	*WAT C HEYE	GENI C	BUSTI C
PRO C AINE	SPE C IMEN	TOP C ROSS	*WAT C HFUL	HAVO C	CALCI C
*PRO C HAIN	SPE C IOUS	TOR C HERE	*WAT C HMAN	HEMI C	CALPA C
*PRO C HEIN	SPE C TATE	TOR C HIER	*WAT C HOUT	HUMI C	CANTI C
PRO C LAIM	SPE C TRAL	TRA C HEID	*WEL C OMER	LILA C	CAPRI C
PRO C URAL	SPE C TRUM	*TRA C HOMA	*WIT C HERY	LINA C	C ELIA C
PRO C URER	SPE C ULUM	*TRA C HYTE	*WIT C HING	LOTI C	*C HEBE C
*PUN C HEON	SPI C C ATO	*TRA C KAGE	*WRA C KFUL	LUDI C	*C HEMI C
PUN C TATE	SPI C IEST	*TRA C KING	*WRE C KAGE	LYRI C	C HORI C
PUN C TUAL	SPI C ULUM	*TRA C KMAN	*WRE C KFUL	LYTI C	*C HYMI C
PUN C TURE	STA C CATO	*TRA C KWAY	*WRE C KFUL	MAFI C	CITRI C
*PUR C HASE	*STI C KFUL	TRA C TATE	*ZE C C HINO	MAGI C	C LERI C
*QUA C KERY	STI C KIER	TRA C TILE	*ZIN C KING	MALI C	C LINI C
*QUA C KISH	*STI C KILY	TRA C TION	*ZIR C ONIA	MANI C	C LITI C
*QUA C KISM	STI C KLER	TRE C ENTO	*ZIR C ONI C	MEDI C	C LONI C
*QUI C KSET	*STI C KMAN	TRI C HINA	*ZOO C HORE	MELI C	COC CIC
RAN C HERO	STI C KOUT	TRI C HITE	*ZU C C HINI	MESI C	C OGNA C
RAS C ALLY	*STI C KPIN	TRI C HOID	BLO C	MIMI C	C ORSA C
REA C C EDE	STI C TION	*TRI C HOME	C HI C	MUSI C	C OSMI C
REA C C ENT	STO C CADO	*TRI C KERY	C RO C	PANI C	C RETI C
REA C C EPT	STO C CATA	TRI C KIER	DIS C	PUBI C	C RITI C
REA C C USE	*STO C KADE	*TRI C KILY	FIS C	PUDI C	C ULTI C
REA C TANT	*STO C KCAR	*TRI C KISH	FLI C	PYRI C	C UPRI C
REA C TION	STO C KIER	TRI C OLOR	HUI C	RABI C	C YANI C
REA C TIVE	*STO C KILY	TRI C ORNE	LAI C	REBE C	*C Y C LI C
*REO C CUPY	*STO C KING	TRI C TRA C	MAR C	RELI C	C YSTI C
RES C HOOL	*STO C KISH	*TRI C Y C LE	NAR C	RUNI C	DEIFI C
RES C REEN	STO C KIST	*TRO C HAI C	PYI C	SALI C	*DEZIN C
RES C RIPT	*STO C KPOT	TRO C HILI	SPE C	SERA C	DYADI C
RES C ULPT	STU C C OER	TRO C HLEA	SPI C	SONI C	FABRI C
SA C C ULAR	SUB C ASTE	TRO C HOID	SYN C	STOI C	FENNE C
SA C C ULUS	SUB C AUSE	*TRU C KAGE	TAL C	SUMA C	FERRI C
*SAN C TIFY	*SUB C HIEF	*TRU C KFUL	TOR C	TARO C	FILMI C
SAN C TION	SUB C LASS	*TRU C KING	*ZIN C	TELI C	FISTI C
SAN C TITY	*SUB C LERK	TRU C KLER	*ZOI C	TONI C	FORMI C
SAR C ENET	SUB C UTIS	*TRU C KMAN	BARI C	TOPI C	FROLI C
*SAU C EBOX	SU C C IN C T	*VA C C INEE	BASI C	TORI C	FUNGI C
SAU C EPAN	SU C C INI C	*VA C C INIA	BORI C	TOXI C	FUSTI C
SEA C OAST	*SU C C INYL	VAS C ULAR	BRON C	TRIA C	GALYA C
SEA C RAFT	SU C C ORER	*VAS C ULUM	C ERI C	TUNI C	GARLI C
*SEE CAT C H	SU C C UBUS	*VIN C HE C K	C IVI C	TYPI C	GEODI C
SEI C ENTO	SUI C IDAL	*VIN C IBLE	C ODE C	VATI C	GESTI C
SEL C OUTH	SUL C ATED	*VIN C ULUM	C OLI C	VINI C	GNOMI C
*SHA C KLER	*SUN C HOKE	*VIS C A C HA	C OMI C	*XEBE C	GOTHI C
*SHU C KING	SUR C EASE	*VIS C ERAL	C ONI C	XENI C	GUAIA C
SME C TITE	*SYN C ARPY	VIS C OUNT	C OSE C	XERI C	GWEDU C
*SMO C KING	SYN C LINE	*VIZ C A C HA	C UBI C	YOGI C	HAEMI C
*SNI C KERY	*SYN C YTIA	*VOI C EFUL	C USE C	*ZEBE C	HAPTI C
SOO C HONG	TEA C HING	*VOL C ANI C	C YNI C	BARDI C	HE C TI C
SOR C ERER	TEO C ALLI	*VUL C ANI C	DARI C	BEYLI C	HELIA C
SOU C HONG	TER C ELET	*WAH C ONDA	DOMI C	BIOPI C	HERDI C
SPA C EMAN	*THI C KISH	*WAR C RAFT	DURO C	BIOTI C	HEROI C
SPA C IOUS	*THI C KSET	*WAT C H C RY	FRAN C	BONDU C	*HYDRI C

*HYPNI C	THORI C	DINERI C	PHRENI C	TITANI C	DIDA C TI C
LA C TI C	*THYMI C	DISOMI C	PIRATI C	*TRAFFI C	DIETETI C
LENTI C	TI C TA C	DO C ETI C	PLASTI C	TRIADI C	*DIHYDRI C
LIMBI C	TI C TO C	DRASTI C	*PLUMBI C	TROPHI C	DIMETRI C
LIMNI C	TOLUI C	*DYNAMI C	POLEMI C	VENATI C	DIOPTRI C
LITHI C	TOMBA C	FANATI C	POLITI C	VERIDI C	*DIPHASI C
LUBRI C	TRAGI C	FARADI C	POSTDO C	*VIVIFI C	DIURETI C
LUETI C	TROPI C	FATIDI C	POTAMI C	VO C ALI C	DOMESTI C
MANIA C	VIATI C	FRANTI C	PRA C TI C	*XANTHI C	DRA C ONI C
MANIO C	VITRI C	FUMARI C	PRIAPI C	*YASHMA C	DRAMATI C
MANTI C	*ZIN C I C	*FUTHAR C	PROSAI C	BALSAMI C	*DYSGENI C
MASTI C	*ZODIA C	*FUTHOR C	PRUSSI C	BANAUSI C	*DYSLEXI C
METRI C	*BA C C HI C	GASTRI C	PSALMI C	BARBARI C	FARADAI C
MIOTI C	BALDRI C	GENERI C	*PSY C HI C	BARLEDU C	*FEBRIFI C
MOSAI C	BASILI C	GENETI C	PYRETI C	*BATHETI C	FORENSI C
MU C LU C	*BAWDRI C	GEORGI C	*PYRRHI C	*BEATIFI C	FRENETI C
MYOTI C	BENEFI C	*GLYPTI C	*QUADRI C	*BI C Y C LI C	*FULMINI C
MYSTI C	BENTHI C	GNATHI C	*QUANTI C	*BIOETHI C	GALA C TI C
*MYTHI C	BIBASI C	GNOSTI C	*QUARTI C	BIOGENI C	GALVANI C
NASTI C	BIOPSI C	*GRAPHI C	*QUINTI C	BIOLOGI C	GEODESI C
NITRI C	BIOPTI C	*GYNE C I C	RA C EMI C	*BIPHASI C	GEODETI C
NOETI C	BIVOUA C	*HALAKI C	RAGADI C	*BROMIDI C	GEOPONI C
NORDI C	BORA C I C	HEBETI C	*RHOMBI C	*C AL C IFI C	GERMANI C
NOSTO C	BOTANI C	HEDONI C	*SAPPHI C	C ANNABI C	GERONTI C
PARSE C	BUBONI C	HEMATI C	SATANI C	*CARBAMI C	GIGANTI C
PELVI C	BU C OLI C	HEPATI C	S C ALDI C	C ARBOLI C	*GLY C ONI C
PEPTI C	BULIMI C	HERETI C	S C EPTI C	*C ARYATI C	*HABBINI C
*PHOBI C	BUTYRI C	*JURIDI C	S C IATI C	*C ATHOLI C	*HAEMATI C
PHONI C	C ALORI C	*KERAMI C	SEBA C I C	C ELERIA C	*HAGGADI C
PHOTI C	*C AMBRI C	KINESI C	SEBASI C	*C EPHALI C	*HARMONI C
*PHYSI C	C ARDIA C	KINETI C	SELENI C	*C HIMERI C	HERALDI C
PI C NI C	C AUSTI C	LA C ONI C	SEMATI C	*C HOLERI C	*HERMETI C
PI C RI C	C ENTRI C	LUNATI C	SHELLA C	*C HTHONI C	HIDROTI C
POETI C	C ERAMI C	MALEFI C	SHOEPA C	C LEIDOI C	HIERATI C
PRATI C	C EROTI C	MASONI C	SILI C I C	*C OLUMBI C	HISTORI C
PUBLI C	*C HAMPA C	*MEDEVA C	*SKEPTI C	C OSMETI C	*HOLOZOI C
*PYKNI C	C HLORI C	MELANI C	SME C TI C	*C RESYLI C	HOMEOTI C
*QUINI C	*C HROMI C	MELODI C	SPASTI C	C UNEATI C	*HORRIFI C
RI C RA C	C HRONI C	METOPI C	SPATHI C	*DA C TYLI C	*HYDRONI C
RUBRI C	C LASSI C	MOLLUS C	SPHENI C	DALMATI C	*HYDROPI C
RUSTI C	C LASTI C	*MORPHI C	SPHERI C	DALTONI C	*HYLOZOI C
S C ENI C	C OELIA C	MOTIVI C	SPLENI C	DEMONIA C	*HYPNOTI C
SEPTI C	C OLONI C	MOTORI C	STANNI C	DESERTI C	*HYPOTHE C
SORBI C	C OMATI C	*MUNTJA C	STROBI C	DEUTERI C	*HYSTERI C
STATI C	C OMEDI C	NEMATI C	STYPTI C	DIABETI C	LEPROTI C
STERI C	C OMETI C	NEPHRI C	SUBERI C	DIABOLI C	*LEUKEMI C
SYNDI C	*C RYPTI C	NERITI C	SUBFUS C	DIALOGI C	LIMNETI C
TA C TI C	DEI C TI C	NUMERI C	TABETI C	DIALYTI C	LOGISTI C
TAMBA C	*DELPHI C	*PA C IFI C	TE C HNI C	DIATOMI C	MAGNETI C
TANNI C	DEMONI C	PARETI C	TEREBI C	DIATONI C	*MAGNIFI C
TANRE C	DEMOTI C	PARODI C	TETANI C	*DI C HOTI C	MAIEUTI C
TARMA C	DEONTI C	PAROTI C	THERIA C	*DI C HROI C	*MAJESTI C
TENRE C	DIBASI C	PELAGI C	THERMI C	DI C ROTI C	MANGANI C
THETI C	DIMERI C	PHALLI C	THIONI C	*DI C Y C LI C	MARGARI C

*MECHANIC	NONMUSIC	*PHTRALIC	REPUBLIC	STOMATIC	TELLURIC
MEDALLIC	*NONOHMIC	*PHTRISIC	*RHEMATIC	SUBOPTIC	TERRIFIC
*MELLIFIC	*NONTOXIC	PLATINIC	RHETORIC	*SUBPUBIC	*THEMATIC
MERISTIC	*PACHALIC	PLATONIC	*RHYTHMIC	SUBSONIC	TOREUTIC
MESMERIC	PALLADIC	POLLINIC	ROMANTIC	SUBTONIC	TRIBASIC
METALLIC	*PANDEMIC	*POLYZOIC	RUTHENIC	SUBTOPIC	TRICTRAC
*METHODIC	PANOPTIC	*PONTIFIC	SABBATIC	SUBTUNIC	TRISOMIC
MNEMONIC	PARANOIC	POPLITIC	*SALVIFIC	SUCCINIC	*TROCHAIC
*MOLYBDIC	*PARHELIC	*POSTSYNC	SANDARAC	SULFONIC	TURMERIC
MONASTIC	*PASHALIC	POTASSIC	SANTALIC	SULFURIC	*TYMPANIC
*MORBIFIC	*PATHETIC	*PREMEDIC	SARDONIC	*SYLLABIC	TYRANNIC
*MYOGENIC	PENTOMIC	*PROLIFIC	SEMANTIC	*SYLVATIC	VIBRONIC
NARCOTIC	PERIODIC	*PROXEMIC	SEMIOTIC	*SYMBOLIC	VILLATIC
NEOTERIC	PERIOTIC	PULMONIC	*SIPHONIC	SYNDETIC	*VOLCANIC
NEURITIC	PERISARC	PURPURIC	*SLIVOVIC	*SYNECTIC	*VULCANIC
NEUROTIC	PETROLIC	*PYCNOTIC	*SPAGYRIC	*SYSTEMIC	ZIRCONIC
*NICKELIC	*PHENETIC	*PYKNOTIC	*SPECIFIC	*TAGMEMIC	*ZOOGENIC
NITROLIC	*PHENOLIC	*PYOGENIC	SPONDAIC	TALMUDIC	
NONBASIC	*PHONETIC	*QUIDNUNC	SPORADIC	TECTONIC	
NONIONIC	*PHREATIC	*QUIXOTIC		TELESTIC	

D

DACE	DEAL	*DEXY	DIVA	DOSE	DUAL
DADA	DEAN	DHAK	DIVE	DOSS	DUCE
DADO	DEAR	DHAL	DJIN	DOST	DUCI
DAFF	DEBT	DHOW	DOAT	DOTE	DUCK
DAFT	DECK	DIAL	DOCK	DOTH	DUCT
DAHL	DECO	DICK	DODO	DOTY	DUDE
DAIS	DEED	DIDO	DOER	DOUM	DUEL
DALE	DEEM	DIDY	DOES	DOUR	DUET
DAME	DEEP	DIED	DOFF	DOUX	DUFF
DAMN	DEER	DIEL	DOGE	DOVE	DUIT
DAMP	DEET	DIET	DOGY	DOWN	DUKE
DANG	DEFI	DIKE	DOIT	*DOXY	DULL
DANK	DEFT	DILL	DOJO	DOZE	DULY
DARB	DEFY	DIME	DOLE	*DOZY	DUMA
DARE	DEIL	DINE	DOLL	DRAB	DUMB
DARK	DEKE	DING	DOLT	DRAG	DUMP
DART	DELE	DINK	DOME	DRAM	DUNE
DASH	DELF	DINT	DONA	DRAT	DUNG
DATA	DELL	DIOL	DONE	DRAW	DUNT
DATE	DEME	DIPT	DONG	DRAY	DUPE
DATO	DEMO	DIRE	DOOM	DREE	DURA
DAUB	DEMY	DIRK	DOOR	DREG	DURE
DAUT	DENE	DIRL	DOPA	DREK	DURN
DAVY	DENT	DIRT	DOPE	DREW	DURO
DAWK	DENY	DISC	DOPY	DRIB	DURR
DAWN	DERE	DISH	DORE	DRIP	DUSK
DAWT	DERM	DISS	DORK	DROP	DUTY
DAZE	DESK	DITA	DORM	DRUB	DYAD
DEAD	DEVA	DITE	DORR	DRUM	DYER
DEAF	DEWY	DITZ	DORY	DUAD	DYKE

DYNE	DEITY	DINGE	**DOOMY**	DRIVE	DAEDAL
DACHA	**DEKKO**	DINGO	*DOOZY	DROIT	DAEMON
DADDY	DELAY	**DINGY**	DOPER	DROLL	DAGGER
*DAFFY	DELLY	**DINKY**	**DOPEY**	DRONE	DAGGLE
DAGGA	DELTA	**DIPPY**	**DORKY**	DROOL	**DAGOBA**
DAILY	DELVE	DIODE	**DORMY**	DROOP	**DAHLIA**
DAIRY	DEMIT	DIPSO	DORSA	DROPT	**DAHOON**
DAISY	**DEMOB**	DIRER	DORTY	DROSS	**DAIKER**
DALLY	DEMON	DIRGE	DOSER	**DROUK**	**DAIKON**
DAMAN	DEMOS	DIRTY	DOTAL	DROVE	DAIMEN
DAMAR	DEMUR	DISCI	DOTER	DROWN	DAIMIO
DANCE	DENIM	DISCO	DOTTY	DRUID	DAIMON
DANDY	DENSE	**DISHY**	DOUCE	DRUNK	**DAIMYO**
DANIO	*DEOXY	DISME	**DOUGH**	DRUPE	**DAINTY**
DARER	DEPOT	**DITCH**	DOUMA	DRUSE	**DAKOIT**
DARIC	**DEPTH**	DITSY	DOURA	**DRYAD**	DALASI
DASHI	DERAT	DITTO	DOUSE	DRYER	**DALEDH**
DASHY	DERAY	DITTY	DOVEN	**DRYLY**	**DALETH**
DATER	**DERBY**	*DITZY	**DOWDY**	**DUCHY**	DALLES
DATTO	DERMA	DIVAN	DOWEL	*DUCKY	DALTON
DATUM	DERRY	DIVOT	DOWER	**DUDDY**	**DAMAGE**
DAUBE	**DESEX**	*DIVVY	DOWIE	DULIA	**DAMASK**
DAUNT	DETER	DIWAN	**DOWNY**	DULLY	**DAMMAR**
DAVEN	**DETOX**	DIXIT	**DOWRY**	DULSE	**DAMMED**
DAVIT	DEVEL	*DIZEN	DOWSE	**DUMKA**	**DAMMER**
DAWEN	DEVIL	*DIZZY	**DOXIE**	**DUMMY**	**DAMNED**
DEAIR	DEVON	**DJINN**	DOYEN	**DUMPY**	DAMNER
DEALT	DEWAN	**DOBBY**	**DOYLY**	DUNAM	**DAMPEN**
DEARY	DEWAR	DOBIE	*DOZEN	DUNCE	**DAMPER**
DEASH	*DEWAX	DOBLA	*DOZER	**DUNCH**	**DAMPLY**
DEATH	**DEXIE**	DOBRA	**DRAFF**	**DUNGY**	DAMSEL
DEAVE	DHOLE	DODGE	DRAFT	DUOMO	DAMSON
DEBAR	DHOTI	**DODGY**	DRAIL	DUPER	DANCER
DEBIT	DHUTI	DOEST	DRAIN	DUPLE	DANDER
DEBUG	DIARY	DOETH	**DRAKE**	DURAL	DANDLE
DEBUT	*DIAZO	**DOGEY**	DRAMA	DUROC	DANGER
DEBYE	DICER	DOGGO	**DRANK**	DURRA	DANGLE
DECAF	**DICEY**	**DOGGY**	DRAPE	DURST	**DANISH**
DECAL	*DICKY	DOGIE	DRAVE	DURUM	**DAPHNE**
DECAY	DICOT	DOGMA	DRAWL	DUSTY	**DAPPED**
DECOY	DICTA	DOILY	DRAWN	**DUTCH**	**DAPPER**
DECRY	DICTY	DOING	DREAD	DUVET	**DAPPLE**
DEDAL	DIDIE	DOLCE	DREAM	**DWARF**	DARING
DEEDY	DIDST	DOLLY	DREAR	DWELL	**DARKEN**
DEFAT	DIENE	DOLMA	DRESS	DWELT	**DARKLE**
DEFER	**DIGHT**	DOMAL	DREST	DWINE	**DARKLY**
DEFOG	DIGIT	**DOMIC**	DRIED	**DYING**	DARNED
DEGAS	**DIKER**	DONEE	DRIER	DYNEL	DARNEL
DEGUM	DILDO	DONGA	DRIES	DABBER	DARNER
DEICE	DILLY	DONNA	DRIFT	DABBLE	DARTER
DEIFY	DIMER	DONOR	DRILL	**DACKER**	DARTLE
DEIGN	**DIMLY**	DONSY	DRILY	DACOIT	**DASHER**
DEISM	DINAR	DONUT	**DRINK**	**DACTYL**	DASSIE
DEIST	DINER	DOOLY	DRIPT	DADDLE	**DATARY**

DATCHA	DEFANG	DENTAL	**DEXTRO**	DINGLE	DOBLON
DATING	**DEFEAT**	DENTIL	*DEZINC	DINGUS	DOCENT
DATIVE	DEFECT	DENTIN	DHARMA	DINING	DOCILE
DATURA	**DEFEND**	DENUDE	DHARNA	**DINKEY**	**DOCKER**
DAUBER	**DEFIED**	DEODAR	DHOOLY	**DINKLY**	**DOCKET**
DAUBRY	**DEFIER**	DEPART	DHOORA	**DINKUM**	DOCTOR
DAUTIE	DEFIES	DEPEND	DHOOTI	DINNED	DODDER
DAWTIE	DEFILE	DEPERM	DHURNA	DINNER	**DODGEM**
DAYBED	DEFINE	DEPICT	DIACID	DIOBOL	DODGER
*DAYFLY	DEFLEA	DEPLOY	DIADEM	DIOECY	DOFFER
*DAZZLE	DEFOAM	DEPONE	DIALER	DIOXAN	DOGDOM
DEACON	DEFORM	DEPORT	DIALOG	DIOXIN	DOGEAR
DEADEN	DEFRAY	DEPOSE	DIAMIN	*DIPLEX	DOGGED
DEADLY	DEFUND	DEPUTE	DIAPER	DIPLOE	DOGGER
DEAFEN	DEFUSE	DEPUTY	DIAPIR	DIPNET	DOGIES
DEAFLY	*DEFUZE	DERATE	DIATOM	DIPOLE	DOGLEG
DEARIE	DEGAGE	DERIDE	*DIAZIN	DIPODY	DOGNAP
DEARLY	DEGERM	DERIVE	DIBBER	DIPPED	DOILED
DEARTH	DEGREE	DERMIS	DIBBLE	DIPPER	DOITED
DEASIL	DEGUST	DERRIS	*DIBBUK	DIPSAS	DOLING
DEATHY	DEHORN	DESALT	DICAST	*DIQUAT	DOLLAR
DEBARK	DEHORT	DESAND	DICIER	DIRDUM	DOLLOP
DEBASE	DEICER	DESCRY	DICING	DIRECT	DOLMAN
DEBATE	DEIFIC	DESERT	DICKER	DIRELY	DOLMEN
DEBEAK	DEIXIS	DESIGN	*DICKEY	DIREST	DOLOUR
DEBONE	*DEJECT	DESIRE	DICKIE	DIRHAM	DOMAIN
DEBRIS	DEKARE	DESIST	DICTUM	DIRNDL	DOMINE
DEBTOR	DELATE	DESMID	DIDACT	DISARM	DOMING
DEBUNK	DELEAD	DESORB	DIDDLE	DISBAR	DOMINO
DECADE	DELETE	*DESOXY	DIDDLY	DISBUD	DONATE
DECAMP	DELICT	DESPOT	DIDIES	DISCUS	DONJON
DECANE	DELIME	DETACH	DIETER	DISMAL	DONKEY
DECANT	DELIST	DETAIL	DIFFER	DISMAY	DONNED
DECARE	DELUDE	DETAIN	DIGAMY	DISOWN	DONNEE
DECEIT	DELUGE	DETECT	DIGEST	DISPEL	DONSIE
DECENT	DELUXE	DETENT	DIGGED	DISSED	*DONZEL
DECERN	DELVER	DETEST	DIGGER	DISSES	DOODAD
DECIDE	DEMAND	DETICK	DIGLOT	DISTAL	DOOFUS
DECILE	DEMARK	DETOUR	*DIKDIK	DISTIL	DOOLEE
DECKEL	DEMAST	DEVEIN	DIKTAT	DISUSE	DOOLIE
DECKER	DEMEAN	DEVEST	DILATE	DITHER	*DOOZER
DECKLE	DEMENT	DEVICE	DILLED	DIURON	*DOOZIE
DECOCT	DEMIES	DEVISE	DILUTE	DIVERT	DOPANT
DECODE	DEMISE	DEVOID	DIMITY	DIVEST	DOPIER
DECREE	DEMODE	DEVOIR	DIMMED	DIVIDE	DOPING
DECURY	DEMOTE	DEVOTE	DIMMER	DIVINE	DORADO
DEDANS	DEMURE	DEVOUR	DIMOUT	DIVING	DORBUG
DEDUCE	DENARY	DEVOUT	DIMPLE	*DJEBEL	DORIES
DEDUCT	DENGUE	DEWIER	DIMPLY	DJINNI	DORMER
*DEEJAY	DENIAL	DEWILY	DIMWIT	*DJINNY	DORMIE
DEEPEN	DENIED	DEWLAP	DINDLE	DOABLE	DORMIN
DEEPLY	DENIER	DEWOOL	DINERO	DOBBER	DORPER
DEEWAN	DENIES	DEWORM	DINGER	DOBBIN	DORSAD
DEFACE	DENNED	DEXIES	DINGEY	DOBIES	DORSAL
DEFAME	DENOTE	DEXTER	DINGHY		DORSEL

DORSER	DRIVEN	DURESS	DATEDLY	DECRIED	DEMOTIC
DORSUM	DRIVER	DURIAN	DAUBERY	DECRIER	DEMOUNT
DOSAGE	DROGUE	DURING	DAUNDER	DECROWN	DENDRON
DOSSAL	DROLLY	DURION	DAUNTER	*DECRYPT	*DENIZEN
DOSSEL	DROMON	DURNED	DAUPHIN	DECUMAN	DENNING
DOSSER	DRONER	DUSTER	*DAYBOOK	DECUPLE	DENSIFY
DOSSIL	DRONGO	DUSTUP	*DAYGLOW	DECURVE	DENSITY
DOTAGE	DROOPY	DYABLE	DAYLILY	DEERFLY	DENTINE
DOTARD	DROPSY	DYADIC	DAYLONG	DEFACER	DENTIST
DOTIER	DROSKY	*DYBBUK	DAYMARE	DEFAMER	DENTOID
DOTING	DROSSY	DYEING	DAYROOM	DEFAULT	DENTURE
DOTTED	DROUTH	DYNAST	DAYSIDE	DEFENCE	DENUDER
DOTTEL	DROVER	DYNEIN	DAYSMAN	DEFENSE	DEODAND
DOTTER	DROWND	DYNODE	DAYSTAR	DEFIANT	DEODARA
DOTTLE	DROWSE	DYVOUR	DAYTIME	DEFICIT	DEONTIC
DOUBLE	DROWSY	DABBLER	*DAYWORK	DEFILER	DEORBIT
DOUBLY	DRUDGE	DABSTER	*DAZZLER	DEFINER	DEPAINT
DOUCHE	DRUGGY	DACOITY	DEADEYE	DEFLATE	DEPLANE
DOUGHT	DRUMLY	DADAISM	DEADPAN	DEFLECT	DEPLETE
DOUGHY	DRYISH	DADAIST	DEAFISH	DEFOCUS	DEPLORE
DOURAH	DRYLOT	*DAGLOCK	DEALING	DEFORCE	DEPLUME
DOURLY	DUALLY	DAGWOOD	DEANERY	DEFRAUD	DEPOSAL
DOUSER	DUBBER	*DAKOITY	DEARIES	*DEFROCK	DEPOSER
DOVISH	DUBBIN	DALAPON	DEATHLY	DEFROST	DEPOSIT
DOWERY	DUCKER	DALLIER	DEBACLE	DEFUNCT	DEPRAVE
DOWNER	DUCKIE	DAMAGER	DEBASER	DEGAUSS	DEPRESS
DOWSER	DUCTAL	DAMMING	DEBATER	*DEGLAZE	DEPRIVE
DOYLEY	DUDDIE	*DAMNIFY	*DEBAUCH	DEGRADE	DEPSIDE
*DOZIER	DUDEEN	DAMOSEL	DEBONER	DEHISCE	DERAIGN
*DOZILY	DUDING	*DAMOZEL	*DEBOUCH	DEICIDE	DERIDER
*DOZING	DUDISH	DAMPING	DEBRIDE	DEICING	DERIVER
DRABLY	DUELER	*DAMPISH	DEBRIEF	DEICTIC	DERMOID
DRACHM	DUELLI	DANDIER	DECALOG	DEIFIED	DERNIER
*DRAFFY	DUELLO	DANDIES	DECANAL	DEIFIER	DERRICK
DRAFTY	DUENDE	DANDILY	DECAPOD	DEIFORM	DERVISH
DRAGEE	DUENNA	DANDLER	DECAYER	*DEJECTA	DESCANT
DRAGGY	DUFFEL	DANGLER	DECEASE	DELAINE	DESCEND
DRAPER	DUFFER	DANSEUR	DECEIVE	DELATOR	DESCENT
DRAPEY	DUFFLE	DAPHNIA	DECIARE	DELAYER	DESERVE
DRAWEE	DUGONG	DAPPING	DECIBEL	DELEAVE	DESIRER
DRAWER	DUIKER	DAPSONE	DECIDER	DELIGHT	DESMOID
DRAWLY	DULCET	DARBIES	DECIDUA	DELIMIT	DESPAIR
DREAMT	DUMBLY	DAREFUL	DECIMAL	DELIVER	DESPISE
DREAMY	DUMDUM	DARESAY	*DECKING	DELOUSE	DESPITE
DREARY	DUMPER	DARIOLE	DECLAIM	*DELPHIC	DESPOIL
DREGGY	DUNITE	*DARKISH	DECLARE	DELTOID	DESPOND
DREICH	DUNLIN	DARNING	DECLASS	DELUDER	DESSERT
DREIDL	DUNNED	DARSHAN	DECLINE	DEMAGOG	DESTAIN
DREIGH	DUNNER	DASHEEN	DECODER	DEMERGE	DESTINE
DRENCH	DUOLOG	DASHIER	DECOLOR	DEMERIT	DESTINY
DRESSY	DUPERY	*DASHIKI	DECORUM	DEMESNE	DESTROY
DRIEST	DUPING	DASHPOT	DECOYER	DEMETON	DESUGAR
DRIFTY	*DUPLEX	DASTARD	DECREER	DEMIGOD	DETENTE
DRIPPY	DUPPED	DASYURE	DECRIAL	DEMIREP	DETERGE
DRIVEL	DURBAR	DATABLE	DECRIAL	DEMONIC	DETINUE

DETRACT	DICOTYL	*DIPTYCA	DISTOME	DOORWAY	DRIFTER
DETRAIN	DICTATE	*DIPTYCH	DISTORT	DOPIEST	DRILLER
DETRUDE	DICTIER	DIREFUL	DISTURB	*DORHAWK	DRINKER
*DEUTZIA	DICTION	DIRTBAG	*DISYOKE	DORMANT	DRIPPER
DEVALUE	*DICYCLY	DISABLE	DITCHER	DORMICE	*DRIZZLY
DEVELOP	DIDDLER	DISAVOW	DITHERY	DORNECK	DROMOND
DEVIANT	DIDDLEY	DISBAND	DITHIOL	DORNICK	DRONING
DEVIATE	*DIEBACK	DISCANT	DITTANY	DOSSIER	DRONISH
DEVILRY	DIEHARD	DISCARD	DIURNAL	DOTIEST	DROPLET
DEVIOUS	DIESTER	DISCASE	DIVERSE	DOTTIER	DROPOUT
DEVISAL	DIETARY	DISCEPT	DIVIDER	DOTTILY	DROPPED
DEVISEE	DIETHER	DISCERN	DIVINER	DOTTING	DROPPER
DEVISER	DIFFUSE	DISCOID	DIVISOR	DOTTREL	DROSERA
DEVISOR	DIGAMMA	DISCORD	DIVORCE	DOUBLER	*DROSHKY
DEVOICE	DIGGING	DISCUSS	DIVULGE	DOUBLET	DROUGHT
DEVOLVE	DIGITAL	DISDAIN	DOCETIC	DOUCEUR	DROUTHY
DEVOTEE	*DIGNIFY	DISEASE	*DOCKAGE	*DOUGHTY	DROWNER
DEWATER	DIGNITY	DISEUSE	DODDERY	DOURINE	DRUBBER
*DEWCLAW	*DIGOXIN	DISGUST	DODGERY	DOVECOT	DRUDGER
DEWDROP	DIGRAPH	DISHELM	DODGING	*DOVEKEY	DRUGGET
DEWFALL	DIGRESS	DISHFUL	DODOISM	*DOVEKIE	DRUGGIE
DEWIEST	DILATER	DISHIER	DOESKIN	DOWABLE	DRUMBLE
DEWLESS	DILATOR	DISHPAN	DOGBANE	DOWAGER	DRUMLIN
*DEXTRAL	DILUENT	DISHRAG	DOGCART	DOWNIER	DRUMMED
*DEXTRAN	DILUTER	*DISJECT	DOGEDOM	DOYENNE	DRUMMER
*DEXTRIN	DILUTOR	*DISJOIN	DOGFACE	*DOZENTH	DRUNKEN
DHOOTIE	DILUVIA	DISLIKE	*DOGFISH	*DOZIEST	DRYLAND
DHOURRA	DIMERIC	DISLIMN	DOGGERY	DRABBET	DRYNESS
DHURRIE	DIMETER	DISMAST	DOGGIES	DRABBLE	DRYWALL
DIABASE	DIMMEST	DISMISS	DOGGING	*DRACHMA	DUALISM
DIABOLO	DIMMING	DISOBEY	DOGGISH	DRAFTEE	DUALIST
DIAGRAM	DIMNESS	DISOMIC	DOGGONE	DRAFTER	DUALITY
DIALECT	*DIMORPH	DISPART	DOGGREL	DRAGGER	*DUALIZE
DIALING	DINERIC	DISPEND	DOGLIKE	DRAGGLE	DUBBING
DIALIST	DINETTE	DISPLAY	DOGSLED	DRAGNET	DUBIETY
DIALLED	DINGBAT	DISPORT	DOGTROT	DRAGOON	DUBIOUS
DIALLEL	DINGIES	DISPOSE	DOGVANE	DRAINER	DUCHESS
DIALYSE	DINGILY	DISPUTE	DOGWOOD	DRAMEDY	DUCKIER
*DIALYZE	DINITRO	DISRATE	DOLEFUL	DRAMMED	DUCKIES
DIAMIDE	DINKIER	DISROBE	DOLLIED	DRAPERY	*DUCKPIN
DIAMINE	DINKIES	DISROOT	DOLLIES	DRAPING	DUCTILE
DIAMOND	DINNING	DISRUPT	DOLLISH	DRASTIC	DUCTING
DIAPSID	DIOCESE	DISSAVE	DOLPHIN	DRAUGHT	DUCTULE
*DIARCHY	DIOPTER	DISSEAT	DOMICAL	DRAWBAR	DUDGEON
DIARIES	DIOPTRE	DISSECT	DOMICIL	DRAWING	DUELIST
DIARIST	DIORAMA	DISSENT	DOMINIE	DRAWLER	DUELLED
DIASTEM	DIORITE	DISSERT	DONATOR	DRAYAGE	DUELLER
*DIAZINE	*DIOXANE	DISSING	DONGOLA	DRAYMAN	DUENESS
*DIAZOLE	*DIOXIDE	DISTAFF	DONNERD	DREAMER	*DUKEDOM
DIBASIC	DIPHASE	DISTAIN	DONNERT	DREDGER	*DULCIFY
DIBBING	DIPLOID	DISTANT	DONNING	DREIDEL	DULLARD
DIBBLER	DIPLOMA	DISTEND	DONNISH	DRESSER	DULLISH
DICIEST	DIPNOAN	DISTENT	DOOMFUL	DRIBBLE	DULNESS
DICKENS	DIPPING	DISTICH	DOORMAN	*DRIBBLY	DUMPIER
DICLINY	DIPTERA	DISTILL	DOORMAT	DRIBLET	*DUMPILY

DUMPING	DAMNABLE	*DEBUNKER	DEGASSER	DENOUNCE	DETHRONE
*DUMPISH	DAMNDEST	DEBUTANT	DEGRADER	DENTALIA	*DETICKER
DUNGEON	DAMPENER	DECADENT	DEGREASE	DENTATED	DETONATE
DUNNAGE	DAMPNESS	DECANTER	DEHORNER	DENTICLE	*DETOXIFY
DUNNESS	*DANDRIFF	DECEDENT	DEIFICAL	DENUDATE	DETRITUS
DUNNEST	*DANDRUFF	DECEIVER	*DEIONIZE	DEPARTEE	DEUTERIC
DUNNING	*DANDYISH	*DECEMVIR	*DEJEUNER	DEPICTER	DEUTERON
DUNNITE	*DANDYISM	DECENARY	*DEKAGRAM	DEPICTOR	DEVELOPE
DUOPOLY	DANEGELD	DECENNIA	DELATION	DEPILATE	DEVERBAL
DUOTONE	DANEWEED	DECENTER	*DELEGACY	DEPLORER	DEVIANCE
DUPPING	DANEWORT	DECENTRE	DELEGATE	DEPOLISH	*DEVIANCY
DUPTRAG	DANKNESS	DECIGRAM	DELETION	DEPONENT	DEVIATOR
DURABLE	DANSEUSE	DECIMATE	*DELICACY	DEPORTEE	*DEVILISH
DURAMEN	DARINGLY	*DECIPHER	DELICATE	DEPRAVER	*DEVILKIN
DURANCE	DARKENER	DECISION	DELIRIUM	DEPRIVAL	DEVILLED
DURMAST	DARKNESS	DECISIVE	*DELIVERY	DEPRIVER	*DEVILTRY
*DUSKISH	*DARKROOM	*DECKHAND	DELOUSER	DEPURATE	DEVISING
DUSTBIN	*DARKSOME	DECLARER	DELUSION	*DEPUTIZE	DEVOTION
DUSTIER	DARNDEST	DECLINER	DELUSIVE	DERELICT	DEVOURER
DUSTILY	DASHIEST	DECORATE	DELUSORY	DERINGER	*DEWBERRY
DUSTMAN	*DATABANK	DECOROUS	DELUSTER	DERISION	*DEXTRINE
DUSTOFF	DATABASE	DECOUPLE	*DEMAGOGY	DERISIVE	*DEXTROSE
DUSTPAN	DATELESS	DECREASE	DEMANDER	DERISORY	*DEXTROUS
DUTEOUS	DATELINE	DECREPIT	*DEMARCHE	DERIVATE	DIABETES
DUTIFUL	DAUGHTER	DECRETAL	DEMEANOR	DEROGATE	DIABETIC
DUUMVIR	DAUPHINE	DECURIES	DEMENTIA	DERRIERE	DIABLERY
DUVETYN	*DAWNLIKE	DECURION	DEMERARA	DESALTER	DIABOLIC
DWARVES	*DAYBREAK	DEDICATE	DEMERGER	DESCRIBE	DIACETYL
DWELLER	*DAYDREAM	DEEDLESS	DEMERSAL	DESCRIER	DIACONAL
DWINDLE	*DAYLIGHT	DEEMSTER	*DEMIJOHN	DESELECT	DIAGNOSE
*DYARCHY	DEACONRY	DEEPENER	DEMILUNE	DESERTER	DIAGONAL
DYEABLE	DEADBEAT	DEEPNESS	DEMIURGE	DESERTIC	*DIAGRAPH
*DYEWEED	DEADBOLT	DEERSKIN	DEMIVOLT	DESERVER	DIALLAGE
*DYEWOOD	DEADENER	DEERWEED	DEMOCRAT	DESIGNEE	DIALLIST
*DYNAMIC	DEADFALL	DEERYARD	DEMONESS	DESIGNER	DIALOGER
DYNASTY	DEADHEAD	DEFECTOR	DEMONIAC	DESILVER	DIALOGIC
DYSPNEA	DEADLIER	DEFENDER	DEMONIAN	DESINENT	DIALOGUE
DYSURIA	DEADLIFT	DEFERENT	DEMONISE	DESIROUS	DIALYSER
DABBLING	DEADLINE	DEFERRAL	DEMONISM	DESOLATE	DIALYSIS
*DABCHICK	*DEADLOCK	DEFERRED	DEMONIST	*DESPATCH	DIALYTIC
*DACTYLIC	DEADNESS	DEFERRER	*DEMONIZE	DESPISER	*DIALYZER
DACTYLUS	DEADWOOD	DEFIANCE	DEMOTICS	DESTRIER	DIAMANTE
*DAFFODIL	DEAERATE	DEFILADE	DEMOTING	DESTRUCT	DIAMETER
DAFTNESS	DEAFNESS	DEFINITE	DEMOTION	DESULFUR	DIANTHUS
*DAHABEAH	*DEALFISH	DEFLATER	DEMOTIST	DETACHER	DIAPASON
*DAHABIAH	DEANSHIP	DEFLATOR	DEMPSTER	DETAILER	DIAPAUSE
*DAHABIEH	DEARNESS	*DEFLEXED	DEMURRAL	DETAINEE	DIAPHONE
*DAHABIYA	*DEATHBED	*DEFLOWER	DEMURRED	DETAINER	*DIAPHONY
*DAIQUIRI	*DEATHCUP	DEFOAMER	DEMURRER	DETASSEL	DIARRHEA
*DAISHIKI	*DEATHFUL	DEFOGGER	DENARIUS	DETECTER	DIASPORA
*DAKERHEN	DEBILITY	DEFOREST	DENATURE	DETECTOR	DIASPORE
DALESMAN	DEBONAIR	DEFORMER	*DENAZIFY	DETERGER	DIASTASE
DALMATIC	*DEBOUCHE	*DEFRAYAL	DENDRITE	DETERRED	DIASTEMA
DALTONIC	DEBRUISE	*DEFRAYER	DENDROID	DETERRER	DIASTOLE
DAMEWORT	DEBUGGER	DEFTNESS	DENIABLE	DETESTER	DIATOMIC

DIATONIC	*DIMETHYL	DISGUISE	DIURESIS	DOMINIUM	*DOWNPLAY
DIATRIBE	DIMETRIC	DISHERIT	DIURETIC	DONATION	DOWNPOUR
*DIAZEPAM	DIMINISH	*DISHEVEL	DIVAGATE	DONATIVE	DOWNSIDE
*DIAZINON	*DIMMABLE	DISHIEST	DIVALENT	DONENESS	*DOWNSIZE
DICHASIA	DINGDONG	*DISHLIKE	*DIVEBOMB	DONNERED	*DOWNTICK
*DICHOTIC	DINKIEST	DISHONOR	DIVERTER	DONNIKER	DOWNTROD
*DICHROIC	DINOSAUR	*DISHWARE	DIVIDEND	*DOOMSDAY	DOWNTURN
DICROTAL	DIOBOLON	DISINTER	DIVIDING	DOOMSTER	*DOWNWARD
DICROTIC	DIOCESAN	*DISJOINT	DIVIDUAL	DOORBELL	*DOWNWASH
DICTATOR	DIOECISM	*DISJUNCT	DIVINING	*DOORJAMB	*DOWNWIND
DICTIEST	DIOICOUS	DISKETTE	DIVINISE	*DOORKNOB	DOWSABEL
*DICYCLIC	DIOLEFIN	DISLIKER	*DIVINITY	DOORLESS	*DOXOLOGY
DIDACTIC	DIOPSIDE	DISLODGE	*DIVINIZE	DOORNAIL	*DOZINESS
*DIDACTYL	DIOPTASE	DISLOYAL	DIVISION	DOORPOST	DRABNESS
DIDAPPER	DIOPTRIC	DISMOUNT	*DIVISIVE	DOORSILL	DRACAENA
*DIDYMIUM	*DIPHASIC	DISORDER	DIVORCEE	DOORSTEP	DRACONIC
*DIDYMOUS	*DIPHENYL	*DISPATCH	DIVORCER	DOORSTOP	*DRAFFISH
*DIDYNAMY	DIPLEGIA	DISPENSE	DIVULGER	DOORYARD	DRAFTING
DIECIOUS	*DIPLEXER	DISPERSE	*DIZYGOUS	DOPAMINE	DRAGGIER
DIELDRIN	*DIPLOIDY	DISPIRIT	*DJELLABA	*DOPEHEAD	DRAGGING
*DIEMAKER	DIPLOMAT	DISPLACE	DOCILITY	DOPESTER	DRAGLINE
DIERESIS	DIPLOPOD	DISPLANT	*DOCKHAND	DOPINESS	DRAGONET
*DIESTOCK	DIPLOSIS	DISPLODE	*DOCKLAND	*DORMANCY	DRAGROPE
DIESTRUM	*DIPPABLE	DISPLUME	*DOCKSIDE	DORMIENT	DRAGSTER
DIESTRUS	*DIPSTICK	DISPOSAL	*DOCKYARD	DORMOUSE	DRAINAGE
DIETETIC	DIPTERAL	DISPOSER	DOCTORAL	DORSALLY	DRAMATIC
*DIFFRACT	DIPTERAN	DISPREAD	DOCTRINE	DOSSERET	DRAMMING
*DIFFUSER	DIPTERON	*DISPRIZE	DOCUMENT	DOTATION	*DRAMMOCK
*DIFFUSOR	DIRECTOR	DISPROOF	DODDERER	DOTINGLY	*DRAMSHOP
DIGAMIES	DIRENESS	DISPROVE	*DOGBERRY	DOTTEREL	*DRAUGHTY
DIGAMIST	DIRIMENT	DISPUTER	*DOGESHIP	DOTTIEST	*DRAWBACK
DIGESTER	DISABUSE	*DISQUIET	*DOGFIGHT	DOUBLING	DRAWBORE
DIGESTOR	DISAGREE	DISROBER	*DOGGEDLY	DOUBLOON	*DRAWDOWN
DIGGINGS	DISALLOW	DISSEISE	DOGGEREL	DOUBLURE	DRAWTUBE
DIGITATE	DISANNUL	*DISSEIZE	DOGGIEST	DOUBTFUL	DREADFUL
*DIGITIZE	DISARMER	DISSERVE	DOGGONED	*DOUGHBOY	DREAMFUL
DIHEDRAL	DISARRAY	DISSUADE	DOGHOUSE	DOUGHIER	DREDGING
DIHEDRON	DISASTER	DISTANCE	DOGNAPER	DOUGHNUT	DRENCHER
*DIHYBRID	DISBOSOM	DISTASTE	*DOGSBODY	DOUPIONI	DRESSAGE
*DIHYDRIC	DISBURSE	DISTAVES	DOGTOOTH	DOURNESS	DRESSING
DILATANT	DISCIPLE	DISTINCT	*DOGWATCH	*DOUZEPER	DRIBBLER
DILATATE	DISCLAIM	DISTRACT	DOLDRUMS	DOVECOTE	DRIBBLET
DILATION	*DISCLIKE	DISTRAIN	DOLERITE	*DOVELIKE	DRIFTAGE
DILATIVE	DISCLOSE	DISTRAIT	DOLESOME	DOVETAIL	DRIFTPIN
DILATORY	DISCOLOR	DISTRESS	DOLOMITE	DOWNBEAT	DRILLING
DILIGENT	DISCOUNT	DISTRICT	DOLOROUS	DOWNCAST	DRIPLESS
DILUTION	DISCOVER	DISTRUST	*DOMELIKE	*DOWNCOME	DRIPPING
DILUTIVE	DISCREET	DISULFID	*DOMESDAY	*DOWNFALL	DRIVELER
DILUVIAL	DISCRETE	DISUNION	DOMESTIC	*DOWNHAUL	*DRIVEWAY
DILUVIAN	DISCROWN	DISUNITE	DOMICILE	*DOWNHILL	DROLLERY
DILUVION	DISENDOW	DISUNITY	DOMINANT	DOWNIEST	*DROPHEAD
DILUVIUM	*DISFAVOR	DISVALUE	DOMINATE	DOWNLAND	*DROPKICK
DIMERISM	*DISFROCK	DITHEISM	DOMINEER	*DOWNLINK	DROPPING
*DIMERIZE	DISGORGE	DITHEIST	*DOMINICK	DOWNLOAD	DROPSHOT
DIMEROUS	DISGRACE	DITHERER	DOMINION	*DOWNPIPE	DROPWORT

*DROUGHTY	DURATION	BED BUG	DUD DIE	MA DRAS	RA DIUS
DRUBBING	DURATIVE	BED DED	DUD EEN	MAD URO	*RAD JUM
DRUDGERY	DUSTHEAP	BED DER	DUD ING	*MED FLY	RAD OME
DRUGGIST	DUSTIEST	*BED ECK	DUD ISH	MED IAD	RAD ULA
DRUIDESS	DUSTLESS	BE DELL	FE DORA	MED IAL	RED ACT
DRUIDISM	DUSTLIKE	BED LAM	FID DLE	MED IAN	RED ATE
DRUMBEAT	*DUTCHMAN	BED PAN	FID DLY	*MED ICK	RED BAY
DRUMFIRE	DUTIABLE	BED RID	FID GET	MED INA	RED BUD
*DRUMFISH	DUVETINE	BE DRUG	FOD DER	MED LAR	RED BUG
*DRUMHEAD	*DUVETYNE	BED SIT	FOD GEL	MID AIR	RED CAP
DRUMLIER	DWARFISH	BED UIN	FUD DLE	*MID WAY	RED DED
*DRUMLIKE	*DWARFISM	BE DUMB	GAD DED	MODERN	RED DEN
DRUMMING	DWELLING	BID DEN	GAD DER	MOD EST	RED DER
DRUMROLL	*DYESTUFF	BID DER	GAD FLY	*MOD IFY	RED DLE
DRUNKARD	*DYNAMISM	BOD EGA	GAD GET	MOD ULE	RED EAR
DRUPELET	DYNAMIST	BO DICE	GAD OID	MOD ULO	RED EEM
DRUTHERS	DYNATRON	BOD IED	GID DAP	MUD CAT	RED EFY
DRYPOINT	*DYSGENIC	BOD IFS	GO D DAM	NID GET	RED ENY
DRYSTONE	*DYSLEXIA	BOD ILY	GO D DED	NID IFY	RED EYE
DUBONNET	*DYSLEXIC	BOD ING	GOD OWN	NID ING	RED FIN
*DUCKBILL	*DYSPEPSY	BOD KIN	GOD SON	NOD DED	RED IAL
*DUCKIEST	DYSPNOEA	BUD DER	GOD WIT	NOD DER	RED LEG
*DUCKLING	*DYSTAXIA	BUD DLE	HAD ITH	NOD DLE	RED OCK
*DUCKTAIL	DYSTOCIA	BUD GET	*HAD JEE	NOD OSE	RED ONE
*DUCKWALK	DYSTONIA	BUD GIE	HAD RON	NOD OUS	RED OUT
*DUCKWEED	DYSTOPIA	BUD GIE	HED DLE	NOD ULE	RED OWA
DUCTLESS		CA DDIE	HED GER	NUD EST	RED RAW
*DUCTWORK	LUDE	CAD DIS	HID DEN	NUD GER	RED TOP
*DUDISHLY	NADA	CA DENT	HI DING	NUD ISM	RED UCE
DUECENTO	PADI	CA DGER	HOD DEN	NUD IST	RID DED
DUELLING	REDD	CED ING	HOD DIN	NUD ITY	RID DEN
DUELLIST	RUDD	CE DULA	HUD DLE	NUD NIK	RID DER
DUETTIST	SUDD	COD DED	HY DRIA	PAD AUK	RID DLE
DULCETLY	CODEC	COD DER	*HY DRIC	PAD DER	RID ENT
DULCIANA	CODED	COD DLE	HYD RID	PAD DLE	RID GEL
DULCIMER	GADID	CO DEIA	*JA DISH	PAD NAG	RID GIL
DULCINEA	GO DET	CO DEIN	*JU D DER	PAD OUK	RID ING
DULLNESS	HODAD	CO DGER	*JU D GER	PE DALO	RID LEY
*DUMBBELL	LUDIC	*CO DIFY	*JU D OKA	PE DANT	ROD ENT
*DUMBCANE	MO DEM	CO DING	*KE D DAH	PE DATE	ROD MAN
*DUMBHEAD	MU D DY	COD LIN	KID DER	PE D DLE	RUD DER
DUMBNESS	*NU D ZH	CUD DIE	KID DIE	PE DLAR	RUD DLE
*DUMFOUND	REDID	CUD DLE	KID NAP	PID DLE	RUD EST
*DUMMKOPF	RE DON	CUD DLY	KID NEY	PID DLY	SAD DEN
*DUMPCART	RE DUB	CUD GEL	*KID VID	PID GIN	SAD DHU
DUMPIEST	RE DUX	DAD DLE	LAD DER	PO DITE	SAD DLE
DUMPLING	SIDED	DED ANS	LAD DIE	PO DIUM	SAD ISM
DUNELAND	SO DOM	DED UCT	LA DIES	PO D SOL	SA DIST
DUNGAREE	WI DER	DID ACT	LA DING	*PO DZOL	SE DATE
DUNGHILL	WO DGE	DID DLE	LA DINO	PUD DLE	SE DILE
DUODENUM	BAD DIE	DID DLY	LAD LER	PUD DLY	SE DUCE
DUOLOGUE	BAD GER	DID IES	LAD RON	RAD DLE	SID DUR
DUOPSONY	BAD MAN	DOD DER	LED GER	RAD IAL	SI DING
*DUPLEXER	BE DAMN	DOD GEM	LOD GER	RAD IAN	SID LER
DURABLES	BE DAUB	DOD GER	MAD DED	RA DISH	SOD DED

SO D D EN	BE D POST	D U D GEON	KI D D IES	PE D ICEL	RO D LIKE
SO D IUM	BE D RAIL	FA D DABLE	KI D D ING	PE D ICLE	RO D SMAN
SO D OMY	BE D RAPE	FA D D IER	*KI D D ISH	PE D LARY	RU D D IER
SU D ARY	*BE D ROCK	FA D D ING	*KI D D USH	PE D LERY	RU D D ILY
SU D D EN	BE D ROLL	*FA D D ISH	*KI D LIKE	PE D OCAL	*RU D DOCK
SU D SER	BE D ROOM	FA D D ISM	*KI D SKIN	PI D D LER	RU D ERAL
TE D D ER	BE D SIDE	*FA D D IST	LA D ANUM	*PI D DOCK	RU D ESBY
TE D IUM	BE D SORE	FE D AYEE	LA D LING	PO D AGRA	SA D D LER
TI D BIT	*BE D TICK	FE D ERAL	LA D RONE	PO D LIKE	SA D IRON
TI D D LY	BE D TIME	FI D EISM	LA D YBUG	PU D D ING	SA D NESS
TI D IED	BE D UNCE	FI D EIST	LA D YISH	PU D D LER	SE D ARIM
TI D IER	BE D WAR D	*FI D GETY	LI D LESS	*PU D ENCY	SE D UCER
TI D IES	*BE D WARF	FI D GING	LO D GING	RA D IANT	SI D EARM
TI D ILY	BI D ARKA	GA D D ING	LY D D ITE	RA D IATE	SI D EBAR
TI D ING	BI D D ING	GA D ROON	MA D HOUS	RA D ICAL	SI D ECAR
TO D D LE	BO D HRAN	GA D WALL	MA D RIGA	RA D ICEL	SI D EMAN
VA D OSE	BU D D IED	*GI D D YAP	*MA D ZOON	RA D ICES	SI D EWAY
VO D OUN	BU D D IES	*GI D D YUP	ME D D USA	RA D ICLE	SO D D ING
WA D D ER	BU D D ING	GO D D ESS	*ME D EVAC	*RA D JALE	TA D POLE
WA D D IE	BU D GING	GO D D ING	*ME D IACY	RE D BAIT	TE D IOUS
WA D D LE	BU D LESS	GO D HEA D	ME D IATE	RE D BIR D	TI D D LER
WA D D LY	BU D LIKE	GO D HOO D	MI D CULT	RE D BONE	TI D ERIP
WA D MAL	*BU D WORM	GO D LESS	MI D LAN D	RE D COAT	TI D EWAY
WA D MEL	CA D AVER	GO D LIER	MI D LIFE	RE D D EST	TI D IEST
WA D MOL	CA D DICE	GO D LIKE	MI D LING	RE D D ING	TO D D IES
WA D SET	CA D D ISH	GO D LING	*MI D RIFF	RE D D ISH	TO D D LER
WE D D ER	CA D ELLE	GO D ROON	*MI D SHIP	RE D FISH	VE D ALIA
WE D ELN	CA D ENCE	GO D SEN D	*MI D SIZE	RE D HEA D	VE D ETTE
WE D GIE	*CA D ENCY	GO D SHIP	MI D SOLE	RE D LINE	VI D ETTE
WI D D ER	*CA D ENZA	GU D GEON	*MI D WEEK	RE D NECK	VI D ICON
WI D D IE	CA D MIUM	HA D ARIM	*MI D WIFE	RE D NESS	VI D UITY
WI D D LE	CE D ILLA	HA D D EST	MO D ERNE	RE D OUBT	WA D ABLE
WI D EST	CO D ABLE	*HA D DOCK	MO D ISTE	RE D OUN D	WA D D IE D
WI D GET	CO D D ING	HE D D ING	MO D ULE D	RE D POLL	WA D D IES
WI D ISH	CO D D LER	HE D ONIC	MU D D IE D	RE D RAFT	WA D D ING
YO D LER	CO D EINA	HI D ABLE	MU D FLAT	RE D REAM	WA D D LER
*ZA D D IK	CO D EINE	HI D ALGO	MU D HOLE	RE D RESS	WA D MAAL
*ZO D IAC	*CO D FISH	HI D EOUS	*MU D PACK	RE D RIE D	WA D MOLL
*ZY D ECO	CO D ICES	HI D EOUT	*MU D ROCK	RE D RIES	WE D D ING
BA D GING	CO D ICIL	*HO DAD DY	NO D D IES	RE D RILL	WI D ENER
BA D LAN D	CO D LING	HU D D LER	NO D D ING	RE D RIVE	WI D EOUT
BA D NESS	CO D RIVE	*HY D ATI D	NO D ICAL	RE D ROOT	WI D GEON
BE D D ING	CU D BEAR	HY D RANT	NU D NICK	RE D SKIN	WI D OWER
BE D EMAN	CU D D IES	HY D RASE	PA D D IES	RE D TAIL	YO D ELER
BE D EVIL	CU D D LER	HY D RATE	PA D D ING	RE D UCER	*ZA D D ICK
BE D FAST	CU D WEE D	*HY D RIDE	PA D D LER	RE D WARE	*ZE D OARY
BE D GOWN	D A D AISM	*HY D ROI D	*PA D DOCK	RE D WING	BE D OTTE D
BE D IGHT	D A D AIST	*HY D ROPS	*PA D LOCK	RE D WOO D	BE D SHEET
BE D IRTY	D E D LICE	HY D ROUS	PA D RONE	RI D ABLE	BE D STAN D
*BE D IZEN	D I D D LER	*HY D ROXY	*PA D SHAH	RI D D ING	BE D STEA D
BE D LAMP	D I D D LEY	*JA D EITE	PE D AGOG	RI D D LER	BI D DABLE
BE D LESS	D O D D ERY	*JO D HPUR	PE D D LER	RI D GIER	BO D YSUIT
BE D LIKE	D O D GERY	*JU D OIST	PE D ICAB	RI D GING	BU D D LEIA
BE D MATE	D O D GING	*KA D D ISH		RI D OTTO	*CO D EBOOK
BE D OUIN	D O D OISM			RO D LESS	CO D ESIGN

CO D IRECT	RE D EMAN D	FI D D LY	SO D DE D	*HA D DOCK	TAR D YON
CO D RIVER	*RE D SHIFT	FO D D ER	SO D D EN	HOO D IER	TI D D LER
DO D DERER	RE D START	FOO D IE	SOR D ID	HU D D LER	TOA D IE D
FA D D IEST	RE D UCTOR	FU D D LE	SOR D OR	HUN D RE D	TO D D IES
*GO D CHILD	RI D D ANCE	GA D DE D	STU D LY	*KA D D ISH	TO D D LER
HI D ROTIC	RU D D IEST	GA D D ER	SU D D EN	KI D D IES	TUR D INE
*HY D RACID	SA D D LERY	GI D D AP	TE D DER	KI D D ING	*TWI D D LY
*HY D ROSKI	SA D D LING	GO D D AM	TI D D LY	*KI D D ISH	WA D D IE D
*KI D NAPEE	SI D EBAN D	GO D DE D	TO D D LE	*KI D D USH	WA D D IES
*LA D YBIR D	SI D EWAR D	HE D D LE	WA D D ER	KIN D RE D	WA D D ING
*LA D YHOO D	SO D D ENLY	HI D DEN	WA D D IE	LEA D MAN	WA D D LER
ME D ALIST	SO D OMIST	HO D D EN	WA D D LE	LY D D ITE	WE D D ING
ME D ALLIC	*SO D OMIZE	HO D D IN	WA D D LY	ME D D USA	WOO D IES
ME D IALLY	TI D ELAN D	HON D LE	WE D D ER	MIN D SET	*ZA D D ICK
ME D IANLY	*VI D EOTEX	HU D D LE	WI D D ER	MIS D EE D	*BAI D ARKA
ME D IATOR	*WI D EBAND	*JU D D ER	WI D D IE	MIS D IAL	*BAL D HEA D
ME D ICAI D	BAL D Y	*KE D D AH	WI D D LE	MU D D IE D	BAL D NESS
ME D ICARE	BIN D I	KI D D ER	WOO D IE	NAN D INA	BAL D PATE
ME D ICATE	BUN D T	KI D D IE	*ZA D D IK	NO D D IES	*BAL D RICK
ME D ICINE	CLA D E	LA D D ER	BAL D IES	NO D D ING	BAN D AGER
ME D IOCRE	CON D O	LA D D IE	BAN D IE D	NON D RUG	BAN D ANNA
ME D ITATE	HOO D Y	MA D DE D	BE D D ING	PA D D IES	BAN D EROL
ME D TEVAL	MU D D Y	NO D DE D	BI D D ING	PA D D LER	BAN D ITRY
ME D USOI D	NER D Y	NO D D ER	BIR D ING	PE D D LER	BAN D SMAN
MI D BRAIN	RAN D Y	NO D D LE	BLU D GER	PER D URE	BAU D RONS
*MI D FIEL D	REA D Y	NOO D GE	BON D ING	PI D D LER	BAW D IEST
MI D POINT	WOO D Y	NOR D IC	BU D D IED	*PI D DOCK	BEA D IEST
MI D RANGE	BA D D IE	PA D D ER	BU D D IES	PRE D IVE	*BEA D LIKE
*MI D SIZE D	BE D DE D	PA D D LE	BU D D ING	PU D D ING	BEA D ROLL
MI D STORY	BE D DER	PE D D LE	CA D D ICE	PU D D LER	BEA D SMAN
MO D ALITY	BI D DEN	PI D D LE	CA D D ISH	RAN D IER	*BEA D WORK
MO D ELING	BI D DER	PI D D LY	CLA D IST	REA D IE D	*BEN D WAYS
MO D ELIST	BU D DER	PU D D LE	CO D D ING	RE D D EST	BEN D WISE
MO D ELLE D	BU D DLE	PU D D LY	CO D D LER	RE D D ING	*BER D ACHE
MO D ELLER	CA D D IE	RA D D LE	COR D ING	RE D D ISH	BI D D ABLE
MO D ERATE	CA D D IS	RE D DE D	CU D D IES	REE D ILY	*BIN D WEED
MO D ERATO	CAN D ID	RE D D EN	CU D D LER	REE D MAN	*BIR D BATH
*MO D IFIE D	CAU D AD	RE D D ER	DEO D AN D	RI D D LER	*BIR D CAGE
MO D IOLUS	CHA D AR	RE D D LE	DID D LEY	ROA D BE D	BIR D CALL
MO D ULATE	CHA D OR	RI D DE D	DO D D ERY	RU D D IER	*BIR D FARM
MU D D IEST	CO D DE D	RI D DEN	FA D D IER	RU D D ILY	*BIR D LIKE
MU D GUAR D	CO D D ER	RI D D ER	FA D D ING	SA D D LER	BIR D LIME
MU D SLI D E	CO D D LE	RI D D LE	*FA D D ISH	SAN D D AB	BIR D SEE D
MU D STONE	COY D OG	ROA D EO	FA D D ISM	SAR D ANA	BIR D SEYE
PA D D LING	CU D D IE	ROA D IE	FA D D IST	SEE D BE D	BIR D SHOT
PE D ALLE D	CU D D LE	RU D D ER	FI D D LER	SEE D PO D	BIR D SONG
*PE D D LERY	CU D D LY	RU D D LE	GA D D ING	SO D D ING	BLU D GEON
PE D D LING	DA D DLE	SA D D EN	*GI D D YAP	STU D IE D	BOL D FACE
*PO D OCARP	DI D DLE	SA D D HU	*GI D D YUP	SUN D ECK	BOL D NESS
PU D D LING	DI D D LY	SA D D LE	GO D D ESS	SWI D D EN	BON D MAI D
RA D ICAN D	DO D DER	SEI D EL	GO D D ING		*BOR D EAUX
RA D WASTE	DU D D IE	SEN D UP	HA D D EST		BOR D ERER
RE D AMAGE	FI D D LE	SI D D UR			BRI D ALLY
RE D ECI D E		SMI D GE			BRI D GING
RE D EFECT					BU D D LEIA

BUN D LING	D EED LESS	*HAN D CUFF	HEA D RACE	LOR D LESS	PEN D ULUM
BUR D ENER	D END RITE	*HAN D FAST	HEA D REST	LOR D LIER	PIE D FORT
CAL D ARIA	D END ROID	*HAN D GRIP	HEA D ROOM	LOR D LIKE	PIE D MONT
*CAN D IDLY	DOD D ERER	*HAN D HELD	HEA D SAIL	LOR D LING	PIN D LING
*CAR D AMOM	D OLD RUMS	*HAN D HOLD	*HEA D SHIP	LOR D OSIS	PLE D GEOR
CAR D AMON	D RED GING	*HAN D ICAP	HEA D SMAN	LOR D SHIP	PLE D GING
*CAR D AMUM	D RUD GERY	HAN D IEST	*HEA D STAY	LOU D NESS	PON D ERER
CAR D CASE	D UOD ENUM	HAN D LING	*HEA D WIND	*MAI D HOOD	*POND WEED
CAR D IGAN	FAD D IEST	HAN D LIST	*HEA D WORD	*MAN D RAKE	POW D ERER
CAR D INAL	FAL D ERAL	HAN D LOOM	*HEAD WORK	ME D ALIST	PRA D ITOR
CAR D IOID	FAL D EROL	*HAN D MADE	*HEB D OMAD	ME D ALLIC	PRE D ATOR
CAR D ITIS	FAN D ANGO	*HAN D MAID	HEE D LESS	ME D IALLY	PRE D RILL
CAU D ATED	*FEED BACK	*HAN D OVER	*HER D LIKE	ME D IANLY	PRI D EFUL
CAU D ILLO	*FEED HOLE	HAN D RAIL	HER D SMAN	ME D IATOR	PRO D IGAL
*CHA D ARIM	FEL D SPAR	*HAN D SEWN	HIN D ERER	ME D ICAID	PRO D ROME
CLA D DING	*FOL D AWAY	*HAN D SFUL	HIN D MOST	ME D ICARE	PRO D UCER
CLO D PATE	FOL D BOAT	HAN D SOME	*HOL D BACK	ME D ICATE	PRU D ENCE
CLO D POLE	FOL D EROL	*HAN D WORK	*HOL D FAST	ME D ICINE	PUD D LING
CLO D POLL	FON D LING	*HAN D WRIT	*HOL D OVER	ME D IEVAL	PUN D ITRY
COA D MIRE	FON D NESS	*HAN D YMAN	HOO D IEST	ME D IOCRE	*PYO D ERMA
COE D ITOR	*FOOD WAYS	*HAR D BACK	HOO D LESS	ME D ITATE	*QUA D PLEX
*COL D COCK	FOR D LESS	*HAR D BALL	*HOO D LIKE	ME D USOID	*QUA D RANS
COL D NESS	GAR D ENER	HAR D BOOT	*HOO D WINK	MI D BRAIN	*QUA D RANT
CON D ENSE	GAR D ENIA	HAR D CASE	KIN D LESS	MI D POINT	*QUA D RATE
CON D OLER	GAR D YLOO	HAR D CORE	KIN D LING	MI D RANGE	*QUA D RIGA
CON D ONER	GEN D ARME	HAR D EDGE	KIN D NESS	MI D STORY	*QUA D ROON
CON D UCER	GEO D ESIC	HAR D ENER	LAB D ANUM	MO D ALITY	*QUID D ITY
COR D ELLE	GEO D ETIC	*HAR D HACK	LAN D FALL	MO D ELING	*QUI D NUNC
COR D LESS	GIL D HALL	*HAR D HEAD	LAN D FILL	MO D ELLED	RAN D IEST
*COR D LIKE	GLA D DEST	HAR D IEST	LAN D FORM	MO D ELLER	RAN D OMLY
COR D OVAN	GLA D DING	HAR D LINE	LAN D GRAB	MO D ERATE	*RAN D PICK
COR D UROY	GLA D IATE	HAR D NESS	LAN D LADY	MO D ERATO	REA D DICT
COR D WAIN	GLA D IEST	HAR D NOSE	LAN D LESS	MO D IFIED	REA D IEST
*COR D WOOD	GLA D IOLA	*HAR D SHIP	LAN D LINE	MO D IOLUS	*REA D JUST
CRE D ENDA	GLA D IOLI	*HAR D TACK	LAN D LORD	MO D IOLUS	REE D BIRD
*CRE D ENZA	GLA D NESS	*HAR D WARE	*LAND MARK	MO D ULATE	*REE D BUCK
CRE D IBLE	GLA D SOME	*HAR D WIRE	LAN D MASS	*MOLD WARP	REE D IEST
CRE D ITOR	GOA D LIKE	*HAR D WOOD	LAN D SIDE	*MOR D ANCY	REE D LING
CRU D ITES	*GOL D FISH	*HAV D ALAH	*LAN D SKIP	MU D DIEST	REN D ERER
CUR D IEST	GOO D NESS	*HEA D ACHE	LAN D SLID	MU D GUARD	REN D IBLE
*DAN D RUFF	*GOO D WIFE	*HEA D ACHY	LAN D SLIP	MU D STONE	*REN D ZINA
*DAN D YISH	GOO D WILL	*HEA D BAND	LAN D SMAN	NEE D IEST	RHO D AMIN
*DAN D YISM	*GRA D IENT	*HEA D FISH	LAN D WARD	NEE D LESS	RI D DANCE
*DAY D REAM	GRA D UAND	HEA D GATE	LAR D IEST	NEE D LING	ROA D KILL
D EAD BEAT	GRA D UATE	HEA D GEAR	LAR D LIKE	NON D AIRY	ROA D LESS
D EAD BOLT	GRI D IRON	*HEA D HUNT	LAU D ABLE	NON D ANCE	ROA D SIDE
D EAD ENER	*GRI D LOCK	HEA D IEST	LAU D ANUM	PA D DLING	ROA D STER
D EAD FALL	GUI D ANCE	*HEA D LAMP	LAU D ATOR	PAN D ANUS	*ROAD WORK
D EAD HEAD	*GUI D HEAD	HEA D LAND	LEA D IEST	PAN D ERER	RON D ELET
D EAD LIER	*HAB D ALAH	HEA D LESS	LEA D LESS	*PAN D EMIC	*ROW D YISH
D EAD LIFT	HAN D BALL	HEA D LINE	LEA D SMAN	PAR D ONER	*ROW D YISM
D EAD LINE	HAN D BELL	*HEA D LOCK	*LEA D WORK	*PAN D OWDY	RU D DIEST
*DEAD LOCK	HAN D BILL	HEA D LONG	LEA D WORT	PED D LERY	SAD D LERY
D EAD NESS	*HAN D BOOK	HEA D MOST	LEW D NESS	PE D D LING	
DEADWOOD	HAN D CART	HEA D NOTE	LOA D STAR	*PEN D ENCY	

SA D D LING	SUB D URAL	WIL D LING	BIR D	KIN D	SEN D
SAN D ARAC	SUN D ERER	WIL D NESS	BOL D	LAI D	SHA D
*SAN D BANK	SUN D RESS	*WILD WOO D	BON D	LAN D	SHE D
SAN D BURR	SUN D RIES	*WILD WOO D	BRA D	LAR D	SHO D
*SAN D FISH	SUN D ROPS	WIN D BURN	BRE D	LAU D	SKI D
SAN D IEST	*SVE D BERG	WIN D FALL	BUN D	LEA D	SLE D
SAN D LIKE	SYN D ESIS	*WIN D FLAW	BUR D	LEN D	SNE D
SAN D LING	SYN D ETIC	WIN D GALL	CAI D	LEU D	SOL D
SAN D PEEP	SYN D ROME	WIN D IEST	CAR D	LEW D	SOR D
SAN D PILE	TEN D ANCE	WIN D LASS	**CHA D**	LIE D	SPE D
SAN D SHOE	TEN D ENCE	WIN D LESS	CLA D	LOA D	SPU D
SAN D SOAP	TEN D ENCY	WIN D LING	CLO D	LOR D	STU D
SAN D SPUR	TEN D ERER	WIN D MILL	COE D	LOU D	SU D D
*SAN D WICH	TEN D ERLY	*WIN D PIPE	COL D	MAI D	SUR D
SAN D WORM	*TOA D FISH	*WIN D SOCK	COR D	MEA D	TEN D
SAN D WORT	*TOA D FLAX	*WIN D SURF	CRU D	MEE D	THU D
SAR D ONIC	TOA D LESS	*WIN D WAR D	CUR D	MEL D	TIE D
*SAR D ONYX	*TOA D LIKE	*WIN D WAR D	D EA D	MEN D	TOA D
SEA D ROME	TOA D YISM	WON D ERER	D EE D	MIL D	TOL D
*SEE D CAKE	*TRA D EOFF	WON D ROUS	D IE D	MOL D	TRA D
SEE D CASE	TRA D ITOR	*WOO D BIN D	D UA D	MOO D	TRO D
SEE D IEST	TRA D UCER	WOO D BINE	D YA D	NAR D	TUR D
SEE D LESS	TRU D GEON	*WOO D CHAT	FAR D	NEE D	VEL D
SEE D LIKE	TRU D GING	*WOO D COCK	FEE D	NER D	VEN D
SEE D LING	TWA D DLER	WOO D IEST	FEN D	NUR D	VOI D
SEE D SMAN	TWI D DLER	WOO D LAN D	FEO D	PAI D	WAN D
SEE D TIME	VEN D ETTA	WOO D LESS	FEU D	PAR D	WAR D
*SHA D BLOW	VEN D EUSE	WOO D LORE	FIN D	PEN D	WEE D
*SHA D BUSH	VEN D IBLE	WOO D NOTE	FLE D	PIE D	WEL D
*SHA D CHAN	*VEN D IBLY	WOO D PILE	FOL D	PLE D	WEN D
*SHA D DOCK	*VER D ANCY	*WOO D RUFF	FON D	PLO D	**WHI D**
SHA D IEST	VER D ERER	*WOO D SHE D	FOO D	PON D	WIL D
*SHA D OWER	VER D ITER	*WOO D SHE D	FOR D	POO D	WIN D
*SHA D RACH	VIN D ALOO	WOO D SMAN	FUN D	PRO D	WOA D
SHE D ABLE	VOI D ANCE	*WOO D WIND	GAU D	QAI D	WOL D
SHE D D ING	VOI D NESS	*WOO D WORK	GEL D	QUA D	WOO D
*SHE D LIKE	WAN D ERER	*WOO D WORM	GIL D	QUI D	WOR D
*SHU D DERY	WAN D EROO	*WOR D BOOK	GIR D	QUO D	**WYN D**
*SKY D IVER	*WAR D ENRY	WOR D IEST	GLA D	RAI D	YAL D
SLE D D ING	WAR D RESS	WOR D LESS	GLE D	RAN D	YAR D
*SLI D EWAY	WAR D ROBE	*WOR D PLAY	GOA D	REA D	YAU D
SMI D GEON	WAR D ROOM	*YAR D BIR D	GOL D	RE D D	YEL D
SO D D ENLY	*WAR D SHIP	YAR D LAN D	GOO D	REE D	YIR D
SOL D ERER	WEE D IEST	*YAR D WAN D	GOW D	REN D	YON D
SOL D IERY	WEE D LESS	*YAR D WORK	GRA D	RIN D	BASE D
SPA D EFUL	WEL D LESS		GRI D	ROA D	BEAR D
SPA D ICES	WEL D MENT		GUI D	ROO D	BIEL D
SPA D ILLE	*WHO D UNIT	BAL D	HAN D	RU D D	**BIFI D**
STE D FAST	*WIL D FIRE	BAN D	HAR D	RYN D	**BIPE D**
*STU D BOOK	*WIL D FOWL	BAR D	HEE D	SAI D	**BIPO D**
STU D D ING	*WIL D LAN D	BAU D	HEL D	SAN D	BLAN D
*STU D FISH	*WIL D LIFE	BEA D	HER D	SAR D	BLEE D
STU D IOUS		BEN D	HIN D	SCA D	BLEN D
*STU D WORK		BIN D	HOL D	SCU D	BLIN D
SUB D EPOT			HOO D	SEE D	

BLON D	GEOI D	PAGE D	STAI D	**BEHEA D**	**D AMME D**
BLOO D	GLAN D	PAGO D	STAN D	**BEHEL D**	**D AMNE D**
BLUE D	GLEE D	**PAVI D**	STEA D	**BEHIN D**	**D APPE D**
BOAR D	GONA D	PILE D	STEE D	**BEHOL D**	D ARNE D
BORE D	GOUR D	PINE D	STIE D	BELAU D	**D AYBE D**
BOUN D	GRAN D	PLAI D	STOO D	BESTU D	**D EFEN D**
BOVI D	GREE D	PLEA D	SWAR D	BETTE D	**D EFIE D**
BRAI D	GRIN D	PLIE D	SWOR D	**BEYON D**	**D EFUN D**
BRAN D	GUAR D	POIN D	SYNO D	**BIBBE D**	D ELEA D
BREA D	GUIL D	POLE D	TABI D	**BIFOL D**	**D EMAN D**
BREE D	HALI D	POUN D	TEII D	BINNE D	D ENIE D
BROAD	HOAR D	PRIE D	TEIN D	BITTE D	D ENNE D
BROO D	**HO DA D**	PROU D	TEPI D	**BO DIE D**	**D EPEN D**
BUIL D	**HOME D**	PSEU D	THIR D	**BOGGE D**	D ESAN D
CAIR D	**HUMI D**	**PYOI D**	TIMI D	**BOYAR D**	**D ESMI D**
CANI D	**HYOI D**	RABI D	TIRE D	BRIAR D	D EVOI D
CASE D	*JEHA D	RANI D	TREA D	**BROMI D**	D IACI D
CAUL D	**JERI D**	RAPI D	TREN D	**BUGGE D**	**D IGGE D**
CAVE D	*JIHA D	REA D D	TRIA D	**BUMME D**	D ILLE D
CEBI D	**KNEA D**	REBI D	TRIE D	BURIE D	**D IMME D**
CERE D	LAIR D	RE DI D	TRUE D	BURRE D	D INNE D
CHIL D	**LAKE D**	RESI D	TUMI D	BUSIE D	*D IOXI D
CHOR D	LAME D	RESO D	TWEE D	BUSSE D	**D IPPE D**
CLOU D	LATE D	REWE D	**TYPE D**	BYROA D	**D ISBU D**
CO DE D	LIAR D	RIGI D	VALI D	*BYWOR D	D ISSE D
COUL D	**LIKE D**	ROSE D	**VAPI D**	CANAR D	**D OGGE D**
CREE D	LINE D	ROUN D	VIAN D	**CAN DI D**	D OILE D
CRIE D	LIPI D	SALA D	VIRI D	CANNE D	D OITE D
CROW D	LIVI D	SAPI D	**VIVI D**	**CAPPE D**	D ONNE D
CUPI D	LOVE D	SARO D	WEAL D	**CAPSI D**	D OO DA D
CYCA D	LUCI D	SAYI D	WEIR D	CATTE D	D ORSA D
D REA D	LURI D	SCAL D	WIEL D	**CAU DA D**	D OTAR D
D RIE D	LUTE D	SCEN D	WISE D	**CEBOI D**	D OTTE D
D RUI D	LYAR D	SCOL D	WOAL D	**CERVI D**	**D ROWN D**
D RYA D	MAUN D	SCRO D	WORL D	**CHIEL D**	D UNNE D
FARA D	MENA D	SHAR D	WOUL D	CITIE D	**D UPPE D**
FAUL D	MONA D	SHEN D	WOUN D	CLERI D	D URNE D
FELI D	**MOPE D**	SHER D	WRIE D	COCCI D	**FANNE D**
FETI D	MOUL D	SHIE D	YAIR D	CO D DE D	FANTO D
FIEL D	MOUN D	SHRE D	YAUL D	COGGE D	**FATTE D**
FIEN D	**MOVE D**	SI DE D	YIEL D	**COHEA D**	FECUN D
FIOR D	**MUCI D**	**SKAL D**	*ZOOI D	COLEA D	FERVI D
FIRE D	MURI D	**SKIE D**	**BABIE D**	CONNE D	FETTE D
*FJEL D	**MYOI D**	SLOI D	**BAGGE D**	CONOI D	FINNE D
*FJOR D	**MYSI D**	**SLOJ D**	BALLA D	**COPIE D**	**FITTE D**
FLIE D	NAIA D	SLOY D	BANNE D	**COPPE D**	FOETI D
FLUI D	**NAKE D**	SNOO D	BARIE D	COSIE D	FOGGE D
FOUN D	NALE D	SOLE D	BARRE D	**COWAR D**	FORBI D
FRAU D	NICA D	SOLI D	BATTE D	*COZIE D	FRIEN D
FREE D	NITI D	SOUN D	**BAYAR D**	**CUBOI D**	FRIGI D
FREM D	NOMA D	SPEE D	**BE D DE D**	**CUPPE D**	FUCOI D
FRIE D	NOSE D	SPEN D	**BE D RI D**	CURSE D	FUGGE D
FRON D	NOTE D	SPIE D	**BEGGE D**	CUSPI D	FULGI D
GA DI D		*SQUA D	**BEGIR D**	CYANI D	FUNNE D
GELI D		*SQUI D	**BEGLA D**	CYMOI D	FURRE D

GABBE D	JERRI D	MORBI D	RAPPE D	SACRE D	TOLUI D
GA D DE D	JETTE D	MUCOI D	RATTE D	SAGGE D	TOMCO D
GA D OI D	*JOCUN D	MUGGE D	REBIN D	SAIYI D	TOMME D
GAGGE D	*JUGGE D	MUMME D	RECLA D	SALPI D	TOPPE D
GAMME D	KELOI D	MUSCI D	RECOR D	SAPPE D	TOROI D
GANOI D	KENNE D	*MUSJI D	RE D BU D	SAYYI D	TORPI D
GAPPE D	*KEPPE D	MYRIA D	RE D DE D	SCHRO D	TORRI D
GARRE D	*KEYPA D	*MYXOI D	REFEE D	SCREE D	TOTTE D
GASSE D	*KI D VI D	NAPPE D	REFFE D	SCRIE D	TOWAR D
GELLE D	KITTE D	NAVAI D	REFIN D	SEABE D	TOXOI D
GEMME D	KOBOL D	NEREI D	REFOL D	SECON D	TREPI D
GERUN D	LAGEN D	NETTE D	REFUN D	SECUN D	TRIFI D
GIGGE D	LAGGE D	NIMRO D	REGAR D	SHAIR D	TRIPO D
GINNE D	LAMME D	NITRI D	REGIL D	SHALE D	TUBBE D
GOBBE D	LAMPA D	NO D DE D	RELEN D	SHIEL D	TUNNE D
GO D DE D	LAPPE D	NORME D	REMAN D	SHOUL D	TUPPE D
GRAVI D	*LAZIE D	NUTTE D	REMEN D	SHREW D	TURBI D
GROUN D	LEAVE D	PALLE D	REMIN D	SHROU D	TURGI D
GUMME D	LEGEN D	PALLI D	REMOL D	SIALI D	TUTTE D
GUNNE D	LEGGE D	PANNE D	REPAI D	SINNE D	VANNE D
GUTTE D	LETTE D	PARRE D	REPAN D	SIPPE D	VARIE D
HAGGE D	LEVIE D	PATTE D	REPPE D	SO D DE D	VATTE D
HAIRE D	LIGAN D	PAVEE D	REREA D	SOGGE D	VAWAR D
HALOI D	LILIE D	PEGGE D	RESAI D	SOLAN D	VERBI D
HAMME D	LIMPI D	PENNE D	RESEE D	SOPPE D	VESPI D
HAPPE D	LIPOI D	PENTA D	RESEN D	SOR D I D	VETTE D
HATRE D	LIPPE D	PEPPE D	RESOL D	SOTTE D	VIROI D
HATTE D	*LIQUI D	PEPTI D	RETAR D	SPARI D	VISAR D
*HAZAR D	*LIZAR D	PERIO D	RETOL D	SPREA D	VISCI D
HEMME D	LOBBE D	PETAR D	RETTE D	STOLI D	*VIZAR D
HEMOI D	LOGGE D	PETTE D	REVVE D	STOUN D	WAGGE D
HEPTA D	LOOSE D	*PHYSE D	REWAR D	STRAN D	WANNE D
HERAL D	LOPPE D	PIGGE D	REWEL D	STROU D	WARRE D
HERBE D	LOTTE D	PINNE D	REWIN D	STUPI D	*WEBFE D
HIPPE D	LUGGE D	PIPPE D	REWOR D	SUBBE D	WETTE D
HISPI D	MA D DE D	PITIE D	RIBAL D	SULFI D	*WICKE D
HOGGE D	MAENA D	PITTE D	RIBAN D	SUMME D	WIGGE D
HOLAR D	MALFE D	PLACI D	RIBBE D	SUNNE D	WINNE D
HONIE D	MALTE D	PLATE D	RI D DE D	SUPPE D	WITTE D
HOOPE D	MANNE D	PLEIA D	RIFFE D	SWOUN D	*WIZAR D
HOOVE D	MANTI D	PONGI D	RIGGE D	TABAR D	WONNE D
HORRI D	MAPPE D	PONIE D	RIMME D	TABBE D	WOOLE D
HOTBE D	MARAU D	POPPE D	RIPPE D	TAGGE D	*XYLOI D
HOTRO D	MARRE D	POTTE D	RITAR D	TANNE D	YAPPE D
HOTTE D	*MASJI D	PREME D	ROBAN D	TARRE D	YESSE D
HUGGE D	MATTE D	PSOCI D	ROBBE D	TATTE D	YIPPE D
HUMME D	*MAZAR D	PUGGE D	ROTUN D	TATTE D	*ZONKE D
HUTTE D	ME D IA D	PUNNE D	RUBBE D	TECHE D	*ZYGOI D
*HYBRI D	MELOI D	PUPPE D	RUBIE D	TETRA D	BA D LAN D
HY D RI D	METHO D	PURRE D	RUCHE D	TI D IE D	BAN D IE D
*JAGGE D	MILOR D	PUTRI D	RUGGE D	TINEI D	BARMAI D
*JAMME D	MISA D D	RAGGE D	RUTTE D	TINNE D	BARTEN D
JARRE D	MOBLE D	RAMME D	SABBE D	TIPPE D	BASTAR D
JASSI D	MONIE D	RAMRO D		TOGGE D	BAUSON D
JEREE D	MOPPE D	RANCI D			*BAYWOO D

BEBLOO D	*CHEVIE D	D ENTOI D	FRITTE D	*JETTIE D	MISREA D
BECLOU D	CHILIA D	D EO D AN D	FROGGE D	*JOLLIE D	MISSEN D
*BECROW D	CHINNE D	D ERMOI D	FROSTE D	*JUGHEA D	MISSHO D
BE D WAR D	*CHIPPE D	D ESCEN D	FROWAR D	*KATY D I D	MISTEN D
BEEYAR D	CHLORI D	D ESMOI D	FUNGOI D	*KEFLOO D	MISWOR D
BELACE D	*CHOPPE D	D ESPON D	GABBAR D	*KEYCAR D	MO D ULE D
BELATE D	CHOROI D	D IALLE D	GARLAN D	*KEYWOR D	MONACI D
BELLIE D	*CICHLI D	D IAMON D	GESSOE D	KILORA D	MONEYE D
BELOVE D	CIRSOI D	D IAPSI D	*GIZZAR D	KIN D RE D	MU D D IE D
BEROBE D	CISSOI D	D IEHAR D	GLENOI D	KNEEPA D	MUMMIE D
BESTEA D	CLAMME D	D IPLOI D	GLOBOI D	KNOTTE D	MUSTAR D
*BETAXE D	CLOTTE D	D ISBAN D	GLOCHI D	LABROI D	MYELOI D
BIGHEA D	CLUPEI D	D ISCAR D	GLUTTE D	LAGGAR D	NEGROI D
BIGOTE D	COCCOI D	D ISCOI D	GNARRE D	LALLAN D	NEUROI D
BILOBE D	COFOUN D	D ISCOR D	GOBIOI D	LANATE D	NOCTUI D
BILSTE D	COLLAR D	D ISPEN D	GO D HEA D	LANGUI D	NONACI D
BLATTE D	COLLIE D	D ISTEN D	GO D HOO D	LANIAR D	NONFOO D
BLESSE D	COLLOI D	D OGSLE D	GO D SEN D	LANYAR D	NONPAI D
BLOTTE D	COLORE D	D OGWOO D	GOLIAR D	LATERA D	NONSKE D
BLOWSE D	COMMAN D	D OLLIE D	GORMAN D	LEEWAR D	NONSKI D
*BLOWZE D	COMMEN D	D ONNER D	GRAN D A D	LENTOI D	NONWOR D
BOBSLE D	COMPEN D	D RAMME D	GRINNE D	LEOPAR D	NORLAN D
BOGWOO D	CONCOR D	D ROMON D	GRIPPE D	LEOTAR D	NOTEPA D
BOLLAR D	CONTEN D	D ROPPE D	GUISAR D	LEPORI D	NUTWOO D
BOMBAR D	COPEPO D	D RUMME D	GUMWEE D	LIANOI D	PAGURI D
BOOKEN D	CORNFE D	D RYLAN D	GUMWOO D	LIMITE D	PAN D IE D
*BOWHEA D	COSTAR D	D UELLE D	GURNAR D	LINGCO D	PAROTI D
*BOXWOO D	*COWBIN D	D ULLAR D	HAGGAR D	LINSEE D	PARRIE D
*BOYHOO D	*COWBIR D	*D YEWEE D	HALBER D	LITHOI D	PARTIE D
BRANNE D	*COWHAN D	*D YEWOO D	HALYAR D	LOBATE D	PAYLOA D
BRIGAN D	*COWHER D	FACIEN D	HAPLOI D	LOGWOO D	PEASCO D
BRIMME D	*COWSHE D	FACTOI D	HARRIE D	LOWBRE D	PERACI D
BRIN D E D	CRAMME D	FANCIE D	HATBAN D	LOWLAN D	PERCOI D
BU D DIE D	CRAW D A D	FANFOL D	HAYSEE D	LUNATE D	*PEROXI D
BUGSEE D	CRICOI D	FARMAN D	HELIPA D	*LYCOPO D	PERPEN D
BULLIE D	CRINOI D	FATBIR D	*HEXAPO D	LYRATE D	*PHASMI D
BURSEE D	CROOKE D	FATHEA D	HISTOI D	MALLAR D	PHONIE D
BURWEE D	CROPPE D	FATWOO D	*HOGWEE D	MANGOL D	*PHYTOI D
BUSLOA D	CTENOI D	FENLAN D	HOLLAN D	MANHOO D	PIEBAL D
BUSTAR D	*CUCKOL D	FERRIE D	HOMINI D	MANKIN D	PIGWEE D
*BUZZAR D	CU D WEE D	FIBROI D	*HOPHEA D	MANSAR D	PINFOL D
CAN D IE D	CULICI D	FILARH D	HOPTOA D	MANWAR D	PINGUI D
CARABI D	CULLIE D	FLAC D I D	HOTHEA D	MARRIE D	PINHEA D
CARLOA D	CURRIE D	*FLAMME D	HUN D RE D	MASTOI D	PINWEE D
CAROTI D	CUSTAR D	*FLAPPE D	HUSBAN D	MATTOI D	PITHEA D
CARRIE D	*CYCLOI D	FLATBE D	HYALOI D	*MAYWEE D	PLACAR D
CATBIR D	CYSTOI D	FLATTE D	*HY D ATI D	*MAZZAR D	PLACOI D
CATHEA D	D AGWOO D	*FLIPPE D	*HY D ROI D	MEGAPO D	PLAFON D
CERATE D	D ASTAR D	FLUORI D	*HYPNOI D	MELAME D	PLANNE D
CESTOI D	D ECAPO D	FOOTPA D	*JARHEA D	MERMAI D	PLASMI D
*CHALCI D	D ECRIE D	FORFEN D	*JAYBIR D	MI D LAN D	PLASTI D
*CHAPPE D	D EFRAU D	FORWAR D	*JEOPAR D	MINUEN D	PLATTE D
CHARRE D	D EIFIE D	FOULAR D	*JERREE D	MISBIN D	PLEOPO D
CHATTE D	D ELTOI D	FRACTE D	*JETBEA D	MIS D EE D	PLOTTE D
CHELOI D	D EMIGO D	FRETTE D		MISLEA D	*PLYWOO D

*POCHAR D	RIMLAN D	SPATTE D	TOGATE D	*BACKYAR D	BULLHEA D
POLLAR D	RIPCOR D	SPIROI D	TOWHEA D	*BALD HEA D	BULLWEE D
*POLYPO D	ROA D BE D	SPITTE D	TOWMON D	*BANKCAR D	BUSHLAN D
PONIAR D	ROSEBU D	SPOROI D	TRAMME D	BAREHEA D	*BUZZWOR D
*POPEYE D	SAGGAR D	SPURRE D	TRAPPE D	BARNYAR D	CABALLE D
POPPIE D	SALLIE D	*SQUALI D	TRIACI D	BASSWOO D	*CABOCHE D
PORTEN D	SAPHEA D	STAGGE D	TRICLA D	*BECOWAR D	*CABOSHE D
POTHEA D	SAPWOO D	STARRE D	TRIFOL D	BE D OTTE D	CABSTAN D
POULAR D	SARCOI D	STEMME D	TRIMME D	BE D STAN D	CANALLE D
PREAGE D	SATYRI D	STEPPE D	*TRIOXI D	BE D STEA D	CANCROI D
PREBEN D	SCANNE D	STEROI D	TRIPPE D	BEEBREA D	CANFIEL D
PREBIN D	SCARRE D	STEWAR D	TROLAN D	*BEEFWOO D	CARANGI D
PREMOL D	SCATTE D	STIPEN D	TROTTE D	BEFRIEN D	CAR D IOI D
PREPAI D	SCIURI D	STIRRE D	TWINNE D	BELLBIR D	CAROLLE D
PREPPE D	SCUMME D	STOPPE D	TWITTE D	BENTWOO D	CARTLOA D
PRESOL D	SEABIR D	STORIE D	TWOFOL D	BERINGE D	CARYATI D
PRETEN D	SEAFOO D	STU D IE D	*TYPHOI D	BEROUGE D	CASELOA D
PRIMME D	SEAWAR D	STUMME D	VANWAR D	BESHROU D	CATENOI D
PROBAN D	SEAWEE D	STUNNE D	VISCOI D	BESLAVE D	CAU D ATE D
PROCEE D	SEE D BE D	STYLOI D	WA D D IE D	BESPREA D	CENTROI D
PROPEN D	SEE D PO D	SUBACI D	WARHEA D	*BEWINGE D	*CEPHALA D
PROPPE D	*SHAMME D	SUBARI D	WARLOR D	*BICUSPI D	CERATOI D
PROTEI D	SHINNE D	SUBHEA D	WAXWEE D	*BIFORKE D	*CHARACI D
PROTEN D	*SHIPPE D	SUBTEN D	*WAYWAR D	*BIFORME D	CHEERLE D
PSYLLI D	*SHOPPE D	SUCCEE D	WEARIE D	BILLFOL D	*CHELIPE D
PUTTIE D	SHOTTE D	SULPHI D	WEASAN D	BILLHEA D	*CHENOPO D
PYRALI D	SIALOI D	SUMMAN D	*WEAZAN D	BILLIAR D	*CHIL D BE D
*PYRAMI D	*SICKBE D	SUNBIR D	*WEEKEN D	*BIND WEE D	*CHILOPO D
*QUERIE D	SIGANI D	SUNLAN D	WERGEL D	BIPARTE D	CHOREOI D
*QUINOI D	SIGMOI D	SUNWAR D	WERGIL D	BIR D SEE D	CHORIOI D
*QUITTE D	SILURI D	SUSPEN D	WESSAN D	*BIVALVE D	CHRESAR D
RAGWEE D	SIMIOI D	SWAGGE D	WETLAN D	*BLINKAR D	CILIATE D
RALLIE D	*SIXFOL D	SWANNE D	*WHIPPE D	*BLIZZAR D	CIRRIPE D
REA D IE D	SKINNE D	SWATTE D	WHIRRE D	BLOO D IE D	*CITYFIE D
REBLEN D	*SKIPPE D	*SYLPHI D	*WHIZZE D	BLOO D RE D	*CITYWAR D
REBOAR D	*SKYWAR D	*SYRPHI D	WILLIE D	*BLOWHAR D	*CLOCHAR D
REBOUN D	SLAPPE D	TABANI D	WITHRO D	BLUEBIR D	*CLUBHAN D
REBREE D	SLATTE D	TABBIE D	WOOLLE D	BLUEHEA D	CLUPEOI D
REBUIL D	SLIMME D	TABLOI D	WORRIE D	BLUEWEE D	COALSHE D
RE D BIR D	SLIPPE D	TALIPE D	WORSTE D	BLUEWOO D	COALYAR D
RE D HEA D	SLITTE D	TALLIE D	*XIPHOI D	BOATLOA D	COATTEN D
RE D OUN D	SLOPPE D	TANKAR D	*YCLEPE D	BOATYAR D	*COEXTEN D
RE D RIE D	SLOTTE D	TANYAR D	YEAREN D	BOLTHEA D	*COKEHEA D
RE D WOO D	SLUGGE D	TARRIE D	*ZEBROI D	*BOMBLOA D	COLESEE D
REFOUN D	SLUMME D	TARWEE D	*ZINCKE D	*BOMBYCI D	COLUBRI D
REGRIN D	SLURRE D	*TAXPAI D	*ZINCOI D	BON D MAI D	*COMPLIE D
REPLEA D	SMARAG D	TELFOR D	*ZONATE D	BONEHEA D	*COMPOUN D
RESCIN D	SMUTTE D	TENFOL D	*BABYHOO D	BONEYAR D	*CONCHOI D
RESOUN D	SNAPPE D	TETCHE D	*BACCATE D	BOTRYOI D	CONELRA D
RESPON D	SNIPPE D	THEROI D	*BACKBEN D	*BOXBOAR D	CONFOUN D
RETREA D	SONHOO D	THINNE D	*BACKHAN D	BRACONI D	*COPYREA D
REWOUN D	*SOZZLE D	THYROI D	*BACKLAN D	BRASSAR D	*COPYROL D
REYNAR D	SPANNE D	TIERCE D	*BACKSLI D	BRIN D LE D	CORACOI D
*RHIZOI D	SPAROI D	TOA D IE D	*BACKWAR D	*BROWBAND	*COR D WOO D
RIBBAN D	SPARRE D	TOEHOL D	*BACKWOOD	*BULKHEA D	*CORKWOO D

CORNUTE D	FAIRLEA D	*HAND HEL D	*LA D YBIR D	*MO D IFIE D	PINNATE D
CORONOI D	FALCATE D	*HAND HOL D	*LADYHOO D	*MONKHOO D	PINNIPE D
COTYLOI D	*FARMHAN D	*HAND MAI D	*LAMPYRI D	MONOACI D	PLASMOI D
COVERLI D	*FARMYAR D	*HANGBIR D	LAND LOR D	MOONSEE D	PLAYLAN D
CRANNIE D	*FILMCAR D	*HARD HEA D	LAND SLI D	MOONWAR D	PLICATE D
CRENATE D	FILMLAN D	*HARD HEA D	LAND WAR D	MOORLAN D	PLOWLAN D
*CRIBBLE D	FIREBIR D	*HARDWOO D	LAPBOAR D	*MOPBOAR D	*PLUMIPE D
CRICETI D	*FIREWEE D	*HASHHEA D	LATEWOO D	MORIBUN D	*POKEWEE D
CROPLAN D	*FIREWOO D	*HAULYAR D	LEEBOAR D	MUDGUAR D	POLEWAR D
CUNEATE D	*FISHPON D	*HAWKEYE D	*LEFTWAR D	MULTIFI D	*POLY D IR D
*CUPBOAR D	FISSIPE D	*HAWKWEE D	LEMUROI D	MULTIPE D	*POLYPOI D
CUSSWOR D	*FIVEFOL D	*HAYFIEL D	LIBELLE D	MURAENI D	*PON D WEE D
*CYANAMI D	FLANCAR D	*HEAD BAN D	LIMULOI D	MURIATE D	*PORKWOO D
*CYPRINI D	*FLATHEA D	HEA D LAN D	LINEATE D	MUTINIE D	POSTCAR D
D ANEGEL D	FLATLAN D	*HEA D WIN D	LINEBRE D	*MYRIAPO D	POSTPAI D
D ANEWEE D	*FLAXSEE D	*HEAD WOR D	LIVERIE D	*MYRIOPO D	POTSHAR D
D EA D HEA D	*FOGBOUN D	*HEB DOMA D	LOANWOR D	NAILFOL D	POTSHER D
DEAD WOO D	*FOOTHOL D	HELICOI D	LOCOWEE D	NAILHEA D	PREBOUN D
*D EATHBE D	*FOREFEN D	HEMATOI D	LONGHAN D	NEATHER D	PRECITE D
*D ECKHAN D	*FOREHAN D	*HEMPWEE D	LONGHEA D	*NECKBAN D	PRESCIN D
D EERWEE D	*FOREHEA D	*HIGHBRE D	LOPSI D E D	NINEBAR D	PRETTIE D
D EERYAR D	FORELAN D	*HIGHLAN D	LOVEBIR D	NINEFOL D	PRISMOI D
D EFERRE D	FORESAI D	*HIGHROA D	*LUNKHEA D	NONBRAN D	PROFOUN D
*D EFLEXE D	*FOREWOR D	*HOGSHEA D	LYREBIR D	NONFLUI D	PROPOUN D
D EMURRE D	*FOREYAR D	*HOMEBRE D	*MAGICKE D	NONRATE D	PROTOPO D
D EN D ROI D	*FOURFOL D	HOMELAN D	*MAID HOO D	NONRIGI D	*PROTOXI D
D ENTATE D	*FOXHOUN D	*HOMEWAR D	MAINLAN D	NONSOLI D	PTEROPO D
D ETERRE D	*FREEHAN D	HOMINOI D	MALPOSE D	NONVALI D	*PULPWOO D
D EVILLE D	*FREEHOL D	HONORAN D	MANIFOL D	NOSEBAN D	PURBLIN D
*D IHYBRI D	FREELOA D	HOTBLOO D	*MANYFOL D	NUCLEOI D	PUREBRE D
D IPLOPO D	FURIBUN D	HUMANOI D	MARIGOL D	*PACIFIE D	PYRENOI D
D ISPREA D	GALLIAR D	*HUMIFIE D	MASTHEA D	PAILLAR D	RACEMOI D
D ISULFI D	GANGLAN D	*HY D RACI D	MEATHEA D	PALMATE D	RA D ICAN D
*D IVI D EN D	GAPESEE D	*HYPOACI D	ME D ICAI D	PANELLE D	RAFTERE D
*D OCKHAN D	GARBOAR D	*HYRACOI D	ME D USOI D	PARANOI D	RAILBIR D
*D OCKLAN D	GASIFIE D	*JACQUAR D	MELANOI D	*PARKLAN D	RAILHEA D
*D OCKYAR D	GATEFOL D	*JAILBIR D	METALLE D	PARO D IE D	RAILROA D
D OGGONE D	GEEPOUN D	*JEREMIA D	*MI D FIEL D	PAROTOI D	RAINBAN D
D ONNERE D	GILTHEA D	*JIGGERE D	*MI D SIZE D	PASSBAN D	RAINBIR D
D OORYAR D	GIRLHOO D	*JUNKYAR D	*MILKMAI D	PASSWOR D	RAPESEE D
*D OPEHEA D	GLOBATE D	*KAILYAR D	*MILKSHE D	PEASECO D	RAVELLE D
D OWNLAN D	GOALWAR D	*KALEYAR D	*MILKWEE D	PE D ALLE D	RAWBONE D
D OWNLOA D	GOATHER D	*KEESHON D	*MILKWOO D	PEGBOAR D	REARWAR D
D OWNTRO D	*GO D CHIL D	KERATOI D	MILLEPE D	PELLUCI D	REASCEN D
*D OWNWAR D	GOURMAN D	*KEYBOAR D	MILLIAR D	PENNATE D	RE D EMAN D
*D OWNWIN D	GRA D UAN D	*KILOBAU D	MILLIPE D	PEREOPO D	RE D UVII D
*D ROPHEA D	GRAND DAD	*KINGBIR D	MILLPON D	PERIO D I D	REE D BIR D
*D RUMHEA D	*GRAND KID	*KINGHOO D	MISAWAR D	PETALOI D	REE D BIR D
D RUNKAR D	GROUPOI D	*KINGWOO D	MISBRAN D	PHORONI D	REFERRE D
*D UCKWEE D	GRUELLE D	*KNAPWEE D	MISBUIL D	*PHOSPHI D	REMANNE D
*D UMBHEA D	*GULFWEE D	*KNOTWEE D	MISFIEL D	*PHYLLOI D	REPETEN D
*D UMFOUN D	GUTTATE D	LABELLE D	MISPLEA D	*PILCHAR D	RERECOR D
D UNELAN D	*GYNECOI D	LABIATE D	MISSOUN D	PILEATE D	REREMIN D
FACETTE D	HAIRBAN D	LACERTI D	MISSPEN D	PINELAN D	REREWAR D
*FAHLBAN D	HALLIAR D	LACEWOO D	MO D ELLE D	PINEWOO D	RESINOI D

RESPREA D	SCLEREI D	*SKINHEA D	STINKAR D	TETRACI D	*VIVERRI D
RETHREA D	SCLEROI D	SLIPSHO D	STRIPPE D	TETRAPO D	WATERBE D
RETINOI D	SCOREPA D	SLUGABE D	SUBACRI D	*TETROXI D	*WAVEBAN D
REVEREN D	*SCRAPPE D	SLUGGAR D	SUBBREE D	THEROPO D	*WELLHEA D
REVULSE D	SCURRIE D	SLUMLOR D	SUBFIEL D	THINCLA D	*WHIPCOR D
*RHIZOPO D	SEABOAR D	SNAPWEE D	SUBFLUI D	THOUSAN D	*WI D EBAN D
*RHOMBOI D	*SELFHOO D	SNOWBIR D	*SUBHUMI D	*THYREOI D	*WIFEHOO D
RICEBIR D	*SELFWAR D	SNOWLAN D	SUBTREN D	*TICKSEE D	WIL D LAN D
*RICHWEE D	SEMIARI D	SNOWMOL D	SUBWORL D	TI D ELAN D	*WIL D WOO D
RIVERBE D	SEMIBAL D	*SNOWSHE D	SULCATE D	*TIGHTWA D	*WILLYAR D
*ROCKWEE D	SEMIHAR D	*SOFTHEA D	*SUMPWEE D	TILTYAR D	*WIN D WAR D
ROOTHOL D	SEMIWIL D	*SOFTWOO D	*SUNBAKE D	TIMECAR D	*WOO D BIN D
ROSEWOO D	*SERFHOO D	SOLENOI D	SUNSCAL D	TOOLHEA D	WOO D LAN D
RUBICUN D	SERRANI D	*SOLIQUI D	SUPERA D D	TOOLSHE D	*WOO D SHE D
RUNROUN D	SESAMOI D	SONGBIR D	SUPERBA D	TOTALLE D	*WOO D WIND
SALMONI D	*SHAMMIE D	SOREHEA D	SURFBIR D	TRACHEI D	*WOOLSHE D
SARABAN D	*SHEETFE D	*SOUFFLE D	SURROUN D	TRAMROA D	*WORKLOA D
SASSWOO D	*SHEPHER D	SOURWOO D	*SWANHER D	TRICHOI D	WORMSEE D
SATINPO D	SHETLAN D	SOWBREA D	SYNAPSI D	TRILOBE D	*WORMWOO D
SAUROPO D	SHIPLOA D	SPHENOI D	SYNERGI D	TRIPLOI D	*WRETCHE D
*SCABBAR D	*SHIPYAR D	SPHEROI D	TACHINI D	TROCHOI D	*YAR D BIR D
SCABLAN D	SI D EBAN D	*SPHINGI D	TAGBOAR D	TROLLIE D	YAR D LAN D
*SCAFFOL D	SI D EWAR D	SPLEN D I D	TAILSKI D	TRUEBRE D	*YAR D WAN D
*SCAPHOI D	*SILKWEE D	*SQUIFFE D	TAILWIN D	TUBEROI D	
*SCHIZOI D	SILUROI D	STAGGAR D	TAMARIN D	VERECUN D	
SCIAENI D	SINUSOI D	STAN D AR D	TEABOAR D	*VAGABON D	
SCINCOI D	SISTROI D	STEA D IE D	*TEAKWOO D	VILIPEN D	
SCIUROI D	*SKEWBAL D	STENOSE D	TEENAGE D	*VINEYAR D	

F

FACE	FAUN	FETE	FIST	**FLOW**	FORM
FACT	**FAWN**	FEUD	**FIVE**	FLUB	FORT
FADE	**FAUX**	FIAR	**FIXT**	FLUE	FOSS
FADO	**FAVA**	FIAT	*FIZZ	**FLUX**	FOUL
FAIL	**FAVE**	FICE	FLAB	FOAL	FOUR
FAIN	*FAZE	FICO	FLAG	FOAM	**FOWL**
FAIR	FEAL	FIDO	**FLAK**	FOGY	*FOXY
FAKE	FEAR	**FIEF**	FLAM	**FOHN**	*FOZY
FALL	FEAT	**FIFE**	FLAN	FOIL	FRAE
FALX	**FECK**	FILA	FLAP	FOIN	FRAG
FAME	FEED	FILE	FLAT	FOLD	FRAP
FANE	FEEL	FILL	**FLAW**	**FOLK**	FRAT
FANG	FEET	FILM	**FLAX**	FOND	**FRAY**
FANO	FELL	FILO	FLAY	FONT	FREE
FARD	FELT	FIND	FLEA	FOOD	FRET
FARE	FEME	FINE	FLED	FOOL	FRIT
FARL	FEND	**FINK**	FLEE	FOOT	*FRIZ
FARM	FEOD	FIRE	**FLEW**	FORA	FROE
FARO	FERE	FIRM	**FLEX**	FORB	FROG
FASH	FERN	FIRN	**FLEY**	FORD	FROM
FAST	FESS	FISC	FLIC	FORE	**FROW**
FATE	FETA	**FISH**	FLIP	**FORK**	FRUG

FUCI	FAUNA	FILLE	**FLUKE**	FREER	*FUZEE
FUEL	**FAUVE**	FILLO	*FLUKY	**FREMD**	*FUZIL
FUGU	**FAVOR**	**FILLY**	**FLUME**	FRENA	*FUZZY
FUJI	FAVUS	**FILTH**	**FLUMP**	FRERE	FYTTE
FULL	**FAWNY**	**FILUM**	FLUNG	**FRESH**	FABLER
FUME	FEASE	**FINAL**	**FLUNK**	FRIAR	**FABRIC**
FUMY	FEAST	**FINCH**	FLUOR	FRIED	**FACADE**
FUND	*FEAZE	FINER	**FLUSH**	FRIER	**FACETE**
FUNK	FECAL	FINIS	FLUTE	FRIES	**FACEUP**
FURL	FECES	**FINNY**	**FLUTY**	FRILL	**FACIAL**
FURY	*FEEZE	FIORD	**FLUYT**	FRISE	**FACIES**
FUSE	FEIGN	*FIQUE	*FLYBY	**FRISK**	**FACILE**
FUSS	FEINT	FIRED	**FLYER**	**FRITH**	**FACING**
*FUTZ	FEIST	FIRER	**FLYTE**	FRITT	**FACTOR**
*FUZE	FELID	**FIRRY**	**FOAMY**	*FRITZ	**FACULA**
*FUZZ	FELLA	FIRST	**FOCAL**	*FRIZZ	**FADING**
FYCE	**FELLY**	**FIRTH**	**FOCUS**	**FROCK**	**FAECES**
FYKE	FELON	**FISHY**	FOEHN	FROND	**FAERIE**
FABLE	**FEMME**	**FITCH**	FOGEY	FRONS	**FAGGOT**
FACER	FEMUR	**FITLY**	**FOGGY**	FRONT	FAILLE
FACET	FENCE	**FIVER**	FOGIE	FRORE	**FAIRLY**
FACIA	**FENNY**	*FIXER	FOIST	**FROSH**	*FAJITA
FADDY	FEOFF	*FIXIT	FOLIA	FROST	FAKEER
FADER	FERAL	*FIZZY	FOLIO	**FROTH**	*FAKERY
FADGE	FERIA	*FJELD	**FOLKY**	**FROWN**	**FAKING**
FAENA	**FERLY**	*FJORD	**FOLLY**	*FROZE	**FALCES**
FAERY	FERMI	**FLACK**	FONDU	**FRUIT**	**FALCON**
FAGIN	**FERNY**	FLAIL	**FOOTY**	**FRUMP**	FALLAL
FAGOT	**FERRY**	FLAIR	**FORAM**	**FRYER**	FALLEN
FAINT	FESSE	**FLAKE**	**FORAY**	**FUBSY**	FALLER
FAIRY	FETAL	*FLAKY	**FORBY**	**FUCUS**	**FALLOW**
FAITH	**FETCH**	**FLAME**	**FORCE**	**FUDGE**	FALSIE
FAKER	FETID	**FLAMY**	FORDO	**FUGAL**	FALTER
*FAKEY	FETOR	**FLANK**	FORGE	**FUGGY**	**FAMILY**
FAKIR	FETUS	FLARE	FORGO	FUGIO	**FAMINE**
FALSE	FEUAR	**FLASH**	*FORKY	FUGLE	**FAMING**
FANCY	**FEVER**	**FLASK**	**FORME**	**FUGUE**	**FAMISH**
FANGA	**FIBER**	FLAWY	FORTE	**FULLY**	**FAMOUS**
FANNY	**FIBRE**	*FLAXY	**FORTH**	**FUMER**	**FANDOM**
FANON	**FICHE**	**FLEAM**	**FORTY**	**FUMET**	**FANEGA**
FANUM	FICHU	**FLECK**	**FORUM**	**FUNGI**	FANION
*FAQIR	FICIN	FLEER	FOSSA	**FUNGO**	*FANJET
FARAD	FICUS	FLEET	FOSSE	*FUNKY	**FANNED**
FARCE	**FIDGE**	**FLESH**	FOUND	**FUNNY**	FANNER
FARCI	FIELD	**FLICK**	FOUNT	FURAN	**FANTOD**
FARCY	FIEND	FLIED	**FOVEA**	FUROR	**FANTOM**
FARER	**FIERY**	FLIER	**FOYER**	**FURRY**	*FAQUIR
FARLE	**FIFER**	FLIES	FRAIL	*FURZE	**FARCER**
FATAL	**FIFTH**	FLING	**FRAME**	*FURZY	**FARCIE**
FATLY	**FIFTY**	FLINT	FRANC	FUSEE	**FARDEL**
FATTY	**FIGHT**	FLOUR	**FRANK**	FUSEL	FARFAL
FATWA	FILAR	FLOUT	FRASS	FUSIL	FARFEL
FAUGH	**FILCH**	**FLOWN**	FRAUD	**FUSSY**	FARINA
FAULD	FILER	**FLUFF**	**FREAK**	**FUSTY**	**FARING**
FAULT	FILET	FLUID	FREED	FUTON	**FARMER**

FARROW	FESTAL	FITFUL	FLURRY	FORINT	FROLIC
FASCES	FESTER	FITTED	FLUTER	FORKER	FROSTY
FASCIA	FETIAL	FITTER	FLUTEY	FORMAL	*FROTHY
FASTEN	FETICH	*FIXATE	*FLYBOY	FORMAT	*FROUZY
FATHER	FETING	*FIXITY	FLYING	FORMEE	FROWST
FATHOM	FETISH	*FIXURE	FLYMAN	FORMER	*FROWSY
FATING	FETTED	*FIZGIG	*FLYOFF	FORMIC	*FROWZY
FATTED	FETTER	*FIZZER	*FLYSCH	FORMOL	*FROZEN
FATTEN	FETTLE	*FIZZES	*FLYWAY	FORMYL	FRUGAL
FATTER	FEUDAL	*FIZZLE	FOAMER	*FORNIX	FRUITY
FAUCAL	FIACRE	*FLABBY	FODDER	FORRIT	*FRUMPY
FAUCES	FIASCO	FLACON	FODGEL	FORTES	FRYPAN
FAUCET	FIBBER	FLAGGY	FOEMAN	FORTIS	FUCOID
FAULTY	FIBRIL	FLAGON	FOETAL	*FORWHY	FUCOSE
FAVELA	FIBRIN	FLAKER	FOETID	FOSSIL	FUCOUS
FAVISM	FIBULA	*FLAKEY	FOETOR	FOSTER	FUDDLE
FAVOUR	*FICKLE	FLAMBE	FOETUS	FOUGHT	FUELER
FAWNER	FIDDLE	FLAMEN	*FOGBOW	FOULLY	FUGATO
FEALTY	FIDDLY	FLAMER	FOGDOG	FOURTH	FUGGED
FEARER	FIDGET	FLANGE	FOGGED	FOWLER	FUHRER
FECIAL	FIERCE	*FLAPPY	FOGGER	*FOXIER	FULFIL
*FECKLY	FIESTA	*FLASHY	FOIBLE	*FOXILY	FULGID
FECULA	FIGURE	FLATLY	FOISON	*FOXING	FULHAM
FECUND	FILIAL	FLATUS	FOLATE	FRACAS	FULLAM
FEDORA	FILING	FLAUNT	FOLDER	FRACTI	FULLER
FEEBLE	FILLER	FLAVIN	FOLIAR	FRAISE	FULMAR
FEEDER	FILLET	FLAVOR	FOLIUM	FRAMER	FUMBLE
FEELER	FILLIP	*FLAXEN	FOLKIE	FRAPPE	FUMIER
*FEIJOA	FILMER	FLAYER	*FOLKSY	FRATFR	FUMING
FEIRIE	FILMIC	FLECHE	FOLLES	*FRAZIL	FUNDUS
FEISTY	FILOSE	*FLECKY	FOLLIS	*FREAKY	FUNEST
FELINE	FILTER	FLEDGE	FOLLOW	FREELY	FUNGAL
FELLAH	*FILTHY	FLEDGY	FOMENT	FREEST	FUNGIC
FELLER	FIMBLE	FLEECE	FOMITE	*FREEZE	FUNGUS
FELLOE	FINALE	FLEECH	FONDLE	FRENCH	FUNKER
FELLOW	FINDER	FLEECY	FONDLY	FRENUM	FUNKIA
FELONY	FINELY	FLENCH	FONDUE	*FRENZY	FUNNED
FEMALE	FINERY	FLENSE	FOODIE	FRESCO	FUNNEL
FENCER	FINEST	*FLESHY	FOOTER	FRETTY	FUNNER
FENDER	FINGER	FLETCH	FOOTLE	FRIARY	FURANE
FENNEC	FINIAL	FLEURY	FOOTSY	FRIDGE	FURFUR
FENNEL	FINISH	*FLEXOR	*FOOZLE	FRIEND	FURIES
FERDAM	FINITE	FLIEST	FORAGE	*FRIEZE	FURLER
FERINE	FINNED	FLIGHT	FORBAN	FRIGHT	FURORE
FERITY	FIPPLE	FLIMSY	FORBID	FRIGID	FURRED
FERLIE	FIRING	FLINCH	FORBYE	*FRIJOL	FURROW
FERREL	FIRKIN	FLINTY	FORCER	FRILER	FUSAIN
FERRET	FIRMAN	*FLIPPY	FOREBY	FRILLY	FUSILE
FERRIC	FIRMER	FLOOIE	FOREDO	FRINGE	FUSING
FERRUM	FIRMLY	FLOURY	FOREGO	FRINGY	FUSION
FERULA	FISCAL	FLOWER	FOREST	*FRISKY	FUSSER
FERULE	FISHER	FLUENT	FORGAT	FRIVOL	FUSTIC
FERVID	*FISHLY	*FLUFFY	FORGER	*FRIZER	FUTILE
FERVOR	FISTIC	*FLUKEY	FORGET	*FRIZZY	FUTURE
FESCUE	*FITCHY	*FLUNKY	FORGOT	FROGGY	*FUZING

*FYLFOT	FARCEUR	FELLATE	*FIEFDOM	FISHING	*FLESHLY
PRINGE	FARCING	FELLIES	FIELDER	FISHNET	*FLEXILE
FABLIAU	FARINHA	FELONRY	FIFTEEN	*FISHWAY	*FLEXION
FABLING	FARMING	FELSITE	*FIFTHLY	FISSATE	*FLEXURE
FABULAR	FARNESS	FELSPAR	FIGHTER	FISSILE	*FLICKER
FACIEND	FARRAGO	FELTING	FIGMENT	FISSION	*FLIGHTY
FACTION	FARRIER	FELUCCA	FIGURAL	FISSURE	FLINDER
FACTOID	FARSIDE	FELWORT	FIGURER	FISTFUL	FLINGER
*FACTORY	FARTHER	FEMININE	FIGWORT	FISTULA	*FLIPPED
FACTUAL	FASCINE	FEMORAL	FILAREE	*FITCHEE	FLIPPER
FACTURE	FASCISM	FENAGLE	FILARIA	*FITCHET	FLOATEL
*FACULTY	FASCIST	FENCING	FILBERT	*FITCHEW	FLOKATI
FADABLE	FASHION	FENLAND	*FILCHER	FITMENT	FLOOSIE
FADDIER	FASTING	FENURON	FILEMOT	FITNESS	FLOUTER
*FADDISH	FATALLY	FEODARY	FILIATE	FITTEST	FLOWAGE
FADDISM	*FATBACK	*FEOFFEE	FILIBEG	FITTING	*FLOWERY
FADDIST	FATBIRD	*FEOFFER	FILLIES	*FIXATIF	FLUBBER
FAGOTER	FATEFUL	*FEOFFOR	FILLING	*FIXEDLY	*FLUBDUB
FAIENCE	FATHEAD	FERMATA	*FILMDOM	*FIXINGS	*FLUENCY
FAILING	FATIDIC	FERMENT	FILMIER	*FIXTUTE	FLUIDLY
FAILURE	FATIGUE	FERMION	*FILMILY	FLACDID	*FLUMMOX
FAINTER	FATLESS	FERMIUM	FILMSET	FLAGGER	FLUNKER
FAINTLY	FATLIKE	FERNERY	FIMBRIA	FLAGMAN	*FLUNKEY
FAIRIES	FATLING	FERRATE	FINABLE	FLAMBEE	FLUORID
FAIRING	FATNESS	FERRETY	FINAGLE	FLAMEAU	FLUORIN
FAIRISH	FATTEST	FERRIED	FINALIS	FLAMIER	FLUSHER
*FAIRWAY	FATTIER	FERRIES	FINALLY	FLAMING	FLUSTER
FAITOUR	FATTIES	FERRITE	FINANCE	*FLAMMED	FLUTIER
FALAFEL	FATTILY	FERROUS	*FINBACK	FLANEUR	FLUTING
FALBALA	FATTING	FERRULE	FINDING	FLANGER	FLUTIST
FALCATE	FATTISH	FERTILE	FINESSE	FLANKEN	FLUTTER
*FALLACY	FATUITY	FERVENT	*FINFISH	FLANKER	FLUVIAL
*FALLOFF	FATUOUS	FERVOUR	FINFOOT	FLANNEL	*FLUXION
FALLOUT	FATWOOD	FESTIVE	FINICAL	*FLAPPED	*FLYABLE
*FALSIFY	FAUCIAL	FESTOON	*FINICKY	FLAPPER	*FLYAWAY
FALSITY	FAUTEIL	*FETCHER	FINIKIN	FLASHER	*FLYBELT
FAMULUS	*FAUVISM	*FETLOCK	FINLESS	FLATBED	*FLYBLOW
FANATIC	FAUVIST	FETTING	FINLIKE	FLATCAR	*FLYBOAT
FANCIED	FAVELLA	FEUDARY	*FINMARK	FLATLET	*FLYLEAF
FANCIER	FAVORER	FEUDIST	FINNIER	FLATTED	FLYLESS
FANCIES	*FAZENDA	FEWNESS	FINNING	FLATTEN	*FLYOVER
FANFARE	FEARFUL	FEYNESS	FIREARM	FLATTER	*FLYPAST
FANFOLD	FEASTER	FIANCEE	*FIREBOX	FLATTOP	FLYTIER
FANLIKE	FEATHER	FIBROID	FIREBUG	FLAUNTY	FLYTING
FANNING	FEATURE	FIBROIN	FIREDOG	FLAVINE	*FLYTRAP
FANTAIL	FEBRILE	FIBROMA	*FIREFLY	FLAVONE	FOAMIER
FANTASM	FEDAYEE	FIBROUS	FIRELIT	*FLAVORY	*FOAMILY
FANTAST	FEDERAL	FICTILE	FIREMAN	FLAVOUR	*FOCALLY
FANTASY	FEEDBAG	FICTION	FIREPAN	FLEABAG	FOCUSER
FANWISE	*FEEDBOX	*FICTIVE	FIREPOT	FLEAPIT	FOGGAGE
FANWORT	FEEDLOT	FIDDLER	FIRSTLY	FLEECER	FOGGING
*FANZINE	FEELESS	FIDEISM	*FISHERY	FLEMISH	FOGHORN
FARADAY	FEELING	FIDEIST	*FISHEYE	*FLEMISH	FOGLESS
FARADIC	FEIGNER	*FIDGETY	*FISHGIG	FLENSER	*FOGYISM
*FARAWAY	FELAFEL	FIDGING	FISHIER	FLESHER	FOLACIN

FOLDOUT	FORKIER	*FREEWAY	FUMIEST	FAIRNESS	*FATHERLY
FOLIAGE	FORLORN	*FREEZER	FUMULUS	*FAIRYISM	*FATSTOCK
FOLIATE	FORMANT	FREIGHT	FUNCTOR	*FAITHFUL	FATTENER
FOLIOSE	FORMATE	FRESHEN	FUNERAL	FALCATED	FATTIEST
FOLIOUS	*FORMFUL	FRESHET	FUNFAIR	*FALCHION	FAUBOURG
*FOLKISH	FORMULA	*FRESHLY	FUNGOID	FALCONER	FAVONIAN
*FOLKMOT	FORSAKE	FRESNEL	FUNGOUS	FALCONET	FAVORITE
*FOLKWAY	FORTIES	FRETFUL	FUNICLE	*FALCONRY	FAVOURER
FOLLIES	*FORTIFY	FRETSAW	FUNNEST	FALDERAL	*FAWNLIKE
FONDANT	FORTUNE	FRETTED	FUNNING	FALDEROL	FAYALITE
FONDLER	FORWARD	FRETTER	*FURBISH	*FALLAWAY	FEARLESS
FONTINA	FORWENT	FRIABLE	FURCATE	*FALLBACK	FEARSOME
FOOLERY	FORWORN	FRIBBLE	FURCULA	*FALLFISH	FEASANCE
FOOLISH	*FOSSICK	FRIGATE	FURIOSO	FALLIBLE	FEASIBLE
FOOTAGE	FOUETTE	*FRIJOLE	FURIOUS	FALSETTO	FEASTFUL
*FOOTBOY	FOULARD	FRISEUR	FURLESS	FALTBOAT	*FEATHERY
FOOTIER	FOULING	FRISKER	FURLONG	FALTERER	*FEBRIFIC
FOOTING	FOUNDER	FRISKET	*FURMETY	FAMELESS	*FECKLESS
FOOTLER	FOUNDRY	FRISSON	*FURMITY	FAMILIAL	FECULENT
FOOTMAN	FOURGON	FRITTED	FURNACE	FAMILIAR	*FEDERACY
FOOTPAD	FOVEOLA	FRITTER	FURNISH	*FAMILISM	FEDERATE
FOOTSIE	FOVEOLE	*FRIZZER	FURRIER	*FANCIFUL	*FEEBLISH
*FOOTWAY	FOWLING	*FRIZZLE	FURRILY	FANDANGO	*FEEDBACK
*FOOZLER	*FOWLPOX	*FRIZZLY	FURRING	FANEGADA	*FEEDHOLE
*FOPPERY	*FOXFIRE	FROGEYE	*FURROWY	FANFARON	*FELDSHER
*FOPPISH	*FOXFISH	FROGGED	FURTHER	*FANLIGHT	FELDSPAR
FORAGER	FOXHOLE	FROGMAN	FURTIVE	FANTASIA	*FELICITY
FORAMEN	*FOXHUNT	FROMAGE	FUSCOUS	FANTASIE	FELINELY
FORAYER	*FOXIEST	FRONTAL	FUSIBLE	FARADAIC	FELINITY
FORBADE	*FOXLIKE	FRONTES	FUSILLI	FARADISE	FELLABLE
FORBEAR	*FOXSKIN	FRONTON	FUSSPOT	FARADISM	FELLATIO
FORBODE	*FOXTAIL	FROSTED	FUSTIAN	*FARADIZE	FELLATOR
FORBORE	*FOXTROT	FROUNCE	*FUTHARC	*FARCICAL	FELLNESS
FORCEPS	FRACTAL	FROWARD	*FUTHARK	FAREWELL	*FELLOWLY
FORCING	FRACTED	FROWNER	*FUTHORC	FARINOSE	FELSTONE
FOREARM	FRACTUR	*FROWSTY	*FUTHORK	*FARMHAND	*FELTLIKE
*FOREBAY	FRACTUS	FRUITER	*FUTTOCK	FARMLAND	*FEMINACY
*FOREBYE	FRAENUM	FRUSTUM	FABULIST	*FARMWIFE	FEMININE
FOREGUT	FRAGILE	*FUCHSIA	FABULOUS	*FARMWORK	FEMINISE
FOREIGN	FRAILTY	*FUCHSIN	*FACEDOWN	*FARMYARD	*FEMINISM
FORELEG	FRAKTUR	FUEHRER	FACELESS	FARNESOL	FEMINIST
FOREMAN	FRAMING	FUELLER	FACETIAE	*FAROUCHE	*FEMINITY
*FOREPAW	FRANKER	FUGGING	FACETTED	FARRIERY	*FEMINIZE
FORERUN	*FRANKLY	FUGUIST	*FACIALLY	FARTHEST	*FENCEROW
FORESEE	FRANTIC	FULCRUM	*FACILITY	*FARTHING	*FENCIBLE
FORETOP	FRAUGHT	FULFILL	FACTIOUS	FASCITLE	FENESTRA
FOREVER	FRAYING	FULGENT	*FACTOTUM	FASHIOUS	FENTHION
FORFEIT	*FRAZZLE	FULLERY	FADDIEST	*FASTBACK	*FERACITY
FORFEND	*FRECKLE	FULMINE	*FADEAWAY	FASTBALL	FERETORY
FORGAVE	*FRECKLY	FULNESS	FADELESS	FASTENER	*FEROCITY
FORGERY	FREEBEE	FULSOME	FAGOTING	FASTNESS	FERREOUS
FORGING	FREEBIE	FULVOUS	*FAHLBAND	FASTUOUS	FERRETER
FORGIVE	FREEDOM	FUMARIC	FAINEANT	FATALISM	FERRIAGE
FORGOER	FREEMAN	FUMBLER	FAINTISH	FATALIST	FERRITIN
*FORKFUL	FREESIA	FUMETTE	FAIRLEAD	FATALITY	*FERRYMAN

*FERVENCY	FINISHER	*FLACKERY	*FLEXAGON	FONTANEL	*FORELOCK
FESSWISE	FINITELY	FLAGELLA	*FLEXIBLE	*FOODWAYS	FOREMAST
FESTIVAL	FINITUDE	FLAGGING	*FLEXTIME	*FOOFARAW	*FOREMILK
FETATION	*FINNICKY	FLAGLESS	*FLEXUOSE	*FOOLFISH	FOREMOST
FETERITA	FINNIEST	FLAGPOLE	*FLEXUOUS	*FOOLSCAP	FORENAME
FETIALIS	*FINNMARK	FLAGRANT	*FLICHTER	FOOTBALL	FORENOON
FETICIDE	*FINOCHIO	*FLAGSHIP	*FLICKERY	*FOOTBATH	FORENSIC
*FETOLOGY	*FIREBACK	*FLAMENCO	*FLIMFLAM	FOOTFALL	FOREPART
FETTERER	FIREBALL	FLAMEOUT	*FLINCHER	FOOTGEAR	FOREPAST
FETTLING	FIREBASE	FLAMIEST	*FLINKITE	FOOTHILL	*FOREPEAK
*FEVERFEW	FIREBIRD	FLAMINES	*FLIPPANT	*FOOTHOLD	*FOREPLAY
*FEVERISH	FIREBOAT	FLAMINGO	FLORALLY	FOOTIEST	*FORERANK
FEVEROUS	*FIREBOMB	*FLAMMING	FLOURISH	FOOTLESS	FORESAID
*FIBERIZE	FIREBRAT	FLANCARD	FLOWERER	*FOOTLIKE	FORESAIL
FIBRANNE	*FIRECLAY	FLANERIE	FLOWERET	FOOTLING	FORESEER
FIBRILIA	*FIREDAMP	*FLAPJACK	FLUERICS	*FOOTMARK	*FORESHOW
FIBROSIS	*FIREFANG	FLAPLESS	FLUIDICS	FOOTNOTE	FORESIDE
*FIDELITY	FIREHALL	*FLAPPING	FLUIDISE	*FOOTPACE	*FORESKIN
FIDGETER	FIRELESS	*FLASHGUN	*FLUIDITY	*FOOTPATH	FORESTAL
FIDUCIAL	*FIRELOCK	*FLASHING	*FLUIDIZE	FOOTRACE	FORESTAY
*FIENDISH	*FIREPINK	FLATBOAT	FLUIDRAM	FOOTREST	FORESTER
*FIFTYISH	FIREPLUG	*FLATFISH	*FLUMMERY	FOOTROPE	FORESTRY
FIGEATER	FIREROOM	FLATFOOT	FLUORENE	FOOTSLOG	FORETELL
*FIGHTING	FIRESIDE	*FLATHEAD	FLUORIDE	FOOTSORE	FORETIME
FIGULINE	FIRETRAP	FLATIRON	FLUORINE	FOOTSTEP	FOREWARN
FIGURANT	*FIREWEED	FLATLAND	FLUORITE	FOOTWALL	FOREWENT
FIGURATE	*FIREWOOD	FLATLING	FLUTIEST	FOOTWEAR	*FOREWING
FIGURINE	*FIREWORK	FLATLONG	FLUTTERY	*FOOTWORK	*FOREWORD
FIGURING	*FIREWORM	FLATMATE	*FLUXGATE	FOOTWORN	FOREWORN
FILAGREE	FIRMNESS	FLATNESS	*FLYPAPER	FORBIDAL	*FOREYARD
FILAMENT	*FIRMWARE	FLATTERY	*FLYSPECK	FORBORNE	FORGIVER
FILARIID	*FISCALLY	FLATTEST	*FLYWHEEL	*FORCEFUL	*FORJUDGE
FILATURE	*FISHABLE	FLATTING	FOAMIEST	*FORCIBLE	*FORKBALL
*FILEFISH	*FISHBOLT	FLATTISH	FOAMLESS	*FORCIPES	*FORKIEST
FILICIDE	*FISHBONE	FLATWARE	*FOAMLIKE	FORDLESS	*FORKLESS
*FILIFORM	*FISHBOWL	*FLATWASH	*FOCACCIA	FOREBEAR	*FORKLIFT
FILIGREE	*FISHHOOK	*FLATWAYS	FOCALISE	FOREBODE	*FORKLIKE
FILISTER	FISHIEST	FLATWISE	*FOCALIZE	*FOREBODY	*FORKSFUL
*FILMCARD	FISHLESS	*FLATWORK	FOGBOUND	*FOREBOOM	FORMALIN
FILMGOER	*FISHLIKE	*FLATWORM	*FOGFRUIT	FORECAST	*FORMALLY
FILMIEST	FISHLINE	FLAUNTER	FOILSMAN	FOREDATE	*FORMERLY
FILMLAND	*FISHMEAL	FLAVONOL	*FOLDAWAY	*FOREDECK	FORMLESS
FILTERER	*FISHPOLE	FLAVORER	FOLDBOAT	FOREDOOM	*FORMWORK
FILTRATE	*FISHPOND	*FLAVOURY	FOLDEROL	*FOREFACE	FORRADER
FINAGLER	FISHTAIL	FLAWLESS	*FOLKLIFE	FOREFEEL	*FORSAKER
FINALISM	*FISHWIFE	*FLAXSEED	*FOLKLIKE	*FOREFEND	FORSOOTH
FINALIST	*FISHWORM	FLEABANE	*FOLKLORE	FOREFOOT	FORSPENT
FINALITY	FISSIPED	FLEABITE	*FOLKMOOT	FOREGOER	FORSWEAR
*FINALIZE	FISTNOTE	FLEAWORT	*FOLKMOTE	*FOREHAND	FORTIETH
FINEABLE	FITTABLE	FLECTION	*FOLKTALE	*FOREHEAD	FORTRESS
FINENESS	*FIVEFOLD	FLEECING	FOLLICLE	*FOREHOOF	FORTUITY
FINESPUN	*FIVEPINS	FLESHIER	FOLLOWER	*FOREKNOW	*FORTYISH
FINGERER	*FIXATION	*FLESHING	FOMENTER	*FORELADY	*FORZANDO
*FINICKIN	*FIXATIVE	*FLESHPOT	FONDLING	FORELAND	FOSSETTE
*FINIKING	FLABELLA	*FLETCHER	FONDNESS	*FORELIMB	FOSTERER

*FOUGHTEN	FRISETTE	FURANOSE	BU F FI	LI F TER	TU F OLI
FOULNESS	FRITTING	*FURBELOW	GO F FER	LO F TER	TU F TER
FOUNTAIN	FRIVOLER	FURCRAEA	TA F FY	NI F FER	*WA F ERY
*FOURCHEE	*FRIZETTE	*FURCULUM	TA F IA	PI F FLE	*WA F FIE
*FOURFOLD	*FRIZZIER	FURFURAL	WI F TY	PU F FER	*WA F FLE
*FOURPLEX	*FRIZZILY	FURFURAN	BA F FLE	PU F FIN	WA F TER
FOURSOME	*FRIZZLER	FURIBUND	BE F ALL	RA F FIA	*WI F ELY
FOURTEEN	*FROGFISH	FURLAUND	BE F LAG	RA F FLE	WI F ING
*FOURTHLY	FROGGING	*FURLOUGH	BE F LEA	RA F TER	*ZA F FAR
FOVEOLET	*FROGLIKE	*FURMENTY	BE F OOL	RE F ACE	*ZA F FER
*FOXGLOVE	FRONDEUR	FURRIERY	BE F ORE	RE F ALL	*ZA F FIR
*FOXHOUND	FRONTAGE	FURRIEST	BE F OUL	RE F ECT	*ZA F FRE
*FOXINESS	FRONTIER	FURRINER	BE F RET	RE F EED	*ZO F TIG
*FOZINESS	FRONTLET	FURROWER	BI F ACE	RE F EEL	*BA F FIES
*FRABJOUS	FROSTBIT	FURTHEST	BI F FIN	RE F ELL	*BA F FLER
FRACTION	FROSTING	FURUNCLE	BI F OLD	RE F ILE	*BE F LECK
FRACTURE	FROTTAGE	FUSELADE	BI F ORM	RE F ILL	BI F ILAR
FRAGGING	FROTTEUR	FUSELESS	BO F FIN	RE F ILM	BI F OCAL
FRAGMENT	FROUFROU	*FUSIFORM	BU F FER	RE F IND	*BO F FOLA
FRAGRANT	FRUITAGE	FUSILEER	BU F FET	RE F INE	*BU F FALO
*FRANCIUM	FRUITFUL	FUSILIER	CA F TAN	RE F IRE	*BU F FIER
*FRANKLIN	FRUITIER	FUTILITY	CO F FEE	RE F LET	*BU F FOON
FRAULEIN	FRUITION	FUTURISM	CO F FER	RE F LEW	*CA F FEIN
*FREAKIER	FRUITLET	FUTURIST	CO F FIN	*RE F LEX	*CO F FING
*FREAKILY	*FRUMENTY	FUTURITY	CO F FLE	RE F LOW	*CO F FRET
*FREAKISH	FRUSTULE	P F FT	DE F ACE	*RE F LUX	CO F OUND
*FREAKOUT	*FUCHSINE	P FUI	DE F AME	RE F OLD	DE F ACER
FREEBASE	FUELLING	BA F F	DE F ANG	RE F ORM	DE F AMER
FREEBOOT	*FUELWOOD	BI F F	DE F EAT	RE F UEL	DE F AULT
FREEBORN	FUGACITY	BO F F	DE F ECT	RE F UGE	DE F ENCE
FREEDMAN	FUGITIVE	BU F F	DE F END	RE F UND	DE F ENSE
*FREEFORM	FUGLEMAN	CA F F	DE F IED	RE F USE	DE F IANT
*FREEHAND	*FULLBACK	CO F F	DE F IER	RE F UTE	DE F ICIT
*FREEHOLD	*FULLFACE	CU F F	DE F IES	RI F FED	DE F ILER
FREELOAD	FULLNESS	DA F F	DE F ILE	RI F FLE	DE F INER
FREENESS	*FULMINIC	DO F F	DE F INE	RU F FLE	DE F LATE
FREEWILL	FUMARASE	DU F F	DE F LEA	*RU F FLY	DE F LECT
FREMITUS	FUMARATE	GA F F	DE F OAM	RU F OUS	DE F OCUS
FRENETIC	FUMAROLE	GU F F	DE F ORM	SA F ARI	DE F ORCE
FRENULUM	*FUMATOKY	HU F F	DE F RAY	SA F EST	DE F RAUD
*FRENZILY	FUMELESS	*JI F F	DE F UND	SA F ETY	*DE F ROCK
*FREQUENT	*FUMELIKE	LU F F	DE F USE	SA F ROL	DE F ROST
FRESCOER	FUMIGANT	MI F F	*DE F UZE	SI F AKA	DE F UNCT
*FRESHMAN	FUMIGATE	MU F F	DI F FER	SI F TER	DI F FUSE
FRETLESS	*FUMINGLY	PU F F	DO F FER	SO F FIT	FI F TEEN
FRETSOME	*FUMITORY	RA F F	DU F FEL	SO F TEN	*FI F THLY
FRETTING	FUNCTION	RI F F	DU F FLE	SO F TIE	*HA F NIUM
*FRETWORK	FUNERARY	RU F F	GA F FER	SO F TLY	*HU F FISH
*FRIBBLER	FUNEREAL	TE F F	GO F FER	SU F FER	LE F TISH
FRICANDO	FUNGIBLE	TI F F	*GU F FAW	*SU F FIX	LE F TISM
FRICTION	FUNICULI	TO F F	HA F TER	TA F FIA	LE F TIST
*FRIENDLY	*FUNNYMAN	TU F F	HE F TER	TI F FIN	LI F EFUL
*FRIGHTEN		WA F F	*KA F FIR	TO F FEE	LI F EWAY
FRILLING		YA F F	KA F TAN	TU F FET	LI F TMAN
*FRIPPERY					

*LI F TO F F	CO F FER	*CO F FRET	CON F RONT	*MIS F AITH	SNI F FIER
LO F TIER	CO F FIN	*COW F LAP	CON F UTER	*MIS F OCUS	*SNI F FILY
LO F TILY	CO F FLE	*COW F LOP	*CU F F LESS	*MIS F RAME	*SNI F FISH
*MA F FICK	CON F IT	DI F FUSE	*DA F FODIL	*MO F FETTE	SNI F F IER
*MU F FLER	DI F FER	*HU F FISH	DEA F NESS	*MOU F LON	*SNU F FBOX
*RA F FISH	DO F FER	*MA F FICK	*DEI F ICAL	*NEW FOUND	SNU F FIER
RA F FLER	DOO F US	MUD F LAT	*DI F FRACT	NON F ATTY	*SNU F FILY
RE F ENCE	DU F FEL	NON F ACT	*DI F FUSER	NON F INAL	SNU F FLER
RE F EREE	DU F FLE	NON F UEL	*DI F FUSOR	NON F LUID	SOL F EGGI
RE F FING	DUP F ER	PRE F ADE	*DIS F AVOR	NON F OCAL	*SOU F FLED
RE F IGHT	GA F FER	PRE F ILE	*DIS F ROCK	*PAR F LESH	*SPI F FING
RE F INER	GO F FER	PRE F IRE	*DOG F IGHT	*PAR F OCAL	*STI F FISH
RE F LATE	*GU F FAW	*RA F FISH	*DRA F FISH	*PER F ECTA	*STU F FING
RE F LECT	*KA F FIR	RE F FING	DRA F TING	*PER F ECTO	SUB F IELD
RE F LIES	*MED F LY	RI F FING	DRI F TAGE	*PER F ORCE	SUB F LOOR
RE F LOAT	MUG F UL	RI F FLER	DRI F TPIN	*PER F UMER	SUB F LUID
RE F OCUS	NI F FER	RU F FIAN	*DUM FOUND	PIL F ERER	*SUB F RAME
RE F ORGE	NON F AN	RU F FLER	FAN F ARON	*PRE F ACER	SU F FERER
RE F OUND	PAN F RY	SA F FRON	*F OG F RUIT	*PRE F IGHT	SU F FLATE
RE F RACT	PI F FLE	SUB F ILE	*FOO FARAW	*PRE F IXAL	*SU F FICER
RE F RAIN	PU F FER	SU F FARI	F UR F URAL	*PRE F LAME	*SU F FIXAL
RE F RAMT	PU F FIN	*SU F FICE	F UR F URAN	*PRE F OCUS	*SU F FRAGE
RE F RESH	RA F FIA	SU F FUSE	GON F ALON	*PRE F RANK	SUL F INYL
RE F RONT	RA F FLE	SYN F UEL	GON F ANON	PRO F ANER	SUL F ONAL
RE F UGEE	REF FED	TA F FETA	GOO F BALL	PRO F ILER	SUL F ONIC
RE F USAL	RI F FED	*WA F FLER	*GRA F FITO	PRO F ITER	SUL F ONYL
RE F USER	RI F FLE	BEE F IEST	GRA F TAGE	PRO F OUND	SUL F URET
RE F UTAL	ROL FER	BEE F LESS	*GRU F FIER	*PU F FBALL	SUL F URIC
RE F UTER	RU F FLE	*BEE FWOOD	*GRU F FILY	PUR F LING	SUL F URYL
RI F FING	SO F FIT	*BOU F ANT	*GRU F FISH	*REA F FIRM	SUR F ACER
RI F FLER	SU F FER	*BOW FRONT	GUL F IEST	*RIF F RAFF	SUR F BIRD
RI F FLER	TA F FIA	*BU F FIEST	*GUL F LIKE	ROO F LESS	SUR F BOAT
RI F LERY	TI F FIN	*CA F FEINE	*GUL F WEED	ROO F LIKE	*SUR F FISH
RI F LING	TIT FER	*CAL F SKIN	*GUN F IGHT	ROO F LINE	SUR F IEST
RU F FIAN	TO F FEE	*CAN F IELD	GUN F LINT	ROO F TREE	*SUR F LIKE
RU F FLER	TU F FET	*CAT F IGHT	*HAL F BACK	RU F F LIER	SWI F TLET
SA F FRON	*WA F FIE	*COE F FECT	*HAL F BEAK	*RU F FLIKE	TA F FAREL
SA F ROLE	*WA F FLE	*COI F FEUR	*HAL F LIFE	*RU F FLING	TA F FEREL
SI F TING	*ZA F FAR	*COI F FURE	HAL F NESS	*SCA F FOLD	TA F FRAIL
SO F TIES	*ZA F FER	*COM F IEST	*HAL F TIME	*SCO F FLAW	TRI F ECTA
SO F TISH	*ZA F FIR	CON F ERVA	HAL F TONE	*SCU F FLER	TRI F LING
SU F FARI	*ZA F FRE	*CON F FTTO	*HAW F INCH	SEA F ARER	TRI F OCAL
*SU F FICE	*BA F FIES	CON F IDER	*HAY F IELD	SEA FLOOR	TRI F ORIA
SU F FUSE	*BA F FLER	CON F INER	*HOO F BEAT	SEA F RONT	TUR F IEST
TA F FETA	BED F RAM	CON F LATE	HOO F LESS	SEL F HEAL	TUR F LESS
*WA F FLER	BEE F ALO	*CON F LICT	*HOO F LIKE	*SEL F HOOD	*TUR F LIKE
WA F TAGE	BIG FOOT	*CON F OCAL	*KA F FIYEH	SEL F LESS	*WA F FLING
WA F TURE	*BO F FOLA	CON F OUND	*KE F FIYEH	SEL F NESS	*WAI F LIKE
*WI F EDOM	*BU F FALO	CON F RERE	*KIN FOLKS	*SEL F SAME	WAR F ARIN
BA F FLE	*BU F FIER		LEA F IEST	*SEL F WARD	*WAY F ARER
BI F FIN	*BU F FOON		LEA F LESS	*SER F HOOD	*WHI F FLER
BO F FIN	*CA F FEIN		*LEA F LIKE	*SER F LIKE	*WOL F FISH
BU F FER	*CO F FING		*LEA FWORM	*SHA F TING	*WOL F LIKE
BU F FET			*MEN FOLKS	*SHU F FLER	
CO F FEE			*MID F IELD	SI F FLEUR	BA F F

BAR F	LOO F	CLI F F	STU F F	*CASTO F F	*WHEREO F
BEE F	LU F F	DECA F	SWAR F	DEBRIE F	WITLOO F
BI F F	MI F F	DRA F F	THIE F	DISTA F F	*BLASTO F F
BO F F	MU F F	DWAR F	WHAR F	DUSTO F F	*BODYSUR F
BU F F	NAI F	FEO F F	*WHI F F	*FALLO F F	*BRUSHO F F
BUM F	NEI F	FLU F F	WHOO F	*FIXATI F	*CALCTU F F
CA F F	PEL F	GANE F	BEGUL F	*FLYLEA F	*CHECKO F F
CAL F	POO F	GANO F	BEHOO F	*HANDO F F	*DANDRI F F
CHE F	POU F	GLI F F	BELIE F	HERSEL F	*DANDRU F F
CLE F	PRO F	GONE F	CUTO F F	*HIMSEL F	DISPROO F
CO F F	PU F F	GONI F	*FLYO F F	HISSEL F	*DUMMKOP F
COO F	RA F F	GONO F	GONI F F	*JUMPO F F	*DYESTU F F
CU F F	REE F	GRIE F	HEREO F	*KICKO F F	*FOREHOO F
CUI F	RFI F	GRI F F	*KHALI F	LEADO F F	*HANDCU F F
CUR F	RI F F	GRU F F	LAYO F F	*LIFTO F F	*KERCHIE F
DA F F	ROL F	*HOW F F	MASSI F	*MASTI F F	*KNOCKO F F
DEA F	ROO F	KALI F	MYSEL F	*MIDRI F F	LANGLAU F
DEL F	RU F F	KENA F	*PAYO F F	NONSEL F	LONGLEA F
DO F F	SEI F	KLOO F	PILA F F	*PICKO F F	MEATLOA F
DU F F	SEL F	MOTI F	PUTO F F	*PLAYO F F	*MISCHIE F
F IE F	SER F	PILA F	REBU F F	*PONTI F F	*MOONCAL F
GA F F	SUR F	POU F F	RELIE F	*RAKEO F F	*RI F FRA F F
GOL F	TE F F	PROO F	REROO F	RESTA F F	SANSERI F
GOO F	TI F F	*QUA F F	RIPO F F	RESTU F F	SEMIDEA F
GU F F	TO F F	*QUI F F	RUBO F F	SENDO F F	SHINLEA F
GUL F	TRE F	SCAR F	RUNO F F	SHADOO F	*STANDO F F
HAA F	TU F F	SCO F F	SCLA F F	SHEREE F	*SUBCHIE F
HAL F	TUR F	SCU F F	SCRU F F	*SHOWO F F	SUNPROO F
HOO F	WA F F	SCUR F	SETO F F	*SHUTO F F	TIPSTA F F
HOW F	WAI F	SERI F	SHADU F	*SPINO F F	*TRADEO F F
HU F F	WOL F	SHEA F	SHARI F	SPORTI F	*WEREWOL F
*JI F F	WOO F	SHEL F	SHERI F	SUNROO F	*WETPROO F
KAI F	YA F F	*SKI F F	*SHRO F F	*TAKEO F F	*WINDSUR F
KEE F	*ZAR F	SLU F F	TARI F F	THEREO F	*WOODRU F F
KER F	BLU F F	SNI F F	TIPO F F	THYSEL F	YOURSEL F
KHA F	BRIE F	SNU F F	*BAILI F F	TURNO F F	
KIE F	CALI F	SPOO F	*BEDWAR F	*WAVEO F F	
LEA F	*CHA F F	STA F F	*BLOWO F F	*WERWOL F	
LIE F	CHIE F	STI F F	*BOILO F F		
LOA F	*CHU F F		*CAITI F F		

G

GABY	GAMA	GARB	GAWK	GENS	GIFT
GADI	GAMB	GASH	GAWP	GENT	GIGA
GAFF	GAME	GASP	GAZE	GENU	GILD
GAGA	GAMP	GAST	GEAR	GERM	GILL
GAGE	GAMY	GATE	GECK	GEST	GILT
GAIN	GANE	GAUD	GEEK	GETA	GIMP
GALA	GANG	GAUM	GEEZ	GEUM	GINK
GALE	GAOL	GAUN	GELD	GHAT	GIRD
GALL	GAPE	GAUR	GELT	GHEE	GIRL
	GAPY	GAVE	GENE	GIBE	GIRN

GIRO	GREW	GANEV	GHYLL	GLOST	GRAPE
GIRT	GREY	GANJA	GIANT	GLOUT	GRAPH
GIST	GRID	GANOF	GIBER	GLOVE	GRAPY
GIVE	GRIG	GAPER	GIDDY	*GLOZE	GRASP
GLAD	GRIM	GAPPY	GIGAS	GLUER	GRASS
GLED	GRIN	GARNI	GIGHE	GLUEY	GRATE
GLEE	GRIP	GARTH	GIGOT	GLUME	GRAVE
GLEG	GRIT	GASSY	GIGUE	GLUON	GRAVY
GLEN	GROG	GATOR	GILLY	GLYPH	*GRAZE
GLEY	GROT	GAUDY	GIMEL	GNARL	GREAT
GLIA	GROW	GAUGE	GIMME	GNARR	GREBE
GLIB	GRUB	GAULT	GIMPY	GNASH	GREED
GLIM	GRUE	GAUNT	GINNY	GNAWN	GREEK
GLOB	GRUM	GAUSS	GIPON	GNOME	GREEN
GLOM	GUAN	*GAUZE	GIPSY	GOBAN	GREET
GLOP	GUAR	*GAWKY	GIRLY	GODET	GREGO
GLOW	GUCK	GAVEL	GIRON	GODLY	GRIDE
GLUE	GUDE	GAVOT	GIRSH	GOFER	GRIEF
GLUG	GUFF	*GAWSY	GIRTH	GOING	GRIFF
GLUM	GUID	GAYAL	GISMO	GOLEM	GRIFT
GLUT	GULF	GAYLY	GIVEN	GOLLY	GRILL
GNAR	GULL	*GAZAR	GIVER	GOMBO	GRIME
GNAT	GULP	*GAZER	*GIZMO	GONAD	GRIMY
GNAW	GUNK	*GAZER	GLACE	GONEF	GRIND
GOAD	GURU	GECKO	GLADE	GONER	GRIOT
GOAL	GUSH	GEEKY	GLADY	GONIA	GRIPE
GOAT	GUST	GEESE	GLAIR	GONIF	GRIPT
GOBO	GYBE	GEEST	GLAND	GONOF	GRIPY
GOBY	GYRE	GELEE	GLANS	*GONZO	GRIST
GOER	GYRI	GELID	GLARE	GOODY	GRITH
GOGO	GYRO	GEMMA	GLARY	GOOEY	GROAN
GOLD	GYVE	GEMMY	GLASS	GOOFY	GROIN
GOLF	GABBY	GEMOT	*GLAZE	GOONY	GROOM
GONE	GABLE	GENET	*GLAZY	GOOPY	GROPE
GONG	GADDI	GENIC	GLEAM	GOOSE	GROSS
GOOD	GADID	GENIE	GLEAN	GOOSY	*GROSZ
GOOF	GAFFE	GENII	GLEBA	GORAL	GROUP
GOOK	GAGER	GENIP	GLEBE	GORGE	GROUT
GOON	GAILY	GENOA	GLEDE	GORSE	GROVE
GOOP	GALAH	GENOM	GLEED	GORSY	GROWL
GORE	GALAX	GENRE	GLEEK	GOUGE	GROWN
GORP	GALEA	GENRO	GLEET	GOURD	GRUEL
GORY	GALLY	GENUS	GLIAL	GOUTY	GRUFF
GOSH	GALOP	GEODE	GLIDE	GOWAN	GRUME
GOUT	GAMAY	GEOID	GLIFF	GOWD	GRUMP
GOWD	GAMBA	GERAH	GLIME	GOWK	GRUNT
GOWK	GAMBE	GERMY	GLINT	GOWN	GUACO
GOWN	GAMER	GESSO	*GLITZ	GRAB	GUANO
GRAB	GAMEY	GESTE	GLOAM	GRAD	GUARD
GRAD	GAMIC	GETUP	GLOAT	GRAM	GUAVA
GRAM	GAMIN	GHAST	GLOBE	GRAN	GUESS
GRAN	GAMMA	GHAUT	GLOGG	GRAT	GUEST
GRAT	GAMMY	*GHAZI	GLOOM	GRANA	GUIDE
GRAY	GAMUT	GHOST	GLORY	GRAND	GUILD
GREE	GANEF	GHOUL	GLOSS	GRANT	GUILE

GUILT	*GALAXY	GARVEY	GERMEN	GLEETY	GOLDEN
GUIRO	GALENA	GASBAG	GERUND	GLIDER	GOLFER
GUISE	GALERE	GASCON	GESTIC	GLIOMA	GOLOSH
GULAG	GALIOT	GASIFY	GETTER	GLITCH	GOMUTI
GULAR	GALLET	GASKET	GEWGAW	*GLITZY	GONIFF
GULCH	GALLEY	GASKIN	GEYSER	GLOBAL	GONION
GULES	GALLON	GASLIT	GHARRI	GLOBBY	GONIUM
GULFY	GALLOP	GASMAN	GHARRY	GLOBIN	GONOPH
GULLY	GALLUS	GASPER	GHERAO	GLOMUS	GOOBER
GULPY	GALOOT	GASSED	GHETTO	GLOOMY	GOODBY
GUMBO	GALORE	GASSER	GHIBLI	GLOPPY	GOODLY
GUMMA	GALOSH	GASSES	GHOSTY	GLORIA	GOOGLY
GUMMY	GALYAC	GASTER	GIAOUR	GLOSSA	GOOGOL
GUNNY	GALYAK	GATEAU	GIBBER	GLOSSY	GOOIER
GUPPY	GAMBIA	GATHER	GIBBET	GLOVER	GOONEY
GURGE	GAMBIR	GATING	GIBBON	GLOWER	GOONIE
GURRY	GAMBIT	GAUCHE	GIBLET	GLUCAN	GOORAL
GURSH	GAMBLE	GAUCHO	GIBSON	GLUING	GOOSEY
GUSHY	GAMBOL	GAUGER	GIDDAP	GLUMPY	GOPHER
GUSSY	GAMELY	GAVAGE	GIGGED	GLUNCH	GORGER
GUSTO	GAMEST	GAVIAL	GIGGLE	GLUTEI	GORGET
GUSTY	GAMETE	GAWKER	GIGGLY	GLUTEN	GORGON
GUTSY	GAMIER	GAWPER	GIGLET	GLYCAN	GORHEN
GUTTA	GAMILY	GAWSIE	GIGLOT	GLYCIN	GORIER
GUTTY	GAMINE	GAYETY	GIGOLO	GLYCOL	GORILY
GUYOT	GAMING	*GAZABO	GILDER	*GLYCYL	GORING
GYPSY	GAMMED	*GAZEBO	GILLER	GNARLY	GOSPEL
GYRAL	GAMMER	*GAZING	GILLIE	GNATTY	GOSSAN
GYRON	GAMMON	*GAZUMP	GIMBAL	GNAWER	GOSSIP
GYRUS	GANDER	GEEGAW	GIMLET	GNEISS	GOTHIC
GABBED	GANGER	*GEEZER	GIMMAL	GNOMIC	GOTTEN
GABBER	GANGLY	GEISHA	GIMMIE	GNOMON	GOUGER
GABBLE	GANGUE	GELADA	GINGAL	GNOSIS	GOURDE
GABBRO	*GANJAH	GELANT	GINGER	GOALIE	GOVERN
GABIES	GANNET	GELATE	GINGKO	GOANNA	GRABBY
GABION	GANOID	GELATI	GINKGO	GOATEE	GRABEN
GABOON	GANTRY	GELATO	GINNED	GOBANG	GRADER
GADDED	GAOLER	GELDER	GINNER	GOBBED	GRADIN
GADDER	GAPING	GELLED	GIPPER	GOBBET	GRADUS
GADFLY	GAPPED	GEMMED	GIRDER	GOBBLE	GRAHAM
GADGET	GARAGE	GEMOTE	GIRDLE	GOBIES	GRAINY
GADOID	GARBLE	GENDER	GIRLIE	GOBLET	GRAMME
GAFFER	GARCON	GENERA	GITANO	GOBLIN	GRANGE
GAGAKU	GARDEN	GENEVA	GITTIN	GOBONY	GRANNY
GAGGED	GARGET	GENIAL	GIVING	GODDAM	GRANUM
GAGGER	GARGLE	GENIUS	GLACIS	GODDED	GRAPPA
GAGGLE	GARISH	GENTES	GLADLY	GODOWN	GRASSY
GAGING	GARLIC	GENTIL	GLAIRE	GODSON	GRATER
GAGMAN	GARNER	GENTLE	GLAIRY	GODWIT	GRATIN
GAIETY	GARNET	GENTOO	GLAIVE	GOFFER	GRATIS
GAINER	GAROTE	GENTRY	GLAMOR	GOGGLE	GRAVEL
GAINLY	GARRED	GEODIC	GLANCE	GOGGLY	GRAVEN
GAINST	GARRET	GERBIL	GLASSY	GOGLET	GRAVER
GAITER	GARRON	GERENT	*GLAZER	GOITER	GRAVID
GALAGO	GARTER	GERMAN	GLEAMY	GOITRE	GRAYLY

*GRAZER	GUGLET	GALIPOT	GASTRIN	GESTURE	GLEANER
GREASE	GUIDER	GALLANT	GATEMAN	GETAWAY	GLEEFUL
GREASY	GUIDON	GALLATE	GATEWAY	GETTING	GLEEMAN
GREAVE	GUILTY	GALLEIN	GAUDERY	GHARIAL	GLENOID
GREEDY	GUIMPE	GALLEON	GAUFFER	GHASTLY	GLEYING
GREENY	GUINEA	GALLERY	GAUNTRY	GHILLIE	GLIADIN
GREIGE	GUITAR	GALLETA	GAVOTTE	GHOSTLY	GLIMMER
GRELAG	GULDEN	GALLFLY	*GAWKIER	GHOULIE	GLIMPSE
GREMMY	GULLET	GALLIUM	*GAWKIES	GIBBING	GLISTEN
GREYLY	GULLEY	GALLNUT	*GAWKISH	GIBBOSE	GLISTER
GRIEVE	GULPER	GALLOON	GAYNESS	GIBBOSE	*GLITCHY
GRIFFE	GUMMED	GALLOOT	*GAZANIA	GIBBOUS	GLITTER
GRIGRI	GUMMER	GALLOUS	*GAZELLE	*GIDDYAP	GLOATER
GRILLE	GUNDOG	GALLOWS	*GAZETTE	*GIDDYUP	GLOBATE
GRILSE	GALOSHE	GALOSHE	*GEARBOX	GIGABIT	GLOBOID
GRIMLY	GUNNED	*GALUMPH	GEARING	GIGATON	GLOBOSE
GRINCH	GUNNEL	GAMBADE	GELATIN	GIGGING	GLOBOUS
GRINGO	GUNNEN	GAMBADO	GELDING	GIGGLER	GLOBULE
GRIPER	GUNNER	GAMBIER	GELLANT	GILBERT	GLOCHID
GRIPEY	GUNSEL	GAMBLER	GELLING	GILDING	GLONION
GRIPPE	GURGLE	GAMBOGE	GEMINAL	GILLNET	GLORIED
GRIPPY	GURNET	GAMBREL	GEMLIKE	*GIMMICK	GLORIES
GRISLY	GURNEY	GAMELAN	GEMMATE	GIMPIER	GLORIFY
GRISON	GUSHER	GAMIEST	GEMMIER	GINGALL	GLOSSER
GRITTY	GUSSET	GAMMIER	*GEMMILY	GINGELI	GLOTTIS
GRIVET	GUSSIE	GAMMING	GEMMING	GINGELY	*GLOWFLY
GROCER	GUTTED	GANACHE	GEMMULE	GINGERY	GLUCOSE
GROGGY	GUTTER	GANGLIA	GENERAL	GINGHAM	GLUEPOT
GROOVE	GUTTLE	GANGREL	GENERIC	GINGILI	GLUTEAL
GROOVY	*GUZZLE	*GANGWAY	GENESIS	GINGIVA	GLUTEUS
GROPER	GWEDUC	GANTLET	GENETIC	GINNING	GLUTTED
GROTTO	GYPPER	GAPOSIS	GENETTE	GINSENG	GLUTTON
GROUCH	GYPSUM	GAPPING	GENIPAP	GIPPING	GLYCINE
GROUND	GYRASE	GARBAGE	GENITAL	GIRAFFE	*GLYPTIC
GROUSE	GYRATE	GARBLER	GENITOR	GIRASOL	GNARRED
GROUTY	GYRENE	GARBOIL	GENOISE	GIRDLER	GNATHAL
GROVEL	GYRING	GARDANT	GENSENG	GIRLISH	GNATHIC
GROWER	GYROSE	GARFISH	GENTEEL	GIROSOL	GNAWING
GROWLY	GABBARD	GARGLER	GENTIAN	GISARME	*GNOCCHI
GROWTH	GABBART	GARIGUE	GENTILE	GITTERN	GNOMISH
GROYNE	GABBIER	GARLAND	GENUINE	*GIZZARD	GNOMIST
GRUBBY	GABBING	GARMENT	GEODESY	*GJETOST	GNOSTIC
GRUDGE	GABBLER	GARNISH	*GEODUCK	GLACIAL	GOATISH
*GRUFFY	GABELLE	GAROTTE	*GEODUCK	GLACIER	GOBBING
GRUGRU	GABFEST	GARPIKE	GEOLOGY	GLADDEN	GOBBLER
GRUMPY	GADDING	GARRING	GEORGIC	GLADDER	GOBIOID
GRUNGE	GADROON	GARROTE	GERBERA	GLADIER	GOBONEE
GRUNGY	GADWALL	GASEOUS	GERENUK	GLAIKET	GODDESS
GRUTCH	GAGGING	GASKING	GERMANE	GLAIKIT	GODDING
GUAIAC	GAGSTER	GASLESS	GERMIER	GLAMOUR	GODHEAD
GUANAY	GAHNITE	GASOHOL	GERMINA	GLANCER	GODHOOD
GUANIN	GAINFUL	GASSING	GESSOED	GLASSIE	GODLESS
GUENON	GAINSAY	GASTRAL	GESTALT	*GLAZIER	GODLIER
*GUFFAW	GALABIA	GASTREA	GESTAPO	*GLAZING	GODLIKE
GUGGLE	GALILEE	GASTRIC	GESTATE	GLEAMER	GODLING

GODROON	GRANDLY	GRIFFON	GUANASE	GYPLURE	GARDENIA
GODSEND	GRANDMA	GRIFTER	GUANINE	GYPSTER	GARDYLOO
GODSHIP	GRANDPA	GRILLER	GUARANI	GYRATOR	GARGANEY
GOGGLER	GRANGER	GRIMACE	GUARDER	GABBIEST	GARGOYLE
GOLDARN	GRANITA	GRIMIER	GUAYULE	GADABOUT	GAROTTER
GOLDBUG	GRANITE	GRIMING	GUDGEON	GADARENE	GARRISON
GOLDEYE	GRANNIE	GRIMMER	GUERDON	GADGETRY	GARROTER
GOLDURN	GRANOLA	GRINDER	GUESSER	*GADZOOKS	GARROTTE
GOLFING	GRANTEE	GRINNED	GUILDER	GAINLESS	GASALIER
GOLIARD	GRANTER	GRINNER	GUIPURE	GALABIYA	GASELIER
GOLOSHE	GRANTOR	GRIPIER	GUISARD	GALACTIC	GASHOUSE
GOMERAL	GRANULE	GRIPING	GULFIER	GALANGAL	GASIFIED
GOMEREL	GRAPERY	GRIPMAN	GUMBOIL	GALAVANT	GASIFIER
GOMERIL	*GRAPHIC	GRIPPED	GUMBOOT	GALBANUM	GASIFORM
GONDOLA	GRAPIER	GRIPPER	GUMDROP	GALENITE	GASLIGHT
GOODBYE	GRAPLIN	GRIPPLE	GUMLESS	GALIVANT	GASOGENE
GOODIES	GRAPNEL	GRISKIN	GUMLIKE	GALLEASS	GASOLENE
GOODISH	GRAPPLE	GRISTLE	GUMMIER	GALLERIA	GASOLIER
GOODMAN	GRASPER	GRISTLY	GUMMING	GALLIARD	GASOLINE
GOOIEST	GRATIFY	*GRIZZLE	GUMMITE	GALLOPER	GASTIGHT
*GOOMBAH	GRATING	*GRIZZLY	GUMMOSE	GALOPADE	GASTNESS
*GOOMBAY	GRAUPEL	GROANER	GUMMOUS	GALVANIC	GASTRAEA
*GORCOCK	GRAVELY	GROCERY	GUMSHOE	GAMASHES	GASTRULA
GORGING	GRAVEST	GROGRAM	GUMTREE	GAMBESON	*GASWORKS
GORIEST	GRAVIDA	GROMMET	GUMWEED	GAMBUSIA	GATEFOLD
GORILLA	GRAVIES	GROOMER	GUMWOOD	*GAMECOCK	GATELESS
GORMAND	GRAVING	GROOVER	GUNBOAT	GAMENESS	GATELIKE
*GOSHAWK	GRAVITY	GROSSER	GUNFIRE	GAMESMAN	GATEPOST
GOSLING	*GRAVLAX	GROSSLY	GUNLESS	GAMESOME	GATHERER
GOSPORT	GRAVURE	*GROUCHY	GUNLOCK	GAMESTER	GAUNTLET
GOSSIPY	GRAYISH	GROUPER	GUNNERY	GAMINESS	*GAVELOCK
GOSSOON	GRAYLAG	GROUPIE	GUNNING	GAMMADIA	*GAYWINGS
GOTHITE	GRAYOUT	GROUSER	GUNPLAY	GAMMIEST	*GAZOGENE
GOUACHE	*GRAZIER	GROUTER	GUNROOM	GAMMONER	*GAZPACHO
GOULASH	*GRAZING	GROWLER	GUNSHIP	GAMODEME	*GAZUMPER
GOURAMI	GREASER	GROWNUP	GUNSHOT	GANGLAND	GEARCASE
GOURMET	GREATEN	*GROWTHY	GUNWALE	GANGLIAL	GEARLESS
GRABBER	GREATLY	GRUBBER	GURGLET	GANGLIAR	GEEPOUND
GRABBLE	*GRECIZE	GRUDGER	GURNARD	GANGLIER	GELATINE
GRACILE	GREENIE	GRUELER	GUSTIER	GANGLING	GELATING
GRACING	GREENLY	*GRUFFLY	GUSTILY	GANGLION	GELATION
GRACKLE	GREENTH	GRUMBLE	GUTLESS	*GANGPLOW	GELIDITY
GRADATE	GREETER	GRUMMER	GUTLIKE	GANGRENE	GELSEMIA
GRADINE	GREISEN	GRUMMET	GUTSILY	GANGSTER	GEMINATE
GRADING	GREMIAL	GRUMOSE	GUTTATE	GANISTER	GEMMIEST
GRADUAL	GREMLIN	GRUMOUS	GUTTERY	GANTLINE	*GEMOLOGY
GRAFTER	GREMMIE	*GRUMPHY	GUTTIER	GANTLOPE	*GEMSBUCK
GRAINER	GRENADE	GRUNION	GUTTING	*GANYMEDE	GEMSTONE
GRAMARY	GREYHEN	GRUNTER	GUTTLER	GAPESEED	GENDARME
GRAMMAR	GREYISH	GRUNTLE	GUYLINE	*GAPEWORM	GENERATE
GRAMPUS	GRIBBLE	GRUSHIE	*GUZZLER	*GAPINGLY	GENEROUS
GRANARY	GRIDDER	GRUTTEN	*GWEDUCK	*GARBANZO	GENETICS
GRANDAD	GRIDDLE	GRUYERE	GYMNAST	GARBLESS	GENITALS
GRANDAM	GRIEVER	*GRYPHON	GYNECIA	GARBOARD	GENITIVE
GRANDEE	GRIFFIN	GUANACO	*GYNECIC	GARDENER	GENITURE

GENOCIDE	GLABRATE	*GLYCONIC	GRACIOUS	GRIMMEST	GUMMIEST
GENOTYPE	GLACIATE	*GLYCOSYL	GRADIENT	GRIMNESS	GUMMOSIS
GENTRICE	GLADDEST	GNARRING	GRADUAND	GRINDERY	GUMPTION
*GENTRIFY	GLADDING	GNATHION	GRADUATE	GRINNING	*GUNFIGHT
GEODESIC	GLADIATE	GNATHITE	*GRAECIZE	GRIPIEST	GUNFLINT
GEODETIC	GLADIEST	GNATLIKE	*GRAFFITO	GRIPPIER	GUNMETAL
GEOGNOSY	GLADIOLA	GNOMICAL	GRAFTAGE	GRIPPING	*GUNNYBAG
GEOLOGER	GLADIOLI	GOADLIKE	GRAMARYE	*GRIPSACK	GUNPAPER
*GEOMANCY	GLADNESS	GOALLESS	*GRAMERCY	GRISEOUS	GUNPOINT
GEOMETER	GLADSOME	GOALPOST	GRANDAME	GRISETTE	GUNSMITH
GEOMETRY	GLANDERS	GOALWARD	GRANDDAD	*GRIZZLER	*GUNSTOCK
*GEOPHAGY	GLANDULE	*GOATFISH	GRANDDAM	GROGGERY	GURUSHIP
GEOPHONE	GLASNOST	GOATHERD	GRANDEUR	*GROGSHOP	GUSTABLE
*GEOPHYTE	GLASSFUL	GOATLIKE	*GRANDKID	GROMWELL	GUSTIEST
GEOPONIC	GLASSIFR	GOATSKIN	GRANDSIR	*GROSBEAK	GUSTLESS
GEOPROBE	GLASSILY	*GODCHILD	GRANDSON	GROSCHEN	GUTTATED
*GEOTAXIS	GLASSINE	GODLIEST	GRANULAR	GROUNDER	GUTTIEST
GERANIAL	GLASSMAN	GOETHITE	*GRAPHEME	GROUPING	GUTTURAL
GERANIOL	GLAUCOMA	GOLCONDA	GRAPHITE	GROUPOID	*GYMKHANA
GERANIUM	GLAUCOUS	*GOLDFISH	GRAPIEST	GROVELER	GYMNASIA
GERARDIA	*GLAZIERY	GOLGOTHA	GRAPLINE	*GRUBWORM	GYNAECEA
GERBILLE	GLEANING	GOLLIWOG	GRAPPLER	GRUELING	GYNAECIA
GERMARIC	GLEESOME	*GOLLYWOG	GRATEFUL	GRUELLED	*GYNANDRY
GERMFREE	GLEGNESS	GOMBROON	GRATINEE	GRUELLER	*GYNARCHY
GERMIEST	GLIADINE	GONENESS	GRATUITY	GRUESOME	*GYNECIUM
GERMINAL	GLIBNESS	GONFALON	GRAVAMEN	*GRUFFIER	*GYNECOID
GERONTIC	GLIMPSER	GONFANON	*GRAVELLY	*GRUFFILY	*GYNIATRY
GESNERIA	GLISSADE	GONGLIKE	GRAVITAS	*GRUFFISH	GYNOECIA
GESTICAL	GLITTERY	GONIDIUM	GRAVITON	GRUMBLER	GYPSEIAN
GESTURAL	GLOAMING	GONOCYTE	*GRAVLAKS	GRUMMEST	GYPSEOUS
*GHASTFUL	GLOBATED	GONOPORE	*GRAYBACK	*GRUMPHIE	*GYPSYDOM
GHOSTING	GLOBULAR	GOODNESS	*GRAYFISH	*GRUMPISH	*GYPSYISH
GIANTESS	GLOBULIN	*GOODWIFE	GRAYLING	GUACHARO	*GYPSYISM
GIANTISM	GLOOMFUL	GOODWILL	GRAYMAIL	GUAIACOL	GYRATION
GIBBSITE	GLOOMING	GOOFBALL	GRAYNESS	GUAIACUM	*GYRATORY
*GIFTEDLY	GLORIOLE	GORBELLY	*GRAZIOSO	GUAIOCUM	GYROIDAL
GIFTLESS	GLORIOUS	*GORBLIMY	GREEGREE	GUANIDIN	GYROSTAT
*GIFTWARE	GLOSSARY	GORGEOUS	GREENERY	GUARANTY	
*GIGABYTE	GLOSSEME	GORGERIN	*GREENFLY	GUARDANT	N G WEE
GIGANTIC	GLOSSIER	GORINESS	GREENIER	GUARDIAN	N G
GIGAWATT	GLOSSIES	GORMLESS	GREENING	GUERIDON	ULTRUM
GILDHALL	GLOSSINA	GOSPELER	GREENISH	GUERILLA	FU G U
GILTHEAD	*GLOWWORM	GOSSAMER	GREENLET	GUERNSEY	HO G G
*GIMCRACK	*GLOXINIA	GOSSIPER	*GREENWAY	GUIDANCE	JA G G
*GIMMICKY	GLUCAGON	GOSSIPRY	GREETING	*GUIDEWAY	MI G G
GIMPIEST	GLUCINUM	GOSSYPOL	GREWSOME	GUILEFUL	MU G G
GINGELEY	GLUELIKE	GOURMAND	GREYNESS	*GUITQUIT	NO G G
GINGELLY	GLUMNESS	GOVERNOR	GRIDIRON	GULFIEST	VI G A
GINGERLY	GLUTELIN	GOWNSMAN	*GRIDLOCK	*GULFLIKE	VU G G
GINGILLI	GLUTTING	GRABBIER	GRIEVANT	*GULF-	YE G G
GIRASOLE	GLUTTONY	GRABBING	GRIEVOUS	WEED	CA G ER
GIRLHOOD	GLYCERIN	GRABBLER	GRILLADE	GULLABLE	DAG G A
*GIVEAWAY	GLYCEROL	GRACEFUL	GRILLAGE	GULLIBLE	KU G EL
*GIVEBACK	*GLYCERYL	GRACILIS	GRIMACER	GULOSITY	LI G ER
GLABELLA	*GLYCOGEN	GRACIOSO	GRIMIEST	GUMBOTIL	LU G ER

MO G GY	DI G AMY	*JA G GER	NA G GER	RI G GED	WI G WAG
NA G GY	DI G EST	JA G UAR	NE G ATE	RI G GER	*WI G WAM
PA G ER	DI G GED	*JI G GER	NI G GLE	RI G HTO	YO G INI
SA G GY	DI G GER	*JI G GLE	NO G GIN	RI G HTY	YO G URT
VU G GY	DI G LOT	*JI G GLY	NU G GET	RI G OUR	*ZI G ZAG
WI G GY	DO G DOM	*JI G SAW	PA G ING	RU G GED	*ZY G OID
BA G ASS	DO G EAR	*JO G GER	PA G ODA	RU G GER	*ZY G OMA
BA G FUL	DO G GED	*JO G GLE	*PE G BOX	RU G OLA	*ZY G OTE
BA G GED	DO G GER	JU G ATE	PE G GED	RU G OSA	BA G ASSE
BA G GER	DO G LEG	*JU G FUL	PI G EON	RU G OSE	BA G GAGE
BA G GIE	DO G NAP	*JU G GED	PI G GED	RU G OUS	BA G GING
BA G MAN	DU G ONG	JU G ULA	PI G GIE	SA G BUT	BA G PIPE
BA G NIO	FA G GOT	KE G LER	PI G GIN	SA G EST	BA G SFUL
BA G UET	FI G URE	LA G END	PI G LET	SA G GAR	*BA G WORM
BA G WIG	*FO G BOW	LA G GED	PI G NUS	SA G GED	BE G GARY
BE G ALL	FO G DOG	LA G GER	PI G NUT	SA G GER	BE G GING
*BE G AZE	FO G GED	LA G OON	PI G OUT	SE G GAR	BE G LOOM
BE G GAR	FO G GER	LA G UNA	PI G PEN	SI G HER	BE G ONIA
BE G GED	FU G ATO	LA G UNE	PI G STY	SI G LOS	BE G ORAH
BE G IRD	FU G GED	LE G ACY	PO G IES	SI G NAL	BE G ORRA
BE G LAD	GA G AKU	LE G ATE	PO G ROM	SI G NEE	BE G RIME
BE G ONE	GA G GED	LE G ATO	PU G GED	SI G NER	BE G ROAN
BE G RIM	GA G GER	LE G END	PU G GRY	SI G NET	BE G UILE
BE G ULF	GA G GLE	LE G GED	PU G REE	SI G NOR	BE G UINE
BI G AMY	GA G ING	LE G GIN	RA G BAG	SO G GED	BI G FOOT
BI G EYE	GA G MAN	LE G ION	RA G GED	SU G ARY	BI G GEST
BI G GER	GI G GED	LE G IST	RA G GEE	TA G GED	BI G GETY
BI G GIE	GI G GLE	LE G MAN	RA G GLE	TA G GER	BI G GING
BI G GIN	GI G GLY	LE G ONG	RA G ING	TA G RAG	BI G GISH
BI G WIG	GI G LET	LE G UME	RA G LAN	TE G MEN	BI G GITY
BO G GED	GI G LOT	LI G AND	RA G MAN	TI G HTS	BI G HEAD
BO G GLE	GI G OLO	LI G ASE	RA G OUT	TI G LON	BI G HORN
BO G IES	GO G GLE	LI G ATE	RA G TAG	TO G ATE	BI G NESS
BU G EYE	GO G GLY	LI G NIN	RA G TOP	TO G GED	BI G OTED
BU G GED	GO G LET	LI G ULA	RE G AIN	TO G GLE	BI G OTRY
BU G GER	GU G GLE	LI G ULE	RE G ALE	TU G GER	BO G BEAN
BU G LER	GU G LET	LI G URE	RE G ARD	TU G RIK	BO G GIER
BU G SHA	HA G BUT	LO G GED	RE G AVE	VA G ARY	BO G GING
BY G ONE	HA G DON	LO G GER	RE G EAR	VA G ILE	BO G GISH
CA G IER	HA G GED	LO G GIA	RE G ENT	VA G INA	BO G GLER
CA G ILY	HA G GIS	LO G ILY	RE G GAE	VA G ROM	BO G WOOD
CA G ING	HA G GLE	LO G ION	RE G ILD	VE G ETE	*BO G YISM
CO G ENT	HE G ARI	*LO G JAM	RE G IME	VE G GIE	*BO G YMAN
CO G GED	HE G IRA	LO G WAY	RE G INA	VI G OUR	BU G ABOO
CO G ITO	HI G GLE	LU G GED	RE G ION	WA G GED	BU G BANE
CO G NAC	*HI G HLY	LU G GER	RE G IUS	WA G GER	BU G BEAR
*CO G WAY	*HI G HTH	LU G GIE	RE G IVE	WA G GLE	BU G GERY
CY G NET	HO G GED	MA G NET	RE G LET	WA G GLY	BU G GING
DA G GER	HO G GER	ME G ASS	RE G LOW	WA G GON	BU G LOSS
DA G GLE	HO G NUT	*MI G HTY	RE G LUE	WA G ING	BU G SEED
DA G OBA	HO G TIE	MI G NON	RE G NAL	WI G EON	CA G EFUL
DE G AGE	HU G EST	MO G GIE	RE G NUM	WI G GED	CA G IEST
DE G ERM	HU G GED	MU G FUL	RE G RET	WI G GLE	CI G ARET
DE G REE	HU G GER	MU G GEE	RE G REW	WI G GLY	*CO G ENCY
DE G UST	*JA G GED	NA G ANA	RE G ROW	WI G LET	CO G GING

CO G NATE	HA G GADA	LO G ANIA	PI G NOLI	SA G UARO	NA G GY
CO G NISE	HA G GARD	LO G BOOK	PI G SKIN	SE G ETAL	SA G GY
*CO G NIZE	HA G GING	LO G GATS	PI G SNEY	SE G MENT	VU G GY
*DA G LOCK	*HA G GISH	LO G GETS	PI G WEED	SI G ANID	WI G GY
DA G WOOD	HA G GLER	LO G GIER	PO G HORN	SI G HTER	WOD G E
DE G AUSS	HA G RIDE	LO G GING	PO G ONIA	SI G HTLY	BA G GED
*DE G LAZE	HE G UMEN	LO G ICAL	PO G ONIP	SI G MOID	BA G GER
DE G RADE	*HI G HBOY	LO G IEST	PU G AREE	SI G NAGE	BA G GIE
DI G AMMA	*HI G HWAY	LO G ROLL	PU G GIER	SI G NIFY	BE G GAR
DI G GING	*HO G BACK	LO G WOOD	PU G GING	SI G NIOR	BE G GED
DI G ITAL	*HO G FISH	LU G CAIL	PU G GISH	SI G NORA	BI G GER
*DI G NIFY	*HO G LIKE	LU G GAGE	*PU G MARK	SI G NORE	BI G GIE
DI G NITY	HO G MANE	LU G GING	RA G GEDY	SI G NORY	BI G GIN
*DI G OXIN	HO G NOSE	LU G WORM	RA G GIES	SU G GEST	BIN G ER
DI G RAPH	*HO G WASH	MA G NETO	RA G GING	TA G GING	BIO G AS
DI G RESS	*HO G WEED	*MA G NIFY	RA G TIME	TA G LIKE	BO G GED
DO G BANE	HU G EOUS	ME G AHIT	RA G WEED	TA G MEME	BO G GLE
DO G CART	HU G GING	ME G ALIT	RA G WORT	TE G ULAR	BOO G EY
DO G EDOM	HY G EIST	ME G APOD	RE G ALER	TE G UMEN	BU G GED
DO G FACE	HY G IENE	ME G AVOL	RE G ALIA	TI G HTEN	BU G GER
*DO G FISH	*JA G GARY	ME G AWAT	RE G ALLY	TI G RISH	BUN G EE
DO G GERY	*JA G GERY	ME G ILLA	RE G ATTA	TI G RESS	CO G GED
DO G GIES	*JA G GING	*ME G ILPH	RE G AUGE	TO G ATED	DAG G ER
DO G GING	*JA G LESS	MI G NONN	RE G ENCY	TO G GERY	DAG G LE
DO G GISH	*JI G ABOO	MI G RAIN	RE G IMEN	TO G GING	DI G GED
DO G GONE	*JI G GING	MU G GIES	*RE G LAZE	TO G GLER	DI G GER
DO G GREL	*JO G GLER	MU G GING	RE G LOSS	TU G BOAT	DIN G ER
DO G LIKE	*JU G GING	NA G GING	RE G NANT	TU G GING	DOD G EM
DO G SLED	*JU G GLER	NE G ATON	RE G ORGE	TU G LESS	DO G GED
DO G TROT	*JU G HEAD	NE G ATOR	RE G OSOL	VA G RANT	DO G GER
DO G VANE	*JU G SFUL	NE G LECT	RE G RADE	VE G ETAL	DRU G GY
DO G WOOD	*JU G ULUM	NE G LIGE	RE G RAFT	VO G UISH	*FIZ G IG
FA G OTER	*JU G VLAR	NE G ROID	RE G RANT	WA G ERER	FO G GED
FI G HTER	KE G ELER	NE G RONI	RE G RATE	*WA G GERY	FO G GER
FI G MENT	KE G LING	*NI G HTY	RE G REEN	WA G GING	FU G GED
FI G URAL	LA G GARD	NI G GLER	RE G REET	*WA G GISH	GA G GED
FI G URER	LA G GING	NI G HTIE	RE G RESS	WA G ONER	GA G GER
FI G WORT	LE G ALLY	NI G HTLY	RE G RIND	WA G SOME	GA G GLE
FO G GAGE	LE G ATEE	NI G RIFY	RE G ROOM	WA G TAIL	GI G GED
FO G GING	LE G ATOR	NO G GING	RE G ROUP	*WI G GERY	GI G GLE
FO G LESS	LE G GIER	*PA G EBOY	RE G ULAR	WI G GIER	GI G GLY
*FO G YISM	LE G GING	PA G EANT	RE G ULUS	WI G GING	GO G GLE
FU G GING	LE G HORN	PA G URID	RI G GING	WI G GLER	GO G GLY
FU G UIST	LE G IBLE	PE G GING	RI G HTER	WI G LESS	GU G GLE
GA G GING	LE G LESS	PE G LESS	RI G HTLY	*WI G LIKE	HA G GED
GA G STER	LE G LIKE	PE G LIKE	RI G IDLY	YE G GMAN	HA G GIS
GI G ABIT	LE G ROOM	PI G BOAT	RO G UERY	YO G HURT	HA G GLE
GI G ATON	LE G UMIN	*PI G FISH	RO G UISH	*ZY G OSIS	HAN G UL
GI G GING	*LE G WORK	PI G GERY	RU G GING	BOO G Y	HI G GLE
GI G GLER	LI G HTEN	PI G GIER	RU G LIKE	DAG G A	HO G GED
GO G GLER	LI G HTER	PI G GIES	SA G AMAN	DIN G E	HO G GER
HA G ADIC	LI G HTLY	PI G GING	SA G GARD	DON G A	HU G GED
HA G BORN	LI G NIFY	PI G GISH	SA G GIER	GLO G G	HU G GER
*HA G BUSH	LI G NITE	PI G LIKE	SA G GING	KLU G E	*JA G GED
*HA G FISH	LI G ROIN	PI G MENT	SA G IEST	MO G GY	*JA G GER

*JAN G LY	WA G G LY	HAN G TA G	SA G G ING	CIN G ULUM	FUN G IBLE
*JI G G ER	WA G G ON	HED G IN G	SEA G ULL	*COA G ENCY	G AD G ETRY
*JI G G LE	WI G G ED	HU G G ING	SER G ING	COA G ULUM	G AN G LAND
*JI G G LY	WI G G LE	*JA G G ARY	STA G ING	CON G ENER	G AN G LIAL
*JO G G ER	WI G G LY	*JA G G ERY	SUB G OAL	CON G LOBE	G AN G LIAR
*JO G G LE	*ZIN G ER	*JA G G ING	SU G G EST	CON G RATS	G AN G LIER
*JU G G ED	BAD G ING	*JI G G ING	SUR G ING	CON G RESS	G AN G LING
LA G G ED	BA G G AGE	*JO G G LER	SWA G G IE	CRA G SMAN	G AN G LION
LA G G ER	BA G G ING	*JU G G ING	SWA G ING	CUD G ELER	*GAN G PLOW
LE G G ED	BE G G ARY	*JU G G LER	TA G G ING	CUT G RASS	G AN G RENE
LE G G IN	BE G G ING	LA G G ARD	TO G G ERY	DAU G HTER	G AN G STER
LO G G ED	BEI G NET	LA G G ING	TO G G ING	DIA G NOSE	G AR G ANEY
LO G G ER	BER G ERE	LAR G EST	TRI G RAM	DIA G ONAL	G AR G OYLE
LO G G IA	BI G G EST	LE G G IER	TU G G ING	*DIA G RAPH	G EO G NOSY
LU G G ED	BI G G ETY	LE G G ING	VER G ING	DIG G INGS	G IN G ELEY
LU G G ER	BI G G ISH	LOD G ING	*WA G G ERY	DIN G DONG	G IN G ELLY
LU G G IE	BI G G ITY	LO G G ATS	*WA G G ISH	DIS G OR G E	G IN G ILLI
MO G G IE	BO G G IER	LO G G ETS	*WI G G ERY	DIS G RACE	G LE G NESS
MOR G AN	BO G G ING	LO G G IER	WI G G IER	DIS G UISE	G OLG OTHA
MU G G EE	BO G G ISH	LO G G ING	WI G G ING	*DO G G EDLY	G ON G LIKE
NA G G ER	BO G G LER	LON G IES	WI G G LER	DO G G EREL	G OR G EOUS
NI G G LE	BUD G ING	LON G ING	WIN G TIP	DO G G IEST	G OR G ERIN
NO G G IN	BU G G ERY	LU G G AGE	YE G G MAN	DO G G ONED	G RO G G ERY
NON G AY	BU G G ING	LU G G ING	*BAD G ERLY	*DOU G HBOY	*G RO G SHOP
NU G G ET	CLO G G ER	LUN G FUL	BAN G TAIL	*DOU G HIFR	*HA G G ADAH
PE G G ED	CO G G ING	LUN G ING	BAR G ELLO	*DOU G HNUT	*HA G G ADIC
PI G G ED	DI G G ING	MER G ING	BAR G EMAN	DRA G G IER	*HAN G FIRE
PI G G IE	DIN G IES	MU G G IES	BAR G HEST	DRA G G ING	HAN G NEST
PI G G IN	DOD G ING	MU G G ING	BAR G UEST	DRA G ONET	*HED G EHO G
PU G G ED	DO G G ERY	NA G G ING	*BE G G ARLY	DRA G ROPE	*HED G EPI G
PU G G RY	DO G G IES	*NI G G HTY	BER G AMOT	DRA G STER	*HEI G HTEN
PUN G LE	DO G G ING	NO G G ING	BIO G ENIC	DRU G G IST	*HU G G ABLE
RA G G ED	DO G G ISH	PAN G ENE	BON G OIST	DUN G AREE	*HUN G OVER
RA G G EE	DO G G ONE	PAR G ING	*BOO G YMAN	DUN G HILL	IAN G SHAN
RA G G LE	DO G G REL	PE G G ING	*BOU G HPOT	*DYS G ENIC	*JA G G HERY
RE G G AE	DRU G G IE	PI G G ERY	BOU G HTEN	FID G ETER	*JAR G ONEL
RI G G ED	FID G ING	PI G G IER	BRA G G ART	FIN G ERER	*JI G G ERED
RI G G ER	FO G G AGE	PI G G IES	BRA G G EST	FLA G ELIA	*JIN G OISM
RU G G ED	FO G G ING	PI G G ING	BRA G G ING	FLA G G ING	*JON G LEUR
RU G G ER	FOR G ING	PI G G ISH	BRI G HTEN	FLA G LINE	*JUD G MENT
SA G G AR	FU G G ING	PLU G OLA	BRO G UERY	FLA G POLE	*JU G G LERY
SA G G ED	GA G G ING	PU G G IER	BRO G UISH	FLA G RANT	*JU G G LING
SA G G ER	GI G G ING	PU G G ING	BUD G ETER	*FLA G SHIP	KAN G AROO
SE G G AR	GI G G LER	PU G G ISH	BUN G ALOW	*FOR G IVER	KED G EREE
SO G G ED	GO G G LER	PUR G ING	BUN G HOLE	*FOU G HTEN	*KIN G BIRD
SYN G AS	GOR G ING	RA G G EDY	BUN G LING	FOX G LOVE	*KIN G BOLT
TA G G ED	HA G G ADA	RA G G IES	BUR G LARY	FRA G G ING	*KIN G FISH
TA G G ER	HA G G ARD	RA G G ING	BUR G ONET	FRA G MENT	*KIN G HOOD
TO G G ED	HA G G ING	RID G ING	BUR G RAVE	FRA G RANT	KIN G LESS
TO G G LE	*HA G G ISH	RI G G ING	*BUR G UNDY	*FRI G G ERY	*KIN G LIKE
TU G G ER	HA G G LER	RIN G GIT	CHI G ETAI	*FRI G HTEN	*KIN G POST
VE G G IE	HAN G DOG	ROU G ING	*CHU G ALUG	*FRO G FISH	*KIN G SHIP
WA G G ED	HAN G ING	RU G G ING		*FRO G LIKE	*KIN G SIDE
WA G G ER		SA G G ARD			*KIN G WOOD
WA G G LE		SA G G IER			

*KNI G HTLY	NON G REEN	SAR G ASSO	TON G UIN G	FAN G	SWA G
LAN G LAUF	NON G UILT	SEA G OIN G	TOU G HIES	FLA G	SWI G
LAN G RA G E	NUT G RASS	SEI G NEUR	*TOU G HISH	FRA G	THU G
LAN G SYNE	PAN G OLIN	SEI G NIOR	TRA G ICAL	FRI G	TIN G
LAN G UA G E	*PAY G RADE	SEI G NORY	TRA G OPAN	FRO G	TON G
LAR G ANDO	PEI G NOIR	SER G EANT	TRI G G EST	FRU G	TRI G
LAU G HIN G	PI G G IEST	SHA G REEN	TRI G G IN G	GAN G	TUN G
LAU G HTER	PIN G RASS	SHI G ELLA	TRI G ONAL	G LE G	TWI G
*LAW G IVER	PLA G IARY	SIN G SON G	TRI G RAPH	G LU G	VAN G
LE G G IERO	PLA G UIN G	SIN G ULAR	TUN G STEN	G ON G	VU G G
LE G G IEST	PLI G HTER	SLO G G IN G	TUR G ENCY	G RI G	WHI G
LIE G EMAN	PLU G LESS	SLU G ABED	TWI G LESS	G RO G	WIN G
LIN G ERER	*PLU G U G LY	SLU G FEST	VAN G UARD	HAN G	YAN G
LIN G ERIE	POI G NANT	SLU G GARD	*VEN G EFUL	HO G G	YE G G
LIN G IEST	PRE G G ERS	SLU G G IN G	VER G ENCE	HON G	ZIN G
LIN G UINE	PRE G NANT	SLU G G ISH	VIR G INAL	HUN G	BEFO G
LIN G UINI	*PRI G G ISH	SMU G G LER	WA G G ONER	JA G G	BEIN G
LIN G UIST	PRI G G ISM	SMU G NESS	*WAY G OIN G	KIN G	BEWI G
LOD G MENT	PRO G ERIA	SNA G LIKE	WEI G ELIA	LAN G	BHAN G
LON G BOAT	PRO G G IN G	SNI G G LER	*WEI G HMAN	LIN G	BOIN G
LON G ERON	PRO G NOSE	SNU G G EST	*WEI G HTER	LON G	BOUR G
LON G HAIR	PRO G RADE	SNU G G IES	WI G G IEST	LUN G	BRIN G
LON G HAND	PRO G RESS	SNU G G IN G	*WIN G BACK	MI G G	CHAN G
LON G HEAD	PU G G AREE	SNU G NESS	WIN G DIN G	MU G G	CLAN G
LON G HORN	PU G G IEST	SON G BIRD	*WIN G EDLY	NO G G	CLIN G
LON G LEAF	*PUN G ENCY	*SON G BOOK	WIN G IEST	PAN G	CLUN G
LON G LINE	*PYO G ENIC	SON G FEST	WIN G LESS	PEA G	COHO G
LON G NESS	*QUA G MIRE	SON G LESS	*WIN G LIKE	PIN G	COLO G
LON G SHIP	*QUA G MIRY	SON G LIKE	*WIN G OVER	PLU G	CUIN G
LON G SOME	RAN G BIRD	SON G STER	WIN G SPAN	PON G	DEBU G
LON G SPUR	RAN G NAIL	*SPA G YRIC	WRI G G LER	PRI G	DEFO G
LON G TIME	RAY G RASS	SPY G LASS	*ZI G G URAT	PRO G	DOIN G
LON G UEUR	REI G NITE	*SRA G BARK	*ZOO G ENIC	PUN G	DYIN G
*LON G WAYS	RIB G RASS	STA G EFUL	*ZOO G LOEA	QUA G	FLIN G
LON G WISE	RID G IEST	STA G IEST		RAN G	FLUN G
*LUN G FISH	RID G LIN G	STA G NANT		RIN G	GLO G G
LUN G WORM	*RIN G BARK	STA G NATE		RUN G	G OIN G
LUN G WORT	RIN G BOLT	STA G G ERY		SAN G	G ULA G
MA G ICIAN	RIN G BONE	STA G G IN G	BAN G	SCA G	HYIN G
MA G ISTER	RIN G DOVE	STA G IEST	BER G	SHA G	KIAN G
MA G NESIA	RIN G HALS	STA G NANT	BON G	SHO G	KLON G
MA G NETIC	RIN G LIKE	STA G NATE	BRA G	SIN G	LIAN G
MA G NOLIA	*RIN G NECK	STE G ODON	BRI G	SKA G	LYIN G
*MAN G ABEY	RIN G SIDE	SUB G ENRE	BUN G	SKE G	PIRO G
MAN G OVER	RIN G TAIL	SUB G ENUS	BUR G	SLA G	PRAR G
*MED G EHO G	RIN G TOSS	SUB G RADE	CHU G	SLO G	PRON G
*MED G EHOP	RIN G WORM	*SUB G RAPH	CLA G	SLU G	RENI G
MIS G RADE	ROU G HAGE	SUB G ROUP	CLO G	SMO G	REPE G
*MYO G ENIC	*ROU G HDRY	SUN G LASS	CRA G	SMU G	RERI G
*MYO G RAPH	*ROU G HHEW	SUR G ICAL	DAN G	SNA G	RETA G
NAR G HILE	*ROU G HISH	SWA G G IN G	DIN G	SNO G	RUIN G
NAR G ILEH	ROU G HLE G	TAI G LACH	DON G	SNU G	SCRA G
NEI G HBOR	RYE G RASS	TEI G LACH	DRA G	SON G	SHRU G
NON G ATAL	SAN G AREE	*THU G G ERY	DRE G	STA G	SLAN G
NON G LARE	SAN G UINE	*THU G G ISH	DUN G	SUN G	SLIN G

SLUN G	CAVIN G	*G AZIN G	MIDLE G	REHAN G	TIRIN G
SPAN G	CERIN G	G IVIN G	MIMIN G	REHUN G	TOKIN G
SPRA G	CITIN G	G LUIN G	MININ G	RICIN G	TOLIN G
SPRI G	CODIN G	G OBAN G	MIRIN G	RIDIN G	TONIN G
SPRU G	COMIN G	G ORIN G	MOPIN G	RILIN G	TOPIN G
*SQUE G	CONIN G	G RELA G	MOVIN G	RIMIN G	TOTIN G
STAI G	COPIN G	G UNDO G	MULIN G	RIPIN G	TRUIN G
STAN G	CORIN G	G YRIN G	MURIN G	RISIN G	TUBIN G
STIN G	COTIN G	HALIN G	MUSIN G	RIVIN G	TUNIN G
STUN G	COVIN G	HARIN G	MUSKE G	ROPIN G	TYPIN G
SUIN G	COYDO G	HATIN G	MUTIN G	ROSIN G	VICIN G
SWAN G	CUBIN G	HAVIN G	NAMIN G	ROVIN G	VIKIN G
SWIN G	CURIN G	HAYIN G	NIDIN G	ROWIN G	VININ G
SWUN G	CYBOR G	*HAZIN G	NOSIN G	RULIN G	VISIN G
THIN G	DARIN G	HIDIN G	NOTIN G	SANIN G	VOTIN G
THON G	DATIN G	HIRIN G	NUTME G	SARON G	WADIN G
TWAN G	DEFAN G	HOLIN G	PACIN G	SATAN G	WA G IN G
TYIN G	DIALO G	HOMIN G	PADNA G	SATIN G	WAKIN G
VYIN G	DICIN G	HONIN G	PA G IN G	SAVIN G	WALIN G
WHAN G	DININ G	HOPIN G	PALIN G	SAWLO G	WANIN G
WRAN G	DIVIN G	HOSIN G	PARAN G	SAYIN G	WARIN G
WRIN G	DO G LE G	HOTDO G	PARIN G	SEABA G	WAVIN G
WRON G	DOLIN G	HUMBU G	PAVIN G	SEADO G	*WAXIN G
WRUN G	DOMIN G	*HYPIN G	PENAN G	SEEIN G	WIFIN G
YOUN G	DOPIN G	*JAPIN G	PHOTO G	SERIN G	WI G WA G
BA G WI G	DORBU G	*JOKIN G	PIEIN G	SEWIN G	WILIN G
BAKIN G	DOTIN G	KALON G	PIKIN G	SIDIN G	WININ G
BALIN G	*DOZIN G	KITIN G	PILIN G	SIPIN G	WIPIN G
BANDO G	DUDIN G	LACIN G	PINAN G	SIRIN G	WIRIN G
BANIN G	DU G ON G	LADIN G	PININ G	SITIN G	WISIN G
BARIN G	DUOLO G	LAKIN G	PIPIN G	*SIZIN G	WITIN G
BARON G	DUPIN G	LAMIN G	POKIN G	SKIIN G	WIVIN G
BASIN G	DURIN G	LAPDO G	POLIN G	SLUIN G	YOKIN G
BATIN G	DYEIN G	LASIN G	POSIN G	SOLIN G	*ZAFTI G
BECLO G	FACIN G	LAVIN G	PROLE G	SORIN G	*ZI G ZA G
BEDBU G	FADIN G	LAWIN G	PROLO G	SPRAN G	*ZOFTI G
BEDRU G	FAKIN G	*LAZIN G	PULIN G	SPRIN G	*ZONIN G
BEFLA G	FAMIN G	LE G ON G	PUTLO G	SPRUN G	*BACKIN G
BELON G	FARIN G	LIKIN G	*QUAHO G	STALA G	*BACKLO G
BIDIN G	FATIN G	LIMIN G	*QUOHO G	STRAN G	BAD G IN G
BI G WI G	FETIN G	LININ G	RACIN G	STRIN G	BA G G IN G
BIKIN G	FILIN G	LIVIN G	RA G BA G	STRON G	BANKIN G
BITIN G	FIRIN G	LOSIN G	RA G IN G	STRUN G	BANNIN G
BLUIN G	*FIZ G I G	LOVIN G	RA G TA G	SUNDO G	BANTEN G
BODIN G	FLYIN G	LOWIN G	RAKIN G	TA G RA G	BAR G IN G
BONIN G	FO G DO G	LURIN G	RAPIN G	TAKIN G	BARRIN G
BORIN G	*FOXIN G	LUTIN G	RARIN G	TAMIN G	BASTIN G
BOWIN G	FUMIN G	LYSIN G	RASIN G	TAPIN G	BATHIN G
BOWLE G	FUSIN G	MACIN G	RATBA G	TARIN G	BATTIN G
*BOXIN G	*FUZIN G	MAKIN G	RATIN G	TAUTO G	BATWIN G
BUSIN G	GA G IN G	MASKE G	RAVIN G	THRON G	BEADIN G
CA G IN G	G AMIN G	MATIN G	*RAZIN G	TIDIN G	BEANBA G
CANIN G	G APIN G	MAYIN G	REDBU G	TILIN G	BEARHU G
CARIN G	G ASBA G	*MAZIN G	REDIN G	TIMIN G	BEARIN G
CASIN G	G ATIN G	METIN G	REDLE G	TININ G	BEATIN G

BEDDIN G	CAPPIN G	DI G G IN G	FRAMIN G	*HAPPIN G	LADLIN G	
BE G G IN G	CARDIN G	DIMMIN G	FRAYIN G	HARPIN G	LADYBU G	
BELTIN G	CARLIN G	DINNIN G	FU G G IN G	HATTIN G	LA G G IN G	
BELYIN G	CARPIN G	DIPPIN G	FUNNIN G	*HAWKIN G	LAMMIN G	
BETTIN G	CARVIN G	DIRTBA G	FURLON G	HEADIN G	LANCIN G	
BIBBIN G	CASTIN G	DISHRA G	FURRIN G	HEARIN G	LANDIN G	
BIDDIN G	CATALO G	DISSIN G	G ABBIN G	HEAVIN G	LAPPIN G	
BI G G IN G	CATLIN G	DOD G IN G	G ADDIN G	HED G IN G	LAPWIN G	
BILLBU G	CATTIN G	DO G G IN G	GA G G IN G	HEELIN G	LASHIN G	
BILLIN G	CAUSIN G	DONNIN G	G AMMIN G	HELPIN G	LASTIN G	
BILTON G	CEILIN G	DOTTIN G	G APPIN G	HEMA G O G	LATHIN G	
BINDIN G	*CHAFIN G	DRAPIN G	G ARRIN G	*HEMMIN G	LEADIN G	
BINNIN G	CHARIN G	DRAWIN G	G ASKIN G	HERRIN G	LEANIN G	
BIRDIN G	CHASIN G	DRONIN G	G ASSIN G	HILDIN G	LEASIN G	
BIRLIN G	*CHIMIN G	DUBBIN G	G EARIN G	*HIPPIN G	LEAVIN G	
BITTIN G	*CHOKIN G	DUCTIN G	G ELDIN G	HISSIN G	LE G G IN G	
BLAMIN G	CHORIN G	DUMPIN G	G ELLIN G	HOLDIN G	LEMMIN G	
BLUEIN G	CLONIN G	DUNNIN G	G EMMIN G	*HOMBUR G	LETTIN G	
BOATIN G	CLOSIN G	DUPPIN G	G ENSEN G	HOMOLO G	LICKIN G	
BOBBIN G	COAMIN G	DUPTRA G	G ETTIN G	*HOPPIN G	LINSAN G	
BO G G IN G	COATIN G	FABLIN G	G IBBIN G	HORSIN G	LIPPIN G	
BOMBIN G	CODDIN G	FAILIN G	GI G G IN G	HOTTIN G	LISTIN G	
BONDIN G	CODLIN G	FAIRIN G	G ILDIN G	HOUSIN G	LOADIN G	
BOOKIN G	*COFFIN G	FANNIN G	G INNIN G	HU G G IN G	LOANIN G	
BOOTLE G	CO G G IN G	FARCIN G	G INSEN G	*HUMMIN G	LOBBIN G	
BOWLIN G	CONNIN G	FARMIN G	G IPPIN G	HUNTIN G	LOD G IN G	
BRACIN G	COOKIN G	FASTIN G	*G LAZIN G	HURLIN G	LO G G IN G	
BRAKIN G	COPPIN G	FATLIN G	G LEYIN G	*HUSKIN G	LON G G IN G	
BRAVIN G	CORDIN G	FATTIN G	G NAWIN G	HUTTIN G	LOOSIN G	
*BRAZIN G	COWLIN G	FEEDBA G	G OBBIN G	*JABBIN G	LOPPIN G	
BREWIN G	CRANIN G	FEELIN G	G ODDIN G	*JACKLE G	LORDIN G	
BRIBIN G	CRANNO G	FELTIN G	G ODLIN G	*JA G G IN G	LOTTIN G	
BRININ G	CRAVIN G	FENCIN G	G OLDBU G	*JAMMIN G	LOVEBU G	
BROKIN G	CUNNIN G	FETTIN G	G OLFIN G	*JARRIN G	LU G G IN G	
BRUTIN G	CUPPIN G	FID G IN G	G OR G IN G	*JESTIN G	LUN G IN G	
BUDDIN G	CURBIN G	FILIBE G	G OSLIN G	*JETTIN G	MADDIN G	
BUD G IN G	CURLIN G	FILLIN G	G RACIN G	*JIBBIN G	*MAHJON G	
BU G G IN G	CURSIN G	FINDIN G	G RADIN G	*JI G G IN G	MAHUAN G	
BULLDO G	CURVIN G	FINNIN G	G RATIN G	*JOBBIN G	MAILBA G	
BUMMIN G	CUTTIN G	FIREBU G	G RAVIN G	*JOININ G	MAILIN G	
BUNTIN G	*CYCLIN G	FIREDO G	G RAYLA G	*JOTTIN G	MANNIN G	
BURNIN G	*CYMLIN G	*FISH G I G	*G RAZIN G	*JU G G IN G	MAPPIN G	
BURRIN G	DAMMIN G	FISHIN G	G RIMIN G	*KAMPON G	MARKIN G	
BUSHIN G	DAMPIN G	FITTIN G	G RIPIN G	KARTIN G	MARLIN G	
*BUSHPI G	DAPPIN G	FLAMIN G	G UMMIN G	KEEPIN G	MARRIN G	
BUSSIN G	DARNIN G	FLEABA G	G UNNIN G	KE G LIN G	MASKIN G	
*BUZZWI G	DAYLON G	FLUTIN G	G UTTIN G	KENNIN G	MATTIN G	
CABBIN G	DEALIN G	FLYTIN G	HA G G IN G	*KEPPIN G	MEANIN G	
CABLIN G	DECALO G	FO G G IN G	HALVIN G	KIDDIN G	MEETIN G	
*CACHIN G	*DECKIN G	FOOTIN G	*HAMBUR G	KILLIN G	MENDIN G	
CALLIN G	DEICIN G	FORCIN G	*HAMMIN G	KILTIN G	MER G IN G	
CAMPIN G	DEMA G O G	FORELE G	HANDBA G	*KIPPIN G	METRIN G	
CAMPON G	DENNIN G	FOR G IN G	HAN G DO G	KITLIN G	*MILCHI G	
CANNIN G	DIALIN G	FOULIN G	HAN G IN G	KITTIN G	MILLIN G	
CANTDO G	DIBBIN G	FOWLIN G	HAN G TA G	*KNOWIN G	MOLDIN G	

MONOLO G	PIPPIN G	RIPPIN G	SIPPIN G	TEASIN G	WHORIN G
MOORIN G	PITTIN G	ROARIN G	SITTIN G	TENSIN G	*WICKIN G
MOPPIN G	PLACIN G	ROBBIN G	SKATIN G	TESTIN G	WI G G IN G
MORNIN G	PLANIN G	ROLLIN G	SLATIN G	THEOLO G	WILDIN G
MOUSIN G	PLATIN G	ROOFIN G	SLAVIN G	TICKIN G	WILLIN G
MUDDIN G	PLUMIN G	ROTTIN G	SLIDIN G	TINNIN G	WINCIN G
MU G G IN G	POPPIN G	ROU G IN G	SLIMIN G	TINTIN G	WINDBA G
MUMMIN G	POSTBA G	ROUTIN G	SMITIN G	TIPPIN G	WINDIN G
MUNTIN G	POSTIN G	RUBBIN G	SMOKIN G	TITHIN G	WINNIN G
MUSTAN G	POTTIN G	RUCHIN G	SOARIN G	TO G G IN G	WITHIN G
NA G G IN G	PRATIN G	RU G G IN G	SODDIN G	TOMMIN G	WITLIN G
NAMETA G	PREPRE G	RUNNIN G	SOLVIN G	TOOLIN G	WITTIN G
NAPPIN G	PRESON G	RUSHIN G	SOPPIN G	TOPPIN G	WONNIN G
NECKIN G	PRICIN G	RUTTIN G	SPACIN G	TOTTIN G	WORDIN G
NERVIN G	PRIMIN G	SABBIN G	SPADIN G	TOURIN G	*WORKBA G
NETTIN G	PROBAN G	SACKIN G	SPAEIN G	TRACIN G	*WORKIN G
NIMMIN G	PROLON G	SACRIN G	SPARIN G	TREPAN G	WRITIN G
NIPPIN G	PROSIN G	SA G G IN G	SPICIN G	TRICIN G	*YAPPIN G
NODDIN G	PROVIN G	SAILIN G	SPIKIN G	TUBBIN G	*YAWPIN G
NO G G IN G	PRUNIN G	SALTIN G	SPILIN G	TU G G IN G	YEALIN G
NONDRU G	PUDDIN G	SALVIN G	SPIRIN G	TUNNIN G	YESSIN G
NOONIN G	PU G G IN G	SANDBA G	SPITIN G	TUPPIN G	*YIPPIN G
NOSEBA G	PULSIN G	SANDHO G	SPUMIN G	TURNIN G	*ZIPPIN G
NOTHIN G	PUNNIN G	SAPLIN G	STA G IN G	TUTTIN G	*BABBLIN G
NURSIN G	PUPPIN G	SAPPIN G	STANIN G	TWININ G	BALLYRA G
NUTTIN G	PUR G IN G	SAUCIN G	STARIN G	VANNIN G	BANTLIN G
*PACKIN G	PURRIN G	SCALIN G	STATIN G	VATTIN G	*BECOMIN G
PADDIN G	PURSIN G	SCARIN G	STOKIN G	VEILIN G	BEESWIN G
PAIRIN G	PUTTIN G	SCORIN G	STONIN G	VEININ G	BIRDSON G
PALLIN G	*QUAHAU G	SCUMBA G	STOPIN G	VER G IN G	BITEWIN G
PANNIN G	*QUOTIN G	SEATIN G	STORIN G	VERSIN G	*BLACKIN G
PAR G IN G	RA G G IN G	SEEMIN G	STYLIN G	VESTIN G	*BLACKLE G
PARKIN G	RAILIN G	SEISIN G	SUBBIN G	VETTIN G	BLASTIN G
PARLIN G	RAISIN G	*SEIZIN G	SUBRIN G	VIEWIN G	BLATTIN G
PARRIN G	RAMMIN G	SEMILO G	SUITIN G	VOICIN G	BLEEDIN G
PARSIN G	RANKIN G	SENSIN G	SUMMIN G	WADDIN G	BLESSIN G
PARTIN G	RAPPIN G	SER G IN G	SUNNIN G	WA G G IN G	BLOODIN G
PASSIN G	RATTIN G	SERVIN G	SUPPIN G	WAITIN G	BLOTTIN G
PASTIN G	READIN G	SETTIN G	SURFIN G	*WALKIN G	BOARDIN G
PATTIN G	REDDIN G	SHADIN G	SUR G IN G	WANNIN G	BRA G G IN G
PEACIN G	REDWIN G	*SHAKIN G	SWA G IN G	WARNIN G	BRAIDIN G
PEDA G O G	REEDIN G	SHAMIN G	SWIVIN G	WARRIN G	BRANNIN G
PEELIN G	REFFIN G	SHAPIN G	SYNA G O G	WARTHO G	*BREAKIN G
PE G G IN G	RETTIN G	SHARIN G	TABBIN G	WASHIN G	BREEDIN G
PENNIN G	RETYIN G	SHAVIN G	TABLIN G	WASHRA G	BRID G IN G
PEPPIN G	REVVIN G	SHEBAN G	TA G G IN G	WASTIN G	BRIEFIN G
PERIWI G	RIBBIN G	SHINDI G	TAILIN G	*WAXWIN G	*BRIMMIN G
PETTIN G	RIDDIN G	SHININ G	TALKIN G	*WEBBIN G	BRISLIN G
PFENNI G	RID G IN G	SHORTIN G	TANNIN G	WEDDIN G	*BRONZIN G
PHONIN G	RIFFIN G	SHOVIN G	TAPPIN G	WELTIN G	BUILDIN G
*PICKIN G	RIFLIN G	SHOWIN G	TARRIN G	WESTIN G	BULLFRO G
PIECIN G	RI G G IN G	SIAMAN G	TASTIN G	WETTIN G	BULLRIN G
PI G G IN G	RIMMIN G	SIBLIN G	TATTIN G	WHALIN G	BULLYRA G
PINKIN G	RINNIN G	SIFTIN G	TAUTAU G	WHININ G	*BUMBLIN G
PINNIN G	RINSIN G	SINNIN G	*TAXYIN G	WHITIN G	BUNDLIN G

BUN G LIN G	DRESSIN G	G RIPPIN G	NEEDLIN G	REEDLIN G	*SHOPPIN G
CA G ELIN G	DRILLIN G	G ROUPIN G	NESTLIN G	REFININ G	SHOTTIN G
*CAJOLIN G	DRIPPIN G	G RUELIN G	NIDERIN G	RESPRAN G	*SHOWRIN G
*CAPRIFI G	DROPPIN G	*G UNNYBA G	NONBEIN G	RESPRIN G	*SHRIVIN G
*CAULKIN G	DRUBBIN G	HANDLIN G	NONCLIN G	RESTRIN G	*SHUCKIN G
CENTRIN G	DRUMMIN G	*HATCHIN G	NONUSIN G	RESTRUN G	SHUTTIN G
*CHANCIN G	*DUCKLIN G	HEADLON G	NORTHIN G	RETIRIN G	SIDELIN G
*CHAPPIN G	DUELLIN G	*HED G EHO G	NURSLIN G	REVERIN G	SIDELON G
*CHARMIN G	DUMPLIN G	*HED G EPI G	PADDLIN G	*REVIVIN G	SI G HTIN G
CHARRIN G	DWELLIN G	HIRELIN G	PAINTIN G	RID G LIN G	SIN G SON G
CHATTIN G	*FARTHIN G	HOARDIN G	PANELIN G	RIESLIN G	SKILLIN G
*CHILDIN G	FAUBOUR G	*HUMBLIN G	PARADIN G	RIPPLIN G	*SKIMMIN G
*CHILIDO G	FETTLIN G	*HYDRA G O G	PARASAN G	*ROCKLIN G	SKINNIN G
CHINNIN G	*FI G HTIN G	*JELUTON G	PARAWIN G	ROSESLU G	SKIORIN G
*CHIPPIN G	FI G URIN G	*JU G G LIN G	PEDDLIN G	ROU G HLE G	*SKIPPIN G
CHITLIN G	*FINIKIN G	KAOLIAN G	PETTIFO G	*RUFFLIN G	SKIRTIN G
CHOOSIN G	*FIREFAN G	*KAYAKIN G	*PHILABE G	RUMBLIN G	SLABBIN G
*CHOPPIN G	FIREPLU G	KINDLIN G	*PHILIBE G	RUSTLIN G	SLAPPIN G
*CHROMIN G	FLA G G IN G	KNITTIN G	PHRASIN G	SADDLIN G	SLASHIN G
*CHU G ALU G	*FLAMMIN G	KNOTTIN G	PILOTIN G	SALADAN G	SLATTIN G
CHURNIN G	*FLAPPIN G	LACEWIN G	*PINCHBU G	SANDLIN G	SLEDDIN G
CIRCLIN G	*FLASHIN G	LALLY G A G	PINDLIN G	SAVA G IN G	SLEEPIN G
CLADDIN G	FLATLIN G	LAU G HIN G	PLA G UIN G	SCALAWA G	SLIMMIN G
*CLAMMIN G	FLATLON G	LAYERIN G	PLAITIN G	SCANNIN G	SLIPPIN G
CLEARIN G	FLATTIN G	LEAPFRO G	*PLANKIN G	SCARRIN G	SLITTIN G
*CLIPPIN G	FLEECIN G	LEARNIN G	PLANNIN G	SCATTIN G	SLO G G IN G
CLOTHIN G	*FLESHIN G	*LEFTWIN G	PLANTIN G	SCOLDIN G	SLOPPIN G
CLOTTIN G	FONDLIN G	LE G ATIN G	PLATTIN G	SCOURIN G	SLOTTIN G
*CLUBBIN G	FOOTLIN G	LIFELON G	PLEADIN G	SCOUTIN G	SLUBBIN G
COASTIN G	FOOTSLO G	LI G HTIN G	PLED G IN G	SCRAPIN G	SLU G G IN G
COHERIN G	*FOREWIN G	LIVELON G	PLOTTIN G	*SCUMMIN G	SLUMMIN G
COLORIN G	FRA G G IN G	LOATHIN G	*PLUMBIN G	*SCUPPAU G	SLURRIN G
*COUCHIN G	FRETTIN G	LOLLY G A G	POLLIWO G	SEA G OIN G	*SMOCKIN G
COUPLIN G	FRILLIN G	LORDLIN G	*POLLYWO G	SECURIN G	SMUTTIN G
COURSIN G	FRITTIN G	LUSTRIN G	POSTDRU G	SEEDLIN G	SNAPPIN G
COVERIN G	FRO G G IN G	*LYNCHIN G	*PREPPIN G	SELAPAN G	SNIPPIN G
*CRACKIN G	FROSTIN G	*MAHJON G G	PRESSIN G	SETTLIN G	SNU G G IN G
CRESTIN G	FUELLIN G	MANTLIN G	*PRICKIN G	*SHAFTIN G	SOANNIN G
*CRIBBIN G	G AN G LIN G	MANURIN G	*PRIMMIN G	*SHAMMIN G	SOOCHON G
*CROPPIN G	G ELATIN G	MARBLIN G	PRINTIN G	SHANTUN G	SOOTHIN G
CROSSIN G	G HOSTIN G	*MEALYBU G	PRO G G IN G	SHEALIN G	SOUARIN G
CRUISIN G	*G LADDIN G	MED G EHO G	*PROPPIN G	SHEARIN G	SOUCHON G
CURRYIN G	G LEANIN G	MIDDLIN G	PUDDLIN G	*SHEEPDO G	SOUNDIN G
*CYMBLIN G	G LOAMIN G	MINUTIN G	PURFLIN G	SHEETIN G	SOUTHIN G
DABBLIN G	G LOOMIN G	MISDOIN G	*QUANDAN G	*SHELVIN G	*SPANKIN G
DEMOTIN G	G LUTTIN G	MISLYIN G	*QUANDON G	*SHEMMIN G	SPARLIN G
DEVISIN G	G NARRIN G	MODELIN G	*QUANTON G	SHIELIN G	SPARRIN G
DIN G DON G	G OLLIWO G	*MONEYBA G	*QUILLIN G	SHILLIN G	SPATTIN G
DIVIDIN G	*G OLLYWO G	MOTORIN G	*QUILTIN G	*SHIMMIN G	*SPEAKIN G
DIVININ G	G RABBIN G	MOULDIN G	*QUISLIN G	SHINNIN G	SPEEDIN G
DOUBLIN G	G RAYLIN G	MOUNTIN G	*QUITTIN G	*SHIPPIN G	SPEERIN G
DRAFTIN G	G REENBU G	MOURNIN G	RALLYIN G	SHIRRIN G	SPELLIN G
DRA G G IN G	G REENIN G	MUTININ G	RATTLIN G	SHIRTIN G	SPHERIN G
DRAMMIN G	G REETIN G	*MYSTA G O G	RAVELIN G	SHITTIN G	*SPIFFIN G
DRED G IN G	G RINNIN G	NAETHIN G	RAVENIN G	SHOOTIN G	SPITTIN G

SPON G IN G	STIRRIN G	SWEETIN G	TRAPPIN G	TWISTIN G	*WHIRRIN G
SPOOLIN G	*STOCKIN G	SWELLIN G	TRAVELO G	TWITTIN G	*WHIZBAN G
SPOONIN G	STOPPIN G	*SWIMMIN G	TRIFLIN G	VAPORIN G	*WHIZZIN G
SPOTTIN G	STRAVAI G	SWIN G IN G	TRI G G IN G	VAULTIN G	WILDLIN G
SPRNNIN G	STRIDIN G	*TACKLIN G	TRIMMIN G	*WAFFLIN G	WIN G DIN G
SPURRIN G	STRIPIN G	TA G ALON G	TRIPLIN G	WAISTIN G	*WITCHIN G
STABLIN G	STUBBIN G	*TEACHIN G	TRIPPIN G	*WAKENIN G	*WRAPPIN G
STA G G IN G	STUDDIN G	TEETHIN G	TRITHIN G	*WATCHDO G	*WRECKIN G
STANDIN G	*STUFFIN G	*THIEVIN G	TROLLIN G	WATERDO G	*WRITHIN G
STARLIN G	STUMMIN G	*THINKIN G	TROTTIN G	WATERIN G	*YACHTIN G
STARRIN G	STUNNIN G	THINNIN G	TROUPIN G	WATERLO G	YEANLIN G
STEADIN G	*SUCKLIN G	TINKLIN G	*TRUCKIN G	*WAY G OIN G	YEARLIN G
STEALIN G	*SVEDBER G	TON G UIN G	TRUD G IN G	*WEAKLIN G	YEARLON G
STEEVIN G	*SWABBIN G	*TORQUIN G	TRUSSIN G	WEANLIN G	YEARNIN G
STEMMIN G	SWA G G IN G	TOWELIN G	TUMBLIN G	*WEEKLON G	*ZINCKIN G
STEPPIN G	SWANNIN G	*TRACKIN G	TURTLIN G	*WHEELIN G	
STERLIN G	SWATTIN G	TRAININ G	TWILLIN G	*WHETTIN G	
*STINKBU G	SWEEPIN G	TRAMMIN G	TWINNIN G	*WHIPPIN G	

H

HAAF	HARP	HERD	HOLK	HULA	HAMAL
HAAR	HART	HERE	HOLM	HULK	*HAMMY
HABU	HASH	HERL	HOLP	HULL	*HAMZA
HACK	HASP	HERM	HOLS	HUMP	HANCE
HADE	HAST	HERN	HOLT	HUNG	HANDY
*HADJ	HATE	HERO	HOLY	HUNH	*HANKY
HAEM	HATH	HERS	HOME	HUNK	HANSA
HAEN	HAUL	HEST	HOMO	HUNT	HANSE
HAET	HAUT	HETH	HOMY	HURL	HAOLE
HAFT	HAVE	HICK	HONE	HURT	*HAPAX
HAHA	HAWK	HIDE	HONG	HUSH	HAPLY
HAIK	*HAZE	HIGH	HONK	HUSK	*HAPPY
HAIL	*HAZY	HIKE	HOOD	HWAN	HARDS
HAIR	HEAL	HILA	HOOF	HYLA	HARDY
HAJI	HEAP	HILI	HOOK	HYMN	HAREM
*HAJJ	HEAR	HILL	HOOP	HYPO	HARPY
HAKE	HEAT	HILT	HOOT	HYTE	HARRY
HALE	HECK	HIND	HOPE	HABIT	HARSH
HALF	HEED	HIRE	HORA	HACEK	HASTE
HALL	HEEL	HISN	HOSE	HADAL	HATCH
HALM	HEFT	HISS	HOST	*HADJI	HATER
HALO	HEIL	HIST	HOUR	HADST	HAUGH
HALT	HEIR	HIVE	HOVE	*HAFIZ	HAULM
HAME	HELD	HOAR	HOWE	HAIKU	HAUNT
HAND	HELL	HOAX	HOWF	HAIRY	HAUTE
HANG	HELM	HOBO	HOWK	*HAJJI	HAVOC
HANK	HELO	HOCK	HOWL	HALER	HAWSE
HANT	HELP	HOER	HOYA	HALID	HAYER
HARD	HEME	HOGG	HUCK	HALLO	*HAZAN
HARE	HEMP	HOKE	HUFF	HALMA	*HAZEL
HARL	HENT	HOLD	HUGE	HALVA	*HAZER
HARM	HERB	HOLE	HUIC	HALVE	HEADY

HEART	HOICK	*HUMPY	HALLOT	HAULMY	HEPTAD
HEAVE	HOISE	HUMUS	*HALLUX	HAUNCH	HERALD
HEAVY	HOIST	HUNCH	HALOID	HAUSEN	HERBAL
HEDER	*HOKEY	*HUNKY	HALTER	HAVING	HERBED
HEDGE	*HOKKU	HURDS	*HALUTZ	HAVIOR	HERDER
HEDGY	HOKUM	HURLY	*HALVAH	*HAWKER	HERDIC
*HEEZE	HOLEY	HURRY	HALVES	*HAWKEY	HEREAT
HEFTY	HOLLA	HURST	HAMATE	*HAWKIE	HEREIN
HEIGH	HOLLO	*HUSKY	HAMAUL	HAWSER	HEREOF
HEIST	HOMED	HUSSY	HAMLET	HAYING	HEREON
HELIO	HOMER	HUTCH	HAMMAL	*HAYMOW	HERESY
*HELIX	HOMEY	*HUZZA	HAMMED	*HAZARD	HERIOT
HELLO	HONAN	HYDRA	HAMMER	*HAZIER	HERMIT
HELOT	HONDA	HYDRO	HAMPER	*HAZILY	HERNIA
HELVE	HONER	HYENA	*HAMZAH	*HAZING	HEROIC
HEMAL	HONEY	HYING	HANDLE	*HAZZAN	HEROIN
HEMIC	*HONKY	HYMEN	HANGAR	HEADER	HERPES
HEMIN	HONOR	HYOID	HANGER	HEALER	HETERO
*HEMPY	HOOCH	HYPER	HANGUL	HEALTH	*HEXADE
HENCE	HOODY	*HYPHA	HANGUP	HEARER	*HEXANE
HENNA	HOOEY	*HYRAX	HANIWA	HEARSE	*HEXONE
HENRY	HOOKA	HYSON	HANKER	HEARTH	*HEXOSE
HERBY	*HOOKY	HABILE	HANKIE	HEARTY	HEYDAY
HERES	HOOLY	HABOOB	HANSEL	*HEATHY	*HEYDEY
HERMA	HOPER	*HACKEE	HANSOM	HEAUME	HIATUS
HERON	*HOPPY	*HACKER	HANTLE	HEAVEN	*HICCUP
HERRY	HORAH	*HACKIE	HAPPED	HEAVER	*HICKEY
*HERTZ	HORAL	*HACKLE	HAPPEN	*HECKLE	HIDDEN
HEUGH	HORDE	*HACKLY	HAPTEN	HECTIC	HIDING
HEWER	HORNY	*HADJEE	HAPTIC	HECTOR	HIEMAL
*HEXAD	HORSE	HADRON	HARASS	HEDDLE	HIGGLE
*HEXER	HORST	HAEMAL	HARBOR	HEDGER	*HIGHLY
*HEXYL	HORSY	HAEMIC	HARDEN	HEEDER	*HIGHTH
HIDER	HOSEL	HAEMIN	HARDLY	*HEEHAW	*HIJACK
HIGHT	HOSTA	HAERES	HAREEM	HEELER	HILLER
HIKER	HOTCH	HAFTER	HARING	HEFTER	HILLOA
HILAR	HOTEL	HAGBUT	HARLOT	HEGARI	HINDER
HILLO	HOTLY	HAGDON	HARMER	HEGIRA	HINGER
HILLY	HOUND	HAGGED	HARMIN	HEIFER	HIPPED
HILUM	HOURI	HAGGIS	HARPER	HEIGHT	HIPPER
HILUS	HOUSE	HAGGLE	HARPIN	HEINIE	HIPPIE
HINGE	HOVEL	HAILER	HARROW	HEISHI	HIRING
HINNY	HOVER	HAIRDO	HARTAL	*HEJIRA	HIRPLE
HIPPO	*HOWFF	HAIRED	HASLET	HELIAC	HIRSEL
*HIPPY	HOYLE	*HAKEEM	HASSEL	HELIUM	HIRSLE
HIRER	*HUBBY	HALALA	HASSLE	HELLER	HISPID
HISSY	*HUFFY	HALEST	HASTEN	HELMET	HISSER
HITCH	HUGER	HALIDE	*HATBOX	HELPER	HITHER
HOAGY	*HULKY	HALING	HATFUL	HEMMED	HOAGIE
HOARD	HULLO	HALITE	HATING	HEMMER	HOARSE
HOARY	HUMAN	HALLAH	HATPIN	HEMOID	*HOAXER
*HOBBY	HUMIC	HALLEL	HATRED	HEMPEN	HOBBIT
HOCUS	HUMID	HALLOA	HATTED	HEMPIE	HOBBLE
HODAD	HUMOR	HALLOO	HATTER	HENBIT	HOBNOB
HOGAN	*HUMPH		HAULER	HEPCAT	

*HOCKER	HOOTCH	HUNTER	HAIRIER	HARBOUR	*HAYCOCK
*HOCKEY	HOOTER	HURDLE	HAIRNET	HARDHAT	*HAYFORK
HODDEN	HOOVED	HURLER	HAIRPIN	HARDIER	HAYLAGE
HODDIN	HOOVES	HURLEY	*HALACHA	HARDIES	*HAYLOFT
HOGGED	HOPING	HURRAH	*HALAKHA	HARDILY	*HAYRACK
HOGGER	HOPPLE	HURRAY	*HALAKIC	HARDPAN	*HAYRICK
HOGNUT	HORARY	HURTER	HALALAH	HARDSET	HAYRIDE
HOGTIE	HORNET	HURTLE	*HALAVAH	HARDTOP	HAYSEED
HOIDEN	HORRID	HUSKER	HALBERD	HARELIP	*HAYWARD
HOLARD	HORROR	HUSSAR	HALBERT	HARIANA	*HAYWIRE
HOLDEN	HORSEY	HUSTLE	*HALCYON	HARICOT	*HAZELLY
HOLDER	HORSTE	HUTTED	*HALFWAY	*HARIJAN	*HAZIEST
HOLDUP	HOSIER	*HUTZPA	HALIBUT	*HARMFUL	HEADIER
HOLIER	HOSING	*HUZZAH	HALIDOM	HARMINE	HEADILY
HOLIES	HOSTEL	HYAENA	HALITUS	*HARMONY	HEADING
HOLILY	HOSTLY	*HYBRID	HALLOTH	HARNESS	HEADMAN
HOLING	HOTBED	HYBRIS	*HALLWAY	HARPIES	HEADPIN
HOLISM	*HOTBOX	HYDRIA	HALOGEN	HARPING	HEADSET
HOLIST	HOTDOG	*HYDRIC	HALVERS	HARPIST	*HEADWAY
HOLLER	HOTROD	HYDRID	HALVING	HARPOON	*HEALTHY
HOLLOA	HOTTED	HYETAL	HALYARD	HARRIED	HEARING
HOLLOO	HOTTER	HYMNAL	HAMBONE	HARRIER	HEARKEN
HOLLOW	HOUDAH	*HYPHEN	*HAMBURG	HARRIES	HEARSAY
HOLPEN	HOURLY	*HYPING	*HAMMADA	HARSHEN	HEARTEN
HOMAGE	HOUSEL	*HYPNIC	HAMMIER	*HARSHLY	HEATHEN
HOMBRE	HOUSER	HYSSOP	*HAMMILY	HARSLET	HEATHER
HOMELY	*HOWDAH	HABITAN	*HAMMING	*HARUMPH	HEAVIER
HOMIER	HOWLER	HABITAT	*HAMMOCK	HARVEST	HEAVIES
HOMILY	HOWLTT	HABITUE	HAMSTER	*HASHISH	HEAVING
HOMING	HOYDEN	HABITUS	HAMULUS	*HASSOCK	HEBETIC
HOMINY	*HUBBLY	*HACHURE	HANAPER	HASTATE	*HECKLER
HOMMOS	*HUBBUB	*HACKBUT	HANDBAG	HASTING	HECTARE
HONCHO	*HUBCAP	*HACKLER	HANDCAR	HATABLE	HEDGING
HONDLE	HUBRIS	*HACKMAN	HANDFUL	HATBAND	HEDONIC
HONEST	*HUCKLE	*HACKNEY	HANDGUN	*HATCHEL	HEEDFUL
HONIED	HUDDLE	*HACKOUT	HANDIER	*HATCHER	HEELING
HONING	HUGEST	*HACKSAW	HANDILY	*HATCHET	HEGUMEN
HONKER	HUGGED	HADARIM	HANDLER	HATEFUL	*HEIGHTH
*HONKEY	HUGGER	HADDEST	*HANDOFF	HATLESS	*HEIMISH
HONKIE	HUIPIL	*HADDOCK	HANDOUT	HATLIKE	HEINOUS
HONOUR	HULLER	HAEMOID	HANDSAW	*HATRACK	HEIRDOM
HOODIE	HULLOA	*HAFNIUM	HANDSEL	HATSFUL	HEIRESS
HOODOO	HUMANE	HAGADIC	HANDSET	HATTING	HEISTER
HOOFER	HUMATE	HAGBORN	HANGDOG	*HAUBERK	HEKTARE
*HOOKAH	HUMBLE	*HAGBUSH	HANGING	*HAUGHTY	HELIAST
*HOOKEY	*HUMBLY	*HAGFISH	HANGMAN	HAULAGE	HELICAL
*HOOKUP	HUMBUG	HAGGADA	HANGOUT	HAULIER	HELICES
HOOLIE	HUMMED	HAGGARD	HANGTAG	HAUNTER	HELICON
HOOPED	HUMMER	HAGGING	HANUMAN	*HAUTBOY	HELIPAD
HOOPER	HUMMUS	*HAGGISH	HAPLESS	HAUTEUR	*HELLBOX
HOOPLA	HUMOUR	HAGGLER	HAPLITE	HAVARTI	HELLCAT
HOOPOE	HUMVEE	HAGRIDE	HAPLOID	HAVEREL	HELLERI
HOOPOO	HUNGER	*HAHNIUM	HAPLONT	HAVIOUR	*HELLERY
HOORAH	HUNGRY	HAIRCAP	*HAPPING	*HAWKING	HELLISH
HOORAY	HUNKER	HAIRCUT	HAPTENE	*HAWKISH	HELLUVA

HELOTRY	*HIMSELF	HOLSTER	HOUNDER	*HYMNODY	*HANDBOOK
*HELPFUL	HINDGUT	*HOLYDAY	HOUSING	*HYPERON	HANDCART
HELPING	HIPBONE	HOMAGER	HOVERER	*HYPNOID	*HANDCUFF
HEMAGOG	HIPLESS	HOMIEST	*HOWBEIT	*HYPOGEA	*HANDFAST
HEMATAL	*HIPLIKE	*HOMBURG	*HOWEVER	*HYPONEA	*HANDGRIP
HEMATIC	HIPLINE	*HOMEBOY	HUDDLER	*HYPOXIA	*HANDHELD
HEMATIN	HIPNESS	HOMINES	*HUFFISH	HABANERA	*HANDHOLD
HEMIOLA	HIPPEST	HOMINID	HUGEOUS	*HABBINIC	*HANDICAP
HEMLINE	HIPPIER	*HOMMOCK	HUGGING	*HABDALAH	HANDIEST
*HEMLOCK	*HIPPING	HOMOLOG	*HUMANLY	HABITANT	HANDLING
*HEMMING	*HIPPISH	*HOMONYM	HUMBLER	HABITUAL	HANDLIST
HEMPIER	*HIPSHOT	*HOMOSEX	*HUMDRUM	HABITUDE	HANDLOOM
HENBANE	HIPSTER	HONESTY	HUMERAL	HACIENDA	*HANDMADE
HENCOOP	HIRABLE	HONOREE	HUMERUS	*HACKWORK	*HANDMAID
HENLIKE	HIRCINE	HONORER	*HUMIDLY	HAEMATAL	*HANDOVER
HENNERY	HIRSUTE	HOODIER	HUMIDOR	*HAEMATIC	*HANDPICK
*HENPECK	HIRUDIN	HOODLUM	*HUMMING	HAEMATIN	HANDRAIL
HEPARIN	HISSELF	HOOKIER	*HUMMOCK	*HAFTARAH	*HANDSEWN
HEPATIC	HISSING	HOOKIES	HUMORAL	*HAFTORAH	*HANDSFUL
HEPTANE	HISTOID	HOOKLET	HUNDRED	HAGADIST	HANDSOME
HEPTOSE	HISTONE	HOOSGOW	HUNNISH	*HAGBERRY	*HANDWORK
HERBAGE	HISTORY	*HOPEFUL	HUNTING	*HAGGADAH	*HANDWRIT
HERBIER	*HITCHER	*HOPHEAD	HURDIES	*HAGGADIC	*HANDYMAN
HERDMAN	HITLESS	HOPLITE	HURDLER	HAIRBALL	*HANGBIRD
HEREDES	HOARDER	*HOPPING	HURLING	HAIRBAND	*HANGFIRE
HERETIC	HOARIER	*HOPSACK	HURRIER	HAIRIEST	HANGNAIL
HERITOR	HOARILY	HOPTOAD	HURTFUL	HAIRLESS	HANGNEST
HEROINE	HOARSEN	HORDEIN	HUSBAND	*HAIRLIKE	*HANGOVER
HEROISM	*HOATZIN	*HORIZON	*HUSHABY	HAIRLINE	*HANKERER
*HEROIZE	HOBBIES	HORNIER	*HUSHFUL	*HAIRLOCK	*HAPLOIDY
HERONRY	HOBBLER	HORNILY	HUSKIER	*HAIRWORK	*HAPTICAL
HERRING	*HOBLIKE	HORNIST	HUSKIES	*HAIRWORM	HARANGUE
HERSELF	HOBNAIL	HORNITO	*HUSKILY	*HALAKIST	HARASSER
HESSIAN	HOBOISM	HORRENT	*HUSKING	*HALAKOTH	HARBORER
HESSITE	*HODADDY	*HORRIFY	HUSTLER	HALATION	*HARDBACK
HETAERA	*HOECAKE	HORSIER	*HUSWIFE	*HALAZONE	HARDBALL
HETAIRA	HOEDOWN	HORSILY	HUTLIKE	HALENESS	HARDBOOT
*HEXAGON	HOELIKE	HORSING	HUTMENT	*HALFBACK	HARDCASE
*HEXAPLA	*HOGBACK	HOSANNA	HUTTING	*HALFBEAK	HARDCORE
*HEXAPOD	*HOGFISH	HOSIERY	*HUTZPAH	*HALFLIFE	HARDEDGE
*HEXEREI	*HOGLIKE	HOSPICE	HYALITE	HALFNESS	HARDENER
*HEXOSAN	HOGMANE	HOSTAGE	HYALOID	*HALFTIME	*HARDHACK
*HIBACHI	HOGNOSE	HOSTESS	*HYDATID	HALFTONE	*HARDHEAD
*HICKORY	*HOGWASH	HOSTILE	HYDRANT	HALIDOME	HARDIEST
HIDABLE	*HOGWEED	HOSTLER	HYDRASE	HALLIARD	HARDLINE
HIDALGO	HOISTER	*HOTCAKE	HYDRATE	*HALLMARK	HARDNESS
HIDEOUS	HOLDALL	HOTFOOT	*HYDRIDE	HALLOWER	HARDNOSE
HIDEOUT	HOLDING	HOTHEAD	*HYDROID	*HALOLIKE	*HARDSHIP
*HIGHBOY	HOLDOUT	HOTLINE	*HYDROPS	HAMARTIA	*HARDTACK
*HIGHWAY	HOLIBUT	HOTNESS	HYDROUS	*HAMMERER	*HARDWARE
*HIJINKS	HOLIDAY	HOTSHOT	*HYDROXY	*HAMMIEST	*HARDWIRE
HILDING	HOLIEST	HOTSPUR	HYGEIST	*HAMPERER	*HARDWOOD
HILLIER	HOLLAND	HOTTEST	HYGIENE	HANDBALL	HAREBELL
*HILLOCK	HOLLIES	HOTTING	*HYMNARY	HANDBELL	*HARELIKE
HILLTOP	HOLMIUM	HOTTISH	*HYMNIST	HANDBILL	*HARKENER

HARLOTRY	HEADRACE	HEMATEIN	HIDROSTS	HOLSTEIN	HOPELESS
HARMLESS	HEADREST	HEMATINE	HIDROTIC	*HOLYTIDE	*HORNBEAM
*HARMONIC	HEADROOM	HEMATITE	*HIERARCH	*HOMEBODY	HORNBILL
HARRIDAN	HEADSAIL	HEMATOID	HIERATIC	*HOMEBRED	*HORNBOOK
HARROWER	*HEADSHIP	*HEMATOMA	*HIGHBALL	HOMELAND	HORNFELS
*HARRUMPH	HEADSMAN	*HEMIPTER	*HIGHBORN	HOMELESS	HORNIEST
*HARUSPEX	*HEADSTAY	*HEMOCOEL	*HIGHBRED	*HOMELIKE	HORNLESS
*HASHEESH	*HEADWIND	*HEMOCYTE	*HIGHBROW	*HOMEMADE	*HORNLIKE
*HASHHEAD	*HEADWORD	*HEMOLYZE	*HIGHBUSH	*HOMEOBOX	*HORNPIPE
HASTEFUL	*HEADWORK	HEMOSTAT	*HIGHJACK	*HOMEOTIC	HORNPOUT
HASTENER	*HEATEDLY	*HEMPIEST	*HIGHLAND	*HOMEPORT	HORNTAIL
*HATCHECK	HEATLESS	*HEMPWEED	*HIGHLIFE	*HOMEROOM	*HORNWORM
*HATCHERY	*HEAVENLY	*HENCHMAN	*HIGHNESS	*HOMESICK	HORNWORT
*HATCHING	*HEAVYSET	*HENEQUEN	*HIGHROAD	HOMESITE	HOROLOGE
*HATCHWAY	*HEBDOMAD	*HENEQUIN	*HIGHSPOT	*HOMESPUN	*HOROLOGY
HATEABLE	HEBETATE	HENHOUSE	*HIGHTAIL	*HOMESTAY	HORRIBLE
*HATMAKER	HEBETUDE	*HENIQUEN	*HIJACKER	*HOMETOWN	*HORRIBLY
HATTERIA	*HEBRAIZE	*HEPATICA	HILARITY	*HOMEWARD	*HORRIFIC
*HAULYARD	*HECATOMB	*HEPATIZE	HILLIEST	*HOMEWORK	HORSECAR
HAUSFRAU	*HECTICAL	*HEPATOMA	HILLSIDE	*HOMICIDE	*HORSEFLY
HAUTBOIS	*HEDGEHOG	HEPTAGON	HILTLESS	HOMILIST	HORSEMAN
*HAVDALAH	*HEDGEHOP	*HEPTARCH	HIMATION	HOMINIAN	HORSIEST
*HAVELOCK	*HEDGEPIG	HERALDIC	HINDERER	HOMINIES	HOSANNAH
*HAVOCKER	*HEDGEROW	*HERALDRY	HINDMOST	*HOMININE	*HOSEPIPE
*HAWFINCH	HEDONICS	HERBARIA	*HIPPARCH	*HOMINIZE	HOSPITAL
*HAWKBILL	HEDONISM	HERBIEST	*HIPPIEST	HOMINOID	HOSPITIA
*HAWKEYED	HEDONIST	HERBLESS	HIRAGANA	*HOMOGONY	HOSPODAR
*HAWKLIKE	HEEDLESS	*HERBLIKE	HIRELING	*HOMOLOGY	HOTBLOOD
*HAWKMOTH	HEELBALL	HERCULES	HISTAMIN	*HOMONYMY	*HOTCHPOT
*HAWKNOSE	HEELLESS	*HERDLIKE	HISTIDIN	HONEWORT	HOTELDOM
*HAWKSHAW	*HEGEMONY	HERDSMAN	HISTOGEN	*HONEYBEE	HOTELIER
*HAWKWEED	HEGUMENE	*HEREDITY	HISTORIC	*HONEYBUN	HOTELMAN
*HAWTHORN	*HEGUMENY	HEREINTO	HITHERTO	*HONEYDEW	HOTHOUSE
*HAYFIELD	*HEIGHTEN	*HERETRIX	HIVELESS	*HONEYFUL	HOTPRESS
*HAYMAKER	HEIRLESS	HEREUNTO	*HIZZONER	HONORAND	*HOUSEBOY
*HAYSTACK	HEIRLOOM	HEREUPON	*HOACTZIN	HONORARY	*HOUSEFLY
*HAZELHEN	*HEIRSHIP	*HEREWITH	HOARDING	HONOURER	HOUSEFUL
*HAZELNUT	HELIACAL	HERITAGE	HOARIEST	HOODIEST	HOUSEMAN
*HAZINESS	*HELICITY	*HERITRIX	*HOBBYIST	HOODLESS	HOUSETOP
*HEADACHE	HELICOID	*HERMETIC	*HOCKSHOP	*HOODLIKE	*HOWITZER
*HEADACHY	*HELICOPT	*HERMITRY	*HOGMANAY	*HOODWINK	*HUARACHE
*HEADBAND	HELILIFT	HERNIATE	*HOGMENAY	*HOOFBEAT	*HUARACHO
*HEADFISH	HELIPORT	HEROICAL	*HOGSHEAD	*HOOFLESS	*HUCKSTER
HEADGATE	HELISTOP	HERSTORY	*HOKINESS	*HOOFLIKE	HUGENESS
HEADGEAR	HELLBENT	HESITANT	*HOKYPOKY	*HOOKIEST	*HUGGABLE
*HEADHUNT	HELLFIRE	HESITATE	*HOLDBACK	*HOOKLESS	*HUISACHE
HEADIEST	*HELLKITE	*HEXAGRAM	*HOLDFAST	*HOOKLIKE	HUMANISE
*HEADLAMP	*HELMINTH	*HEXAMINE	*HOLDOVER	*HOOKNOSE	*HUMANISM
HEADLAND	HELMLESS	*HEXAPODY	HOLELESS	*HOOKWORM	*HUMANIZE
HEADLESS	*HELMSMAN	*HEXARCHY	HOLINESS	HOOLIGAN	HUMANOID
HEADLINE	HELOTAGE	HIBERNAL	*HOLOGAMY	HOOPLESS	*HUMBLEST
*HEADLOCK	HELOTISM	*HIBISCUS	HOLOGRAM	*HOOPLIKE	*HUMBLING
HEADLONG	HELPLESS	*HICCOUGH	*HOLOGYNY	HOOPSTER	*HUMIDIFY
HEADMOST	*HELPMATE	*HIDEAWAY	*HOLOTYPE	*HOOSEGOW	*HUMIDITY
HEADNOTE	*HELPMEET	HIDELESS	*HOLOZOIC	*HOOSEGOW	*HUMIFIED

*HUMILITY	B H UT	S H IV	*C H AFF	*C H IVY	S H ADE
*HUMMABLE	C H AD	S H MO	C H AIN	*C H OCK	S H ADY
*HUMORFUL	C H AM	S H OD	C H AIR	C H OIR	S H AFT
HUMORIST	C H AO	S H OE	C H ALK	C H OKE	S H AKE
HUMOROUS	C H AP	S H OG	C H AMP	*C H OKY	S H AKO
*HUMPBACK	C H AR	S H OO	C H ANG	C H OLO	*S H AKY
*HUMPLESS	C H AT	S H OP	C H ANT	C H OMP	S H ALE
*HUNGOVER	C H AW	S H OT	C H AOS	C H OOK	S H ALL
HURTLESS	C H AY	S H OW	C H APE	C H ORD	S H ALT
*HUSKIEST	C H EF	S H RI	C H APT	C H ORE	S H ALY
*HUSKLIKE	C H EW	S H UL	C H ARD	C H OSE	S H AME
HUSTINGS	*C H EZ	S H UN	C H ARE	C H OTT	S H ANK
*HYACINTH	C H IA	S H UT	C H ARK	*C H UCK	S H APE
*HYALOGEN	C H IC	T H AE	C H ARM	C H UFA	S H ARD
*HYDRACID	C H IN	T H AN	C H ARR	*C H UFF	S H ARE
*HYDRAGOG	C H IP	T H AT	C H ART	C H URL	S H ARN
*HYDRANTH	C H IT	T H AW	C H ARY	C H URN	S H ARP
*HYDRATOR	C H ON	T H EE	C H ASE	C H URR	S H AUL
*HYDROGEL	C H OP	T H EM	C H ASM	C H UTE	S H AWL
*HYDROGEN	C H OW	T H EN	C H EAP	C H YLE	S H AWM
*HYDROMEL	C H UB	T H EW	C H EAT	*C H YME	S H AWN
*HYDRONIC	C H UG	T H EY	C H EEK	D H OLE	S H AWN
*HYDROPIC	C H UM	T H IN	C H EEP	D H OTI	S H EAF
*HYDROPSY	D H AK	T H IO	C H EER	D H UTI	S H EAL
*HYDROSKI	D H AL	T H IR	C H ELA	G H AUT	S H EAR
*HYDROSOL	D H OW	T H IS	C H ERT	*G H AZI	S H EEN
*HYDROXYL	G H AT	T H OU	*C H ESS	G H OST	S H EEP
*HYGIEIST	G H EE	T H RO	C H EST	G H OUL	S H EER
*HYLOZOIC	K H AF	T H RU	C H ETH	G H YLL	S H EET
*HYMENEAL	K H AN	T H UD	*C H EVY	K H ADI	S H EIK
*HYMENIUM	K H AT	T H UG	*C H EWY	*K H AKI	S H ELF
*HYMNBOOK	K H ET	T H US	C H IAO	*K H APH	S H ELL
*HYMNLESS	P H AT	W H AM	*C H ICK	K H EDA	S H END
*HYMNLIKE	P H EW	W H AP	C H ICO	*K H ETH	S H EOL
*HYOSCINE	*P H IZ	W H AT	C H IDE	K H OUM	S H ERD
*HYPERGOL	P H ON	W H EE	C H IEF	P H AGE	S H IED
*HYPEROPE	P H OT	W H EN	C H IEL	P H ASE	S H IES
*HYPHEMIA	P H UT	W H ET	C H ILD	P H IAL	S H IFT
*HYPNOSIS	R H EA	W H EW	C H ILE	*P H LOX	S H ILL
*HYPNOTIC	R H US	W H EY	C H ILI	P H ONE	S H ILY
*HYPOACID	S H AD	W H ID	C H ILL	P H ONO	S H INE
*HYPODERM	S H AG	W H IG	C H IMB	P H ONY	S H INY
*HYPOGEAL	S H AH	W H IM	C H IME	P H OTO	S H IRE
*HYPOGEAN	S H AM	W H IN	C H IMP	*P H PHT	S H IRK
*HYPOGENE	S H AT	W H IP	C H INA	P H YLA	S H IRR
*HYPOGEUM	S H AW	W H IR	C H INE	P H YLE	S H IRT
*HYPOGYNY	S H AY	W H IT	C H INK	*Q H AST	S H IST
*HYPONOIA	S H EA	*W H IZ	C H INO	R H EUM	S H IVA
*HYPOPNEA	S H ED	W H OA	C H IRK	R H INO	S H IVE
*HYPOPYON	S H EW	W H OM	C H IRM	R H OMB	S H LEP
*HYPOTHEC	S H IM	W H OP	C H IRO	R H UMB	S H OAL
*HYRACOID	S H IN	B H ANG	C H IRP	R H YME	S H OAT
HYSTERIA	S H IP	B H OOT	C H IRR	R H YTA	S H OCK
*HYSTERIC	S H IT	C H AFE	C H IVE	S H ACK	S H OER

*S H OJI	T H ORN	W H ORT	C H ABLIS	*C H ILIDOG	CO H EIR
S H ONE	T H ORO	W H OSE	*C H ALLA H	C H ITOSAN	CO H ERE
S H OOK	T H ORP	W H OSO	*C H ALOT H	*C HLOASMA	CO H ORT
S H OOL	T H OSE	*W H UMP	C H APATI	*C H OCKFUL	CO H OS H
S H OON	T H RAW	C H ADAR	*C H ARLEY	*C H UGALUG	CO H OST
S H OOT	T H REE	C H ADOR	C H ARLIE	*C H UTZPA H	CO H UNE
S H ORE	T H REW	C H ALAH	C H ATTED	G H OSTING	DA H LIA
S H ORL	T H RIP	C H ALEH	*C H AZZAN	*P H ILTRUM	DA H OON
S H ORN	T H ROB	C H ALLA	*C H EERLY	P H ORONID	DE H ORN
S H ORT	T H ROE	C H EAPO	*C H EETA H	*P HTH ALIC	DE H ORT
S H OTE	T H ROW	C H ETAH	*C H ERIS H	*P HTH ALIN	FU H RER
S H OTT	T H RUM	C H EVRE	C H ETRUM	*P HT H ISIC	*JO H NNY
S H OUT	*T H UJA	C H ICANO	C H ICANO	*P HT H ISIS	KA H UNA
S H OVE	T H UNK	*C H INC H	*C H ICKEE	*S HADBUS H	*MA H ZOR
S H OWN	T H URL	*C H IPPY	C H OLENT	*S HADRACH	MI H RAB
S H OWY	T H UYA	C H IRAL	*C H OMPER	S H EARING	RE H ANG
S H OYU	T H YME	*C H LINK	*C H UDDA H	*S H EDLIKE	RE H AS H
S H RED	T H YMI	C H OANA	D H URRIE	S H EENFUL	RE H EAR
S H REW	*T H YMY	*C H URC H	G H ARIAL	*S H EEPCOT	RE H EAT
S H RUB	*W H ACK	*K H EDAH	G H OULIE	*S H EEPIS H	RE H EEL
S H RUG	W H ALE	*P H OBIC	*K H IRKA H	S H IITAKE	RE H IRE
S H UCK	W H AMO	P H YLLO	*P H ARAO H	*S H MALTZY	RE H UNG
S H UNT	W H ANG	*P H YSED	P H ENATE	S H OELESS	SC H EMA
S H US H	W H ARF	S H ALEY	*P H ENOXY	S H OOTOUT	SC H EME
S H UTE	W H AUP	S H AMOS	P H OEBUS	S H ORTIS H	SC H ISM
S H YER	W H EAL	S H ANNY	P H ONIED	S H OWERER	SC H IST
S H YLY	W H EAT	S H AUG H	S H ANTI H	*S H OWRING	*SC H IZO
T H ACK	W H EEL	S H EAT H	S H IATSU	*S H REWIS H	*SC H IZY
T H ANE	W H EEN	*S H EIK H	*S H IATZU	S H REWIS H	SC H LEP
T H ANK	W H EEP	S H EILA	*S H ICKER	*T H ICKIS H	SC H MOE
T H ARM	*W H ELK	S H ELTA	S H IKKER	*T H IEVIS H	*SC H NOZ
T H EBE	W H ELM	S H ERPA	S H ITAKE	T H INNIS H	SC H OOL
T H EFT	W H ELP	S H EUC H	S H ITTA H	*T HOROUG H	SC H ORL
T H EGN	W H ERE	S H EUG H	*S H LUMPY	*T H UGGIS H	*SC H RIK
T H EIN	*W H IC H	S H IBA H	*S H MALTZ	*T H YMOSIN	SC H ROD
T H EIR	*W H IFF	S H LEPP	*S H MOOZE	W H ATNESS	*SC H TIK
T H EME	W H ILE	S H LUMP	*S H OWBIZ	*W H EYLIKE	SC H UIT
T H ERE	W H INE	S H MEAR	T H ISTLY	*W H IPLAS H	SC H USS
T H ERM	W H INY	S H NOOK	T H ROUG H	RE H AB	SP H ENE
T H ESE	W H IPT	T HATC H	W HATSIS	BE H ALF	SP H ERE
T H ETA	W H IRL	*W H ITIS H	*W H ITIS H	BE H AVE	SP H ERY
T H EWY	W H IRR	S H NOOK	*W H ORIS H	*SP H INX	*SP H INX
T H ICK	W H IS H	T HATC H	*C H AINSAW	BE H EAD	TA H INI
T H IEF	*W H ISK	T H LIMB	*C H ALAZIA	BE H ELD	TA H SIL
T H IGH	W H IST	T H LIMP	*C H ALLOT H	BE H EST	VA H INE
T H ILL	W H ITE	T H OUG H	*C H APATTI	BE H IND	WA H INE
T H INE	W H ITY	T H RAS H	*C H APPATI	BE H OLD	BA H ADUR
T H ING	*W H IZZ	T H RES H	*C HATC H KA	BE H OOF	*BE H AVER
T H INK	W H OLE	T H RUS H	BE H OOF	BE H OVE	*BE H OOVE
T H IOL	*W H OMP	*W HACKO	*C H EAPIS H	BE H OWL	BO H EMIA
T H IRD	W H OOF	*W H AMMO	C H EERLED	*BO H UNK	CO H ABIT
T H IRL	W H OOP	W H INGE	*C H ELIPED	CA H IER	CO H ERER
T H OLE	W H ORE	*W H OOS H	*C H ICKORY	CA H OOT	DE H ISCE
T H ONG	W H ORL	*W H YDA H	*C H ILDIS H	CO H EAD	GA H NITE

*H A H NIUM	*BUS H WA H	*CAS H MERE	*H IG H BRED	NEP H RITE	RUT H ENIC	
*LE H AYIM	*FOX H UNT	CAT H EDRA	*H IG H BROW	NIG H NESS	RUT H LESS	
MA H ARAN	GAT H ERE	CAT H ETER	*H IG H BUS H	*NIG H TCAP	SAW H ORSE	
*MA H JONG	*H AS H IS H	*CAT H EXIS	*H IG H JACK	NIG H TIES	SIG H LESS	
*PA H LAVI	*JAR H EAD	*CAT H OLIC	*H IG H LAND	*NIG H TJAR	*SIG H LIKE	
RE H INGE	*LIT H IFY	CAT H OUSE	*H IG H LIFE	*NON HARDY	SIG H TING	
RE H OUSE	LIT H OID	*CEP H ALAD	*H IG H NESS	NON H UMAN	SIG H TSEE	
SA H IWAL	LUT H IER	*CEP H ALIC	*H IG H ROAD	*NUT HATCH	SIP H ONAL	
SA H UARO	MES H IER	*CEP H ALIN	*H IG H SPOT	NUT H OUSE	*SIP H ONIC	
*SC H APPE	MES H UGA	*C H T H ONIC	*H IG H TAIL	*PAC HADOM	SIT H ENCE	
SC H EMER	MOT H ALL	COT H URNI	H IT H ERTO	*PAC H ALIC	*SUB H UMAN	
*SC H ERZO	MUD H OLE	CUS H IEST	H OT H OUSE	*PAC H INKO	*SUB H UMID	
*SC H IZZY	NON H EME	*CUS H IONY	*H YP H EMIA	*PAC H OULI	SUC H LIKE	
*SC H LEPP	NON H OME	DAS H IEST	*KAS H RUT H	*PAN H UMAN	SUC H NESS	
*SC H LOCK	PIS H OGE	DET H RONE	*KEP H ALIN	PAR H ELIA	*SYP H ILIS	
*SC H LUMP	RES H AVE	*DIC H OTIC	*KYP H OSIS	*PAR H ELIC	TAC H INID	
*SC H MALZ	RES H INE	*DIC H ROIC	LAT H ERER	PAS H ADOM	*TAC H ISME	
SC H MEAR	RES H ONE	*DIP H ASIC	LAT H IEST	*PAS H ALIC	TAC H ISTE	
SC H MEER	SON H OOD	*DIP H ENYL	*LAT H WORK	*PAS H ALIK	TAP H OUSE	
SC H MOOS	*TAC H YON	DIS H ERIT	*LEC H AYIM	*PAT H ETIC	TEA H OUSE	
*SC H MUCK	*TUG H RIK	DIS H IEST	LET H ALLY	PAT H LESS	TEP H RITE	
SC H NAPS	*ZIT H ERN	*DIS H EVEL	*LET H ARGY	PAT H OGEN	*TIG H TWAD	
*SC H NOOK	*BAC H ELOR	DIS H IEST	LIC H ENIN	*P H T H ALIC	TIT H ABLE	
*SC H NOZZ	BAG H OUSE	*DIS H LIKE	*LIG H TFUL	*P H T H ALIN	TIT H ONIA	
*SC H TICK	*BAT H ETIC	DIS H ONOR	LIG H TING	*P H T H ISIC	TRI H EDRA	
SP H ENIC	BAT H LESS	*DIS H WARE	*LIG H TIS H	*P H T H ISIS	WAR H ORSE	
SP H ERAL	*BAT H ROBE	DIT H EISM	LIT H ARGE	PIS H OGUE	*WAS H ABLE	
SP H ERIC	*BAT H ROOM	DIT H EIST	LIT H EMIA	PIT H LESS	*WASH BOWL	
ST H ENIA	BAU H INIA	DIT H ERER	LIT H OSOL	POS H NESS	WAS H IEST	
*VE H ICLE	*BEC H AMEL	DOG H OUSE	LOT H ARIO	POT H OUSE	*WASH ROOM	
BOT H Y	*BEC H ANCE	FAS H IOUS	LOT H SOME	PRE H UNAN	*WIS H BONE	
DAS H I	*BES H ADOW	*FAT H ERLY	LUS H NESS	*PRO H IBIT	WIS H LESS	
LAT H I	*BES H IVER	*FIG H TING	*MAC H ISMO	*PUS H BALL	*WITH DRAW	
MIC H E	BES H ROUD	*FIS H BOLT	*MEC H ANIC	*PUS H CART	WIT H ERER	
*MYT H Y	BET H ESDA	*FIS H BONE	*MEP H ITIS	*PUS H DOWN	*WITH H OLD	
NAC H O	*BIC H ROME	*FIS H BOWL	MES H IEST	PUS H IEST	WIT H IEST	
SUS H I	*BIP H ASIC	*FIS H HOOK	*MES H UGA H	*PUS H OVER	*YAC H TING	
WAS H Y	*BIP H ENYL	FIS H IEST	*MES H UGGA	RAC H ILLA	*YAC H TMAN	
*YEC H Y	*BOE H MITE	*FIS H LESS	*MES H WORK	RAC H ITIS	*YES H IVA H	
BUS H WA	*BON H OMIE	*FIS H LIKE	MET H INKS	RAS H NESS	*YOG H OURT	
*H IG H T H	*BOS H VARK	FIS H LINE	*MET H ODIC	REC H ANGE		
*JUB H A H	*BOT H RIUM	*FIS H MEAL	*MET H OXYL	REC H ARGE	BAC H	
LEC H WE	BUG H OUSE	*FIS H POLE	*MET H YLAL	REC H OOSE	BAS H	
LOC H AN	*BUS H FIRE	*FIS H POND	*MIS H MAS H	RED H ORSE	BAT H	
NAC H AS	BUS H GOAT	FIS H TAIL	*MIS H MOS H	REP H RASE	BET H	
NAC H ES	BUS H IEST	*FIS H WIFE	RES H APER	BLA H		
NOT H ER	BUS H LAND	*FIS H WORM	*MOT H ERLY	RET H READ	BOT H	
*QUO H OG	BUS H LESS	*FOX H OUND	*MOT H LIKE	RIC H NESS	BUS H	
REC H EW	*BUS H LIKE	*FUC H SINE	*MUCHACHO	*RIC H WEED	CAP H	
RUC H ED	*CAC H ALOT	GAS H OUSE	*MUC H NESS	*RIG H TFUL	CAS H	
TEC H IE	*CAC H EPOT	*H AS H EES H	*MUS H ROOM	RIG H TIES	DAS H	
WUT H ER	*CAC H EXIA	*H AS H HEAD	*MYT H ICAL	RIG H TIST	DIS H	
BAT H MAT	*CAC H UCHA	H EN H OUSE	*NAP H T H OL	RUS H IEST	DOT H	
BOD H RAN	*CAS H BOOK	*H IG H BALL	NAT H LESS	*RUS H LIKE	FASH	
*BUS H PIG	CAS H LESS	*H IG H BORN	*NEP H RISM		FIS H	

GAS H	SUC H	CRUS H	KETC H	*PUJA H	TILT H
GOS H	SUG H	CUIS H	KNIS H	PUNC H	TOOT H
GUS H	SYP H	CULC H	LAIC H	*QUAS H	TORA H
H AS H	TAC H	CURC H	LAIG H	*QUOT H	TORC H
HAT H	TET H	CUTC H	LAIT H	*QURS H	TOUC H
H ET H	TOP H	DEAS H	LARC H	*RAJA H	TOUG H
HIG H	TOS H	DEAT H	LATC H	RALP H	TRAS H
H UN H	TUS H	DEPT H	LAUG H	RANC H	TROT H
H US H	VUG H	DIRT H	LEAC H	RATC H	TRUT H
JOS H	WAS H	DITC H	LEAS H	RAYA H	VETC H
KAP H	WIC H	DOET H	LEEC H	REAC H	VOUC H
KIT H	WIS H	DOUG H	LETC H	RERC H	WATC H
KOP H	WIT H	DUNC H	LOAC H	ROAC H	WAUG H
LAK H	*WYC H	DUTC H	LOAT H	ROTC H	WEIG H
LAS H	YEA H	FAIT H	LOTA H	ROUG H	WELC H
LAT H	YEC H	FAUG H	LOUG H	ROUT H	WELS H
LEC H	YOD H	FETC H	LUNC H	ROWT H	WENC H
LIC H	YOG H	FIFT H	LURC H	SAIT H	*W HIC H
LOC H	YUC H	FILC H	*LYMP H	SANG H	W HIS H
LOT H	BAIT H	FILT H	LYNC H	SAUC H	WIDT H
LUS H	BATC H	FINC H	MARC H	SAUG H	WINC H
MAC H	BEAC H	FIRT H	MARS H	SELA H	WITC H
MAS H	BEEC H	FITC H	MATC H	S H US H	WOOS H
MAT H	BELC H	FLAS H	MILC H	*SIXT H	WORT H
MES H	BENC H	FLES H	MIRT H	SKOS H	WRAT H
MET H	BERT H	FLUS H	MONT H	SLAS H	WROT H
MOT H	BIMA H	FORT H	MOOC H	SLOS H	*YECC H
MUC H	BIRC H	FRES H	MORP H	SLOT H	YIRT H
MUS H	BITC H	FRIT H	MOUC H	SLUS H	YOUT H
MYT H	BLUS H	FROS H	MOUT H	SMAS H	*YUCC H
NIG H	BOOT H	FROT H	MULC H	SMIT H	*ZILC H
NOS H	BOTC H	GALA H	MUNC H	SNAS H	BANIS H
PAS H	BOUG H	GART H	MUST H	SNAT H	BLANC H
PAT H	BRAC H	GERA H	MUTC H	SOOT H	BLEAC H
PEC H	BRAS H	GIRS H	MYNA H	SOUG H	BLENC H
PIS H	BROT H	GIRT H	MYRR H	SOUT H	BLOTC H
PIT H	BRUG H	GLYP H	NATC H	STAP H	BLUIS H
POO H	BRUS H	GNAS H	NEAT H	STAS H	BOYIS H
POS H	BUMP H	GRAP H	NEIG H	STIC H	BRANC H
PUG H	BUNC H	GRIT H	NORT H	SUBA H	BREAC H
PUS H	BURG H	GULC H	NOTC H	SURA H	BREAT H
*QOP H	BUTC H	GURS H	*NYMP H	SWAS H	BREEC H
RAS H	CATC H	H ARS H	PARC H	SWAT H	BROAC H
RAT H	C HET H	HATC H	PATC H	SWIS H	BROOC H
RES H	CINC H	HAUG H	PEAC H	SWIT H	BRUNC H
RIC H	CLAC H	H EIG H	PERC H	SYLP H	CALAS H
RUS H	CLAS H	H EUG H	PINC H	SYNC H	CALIP H
RUT H	CLOT H	H ITC H	PITC H	SYNT H	CAROC H
SAS H	COAC H	H OOC H	PLAS H	TEAC H	CASBA H
S HA H	CONC H	H ORA H	PLUS H	TEET H	CERIP H
SIG H	COOC H	H OTC H	POAC H	TENC H	C HALA H
SIN H	COUC H	*H UMP H	POOC H	TENT H	C HALE H
SIT H	COUG H	H UNC H	PORC H	TEUC H	C HETA H
SOP H	COUT H	H UTC H	POUC H	TEUG H	*C HINC H
SOT H	CRAS H	KENC H	*PSYC H	T HIG H	*C HOUG H

CHOUSH	HALLAH	MULLAH	*SHIVAH	WARMTH	*CHALOTH
*CHURCH	*HALVAH	NAUTCH	SIRRAH	WEALTH	*CHEETAH
CLENCH	*HAMZAH	NEWISH	SKEIGH	*WHIDAH	*CHERISH
CLINCH	HAUNCH	NULLAH	*SKETCH	*WHOOSH	*CHUDDAH
CLOUGH	HEALTH	OARAPH	SLATCH	*WHYDAH	*CLAYISH
CLUTCH	HEARTH	PAINCH	SLEIGH	WIDISH	*COCKISH
COHOSH	*HIGHTH	PALISH	SLEUTH	WINISH	*CODFISH
COMETH	*HOOKAH	PARDAH	SLOUCH	WRAITH	COLDISH
COOLTH	HOORAH	PARIAH	SLOUGH	WREATH	COOLISH
COPRAH	HOOTCH	PARTSH	SMIRCH	WRENCH	*COWFISH
COYISH	HOUDAH	PAUNCH	SMOOCH	WRETCH	CRAUNCH
CRANCH	*HOWDAH	PERISH	SMOOTH	*ZENITH	*CUBBISH
CRATCH	HURRAH	PLANCH	SNATCH	*ZEROTH	CULTISH
CREESH	*HUZZAH	PLEACH	SNEESH	*ZIBETH	CURRACH
CROTCH	*JADISH	PLENCH	SNITCH	*ZILLAH	CURRAGH
CROUCH	*JARRAH	PLINTH	SPEECH	*ZIZITH	CURRISH
CRUNCH	*JOSEPH	POLISH	SPILTH	*BABYISH	*DAMPISH
CRUTCH	*JUBBAH	POPISH	SPLASH	BALDISH	*DARKISH
CULTCH	*JUBHAH	POTASH	SPLOSH	*BATFISH	DEAFISH
CURAGH	*KALIPH	PREACH	*SQUASH	BEAMISH	*DEBAUCH
DALETH	*KASBAH	PRUTAH	*SQUISH	BEARISH	DERVISH
DANISH	*KEBLAH	PUNISH	*SQUUSH	BEGORAH	DIGRAPH
DEARTH	*KEDDAH	*PUNKAH	STANCH	BENEATH	*DIMORPH
DETACH	*KHEDAH	PURDAH	STARCH	BESEECH	*DIPTYCH
DOVISH	KIAUGH	PUTSCH	STENCH	BETROTH	DISTICH
DREICH	*KIBBEH	*QUAICH	STITCH	*BEWITCH	*DOGFISH
DREIGH	*KIBLAH	*QUAIGH	STRATH	BIGGISH	DOGGISH
DRENCH	*KIBOSH	*QUENCH	SUCCAH	BISMUTH	DOLLISH
DROUTH	*KIRSCH	*QUITCH	*SUKKAH	BLEMISH	DONNISH
DRYISH	*KITSCH	*QURUSH	SUMACH	BLUEISH	*DOZENTH
DUDISH	*KLATCH	RADISH	SUNNAH	BOARISH	DRONISH
FAMISH	*KVETCH	RAKISH	SWART H	BOGGISH	DULLISH
FELLAH	*KYBOSH	RAUNCH	SWATCH	BOOBISH	*DUMPISH
FETICH	LAMEDH	RAVISH	SWITCH	*BOOKISH	*DUSKISH
FETISH	LATISH	RAWISH	SWOOSH	BOORISH	*FADDISH
FINISH	LAUNCH	REHASH	TEMPEH	BOROUGH	FAIRISH
FLEECH	LAVISH	RELISH	TERAPH	*BOXFISH	FATTISH
FLENCH	LENGTH	REWASH	THATCH	BREADTH	*FINFISH
FLETCH	LOOFAH	RUPIAH	THOUGH	BRINISH	*FLEMISH
FLINCH	LOWISH	SAMECH	THRASH	BRUTISH	*FOLKISH
*FLYSCH	MARISH	*SAMEKH	THRESH	*BUCKISH	FOOLISH
FOURTH	MATSAH	SCARPH	THRUSH	BULLISH	*FOPPISH
FRENCH	*MATZAH	SCORCH	TONISH	BULRUSH	*FOXFISH
GALOSH	*MATZOH	SCOTCH	TOROTH	BURNISH	*FURBISH
*GANJAH	MENSCH	SCOUTH	TOYISH	*BUSHWAH	FURNISH
GARISH	*MIKVAH	SCUTCH	TREFAH	CADDISH	*GALUMPH
GLITCH	*MIKVEH	SEARCH	TRENCH	*CAPOUCH	GARFISH
GLUNCH	MINISH	SERAPH	TROUGH	CARLISH	GARNISH
GOLOSH	MODISH	SHAUGH	TROWTH	CAROACH	*GAWKISH
GONOPH	MOLLAH	SHEATH	TUSSAH	CARROCH	GIRLISH
GRINCH	MOLOCH	SHEIKH	TUSSEH	*CARWASH	GNOMISH
GROUCH	MONISH	SHEUCH	TWITCH	CATARRH	GOATISH
GROWTH	MOOLAH	SHEUGH	VANISH	CATTISH	GOODISH
GRUTCH	MOPISH	SHIBAH	WALLAH	*CHALLAH	*GOOMBAH
HADITH	MULISH				

GOULAS H	MONARC H	RUTTIS H	TURBIT H	BROADIS H	FLOURIS H
GRAYIS H	*MONKIS H	SABBAT H	TURPET H	BROGUIS H	*FOOLFIS H
GREENT H	MOONIS H	SALTIS H	*TWELFT H	*BROWNIS H	*FOOTBAT H
GREYIS H	MOORIS H	*SAWFIS H	*VAMPIS H	BULLRUS H	*FOOTPAT H
*H AGBUS H	*MUDFIS H	SCRAIC H	VARNIS H	*CABBALA H	FORSOOT H
*H AGFIS H	NEBBIS H	SCRAIG H	*VERMUT H	*CALABAS H	FORTIET H
*H AGGIS H	NEOLIT H	SCRÁTC H	VOGUIS H	*CALIPAS H	*FORTYIS H
H ALALA H	NOMARC H	SCREEC H	*WAGGIS H	*CARRITC H	*FREAKIS H
*H ALAVA H	NONCAS H	SCROOC H	*WAMPIS H	*CARTOUC H	*FROGFIS H
H ALLOT H	NONSUC H	SCRUNC H	*WARMIS H	*CAVEFIS H	*FURLOUG H
*H ARUMP H	NOURIS H	SELFIS H	*WARPAT H	*CENOTAP H	*GOATFIS H
*H AS H IS H	NUNNIS H	SERFIS H	*WEAKIS H	*C H ALLOT H	*GOLDFIS H
*H AWKIS H	*PADS H A H	SEVENT H	WEARIS H	*C H EAPIS H	*GRAYFIS H
*H EIG H T H	*PANFIS H	S H ANTI H	WENNIS H	*C H ILDIS H	GREENIS H
*H EIMIS H	*PEAKIS H	S H ITTA H	WETTIS H	*C H UTZPA H	*GRUFFIS H
H ELLIS H	*PECKIS H	*SICKIS H	*W H ITIS H	CLANNIS H	*GRUMPIS H
*H IPPIS H	*PEEVIS H	*SKREEG H	*W H ORIS H	*CLERKIS H	GUNSMIT H
*H OGFIS H	*PERKIS H	*SKREIG H	WILDIS H	*CLIQUIS H	*GYPSYIS H
*H OGWAS H	PETTIS H	SLAVIS H	*WIMPIS H	*CLOWNIS H	*H ABDALA H
H OTTIS H	*P H ARAO H	SLOWIS H	*WISPIS H	*CLUBBIS H	*H AFTARA H
*H UFFIS H	*PIBROC H	SOFTIS H	*WOLFIS H	*CLUMPIS H	*H AFTORA H
H UNNIS H	*PIGFIS H	SOTTIS H	*WORMIS H	*COALFIS H	*HAGGADA H
*H UTZPA H	PIGGIS H	SOURIS H	WOTTET H	*COPPERA H	*H ALAKOT H
*JACINT H	*PINFIS H	SPINAC H	*XERARC H	*CORONAC H	*HAS H EES H
*JEWFIS H	*PINKIS H	SPLOTC H	*ZANYIS H	*CRANKIS H	*H AVDALA H
*KADDIS H	PLANIS H	*SQUELC H	*ZAPTIA H	*CRAWFIS H	*H AWFINC H
*K H IRKA H	PLENIS H	*SQUINC H	*ZAPTIE H	*CRAYFIS H	*H AWKMOT H
*KIDDIS H	POORIS H	*SQUOOS H	*BACKLAS H	*CROMLEC H	*H EADFIS H
*KIDDUS H	POTLAC H	STAUNC H	*BACKRUS H	*DA H ABEA H	*H ELMINT H
*KLATSC H	*PREWAS H	STEALT H	*BACKWAS H	*DA H ABIA H	*H EPTARC H
*KURBAS H	PRUDIS H	STENGA H	*BADMOUT H	*DA H ABIE H	*H EREWIT H
LADYIS H	PUBLIS H	STOMAC H	*BAKS H IS H	*DANDYIS H	*H ICCOUG H
LARGIS H	*PUCKIS H	STONIS H	*BEDRENC H	*DEALFIS H	*H IERARC H
LARKIS H	PUGGIS H	STRETC H	BEGORRA H	DEPOLIS H	*H IG H BUS H
*LAZYIS H	*PUNKIS H	STYLIS H	*BE H EMOT H	*DESPATC H	*H IPPARC H
LEFTIS H	*PUPFIS H	SUCCOT H	*BEQUEAT H	*DEVILIS H	H OSANNA H
LONGIS H	*QUAMAS H	SUNBAT H	*BESCORC H	*DIAGRAP H	*H YACINT H
LOUDIS H	*RAFFIS H	SUNFIS H	*BESMIRC H	DIMINIS H	*H YDRANT H
LOUTIS H	RAMMIS H	SWINIS H	*BESMOOT H	*DISPATC H	*JACKFIS H
LUMPIS H	RANKIS H	TALLIS H	*BIGMOUT H	DOGTOOT H	*KABBALA H
MADDIS H	RASPIS H	TALLIT H	*BILLFIS H	*DOGWATC H	*KAFFIYE H
*MAMMOT H	RATFIS H	TANNIS H	*BIRDBAT H	*DOWNWAS H	*KAS H RUT H
MANNIS H	RATTIS H	TARBUS H	*BLACKIS H	*DRAFFIS H	*KEFFIYE H
*MATZOT H	REBIRT H	TARNIS H	BLANDIS H	*DRUMFIS H	*KEYPUNC H
*MAWKIS H	REDDIS H	TARTIS H	*BLEAKIS H	*DWARFIS H	*KINGFIS H
*MAYBUS H	REDFIS H	TEREFA H	*BLOCKIS H	FAINTIS H	*KREPLAC H
*MEGILP H	REFRES H	T H ROUG H	BLONDIS H	*FALLFIS H	*KRYOLIT H
MENORA H	REMATC H	TIGRIS H	*BLOWFIS H	*FEEBLIS H	*LADYFIS H
MESARC H	REPATC H	TOADIS H	*BLUEFIS H	*FEVERIS H	LANGUIS H
MESSIA H	RETEAC H	TONNIS H	*BOARFIS H	*FIENDIS H	*LIG H TIS H
*MEZUZA H	RETOUC H	TOWNIS H	*BONEFIS H	*FIFTYIS H	LIONFIS H
MIDRAS H	REWEIG H	*TOWPAT H	*BRACKIS H	*FILEFIS H	LITTLIS H
*MITSVA H	ROGUIS H	TRÍUMP H	BRAINIS H	*FLATFIS H	LIVERIS H
*MITZVA H	ROMPIS H	TUNDIS H	BRANDIS H	FLATTIS H	*LOGOMAC H
*MOBBIS H	RUBBIS H	TURBET H	BRASSIS H	*FLATWAS H	*LUMPFIS H

*LUNGFIS H	*PARAS H A H	RELAUNC H	*S H AMMAS H	STRENGT H	TOVARIS H
*MASTABA H	*PARFLES H	REPOLIS H	*S H EEPIS H	*STUDFIS H	*TRAMPIS H
MEGALIT H	*PARRITC H	*REPROACH H	S H ORTIS H	*SUBEPOC H	*TRIBRAC H
MEGILLA H	PEARLAS H	RESEARC H	*S H REWIS H	*SUBGRAP H	*TRICKIS H
*MES H UGA H	*PENTARC H	*RESKETC H	SISSYIS H	*SUCKFIS H	*TRIGLYP H
*MIDMONT H	PERIANT H	RESMOOT H	*SIXTIET H	*SUNPORC H	TRIGRAP H
*MIDWATC H	*PIPEFIS H	RESTITC H	*SIXTYIS H	*SURFFIS H	*TRIMORP H
*MILKFIS H	*PLUMPIS H	RETRENC H	*SKIRMIS H	*SWAMPIS H	*TRIPTYC H
*MISFAIT H	*POLYMAT H	*ROCKFIS H	*SKITTIS H	SWEETIS H	TRISTIC H
*MIS H MAS H	POORTIT H	ROSEBUS H	SLAPDAS H	TAIGLAC H	*TZITZIT H
*MIS H MOS H	*POTLATC H	ROSEFIS H	*SLOBBIS H	TARBOOS H	*VANQUIS H
*MISMATC H	*PRANKIS H	*ROUG H IS H	SLUGGIS H	TEIGLAC H	*VAPORIS H
*MISPATC H	*PRECRAS H	ROUNDIS H	SMALLIS H	TELEPAT H	*VERANDA H
*MISTEAC H	*PRELUNC H	*ROWDYIS H	*SNAPPIS H	TETRARC H	*VERMOUT H
*MISTOUC H	*PREPUNC H	SAGANAS H	*SNIFFIS H	*T H ICKIS H	*VIGORIS H
*MONKFIS H	*PRIGGIS H	SAILFIS H	*SNOBBIS H	*T H IEVIS H	*WARMOUT H
MONOLIT H	*PURPLIS H	SALTBUS H	SNOUTIS H	T H INNIS H	WATERIS H
MONTEIT H	*QUACKIS H	*SANDFIS H	*SNOWBUS H	*T H OROUG H	*WEAKFIS H
*MOONFIS H	*QUALMIS H	*SANDWIC H	*SPARKIS H	*T H UGGIS H	*W H IPLAS H
*MUSQUAS H	*QUEERIS H	SAVANNA H	*SPOOKIS H	*TICKLIS H	*WOLFFIS H
*MYOGRAP H	*QUIPPIS H	SAWTOOT H	*SQUARIS H	TIGERIS H	*WOMANIS H
NARGILE H	*QUIRKIS H	*SCAMPIS H	*SQUIRIS H	TILEFIS H	WOSTTET H
*NEOMORP H	RAINWAS H	SCROOTC H	STABLIS H	TINSMIT H	*XENOLIT H
NONESUC H	*RARRUMP H	*SEABEAC H	STANDIS H	*TOADFIS H	*YES H IVA H
NONTRUT H	REATTAC H	*SEECATC H	STEEPIS H	*TOADYIS H	*YOKELIS H
*NUMBFIS H	*REBRANC H	SELCOUT H	*STIFFIS H	TOLBOOT H	*YOUNGIS H
*NUT H ATC H	REFINIS H	*SEMI H IG H	*STOCKIS H	TOPNOTC H	*ZOOMORP H
*PADIS H A H	REGOLIT H	*S H ADBUS H	STOUTIS H	*TOUG H IS H	
PAGANIS H	*REGROWT H	*S H ADRAC H	STRAMAS H	*TOVARIC H	

J

*JACK	JEHU	JOEY	*JUNK	JAPER	*JIMMY
JADE	JELL	JOHN	JUPE	JAUNT	*JIMPY
JAGG	JEON	JOIN	JURA	*JAWAN	JINGO
JAIL	*JERK	*JOKE	JURY	*JAZZY	JINNI
*JAKE	JESS	*JOKY	JUST	JEBEL	*JIVER
*JAMB	JEST	JOLE	JUTE	*JEHAD	*JIVEY
JANE	JETE	JOLT	JABOT	*JELLY	JNANA
JAPE	JIAO	JOSH	JACAL	*JEMMY	*JOCKO
JARL	*JIBB	JOSS	*JACKY	*JENNY	JOINT
JATO	JIBE	JOTA	JAGER	JERID	JOIST
*JAUK	*JIFF	*JOUK	*JAGGY	*JERKY	*JOKER
JAUP	JILL	JOWL	JAGRA	*JERRY	*JOLLY
JAVA	JILT	JUBA	*JAKES	JESSE	*JOLTY
*JAZZ	*JIMP	JUBE	JALAP	JETON	JONES
JEAN	*JINK	JUDO	JALOP	*JETTY	JORAM
JEEP	JINN	JUGA	*JAMBE	*JEWEL	JORUM
JEER	*JINX	*JUJU	*JAMMY	JIBER	*JOTTY
*JEEZ	JIVE	*JUKE	*JANTY	*JIFFY	JOUAL
JEFE	*JOCK	*JUMP	JAPAN	*JIHAD	JOULE

JOUST	*JAZZER	*JOYPOP	*JARRING	*JOINERY	*JAILBIRD
*JOWAR	JEERER	*JUBBAH	*JARSFUL	*JOINING	*JALAPENO
*JOWLY	*JEJUNA	*JUBHAH	*JASMINE	JOINTER	*JALOUSIE
JUDAS	*JEJUNE	*JUBILE	*JAVELIN	*JOINTLY	*JAMBOREE
JUDGE	JENNET	*JUDDER	*JAWBONE	*JOKIEST	*JANIFORM
JUGAL	*JERBOA	*JUDGER	*JAWLIKE	*JOLLIED	*JANISARY
*JUGUM	JEREED	*JUDOKA	*JAWLINE	JOLLIER	*JANIZARY
JUICE	*JERKER	JUGATE	*JAYBIRD	JOLLIES	*JAPANIZE
*JUICY	*JERKIN	*JUGFUL	*JAYWALK	*JOLLIFY	*JAPANNER
JULEP	JERRID	*JUGGED	*JAZZMAN	*JOLLITY	*JAPINGLY
*JUMBO	*JERSEY	*JUGGLE	JEALOUS	*JONQUIL	*JAPONICA
*JUMPY	JESTER	JUGULA	*JEEPERS	JOSTLER	*JARGONEL
JUNCO	JESUIT	*JUICER	*JEEPNEY	*JOTTING	*JAROSITE
*JUNKY	*JETSAM	*JUJUBE	*JEJUNAL	JOURNAL	*JAROVIZE
JUNTA	*JETSOM	*JUMBAL	*JEJUNUM	*JOURNEY	*JAUNDICE
JUNTO	JETTED	*JUMBLE	*JELLABA	JOUSTER	*JAVELINA
JUPON	JETTON	*JUMPER	*JELLIFY	*JOYANCE	*JAWBONER
JURAL	*JEZAIL	JUNGLE	*JEMADAR	*JOYLESS	*JAZZLIKE
JURAT	*JIBBER	*JUNGLY	*JEMIDAR	*JOYRIDE	*JEALOUSY
JUREL	*JICAMA	JUNIOR	*JEOPARD	*JUBILEE	*JEJUNITY
JUROR	*JIGGER	*JUNKER	*JERKIES	*JUDOIST	*JELUTONG
*JUTTY	*JIGGLE	*JUNKET	*JERREED	*JUGGING	*JEOPARDY
*JABBER	*JIGGLY	*JUNKIE	JESSANT	*JUGGLER	*JEREMIAD
*JABIRU	*JIGSAW	JURANT	*JESTFUL	*JUGHEAD	*JEROBOAM
*JACANA	JILTER	JURIES	*JESTING	*JUGSFUL	*JERRICAN
*JACKAL	*JIMINY	JURIST	*JETBEAD	*JUGULAR	*JERRYCAN
*JACKER	JINGAL	JUSTER	*JETLIKE	*JUGULUM	*JESUITRY
*JACKET	*JINGKO	JUSTLE	*JETPORT	*JUJITSU	*JETLINER
*JADISH	JINGLE	*JUSTLY	*JETTIED	*JUJUISM	*JETTIEST
JAEGER	*JINGLY	*JABBING	JETTIER	*JUJUIST	*JETTISON
*JAGGED	*JINKER	*JACAMAR	JETTIES	*JUJUTSU	*JEWELLER
*JAGGER	JINNEE	*JACINTH	*JETTING	*JUKEBOX	*JIGGERED
JAGUAR	*JITNEY	*JACKASS	*JEWELER	*JUMBLER	*JINGOISM
JAILER	JITTER	*JACKDAW	*JEWELRY	*JUMBUCK	*JINGOIST
JAILOR	*JOBBER	*JACKIES	*JEWFISH	*JUMPOFF	*JIPIJAPA
*JALOPY	*JOCKEY	*JACKLEG	*JEZEBEL	*JUNIPER	*JIUJITSU
*JAMMED	*JOCOSE	*JACKPOT	*JIBBING	*JUNKMAN	*JIUJUTSU
*JAMMER	*JOCUND	*JACOBIN	*JIBBOOM	*JURIDIC	*JOCKETTE
JANGLE	*JOGGER	*JACOBUS	*JIGGING	*JURYMAN	*JOCOSITY
*JANGLY	*JOGGLE	*JACONET	JILLION	*JUSSIVE	*JOHANNES
*JAPERY	*JOHNNY	*JADEITE	*JIMJAMS	*JUSTICE	*JOHNBOAT
*JAPING	JOINER	*JAGGARY	*JIMMINY	*JUSTIFY	*JOINTURE
*JARFUL	*JOJOBA	*JAGGERY	*JINGALL	*JUVENAL	*JOKESTER
JARGON	*JOKIER	*JAGGING	*JINGLER	*JABBERER	*JOKINESS
JARINA	*JOKING	*JAGLESS	*JITTERY	*JACINTHE	*JOKINGLY
*JARRAH	JOLTER	*JALAPIN	*JIVEASS	*JACKAROO	*JOLLIEST
JARRED	JORDAN	*JALOPPY	JOANNES	*JACKBOOT	*JONGLEUR
*JARVEY	*JOSEPH	*JAMBEAU	*JOBBERY	*JACKEROO	*JOVIALTY
*JASMIN	*JOSHER	*JAMMIES	*JOBBING	*JACKFISH	*JOYRIDER
*JASPER	JOSTLE	*JAMMING	*JOBLESS	*JACKROLL	*JOYSTICK
JASSID	*JOUNCE	*JANGLER	*JOBNAME	*JACKSTAY	*JUBILANT
*JAUNCE	*JOUNCY	JANITOR	*JOCULAR	*JACQUARD	*JUBILATE
*JAUNTY	*JOVIAL	*JARGOON	*JODHPUR	*JACULATE	*JUDGMENT
*JAYGEE	*JOYFUL	*JARHEAD	*JOGGLER	*JAGGHERY	*JUDICIAL
*JAYVEE	*JOYOUS	*JARLDOM	*JOINDER	*JAILBAIT	*JUGGLERY

*JUGGLING	MO J O	SE J ANT	*MA J ESTY	*BAN J AX	*MAH J ONGG
*JUGULATE	PU J A	*BE J ESUS	*MA J ORAM	*FEI J OA	*MIS J UDGE
*JULIENNE	*PU J AH	*BE J EWEL	*MA J ORLY	*GAN J AH	*NON J UROR
*JUNCTION	*CA J OLE	*CA J APUT	*MO J ARRA	*VEE J AY	*PER J URER
*JUNCTURE	*CO J OIN	*CA J OLER	*PY J AMAS	*NON J URY	*PRE J UDGE
*JUNKETER	*DE J ECT	*CA J UPUT	*RE J OICE	*BAN J OIST	*SER J EANT
*JUNKYARD	*FA J ITA	*DE J ECTA	*RE J UDGE	*BEN J AMIN	*SKI J ORER
*JURATORY	*HE J IRA	*HI J INKS	SE J EANT	*CON J UGAL	*VER J UICE
*JUSTNESS	*HI J ACK	*JE J UNAL	SO J OURN	*CON J UNCT	
*JUVENILE	*JO J OBA	*JE J UNUM	*BE J ABERS	*CON J URER	*HAD J
	*JE J UNA	*JU J ITSU	*BE J EEZUS	*CON J UROR	*HA J J
	*JE J UNAL	*JU J UISM	*RE J ACKET	*DIS J OINT	*SVARA J
D J IN	*JE J UNE	*JU J UIST	*RE J UGGLE	*DIS J UNCT	*SWARA J
D J INN	*JU J UBE	*JU J UTSU	*PA J AMAED	*FOR J UDGE	
*F J ELD	*PA J AMA	*KA J EPUT	NIN J A	*J IU J ITSU	
*F J ORD	*RE J ECT	*MA J AGUA	RIO J A	*J IU J UTSU	
*HA J J	RE J OIN				

K

KAAS	KENT	KIWI	KABAB	KEMPT	KITTY
KADI	KEPI	KNAP	KABAR	KENAF	KLONG
KAGU	KEPT	KNAR	KABOB	KENCH	KLOOF
KAIF	KERB	KNEE	KAFIR	KENDO	KLUGE
KAIL	KERF	KNEW	KAIAK	KERNE	*KLUTZ
KAIN	KERN	KNIT	KALAM	KERRY	*KNACK
KAKA	KETO	KNOB	KALIF	KETCH	KNAUR
KAKI	KHAF	KNOP	KALPA	KETOL	KNAVE
KALE	KHAN	KNOT	*KAMIK	KEVEL	KNEAD
KAME	KHAT	KNOW	*KANJI	KEVIL	KNEEL
KAMI	KHET	KNUR	*KAPOK	KHADI	KNELT
KANA	KIBE	KOAN	KAPPA	*KHAKI	KNIFE
KANE	KICK	KOBO	KAPUT	*KHAPH	KNISH
KAON	KIEF	KOEL	KARAT	KHEDA	*KNOCK
KAPA	KIER	KOHL	KARMA	*KHETH	KNOLL
KAPH	KILL	KOLA	KAROO	KHOUM	KNOSP
KARN	KILN	KOLO	KARST	KIANG	KNOUT
KART	KILO	KONK	KASHA	KIBBE	KNOWN
KAVA	KILT	KOOK	KAURI	KIBBI	KNURL
KAYO	KINA	KOPH	KAURY	KIBEI	KOALA
KBAR	KIND	KORE	*KAYAK	KIBLA	KOINE
KECK	KINE	KOSS	*KAZOO	*KICKY	*KOOKY
KEEF	KING	KOTO	KEBAB	KIDDO	*KOPEK
KEEK	KINK	KRIS	KEBAR	KIDDY	*KOPJE
KEEL	KINO	KUDO	KEBOB	KILIM	KOPPA
KEEN	KIRK	KUDU	KEDGE	KILTY	KORAT
KEEP	KIRN	KURU	KEEVE	KININ	KOTOW
KEET	KISS	KVAS	KEFIR	*KINKY	KRAAL
KEIR	KIST	*KYAK	KELEP	KIOSK	KRAFT
KELP	KITE	KYAR	KELIM	KISSY	KRAIT
KEMP	KITH	KYAT	KELLY	KITER	KRAUT
KENO	KIVA	KYTE	KELPY	KITHE	KREEP

KRILL	KEGLER	KISMAT	KAINITE	*KICKOFF	KNITTER
KRONA	KELOID	KISMET	*KAJEPUT	KIDDIES	*KNOBBLY
KRONE	KELPIE	KISSER	KALENDS	KIDDING	*KNOCKER
KROON	KELSON	KITING	*KALIMBA	*KIDDISH	KNOLLER
KRUBI	KELTER	*KITSCH	*KAMPONG	*KIDDUSH	KNOTTED
*KUDZU	KELVIN	KITTED	KAMSEEN	*KIDLIKE	KNOTTER
KUGEL	KENNED	KITTEL	KANTELE	*KIDSKIN	*KNOWING
KUKRI	KENNEL	KITTEN	KAOLINE	KIESTER	*KNUCKLE
KULAK	*KEPPED	KITTLE	*KARAKUL	KILLDEE	*KNUCKLY
KUMYS	KEPPEN	*KLATCH	*KARAOKE	*KILLICK	*KOKANEE
KURTA	KERMES	*KLAXON	KARTING	KILLING	*KOLACKY
KUSSO	KERMIS	*KLEPHT	*KASHMIR	*KILLJOY	KOLBASI
KVASS	KERNEL	KLUDGE	KASHRUT	*KILLOCK	*KOLKHOS
*KYACK	KERRIA	*KLUTZY	KATCINA	KILOBAR	*KOLKHOZ
*KYLIX	KERSEY	KNAWEL	*KATHODE	KILOBIT	*KOMATIK
KYRIE	KETENE	KNIFER	*KATYDID	KILORAD	KOTOWER
*KYTHE	KETONE	KNIGHT	*KAYAKER	KILOTON	KOUMISS
*KABAKA	KETOSE	KNIVES	*KEBBOCK	KILTING	*KOUMYSS
KABALA	KETTLE	*KNOBBY	*KEBBUCK	*KIMCHEE	*KOUPREY
*KABAYA	*KEYPAD	KNOLLY	KEELAGE	KINDLER	KREMLIN
*KABIKI	KEYSET	KNOTTY	KEELSON	KINDRED	*KREUZER
*KABUKI	*KEYWAY	KNOWER	KEEPING	KINESIC	*KRIMMER
*KAFFIR	*KHALIF	KNURLY	KEESTER	KINESIS	KRULLER
KAFTAN	*KHAZEN	KOBOLD	KEGELER	KINETIC	*KRYPTON
KAHUNA	*KHEDAH	*KOLHOZ	KEGLING	KINETIN	*KUMQUAT
KAINIT	KIAUGH	*KOLKOZ	KEISTER	*KINFOLK	*KUNZITE
KAISER	*KIBBEH	KOODOO	KEITLOA	*KINGCUP	*KURBASH
*KAKAPO	KIBBLE	KOOKIE	KENNING	*KINGDOM	*KVETCHY
KALIAN	*KIBITZ	*KOPECK	KENOSIS	KINGLET	KYANISE
*KALIPH	*KIBLAH	KOPPIE	*KEPPING	KINGPIN	KYANITE
KALIUM	*KIBOSH	KORUNA	*KERAMIC	*KINSHIP	*KYANIZE
KALMIA	*KICKER	KOSHER	KERATIN	KINSMAN	*KABBALAH
KALONG	*KICKUP	KOUMIS	*KERCHOO	*KIPPING	*KABELJOU
*KALPAK	KIDDER	*KOUMYSS	KERMESS	KIPSKIN	*KAFFIYEH
KAMALA	KIDDIE	KOUROS	KERNITE	*KIRKMAN	*KAILYARD
KAMSIN	KIDNAP	KOUSSO	KEROGEN	KIRMESS	KAISERIN
KANBAN	KIDNEY	*KOWTOW	*KERYGMA	KISTFUL	*KAKEMONO
KANTAR	*KIDVID	KRAKEN	KESTREL	*KITCHEN	*KAKIEMON
KAOLIN	KILLER	KRATER	*KETCHUP	KITHARA	*KALEWIFE
KAPUTT	KILLIE	KRONOR	KETOSIS	KITLING	*KALEYARD
KARATE	KILTER	KRONUR	*KEYCARD	KITTIES	*KALIFATE
KAROSS	KILTIE	KRUBUT	*KEYHOLE	KITTING	KALLIDIN
*KASBAH	*KIMCHI	*KUCHEN	KEYLESS	*KLATSCH	*KALYPTRA
KASHER	KIMONO	KULTUR	KEYNOTE	KLAVERN	KAMAAINA
KATION	KINASE	KUMISS	KEYSTER	KLEAGLE	*KAMACITE
KAVASS	KINDLE	KUMMEL	*KEYWORD	*KLEZMER	*KAMIKAZE
KAYLES	KINDLY	KURGAN	*KHADDAR	KLISTER	KANGAROO
KEBBIE	KINEMA	*KUVASZ	*KHALIFA	*KNACKER	KAOLIANG
*KEBLAH	KINGLY	*KVETCH	*KHAMSIN	*KNAPPER	*KARYOTIN
*KECKLE	KIPPEN	*KWACHA	KHANATE	*KNAVERY	*KASHRUTH
*KEDDAH	KIPPER	*KWANZA	*KHEDIVE	KNEADER	KATAKANA
KEENER	KIRSCH	*KYBOSH	*KHIRKAH	*KNEECAP	*KATCHINA
KEENLY	KIRTLE	*KABBALA	*KIBBITZ	KNEELER	KAVAKAVA
KEEPER	*KISHKA	*KACHINA	*KIBBUTZ	KNEEPAD	*KAYAKING
	*KISHKE	*KADDISH	*KICKIER	KNESSET	*KAZACHOK

*KAZATSKI	KINGSIDE	S K EET	*FA K ERY	*RI K SHAW	*ZAI K AI
*KAZATSKY	*KINGWOOD	S K EIN	FA K ING	SO K EMAN	*BAC K FIT
KEDGEREE	*KINKAJOU	S K ELM	*HA K EEM	*TA K EOFF	*BOO K FUL
KEELBOAT	*KINSFOLK	S K ELP	*JO K IER	TA K EOUT	BRO K ING
*KEELHALE	*KIPPERER	S K ENE	*JO K ING	TE K TITE	*COO K TOP
*KEELHAUL	*KIRIGAMI	S K IED	*K A K APO	*TO K AMA K	FLO K ATI
KEELLESS	*KITELIKE	S K IER	LA K ING	*TO K OMA K	*K IC K IER
KEENNESS	*KLYSTRON	S K IES	LE K VAR	*WA K ANDA	LAR K ISH
*KEEPSAKE	*KNACKERY	S K IEY	LI K ELY	*WA K EFUL	*MIS K IC K
*KEESHOND	*KNAPSACK	*S K IFF	LI K EST	WA K ENER	*PEC K ISH
*KEFFIYEH	*KNAPWEED	S K ILL	LI K ING	*ZI K URAT	*PIC K LOC
KENOTRON	*KNEEHOLE	S K IMO	LI K UTA	*CA K EWALK	*PUN K ISH
*KEPHALIN	*KNEESOCK	S K IMP	*MI K VAH	*CO K EHEAD	*RAC K FUL
KERATOID	*KNICKERS	S K INK	*MI K VEH	*HO K INESS	RAN K ING
KERATOMA	*KNIGHTLY	S K INT	*MU K LU K	*JO K INESS	*SHI K K ER
KERATOSE	KNITTING	S K IRL	*MU K TU K	*K A K IEMON	SIC K OUT
*KERCHIEF	*KNITWEAR	S K IRR	NE K TON	*MA K EOVER	TIN K LER
KEROSENE	*KNOCKOFF	S K IRT	*PA K EHA	*PY K NOSIS	*TOP K IC K
KEROSINE	*KNOCKOUT	S K ITE	*PI K A K E	*PY K NOTIC	*BACKACHE
*KERPLUNK	*KNOTHOLE	S K IVE	PI K ING	*TA K EAWAY	*BAC K BEAT
*KEYBOARD	KNOTLESS	S K OAL	PO K IER	*YA K ITORI	*BAC K BEND
*KEYNOTER	*KNOTLIKE	S K OSH	PO K IES	*YO K OZUNA	*BAC K BITE
*KEYPUNCH	KNOTTING	S K ULK	*PO K ILY	*ZI K K URAT	*BAC K BONE
*KEYSTONE	*KNOTWEED	S K ULL	PO K ING	DE K K O	*BAC K CAST
*KHAMSEEN	*KNUCKLER	S K UNK	*PY K NIC	DOR K Y	*BAC K CHAT
*KIBITZER	*KOHLRABI	*S K YEY	RA K ING	*FOL K Y	*BAC K DATE
*KICKBACK	KOLBASSI	*S K YBOX	RA K ISH	GEE K Y	*BAC K DOOR
*KICKBALL	*KOLINSKI	S K YLIT	RE K NIT	*K IC K Y	*BAC K DROP
*KICKIEST	*KOLINSKY	*S K YHOO K	*SU K K AH	MIN K E	*BAC K FILL
*KICKSHAW	*KOMONDOR	*S K YJAC K	TA K AHE	NAR K Y	*BAC K FIRE
*KIDNAPEE	*KOWTOWER	*S K YWAL K	TA K ING	SAR K Y	*BAC K FLOW
*KIDNAPER	*KREPLACH	*SK EWBACK	TA K ING	SIC K O	*BAC K HAND
KIELBASA	*KREUTZER	*S K IPJACK	TO K ING	SIL K Y	*BAC K HAUL
KILLDEER	*KRUMHORN	TA K A	TS K TS K	SOC K O	*BAC K LAND
KILOBASE	*KRYOLITE	BI K IE	VA K EEL	TRI K E	*BAC K LASH
*KILOBAUD	*KRYOLITH	CA K EY	VI K ING	WAC K O	*BAC K LESS
*KILOBYTE	KURTOSIS	DE K K O	*WA K I KI	*YUC K Y	*BAC K LIST
*KILOGRAM	S K AG	*FA K EY	WA K ING	*CHA K RA	*BAC K MOST
KILOMOLE	S K AT	K U K RI	*WI K IUP	*CRI K EY	*BAC K PAC K
*KILOVOLT	S K EE	SO K OL	*YA K K ER	DAI K ON	*BAC K REST
*KILOWATT	S K EG	TO K ER	YO K ING	*FLA K EY	*BAC K ROOM
KINDLESS	S K EP	YI K ES	*BA K LAVA	FOL K IE	*BAC K RUSH
KINDLING	S K EW	*BA K ERY	*BA K LAWA	NEC K ER	*BAC K SEAT
KINDNESS	S K ID	BA K ING	*BI K EWAY	PIN K EN	*BAC K SIDE
KINESICS	S K IM	BE K ISS	*DA K OITY	PIN K ER	*BAC K SLAP
KINETICS	S K IN	BI K ING	*DU K EDOM	PIN K EY	*BAC K SLID
*KINFOLKS	S K IP	BI K INI	HE K TARE	PUN K ER	*BAC K SPIN
*KINGBIRD	S K IT	DA K OIT	*JO K IEST	*QUO K K A	*BAC K STAY
*KINGBOLT	S K UA	DE K ARE	*JU K EBOX	RUC K LE	*BAC K STOP
*KINGFISH	S K IT	DA K OIT	*K O K ANEE	RYO K AN	*BAC K WARD
*KINGHOOD	S K UA	DE K ARE	LI K ABLE	SIC K EE	*BAC K WASH
KINGLESS	S K ALD	*DI K DI K	*PI K E K AN	SIC K IE	*BAC K WOOD
*KINGLIKE	S K ATE	*DI K DIX	PO K IEST	*SPI K EY	*BAC K WRAP
*KINGPOST	S K EAN	DI K TAT	*RA K EOFF	*SU K K AH	*BAC K YARD
*KINGSHIP	S K EEN	FA K EER	RI K ISHA	*YA K K ER	BAL K LINE

*BAN K BOO K
*BAN K CARD
BAN K NOTE
BAN K ROLL
*BAN K RUPT
*BAN K SIDE
BAR K LESS
*BAS K ETRY
*BEC K ONER
*BIC K ERER
*BOO K CASE
*BOO K LICE
BOO K LORE
*BOO K MAR K
*BOO K RAC K
BOO K REST
*BOO K SHOP
*BOO K WORM
*BRA K EAGE
*BRA K EMAN
*BUC K AROO
*BUC K AYRO
*BUC K BEAN
*BUC K EROO
*BUC K SHEE
*BUC K SHOT
*BUC K S K IN
*BUC K TAIL
*BUL K HEAD
*BUN K KATE
*COC K ATOO
*COC K APOO
*COC K BILL
*COC K BOAT
*COC K CROW
*COC K EREL
*COC K IEST
*COC K LI K E
*COC K LOFT
*COC K SHUT
*COC K SPUR
*COC K SURE
*COC K TAIL
*COO K BOO K
COO K LESS
*COO K SHOP
*COO K WARE
COR K IEST
*COR K LI K E
*COR K WOOD
DAN K NESS
DAR K ENER
DAR K NESS
*DAR K ROOM
*DAR K SOME

*DEC K HAND
DIN K IEST
DIS K ETTE
*DOC K HAND
*DOC K LAND
*DOC K SIDE
*DOC K YARD
*DUC K BILL
*DUC K IEST
*DUC K LING
*DUC K TAIL
*DUC K WAL K
*DUC K WEED
*FEC K LESS
*FOL K LIFE
*FOL K LI K E
*FOL K LORE
*FOL K MOOT
*FOL K MOTE
*FOL K TALE
*FOR K BALL
*FOR K IEST
*FOR K LESS
*FOR K LIFT
*FOR K LI K E
*FOR K SFUL
*GYM K HANA
*HAC K WOR K
*HAN K ERER
*HAR K ENER
*HAW K EYED
*HAW K BILL
*HAW K LI K E
*HAW K MOTH
*HAW K NOSE
*HAW K SHAW
*HAW K WEED
*HOC K SHOP
*HOO K LESS
*HOO K NOSE
*HOO K WORM
*HUC K STER
*HUS K IEST
*HUS K LI K E
*JAC K AROO
*JAC K BOOT
*JAC K EROO
*JAC K FISH
*JAC K ROLL
*JAC K STAY
*JOC K ETTE
*JUN K ETER
*JUN K YARD
*K IC K BAC K
*K IC K BALL

*K IC K IEST
*K IC K SHAW
*K IN K AJOU
*LAC K ADAY
LAR K IEST
LAR K SOME
LAR K SPUR
LEA K LESS
LEU K EMIA
*LEU K EMIC
LEU K OSIS
*LIC K SPIT
LIN K SMAN
*LIN K WOR K
*LOC K DOWN
*LOC K STEP
*LOO K DOWN
*LUN K HEAD
*MAC K EREL
*MAC K INAW
*MAR K DOWN
*MAR K EDLY
*MAR K HOOR
*MAR K SMAN
*MAS K LI K E
*MIL K FISH
*MIL K MAID
*MIL K SHED
*MIL K WEED
*MIL K WOOD
*MIL K WORT
*MON K FISH
*MON K HOOD
*MUC K IEST
*MUC K LUC K
*MUC K LUC K
*MUC K RA K E
*MUC K WORM
*MUS K ETRY
*NEC K BAND
*NEC K LACE
NEC K LESS
*NEC K LI K E
NEC K LINE
*NEC K WEAR
*NIC K ELIC
*NIC K NAC K
*NIC K NAME
*PAC K AGER
*PAC K NESS
*PAC K SAC K
*PAR K LAND
*PAR K LI K E
PEA K IEST
PEA K LESS

*PEA K LI K E
*PEE K ABOO
*PEN K NIFE
*PIC K ADIL
*PIC K EREL
*PIC K ETER
*PIC K IEST
*PIC K LOC K
*PIC K WIC K
PIN K NESS
PIN K ROOT
*POC K ETER
*POC K MAR K
POR K IEST
*POR K WOOD
*PUC K ERER
*RAC K WOR K
RAN K NESS
REC K LESS
REC K ONER
*RES K ETCH
*RIC K RAC K
*RIC K SHAW
RIS K LESS
*ROC K ABYE
*ROC K AWAY
ROC K ETER
*ROC K ETRY
*ROC K FALL
*ROC K FISH
*ROC K LI K E
*ROC K LING
ROC K ROSE
*ROC K WEED
*ROC K WOR K
*RUC K SAC K
*SAC K LI K E
*SAC K SFUL
*SHA K EOUT
*SHA K IEST
*SHI K AREE
SIC K ENER
*SIC K ERLY
SIC K NESS
*SIC K ROOM
SIL K IEST
*SIL K LI K E
*SIL K WEED
*SIL K WORM
*SIN K HOLE
*SMO K EPOT
SNA K EBIT
SOC K LESS
SPI K ELET
STA K EOUT

STO K ESIA
*SUC K FISH
*SUC K LING
TAC K IEST
TAC K LESS
*TAC K LING
TAL K ABLE
*TAN K LI K E
*TAS K WOR K
*TEA K WOOD
*TIC K LISH
*TIC K SEED
*TIC K TAC K
*TIC K TOC K
TIN K ERER
TIN K LING
*TUC K AHOE
*TUC K SHOP
TUS K LESS
*TUS K LI K E
*VAL K YRIE
*WAL K AWAY
*WAL K OVER
*WAL K YRIE
*WEA K ENER
*WEA K FISH
*WEA K LING
*WEA K NESS
*WEA K SIDE
*WEE K LONG
*WOR K ABLE
*WOR K ADAY
*WOR K BOAT
*WOR K BOO K
*WOR K FARE
*WOR K FOL K
*WOR K LESS
*WOR K LOAD
*WOR K MATE
*WOR K SHOP
*WOR K WEE K
*ZI K KURAT

BAC K
BAL K
BAN K
BAR K
BAS K
BEA K
BEC K
BIL K
BIR K
BIS K
BOC K
BON K

BOO K
BOS K
BUC K
BUL K
BUN K
BUS K
CAL K
CAR K
CAS K
COC K
CON K
COO K
COR K
CUS K
DAN K
DAR K
DAW K
DEC K
DES K
DHA K
DIC K
DIN K
DIR K
DOC K
DOR K
DRE K
DUC K
DUS K
FEC K
FIN K
FLA K
FOL K
FOR K
FUN K
GAW K
GEC K
GEE K
GIN K
GOW K
GUC K
GUN K
HAC K
HAN K
HAW K
HEC K
HIC K
HOC K
HOL K
HON K
HOO K
HOW K
HUC K
HUL K
HUN K
HUS K

*JAC K	PIN K	YER K	DRUN K	SLEE K	TUPI K
*JAU K	POC K	YEU K	FLAC K	SLIC K	TWEA K
*JER K	POR K	YOC K	FLAN K	SLIN K	*WHAC K
*JIN K	PUC K	YOL K	FLAS K	SLUN K	*WHEL K
*JOC K	PUN K	YUC K	FLEC K	SMAC K	*WHIS K
*JOU K	RAC K	*ZER K	FLIC K	SMEE K	WRAC K
*JUN K	RAI K	*ZON K	FLUN K	SMER K	WREA K
K EC K	RAN K	BATI K	FRAN K	SMIR K	WREC K
K EE K	REC K	BAUL K	FREA K	SMOC K	WRIC K
K IC K	REE K	BLAC K	FRIS K	SNAC K	YAPO K
K IN K	RIC K	BLAN K	FROC K	SNAR K	BATTI K
K IR K	RIN K	BLEA K	GLEE K	SNEA K	*BEDEC K
K ON K	RIS K	BLIN K	GREE K	SNEC K	*BEMOC K
K OO K	ROC K	BLOC K	HACE K	SNIC K	BETOO K
*K YA K	ROO K	BRAN K	HOIC K	SNOO K	*BEYLI K
LAC K	RUC K	BREA K	K AIA K	SNUC K	*BIPAC K
LAN K	RUS K	BRIC K	*K AMI K	SPAN K	*BOHUN K
LAR K	SAC K	BRIN K	*K APO K	SPAR K	*BYTAL K
LEA K	SAN K	BRIS K	*K AYA K	SPEA K	CARAC K
LEE K	SAR K	BROC K	K IOS K	SPEC K	*CHABU K
LIC K	SEE K	BROO K	*K NAC K	SPIC K	*COPEC K
LIN K	SIC K	BRUS K	*K NOC K	SPOO K	*CROJI K
LOC K	SIL K	CAUL K	*K OPE K	SPUN K	DAMAS K
LOO K	SIN K	CHAL K	K ULA K	STAC K	DEBAR K
LUC K	SOA K	CHEE K	*K YAC K	STAL K	DEBEA K
LUN K	SOC K	*CHIC K	*MUJI K	STAN K	DEBUN K
LUR K	SOO K	CHIN K	PLAC K	STAR K	DEMAR K
MAC K	SOU K	CHIR K	PLAN K	STEA K	DETIC K
MAR K	SPI K	CHOO K	PLON K	STEE K	*DIBBU K
MAS K	SUC K	*CHOC K	PLUC K	STIC K	*DI K DI K
MEE K	SUL K	*CHUC K	PLUN K	STIN K	*DYBBU K
MER K	SUN K	CHUN K	PRAN K	STIR K	GALYA K
MIC K	TAC K	CLAC K	PRIC K	STOC K	*HIJAC K
MIL K	TAL K	CLAN K	PRIN K	STOO K	*K ALPA K
MIN K	TAS K	CLEE K	PULI K	STOR K	*K OPEC K
MIR K	TEA K	CLER K	*QUAC K	STUC K	*MEDIC K
MOC K	TIC K	CLIC K	*QUAR K	STUN K	*MOUJI K
MON K	TOO K	CLIN K	*QUIC K	SWAN K	*MU K LU K
MOS K	TRE K	CLOA K	*QUIR K	SWIN K	*MU K TU K
MUC K	TUC K	CLOC K	REIN K	TALU K	*MUZHI K
MUR K	TUR K	CLON K	SAME K	TARO K	*MUZJI K
NAR K	TUS K	CLUC K	SCUL K	THAC K	NAMLU K
NEC K	WAC K	CLUN K	SHAC K	THAN K	NUDNI K
NEU K	WAL K	CRAC K	SHAN K	THIC K	PADAU K
NIC K	WAR K	CRAN K	SHAR K	THIN K	PADOU K
NOC K	WAU K	CREA K	SHEI K	THUN K	REBEC K
NOO K	WEA K	CREE K	SHIR K	TORS K	REBOO K
PAC K	WEE K	CRIC K	SHOC K	TRAC K	RECOC K
PAI K	WIC K	CROA K	SHOO K	TRAI K	RECOO K
PAR K	WIN K	CROC K	SHUC K	TRAN K	RECOR K
PEA K	WON K	CROO K	SIAN K	TRIC K	REDOC K
PEC K	WOR K	CRUC K	S K IN K	TROA K	RELIN K
PEE K	YAC K	DRAN K	S K UL K	TROC K	RELOO K
PER K	YAN K	DRIN K	S K UN K	TRUC K	REMAR K
PIC K	YEL K	DROU K	SLAC K	TRUN K	REPAC K

REPAR K	*BITTOC K	*HATRAC K	*PADLOC K	SUNDEC K	*BUSHBUC K
REPER K	*BLAUBO K	*HAUBER K	PARTOO K	TANBAR K	*BUSYWOR K
RERAC K	*BLESBO K	*HAYCOC K	*PAYBAC K	*TIEBAC K	*CA K EWAL K
RESEE K	*BONNOC K	*HAYFOR K	*PEACOC K	TINWOR K	*CASEBOO K
RESOA K	*BOYCHI K	*HAYRAC K	*PETCOC K	TITLAR K	*CASEWOR K
RETAC K	*BULLOC K	*HAYRIC K	*PIDDOC K	*TO K AMA K	*CASHBOO K
RETOO K	*BULWAR K	*HEMLOC K	*PINWOR K	*TO K OMA K	*CHAPBOO K
REWOR K	*BURDOC K	*HENPEC K	*POLLAC K	*TOMBAC K	*CHARLOC K
*RHEBO K	BURLES K	*HILLOC K	*POLLOC K	*TOP K IC K	*CHIPMUC K
*SANJA K	*BUTTOC K	*HOGBAC K	*POTHOO K	*TOPWOR K	*CHIPMUN K
*SCHRI K	BUYBAC K	*HOMMOC K	*POTLUC K	*TRIPAC K	*CLAYBAN K
*SCHTI K	*CALPAC K	*HOPSAC K	*PREBOO K	TUSSOC K	*COALSAC K
SCREA K	*CAPROC K	*HUMMOC K	*PRECOO K	TUSSUC K	*COATRAC K
*SHLOC K	*CARRAC K	*JAYWAL K	PREDUS K	*TZADDI K	*CODEBOO K
*SHMUC K	*CARSIC K	*JUMBUC K	*PREPAC K	*WAESUC K	*COLDCOC K
SHNOO K	*CASSOC K	*K EBBOC K	*PREROC K	*WARLOC K	*COMEBAC K
SHRAN K	*CATWAL K	*K EBBUC K	PRESOA K	*WARWOR K	*COO K BOO K
SHRIE K	*CHABOU K	*K ILLIC K	*PREWOR K	*WAXWOR K	*COPYBOO K
SHRIN K	*CHAMPA K	*K ILLOC K	*PUGMAR K	*WEDLOC K	*COPYDES K
SHRUN K	*CHEWIN K	*K INFOL K	RANSAC K	*WETBAC K	*CORNHUS K
*SHTIC K	*CHIBOU K	*K OMATI K	RATFIN K	*WINNOC K	*CREWNEC K
*SQUAW K	*CHINOO K	*LAVROC K	*RECHEC K	*WRYNEC K	*CRIBWOR K
*SQUEA K	*COMATI K	*LAWBOO K	REDNEC K	*YASHMA K	*DABCHIC K
STREA K	*COSSAC K	*LEGWOR K	REITBO K	*ZADDIC K	*DATABAN K
STREE K	*COWLIC K	LENTIS K	RESPEA K	*BAC K PAC K	*DAYBREA K
STRIC K	*CUTBAC K	*LIMBEC K	RESTAC K	*BALDRIC K	*DEADLOC K
STROO K	*CUTBAN K	LOGBOO K	RESTOC K	*BALLHAW K	*DIESTOC K
STRUC K	*CUTWOR K	*MAFFIC K	RETHIN K	*BALLPAR K	*DIPSTIC K
SUSLI K	*DAGLOC K	*MAMMOC K	RETRAC K	*BAN K BOO K	*DISFROC K
TAMBA K	*DAYBOO K	*MANPAC K	*RIMROC K	*BAREBAC K	*DOMINIC K
*THWAC K	*DAYWOR K	*MATTOC K	*ROEBUC K	BARESAR K	*DOWNLIN K
TOMBA K	*DEFROC K	*MENFOL K	ROLLIC K	BASILIS K	*DOWNTIC K
TS K TS K	DERRIC K	*MIDWEE K	*ROWLOC K	*BEADWOR K	*DRAMMOC K
TUGRI K	*DIEBAC K	*MISCOO K	*RUDDOC K	*BENEDIC K	*DRAWBAC K
*YAPOC K	DORNEC K	*MIS K IC K	*RUNBAC K	*BILLHOO K	*DROP K IC K
*YASMA K	DORNIC K	*MISMAR K	*SAWBUC K	*BITSTOC K	*DUC K WALK
*ZADDI K	*FATBAC K	MISTEU K	*SCHLOC K	*BLESBUC K	*DUCTWOR K
*ZEBEC K	*FETLOC K	MISTOO K	*SCHMUC K	*BLOWBAC K	*FALLBAC K
*BANG K O K	*FINBAC K	MUDLAR K	*SCHNOO K	*BLUEBOO K	*FARMWOR K
*BANNOC K	*FINMAR K	*MUDPAC K	*SCHTIC K	*BLUEJAC K	*FASTBAC K
*BARRAC K	*FOSSIC K	*MUDROC K	*SEACOC K	*BLUETIC K	*FATSTOC K
*BASHLY K	*FUTHAR K	*MULLOC K	SEAMAR K	*BOATHOO K	*FEEDBAC K
*BAWCOC K	*FUTHOR K	MULLUS K	SEASIC K	BOBOLIN K	*FINNMAR K
BEATNI K	*FUTTOC K	*MUNTJA K	*SETBAC K	*BODYWOR K	*FIREBAC K
*BECHAL K	*GEMSBO K	NETWOR K	SHASLI K	*BONTEBO K	*FIRELOC K
*BECLOA K	*GEODUC K	*NIBLIC K	*SHYLOC K	*BOO K MARK	*FIREPIN K
*BEDROC K	GERENU K	*NITPIC K	*S K YHOO K	*BOO K RACK	*FIREWOR K
*BEDTIC K	*GIMMIC K	NONBAN K	*S K YJAC K	*BOONDOC K	*FISHHOO K
*BEFLEC K	*GORCOC K	NONBOO K	*S K YLAR K	*BOOTJAC K	*FLAPJAC K
BELLEE K	*GOSHAW K	NONPEA K	*S K YWAL K	*BOOTLIC K	*FLATWOR K
BERSER K	GUNLOC K	NONWOR K	*SOYMIL K	*BOSCHBO K	*FLYSPEC K
*BESPEA K	*GWEDUC K	NUDNIC K	SPELUN K	*BOSHVAR K	*FOOTMAR K
*BETHAN K	*HADDOC K	NUNATA K	SPUTNI K	*BOYCHIC K	*FOOTWOR K
*BETHIN K	*HAMMOC K	*NUTPIC K	SUBTAS K	*BUHLWOR K	*FOREDEC K
*BIBCOC K	*HASSOC K	*PADDOC K	*SUNBAC K	*BULLNEC K	*FORELOC K

*FOREMIL K	*HOLDBAC K	*MISTHIN K	*PREFRAN K	*SHELLAC K	*TASKWORK
*FOREPEA K	*HOMESIC K	*MOBSTIC K	*PRINCOC K	*SHERLOC K	*TEAMWOR K
*FORERAN K	*HOMEWOR K	*MOONWAL K	*PULLBAC K	*SHOEPAC K	TELEMAR K
*FORMWOR K	*HOODWIN K	*MOORCOC K	*RACKWORK	*SHOPTAL K	*TEXTBOO K
*FRETWOR K	*HUMPBAC K	*MOSSBAC K	*REAPHOO K	*SIDEKIC K	*TICKTAC K
*FULLBAC K	*HYMNBOO K	*MUCKLUC K	REATTAC K	*SIDEWAL K	*TICKTOC K
*GAMECOC K	*JOYSTIC K	NAINSOO K	*REDBRIC K	*SITZMAR K	*TIDEMAR K
*GAVELOC K	*KAZACHO K	*NEWSPEA K	*REDSHAN K	*SKEWBAC K	*TIMEWOR K
*GEMSBUC K	*KERPLUN K	*NICKNAC K	*REEDBUC K	*SKIPJAC K	*TIPSTOC K
*GIMCRAC K	*KICKBAC K	*NONBLAC K	*REEMBAR K	*SLAPJAC K	*TOMAHAW K
*GRAYBAC K	*KINSFOL K	NONSTIC K	*REFUSNI K	*SLOPWOR K	*TOWNFOL K
*GRIDLOC K	*KNAPSAC K	NOTEBOO K	RESTRUC K	*SLOTBAC K	*TRAPROC K
*GRIPSAC K	*KNEESOC K	*PACKSAC K	*RICKRAC K	*SNAPBAC K	*TUBEWOR K
*GROSBEA K	*LACEWOR K	*PASHALI K	*RINGBAR K	*SNOWBAN K	*WHITRAC K
*GUNSTOC K	*LANDMAR K	*PASSBOO K	*RINGNEC K	*SNOWPAC K	*WINDSOC K
*HACKWOR K	*LATHWOR K	*PAYCHEC K	*ROADWOR K	*SOAPBAR K	*WINGBAC K
*HAIRLOC K	*LAVEROC K	*PEACENI K	*ROCKWOR K	*SOFTBAC K	*WIREWOR K
*HALFBAC K	*LEADWOR K	*PICKLOC K	*ROLLBAC K	*SONGBOO K	*WOODCOC K
*HALFBEA K	*LIFEWOR K	*PICKWIC K	*ROORBAC K	STEENBO K	*WOODLAR K
*HALLMAR K	*LIMERIC K	*PIGSTIC K	*ROPEWAL K	STEINBO K	*WOODWOR K
*HANDBOO K	*LINKWOR K	*PINCHEC K	*RUCKSAC K	*STOPBAN K	*WOOLPAC K
*HANDPIC K	LINSTOC K	*PINPRIC K	*SALTWOR K	*STOPCOC K	*WOOLSAC K
*HANDWOR K	*LIPSTIC K	*PIROZHO K	*SANDBAN K	*STUDBOO K	*WOOLWOR K
*HARDBAC K	*LOPSTIC K	*PLAYBAC K	*SCATBAC K	*STUDWOR K	*WORDBOO K
*HARDTAC K	*LOVELOC K	*PLAYBOO K	*SEATWOR K	*SUBBLOC K	*WORKBOO K
*HATCHEC K	*LOVESIC K	*PLOWBAC K	SELAMLI K	*SUBCLER K	*WORKFOL K
*HAVELOC K	*MAVERIC K	*POCKMAR K	*SHADDOC K	*SUNBLOC K	*WORKWEE K
*HAYSTAC K	*MEGABUC K	*POLITIC K	*SHAGBAR K	*SWAYBAC K	*YARDWOR K
*HEADLOC K	*MILLWOR K	*PORTAPA K	*SHAMROC K	*TAILBAC K	*YEARHOO K
*HEADWOR K	*MINIPAR K	*POSTMAR K	*SHASHLI K	*TAMARAC K	*ZWIEBAC K
*HIGHJAC K	*MISSPEA K	*PRECHEC K	*SHELDUC K	TAMARIS K	

L

LACE	LANE	*LAZY	LEPT	LIFT	LION
LACK	LANG	LEAD	LESS	LIKE	LIRA
LACY	LANK	LEAF	LEST	LILT	LISP
LADE	LARD	LEAK	LEUD	LILY	LIST
LADY	LARI	LEAL	LEVO	LIMA	LITE
LAIC	LARK	LEAN	LEVY	LIMB	LITU
LAID	LASE	LEAP	LEWD	LIME	LIVE
LAIN	LASH	LEAR	LIAR	LIMN	LOAD
LAIR	LASS	LECH	LICE	LIMO	LOAF
LAKE	LAST	LEEK	LICH	LIMP	LOAM
LAKH	LATE	LEER	LICK	LIMY	LOAN
LAKY	LATH	LEET	LIDO	LINE	LOBE
LALL	LATI	LEFT	LIED	LING	LOBO
LAMA	LAUD	LEHR	LIEF	LINK	LOCA
LAMB	LAVA	LEND	LIEN	LINN	LOCH
LAME	LAVE	LENO	LIER	LINO	LOCI
LAMP	LAWN	LENS	LIEU	LINT	LOCK
LAND	LAZE	LENT	LIFE	LINY	LOCO

LODE	**LUTZ**	LATHI	LIANG	LIVRE	LOWSE
LOFT	**LUXE**	**LATHY**	LIARD	**LLAMA**	LOYAL
LOGE	LWEI	LAUAN	LIBEL	**LLANO**	LUCES
LOGO	**LYNX**	LAUGH	LIBER	**LOACH**	LUCID
LOGY	LYRE	LAURA	LIBRA	**LOAMY**	**LUCKY**
LOIN	LYSE	LAVER	LIBRI	LOATH	LUCRE
LOLL	LAARI	***LAXLY**	**LICHI**	LOBAR	LUDIC
LONE	LABEL	LAYER	**LICHT**	**LOBBY**	**LUFFA**
LONG	LABIA	**LAZAR**	LICIT	LOCAL	LUGER
LOOF	LABOR	**LEACH**	LIDAR	LOCUM	LUMEN
LOOK	LABRA	LEADY	LIEGE	LOCUS	**LUMPY**
LOOM	LACER	**LEAFY**	LIEVE	LODEN	LUNAR
LOON	**LACEY**	**LEAKY**	LIFER	LODGE	**LUNCH**
LOOP	LADEN	LEANT	LIGAN	LOESS	LUNET
LOOT	LADER	LEAPT	LIGER	**LOFTY**	LUNGE
LOPE	LADLE	LEARN	LIGHT	LOGAN	LUNGI
LORD	LAEVO	LEARY	**LIKED**	**LOGGY**	LUPIN
LORE	LAGAN	LEASE	LIKEN	LOGIA	LUPUS
LORN	LAGER	LEASH	LIKER	LOGOS	**LURCH**
LORY	LAHAR	LEAST	LILAC	LOLLY	LURER
LOSE	**LAICH**	LEAVE	LIMAN	LONER	LURID
LOSS	LAIGH	**LEAVY**	LIMBA	LONGE	LUSTY
LOST	LAIRD	LEBEN	LIMBI	**LOOBY**	LUSUS
LOTA	LAITH	LEDGE	LIMBO	LOOEY	LUTEA
LOTH	LAITY	**LEDGY**	**LIMBY**	LOOFA	LUTED
LOTI	**LAKED**	LEECH	LIMEN	LOOIE	LYARD
LOUD	LAKER	LEERY	LIMES	LOONY	LYART
LOUP	**LAMBY**	**LEFTY**	**LIMEY**	**LOOPY**	LYASE
LOUR	LAMED	LEGAL	LIMIT	LOOSE	**LYCEA**
LOUT	LAMER	LEGER	LINAC	LOPER	**LYCEE**
LOVE	LAMIA	LEGES	LINDY	**LOPPY**	LYING
LOWE	LANAI	**LEGGY**	LINED	LORAL	***LYMPH**
LOWN	LANCE	LEGIT	LINEN	LORAN	**LYNCH**
LUAU	**LANKY**	LEHUA	LINER	LORIS	**LYRIC**
LUBE	LAPEL	LEMAN	LINEY	LORRY	LYSIN
LUCE	LAPIN	LEMMA	LINGA	LOSEL	LYSIS
LUCK	LAPIS	LEMON	LINGO	LOSER	LYSSA
LUDE	LAPSE	LEMUR	LINGY	LOSSY	**LYTIC**
LUES	**LARCH**	LENES	LININ	LOTAH	LYTTA
LUFF	LARDY	LENIS	**LINKY**	LOTIC	LAAGER
LUGE	LAREE	LENSE	LINTY	LOTOS	LABIAL
LULL	LARES	LENTO	LINUM	LOTTE	LABILE
LULU	LARGE	LEONE	LIPID	LOTTO	**LABIUM**
LUMP	LARGO	LEPER	LIPIN	LOTUS	LABOUR
LUNA	**LARKY**	**LETCH**	**LIPPY**	LOUGH	LABRET
LUNE	LARUM	LETHE	LISLE	LOUIE	**LABRUM**
LUNG	LARVA	LETUP	LITAS	LOUIS	**LACHES**
LUNK	LASER	LEVEE	LITER	LOUPE	LACIER
LUNT	LASSO	LEVEL	LITHE	LOURY	**LACILY**
LUNY	**LATCH**	LEVER	LITHO	LOUSE	LACING
LURE	LATED	LEVIN	LITRE	LOUSY	**LACKER**
LURK	LATEN	LEWIS	LIVEN	LOVED	***LACKEY**
LUSH	LATER	**LEXIS**	LIVER	LOVER	**LACTAM**
LUST	**LATEX**	LIANA	LIVES	LOWER	**LACTIC**
LUTE	LATHE	LIANE	LIVID	**LOWLY**	LACUNA

LACUNE	LASHER	**LECHWE**	LIGNIN	LITANY	LOONEY
LADDER	LASING	LECTIN	LIGULA	**LITCHI**	LOOPER
LADDIE	LASSIE	LECTOR	LIGULE	LITHIA	*LOOSED
LADIES	LASTER	LEDGER	LIGURE	**LITHIC**	LOOSEN
LADING	LASTLY	**LEEWAY**	**LIKELY**	LITMUS	LOOSER
LADINO	LATEEN	**LEGACY**	**LIKEST**	LITTEN	LOOTER
LADLER	LATELY	LEGATE	**LIKING**	LITTER	**LOPPED**
LADRON	LATENT	LEGATO	**LIKUTA**	LITTLE	**LOPPER**
LAGEND	LATEST	LEGEND	LILIED	**LIVELY**	*LOQUAT
LAGGED	LATHER	LEGGED	**LIMBER**	**LIVERY**	**LORDLY**
LAGGER	LATIGO	LEGGIN	**LIMBIC**	LIVEST	LOREAL
LAGOON	LATINO	LEGION	**LIMBUS**	LIVIER	LORICA
LAGUNA	LATISH	LEGIST	LIMIER	**LIVING**	LORIES
LAGUNE	LATRIA	LEGMAN	LIMINA	**LIVYER**	LOSING
LAKING	LATTEN	LEGONG	LIMING	*LIZARD	LOTION
LALLAN	LATTER	LEGUME	**LIMMER**	LOADER	LOTTED
LAMBDA	LATTIN	**LEKVAR**	LIMNER	LOAFER	**LOUCHE**
LAMBER	LAUDER	LENDER	**LIMNIC**	LOANER	LOUDEN
LAMBIE	LAUNCE	**LENGTH**	**LIMPER**	LOATHE	**LOUDLY**
LAMEDH	LAUNCH	LENITY	LIMPET	LOAVES	LOUNGE
LAMELY	LAUREL	LENTEN	**LIMPID**	LOBATE	**LOUNGY**
LAMENT	**LAVABO**	LENTIC	**LIMPLY**	LOBBED	LOUVER
LAMEST	**LAVAGE**	LENTIL	**LIMPSY**	**LOBBER**	LOUVRE
LAMINA	LAVEER	LEPTON	LINAGE	LOBULE	**LOVAGE**
LAMING	**LAVING**	LESION	LINDEN	LOCALE	**LOVELY**
LAMMED	**LAVISH**	LESSEE	LINEAL	LOCATE	**LOVING**
LAMPAD	**LAWFUL**	LESSEN	LINEAR	**LOCHAN**	LOWBOY
LAMPAS	LAWINE	LESSER	LINEUP	**LOCHIA**	**LOWERY**
LANATE	**LAWING**	LESSON	LINGAM	**LOCKER**	**LOWING**
LANCER	**LAWMAN**	LETHAL	LINGER	**LOCKET**	LOWISH
LANCET	**LAWYER**	LETTED	LINGUA	**LOCKUP**	LUBBER
LANDAU	*LAXITY	LETTER	LINIER	LOCULE	**LUBRIC**
LANDER	**LAYMAN**	LEUCIN	LINING	LOCUST	LUCENT
LANELY	*LAYOFF	**LEUKON**	**LINKER**	LODGER	LUCERN
LANGUE	*LAZIED	LEVANT	**LINKUP**	LOFTER	**LUCKIE**
LANGUR	**LAZIER**	**LEVIED**	LINNET	LOGGED	LUETIC
LANNER	*LAZIES	LEVIER	LINSEY	LOGGER	LUGGED
LANOSE	*LAZILY	LEVIES	LINTEL	LOGGIA	LUGGER
LANUGO	*LAZING	**LEVITY**	LINTER	LOGIER	LUGGIE
LAPDOG	*LAZULI	*LEXEME	LINTOL	**LOGILY**	LUMBAR
LAPFUL	**LEACHY**	LIABLE	LIPASE	LOGION	**LUMBER**
LAPPED	LEADEN	LIAISE	LIPIDE	LOITER	*LUMMOX
LAPPER	LEADER	**LIBBER**	LIPOID	LOLLER	LUMPEN
LAPPET	LEAGUE	LIBIDO	**LIPOMA**	LOLLOP	**LUMPER**
LAPTOP	LEAKER	LIBLAB	**LIPPED**	LOMEIN	LUNACY
LANNER	LEALTY	**LICHEE**	**LIPPEN**	LOMENT	LUNATE
LANOUS	LEANER	**LICHEN**	**LIPPER**	LONELY	LUNGAN
LARDER	LEAPER	**LICKER**	*LIQUID	LONGAN	LUNGEE
LARDON	LEARNT	LICTOR	*LIQUOR	LONGER	LUNGER
LARIAT	LEASER	LIENAL	LISPER	**LONGLY**	LUNGYI
LARINE	**LEAVED**	LIERNE	LISSOM	LOOFAH	LUNIER
LARKER	LEAVEN	LIFTER	LISTEE	LOOKER	LUNIES
LARRUP	LEAVER	LIGAND	LISTEL	**LOOKUP**	LUNKER
*LARYNX	LEAVES	LIGASE	LISTEN		LUNULA
LASCAR	**LECHER**	LIGATE	LISTER		LUNULE

LUPINE	**LAMBERT**	LATRINE	***LEHAYIM**	**LIGNIFY**	**LITTERY**
LUPOUS	***LAMBKIN**	LATTICE	LEISTER	LIGNITE	**LITURGY**
LURDAN	**LAMBIER**	**LAUGHER**	LEISURE	LIGROIN	**LIVABLE**
LURING	LAMELLA	LAUNDER	**LEMMING**	**LIKABLE**	**LIVENER**
LURKER	**LAMMING**	**LAUNDRY**	**LEMPIRA**	**LIMACON**	LOADING
LUSTER	**LAMPERS**	**LAUWINE**	LEMURES	**LIMBATE**	LOANING
LUSTRA	**LAMPION**	***LAVROCK**	**LENGTHY**	***LIMBECK**	**LOATHER**
LUSTRE	**LAMPOON**	***LAWBOOK**	LENIENT	**LIMBIER**	**LOATHLY**
LUTEAL	**LAMPREY**	**LAWLESS**	LENSMAN	**LIMEADE**	**LOBATED**
LUTEIN	LAMSTER	**LAWLIKE**	LENTIGO	LIMIEST	**LOBBING**
LUTEUM	LANATED	**LAWSUIT**	**LENTISK**	LIMINAL	**LOBBYER**
LUTING	**LANCING**	**LAXNESS**	LENTOID	**LIMITED**	**LOBEFIN**
LUTIST	LANDING	***LAYAWAY**	LEONINE	LIMITER	LOBELIA
LUXATE	**LANDMAN**	**LAYETTE**	**LEOPARD**	LIMITES	LOBSTER
***LUXURY**	**LANDMEN**	**LAYOVER**	LEOTARD	***LIMPKIN**	**LOBWORM**
LYCEUM	**LANEWAY**	***LAZARET**	**LEPORID**	**LIMPSEY**	**LOCALLY**
LYCHEE	LANGREL	***LAZIEST**	LEPROSE	LIMULUS	**LOCATFR**
LYRATE	LANGUET	***LAZYISH**	**LEPROSY**	LINABLE	**LOCATOR**
LYRISM	LANGUID	**LEACHER**	LEPROUS	LINALOL	**LOCKAGE**
LYRIST	LANGUOR	LEADIER	LESBIAN	LINDANE	***LOCKBOX**
LYSATE	LANIARD	LEADING	**LETDOWN**	LINEAGE	***LOCKJAW**
LYSINE	**LANIARY**	**LEADMAN**	LETTING	LINEATE	**LOCKNUT**
LYSING	LANITAL	**LEADOFF**	LETTUCE	LINECUT	**LOCKOUT**
LABARUM	LANOLIN	**LEAFAGE**	LEUCINE	LINEMAN	***LOCKRAM**
LABELER	LANTANA	**LEAFIER**	LEUCITE	**LINGCOD**	**LOCOISM**
LABELLA	LANTERN	**LEAFLET**	**LEUCOMA**	LINGIER	LOCULAR
LABIATE	**LANYARD**	LEAGUER	**LEUKOMA**	LINGUAL	LOCULUS
LABORER	**LAPIDES**	**LEAKAGE**	**LEVATOR**	LINIEST	LOCUSTA
LABROID	**LAPPING**	LEANING	**LEVELER**	LINKAGE	**LODGING**
LACIEST	**LAPWING**	LEARIER	**LEVELLY**	***LINKBOY**	**LOFTIER**
LACONIC	**LARCENY**	LEARNER	**LEVERET**	LINKMAN	**LOFTILY**
***LACQUER**	LARDIER	LEASING	**LEVULIN**	LINOCUT	LOGANIA
***LACQUEY**	LARDOON	**LEATHER**	***LEXICAL**	LINSANG	**LOGBOOK**
LACTARY	LARGESS	**LEAVING**	***LEXICON**	LINSEED	LOGGATS
LACTASE	**LARGEST**	***LECHERY**	LIAISON	LINTIER	LOGGETS
LACTATE	**LARGISH**	LECTERN	LIANOID	LINURON	**LOGGING**
LACTEAL	**LARKIER**	LECTION	LIBELEE	LIONESS	**LOGICAL**
LACTEAN	**LARKISH**	LECTURE	LIBELER	LIONISE	LOGIEST
LACTONE	LASAGNA	**LEEWARD**	LIBERAL	***LIONIZE**	LOGROLL
LACTOSE	LASAGNE	**LEFTIES**	**LIBERTY**	LIPLESS	**LOGWOOD**
LACUNAR	**LASHING**	**LEFTISH**	**LIBRARY**	LIPLIKE	LOLLIES
LADANUM	**LASHINS**	**LEFTISM**	LIBRATE	LIPPING	**LONGBOW**
LADLING	**LASHKAR**	**LEFTIST**	**LICENCE**	***LIQUATE**	LONGIES
LADRONE	LASSOER	**LEGALLY**	LICENSE	***LIQUEFY**	LONGING
LADYBUG	LASTING	LEGATEE	LICENTE	***LIQUEUR**	**LONGISH**
LADYISH	LATAKIA	LEGATOR	***LICHTLY**	***LIQUIFY**	**LOOKOUT**
***LADYKIN**	**LATCHET**	LEGGIER	**LICKING**	LISENTE	LOOSEST
LAGGARD	**LATENCY**	**LEGGING**	LIDLESS	LISSOME	LOOSING
LAGGING	LATERAD	**LEGHORN**	**LIFEFUL**	LISTING	**LOPPING**
LAICISE	LATERAL	**LEGIBLE**	**LIFEWAY**	LITERAL	LORDING
LAICISM	**LATHERY**	LEGLESS	***LIFTMAN**	***LITHIFY**	**LORDOMA**
***LAICIZE**	**LATHIER**	**LEGLIKE**	***LIFTOFF**	**LITHIUM**	LORGNON
LALIAND	**LATHING**	**LEGROOM**	**LIGHTEN**	**LITHOID**	LORIMER
LAMBAST	LATICES	**LEGUMIN**	**LIGHTER**	LITORAL	LORINER
LAMBENT	LATOSOL	***LEGWORK**	**LIGHTLY**	LITOTES	**LOTTERY**

LOTTING	LABDANUM	LANCELET	LATHIEST	LEFTOVER	LIBELIST
LOUDISH	LABELLED	LANCIERS	*LATHWORK	*LEFTWARD	LIBELLED
LOUTISH	LABELLER	LANDFALL	LATINITY	*LEFTWING	LIBELLEE
LOVABLE	LABELLUM	LANDFILL	*LATINIZE	LEGALESE	LIBELLER
LOVEBUG	LABIALLY	LANDFORM	LATITUDE	LEGALISE	LIBELOUS
LOWBALL	LABIATED	LANDGRAB	LATTERLY	LEGALISM	LIBERATE
LOWBORN	LABILITY	LANDLADY	LAUDABLE	LEGALIST	LIBRETTO
LOWBRED	LABORITE	LANDLESS	LAUDANUM	LEGALITY	LICENCEE
*LOWBROW	LABOURER	LANDLINE	LAUDATOR	*LEGALIZE	LICENCER
LOWDOWN	LABRADOR	LANDLORD	LAUGHING	LEGATINE	LICENSEE
LOWLAND	LABRUSCA	*LANDMARK	LAUGHTER	LEGATING	LICENSER
LOWLIFE	LABURNUM	LANDMASS	LAUNCHER	LEGATION	LICENSOR
LOWNESS	LACELESS	LANDSIDE	LAUREATE	LEGENDRY	LICHENIN
LOYALLY	LACELIKE	*LANDSKIP	LAVALAVA	LEGERITY	*LICKSPIT
LOYALTY	LACERATE	LANDSLID	LAVALIER	LEGGIEST	LICORICE
*LOZENGE	LACERTID	LANDSLIP	*LAVALIKE	LEGGIERO	LIEGEMAN
LUCARNE	LACEWING	LANDSMAN	LAVATION	*LEKYTHOS	LIENABLE
LUCENCE	LACEWOOD	LANDWARD	LAVATORY	*LEKYTHUS	LIENTERY
LUCENCY	*LACEWORK	LANGLAUF	LAVENDER	LEMNISCI	LIFEBOAT
LUCERNE	LACINESS	LANGRAGE	*LAVEROCK	LEMONADE	LIFELESS
LUCIFER	*LACKADAY	LANGSHAN	LAVISHER	LEMURINE	*LIFELIKE
LUGGAGE	LACONISM	LANGSYNE	*LAWGIVER	LEMUROID	LIFELONG
LUGGING	LACRIMAL	LANGUAGE	*LAWMAKER	LENGTHEN	LIFETIME
LUGSAIL	LACROSSE	LANGUISH	LAXATION	LENIENCE	*LIFEWORK
LUGWORM	LACTEOUS	LANKNESS	*LAXATIVE	LENIENCY	LIFTGATE
LULLABY	LACUNOSE	LANNERET	LAYABOUT	LENITION	LIGAMENT
LUMBAGO	LADLEFUL	LANOLINE	LAYERAGE	LENITIVE	LIGATION
LUMPISH	*LADYBIRD	LANOSITY	LAYERING	LENTANDO	LIGATURE
LUNATED	*LADYFISH	LANTHORN	*LAYWOMAN	LENTICEL	*LIGHTFUL
LUNATIC	*LADYHOOD	LAPBOARD	*LAZINESS	LEPIDOTE	LIGHTING
LUNCHER	*LADYLIKE	LAPIDARY	*LAZULITE	LEPORINE	*LIGHTISH
LUNETTE	*LADYLOVE	LAPIDATE	*LAZURITE	LEPROTIC	LIGNEOUS
LUNGFUL	*LADYPALM	*LAPIDIFY	LEACHATE	LETHALLY	LIGROINE
LUNGING	*LADYSHIP	LAPIDIST	LEADIEST	*LETHARGY	LIKEABLE
LUNIEST	LAETRILE	LAPILLUS	LEADLESS	LETTERER	LIKENESS
LUPANAR	LAGNAPPE	LARBOARD	LEADSMAN	LEUCEMIA	*LIKEWISE
LUPULIN	LAITANCE	LARCENER	*LEADWORK	LEUKEMIA	LILLIPUT
LURCHER	LAKEPORT	LARDIEST	LEADWORT	*LEUKEMIC	LIMACINE
LUSTFUL	LAKESIDE	LARDLIKE	LEAFIEST	LEUKOSIS	LIMBIEST
LUSTIER	LALLYGAG	LARGANDO	LEAFLESS	LEVANTER	LIMBLESS
LUSTILY	LAMASERY	LARGESSE	*LEAFLIKE	LEVELLER	LIMEKILN
LUSTRAL	LAMBASTE	LARKIEST	*LEAFWORM	LEVERAGE	LIMELESS
LUSTRUM	*LAMBENCY	LARKSOME	LEAKLESS	LEVIABLE	*LIMERICK
LUTEOUS	LAMBIEST	LARKSPUR	LEANNESS	LEVIGATE	LIMINESS
LUTHIER	*LAMBKILL	LARRIGAN	LEAPFROG	LEVIRATE	LIMITARY
LUTHERN	*LAMBLIKE	LARRIKIN	LEARIEST	LEVITATE	LIMNETIC
*LYCHNIS	*LAMBSKIN	LARRUPER	LEARNING	LEVODOPA	LIMONENE
*LYCOPOD	LAMENESS	*LATCHKEY	LEATHERN	*LEVOGYRE	LIMONITE
LYDDITE	LAMENTER	LATEENER	LEATHERY	LEVULOSE	LIMPNESS
LYINGLY	LAMINATE	LATENESS	*LECHAYIM	LEWDNESS	LIMULOID
LYNCEAN	LAMINOSE	LATENTLY	LECITHIN	LEWISITE	LINALOOL
*LYNCHER	LAMINOUS	LATERITE	LECTURER	LEWISSON	*LINCHPIN
LYRATED	LAMISTER	*LATERIZE	*LECYTHIS	LIBATION	LINEABLE
LYRICAL	LAMPPOST	LATEWOOD	*LECYTHUS	LIBECCIO	LINEBRED
LYSOGEN	*LAMPYRID	LATHERER	LEEBOARD	LIBELANT	LINEATED

LINELESS	LOBELINE	*LONGWAYS	LUSCIOUS	C L OD	P L OP
LINELIKE	LOBLOLLY	LONGWISE	LUSHNESS	C L OG	P L OT
LINESMAN	*LOBOTOMY	*LOOKDOWN	LUSTIEST	C L ON	P L OW
LINGERER	*LOBSTICK	LOOPHOLE	LUSTRATE	C L OP	P L OY
LINGERIE	LOCALISE	LOOSENER	LUSTRING	C L OT	P L UG
LINGIEST	LOCALISM	LOPSIDED	LUSTROUS	C L OY	P L UM
LINGUINE	LOCALIST	*LOPSTICK	LUTANIST	C L UB	P L US
LINGUINI	LOCALITE	LORDLESS	LUTECIUM	C L UE	S LAB
LINGUIST	LOCALITY	LORDLIER	*LUTEFISK	F LAB	S LAG
LINIMENT	*LOCALIZE	LORDLIKE	LUTENIST	F LAG	S LAM
LINKSMAN	LOCATION	LORDLING	LUTEOLIN	F LAK	S LAP
*LINKWORK	LOCATIVE	LORDOSIS	LUTETIUM	F LAM	S LAT
LINOLEUM	*LOCKDOWN	LORDSHIP	*LUXATION	F LAN	S LAW
LINSTOCK	*LOCKSTEP	LORICATE	*LYCOPENE	F LAP	S LAY
LINTIEST	*LOCOFOCO	LORIKEET	*LYMPHOMA	F LAT	S LED
LINTLESS	LOCOMOTE	LORNNESS	*LYNCHING	F LAW	S LEW
LIONFISH	LOCOWEED	LOSINGLY	*LYNCHPIN	F LAX	S LIM
*LIONIZER	LOCULATE	LOSTNESS	*LYOPHILE	F LAY	S LIP
*LIPOCYTE	LOCUTION	LOTHARIO	LYREBIRD	F LEA	S LIT
LIPOSOME	LOCUTORY	LOTHSOME	LYRICISE	F LED	S LOB
*LIPSTICK	LODESTAR	LOUDNESS	*LYRICISM	F LEE	S LOE
*LIQUIDLY	LODGMENT	LOVEABLE	LYRICIST	F LEW	S LOG
LIRIPIPE	LODICULE	LOVEBIRD	*LYRICIZE	F LEX	S LOP
LISTENER	LOFTIEST	LOVELESS	*LYRIFORM	F LEY	S LOT
LISTLESS	LOFTLESS	LOVELIER	*LYSOGENY	F LIC	S LOW
LITERACY	LOGICIAN	LOVELIES	LYSOSOME	F LIP	S LUB
LITERARY	LOGICISE	LOVELILY	*LYSOZYME	F LIP	S LUF
LITERATE	*LOGICIZE	*LOVELOCK		F LUE	S LUG
LITERATI	LOGINESS	LOVELORN	B LAB	F LUX	S LUM
LITHARGE	LOGISTIC	*LOVESICK	B LAE	G LAD	S LUR
LITHEMIA	LOGOGRAM	LOVESOME	B LAH	G LED	S LUT
LITHOSOL	*LOGOMACH	LOVEVINE	B LAM	G LEE	B LACK
LITIGANT	LOGOTYPE	*LOVINGLY	B LAT	G LEG	B LADE
LITIGATE	*LOGOTYPY	LOWLIFER	B LAW	G LEN	B LAIN
LITTERER	LOITERER	*LOWLIGHT	B LEB	G LEY	B LAME
LITTLISH	LOLLIPOP	LOWRIDER	B LET	G LIA	B LAND
LITTORAL	LOLLYGAG	LOYALISM	B LIN	G LIB	B LANK
LIVEABLE	*LOLLYPOP	LOYALIST	B LIP	G LIM	B LARE
LIVELONG	LOMENTUM	LUBRICAL	B LOB	G LOB	B LASE
LIVENESS	LONENESS	LUCIDITY	B LOC	G LOM	B LAST
LIVERIED	LONESOME	LUCKLESS	B LOT	G LOP	B LATE
LIVERISH	LONGBOAT	LUCULENT	B LOW	G LOW	*B LAZE
LIVETRAP	LONGERON	*LUKEWARM	B LUB	G LUG	B LEAK
*LIVIDITY	LONGHAIR	LUMBERER	B LUE	G LUH	B LEED
*LIVINGLY	LONGHAND	LUMINARY	B LUR	G LUM	B LEEP
*LIXIVIUM	LONGHEAD	LUMINIST	C LAD	G LUT	B LEND
LOADSTAR	LONGHORN	LUMINOUS	C LAG	P LAN	B LENT
LOAMLESS	LONGLEAF	*LUMPFISH	C LAM	P LAT	B LESS
LOANWORD	LONGLINE	LUNARIAN	C LAN	P LAY	B LEST
LOATHFUL	LONGNESS	LUNATION	C LAP	P LEA	B LEAR
LOATHING	LONGSHIP	LUNCHEON	C LAW	P LEB	B LEAT
LOBATION	LONGSOME	*LUNGFISH	C LAY	P LED	B LIMP
*LOBBYGOW	LONGSPUR	LUNGWORM	C LEF	P LEW	B LIMY
*LOBBYISM	LONGTIME	LUNGWORT	C LEW	P LIE	B LIND
*LOBBYIST	LONGUEUR	*LUNKHEAD	C LIP	P LOD	B LINI

B L INK	C L OMP	F L UYT	P L ANE	S L OSH	BU L GER
B LISS	C L ONE	*F L YBY	P L ANK	S L OTH	BU L GUR
B LITE	C L ONK	F L YER	P L ANT	S L OYD	BU L LET
*B LITZ	C L OOT	F L YTE	P L ASH	S L UFF	BY L INE
B LOAT	C L OSE	G L ACE	P L ASM	S L UMP	CALAMI
B LOCK	C L OTH	G L ADE	P L ATE	S L UNG	CA L ASH
B LOKE	C L OUD	G L ADY	P L ATY	S L UNK	CA L CAR
B LOND	C L OUR	G L AIR	P L AYA	S L URB	CA L CES
B LOOD	C L OUT	G L AND	*P L AZA	S L URP	CA L CIC
B LOOM	C L OVE	G L ANS	P L EAD	S L USH	CA L ESA
B LOOP	C L OWN	G L ARE	P L EAT	S L YPE	CA L ICO
B LOWN	*C L OZE	G L ARY	P L EBE	BA L ATA	CA L IPH
B LOWY	C L UCK	G L ASS	P L ENA	BA L BOA	CA L KER
B LUER	C L UMP	*G L AZE	P L ICA	BA L DLY	CA L KIN
B LUET	C L UNG	*G L AZY	P L IED	BA L EEN	CAL L AN
B LUEY	C L UNK	G L EAM	P L IER	BA L KER	CAL L ER
B LUFF	F L ACK	G L EAN	P L IES	BAL L AD	CAL L ET
B LUMP	F L AIL	G L EBA	P L INK	BAL L ER	CAL L OW
B LUNT	F L AIR	G L EBE	P L ONK	BAL L ET	CAL L US
B LURB	F L AKE	G L EDE	P L UCK	BAL L ON	CA L ORY
B LURT	*F L AKY	G L EED	P L UMB	BAL L OT	CA L PAC
B LUSH	F L AME	G L EEK	P L UME	BA L SAM	CA L VES
B LYPE	F L AMY	G L EET	P L UMP	BE L ADY	CE L ERY
C L ACH	F L ANK	G L IAL	P L UMY	BE L AUD	CE L IAC
C L ACK	F L ARE	G L IDE	P L UNK	BE L DAM	CE L LAR
C L ADE	F L ASH	G L IFF	P L USH	BE L EAP	CI L ICE
C L AIM	F L ASK	G L IME	P L YER	BE L FRY	CI L IUM
C L AMP	F L AWY	G L OAM	S L ACK	BE L IED	COLDLY
C L ANG	*F L AXY	G L OAT	S L AIN	BE L IEF	CO L EAD
C L ANK	F L EAM	G L OBE	S L AKE	BE L IER	CO L EUS
C L ARO	F L ECK	G L OGG	S L ANG	BE L IES	CO L LAR
C L ARY	F L EER	G L OOM	S L ANK	BE L IKE	CO L LET
C L ASH	F L EET	G L ORY	S L ANT	BE L IVE	CO L LIE
C L ASP	F L ESH	G L OSS	S L ASH	BE L LOW	CO L LOP
C L ASS	F L ICK	G L OST	S L ATE	BE L ONG	CO L ONE
C L AST	F L IED	G L OUT	S L ATY	BE L TER	CO L ONI
C L AVI	F L IER	G L OVE	S L EEK	BE L UGA	CO L ONY
C L EAN	F L IES	*G L OZE	S L EEP	BI L BOA	CO L OUR
C L EAR	F L ING	G L UER	S L EET	BI L KER	CO L TER
C L EEK	F L INT	G L UEY	S L EPT	BIL L ER	CO L UGO
C L EFT	F L OUR	G L UON	S L ICE	BIL L ET	CO L URE
C L EPE	F L OUT	G L YPH	S L ICK	BIL L IE	CU L LAY
C L ERK	F L OWN	K L ONG	S L IDE	BIL L ON	CU L LER
C L ICK	F L UFF	K L OOF	S L IER	BI L LOW	CU L LET
C L IFF	F L UID	K L UGE	S L ILY	BO L ERO	CU L LIS
C L IFT	F L UKE	*K L UTZ	S L IME	BO L ETE	CU L TCH
C L IMB	*F L UKY	L L AMA	S L IMY	BO L IBE	CU L TIC
C L IME	F L UME	L L ANO	S L ING	*BO L LIX	CU L TUS
C L INE	F L UMP	P L ACE	S L INK	*BO L LOX	CU L VER
C L ING	F L UNG	P L ACK	S L IPE	BO L SHY	DALASI
C L INK	F L UNK	P L AGE	S L IPT	BO L TER	DA L EDH
C L IPT	F L UOR	P L AID	S L OID	BU L BEL	DA L ETH
C L OAK	F L USH	P L AIN	S L OJD	BU L BIL	DAL L ES
C L OCK	F L UTE	P L AIT	S L OOP	BU L BUL	DAL TON
C L OMB	F L UTY		S L OPE		DE L EAD

DE L ETE	GA L ERE	**HO L ILY**	MIL LET	**PIL LOW**	SA L AAM
DE L ICT	GAL LET	**HO L ING**	**MIL NEB**	PIL OSE	SA L AMI
DE L IME	**GA L LEY**	**HO L ISM**	MIL ORD	PIL OUS	SA L ARY
DE L IST	GAL LON	HOL IST	MIL TER	PIL ULE	**SA L IFY**
DE L UDE	GAL LOP	HOL LER	MOL DER	POL DER	SA L INA
DE L UGE	GAL LUS	HOL LOA	MOL EST	***PO L EAX**	SA L INE
DE L UXE	GA L ORE	HOL LOO	MOL INE	POL EIS	SA L IVA
DE L VER	**GAL OSH**	**HOL LOW**	MOL LIE	**PO L EYN**	SA L LET
D I LATE	**GA L YAK**	**HOL PEN**	MOL TEN	**PO L ICE**	SA L LOW
DIL L ED	GELADA	HUL LER	MOL TER	**PO L ICY**	SA L MON
DO L LAR	GELANT	HUL LOA	MUL ETA	POL ING	SA L OON
DO L LOP	GEL ATE	***JA L OPY**	MUL ING	**PO L ISH**	SA L OOP
DO L MAN	GELATI	**JIL TER**	MUL LAH	POL ITE	SA L PID
DO L MEN	GELATO	**JO L TER**	MUL LER	**PO L ITY**	SA L TER
DO L OUR	GEL DER	KA L IAN	MUL LET	POL LEE	SA L TIE
DU L CET	GEL L ED	***KA L IPH**	NEL LIE	POL LEN	**SA L UKI**
FA L CES	GIL DER	KA L IUM	NEL SON	POL LER	SA L UTE
FA L CON	GIL LER	KAL MIA	NIL GAI	***PO L LEX**	SA L VER
FAL LAL	GIL LIE	KA L ONG	NIL GAU	**PO L YPI**	SA L VIA
FAL LEN	GOL DEN	***KA L PAK**	NUL LAH	PUL LER	SA L VOR
FAL LER	**GOL FER**	KEL OID	**PA L ACE**	PUL LET	SC L AFF
FA L LOW	**GOL OSH**	**KEL PIE**	PAL AIS	**PUL LEY**	SC L ERA
FAL SIE	GUL LET	KEL SON	PAL ATE	**PUL LUP**	SE L DOM
FAL TER	**GUL LEY**	**KEL TER**	**PALE LY**	**PUL PAL**	SE L ECT
FE L INE	GUL PER	**KEL VIN**	PAL EST	**PUL PER**	SE L LER
FE L LAH	HALALA	KIL LER	**PA L ISH**	**PUL PIT**	SE L SYN
FEL LER	HALATE	KIL LIE	PAL LED	***PUL QUE**	SE L VES
FE L LOW	**HA L IDE**	KIL TER	PAL LOR	PUL SAR	**SH L EPP**
FE L ONY	**HA L ING**	**KIL TIE**	PAL LET	PUL SER	***SH L OCK**
FIL IAL	HALITE	***KO L HOZ**	PAL LIA	RAL LYE	**SH L UMP**
FIL LER	**HAL LAH**	***KO L KOZ**	PAL LID	RE LACE	SI L AGE
FIL LET	HAL LEL	KUL TUR	PAL MAR	RE LATE	SI L ANE
FIL L IP	HAL LOA	LAL LAN	**PAL MAR**	RE LAUR	SI L ENI
FIL MER	HAL LOO	LIL IED	**PAL MER**	RE LEND	SI L ENT
FIL MIC	HAL LOT	LOL LER	**PAL PAL**	RE LENT	SI L ICA
FIL OSE	**HA L LOW**	LOL LOP	**PAL PUS**	RE LEVE	**SI L KEN**
FIL TER	***HA L LUX**	MAL ATE	PAL TER	RE LICT	SI L LER
*FIL THY	**HA L OID**	MAL GRE	**PAL TRY**	RE LIED	SI L VAN
FO L ATE	HAL TER	MAL IGN	PEL AGE	RE LIEF	SI L VER
FO L DER	***HA L UTZ**	MAL INE	PEL ITE	RE LIER	SO L ACE
FO L IAR	***HA L VAH**	MAL LEE	PEL LET	RE LIES	SO L AND
FO L IUM	**HAL VES**	MAL LEI	**PEL MET**	RE LINE	SO L ANO
FO L KIE	HEL IAC	MAL LET	PELOTA	**RE LINK**	SO L ATE
*FO L KSY	**HEL IUM**	MALOTI	PEL TER	RE LISH	SO L DAN
FOL LES	HEL LER	MALTED	**PEL TRY**	RE LIST	SO L DER
FOL LIS	**HEL MET**	MALTOL	**PEL VIC**	RE LIVE	SO L ELY
FO L LOW	**HEL PER**	MEL DER	**PEL VIS**	RE LOAD	SO L EMN
FUL FIL	HIL LER	MEL OID	**PH L EGM**	RE LOAN	SO L EUS
FUL GID	HIL LOA	MEL TER	**PH L OEM**	**RE LOOK**	SO L GEL
FUL LAM	**HO L ARD**	MEL TON	**PIL AFF**	RE LUCT	SO L IDI
FUL LER	**HO L DEN**	MIL ADI	PIL EUM	RE LUME	SO L ING
FUL MAR	**HO L DER**	MIL AGE	PIL EUP	RIL LET	SO L ION
GALAGO	**HO L DUP**	MIL DEN	PIL EUS	ROL FER	SO L UTE
*GA L AXY	HOL IER	MIL IEU	**PIL FER**	ROL LER	SO L VER
GALENA	HOL IES	MIL LER	PIL ING	RU LING	SP L AKE
			PIL LAR		

SPLASH	VALVAR	BALDRIC	BULLISH	CHLORIN	DILUTER
SPLEEN	VELATE	BALEFUL	*BULLOCK	CILIARY	DILUTOR
SPLENT	VELLUM	BALLADE	BULLOUS	CILIATE	DILUVIA
SPLICE	VELOCE	BALLAST	BULLPEN	COLDISH	DOLEFUL
SPLINE	VELOUR	BALLIES	BULRUSH	COLICIN	DOLLIED
SPLINT	VELURE	BALLING	*BULWARK	*COLICKY	DOLLIES
SPLORE	VELVET	BALLOON	BYLINER	COLITIS	DOLLING
SPLOSH	VILLUS	BALLUTE	CALAMAR	COLLAGE	DOLLISH
SULCUS	VOLANT	BALNEAL	CALAMUS	COLLARD	DOLPHIN
SULDAN	VOLERY	BALONEY	CALANDO	COLLATE	*DULCIFY
SULFID	VOLLEY	BELABOR	CALCINE	COLLECT	DULLARD
SULFUR	VOLOST	BELACED	CALCIUM	COLLEEN	DULLISH
SULKER	VOLUTE	BELATED	CALDERA	COLLEGE	DULNESS
SULLEN	*VOLVOX	BELCHER	CALDRON	COLLIDE	FALAFEL
SULPHA	VULGAR	BELDAME	CALECHE	COLLIED	FALBALA
SULTAN	VULGUS	BELIEVE	CALENDS	COLLIER	FALCATE
SULTRY	WALING	BELLBOY	CALIBER	COLLIES	*FALLACY
SYLVAN	WALKER	BELLEEK	CALIBRE	COLLINS	*FALLOFF
SYLVIN	*WALKUP	BELLHOP	CALICES	COLLOID	FALLOUT
TALCUM	WALLAH	BELLMAN	CALICHE	COLLUDE	*FALSIFY
TALENT	WALLET	BELOVED	CALICLE	COLOBUS	FALSITY
TALION	WALLIE	BELTING	CALIPEE	COLOGNE	FELAFEL
TALKER	WALLOP	BELYING	CALIPER	COLONEL	FELLATE
TALKIE	WALLOW	BILAYER	CALLANT	COLONIC	FELLIES
TALLIS	WALNUT	BILIARY	CALLBOY	COLONUS	FELONRY
TALLIT	WALRUS	BILIOUS	CALLING	COLORED	FELSITE
TALLOL	WELDER	BILLBUG	CALLOSE	COLORER	FELSPAR
TALLOW	WELDOR	BILLIES	CALLOUS	COLUMEL	FELTING
TALUKA	WELKIN	BILLING	CALOMEL	CULICID	FELUCCA
TELEDU	WELLIE	BILOBED	CALORIC	CULLIED	FELWORT
TELEGA	WELTER	BILSTED	CALORIE	CULLIES	FILAREE
TELFER	WILDER	BILTONG	CALOTTE	CULLION	FILARIA
TELIAL	WILDLY	BOLETUS	CALOYER	CULOTTE	FILBERT
TELIUM	WILFUL	BOLIVAR	*CALPACK	CULPRIT	*FILCHER
TELLER	WILIER	BOLIVIA	CALTRAP	CULTISH	FILEMOT
TELOME	WILILY	BOLLARD	CALTROP	CULTISM	FILIATE
TELSON	WILING	BOLOGNA	CALUMET	CULTIST	FILIBEG
TILLER	WILLER	BOLONEY	CALUMNY	CULTURE	FILLIES
TILTER	WILLET	BOLSHIE	*CALVARY	CULVERT	FILLING
TOLANE	WILLOW	BOLSTER	CALYCES	DALAPON	*FILMDOM
TOLEDO	WOLFER	BULBLET	CALYCLE	DALLIER	FILMIER
TOLLER	WOLVER	BULBOUS	CALYPSO	DELAINE	*FILMILY
TOLUIC	WOLVES	BULIMIA	*CALZONE	DELATOR	FILMSET
TOLUID	*XYLENE	BULIMIC	CELADON	DELAYER	FOLACIN
TOLUOL	*XYLOID	BULKAGE	CELESTA	DELEAVE	FOLDOUT
TOLUYL	*XYLOSE	BULLACE	CELESTE	DELIGHT	FOLIAGE
TULADI	YCLEPT	BULLBAT	CELLIST	DELIMIT	FOLIATE
VALGUS	YELLER	BULLDOG	CELLULE	DELIVER	FOLIOSE
VALINE	YELLOW	BULLIED	CELOSIA	DELOUSE	FOLIOUS
VALISE	YELPER	BULLIES	*CHLAMYS	*DELPHIC	*FOLKISH
VALLEY	*ZILLAH	BULLION	CHLORAL	DELTOID	*FOLKMOT
VALOUR	BALANCE		CHLORIC	DELUDER	*FOLKWAY
VALUER	BALCONY		CHLORID	DILATER	FOLLIES
VALUTA	BALDIES			DILATOR	FULCRUM
VALVAL	BALDISH			DILUENT	FULFILL

FU L GENT	*HA L LWAY	*KI L LJOY	MU L LEIN	PO LEMIC	SAL LIER
FU L LERY	HA LOGEN	*KO LACKY	MU L LION	PO LENTA	SAL LIES
FU L MINE	HA L VERS	KO L BASI	MU L LITE	PO LITIC	SAL LOWY
FU L NESS	HA L VING	*KO L KHOS	*MU L LOCK	*PO L LACK	SAL PIAN
FU L SOME	HA L YARD	*KO L KHOZ	MU LTURE	PO L LARD	*SA L PINX
FU L VOUS	HE LIAST	LA L LAND	NE LUMBO	POL LIST	SAL SIFY
GA LABIA	HE LICAL	LO L LIES	NIL GHAI	PO L LUTE	SALTANT
GA LATEA	HE LICES	LU L LABY	NIL GHAU	PO LOIST	*SA LTBOX
GA LILEE	HE LICON	MA LACCA	NUL LIFY	PO LYCOT	SAL TERN
GA LIPOT	HE LIPAD	MA LAISE	NUL LITY	PO LYENE	SAL TIER
GA L LANT	*HE L LBOX	MA LAMUT	NY L GHAI	PO LYGON	SALTILY
GA L LATE	HE L LCAT	MA LANGA	NY L GHAU	PO LYMER	SAL TINE
GA L LEIN	HE L LERI	MA LAPER	PA LABRA	*PO LYNYA	SAL TING
GA L LEON	HE L LERY	MA LAPRO	PA LADIN	PO LYOMA	SAL TIRE
GA L LERY	HE L LISH	MA LARIA	PA LATA L	*PO LYPOD	SAL TISH
GA L LETA	HE L LUVA	*MA LARKY	PA LAVER	*PO LYPOD	SAL TPAN
GA L LFLY	HE LOTRY	MA LAROM	*PA LAZZO	PO LYPUS	SAL UTER
GA L LIOT	*HE L PFUL	MA LEATE	PA LETOT	PUL LING	SAL VAGE
GA L LIUM	HE L PING	MA LEDIC	PA LETTE	PUL LMAN	SAL VING
GA L LNUT	HI L DING	MA LEMIU	PA LIEST	PUL LOUT	SE LENIC
GA L LOON	HI L LIER	MA LEMUT	PA LIKAR	PUL PIER	SE LFDOM
GA L LOOT	*HI L LOCK	MA LENES	PAL LIA L	PULPILY	SE LFISH
GA L LOUS	HI L LTOP	MA LIGNE	PAL LIER	PUL SANT	SEL LOUT
GA L LOWS	HO LDAL L	MA LIGN L	PA L LING	PUL SATE	*SE L TZER
GA L LYAC	HO L DING	MA LIHIN	PAL LIUM	PUL SING	SE LVAGE
GA LOSHE	HO L DOUT	MA LINGE	PA L MARY	PUL SION	*SH LUMPY
*GA LUMPH	HO L IBUT	MA LISON	PA L MATE	PY LORUS	SiL ENCE
GE LATIN	HO LIDAY	MA L LEUS	PA L MIER	RA L LIED	SIL ENTS
GE L DING	HO LIEST	MA L POSE	PA L MIST	RA L LIER	SIL ENUS
GE L LANT	HO L LAND	MA LTASE	PA L MYRA	RA L LINE	SIL ICLE
GE L LING	HO L LIES	MA LTIER	PA LOOKA	RE LABEL	SiL ICON
GI L BERT	HO L MIUM	MA LTIES	PA L PATE	RE LAPSE	SIL URID
GI L DING	HO L STER	MA LTOSE	PA LSHIP	RE LATER	SIL VERN
GI L LNET	*HO L YDAY	ME LAMED	PA LUDA L	RE LATOR	SIL VERY
GO L DARN	*JA LAPIN	ME LANIN	PE LAGIC	RE LAXIN	SIL VICS
GO L DBUG	*JA LOPPY	MELILIT	PE LICAN	RE LEARN	SI L ESIA
GO L DEYE	*JE L LABA	MELILOT	PE LISSE	RE LEASE	*SI L IQUA
GO L DURN	*JE L LIFY	ME LINIT	PE LORIA	RE LIANT	*SI L IQUE
GO L FING	JIL LION	ME LODIC	PE LORUS	RE LIEVE	SO LACER
GO LIARD	*JO L LIED	ME LODIE	PE LTAST	RE LIEVO	SO LANIN
GO L OSHE	JO L LIER	*MIL CHIG	PE LTATE	RE LIGHT	SO LANUM
GU L FIER	JO L LIES	*MIL DEWY	*PH L EGMY	*RE LIQUE	SO LARIA
*HA LACHA	*JO L LIFY	MIL FOIL	PI LEATE	RI LIEVO	SO LATIA
*HA LAKHA	*JO L LITY	MILITIA	PI LEOUS	RI L LING	SO L DIER
*HA LAKIC	KA LENDS	*MILKILY	PI LGRIM	RO L LICK	SO LERET
HA LA LAH	*KA L IMBA	*MILKMAN	PI L LAGE	RO L LING	SO L FEGE
*HA LAVAH	KIL LDEE	*MILKSOP	*PIL LBOX	RO L LMOP	SO LICIT
HA L BERD	KIL LING	MIL LIER	PIL LION	ROL LOUT	SO LIDLY
HA L BERT	*KI L LOCK	MIL LINE	PI L LORY	ROL LTOP	SO LIDUS
*HA L CYON	KI LOBAR	MIL LION	*PI L LOWY	RO L LWAY	SO LITON
*HA L FWAY	KI LOBIT	MIL LRUN	PI LSNER	SALABLE	SO LOIST
HA LIBUT	KI LORAD	MIL REIS	PO LARON	*SA L CHOW	SO LUBLE
HA LIDOM	KI LOTON	MOL LIES	*PO LEAXE	SA LICIN	SO LUBLY
HA LITUS	KI L TING	*MOL LIFY	PO LECAT	SA LIENT	SO LVATE
HA L LOTH	*KI L LICK	MU LATTO	PO LECAT	SAL LIED	SO LVENT

SO L VING	TO L LMAN	WI L LIES	CA L AMARI	*FU L LBACK	MI L DNESS
*SP L ASHY	TO L LWAY	WI L LING	CA L DARIA	*FU L LFACE	MI L EPOST
SP L EENY	TO L UATE	*WI L LOWY	CA L ENDAL	FU L LNESS	MI L ESIMO
SP L ENIA	TO L UENE	*WO L FISH	CA L LALOO	GA L ABIYA	MI L IARIA
SP L ENIC	TO L UIDE	*WO L FRAM	*CAL LBACK	GA L ANGAL	MI L ITANT
SP L ICER	TO LUO LE	*XY L IDIN	CA L LIPEE	GA L LERIA	MI L ITARY
SP L ODGE	TY L OSIN	*XY L ITOL	CA L LIPER	GA L LIARD	MI L ITATE
SP L OTCH	VA L ANCE	*YC L EPED	*CA L ORIZE	GA L LOPER	MI L KIEST
SP L URGE	VA L ENCE	*YE L LOWY	*CA L OTYPE	GE L ATING	*MI L KSHED
SP L URGY	*VA L ENCY	*ZE L KOVA	*CA L YCEAL	GIL DHA L L	*MIL LCAKE
SU L CATE	VA L IANT	*ZI L LION	CE L LARER	GO L LIWOG	MI L LEPED
SU L FATE	VA L IDLY	BA L LGAME	CE L LARET	*GOL LYWOG	MI L LIARD
SU L FIDE	VA L LATE	*BAL LHAWK	CE L LMATE	GUL LABLE	MI L LIARE
SU L FITE	VA L ONIA	BA L LISTA	CE L LULAR	GUL LIBLE	MI L LIARY
SU L FONE	VA L UATE	BA L LONET	*CO L DCOCK	*HA L AZONE	MI L LIBAR
SU L FURY	VA L VATE	BA L LONNE	CO L EADER	HA L LIARD	MI L LIEME
SU L LAGE	VA L VULA	BA L LOTER	CO L LAGEN	*HAL LMARK	MI L LIGA L
SU L PHID	VA L VULE	*BA L LPARK	CO L LAPSE	HAL LOWER	MI L LIGA L
SU L PHUR	VE L AMEN	BA L LROOM	CO L LARET	HE L IACAL	*MIL LILUX
SU L TANA	VE L IGER	*BAL LYHOO	CO L LEGER	HE L ILIFT	*MIL LIMHO
SY L LABI	VE L ITES	BA L LYRAG	CO L LEGIA	HE L LBENT	MI L LINER
*SY L PHID	VE L OUTE	BA L MORAL	CO L LIDER	*HEL LKITE	*MIL LIOHM
SY L VINE	VI L AYET	BE L LBIRD	CO L LIERY	HIL LIEST	MI L LIPED
SY L VITE	VI L LAGE	BE L LOWER	CO L LOGUE	HIL LSIDE	MI L LIREM
TA L ARIA	VI L LAIN	BE L LPULL	*COL LOQUY	*HOL OGAMY	MI L LPOND
TA L IFED	VI L LEIN	BE L LWORT	CO L LUDER	*JA L APENO	MI L LRACE
TA L IPES	*VI L LIFY	*BE L LYFUL	CO L LUVIA	*JO L LIEST	*MIL LWORK
TA L IPOT	VO L ANTE	BI L ABIAL	CO L LYRIA	KA L LIDIN	MO L ALITY
TA L KING	VO L CANO	BI L LETER	CO L OBOMA	KIL LDEER	MO L ARITY
TA L LAGE	VO L LIME	*BI L LFISH	CO L ONIAL	KI L OBASE	MO L ASSES
TA L LBOY	VO L TAGE	BI L LFOLD	CO L ORFUL	*KILOBAUD	MO L DIEST
TA L LIED	VO L UBLE	BI L LHEAD	*CO L ORIZE	*KI L OBYTE	MO L ECULE
TA L LIER	VO L UTIN	*BI L LHOOK	CO L ORMAN	KO L BASSI	MO L EHILL
TA L LIES	VU L GATE	BI L LIARD	CO L OSSAL	LA L LYGAG	MO L ESKIN
TA L LISH	VU L PINE	*BI L LYCAN	CU L TURAL	LIL LIPUT	MO L ESTER
TA L LITH	VU L TURE	*BO L LOCKS	DE L OUSER	LOL LIPOP	MU L ETEER
TA L LOWY	*WA L KING	*BOL LWORM	DI L UVIAL	LOL LYGAG	MU L LIGAN
TA L LYHO	WA L KOUT	BO L THOLE	DU L LNESS	*LOL LYPOP	MU L TIAGE
TA L OOKA	*WA L KWAY	*BU L LDOZE	FA L DERAL	MA L LEOLI	MU L TICAR
TE L AMON	WA L LABY	BU L LETIN	FA L DEROL	MA L TREAT	MU L TIFID
TE L EMAN	WA L LEYE	BU L LFROG	*FA L LAWAY	MA L TSTER	MU L TIPED
TE L EOST	WA L LIES	BU L LHEAD	*FAL LBACK	MA L VASIA	*MU L TIPLY
TE L ERAN	*WA L TZER	BU L LHORN	*FAL LFISH	ME L AMINE	MU L TITON
TE L ESIS	*WE L CHER	BU L LIEST	FAL L LIKE	ME L ANIAN	MU L TIUSE
TE L FORD	WE L COME	*BUL LNECK	*FE L DSHER	ME L ANISM	MY L ONITE
TEL L IES	WE L FARE	BU L LNOSE	FE L LABLE	ME L ANITE	PA L ATIAL
TE L PHER	WE L LIES	BU L LPOUT	FE L LATOR	ME L ANOID	*PA L AZZOS
TI L APIA	WE L SHER	BU L LRING	FE L LNESS	ME L ANOMA	PA L EOSOL
TI L LAGE	WE L TING	BU L LRUSH	*FEL LOWLY	ME L ANOUS	*PA L IMONY
TI L LING	WI L DCAT	BU L LSHIT	*FE L TLIKE	*ME L LIFIC	PA L LADIA
TI L LITE	WI L DING	BU L LSHOT	FO L DEROL	ME L ODEON	PA L LADIC
TO L IDIN	WI L DISH	BU L LWEED	FO L LICLE	ME L ODICA	PA L LIATE
TO L LAGE	WI L IEST	*BU L LWHIP	FO L LOWER	ME L ODIST	PA L LIEST
TO L LBAR	WI L LFUL	*BUL LYBOY		ME L TDOWN	PE L LAGRA
TO L LING	WI L LIED	BUL LYRAG			

PEL LETAL	VOL LEYER	DOL LOV	MOB LED	WAL LOW	COL LEEN
PEL LICLE	WAL LAROO	FAL LAL	MOL LIE	WEL LIE	COL LEGE
PEL LMELL	WAL LOPER	FAL LEN	MUL LEN	WIL LER	COL LIDE
PEL LUCID	WAL LOWER	FAL LER	MUL LER	WIL LET	COL LIED
PILE LESS	*WEL LADAY	FA LLOW	MUL LET	WIL LOW	COL LIER
POL LINIA	*WEL LAWAY	FE LLAH	NEL LIE	WOO LED	COL LIES
POL LINIC	WEL LBORN	FE LLER	NUL LAH	YEL LER	COL LIMN
POL LIWOG	*WEL LCURB	FIL LER	PAB LUM	YEL LOW	COL LINS
POL LSTER	WEL LDOER	FIL LET	PAL LED	*ZIL LAH	COL LOID
*PO LL YWOG	*WEL LHEAD	FIL LIP	PAL LET	BAL LADE	COL LUDE
*PUL LBACK	WEL LHOLE	FOL LES	PAL LIA	BAL LAST	CUL LIED
PUL LOVER	WEL LNESS	FO LLIS	PAL LID	BAL LIES	CUL LIES
PULPOLIS	WEL LSITE	FOL LOW	PAL LOR	BAL LING	CUL LION
RAL LYING	*WILDFOWL	FUL LAM	PEL LET	BAL LOON	*CYC LERY
RAL LYIST	WILDLAND	FUL LER	PHY LLO	BAL LUTE	DAL LIER
RE LIABLY	WIL LIWAU	GAL LET	PIL LAR	BEL LBOY	DOL LIED
ROL LAWAY	*WIL LIWAW	GAL LEY	PIL LOW	BEL LEEK	DOL LIES
*ROL LBACK	WIL LOWER	GAL LON	POL LEE	BEL LHOP	DOL LING
*ROL LICKY	*WIL LYARD	GAL LOP	POL LEN	BEL LMAN	DOL LISH
ROL LOVER	*WIL LYWAW	GAL LUS	POL LER	BIB LIST	DRY LAND
SE LFHEAL	BAL LAD	GEL LED	*POL LEX	BIL LBUG	DUL LARD
SH LEMIEL	BAL LER	GIL LER	PUL LER	BIL LIES	DUL LISH
SI LICIER	BAL LET	GIL LIE	PUL LET	BIL LING	*FAL LACY
SI LICILY	BAL LON	GUL LET	PUL LEY	BIL LION	*FAL LOFF
SI LICULA	BAL LOT	GUL LEY	PUL LUP	*BOIL OFF	FAL LOUT
SIL LABUD	BE LLOW	HAL LAH	RAL LYE	BOL LARD	FEL LATE
SIL LIBUB	BIL LER	HAL LEL	REP LOT	*BOWL FUL	FEL LIES
SI LVICAL	BIL LET	HAL LOA	RIL LET	BRA LESS	FEN LAND
SO LATION	BIL LIE	HAL LOO	ROL LER	BUL LACE	FIL LIES
SOL LERET	BIL LON	HAL LOT	SAL LET	BUL LATE	FIL LING
SP LENIAL	BIL LOW	HAL LOW	SAL LOW	BUL LBAT	FLY LESS
SP LURGER	*BOL LIX	*HAL LUX	SEL LER	BUL LDOG	FOL LIES
SU LFINYL	*BOL LOX	HEL LER	SHA LEY	BUL LIED	FUL LERY
SU LFONAL	BUL LET	HIL LER	SHE LTA	BUL LIER	GAL LANT
SU LFONYL	CAL LAN	HIL LOA	SIA LID	BUL LIES	GAL LATE
SU LFURYL	CAL LER	HOL LER	SIL LER	BUL LION	GAL LEIN
*SY LLABIC	CAL LET	HOL LOA	SKY LIT	BUL LISH	GAL LEON
SY LLABLE	CA LLOW	HOL LOO	SMI LEY	*BUL LOCK	GAL LERY
*SY LLABUB	CAL LUS	HUL LER	SUB LOT	BUL LOUS	GAL LETA
SY LLABUS	CAP LET	HUL LOA	SUL LEN	BUL LPEN	GAL LFLY
TA LLNESS	CHAL LA	KIL LER	TAL LIS	BUS LOAD	GAL LIOT
TA LLYMAN	COL LAR	KIL LIE	TAL LIT	CAB LING	GAL LIUM
TE LEPATH	COL LET	LAL LAN	TAL LOL	CAL LANT	GAL LNUT
TE LESTIC	COL LIE	LIB LAB	TAL LOW	CAL LBOY	GAL LOON
*TE LETEXT	COL LOP	LOL LER	TEL LER	CAL LING	GAL LOOT
TE LLTALE	COO LTH	LOL LOP	TIL LER	CAL LOSE	GAL LOUS
TE LLURIC	CUL LAY	MAG LEV	TOL LER	CAL LOUS	GAL LOWS
TO LLGATE	CUL LER	MAL LEE	VAL LEY	CEL LIST	GAL LYAC
TU LLIBEE	CUL LET	MAL LEI	VEL LUM	CEL LULE	GEL LANT
*VA LKYRIE	CUL LIS	MAL LET	VIL LUS	CHO LENT	GEL LING
VE LLEITY	DAL LES	MER LOT	VOL LEY	COA LIER	GIL LNET
VIL LADOM	DIL LED	MIL LER	WAL LAH	COL LAGE	GUY LINE
VIL LAGER	DOL LAR	MIL LET	WAL LET	COL LARD	GYP LURE
VIL LAINY			WAL LIE	COL LATE	HAL LOTH
VIL LATIC			WAL LOP	COL LECT	*HAL LWAY

*HEL L BOX	PIG L IKE	TAL L IES	*BEF L OWER	CHE L ATOR	DIA L LIST
HEL L CAT	PIL L AGE	TAL L ISH	BEG L AMOR	*CHE L IPED	DIA L OGER
HEL L ERI	*PIL L BOX	TAL L ITH	BEL L BIRD	*CHI L DBED	DIA L OGIC
HEL L ERY	PIL L ION	TAL L OWY	BEL L OWER	*CHI L DING	DIA L OGUE
HEL L ISH	PIL L ORY	TEA L IKE	BEL L PULL	*CHI L DISH	DIA L YSER
HEL L UVA	*PIL L OWY	TEL L IES	BEL L WORT	CHI L DREN	DIA L YSIS
HIL L IER	POD L IKE	TIE L ESS	BES L AVED	CHI L IASM	DIA L YTIC
*HIL L OCK	*POL L ACK	TIL L AGE	BIL L ETER	CHI L IAST	*DIA L YZER
HIL L TOP	POL L ARD	TIL L ING	*BIL L FISH	*CHI L IDOG	DIE L DRIN
HIP L INE	POL L IST	TIL L ITE	BIL L FOLD	CHI L OPOD	DIO L EFIN
HOL L AND	*POL L OCK	TOI L FUL	BIL L HEAD	*CHO L ERIC	DIP L EGIA
HOL L IES	POL L UTE	TOL L AGE	*BIL L HOOK	COA L ESCE	*DIP L EXER
HOT L INE	POT L INE	TOL L BAR	BIL L IARD	*COA L FISH	*DIP L OIDY
*JEL L ABA	POU L TER	TOL L ING	*BIL L YCAN	COA L HOLE	DIP L OMAT
*JEL L IFY	PRE L IFE	TOL L MAN	BIO L OGIC	COA L IEST	DIP L OPOD
JET L IKE	PRE L OAD	TOL L WAY	*BOL L OCKS	COA L LESS	DIP L OSIS
JIL L ION	PUL L ING	TOP L INE	*BOL L WORM	COA L SACK	DIS L IKER
*JOL L IED	PUL L MAN	VAL L ATE	*BOW L LIKE	COA L YARD	DIS L ODGE
JOL L IER	PUL L OUT	VIL L AGE	*BUH L WORK	COL L AGEN	DIS L OYAL
JOL L IES	RAI L BUS	VIL L AIN	BUI L DING	COL L APSE	*DJE L LABA
*JOL L IFY	RAI L CAR	VIL L EIN	*BUL L DOZE	COL L ARET	DRI L LING
*JOL L ITY	RAL L IED	*VIL L IFY	BUL L ETIN	COL L ATOR	DRO L LERY
KIL L DEE	RAL L IER	VOL L IME	BUL L FROG	COL L EGER	DUE L LIST
*KIL L ICK	RAL L INE	WAI L FUL	BUL L HEAD	COL L EGIA	DUL L NESS
KIL L ING	RAY L IKE	*WAL L ABY	BUL L HORN	COL L IDER	DUO L OGUE
*KIL L JOY	REB L END	WAL L EYE	BUL L IEST	COL L IERY	*DUP L EXER
*KIL L OCK	RED L INE	WAL L IES	*BUL L NECK	COL L OGUE	DWE L LING
LAD L ING	REP L EAD	WIL L FUL	BUL L NOSE	*COL L OQUY	*DYS L EXIA
LAL L AND	REP L UMB	WIL L IED	BUL L POUT	COL L UDER	*DYS L EXIC
LOL L IES	RES L ATE	WIL L IES	BUL L RING	COL L UVIA	*FAH L BAND
LUL L ABY	RIL L ING	WIL L ING	BUL L RUSH	COL L YRIA	*FAL L AWAY
MAL L EUS	ROL L ICK	*WIL L OWY	*BUL L SHIT	COO L DOWN	*FAL L BACK
*MAP L IKE	ROL L ING	WIN L ESS	BUL L SHOT	COO L NESS	*FAL L FISH
MID L IFE	ROL L MOP	WOO L HAT	BUL L WEED	COP L ANAR	FAL L IBLE
MIL L IER	ROL L OUT	WOO L LED	*BUL L WHIP	COU L DEST	FAN L IGHT
MIL L INE	ROL L TOP	*YEL L OWY	*BUL L YBOY	COU L ISSE	FEL L ABLE
MIL L ION	ROL L WAY	*ZIL L ION	BUL L YRAG	CUR L ICUE	FEL L ATIO
MIL L RUN	SAL L IED	*ZIP L ESS	*CAB L EWAY	*CUR L YCUE	FEL L ATOR
MOL L IES	SAL L IER	BAI L MENT	CAL L ALOO	*CYC L AMEN	FEL L NESS
*MOL L IFY	SAL L IES	BAI L SMAN	*CAL L BACK	*CYC L ECAR	*FEL L OWLY
MUL L EIN	SAL L OWY	BAL L GAME	CAL L IPEE	*CYC L ICAL	FOI L SMAN
MUL L ION	SCA L EUP	*BAL L HAWK	CAL L IPER	*CYC L ITOL	FOL L ICLE
MUL L ITE	SCA L PEL	BAL L ISTA	CAL L IOPE	DAY L IGHT	FOL L OWER
*MUL L OCK	*SCH L UMP	BAL L ONET	CAU L DRON	*DEA L FISH	*FOO L FISH
NET L ESS	SEL L OUT	BAL L ONNE	CAU L ICLE	DEC L ARER	*FOO L SCAP
NUC L EAL	SKI L FUL	BAL L OTER	*CAU L KING	DEC L ASSE	FOU L NESS
NUL L IFY	SOU L FUL	*BAL L PARK	CEL L ARET	DEC L INER	FRI L LING
NUL L ITY	SPI L MIN	BAL L ROOM	CEL L MATE	DEF L ATER	FUE L LING
PAI L FUL	SUB L INE	*BAL L YHOO	CEL L ULAR	DEF L ATOR	FUG L EMAN
PAL L IAL	SUL L AGE	BAL L YRAG	CHA L DRON	*DEF L EXED	*FUL L BACK
PAL L IER	SYL L ABI	BAR L EDUC	CHA L LIES	*DEF L OWER	*FUL L FACE
PAL L ING	TAI L FAN	BDE L LIUM	*CHA L AZIA	DEP L ORER	FUL L NESS
PAL L IUM	TAL L AGE	BEC L AMOR	*CHA L LOTH	DIA L LAGE	*FUR L OUGH
*PAV L OVA	TAL L IED	*BEC L OTHE	DIA L LAGE		GAL L EASS
PED L ERY	TAL L IER				

GAL L ERIA	*LOW LIGHT	PEL L MEL L	*QUI L LAJA	SHI L LING	TAI L LIKE
GAL L IARD	MAL LEOLI	PEL L UCID	*QUI L LING	SIA LIDAN	TAI L PIPE
GAL L OPER	*MEAL WORM	PEN LIGHT	*QUI L TING	SIL LABUB	TAI L RACE
GAS L IGHT	*MEA LYBUG	PER L UDER	RAC LETTE	SIL L IBUB	TAI L SKID
GEO L OGER	*ME L LIFIC	PHA LANGE	RAIL BIRD	SKE LETON	TAI L SPIN
GIR L HOOD	*MIL L CAKE	PHAL L ISM	RAIL HEAD	SKI L LESS	TAI L WIND
GOAL LESS	MIL L EPED	PHAL L IST	RAIL LERY	SKI L LING	TAL L NESS
GOA L POST	MIL L IARD	PHE LONIA	RAIL ROAD	*SKIL L FUL	TAL L YMAN
GOA L WARD	MIL L IARE	*PHI L ABEG	RAL L YING	*SKUL L CAP	TAR LETAN
GOD L IEST	MIL L IARY	*PHI L IBEG	RA L L YIST	*SKY LIGHT	TEL L TALE
GO L LIWOG	MIL L IBAR	*PHI L OMEL	REA LISER	SMAL LAGE	TEL L URIC
*GOL LYWOG	MIL L IEME	*PHI L TRUM	*REA L IZER	SMA L LISH	THA LAMUS
GRI L LADE	MIL L IGAL	*PHY LAXIS	REA L NESS	*SMAL LPOX	THA L LIUM
GRI L LAGE	*MIL LILUX	*PHY L ESIS	REC LINER	SMA LTINE	THE LITIS
GUI L EFUL	*MIL LIMHO	*PHY L LARY	REC LOTHE	SMA LTITE	THO LEPIN
GUL LABLE	MIL LIME	*PHY L LITE	REF LOWER	SME LTERY	TOI LETTE
GUL LIBLE	*MIL LIOHM	*PHY L LODE	REF LUENT	SOIL LESS	TOL L GATE
HAL L IARD	MIL LINE	*PHY L LOID	REP LACER	SOL LERET	TOO L HEAD
*HAL LMARK	*MIL LIOHM	*PHY L LOME	REP LEDGE	SPA L PEEN	TOO L LESS
HAL LOWER	MIL L IPED	PIC L ORAM	REP LEVIN	SPE LAEAN	TOO L ROOM
*HAP L OIDY	MIL L IREM	PO L LINIA	REP LICON	SPE L LING	TOO L SHED
HAR L OTRY	*MIL L WORK	PO L LINIC	REP LUNGE	SPI L LAGE	*TOP LOFTY
*HAU L YARD	MIS LABEL	PO L LIWOG	RIF LEMAN	*SPIL LWAY	TRI L LION
HEE L BALL	MUL L IGAN	PO L LSTER	ROL LAWAY	SPO LIATE	TRI L LIUM
HEE L LESS	NAIL FOLD	*POL LYWOG	*ROL LBACK	STAL LION	TRI LOBAL
HE L L BENT	NAI L HEAD	POO L HAL L	*ROL LICKY	STA LWART	TRI LOBED
HE L L FIRE	NEG LIGEE	POO L ROOM	ROL LOVER	STEL LATE	TRO L LIED
*HEL LKITE	*NEW LYWED	POO L SIDE	ROU LETTE	STE L LIFY	TRO L LIES
HIL LIEST	NGU L TRUM	POP LITIC	SAIL BOAT	STI L BENE	TRO L LING
HIL LSIDE	NIE L LIST	*POT LACHE	SAIL FISH	STI L BITE	TUL L IBEE
HOO LIGAN	NOB LEMAN	*POT LATCH	SCA LABLE	STI LETTO	*TWE LVEMO
*HYA LOGEN	NOB LESSE	POU LARDE	SCA LAWAG	STI L LMAN	*TWI LIGHT
*JAI LBAIT	NON LABOR	POU LTICE	SCA LENUS	STO LPORT	TWI L LING
*JAI LBIRD	NON LEAFY	PRE LEGAL	SCA LEPAN	STU LTIFY	VAR LETRY
*JEA LOUSY	NON LEGAL	PRE LIMIT	SCA LIEST	STY LISER	VAU LTING
*JET LINER	NON LOCAL	*PRE LUNCH	SCA L LION	*STY LIZER	*VEI LEDLY
*JOL LIEST	NUC LEASE	PRO LABOR	SCH LIERE	SUB LEASE	*VEI LLIKE
*KAI LYARD	NUC LEATE	PRO LAMIN	*SCH LOCKY	SUB LEVEL	VEL LEITY
KA L LIDIN	NUC LEOID	PRO LAPSE	SCI LICET	SUB LIMER	VIL LADOM
KAO LIANG	NUC LEOLE	*PRO LIFIC	SCO LDING	SUB LUNAR	VIL LAGER
KEE LBOAT	NUC LEOLI	PRO LOGUE	SCO LIOMA	SUN LIGHT	VIL LAINY
*KEE LHALE	PAI L LARD	PRO LONGE	SCU L LERY	SWEL LING	VIL LATIC
*KEE LHAUL	PA L LADIA	PSA LMIST	SCU L LION	*SYL LABIC	VIO LABLE
KEE L LESS	PA L LADIC	*PSA LMODY	SCU L PTOR	SYL LABLE	VIO LATER
KIE L BASA	PA L LETTE	PSA LTERY	SEA L LIKE	SYL LABUB	VIO LATOR
KIL L DEER	PA L LIATE	PSI LOCIN	SEA L SKIN	SYL LABUS	VIO LENCE
*KOH LRABI	PA L LIEST	PSI LOSIS	SHA LIEST	TAB LEFUL	VOL LEYER
LAD LEFUL	PAR LANCE	*PSY LLIUM	SHA L LOON	TAB LETOP	WAI LSOME
LAL LYGAG	PAR LANDO	PUB LICAN	*SHE LDUCK	*TAIL BACK	WAL LAROO
LIL LIPUT	PAR LANTE	*PUB LICLY	*SHE LFFUL	TAIL BONE	WAL LOPER
LOB LOL LY	PAU LDRON	*PUL LBACK	*SHE LLACK	TAIL COAT	WAL LOWER
LO L LYPOP	PE L LAGRA	PUL LOVER	*SHE LVING	TAIL GATE	*WAY LAYER
LO L LYGAG	PE L LETAL	PYE LITIS	SHI LINGI	TAIL LAMP	WEL LADAY
*LOL LYPOP	PE L LICLE	*QUA LMISH	SHI L LALA	TAIL LESS	*WEL LAWAY
LOW LIFER	PE L LICLE	*QUI L LAIA	SHI L LALA	TAIL LEUR	WEL L BORN

*WELLCURB	DIAL	LULL	TELL	CEORL	GYRAL
WELLDOER	DIEL	MAIL	TILL	CHILL	HADAL
*WELLHEAD	DILL	MALL	TIRL	CHURL	HAMAL
WELLHOLE	DIOL	MARL	TOIL	CIBOL	*HAZEL
WELLNESS	DIRL	MAUL	TOLL	CIVIL	HEMAL
WELLSITE	DOLL	MEAL	TOOL	COMAL	*HEXYL
*WHALEMAN	DUAL	MELL	VAIL	COPAL	HORAL
WILLIWAU	DUEL	MERL	VEAL	CORAL	HOSEL
*WILLIWAW	DULL	MEWL	VEIL	CRAAL	HOTEL
WILLOWER	FAIL	MILL	VIAL	CRAWL	HOVEL
*WILLYARD	FALL	MOIL	VILL	CREEL	JACAL
WILLYART	FARL	MOLL	VIOL	CRUEL	JEBEL
*WILLYWAW	FEAL	MOOL	VIRL	CUPEL	*JEWEL
WOOLFELL	FEEL	MULL	WAIL	CYMOL	JOUAL
*WOOLLIKE	FELL	NAIL	WALL	DECAL	JUGAL
*WOOLPACK	FILL	NILL	WAUL	DEDAL	JURAL
*WOOLSACK	FOAL	NOEL	WAWL	DEVEL	JUREL
*WOOLSHED	FOIL	NULL	WEAL	DEVIL	KETOL
*WOOLSKIN	FOOL	NURL	WEEL	DOMAL	KEVEL
*WOOLWORK	FOUL	PAIL	WELL	DOTAL	KEVIL
WOULDEST	FOWL	PALL	WILL	DOWEL	KNEEL
*ZEALOTRY	FUEL	PAWL	WOOL	DRAIL	KNOLL
*ZOOLATER	FULL	PEAL	YAWL	DRAWL	KNURL
*ZOOLATRY	FURL	PEEL	YELL	DRILL	KRAAL
	GALL	PIAL	YILL	DROLL	KRILL
BAAL	GAOL	PILL	YOWL	DROOL	KUGEL
BAIL	GILL	POLL	ZEAL	DURAL	LABEL
BALL	GIRL	POOL	ZILL	DWELL	LAPEL
BAWL	GOAL	PULL	BABEL	DYNEL	LEGAL
BELL	GULL	PURL	BABUL	FATAL	LEVEL
BILL	HAIL	RAIL	BAGEL	FECAL	LIBEL
BIRL	HALL	REAL	BANAL	FERAL	LOCAL
BOIL	HARL	REEL	BASAL	FETAL	LORAL
BOLL	HAUL	RIAL	BASIL	FINAL	LOSEL
BOWL	HEAL	RIEL	BEDEL	FLAIL	LOYAL
BUHL	HEEL	RILL	BERYL	FOCAL	MAILL
BULL	HEIL	ROIL	BETEL	FOSEL	MEDAL
BURL	HELL	ROLL	BEVEL	FRAIL	METAL
BYRL	HERL	ROTL	*BEZEL	FRILL	MIAUL
CALL	HILL	SAIL	*BEZIL	FUGAL	MODAL
CARL	HOWL	SALL	BINAL	FUSIL	MODEL
CAUL	HULL	SAUL	BORAL	*FUZIL	MOGUL
CEIL	HURL	SEAL	BOTEL	GAVEL	MOHEL
CELL	JAIL	SEEL	BOWEL	GAYAL	MOLAL
COAL	JARL	SELL	BRAIL	GHOUL	MORAL
COIL	JELL	SHUL	BRAWL	GHYLL	MOREL
COOL	JILL	SIAL	BRILL	GIMEL	MOTEL
COWL	JOWL	SILL	BROIL	GLIAL	MURAL
CULL	KAIL	SOIL	BUBAL	GNARL	NASAL
CURL	KEEL	SOUL	BUTYL	GORAL	NATAL
DAHL	KILL	TAEL	CABAL	GRAAL	NAVAL
DEAL	KOEL	TAIL	CAMEL	GRAIL	NAVEL
DEIL	KOHL	TALL	CANAL	GRILL	NEROL
DELL	LEAL	TEAL	CAROL	GROWL	NEWEL
DHAL	LOLL	TEEL	CAVIL	GRUEL	NICOL

NIDAL	SHELL	TRAIL	BRASIL	CUPFUL	*FRAZIL
NIHIL	SHEOL	TRAWL	*BRAZIL	CURTAL	*FRIJOL
NIVAL	SHIEL	TRIAL	BRIDAL	*CYMBAL	FRIVOL
NODAL	SHILL	TRILL	BRUMAL	DACTYL	FRUGAL
NONYL	SHOAL	TRIOL	BRUTAL	DAEDAL	FULFIL
NOPAL	SHOOL	TROLL	BUCCAL	DAMSEL	FUNGAL
NOTAL	SHORL	TRULL	BULBEL	DARNTL	FUNNEL
NOVEL	SIBYL	TUBAL	BULBIL	DEASIL	GAMBOL
PANEL	SIGIL	TWILL	BULBUL	DECKEL	GAVIAL
PAPAL	SISAL	TWIRL	BURIAL	DENIAL	GENIAL
PAROL	SKILL	TYPAL	BUSHEL	DENTAL	GENTIL
PEARL	SKIRL	VAGAL	CAMAIL	DENTIL	GERBIL
PEDAL	SKOAL	VENAL	CANCEL	DETAIL	GIMBAL
PENAL	SKULL	VIGIL	CANNEL	DEWOOL	GIMMAL
PERIL	SMALL	VINAL	CAPFUL	DIOBOL	GINGAL
PETAL	SMELL	VINYL	CARCEL	DIRNDL	GLOBAL
PHIAL	SNAIL	VIRAL	CARFUL	DISMAL	GLYCOL
PIBAL	SNARL	VITAL	CARNAL	DISPEL	*GLYCYL
PICAL	SNELL	VOCAL	CARPAL	DISTAL	GOOGOL
PICUL	SNOOL	VOWEL	CARPEL	DISTIL	GOORAL
PIPAL	SOKOL	WEDEL	CARRTL	*DJEBEL	GOSPEL
PIXEL	SOREL	WHEAL	CARTEL	*DONZEL	GRAVEL
PRILL	SOTOL	WHEEL	CARVEL	DORSAL	GROVEL
PROWL	SPAIL	WHIRL	CASUAL	DORSEL	GUNNEL
PUPIL	SPALL	WHORL	CAUDAL	DOSSAL	GUNSEL
QUAIL	SPEEL	WOFUL	CAUSAL	DOSSEL	HAEMAL
QUELL	SPEIL	*XYLOL	CENTAL	DOSSIL	HALLEL
QUILL	SPELL	*XYLYL	CEREAL	DOTTEL	HAMMAL
RATAL	SPIEL	YODEL	CHAPEL	DREIDL	HANGUL
RATEL	SPILL	YOKEL	CHIRAL	DRIVEL	HANSEL
RAVEL	SPOIL	ZONAL	CHISEL	DUCTAL	HASSEL
REBEL	SPOOL	ZORIL	CHITAL	DUFFEL	HATFUL
REFEL	STALL	BABOOL	CHORAL	FACIAL	HERBAL
REGAL	STEAL	BAGFUL	CINEOL	FALLAL	HIEMAL
RENAL	STEEL	BARBAL	CITRAL	FARDEL	HIRSEL
REOIL	STILL	BARBEL	CLINAL	FARFAL	HOSTEL
REPEL	STOOL	BARRFL	*COAXAL	FARFEL	HOUSEL
REVEL	STULL	BEDELL	COCCAL	FAUCAL	HYETAL
RIVAL	SURAL	BEFALL	COEVAL	FECIAL	HYMNAL
RIYAL	SWAIL	BEFOOL	COMPEL	FENNEL	*JACKAL
ROWEL	SWELL	BEFOUL	CONSOL	FERREL	*JARFUL
ROYAL	SWILL	BEGALL	CONSUL	FESTAL	*JEZAIL
RURAL	SWIRL	BEHOWL	CORBEL	FETIAL	JINGAL
SALAL	TAMAL	*BENZAL	CORMEL	FEUDAL	*JOVIAL
SALOL	TEPAL	*BENZOL	CORNEL	FIBRIL	*JOYFUL
SCALL	THILL	*BENZYL	CORRAL	FILIAL	*JUGFUL
SCHUL	THIOL	BETHEL	CREDAL	FINIAL	*JUMBAL
SCOWL	THIRL	BEWAIL	CRENEL	FISCAL	KENNEL
SCULL	THURL	*BIAXAL	CRESOL	FITFUL	KERNEL
SEPAL	TICAL	BOATEL	CRESYL	FODGEL	KITTEL
SERAL	TIDAL	BORDEL	CREWEL	FOETAL	KNAWEL
SHALL	TOLYL	BOREAL	CRURAL	FORMAL	KUMMEL
SHAUL	TONAL	*BOXFUL	CUDGEL	FORMOL	LABIAL
SHAWL	TOTAL		CUNEAL	FORMYL	LAPFUL
SHEAL	TOWEL			FOSSIL	LAUREL

LAWFUL	PEEPUL	REMAIL	SPINAL	VALVAL	BRIMFUL
LENTIL	PENCEL	RENAIL	SPINEL	VANDAL	BRISTOL
LETHAL	PENCIL	RENTAL	SPIRAL	VASSAL	BROTHEL
LIENAL	PENSIL	REPEAL	SPITAL	VATFUL	BUTANOL
LINEAL	PENTYL	REPOLL	SPORAL	VEINAL	BUTYRAL
LINTEL	PETREL	REROLL	SPRAWL	VENIAL	*BUTYRYL
LINTOL	PETROL	RESAIL	*SQUALL	VERBAL	*CACODYL
LISTEL	PEYOTL	RESEAL	*SQUEAL	VERNAL	CAGEFUL
LOREAL	PHENOL	RESELL	*SQUILL	VERSAL	CALOMEL
LUTEAL	PHENYL	RETAIL	STATAL	VESTAL	CAMBIAL
MALTOL	PHONAL	RETELL	STEROL	VINEAL	*CAMPHOL
MAMMAL	PINEAL	RETIAL	STIPEL	VISUAL	CANSFUL
MANFUL	PINNAL	RETOOL	STOMAL	WADMAL	CAPITAL
MANGEL	PISTIL	RETRAL	STROLL	WADMOL	CAPITOL
MANTEL	PISTIL	REVEAL	STROML	WADNEL	CAPORAL
MANUAL	PISTOL	RHINAL	SWIVEL	WAEFUL	CARACAL
MARCEL	PLAGAL	RIDGEL	SYMBOL	WEASEL	CARACOL
MARVEL	*PLEXAL	RIDGIL	TAHSIL	WEEVIL	CARACUL
MEDIAL	*PLEXAL	RITUAL	TALLOL	WILFUL	CARAMEL
MENIAL	PLURAL	RONDEL	TARNAL	WITHAL	CARAVEL
MENSAL	PODSOL	RONNEL	TARSAL	WITTOL	CAREFUL
MENTAL	*PODZOL	RUEFUL	TASSEL	WOEFUL	CARPOOL
MESCAL	POMMEL	RUNNEL	TEASEL	WORMIL	CARRELL
MESIAL	PONTIL	SACRAL	*TEAZEL	*WURZEL	CATCALL
METHYL	PORTAL	SAFROL	TECTAL	BABBOOL	CATTAIL
*MEZCAL	POSTAL	SAMIEL	TELIAL	BAGSFUL	CENSUAL
MICELL	POTFUL	SANDAL	TENAIL	BALEFUL	CENTRAL
MISKAL	PRIMAL	SANTOL	TERCEL	BALNEAL	CERAMAL
MISSAL	PROPEL	SAUREL	TERGAL	BANEFUL	CHANCEL
MISSEL	PROPYL	SCHOOL	TETRYL	BARBELL	CHANNEL
MITRAL	PROTYL	SCHORL	THENAL	*BASHFUL	CHARNEL
MONGOL	PULPAL	SCRAWL	THRALL	*BATFOWL	CHATTEL
MORSEL	PUMMEL	SCROLL	THRILL	*BATHYAL	*CHERVIL
MORTAL	PYRROL	SEIDEL	THYMOL	BECRAWL	CHORDAL
MUGFUL	*QUEZAL	SENDAL	TIMBAL	BEDEVIL	CHORIAL
MUSSEL	*QUINOL	SEPTAL	TINCAL	BEDRAIL	*CHROMYL
MUTUAL	RACIAL	*SEQUEL	TINFUL	BEDROLL	CITADEL
MUTUEL	RADIAL	SERAIL	TINSEL	*BEJEWEL	COAEVAL
NARWAL	RAMTIL	SERIAL	TOLUOL	BENOMYL	COASTAL
NEURAL	RAPPEL	SERVAL	TOLUYL	BENTHAL	*COAXIAL
NICKEL	RASCAL	SEXUAL	TOMDAL	*BENZOYL	CODICIL
NITRIL	REBILL	SHEKEL	TONSIL	BESTIAL	*COEQUAL
NORMAL	REBOIL	*SHEQEL	TOPFUL	*BIAXIAL	COLONEL
NUCHAL	RECALL	SHOVEL	TRAMEL	BIFOCAL	COLUMEL
PALPAL	RECOAL	SHRILL	TRAVEL	BIMETAL	COMICAL
PANFUL	RECOIL	SHTETL	TRIBAL	BIMODAL	CONCEAL
PARCEL	RECTAL	SIGNAL	TRINAL	*BIVINYL	CONGEAL
PARRAL	REDIAL	SIMNEL	TROTYL	BOATFUL	CONICAL
PARREL	REFALL	SINFUL	TROWEL	BOBTAIL	CONTROL
PASCAL	REFEEL	SKATOL	TUBFUL	*BOOKFUL	CORBEIL
PASSEL	REFELL	SNIVEL	TUNNEL	BORNEOL	CORDIAL
PASTEL	REFILL	SOBFUL	TUSSAL	BORSTAL	CORONAL
PASTIL	REFUEL	SOCIAL	TWIBIL	*BOWLFUL	CORONEL
PATROL	REGNAL	SOLGEL	TYMBAL	*BOXHAUL	COSTREL
PAUSAL	REHEEL	SORREL	VAKEEL	BRADAWL	

COTIDA L	FINICA L	HUMERA L	MISDEA L	POITRE L	SAWMI L L
COUNCI L	FISTFU L	HUMORA L	MISDIA L	POTBOI L	SCA L PE L
COUNSE L	F LANNE L	HURTFU L	MISTRA L	POUNDA L	SCANDA L
COWBE L L	F LOATE L	*HUSHFU L	MOANFU L	POUTFU L	SCRIBA L
COWGIR L	F LUVIA L	*JARSFU L	MONGRE L	PREANA L	SCURRI L
CRANIA L	*FORKFU L	*JEJUNA L	MONOFI L	PREBI L L	SEAFOW L
CREOSO L	*FORMFU L	*JESTFU L	MUDSI L L	PREBOI L	SEAGU L L
CRESTA L	*FOXTAI L	*JEZEBE L	MUSEPU L	PRECOO L	SEAWA L L
CRUCIA L	FRACTA L	*JONQUI L	MUSICA L	PREDIA L	SEGETA L
CRUSTA L	FRESNE L	JOURNA L	NAPHTO L	PREMEA L	SEMINA L
CRYSTA L	FRETFU L	*JUGSFU L	NARWHA L	PREPI L L	SENSUA L
CUBICA L	FRONTA L	*JUVENA L	NATURA L	*PREQUE L	SEVERA L
CUPSFU L	FU LFI L L	*KARAKU L	NEEDFU L	PRESE L L	SHRIVE L
CURTAI L	FUNERA L	KESTRE L	NEUTRA L	*PRETZE L	SHTETE L
CYNICA L	GADWA L L	KISTFU L	NITINO L	PREVAI L	SKI L FU L
DAMOSE L	GAINFU L	L ACTEA L	NODICA L	*PUSHFU L	SKINFU L
*DAMOZE L	GAMBRE L	L ANGRE L	NOMBRI L	*QUANTA L	SKYSAI L
DAREFU L	GANGRE L	L ANITA L	NOMINA L	*QUARRE L	SNORKE L
DECANA L	GARBOI L	L ATOSO L	NONFUE L	*QUETZA L	SONGFU L
DECIBE L	GASOHO L	L ATPRA L	NOSTRI L	*RACKFU L	SORORA L
DECRIA L	GASTRA L	*L EXICA L	NUC L EA L	RADICA L	SOU L FU L
DECTMA L	GEMINA L	L IBERA L	NUMERA L	RADICE L	SPACIA L
DEPOSA L	GENERA L	L IFEFU L	NUPTIA L	RATTAI L	SPANCE L
DESPOI L	GENITA L	L IMINA L	NUTGA L L	REAVAI L	SPANIE L
DEVISA L	GENTEE L	L INAL O L	PAGINA L	RECITA L	SPATIA L
DEWFA L L	GHARIA L	L INGUA L	PAI L FU L	REDPO L L	SPECIA L
*DEXTRA L	GINGA L L	L ITERA L	PAINFU L	REDRI L L	SPHERA L
DIA L LE L	GIRASO L	L ITORA L	PA L ATA L	REDTAI L	SPIEGE L
DICOTY L	GIROSO L	L OGICA L	PAL LIA L	REFUTA L	SPONSA L
DIGITA L	G LACIA L	L OGRO L L	PA L UDA L	REFUSA L	SPOUSA L
DIREFU L	G LEEPU L	L OWBA L L	PARASO L	REGOSO L	STAMME L
DISHFU L	G LUTEA L	L UGSAI L	PARBOI L	RE L ABE L	STENCI L
DISTI L L	GNATHA L	L UNGFU L	PARTIA L	REMODE L	STERNA L
DITHIO L	GOMERA L	L USTFU L	PASCHA L	REMOVA L	STIBIA L
DIURNA L	GOMERE L	L USTRA L	*PASQUI L	RENEWA L	STRATA L
DOGGRE L	GOMERI L	L YRICA L	PAYRO L L	REPANE L	STRIGI L
DO L EFU L	GRADUA L	MAGICA L	*PEAFOW L	REPOSA L	STRUDE L
DOMICA L	GRAPNE L	MANDRE L	PEDICE L	RESPE L L	SUBCE L L
DOMICI L	GRAUPE L	MANDRI L	PEDOCA L	RESTFU L	SUBCOO L
DOOMFU L	GREMIA L	MARITA L	PENICI L	RETINA L	SUBDUA L
DOTTRE L	GUMBOI L	MARSHA L	PERORA L	RETINO L	SUBGOA L
DREIDE L	HANDFU L	MARTIA L	PERUSA L	RETRIA L	SUBORA L
DRYWA L L	HANDSE L	MATINA L	PEYTRA L	REVISA L	SUBOVA L
DUTIFU L	*HARMFU L	*MAXIMA L	PEYTRE L	REVIVA L	SUBSOI L
FACTUA L	*HATCHE L	*MAXWE L L	PHRASA L	ROOMFU L	SUNDIA L
FA LAFE L	HATEFU L	MEDICA L	PINBA L L	*RORQUA L	SURREA L
FANTAI L	HATSFU L	MENTHO L	PINITO L	ROSINO L	SURVEI L
FATEFU L	HAVERE L	METICA L	PINTAI L	ROSTRA L	SUTURA L
FAUCIA L	HEEDFU L	MI LFOI L	PIPEFU L	ROUNDE L	*SWAYFU L
FAUTEI L	HE LICA L	MIMICA L	PITFA L L	RUDERA L	SYNFUE L
FEARFU L	*HE L PFU L	MINDFU L	PITIFU L	RUTHFU L	TACTFU L
FEDERA L	HEMATA L	MINERA L	PIVOTA L	*SACKFU L	TACTUAL
FE LAFE L	HOBNAI L	MINIMA L	*P LAYFU L	SAHIWA L	TANKFU L
FEMORA L	HO LDA L L	MISBI L L	P LIMSO L	SATCHE L	TEABOW L
FIGURA L	*HOPEFU L	MISCA L L	P LUVIA L	SAWBI L L	TEARFU L

TEENFU L	*WAMEFU L	B L UEBE L L	CONEPAT L	DREADFU L	G L YCERO L
TENDRI L	WASSAI L	B L UEBI L L	*CONFOCA L	DREAMFU L	*G L YCERY L
TERTIA L	WASTRE L	B L UEGI L L	*CONJUGA L	DRUMRO L L	*G L YCOSY L
TETANA L	*WAXBI L L	*B L USHFU L	CONTRAI L	*DUCKBI L L	GNOMICA L
TEXTUA L	*WAYBI L L	BOASTFU L	CORNBA L L	*DUCKTAI L	GOODWI L L
THEE L O L	WIL L FU L	BOATBI L L	CORNMEA L	*DUMBBE L L	GOOFBA L L
THERMA L	*WISHFU L	BONEMEA L	CORPORA L	DUNGHI L L	GOSSYPO L
THERME L	WISTFU L	BONSPE L L	CORRIVA L	*FAITHFU L	GRACEFU L
*THIAZO L	*XY L ITO L	BONSPIE L	CORTISO L	FA L DERA L	GRATEFU L
THIONY L	*ZESTFU L	*BRACHIA L	COSMICA L	FA L DERO L	GRAYMAI L
TIERCE L	*BACKFI L L	BRANTAI L	COVERA L L	FAMI L IA L	GROMWE L L
TIMBRE L	*BACKHAU L	*BRIMFU L L	*CRACKNE L	*FANCIFU L	GUAIACO L
TINFOI L	BA L MORA L	BROCATE L	CRIMINA L	*FARCICA L	GUI L EFU L
TISSUA L	BANDERO L	*BUCKTAI L	CU L TURA L	FAREWE L L	GUMBOTI L
TOENAI L	BANGTAI L	*CACOMIX L	CUSPIDA L	FARNESO L	GUNMETA L
TOI L FU L	BANKRO L L	CA L ENDA L	CUSTUMA L	FASTBA L L	GUTTURA L
TOMFOO L	BANNERO L	*CA L YCEA L	*CYC L ICA L	FEASTFU L	GYROIDA L
TOPFU L L	BARBICE L	CANNIBA L	*CYC L ITO L	FESTIVA L	HABITUA L
TOPSAI L	BARBITA L	CANTONA L	*DAFFODI L	FIDUCIA L	HAEMATA L
TOPSOI L	BARONIA L	*CARBARY L	DEADFA L L	FIREBA L L	HAIRBA L L
*TOXICA L	BARSTOO L	CARBINO L	*DEATHFU L	FIREHA L L	HANDBA L L
TRAME L L	BASEBA L L	*CARBONY L	DECRETA L	*FISHBOW L	HANDBE L L
TRAMME L	BASINFU L	*CARBOXY L	DEFERRA L	*FISHMEA L	HANDBI L L
TRAVAI L	*BASOPHI L	CARDINA L	DEIFICA L	FISHTAI L	HANDRAI L
TRAYFU L	BEADRO L L	CARNIVA L	DEMERSA L	F L AVONO L	*HANDSFU L
TREFOI L	BEANBA L L	CAROUSA L	DEMURRA L	*F L YWHEE L	HANGNAI L
TRENAI L	*BECHAME L	CAROUSE L	DEPRIVA L	FO L DERO L	*HAPTICA L
TRESSE L	BECUDGE L	CARRYA L L	DETASSE L	FONTANE L	HARDBA L L
TRIVIA L	BEDRIVE L	CASCABE L	DEVERBA L	FOOTBA L L	HAREBE L L
TROCHA L	BE L L PU L L	*CATCHA L L	DIACETY L	FOOTFA L L	HASTEFU L
TROCHI L	*BE L LYFU L	*CATECHO L	DIACONA L	FOOTHI L L	*HAWKBI L L
TROMME L	BERASCA L	CEREBRA L	DIAGONA L	FOOTWA L L	HEADSAI L
TRUNNE L	BESTOWA L	CESSPOO L	DICROTA L	FORBIDA L	*HECTICA L
TRYSAI L	BETRAYA L	*CHARCOA L	*DIDACTY L	*FORCEFU L	HEE L BA L L
TUMBRE L	*BIACETY L	*CHEEKFU L	DIHEDRA L	FOREFEE L	HE L IACA L
TUMBRI L	BIANNUA L	*CHEERFU L	DI L UVIA L	FORESAI L	*HEMOCOE L
TUNEFU L	BICAUDA L	*CHEMICA L	*DIMETHY L	FORESTA L	HEROICA L
TURMOI L	BIDENTA L	*CHESTFU L	DIPTERA L	FORETE L L	HIBERNA L
TWIBI L L	BIENNIA L	*CHOCKFU L	DISANNU L	*FORKBA L L	*HIGHBA L L
TYPICA L	*BIFACIA L	*CINNAMY L	*DISHEVE L	*FORKSFU L	*HIGHTAI L
VANPOO L	BI L ABIA L	C L ERICA L	DIS L OYA L	FREEWI L L	*HONEYFU L
VATICA L	BIMANUA L	C L ODPO L L	DISPOSA L	FRUITFU L	HORNBI L L
VEGETA L	BIMENSA L	*C L UBHAU L	DIVIDUA L	FUNEREA L	HORNTAI L
VENTAI L	*BIMETHY L	COATTAI L	DOCTORA L	FURFURA L	HOSPITA L
VENTRA L	BINAURA L	*COCKBI L L	DOGGERE L	GA L ANGA L	HOUSEFU L
VERMEI L	BINOMIA L	*COCKERE L	DOORBE L L	GANG L IA L	*HUMORFU L
VICINA L	BIOTICA L	*COCKTAI L	DOORNAI L	GERANIA L	*HYDROGE L
VICTUA L	*BIPHENY L	*COGWHEE L	DOORSI L L	GERANIO L	*HYDROME L
VIRTUA L	BIRACIA L	COISTRE L	DOTTERE L	GERMINA L	*HYDROSO L
VITRIO L	BIRADIA L	COISTRI L	DOUBTFU L	GESTICA L	*HYDROXY L
WADMAA L	BIRDCA L L	CO L ONIA L	DOVETAI L	GESTURA L	*HYMENEA L
WADMO L L	*BISEXUA L	CO L ORFU L	*DOWNFA L L	*GHASTFU L	*HYPERGO L
WAGTAI L	*B L AMEFU L	CO L OSSA L	*DOWNHAU L	GI L DHA L L	*HYPOGEA L
WAI L FU L	*B L OWBA L L	COMMUNA L	*DOWNHI L L	G L ASSFU L	*JACKRO L L
*WAKEFU L	B L UEBA L L		DOWSABE L	G L OOMFU L	*JARGONE L

*JUDICIA L	MOONSAI L	PEDESTA L	RAINFA L L	SI L VICA L	SURROYA L
*KEE L HAU L	*MOORFOWL	PE L L ETA L	*RAKEHE L L	SIPHONA L	SURVIVA L
*KICKBA L L	*MOTHBA L L	PE L LMEL L	RASORIA L	*SKI L L FU L	TAB L EFU L
L ACRIMA L	MOTIONA L	PENONCE L	RATIONA L	S L OTHFU L	TAFFARE L
L AD L EFU L	MOURNFU L	PENTANO L	REASSAI L	SNEERFU L	TAFFERE L
*LAMBKI L L	*MOUTHFU L	PERONEA L	REBURIA L	SNOWBA L L	TAFFRAI L
L ANDFA L L	MUSCADE L	PERSONA L	REBUTTA L	SNOWBE L L	TAFFRAI L
L ANDFI L L	MUSCATE L	PETRONE L	REENRO L L	SNOWFA L L	TASTEFU L
L ENTICE L	*MYSTICA L	PETROSA L	REFERRA L	SOFTBA L L	TEETOTA L
*L IGHTFU L	*MYTHICA L	PHENETO L	REMEDIA L	SOMEDEA L	TEGMINA L
L INA L OO L	*NAPHTHO L	*PHI L OME L	REMITTA L	SORBITO L	TEMPORA L
L ITHOSO L	*NAPHTHY L	*PHYSICA L	REPRISA L	SOURBA L L	TERMINA L
L ITTORA L	NATIONA L	*PICKADI L	REPROVA L	SPADEFU L	TERPINO L
L OATHFU L	NAUTICA L	*PICKERE L	*REQUITA L	SPANDRE L	*TEXTURA L
L UBRICA L	NEWSREE L	*PINWHEE L	RESCHOO L	SPANDRI L	*THANKFU L
*MACKERE L	NITROSY L	P LANOSO L	RESIDUA L	SPECTRA L	THETICA L
MACRURA L	*NONEQUA L	P LATEFU L	RESTORA L	SPITBA L L	TRAGICA L
MADRIGA L	NONFINA L	*P LAYBI L L	REVERSA L	SPITEFU L	TRAINFU L
MAINSAI L	NONFOCA L	P LAYGIR L	REVIEWA L	SP L ENIA L	*TRANQUI L
MANDRI L L	NONGATA L	P L IMSO L L	REGIONA L	SPOONFU L	TRAPBA L L
MANGONE L	NONIDEA L	POETICA L	*RHEOPHI L	SPORTFU L	TREENAI L
MANNITO L	NON L EGA L	PONYTAI L	*RIGHTFU L	SPRINGA L	*TRIAXIA L
MANURIA L	NON L OCA L	POO L HA L L	RINGTAI L	SPURGA L L	TRIBUNA L
MARGINA L	NONMETA L	POSTANA L	ROADKI L L	*SQUIRRE L	TRIETHY L
MARSHA L L	NONMODA L	POSTOPA L	*ROCKFA L L	STAGEFU L	TRIFOCA L
MATERIA L	NONMORA L	POSTURA L	ROTOTI L L	STAUNRE L	TRIGONA L
MATERIE L	NONNAVA L	*POWERFU L	RUSTICA L	STAYSAI L	TRI L OBA L
MATERNA L	NONNOVE L	PRAEDIA L	*SACKSFU L	STERICA L	TRINODA L
MEATBA L L	NONPAPA L	PRANDIA L	SAGITTA L	*STICKFU L	TRIPEDA L
MEDIEVA L	NONRIVA L	PRATFA L L	SANTA L O L	STOMATA L	TRISTFU L
MEGADEA L	NONROYA L	*PREAXIA L	SAPROPE L	STRONGY L	TROOPIA L
MEMORIA L	NONRURA L	PREBASA L	SCENICA L	STUNSAI L	TROUPIA L
MENSEFU L	NONTIDA L	*PRECHI L L	SCEPTRA L	*SUBAXIA L	*TRUCKFU L
MENSURA L	NONTONA L	PREDRI L L	*SCOOPFU L	SUBDURA L	*TRUNKFU L
*MERCIFU L	NONVIRA L	*PREFIXA L	SCORNFU L	SUB L EVE L	TRUSTFU L
*MESOPHY L	NONVOCA L	PRE L EGA L	SCRANNE L	SUBNASA L	TRUTHFU L
METHANO L	NOTARIA L	PREMORA L	SEASHE L L	SUBNODA L	TURBINA L
*METHOXY L	NOVERCA L	PRENATA L	SEASONA L	SUBPANE L	TURNHA L L
*METHY LA L	NUDICAU L	PRERENA L	SECTORA L	SUBSHE L L	TURRICA L
METRICA L	NUMSKU L L	PRETRIA L	SE L FHEA L	SUBSKI L L	TUTORIA L
MI L L IGA L	NURTURA L	PRIDEFU L	SENSEFU L	SUBTOTA L	*TYMPANA L
MINSTRE L	NUTSHE L L	PRIMATA L	SENTINE L	SUBVIRA L	VARIETA L
MISENRO L	PA L ATIA L	*PRIMEVA L	SESSPOO L	*SUBVOCA L	VAUNTFU L
MIS L ABE L	PA L EOSO L	PROCURA L	*SHAMEFU L	*SUCCINY L	VENEREA L
MISSPE L L	PANBROI L	PRODIGA L	SHEENFU L	*SUFFIXA L	*VENGEFU L
MISTRIA L	PARA L L EL	PROPENO L	*SHE L FFU L	SUICIDA L	VERTICA L
MOISTFU L	PARENTA L	*PROPENY L	SH L EMIE L	SU L FINY L	VERTICI L
MO L EHI L L	*PARFOCA L	PROPOSA L	SHOEBI L L	SU L FONA L	VESPERA L
*MONACHA L	PARIETA L	PROTOCO L	SHOPGIR L	SU L FONY L	VESTURA L
MONAURA L	PASTORA L	PROUDFU L	*SHOWGIR L	SU L FURY L	VIATICA L
*MONAXIA L	PASTURA L	*PROXIMA L	SHRAPNE L	SUMMITA L	VICARIA L
MONOFUE L	PATAGIA L	*PUFFBA L L	SHRIEVA L	SUPERNA L	VIRGINA L
MONOHU L L	PATERNA L	PUNCTUA L	SIDEHI L L	SUPPOSA L	VISCERA L
MONOMIA L	*PEACEFU L	*PUSHBA L L	SIDEREA L	SUPPOSA L	VISIONA L
MONORAI L	PECTORA L	*QUINIRA L	SIDEWA L L	SURGICA L	*VOICEFU L

WARRAGA L	*WATCHFU L	*WI LDFOW L	WOO LFE L L	*WRECKFU L
WARRIGA L	WEARIFU L	*WINDFA L L	*WORTHFU L	*WRONGFU L
*WASHBOW L	*WHIMBRE L	WINDGA L L	*WRACKFU L	*WROTHFU L
WASTEFU L	*WHIPTAI L	WINDMI L L	*WRATHFU L	*YOUTHFU L

M

MAAR	MEAL	**MINK**	MORN	MADRE	**MARSH**
MABE	MEAN	MINT	MORT	**MAFIA**	**MARVY**
MACE	MEAT	**MINX**	**MOSK**	**MAFIC**	MASER
MACH	MEED	MIRE	MOSS	**MAGIC**	**MASHY**
MACK	**MEEK**	**MIRK**	MOST	**MAGMA**	MASON
MADE	MEET	MIRI	MOTE	MAGOT	MASSA
MAGE	MELD	MIRY	MOTH	MAGUS	MASSE
MAGI	MELL	MISE	MOTT	**MAHOE**	**MASSY**
MAID	MELT	MISO	MOUE	MAILE	**MATCH**
MAIL	MEMO	MISS	MOVE	MAILL	MATER
MAIM	MEND	MIST	**MOXA**	MAIST	**MATEY**
MAIN	MENO	MITE	*MOZO	MATIN	MATIN
MAIR	MENU	MITT	*MAIZE	*MAIZE	MATTE
MAKE	MEOW	**MIXT**	**MUCH**	**MAJOR**	*MATZA
MAKO	MERE	MOAN	**MUCK**	**MAKAR**	*MATZO
MALE	**MERK**	MOAT	**MUFF**	**MAKER**	MAUND
MALL	MERL	**MOCK**	MUGG	MALAR	**MAUVE**
MALM	MESA	MODE	MULE	MALIC	**MAVEN**
MALT	MESH	MODI	MULL	**MALMY**	**MAVIE**
MAMA	MESS	MOIL	**MUMM**	**MALTY**	**MAVIN**
MANA	META	**MOJO**	**MUMP**	**MAMBA**	MAVIS
MANE	METE	**MOKE**	MUMU	**MAMBO**	*MAXIM
MANO	METH	MOLA	MUNI	MAMEY	**MAYBE**
MANY	MEWL	MOLD	MUON	MAMIE	**MAYOR**
MARC	*MEZE	MOLE	MURA	**MAMMA**	MAYST
MARE	MICA	MOLL	MURE	**MAMMY**	*MAZER
MARK	MICE	MOLT	**MURK**	MANGE	MBIRA
MARL	MICK	MOLY	MURR	MANGO	**MEALY**
MART	MIDI	MOME	MUSE	**MANGY**	MEANT
MASH	MIEN	MOMI	MUSH	MANIA	**MEANY**
MASK	**MIFF**	**MONK**	**MUSK**	MANIC	**MEATY**
MASS	MIGG	MONO	MUSS	**MANLY**	**MECCA**
MAST	**MIKE**	MONS	MUST	MANNA	MEDAL
MATE	MILD	MONY	MUTE	MANOR	MEDIA
MATH	MILE	MOOD	MUTT	MANSE	**MEDIC**
MATT	**MILK**	MOOL	MYNA	MANTA	MEDII
MAUL	MILL	MOON	**MYTH**	MANUS	**MEINY**
MAUN	MILO	MOOR	**MACAW**	MAPLE	MELEE
MAUT	MILT	MOOT	MACER	*MAQUI	MELIC
MAXI	MIME	MOPE	**MACHO**	**MARCH**	MELON
MAYA	MINA	**MOPY**	MACLE	MARGE	MENAD
*MAZE	MIND	**MORA**	MACON	MARIA	MENSA
*MAZY	MINE	MORE	MACRO	**MARLY**	MENSE
MEAD	MINI	MORE	**MADAM**	**MARRY**	MENTA
			MADLY	MARSE	

MERCY	MISSY	MOSSY	MUSSY	MALICE	MARGAY
MERGE	MISTY	MOSTE	MUSTH	MALIGN	MARGIN
MERIT	MITER	MOTEL	MUSTY	MALINE	MARINA
MERLE	MITIS	MOTET	MUTCH	MALKIN	MARINE
MERRY	MITRE	MOTEY	MUTER	MALLEE	MARISH
MESHY	MIXER	MOTHY	MUTON	MALLEI	MARKER
MESIC	*MIXUP	MOTIF	*MUZZY	MALLET	MARKET
MESNE	*MIZEN	MOTOR	MYNAH	MALLOW	*MARKKA
MESON	MOCHA	MOTTE	MYOID	MALOTI	MARKUP
MESSY	MODAL	MOTTO	MYOMA	MALTED	MARLIN
METAL	MODEL	MOUCH	MYOPE	MALTHA	MARMOT
METER	MODEM	MOULD	*MYOPY	MALTOL	MAROON
METIS	MODUS	MOULT	MYRRH	MAMLUK	*MARQUE
METRE	MOGGY	MOUND	MYSID	MAMMAL	MARRAM
METRO	MOGUL	MOUNT	*MYTHY	MAMMEE	MARRED
*MEZZO	MOHEL	MOURN	MACACO	MAMMER	MARRER
MIAOU	MOHUR	MOUSE	MACING	MAMMET	MARRON
MIAOW	MOIRA	MOUSY	MACKLE	MAMMIE	MARROW
MIASM	MOIRE	MOUTH	MACRON	MAMMON	MARSHY
MIAUL	MOIST	MOVED	MACULA	MANAGE	MARTEN
MICHE	MOLAL	MOVER	MACULE	MANANA	MARTIN
MICRA	MOLAR	MOVIE	MADAME	MANCHE	MARTYR
MICRO	MOLDY	MOWER	MADCAP	MANEGE	MARVEL
MIDDY	MOLLY	MOXIE	MADDED	MANFUL	MASCON
MIDGE	MOLTO	MUCID	MADDEN	MANGEL	MASCOT
MIDST	MOMMA	MUCIN	MADDER	MANGER	MASHER
*MIFFY	MOMMY	*MUCKY	MADMAN	MANGEY	MASHIE
MIGHT	MOMUS	MUCOR	MADRAS	MANGLE	*MASJID
MILCH	MONAD	MUCRO	MADURO	MANIAC	MASKEG
MILER	MONAS	MUCUS	MAENAD	MANILA	MASKER
MILIA	MONDE	MUDDY	MAFFIA	MANIOC	*MASQUE
MILKY	MONDO	MUDRA	MAFTIR	MANITO	MASSIF
MILLE	MONEY	MUFTI	MAGGOT	MANITU	MASTER
MILPA	MONGO	MUGGY	MAGIAN	MANNAN	MASTIC
MILTY	MONIE	MUHLY	MAGILP	MANNED	*MASTIX
MIMEO	MONTE	*MUJIK	MAGLEV	MANNER	MATING
MIMER	MONTH	MULCH	MAGNET	MANTEL	MATRES
MIMIC	MOOCH	MULCT	MAGNUM	MANTES	MATRON
MINAE	MOODY	MULEY	MAGPIE	MANTIC	MATSAH
MINCE	MOOLA	MULLA	MAGUEY	MANTIS	*MATRIX
MINCY	MOONY	MUMMY	MAHOUT	MANTLE	MATTED
MINER	MOORY	MUNCH	*MAHZOR	MANTRA	MATTER
MINGY	MOOSE	MUNGO	MAIDEN	MANTUA	MATTIN
MINIM	MOPED	MURAL	MAIGRE	MANUAL	MATURE
MINKE	MOPER	MUREX	MAIHEM	MANURE	*MATZAH
MINNY	MOPEY	MURID	MAILER	MAPPED	*MATZOH
MINOR	MORAL	MURKY	MAIMER	MAPPER	*MATZOT
MINTY	MORAY	MURRA	MAINLY	*MANQUE	MAUGER
MINUS	MOREL	MURRE	MAKEUP	MARACA	MAUGRE
MIREX	MORON	MURRY	MAKING	MARAUD	MAULER
MIRKY	MORPH	MUSCA	MAKUTA	MARBLE	MAUMET
MIRTH	MORRO	MUSER	MALADY	MARBLY	MAUNDY
*MIRZA	MORSE	MUSHY	MALATE	MARCEL	*MAXIMA
MISDO	MOSEY	MUSIC	MALFED		*MAXIXE
MISER	MOSSO	MUSKY	MALGRE		*MAYDAY

MAYEST	MENHIR	*MIKVAH	MISSAL	MONODY	MUCOSA
*MAYFLY	MENIAL	*MIKVEH	MISSAY	MONTES	MUCOSE
*MAYHAP	*MENINX	MILADI	MISSEL	MOOLAH	MUCOUS
*MAYHEM	MENSAL	MILADY	MISSET	MOOLEY	MUDCAP
MAYING	MENSCH	MILAGE	MISSIS	MOOTER	MUDDER
*MAYPOP	MENTAL	MILDEN	MISSUS	MOPERY	MUDDLE
MAYVIN	MENTOR	MILDEW	MISTER	MOPIER	MUESLI
*MAZARD	MENTUM	MILIEU	MISUSE	MOPING	MUFFIN
*MAZIER	MERCER	MILIUM	MITHER	MOPISH	MUFFLE
*MAZILY	MERGER	MILKER	MITIER	MOPOKE	MUGFUL
*MAZING	MERINO	MILLER	MITRAL	MOPPED	MUGGAR
*MAZUMA	MERLIN	MILLET	MITTEN	MOPPER	MUGGED
MEADOW	MERLON	MILNEB	*MIZZEN	MOPPET	MUGGEE
MEAGER	MERLOT	MILORD	*MIZZLE	MORALE	MUGGER
MEAGRE	MERMAN	MILTER	*MIZZLY	MORALS	MUGGUR
MEALIE	MESCAL	MIMBAR	MOANER	MORASS	*MUKLUK
MEANER	MESIAL	MIMING	MOBBER	MORBID	*MUKTUK
MEANIE	MESIAN	MIMOSA	MOBCAP	MOREEN	MULETA
MEANLY	MESSAN	MINCER	MOBILE	MORGAN	MULING
MEASLE	MESTEE	MINDER	MOBLED	MORGEN	MULISH
MEASLY	METAGE	MINGLE	MOCKER	MORGUE	MULLAH
MEATUS	METATE	MINIFY	*MOCKUP	MORION	MULLEN
MEDAKA	METEOR	MINIMA	MODERN	MOROSE	MULLER
MEDDLE	METEPA	MINING	MODEST	MORPHO	MULLET
*MEDFLY	METHOD	MINION	*MODIFY	MORRIS	MULLEY
MEDIAD	METHYL	MINISH	MODISH	MORROW	MUMBLE
MEDIAL	METIER	MINIUM	MODIST	MORSEL	*MUMBLY
MEDIAN	METING	MINNOW	MODULE	MORTAL	MUMMED
*MEDICK	METOPE	MINTER	MODULO	MORTAR	MUMMER
MEDICO	METRIC	MINUET	MOGGIE	MORULA	MUMPER
MEDINA	METTLE	MINUTE	MOHAIR	MOSAIC	MUNTIN
MEDIUM	METUMP	MINYAN	MOIETY	MOSHAV	MURDER
MEDLAR	MEWLER	MIOLER	MOLDER	*MOSQUE	MUREIN
MEDLEY	*MEZCAL	MIOSIS	MOLEST	MOSSER	MURINE
MEDUSA	*MEZUZA	MIOTIC	MOLIES	MOSTLY	MURING
MEETER	MIASMA	MIRAGE	MOLINE	MOTHER	MURMUR
MEETLY	MICELL	MIRIER	MOLLAH	MOTILE	*MURPHY
MEGASS	*MICKEY	MIRING	MOLLIE	MOTION	MURREY
MEGILP	MICKLE	MIRROR	MOLOCH	MOTIVE	MURRHA
MEGOHM	MICRON	MISACT	MOLTEN	MOTLEY	MUSCAT
MEGRIM	MIDAIR	MISADD	MOLTER	MOTMOT	MUSCID
MEIKLE	MIDDAY	MISAIM	MOMENT	MOTTLE	MUSCLE
MEINIE	MIDDEN	MISATE	MOMISM	*MOUJIK	MUSCLY
MELDER	MIDDLE	MISCUE	MOMSER	MOULDY	MUSEUM
MELLOW	MIDGET	MISCUT	*MOMZER	MOULIN	MUSHER
MELODY	MIDGUT	MISEAT	MONGER	MOUSER	MUSING
MELOID	MIDLEG	MISERY	MONGOE	MOUSEY	*MUSJID
MELTER	MIDRIB	MISFIT	MONGOL	MOUSSE	MUSKEG
MELTON	*MIDWAY	MISHAP	MONGST	MOUTHY	MUSKET
MEMBER	MIGGLE	MISHIT	MONIED	MOUTON	MUSKIE
MEMOIR	*MIGHTY	MISKAL	MONIES	MOVING	MUSKIT
MEMORY	MIGNON	MISLAY	MONISH	MUCKER	MUSLIN
MENACE	MIHRAB	MISLIE	MONISM	MUCKLE	MUSSEL
MENAGE	MIKADO	MISLIT	MONIST	MUCLUC	MUSTEE
MENDER	MIKRON	MISPEN	*MONKEY	MUCOID	MUSTEE

MUSTER	MADWORT	MANGIER	MARMITE	*MAYWEED	MESALLY
MUTANT	*MADZOON	MANGILY	MARPLOT	*MAZIEST	MESARCH
MUTASE	MAESTRO	MANGLER	*MARQUEE	*MAZURKA	MESEEMS
MUTATE	*MAFFICK	MANGOLD	*MARQUIS	*MAZZARD	MESHIER
MUTEST	MAFIOSO	MANHOLE	MARRANO	MEALIER	MESHUGA
MUTINE	MAGENTA	MANHOOD	MARRIED	MEANDER	*MESQUIT
MUTING	MAGICAL	MANHUNT	MARRIER	MEANIES	MESSAGE
MUTINY	MAGNATE	MANIHOT	MARRIES	MEANING	MESSIAH
MUTISM	MAGNETO	MANIKIN	MARRING	MEASURE	MESSIER
MUTTER	*MAGNIFY	MANILLA	*MARROWY	MEATIER	MESSILY
MUTTON	MAHATMA	MANILLE	MARSALA	MEATILY	MESSMAN
MUTUAL	*MAHJONG	MANIOCA	MARSHAL	MEATMAN	MESTESO
MUTUEL	MAHONIA	MANIPLE	MARTIAL	MEDDLER	MESTINO
MUTULE	MAHUANG	MANITOU	MARTIAN	*MEDEVAC	*MESTIZA
MUUMUU	MAILBAG	MANKIND	MARTINI	*MEDIACY	*MESTIZO
*MUZHIK	*MAILBOX	MANLESS	MARTLET	MEDIANT	METAMER
*MUZJIK	MAILING	MANLIKE	*MARTYRY	MEDIATE	METHANE
*MUZZLE	MAILLOT	MANMADE	MASCARA	MEDICAL	*METHOXY
MYASIS	MAILMAN	MANNING	MASKING	MEDULLA	METICAL
MYCELE	MAINTOP	MANNISH	MASONIC	MEDUSAN	METISSE
MYELIN	*MAJAGUA	MANNITE	MASONRY	MEERKAT	METONYM
MYOPIA	*MAJESTY	MANNOSE	*MASQUER	MEETING	METOPIC
MYOSIN	*MAJORAM	*MANPACK	MASSAGE	MEGABAR	METOPON
MYOSIS	*MAJORLY	MANROPE	MASSEUR	MEGABIT	*METRIFY
MYOTIC	MALACCA	MANSARD	MASSIER	MEGAHIT	METRING
MYRIAD	MALAISE	MANSION	MASSIVE	MEGAPOD	METRIST
MYRICA	MALANGA	MANTEAU	MASTABA	MEGASSE	*MEZQUIT
MYRTLE	MALARIA	MANTLET	MASTERY	MEGATON	*MEZUZAH
MYSELF	*MALARKY	MANTRAP	*MASTIFF	*MEGILPH	MICELLA
MYSOST	MALEATE	MANUARY	MASTOID	MEIOSIS	MICELLE
MYSTIC	MALEFIC	MANUMIT	MATADOR	MELAMED	*MICRIFY
*MYTHIC	MALISON	MANURER	MATCHER	MELANGE	MICROBE
MYTHOS	MALLARD	MANWARD	*MATCHUP	MELANIC	*MICROHM
*MYXOID	MALLEUS	MANWISE	MATELOT	MELANIN	MIDCULT
*MYXOMA	MALMSEY	*MAPLIKE	MATILDA	MELILOT	MIDDIES
MACABER	MALODOR	MAPPING	MATINAL	MELISMA	MIDDLER
MACABRE	MALTASE	MARABOU	MATINEE	MELODIA	MIDIRON
MACADAM	MALTIER	MARANTA	MATLESS	MELODIC	MIDLAND
*MACAQUE	MALTOSE	MARASCA	MATRASS	MELTAGE	MIDLIFE
*MACCHIA	*MAMMARY	MARBLER	MATTERY	MEMENTO	MIDLINE
MACHETE	MAMMATE	MARCATO	MATTING	MENACER	MIDMOST
MACHINE	MAMMIES	MARCHEN	*MATTOCK	*MENAZON	MIDNOON
MACHREE	*MAMMOCK	MARCHER	MATTOID	MENDIGO	MIDRASH
*MACHZOR	*MAMMOTH	MAREMMA	*MATZOON	MENDING	*MIDRIFF
MACRAME	MANACLE	MARENGO	*MATZOTH	*MENFOLK	*MIDSHIP
*MACUMBA	MANAGER	MARGENT	MAUDLIN	MENORAH	*MIDSIZE
MADDEST	MANAKIN	MARIMBA	MAUNDER	MENTHOL	MIDSOLE
MADDING	MANATEE	MARINER	*MAWKISH	MENTION	MIDTERM
MADDISH	MANCHET	MARITAL	*MAXILLA	MERCERY	MIDTOWN
MADEIRA	MANDALA	*MARKHOR	*MAXIMAL	MERCIES	*MIDWEEK
MADNESS	MANDATE	MARKING	*MAXIMIN	MERCURY	*MIDWIFE
MADONNA	MANDOLA	MARLIER	*MAXIMUM	MERGING	MIDYEAR
MADRONA	MANDREL	MARLINE	*MAXWELL	MERISIS	MIGRANT
MADRONE	MANDRIL	MARLING	*MAYBUSH	MERMAID	MIGRATE
MADRONO	*MANGABY	MARLITE	MAYPOLE	MEROPIA	*MILCHIG

*MILDEWY	MISCODE	MISTAKE	MONITOR	MOUILLE	MUNSTER
MILEAGE	MISCOIN	MISTBOW	*MONKERY	MOULAGE	MUNTING
MILFOIL	*MISCOOK	MISTEND	*MONKISH	MOULDER	*MUNTJAC
MILIARY	*MISCOPY	MISTERM	MONOCLE	MOULTER	*MUNTJAK
MILITIA	MISDATE	MISTEUK	MONOCOT	MOUNTER	MUONIUM
MILKIER	MISDEAL	MISTIER	MONOECY	MOURNER	MURIATE
*MILKILY	MISDEED	MISTILY	MONOFIL	MOUSIER	MURICES
*MILKMAN	MISDEEM	MISTIME	MONOLOG	MOUSILY	MURRAIN
*MILKSOP	MISDIAL	MISTOOK	MONOMER	MOUSING	MURRINE
MILLAGE	MISDOER	MISTRAL	MONSOON	MOUTHER	MURTHER
MILLDAM	MISDONE	MISTUNE	MONSTER	MOVABLE	MUSEFUL
MILLIER	MISDRAW	MISTYPE	MONTAGE	*MOVABLY	MUSETTE
MILLIME	MISEASE	MISUSER	MONTANE	MOVIOLA	MUSICAL
MILLINE	MISEDIT	MISWORD	MONTERO	*MOZETTA	MUSKIER
MILLING	MISERLY	*MISYOKE	*MONTHLY	*MUCKIER	*MUSKILY
MILLION	MISFILE	MITERER	MONURON	*MUCKILY	MUSKRAT
MILLRUN	MISFIRE	MITIEST	MOOCHER	MUDDIED	*MUSPIKE
MILREIS	MISFORM	MITOGEN	MOONBOW	MUDDIER	MUSTANG
MIMESIS	MISGIVE	MITOSIS	MOONEYE	MUDDIES	MUSTARD
MIMICAL	MISGROW	*MITSVAH	MOONIER	MUDDILY	MUTABLE
*MIMICRY	MISHEAR	*MITZVAH	MOONILY	MUDDING	MUTAGEN
MINABLE	*MISJOIN	*MIXTURE	MOONISH	MUDDLER	*MUZZIER
MINARET	*MISKEEP	MOANFUL	MOONLET	*MUDFISH	*MUZZILY
MINDFUL	*MISKICK	*MOBBISH	MOONLIT	MUDFLAT	*MUZZLER
MINDSET	*MISKNOW	MOBSTER	MOONSET	MUDHOLE	MYALGIA
MINERAL	MISLAIN	MOCHILA	MOORAGE	MUDLARK	MYCOSIS
MINGIER	MISLEAD	*MOCKERY	MOORHEN	*MUDPACK	MYELINE
MINGLER	MISLIKE	MODELER	MOORIER	*MUDROCK	MYELIOD
MINIBUS	MISLIVE	MODERNE	MOORING	MUDROOM	MYELOMA
MINICAB	*MISMAKE	MODESTY	MOORISH	MUDSILL	MYIASIS
MINICAR	*MISMARK	MODICUM	MOPIEST	MUEDDIN	*MYNHEER
MINIKIN	MISMATE	MODULAR	MOPPING	*MUEZZIN	*MYOLOGY
MINILAB	MISMEET	MODULUS	MORAINE	*MUFFLER	MYOSOTE
MINIMAL	MISMOVE	MOFETTE	MORCEAU	MUGGIER	MYOTOME
*MINIMAX	MISNAME	MOIDORE	MORDANT	MUGGILY	*MYSTERY
MINIMUM	MISPAGE	MOISTEN	MORDENT	MUGGING	*MYSTIFY
MINISKI	MISPART	MOISTLY	MORELLE	MUGGINS	MACARONI
MINIVAN	MISPLAN	*MOJARRA	MORELLO	MUGWORT	MACAROON
MINIVER	MISPLAY	MOLDIER	MORNING	*MUGWUMP	*MACCABAW
MINORCA	MISRATE	MOLDING	MOROCCO	MULATTO	*MACCABOY
MINSTER	MISREAD	MOLLIES	MORPHIA	MULLEIN	*MACCOBOY
MINTAGE	MISRELY	*MOLLIFY	*MORPHIC	MULLION	MACERATE
MINUEND	MISRULE	MOLLUSC	MORPHIN	MULLITE	*MACHISMO
MINUTIA	MISSEAT	MOMENTA	MORRION	MULLOCK	*MACKEREL
MIRACLE	MISSEND	MOMENTO	MORTARY	MULLUSK	*MACKINAW
MIRADOR	MISSHOD	MONACID	MORTICE	MULTURE	MACRURAL
MIRIEST	MISSIES	MONADES	*MORTIFY	MUMBLER	MACRURAN
MISALLY	MISSILE	MONARCH	MORTISE	*MUMMERY	MACULATE
MISAVER	MISSION	MONARDA	MOSSIER	MUMMIED	MADHOUSE
MISBIAS	MISSIVE	*MONAXON	MOSTEST	MUMMIES	MADRIGAL
MISBILL	MISSORT	MONERAN	MOTIVIC	*MUMMIFY	*MADWOMAN
MISBIND	MISSOUT	MONEYED	MOTORIC	MUMMING	MAESTOSO
MISCALL	MISSTEP	MONEYER	MOTTLER	MUNCHER	*MAGAZINE
MISCAST	MISSTOP	MONGREL	MOUFLON	MUNDANE	MAGICIAN
MISCITE	MISSUIT	MONIKER	MOUFLON	MUNNION	*MAGICKED

MAGISTER	MANDATOR	*MARKSMAN	*MAZAEDIA	MELANOUS	METALISE
MAGNESIA	MANDIBLE	MARLIEST	*MAZELIKE	MELILITE	METALIST
MAGNETIC	MANDIOCA	MARMOSET	*MAZINESS	MELINITE	*METALIZE
MAGNETON	MANDOLIN	MAROCAIN	*MAZOURKA	*MELLIFIC	METALLED
*MAGNIFIC	*MANDRAKE	*MARQUESS	MEALIEST	MELODEON	METALLIC
MAGNOLIA	MANDRILL	*MARQUISE	MEALLESS	MELODICA	METAMERE
*MAHARAJA	MANEUVER	MARRIAGE	MEALTIME	MELODIES	*METAPHOR
MAHARANI	*MANGABEY	MARSHALL	*MEALWORM	MELODISE	*METAZOAN
*MAHIMAHI	MANGANIC	MARSUPIA	*MEALYBUG	MELODIST	*METAZOON
*MAHJONGG	MANGIEST	MARTAGON	MEANNESS	*MELODIZE	METERAGE
*MAHOGANY	MANGONEL	MARTINET	MEANTIME	MELTDOWN	METHADON
*MAIDHOOD	MANGROVE	*MARTYRLY	MEASURER	MEMBRANE	METHANOL
MAIEUTIC	MANICURE	*MARYJANE	MEATBALL	MEMORIAL	*METHINKS
MAILLESS	MANIFEST	*MARZIPAN	MEATHEAD	MEMORISE	*METHODIC
MAINLAND	MANIFOLD	MASGACRE	MEATIEST	*MEMORIZE	*METHOXYL
MAINLINE	MANNERLY	*MASKLIKE	MEATLESS	*MEMSAHIB	*METHYLAL
MAINMAST	MANNIKIN	MASSAGER	MEATLOAF	*MENARCHE	METRICAL
MAINSAIL	MANNITOL	MASSCULT	*MECHANIC	*MENFOLKS	METRITIS
MAINSTAY	*MANPOWER	MASSEDLY	MECONIUM	MENHADEN	MEUNIERE
MAINTAIN	MANTELET	MASSETER	MEDALIST	MENIALLY	*MEZEREON
MAIOLICA	MANTILLA	MASSEUSE	MEDALLIC	MENISCUS	*MEZEREUM
*MAJESTIC	MANTISSA	MASSICOT	MEDIALLY	MENOLOGY	*MEZQUITE
*MAJOLICA	MANTLING	MASSIEST	MEDIANLY	MENSEFUL	*MICAWBER
*MAJORITY	MANUALLY	MASSLESS	MEDIATOR	MENSTRUA	MICROBAR
*MAKEBATE	MANUBRIA	*MASTABAH	MEDICAID	MENSURAL	MICROBUS
*MAKEFAST	MANURIAL	MASTERLY	MEDICARE	MENSWEAR	MICRODOT
*MAKEOVER	MANURING	MASTHEAD	MEDICATE	MENTHENE	*MICROLUX
*MAKIMONO	MANWARDS	*MASTICHE	MEDICINE	*MEPHITIS	*MICROMHO
MALAMUTE	*MANYFOLD	MASTITIS	MEDIEVAL	MERCAPTO	*MICRURGY
MALAPERT	*MAPMAKER	MASTLESS	MEDIOCRE	*MERCHANT	MIDBRAIN
MALAPROP	*MAPPABLE	MASTLIKE	MEDITATE	*MERCIFUL	MIDDLING
*MALARKEY	*MAQUETTE	MASTODON	MEDUSOID	MERENGUE	*MIDFIELD
MALAROMA	MARABOUT	MASURIUM	MEEKNESS	MERGENCE	*MIDMONTH
MALEDICT	MARASMUS	*MATCHBOX	MEETNESS	MERIDIAN	*MIDNIGHT
MALEMIUT	MARATHON	MATELESS	*MEGABTYE	MERINGUE	MIDPOINT
MALEMUTE	MARAUDER	MATELOTE	*MEGABUCK	MERISTEM	MIDRANGE
MALENESS	MARAVEDI	MATERIAL	*MEGACITY	MERISTIC	*MIDSHIPS
MALIGNER	MARBLING	MATERIEL	MEGADEAL	MESDAMES	*MIDSIZED
MALIGNLY	*MARCHESA	MATERNAL	MEGADOSE	MESHIEST	*MIDSPACE
MALIHINI	*MARCHESE	*MATESHIP	*MEGADYNE	*MESHUGAH	MIDSTORY
MALINGER	MARGARIC	MATINESS	MEGALITH	*MESHUGGA	*MIDWATCH
MALLEOLI	MARGARIN	MATTEDLY	MEGALOPS	*MESHUGGE	MIGNONNE
MALPOSED	MARGINAL	MATTRASS	MEGAPODE	*MESHWORK	MIGRAINE
MALTIEST	MARGRAVE	MATTRESS	MEGASTAR	MESMERIC	MIGRATOR
MALTREAT	*MARIACHI	MATURATE	MEGAVOLT	MESNALTY	MILDNESS
MALTSTER	MARIGOLD	MATURITY	MEGAWATT	MESOCARP	MILEPOST
MALVASIA	MARINADE	*MAUMETRY	MEGILLAH	MESODERM	MILESIMO
MAMALIGA	MARINARA	MAUSOLEA	MELAMINE	MESOGLEA	MILIARIA
*MAMELUKE	MARINATE	*MAVERICK	MELANIAN	*MESOPHYL	MILITANT
MAMMATUS	MARIPOSA	*MAXICOAT	MELANISM	MESOSOME	MILITARY
MAMMILLA	MARITIME	*MAXIMISE	MELANIST	MESOTRON	MILITATE
MAMMITIS	*MARKDOWN	*MAXIMITE	MELANITE	*MESQUITE	*MILKFISH
MANCIPLE	*MARKEDLY	*MAXIMIZE	*MELANIZE	MESSIEST	MILKIEST
MANDAMUS	MARKETER	*MAYAPPLE	MELANOID	MESSMATE	*MILKMAID
MANDARIN	*MARKHOOR	MAYORESS	MELANOMA	MESSUAGE	*MILKSHED

*MILKWEED	MISCIBLE	MISSENSE	MOISTURE	*MONOPOLY	MORTISER
*MILKWOOD	MISCLAIM	*MISSHAPE	MOLALITY	MONORAIL	MORTMAIN
*MILKWORT	MISCLASS	MISSILRY	MOLARITY	MONOSOME	MORTUARY
*MILLCAKE	MISCOLOR	MISSOUND	MOLASSES	*MONOSOMY	MOSASAUR
MILLEPED	MISCOUNT	MISSPACE	MOLDIEST	MONOTINT	*MOSCHATE
MILLIARD	MISDOING	*MISSPEAK	*MOLDWARP	MONOTONE	*MOSQUITO
MILLIARE	MISDOUBT	MISSPELL	MOLECULE	MONOTONY	*MOSSBACK
MILLIARY	MISDRIVE	MISSPEND	MOLEHILL	*MONOTYPE	MOSSIEST
MILLIBAR	MISENROL	*MISSPOKE	MOLESKIN	*MONOXIDE	MOSSLIKE
MILLIEME	MISENTER	MISSTART	MOLESTER	MONSIEUR	*MOTHBALL
MILLIGAL	MISENTRY	MISSTATE	*MOLYBDIC	MONSTERA	*MOTHERLY
*MILLILUX	MISERERE	MISSTEER	*MOMENTLY	MONTEITH	*MOTHLIKE
*MILLIMHO	MISEVENT	MISSTYLE	MOMENTUM	MONUMENT	MOTILITY
MILLINER	*MISFAITH	MISTAKER	*MONACHAL	MOONBEAM	MOTIONAL
*MILLIOHM	MISFIELD	*MISTEACH	MONADISM	*MOONCALF	MOTIONER
MILLIPED	*MISFOCUS	*MISTHINK	MONANDRY	MOONDUST	MOTIVATE
MILLIREM	*MISFRAME	*MISTHROW	*MONARCHY	*MOONFISH	*MOTIVITY
MILLPOND	MISGAUGE	MISTIEST	MONASTIC	MOONIEST	MOTORBUS
MILLRACE	MISTITLE	MISTITLE	MONAURAL	MOONLESS	MOTORCAR
*MILLWORK	MISGRAFT	*MISTOUCH	*MONAXIAL	MOONLIKE	MOTORDOM
MIMETITE	MISGUESS	MISTRACE	*MONAZITE	MOONPORT	MOTORING
*MIMICKER	MISGUIDE	MISTRAIN	MONECIAN	MOONRISE	MOTORISE
*MINACITY	*MISHMASH	MISTREAT	MONELLIN	MOONSAIL	MOTORIST
MINATORY	*MISHMOSH	MISTRESS	MONETARY	MOONSEED	*MOTORIZE
MINDLESS	MISINFER	MISTRIAL	MONETISE	MOONSHOT	MOTORMAN
MINEABLE	MISINTER	MISTRUST	*MONETIZE	*MOONWALK	*MOTORWAY
MINGIEST	*MISJUDGE	MISTRYST	*MONEYBAG	MOONWARD	MOUCHOIR
*MINIBIKE	MISLABEL	MISTUTOR	*MONEYMAN	MOONWORT	*MOUFFLON
*MINICAMP	MISLAYER	MISUNION	MONGEESE	*MOORCOCK	MOULDING
MINIMISE	MISLEARN	MISUSAGE	MONGOOSE	*MOORFOWL	MOUNTAIN
*MINIMIZE	MISLIGHT	MISVALUE	*MONICKER	MOORIEST	MOUNTING
*MINIPARK	MISLIKER	MISWRITE	MONITION	MOORLAND	MOURNFUL
MINISTER	MISLODGE	MITICIDE	MONITIVE	MOORWORT	MOURNING
MINISTRY	MISLYING	MITIGATE	MONITORY	*MOPBOARD	MOUSIEST
MINORITY	*MISMATCH	MITTIMUS	*MONKFISH	*MOPINGLY	MOUSSAKA
MINSTREL	MISNOMER	*MIXOLOGY	*MONKHOOD	*MOQUETTE	*MOUTHFUL
MINUTING	*MISOGAMY	MNEMONIC	MONOACID	MORALISE	*MOVEABLE
*MIQUELET	*MISOGYNY	MOATLIKE	MONOCARP	MORALISM	*MOVEABLY
MIRINESS	MISOLOGY	MOBILISE	MONOCRAT	MORALIST	MOVELESS
MIRLITON	MISORDER	*MOBILITY	*MONOCYTE	MORALITY	*MOVEMENT
MISADAPT	MISPAINT	*MOBILIZE	MONODIST	*MORALIZE	*MOVIEDOM
MISAGENT	MISPARSE	MOBOCRAT	MONOFUEL	MORATORY	MOVIEOLA
MISALIGN	*MISPATCH	MOCCASIN	*MONOGAMY	*MORBIFIC	*MOVINGLY
MISALTER	MISPLACE	MODALITY	MONOGENY	MORBILLI	*MOZZETTA
MISANDRY	MISPLANT	MODELING	MONOGERM	*MORDANCY	MRIDANGA
*MISAPPLY	MISPLEAD	MODELIST	MONOGLOT	MOREOVER	*MUCHACHO
MISASSAY	MISPOINT	MODELLED	MONOGRAM	*MORESQUE	*MUCHNESS
MISATONE	MISPOISE	MODELLER	*MONOGYNY	MORIBUND	*MUCIDITY
MISAWARD	MISPRINT	MODERATE	MONOHULL	MORONISM	MUCILAGE
MISBEGIN	*MISPRIZE	MODERATO	MONOLITH	MORONITY	*MUCKIEST
MISBEGOT	*MISQUOTE	MODIFIER	MONOLOGY	MOROSITY	*MUCKLUCK
MISBRAND	MISRAISE	MODIOLUS	MONOMIAL	*MORPHEME	*MUCKRAKE
MISBUILD	MISREFER	MODULATE	MONOPODE	*MORPHINE	*MUCKWORM
*MISCARRY	MISROUTE	*MOFFETTE	*MONOPODY	MORTALLY	*MUCOSITY
*MISCHIEF	MISSABLE	MOISTFUL	MONOPOLE	MORTGAGE	MUDDIEST

MUDGUARD	MUTTERER	S MARTASS	CO M MIE	FA MISH	HU M MER
*MUDPUPPY	*MUZZIEST	S MECTITE	CO M MIT	FA MOUS	HU M MUS
MUDSLIDE	*MYCELIUM	S MITHERS	*CO M MIX	FE MALE	HU MOUR
MUDSTONE	*MYCETOMA	TE MP	CO M MON	FI MBLE	HU MVEE
MUENSTER	*MYCOLOGY	WIM P	CO MOSE	FO MENT	HY MNAL
MUGGIEST	MYELITIS	BU MPH	CO MOUS	FU MBLE	*JA M MED
*MULBERRY	MYLONITE	*CO MIX	CO MPEL	FU MIER	*JA M MER
MULETEER	*MYOBLAST	GA MAY	*CO M PLY	FU MING	*JI MINY
MULLIGAN	*MYOGENIC	GAM MY	CU MBER	GA MBIA	*JU MBAL
MULTIAGE	*MYOGRAPH	GIM ME	CU M MER	GA MBIR	*JU MBLE
MULTICAR	*MYOPATHY	*HA M ZA	CU M MIN	GA MBIT	*JU MPER
MULTIFID	*MYOSCOPE	*JA M MY	CY MDAL	GA MBLE	KA MALA
*MULTIJET	MYOSITIS	LA MBY	CY MENE	GA MBOL	KA MSIN
MULTIPED	MYOSOTIS	LI MPA	CY MLIN	GA MELY	*KI M CHI
MULTIPLE	MYOTONIA	MIMEO	CY MOID	GA MEST	KI MONO
*MULTIPLY	*MYRIAPOD	ROMEO	CY MOSE	GA METE	KU MISS
MULTITON	*MYRIOPOD	*WI MPY	CY MOUS	GA MIER	KU M MEL
MULTIUSE	*MYRMIDON	BE MATA	DA MAGE	GA MILY	LA MBDA
*MUNCHIES	*MYSTAGOG	BE MEAN	DA MASK	GA MINE	LA MBIE
*MUNCHKIN	*MYSTICAL	BE MIRE	DAM MAR	GA MING	LA MEDH
MUNDUNGO	*MYSTICLY	BE MIST	DAM MED	GAM MED	LA MELY
MUNGOOSE	*MYSTIQUE	BE MOAN	DAM MER	GAM MER	LA MENT
MUNIMENT	*MYTHICAL	*BE MOCK	DA MNER	GAM MON	LA MEST
MUNITION	*MYXEDEMA	BE MUSE	DA MPEN	GEM MED	LA MINA
MURAENID	*MYXOCYTE	BOMBER	DA MPER	GE MOTE	LA MING
MURALIST		*BO MBAX	DA MPLY	GI MBAL	LA M MED
MURDEREE	S MEW	*BO MBYX	DA MSEL	GI MLET	LA MPAD
MURDERER	S MOG	BU MBLE	DA MSON	GI M MAL	LA MPAS
MURIATED	S MUG	BU MKIN	DE MAND	GI M MIE	LI MBUS
MURICATE	S MUT	BU M MER	DE MARK	GO MUTI	LI MHER
MURMURER	S MACK	BU MMED	DE MAST	GU M MED	LI MIER
MURRELET	S MALL	BU MPER	DE MEAN	GU M MER	LI MINA
MUSCADEL	S MALT	CA MAIL	DE MENT	HA MATE	LI MING
MUSCADET	S MARM	CA MASS	DE MIES	HA MLET	LI M MER
MUSCATEL	S MART	CA MBIA	DE MISE	HA M MAL	LI M MIC
MUSCULAR	S MASH	CA MDER	DE MODE	HA M MED	LI MNER
*MUSHROOM	*S MAZE	CA MERA	DE MOTE	HA M MER	LI MNIC
MUSICALE	S MEAR	CA MION	DE MURE	HA MPER	LI MPET
MUSICLAN	S MEEK	CA MISA	DI MING	HE M MED	LI MPID
MUSINGLY	S MELL	CA MISE	DI MITY	HE M MER	LI MPLY
*MUSKETRY	S MELT	CA MLET	DIM MED	HE MOID	LI MPSY
MUSKIEST	S MERK	CA MPER	DIM MER	HE MPIE	LO MEIN
*MUSQUASH	S MILE	CA MPUS	DI MOUT	HO MAGE	LO MENT
*MUSTACHE	S MIRK	CE MENT	DI MPLE	HO MBRE	LU MBAR
MUSTARDY	S MITE	CO MAKE	DI MPLY	HO MELY	LU MHER
MUTATION	S MITH	CO MATE	DI MWIT	HO MIER	*LU M MOX
*MUTCHKIN	S MOCK	CO MBAT	DO MAIN	HO MILY	LU MPEN
MUTENESS	S MOKE	CO M DER	DO MINE	HO MING	LU MPER
MUTICOUS	S MOKY	CO MEDO	DO MING	HO MINY	*MAM MEY
MUTILATE	S MOLT	CO MEDY	DO MINO	HU MANE	MO MISM
MUTINEER	S MOTE	CO MELY	DU MBLY	HU MATE	MO MSER
MUTINIED	S MIDGE	CO METH	DU M DUM	HU MBLE	*MO M SER
MUTINIES	S MILEY	CO M FIT	DU MPER	*HU MBLY	*MUM BLY
MUTINING	S MILOM	CO MING	FA MILY	HU MBUG	NA MELY
MUTINOUS	S MEDDUM	CO MITY	FA MING	HU M MED	

NAMING	REMOVE	SUMMON	BAMBINO	COMPERE	FUMIEST
NIMBLE	REMUDA	SYMBOL	BEMADAM	COMPETE	FUMULUS
NIMBUS	RIMIER	TAMALE	BIMETAL	COMPILE	GAMBADE
NIMMED	RIMING	TAMARI	BIMODAL	COMPLIN	GAMBADO
NIMROD	RIMMED	TAMBAC	*COMPLEX	COMPLOT	GAMBIER
NOMISM	RIMMER	TAMBAK	BOMBARD	COMPONE	GAMBLER
NUMBAT	RIMOSE	TAMBUR	BOMBAST	COMPORT	GAMBOGE
NUMBER	RIMOUS	TAMEIN	BOMBING	COMPOSE	GAMBREL
NUMBLY	RIMPLE	TAMELY	BUMBLER	COMPOST	GAMELAN
NUMINA	ROMANO	TAMEST	BUMBOAT	COMPOTE	GAMIEST
*NYMPHA	ROMPER	TAMING	BUMMEST	COMPUTE	GAMMIER
*NYMPHO	RUMAKI	TAMMIE	BUMMING	CUMARIN	GAMMING
PAMPER	RUMBLE	TAMPAN	*BUMPKIN	*CUMQUAT	GEMINAL
PIMPLE	RUMBLY	TAMPER	CAMBIAL	*CUMSHAW	GEMLIKE
*PIMPLY	RUMEST	TAMPON	CAMBIST	CUMULUS	GEMMATE
POMACE	RUMMER	TEMPEH	*CAMBIUM	*CYMLING	*GEMMILY
POMADE	RUMOUR	TEMPER	*CAMBRIC	DAMAGER	GEMMING
POMELO	RUMPLE	TEMPLE	CAMELIA	DAMMING	GEMMULE
POMMEE	RUMPLY	TIMBAL	CAMISIA	DAMOSEL	*GEMSBOK
POMMEL	RUMPUS	TIMBER	CAMORRA	*DAMOZEL	*GIMMICK
POMPOM	SAMARA	TIMBRE	*CAMPHOL	DAMPING	GIMPIER
POMPON	SAMBAR	TIMELY	*CAMPHOR	*DAMPISH	GOMERAL
PUMELO	SAMBUR	TIMING	CAMPIER	DEMAGOG	GOMEREL
PUMICE	SAMECH	TOMATO	*CAMPILY	DEMERGE	GOMERIL
PUMMEL	*SAMEKH	TOMBAC	CAMPING	DEMERIT	GUMBOIL
PUMPER	SAMIEL	TOMBAK	CAMPION	DEMESNE	GUMBOOT
RAMATE	SAMITE	TOMBOY	CAMPONG	DEMETON	GUMDROP
RAMAUL	SAMLET	TOMCOD	CEMBALO	DEMIGOD	GUMLIKE
RAMBLE	SAMOSA	TOMMED	COMATIC	DEMIREP	GUMMIER
RAMIFY	SAMPAN	TOMTIT	*COMATIK	DEMONIC	GUMMING
*RAMJET	SAMPLE	TUMBLE	COMBINE	DEMOTIC	GUMMITE
RAMMED	SAMSHU	TUMEFY	COMBUST	DEMOUNT	GUMMOSE
RAMMER	SEMEME	TUMOUR	COMEDIC	DIMERIC	GUMMOUS
RAMOSE	SEMINA	TUMULI	COMETIC	DIMETER	GUMSHOE
RAMOUS	SEMPLE	TUMULT	COMFIER	DIMMEST	GUMTREE
RAMROD	SEMPRE	TYMBAL	COMFORT	DIMNESS	GUMWEED
RAMSON	SHMEAR	TYMPAN	*COMFREY	*DIMORPH	GUMWOOD
RAMTIL	*SHMUCK	VAMOSE	COMICAL	DOMICAL	GYMNAST
REMAIL	SIMIAN	VAMPER	COMITIA	DOMICIL	HAMBONE
REMAIN	SIMILE	VOMICA	COMMAND	DOMINIE	*HAMBURG
REMAKE	SIMLIN	VOMITO	COMMEND	DUMPIER	*HAMMADA
REMAND	SIMMER	WAMBLE	COMMENT	*DUMPILY	HAMMIER
REMARK	SIMNEL	*WAMBLY	COMMIES	DUMPING	*HAMMILY
REMATE	SIMONY	WAMMUS	COMMODE	*DUMPISH	*HAMMING
REMEDY	SIMOOM	*WAMPUM	*COMMOVE	FAMULUS	*HAMMOCK
REMEET	SIMOON	WAMPUS	COMMUNE	FEMINIE	HAMSTER
REMELT	SIMPER	WOMBAT	COMMUTE	FEMORAL	HAMULUS
REMEND	SIMPLE	WOMERA	COMPACT	FIMBRIA	HEMAGOG
REMIND	SOMBER	YAMMER	*COMPANY	FUMARIC	HEMATAL
REMINT	SOMBRE	*ZOMBIE	COMPARE	FUMBLER	HEMATIC
REMISE	SOMITE	*ZYMASE	COMPART	FUMETTE	HEMATIN
REMISS	SUMACH		COMPASS		HEMIOLA
REMOLD	SUMMED		COMPEER		HEMLINE
REMORA	SUMMER		COMPEND		*HEMLOCK
REMOTE	SUMMIT				

*HE M M ING	LE M URES	RA M PAGE	SO M EDAY	*TY M PANY	GI M PIEST
HE M PIER	LI M ACON	RA M PANT	*SO M EHOW	VA M OOSE	GU M MIEST
*HI M SELF	LI M BATE	RA M PART	SO M EONE	VA M PIRE	GU M MOSIS
HO M AGER	*LI M BECK	*RA M PIKE	*SO M EWAY	*VA M PISH	*HA M MERER
*HO M BURG	LI M BIER	RA M PION	SU M LESS	VO M ITER	*HA M MIEST
*HO M EBOY	LI M EADE	RA M POLE	SU M MAND	VO M ITUS	*HO M EOBOX
HO M IEST	LI M IEST	RE M AKER	SU M MARY	*WA M EFOU	*HO M EOTIC
HO M INES	LI M INAL	RE M ARRY	SU M MATE	*WA M EFUL	*HO M EPORT
HO M INID	LI M ITED	RE M ATCH	SU M MERY	*WA M PISH	*HOMEROO M
*HO M MOCK	LI M ITER	RE M ERGE	SU M MING	*WI M PISH	*HO M ESTAY
HO M OLOG	LI M ITES	RE M NANT	SU M MONS	*WO M ANLY	*HO M INIZE
*HO M ONY M	*LI M PKIN	RE M ODEL	SU M PTER	WO M MERA	*HU M ANIS M
*HO M OSEX	LI M PSEY	RE M ORSE	SY M BION	*YA M ALKA	*HY M ENIU M
*HU M ANLY	LI M ULUS	RE M OUNT	SY M BIOT	*YA M ULKA	*KY M OGRA M
HU M BLER	LU M BAGO	RE M OVAL	*SY M PTO M	*ZA M ARRA	LA M BIEST
*HU M DRU M	LU M PISH	RE M OVER	TA M ABLE	*ZA M ARRO	LE M URINE
HU M ERAL	*MAM MARY	RI M FIRE	TA M ANDU	*ZE M STVO	LO M ENTU M
HU M ERUS	*MAM MOCK	RI M IEST	TA M ARAO	*ZO M BIFY	MA M ALIGA
*HU M IDLY	*MAM MOTH	RI M LAND	TA M ARAU	*ZY M OGEN	MA M MATUS
HU M IDOR	*MI M ICRY	RI M LESS	TA M ARIN	*ZY M OSAN	MA M MILLA
*HU M MING	*MUM MERY	RI M MING	TA M ASHA	*ZY M OSIS	MA M MITIS
*HU M MOCK	*MUM MIFY	*RI M ROCK	TA M BALA	*ZY M URGY	ME M BRANE
HU M ORAL	NA M ETAG	RO M AINE	TA M BOUR	BO M BESIN	ME M ORIAL
*HY M NARY	NE M ATIC	RO M ANCE	TA M BURA	CE M ENTU M	ME M ORISE
*HY M NIST	NE M ESIS	RO M AUNT	TA M PALA	*CI M BALO M	MI M ETITE
*HY M NODY	NI M IETY	RO M PISH	TA M PION	CO M ANAGE	MO M ENTU M
*JA M BEAU	NI M MING	RU M BLER	TE M BLOR	*CO M EMBER	MO M ENTU M
*JA M MIES	NO M ARCH	RU M MAGE	TE M PERA	CO M INGLE	NO M ADIS M
*JA M MING	NO M BLES	SA M BHAR	TE M PEST	*COM MANDO	NO M OGRA M
*JE M ADAR	NO M BRIL	SA M BHUR	TE M PLAR	*COM MENCE	*NU M ERACY
*JE M IDAR	NO M INAL	SA M BUCA	TE M PLET	*COM MERCE	NU M MULAR
*JI M JAMS	NO M INEE	*SA M BUKE	TE M PTER	CO M MONER	*PE M MICAN
*JI M MINY	NU M ERAL	SA M ISEN	TE M PURA	*COM MONLY	RA M ENTU M
*JU M BLER	NU M ERIC	SA M OVAR	TI M ARAU	CO M MUNAL	*RA M IFOR M
*JU M BUCK	NU M MARY	SA M PLER	TI M BALE	*CY M ATIU M	*RA M MIEST
*JU M POFF	*NY M PHET	SA M SARA	TI M BREL	*CYMBALOM	RE M ARKET
*KA M PONG	PA M PEAN	SA M URAI	TI M EOUS	*CY M BIDIA	RE M ASTER
KA M SEEN	PA M PERO	SE M ATIC	TI M EOUT	DE M ERARA	RI M INESS
*KI M CHEE	PE M BINA	SE M IDRY	TI M OLOL	DE M ERGER	RO M ANISE
*KO M ATIK	PE M ICAN	SE M IFIT	TI M PANO	DE M ERSAL	RU M MAGER
*KU M QUAT	*PE M PHIX	SE M ILOG	*TI M OTHY	DE M ONIS M	SA M ARIU M
LA M BAST	PI M ENTO	SE M IMAT	*TO M BACK	DI M ERIS M	*SA M IZDAT
LA M BENT	PO M ATUM	SE M INAL	TO M BOLO	*DI M MABLE	SA M PLIS M
LA M BERT	PO M FRET	SE M INAR	TO M FOOL	DO M INIU M	*SH M ALTZY
LA M BIER	PO M PANO	SE M IPRO	TO M MING	*DU M BCANE	SI M PLIST
LA M ELLA	PO M POUS	SE M IRAW	TO M PION	*DU M BHEAD	SU M MABLE
LA M MING	PU M ICER	*SH M ALTZ	TU M BLER	*FA M ILIS M	*SU M MERIY
LA M PERS	PU M MELO	*SH M OOZE	TU M BREL	*FE M INIS M	SU M MITAL
LA M PION	*PU M PKIN	SI M ILAR	TU M BRIL	GA M ESMAN	*SU M MITRY
LA M POON	RA M BLER	SI M IOID	TU M MLER	GA M MADIA	SU M MONER
LA M PREY	RA M EKIN	SI M IOUS	TU M ULAR	GA M MIEST	*SY M METRY
LA M STER	RA M ILIE	SI M ITAR	TU M ULUS	GA M MONER	*SY M PODIA
LE M MING	RA M MIER	*SI M PLEX	TY M PANA	GE M MIEST	*SY M POSIA
LE M PIRA	RA M MING	SI M ULAR	TY M PANI	*GI M MICKY	TI M ELINE
	RA M MISH	*SI M MPLY	TY M PANO		TI M PANU M

TO M ENTU M	NI M MED	*GI M MICK	SU M MAND	*COM MONLY	FLA M INGO
*TOM MYROT	PEL M ET	*GOO M BAH	SU M MARY	COM M UNAL	*FLA M MING
TO M OGRAM	PO M MEE	*GOO M BAY	SU M MATE	COS M ETIC	*FLI M FLA M
*TY M PANIC	PO M MEL	GU M MIER	SU M MERY	COS M ICAL	*FLU M MERY
*TYM PANUM	PUM M EL	GU M MING	SU M MING	COU M ARIN	FOA M IEST
*YAM MERER	RA M MED	GU M MITE	SU M MONS	COU M AROU	FOA M LESS
*ZYM OGRAM	RA M MER	GU M MOSE	TO M MING	*CRA M MING	*FOA M LIKE
DOL M A	RI M MED	GU M MOUS	TU M MLER	*CRA M OISY	FOR M ALIN
DOO M Y	RI M MER	*HA M MADA	WOM M ERA	CRA M POON	*FOR M ALLY
GAM M Y	RU M MER	HA M MIER	*BAD M OUTH	CRE M AINS	*FOR M ERLY
GI M ME	SHA M OS	*HA M MILY	BAL M ORAL	CRE M ATOR	FOR M LESS
HAL M A	SI M MER	*HA M MING	BEA M IEST	CRI M INAL	*FOR M WORK
*JAM M Y	SU M MED	*HA M MOCK	BEA M LESS	*CRO M LECH	FRE M ITUS
PRO M O	SU M MER	*HEI M ISH	*BEA M LIKE	*CRU M BIER	*FRO M ENTY
WHA M O	SU M MIT	*HE M MING	*BED M AKER	*CRUM HORN	*FRU M ENTY
BAY M AN	SU M MON	HOL M IUM	BER M UDAS	DAL M ATIC	*FUL M INIC
BU M MER	TA M MIE	*HOM MOCK	*BES M OOTH	DEE M STER	*FUR M ENTY
CO M MIE	TO M MED	*HU M MING	BES M UDGE	DIA M ANTE	GA M MADIA
CO M MIT	WA M MUS	*HU M MOCK	*BIG M OUTH	DIA M ETER	GA M MIEST
*CO M MIX	*WHA M MO	*JA M MIES	*BIO M ETRY	*DIE M AKER	GA M M ONER
CO M MON	YA M MER	*JA M MING	BLA M ABLE	*DIM M ABLE	GE M M IEST
CU M MER	BAS M ATI	*JI M MINY	*BLA M EFUL	DIS M OUNT	*GEO M ANCY
CU M MIN	*BOO M BOX	LA M MING	BOO M IEST	*DOO M SDAY	GEO M ETER
DAM M AR	BRO M ISM	LE M MING	*BOOM TOWN	DOO M STER	GEO M ETRY
DAM M ED	*BRO M IZE	*MAM MARY	*BRI M FULL	*DOR M ANCY	GER M ANIC
DAM M ER	BU M M EST	*MAM MOCK	BRI M LESS	DOR M IENT	GER M FREE
DI M MED	BU M MING	*MAM MOTH	*BRI M MING	DOR M OUSE	GER M IEST
DI M MER	CAD M IU M	*MIS MAKE	BRO M ELIN	DRA M ATIC	GER M INAL
FIL M ER	*CHE M ISM	*MUM MERY	*BRO M IDIC	DRA M MING	*GI M MICKY
GA M MED	*CHO M PER	*MUM MIFY	CAL M NESS	*DRA M MOCK	GLI M PSER
GA M MER	CLA M MER	NI M MING	*CAP M AKER	*DRA M SHOP	GLU M NESS
GA M MON	CO M MAND	NON M EAT	*CAR M AKER	DRU M BEAT	GNO M ICAL
GE M MED	CO M MEND	NU M MARY	*CHA M BRAY	DRU M FIRE	GOR M LESS
GI M M AL	CO M MENT	*PLU M BUM	*CHA M FRON	*DRU M FISH	GRA M ARYE
GI M MIE	CO M MIES	PRE M ADE	*CHA M PION	*DRUM HEAD	*GRA M ERCY
GU M MED	CO M MODE	PRE M EAL	*CHE M ICAL	DRU M LIER	GRI M ACER
GU M MER	*CO M MOVE	PRE M EET	*CHE M URGY	*DRU M LIKE	GRI M IEST
HA M MAL	CO M MUNE	PRE M IUM	*CHI M AERA	DRU M MING	GRI M MEST
HA M MED	CO M MUTE	PRE M OLD	*CHI M BLEY	DRU M ROLL	GRI M NESS
HA M MER	CON M ATA	PRE M OLT	*CHI M ERIC	*DUM M KOPF	GRO M WELL
HE M MED	COS M ISM	PRO M INE	*CHU M SHIP	FAR M HAND	GRU M BLER
HE M MER	*CRU M BUM	PUM M ELO	*CHY M OSIN	FAR M LAND	GRU M MEST
HO M MOS	DAM M ING	RA M MIER	*CLA M BAKE	*FAR M WIFE	*GRU M PHIE
HU M MED	DI M M EST	RA M MING	*CLA M MING	*FAR M WORK	*GRU M PISH
HU M MER	DRA M EDY	RA M MISH	CLA M ORER	*FAR M YARD	GU M M IEST
HU M MUS	FER M IU M	RI M MING	*CLAM WORM	*FIL M CARD	GU M MOSIS
*JA M MED	*FIL M DOM	RU M MAGE	CLE M ATIS	FIL M GOER	GUN M ETAL
*JA M MER	FRA M ING	SCH M EAR	*CLE M ENCY	FIL M IEST	HAE M ATAL
*JAS M IN	GA M MIER	SCH M EER	*CLU M PISH	FIL M LAND	*HAE M ATIC
KU M M EL	GA M MING	SCU M BAG	*COE M BODY	FIR M NESS	HAE M ATIN
LA M MED	GE M MATE	SLA M MER	*COE M PLOY	*FIR M WARE	*HA M MERER
LI M MER	GE M MIER	SLU M GUM	*COM MANDO	*FLA M ENCO	*HA M MIEST
LI M M IC	*GE M MILY	SLU M IS M	*COM MENCE	FLA M EOUT	HAR M LESS
*LU M MOX	GE M MING	*SOY M ILK	*COM MERCE	FLA M IEST	HAR M ONIC
*MA M MEY	GE M M ULE	SUB M ENU	COM M ONER	FLA M INES	*HAT M AKER

*HAY MAKER	*PLU M BIS M	*SCH M OOZE	SWI M SUIT	*YAR MELKE	MU M M
*HEL M INTH	PLU M BOUS	SCI M ETAR	*SWI M WEAR	*YAR M ULKE	NEE M
HEL M LESS	PLU M ELET	SCI M ITAR	*SYM M ETRY	*YAW M ETER	NEU M
*HELM SMAN	PLU M ERIA	SCI M ITER	*TAG MEMIC	*YEO M ANRY	NOR M
*HER M ETIC	PLU M IEST	*SCU M LIKE	TAL M UDIC	*ZOO M ANIA	PAL M
*HER M ITRY	*PLU M IPED	*SCU M MING	TEA M AKER	*ZOO M ETRY	PER M
*HOG M ANAY	*PLU M LIKE	SEA M IEST	TEA M MATE	*ZOO M ORPH	PLU M
*HOG M ENAY	*PLU M PISH	SEA M LESS	TEA M STER		POE M
*HUM MABLE	*PRE M EDIC	SEA M LIKE	*TEA M WORK	BAL M	PRA M
*KHA M SEEN	PRE M IERE	SEA M OUNT	TEG M ENTA	BAR M	PRI M
*KRUM HORN	PRE M OLAR	SEA M STER	TEG M INAL	BEA M	PRO M
*LAW MAKER	PRE M ORAL	*SHA M ABLE	TER M INAL	BER M	REA M
LOA M LESS	PRE M ORSE	*SHA M EFUL	TER M INUS	BLA M	ROA M
MAM MATUS	PRI M ATAL	*SHAM MASH	TER M LESS	BOO M	ROO M
MAM M ILLA	*PRI M EVAL	*SHA M MIED	TER M TI M E	BRI M	SCA M
MAM M ITIS	PRI M M EST	*SHA M MIES	*THE M ATIC	CAL M	SCU M
*MAP MAKER	*PRI M MING	*SHA M MING	*THU M BNUT	CHA M	SEA M
*MAU M ETRY	PRI M NESS	*SHA M OSIM	*THU M HKIN	CHU M	SEE M
*MID M ONTH	PRI M ROSE	*SHAM ROCK	*THY M JEST	CLA M	SHA M
*M IS MATCH	PRO M ISEE	*SHI M MERY	*THY M OSIN	COR M	SHI M
*MYR M IDON	PRO M ISER	*SHI M MING	TIT M OUSE	CRA M	SKI M
*NAU M ACHY	PRO M ISOR	*SKI M MING	*TOM M YROT	CUL M	SLA M
*NEO M ORPH	PRO M OTER	SLI M IEST	TRA M LESS	DEE M	SLI M
*NEO M YCIN	PRO M PTER	SLI M M EST	TRA M LINE	DER M	SLU M
*NON MAJOR	*PRO M PTLY	SLI M MING	TRA M M ING	DOO M	STE M
NON M ETAL	PRO M ULGE	SLI M NESS	*TRA M PISH	DOR M	STU M
NON M ETRO	PSA M MITE	*SLU M BERY	TRA M PLER	DOU M	SWA M
NON M ODAL	PTO M AINE	SLU M LORD	TRA M ROAD	DRA M	SWI M
NON M ONEY	PUL M ONIC	SLU M M ING	TRE M BLER	DRU M	SWU M
NON M ORAL	PUL M OTOR	SPU M IEST	TRI M ARAN	FAR M	TEA M
NON M USIC	*PYG M YIS M	STA M PEDE	TRI M ETER	FIL M	TEE M
*NOR M ALCY	*QIO M TAIN	STE M LESS	TRI M M EST	FIR M	TER M
NOR M ALLY	RA M M IEST	STE M LIKE	TRI M M ING	FLA M	THE M
NOR M ANDE	*REE M BARK	*STE M MERY	TRI M NESS	FOA M	TOO M
NOR M LESS	*REE M BODY	STE M M ING	*TRI M ORPH	FOR M	TRA M
NOU M ENON	REE M ERGE	STE M WARE	TRI M OTOR	FRO M	TRI M
NUM M ULAR	*REE M PLOY	STO M ACHY	TRO M BONE	GAU M	WAR M
PAL M ATED	REI M PORT	STO M ATAL	*TRU M PERY	GER M	WHA M
PAL M ETTE	REI M POSE	STO M ATIC	TUR M ERIC	GEU M	WHI M
PAL M ETTO	REN M INBI	STO M ODEA	VER M OULU	GLI M	WHO M
PAL M IEST	RES M OOTH	STU M BLER	VER M OUTH	GLO M	WOR M
PAL M ITIN	RHA M NOSE	STU M M ING	*VIO M YCIN	GLU M	YLE M
*PAL M LIKE	*RHE M ATIC	SUB M ERGE	*WAR MAKER	GRA M	*ZOO M
*PAN M IXIA	*RHO M BOID	SUB M ERSE	WAR M NESS	GRI M	BEDI M
*PAN M IXIS	ROO M ETTE	SUM M ABLE	*WAR M OUTH	GRU M	BEGU M
*PE M MICAN	ROO M MATE	*SUM M ITAL	*WHI M BREL	HAE M	BESO M
PER M EANT	RUM M AGER	*SUM M ITRY	*WHOM EVER	HAL M	BLOO M
PER M EASE	SAL M ONID	SUM M ONER	*WIG M AKER	HAR M	BOSO M
PER M EATE	SAR M ENTA	SUR M ISER	*WOR M HOLE	HEL M	BREA M
*PHI M OSIS	*SCA M MONY	SUR M OUNT	WOR M IEST	HER M	BROO M
PLI M SOLE	*SCA M PISH	*SWA M PISH	*WOR M LIKE	HOL M	*BUXO M
PLI M SOLL	*SCH M ALTZ	*SWI M MING	WOR M ROOT	LOA M	CARO M
*PLU M BAGO	*SCH M ALZY	SUR M OUNT	WOR M SEED	LOO M	CECU M
*PLU M BERY	*SCH M ELZE	*SWA M PISH	*WORMWOOD	M AI M	CELO M
*PLU M BING	*SCH M OOSE	*SWI M MING	*YAM M ERER	M AL M	CHAS M

CHIR M	SCRA M	CUBIS M	M AGNU M	SCHIS M	BOSSDO M
CLAI M	SCRI M	CUNDU M	M AIHE M	SCREA M	BOSSIS M
CREA M	SCRU M	CUPRU M	M ARRA M	SCUTU M	*BRECHA M
DATU M	SEBU M	CURTU M	*M AYHE M	SELDO M	BRO M IS M
DEGU M	SEDU M	CUSTO M	M EDIU M	SENSU M	BRUTIS M
DEIS M	SEIS M	DEFOA M	M EGOH M	SEPTU M	*BRUXIS M
DENI M	SERU M	DEFOR M	M EGRI M	*SEXIS M	*BUCKRA M
DREA M	SHAW M	DEGER M	M ENTU M	SHOLO M	*BUDWOR M
DUNA M	SKEL M	DEPER M	M INIU M	SI M OO M	CAD M IU M
DURU M	S M AR M	DESEE M	M ISAI M	SITCO M	CAESIU M
FANU M	SODO M	DEWOR M	M O M IS M	SLALO M	CALCIU M
FILU M	SOLU M	DIADE M	M ONIS M	S M ILO M	*CA M BIS M
FLEA M	SPAS M	DIATO M	M USEU M	SODIU M	*CA M BIU M
FORA M	SPER M	DICTU M	M UTIS M	SPIRE M	CENTRU M
FORU M	STEA M	DINKU M	NANIS M	SPUTU M	CHARIS M
GENO M	STOR M	DIRDU M	NAPAL M	*SQUIR M	*CHEFDO M
GLEA M	STRU M	DIRHA M	NO M IS M	STREA M	*CHE M IS M
GLOA M	SWAR M	DISAR M	NONCO M	SUBGU M	CHETRU M
GLOO M	THAR M	DODGE M	NUDIS M	SYNCO M	CHILLU M
GOLE M	THER M	DOGDO M	PABLU M	SYSTE M	CHRISO M
GROO M	THRU M	DORSU M	PAYNI M	TALCU M	CLONIS M
HARE M	TOTE M	DRACH M	PEPLU M	TANDE M	*COCOYA M
HAUL M	VELU M	DU M DU M	PHENO M	TECTU M	CONFIR M
HILU M	VENO M	FANDO M	PHLEG M	TEDIU M	CONFOR M
HOKU M	VROO M	FANTO M	PHLOE M	TELIU M	COS M IS M
JORA M	WHEL M	FATHO M	*PHYLU M	TERGU M	CRANIU M
JORU M	*XYLE M	FAVIS M	PILEU M	THAIR M	CRISSU M
*JUGU M	*ZIRA M	FERBA M	PISSI M	THEIS M	*CRU M BU M
KALA M	BALSA M	FERRU M	PLENU M	THIRA M	CULTIS M
KELI M	BANTA M	FOLIU M	PODIU M	TRUIS M	CUTWOR M
KHOU M	BARIU M	FRENU M	POGRO M	VACUU M	*CZARDO M
KILI M	BECAL M	FULHA M	PO M PO M	VAGRO M	*CZARIS M
LARU M	BEDLA M	FULLA M	PORIS M	VAROO M	DADAIS M
LINU M	BEGRI M	GODDA M	POSSU M	VELLU M	DAYROO M
LOCU M	BELDA M	GONIU M	PREAR M	VICTI M	DECLAI M
M ADA M	BESEE M	GRAHA M	PRELI M	*WA M PU M	DECORU M
*M AXI M	BEWOR M	GRANU M	PURIS M	WHILO M	DEIFOR M
M IAS M	BIFOR M	GYPSU M	*QUORU M	*WIGWA M	DIAGRA M
M INI M	BOTTO M	*HAKEE M	RACIS M	WISDO M	DIASTE M
M ODE M	BUNKU M	HANSO M	RADIU M	BAALIS M	DISHEL M
NOTU M	CAECU M	HAREE M	RANDO M	*BAGWOR M	DODOIS M
*NUZA M	CARRO M	HELIU M	RANSO M	BAPTIS M	DOGEDO M
PLAS M	CENTU M	HOLIS M	RECTU M	BARROO M	DUALIS M
PRAA M	CERIU M	*JETSA M	REDEE M	*BECHAR M	*DUKEDO M
PRIS M	CESIU M	*JETSO M	REFIL M	BEDROO M	FADDIS M
PROE M	CHIAS M	KALIU M	REFOR M	BEGLOO M	FANTAS M
PSAL M	CHRIS M	LABIU M	REGNU M	BE M ADA M	FASCIS M
*QUAL M	CILIU M	LABRU M	RETEA M	BERSEE M	*FAUVIS M
REAL M	CIVIS M	LACTA M	RETRI M	BESWAR M	FER M IU M
REAR M	COELO M	LINGA M	REWAR M	BIOHER M	FIDEIS M
REHE M	CONDO M	LISSO M	*RHYTH M	BLELLU M	*FIEFDO M
RETE M	CONIU M	*LOGJA M	SACHE M	BLOSSO M	*FIL M DO M
RHEU M	COPAL M	LUTEU M	SACRU M	BLUEGU M	FIREAR M
SAGU M	CORIU M	LYCEU M	SADIS M	*BOGYIS M	*FOGYIS M
SATE M	CRINU M	LYRIS M	SALAA M	BOREDO M	FOREAR M

FRAENU M	NOSTRU M	SOLANU M	BASIDIU M	DECIGRA M	*HAIRWOR M
FREEDO M	PABULU M	SOPHIS M	*BATHROO M	*DEKAGRA M	HANDLOO M
FRUSTU M	PALLIU M	SORGHU M	BDELLIU M	DELIRIU M	HEADROO M
FULCRU M	PANICU M	STADIU M	BIENNIU M	DE M ONIS M	HEDONIS M
GALLIU M	PANTOU M	STANNU M	BIOPLAS M	*DIAZEPA M	HEIRLOO M
GINGHA M	PARONY M	STARDO M	*BIRDFAR M	*DIDY M IU M	HELOTIS M
GRANDA M	PEONIS M	STATIS M	*BLACKGU M	DIESTRU M	*HEXAGRA M
GROGRA M	PERFOR M	STERNU M	BLUESTE M	DILUVIU M	HOLOGRA M
GUNROO M	PHANTO M	STEWBU M	*BOLLWOR M	DI M ERIS M	*HOMEROO M
HADARI M	PHELLE M	STIBIU M	*BOOKWOR M	DIOECIS M	*HOOKWOR M
*HAFNIU M	PIANIS M	*STICKU M	*BOTHRIU M	DISBOSO M	*HORNBEA M
HALIDO M	PIETIS M	STRATU M	BOTULIS M	DISCLAI M	*HORNWOR M
HEIRDO M	PILGRI M	SUNBEA M	*BOYARIS M	DITHEIS M	HOTELDO M
HEROIS M	PINETU M	SUNROO M	*BRACHIU M	DO M INIU M	*HU MANIS M
HOBOIS M	PINWOR M	*SY M PTO M	*BROUGHA M	DRUIDIS M	*HY M ENIU M
HOL M IU M	PLENIS M	*SYNONY M	*BRUNIZE M	DUODENU M	*HYPODER M
*HO M ONY M	*PLU M BU M	TACHIS M	CABALIS M	*DWARFIS M	HYPOGEU M
HOODLU M	PO M ATU M	TANGRA M	CALADIU M	*DYNA MIS M	*JANIFOR M
*HU M DRU M	POPEDO M	TANTRU M	*CAPSICU M	*FACTOTU M	*JEROBOA M
*JARLDO M	PREBOO M	TAPETU M	*CARDA MO M	FAIRYIS M	*JINGOIS M
*JEJUNU M	PREFOR M	TAPROO M	*CARDA MU M	*FA M ILIS M	*KILOGRA M
*JIBBOO M	PRE M IU M	TEAROO M	*CASEWOR M	FARADIS M	*KYMOGRA M
*JUGULU M	PRETER M	TERAOH M	CASTEIS M	FATALIS M	LABDANU M
*JUJUIS M	PRETRI M	TERBIU M	CE M ENTU M	*FE M INIS M	LABELLU M
*KINGDO M	PREWAR M	TETOTU M	CENTRIS M	*FILIFOR M	LABURNU M
LABARU M	PROBLE M	THEORE M	CEREBRU M	FINALIS M	LACONIS M
LADANU M	PROGRA M	THORIU M	*CHADARI M	FIREROO M	*LADYPAL M
LAICIS M	PROTIU M	THULIU M	*CHIEFDO M	*FIREWOR M	LANDFOR M
LEFTIS M	*QUANTU M	TONEAR M	*CHRO MIU M	*FISHWOR M	LAUDANU M
LEGROO M	*QUONDA M	TOPONY M	CIBORIU M	FLATWOR M	*LEAFWOR M
*LEHAYI M	REALIS M	TOURIS M	*CI M BALO M	FLI M FLA M	*LECHAYI M
LITHIU M	REBLOO M	TRANGA M	CINGULU M	FLUIDRA M	LEGALIS M
LOBWOR M	RECLAT M	TRANSO M	*CIVICIS M	*FOREBOO M	LINOLEU M
*LOCKRA M	REDREA M	TRIDUU M	*CLAMWOR M	FOREDOO M	*LIXIVIU M
LOCOIS M	REGROO M	TRIFOR M	CLASSIS M	*FRANCIU M	*LOBBYIS M
LUGWOR M	*REQUIE M	TRIGRA M	*CLERKDO M	*FREEFOR M	LOCALIS M
LUSTRU M	*RHABDO M	TRITIU M	COAGULU M	FRENULU M	LOGOGRA M
MACADA M	RHENIU M	TRIVIU M	COATROO M	*FURCULU M	LO M ENTU M
*M AJORA M	RHODIU M	TROPIS M	*COLIFOR M	*FUSIFOR M	LOYALIS M
*MAXI M U M	ROSTRU M	TSARDO M	COLISEU M	FUTURIS M	*LUKEWAR M
M ETONY M	SANCTU M	TSARIS M	COLORIS M	GALBANU M	LUNGWOR M
*M ICROH M	SARCAS M	*TZARDO M	CONIDIU M	*GAPEWOR M	LUTECIU M
M IDTER M	SCROTU M	*TZARIS M	COREDEE M	GASIFOR M	LUTETIU M
M ILLDA M	SEDARI M	*WAXWOR M	CORE M IU M	GERANIU M	*LYRICIS M
M INI M U M	SELFDO M	*WEBWOR M	CORUNDU M	GIANTIS M	*LYRIFOR M
M ISDEE M	SERFDO M	*WHOLIS M	*CRONYIS M	*GLOWWOR M	M ASURIU M
M ISFOR M	*SHAHDO M	*WIFEDO M	CROSSAR M	GLUCINU M	*MEALWOR M
M ISTER M	SHITTI M	*WOLFRA M	*CUBIFOR M	GONIDIU M	M ECONIU M
M ODICU M	SIDEAR M	YARDAR M	*CUNIFOR M	GRANDDA M	M ELANIS M
M UDROO M	SISTRU M	YTTRIU M	*CY M ATIU M	*GRUBWOR M	M ERISTE M
M UONIU M	SKELLU M	*ZOARIU M	*CYMBALO M	GUAIACU M	M ESODER M
NARCIS M	*SKOOKU M	*ZOECIU M	*CYNICIS M	GUAIOCU M	*M EZEREU M
NATRIU M	SLU M GU M	*BACKROO M	*DANDYIS M	*GYNECIU M	*M ILLIOH M
NIOBIU M	SLU M IS M	BALLROO M	*DARKROO M	*GYPSYDO M	M ILLIRE M
NONFAR M	S M EDDU M	BAROGRA M	*DAYDREA M	*GYPSYIS M	M ISCLAI M

M O M ENTUM	*PASHADO M	PROSAIS M	SAINTDO M	SOLECIS M	*TY M PANU M
M ONADIS M	PATAGIU M	*PSYLLIU M	SALEROO M	SONOGRA M	VANADIU M
M ONOGER M	PECULIU M	*PTYALIS M	SA M ARIU M	*SPANWOR M	*VARIFOR M
M ONOGRA M	*PEDIFOR M	PUDENDU M	SA M PLIS M	SPECTRU M	VARIORU M
M OONBEA M	PENDULU M	PUGILIS M	SANDWOR M	SPECULU M	*VASCULU M
M ORALIS M	*PEPONJU M	*PUPPYDO M	*SAPPHIS M	*SPHAGNU M	*VASIFOR M
M ORONIS M	PERIBLE M	*PYGIDIU M	SATANIS M	SPICULU M	VEGANIS M
M OTORDO M	PERIDER M	*PYG M YIS M	SAVAGIS M	SPLENIU M	VELARIU M
*M OVIEDO M	PERIDIU M	*PYRIFOR M	SCANDIU M	STOICIS M	VENOGRA M
*MUCKWOR M	PERINEU M	*PYXIDIU M	*SCHOLIU M	SUDARIU M	VERATRU M
*MUSHROO M	*PHALLIS M	*QUACKIS M	SCIOLIS M	SUPER M O M	*VERBATI M
*M YCELIU M	*PHANTAS M	*QUEENDO M	SECUNDU M	*SYCONIU M	*VEXILLU M
NABOBIS M	*PHILTRU M	*QUIETIS M	SEDILIU M	TALEYSI M	*VIATICU M
NANOGRA M	*PICIFOR M	RACE M IS M	SELENIU M	TANTALU M	*VIBURNU M
*NAPIFOR M	PICLORA M	RA M ENTU M	*SERAPHI M	*TAPEWOR M	VILLADO M
NATIVIS M	*PICOGRA M	*RA M IFOR M	SERIATI M	TAUTONY M	*VINCULU M
NATURIS M	*PILIFOR M	*REAFFIR M	SETIFOR M	TEETOTU M	VIRILIS M
NEOPLAS M	PIPESTE M	REBELDO M	SETS M IS M	TELEFIL M	VITALIS M
*NEPHRIS M	*PIRIFOR M	REFUGIU M	*SHA M OSI M	TELEGRA M	*VIVARIU M
NEPOTIS M	*PISIFOR M	REHOBOA M	*SHA M OST M	THALLIU M	*VOCALIS M
NEWSROO M	*PLANFOR M	REINFOR M	*SHEIKDO M	THRALDO M	VOLTAIS M
NGULTRU M	PLASTRU M	RENIFOR M	*SHIPWOR M	TI M PANU M	WARDROO M
NIHILIS M	*PLATFOR M	RENOGRA M	*SHKOTZI M	TITANIS M	WAREROO M
NOBELIU M	PLATINU M	RESIDUU M	SHOWROO M	TITANIU M	*WASHROO M
NO M ADIS M	*PLAYROO M	RESTROO M	*SICKROO M	TOADYIS M	*WAVEFOR M
NO M OGRA M	PLECTRU M	RETIFOR M	*SIEROZE M	TOKENIS M	*WHIPWOR M
*PACHADO M	PLEONAS M	RIGHTIS M	SILICIU M	TO M ENTU M	*WHOREDO M
*PACIFIS M	*PLU M BIS M	RIGORIS M	*SILKWOR M	TO M OGRA M	*WIREWOR M
PAEANTS M	POLONIU M	RINGWOR M	SINAPIS M	TOOLROO M	*WOODWOR M
PAGANDO M	POOLROO M	ROBOTIS M	*SKIAGRA M	TOTALIS M	*WORKROO M
PAGANIS M	POPULIS M	ROSARIU M	*SLIPFOR M	TOTE M IS M	*YAHOOIS M
PALUDIS M	*POSTFOR M	ROTIFOR M	*SLOWWOR M	TRIADIS M	*ZO M BIIS M
PARADIG M	PRIAPIS M	*ROWDYIS M	SNOBBIS M	TRILLIU M	*ZOOSPER M
*PARAFOR M	PRIGGIS M	ROYALIS M	SOLARIS M	TRITICU M	*ZY M OGRA M
PARECIS M	PROCLAI M	RUBIDIU M	SOLARIU M	TROILIS M	
*PAROXYS M	PRONOTU M	RURALIS M	SOLATIU M	*TUBIFOR M	

N

NAAN	NAVE	NENE	NICE	NODE	NOOK
NADA	NAVY	NEON	**NICK**	NODI	NOON
NAIF	**NAZI**	NERD	NIDE	NOEL	NOPE
NAIL	NEAP	NESS	NIDI	NOES	NORI
NAME	NEAR	NEST	NIGH	NOGG	NORM
NANA	NEAT	NETT	NILL	NOIL	NOSE
NAOS	**NECK**	NEUK	NINE	NOIR	NOSH
NAPE	NEED	NEUM	NIPA	NOLO	NOSY
NARC	NEEM	NEVE	NISI	NOMA	NOTA
NARD	NEEP	NEWS	NITE	NOME	NOTE
NARK	NEIF	NEWT	**NIXY**	NONA	NOUN
NARY	NEMA	**NEXT**	**NOCK**	NONE	NOUS

NOVA	NICAD	***NYMPH**	NITRID	NULLAH	NINEPIN
NOWT	NICOL	**NACHAS**	NITRIL	**NUMBAT**	NIOBATE
NUDE	NIDAL	**NACHES**	NITWIT	NUMINA	NITINOL
NUKE	NIDUS	NARROW	NOBLER	NUNCIO	***NITPICK**
NULL	NIECE	NARWAL	NOCENT	NUNCLE	NITRATE
NUMB	NIEVE	NASION	NODDED	NURSER	NITRIDE
NURD	NIGHT	NASTIC	NODDER	NUTANT	NITRILE
NURL	NIHIL	NATANT	NODDLE	NUTATE	NITRITE
NABIS	**NINJA**	NATION	NODOSE	NUTLET	NITROSO
NABOB	NINNY	NATIVE	NODOUS	NUTMEG	NITROUS
NACHO	NINON	NATRON	NODULE	NUTRIA	**NONBODY**
NACRE	NINTH	NATTER	NOESIS	NUTTED	NOBLEST
NADIR	NISEI	NATURE	NOETIC	NUTTER	NOCTULE
NAGGY	NISUS	NAUSEA	NOGGIN	***NUZZLE**	NOCTURN
NAIAD	NITER	NAVIES	NONAGE	***NYMPHA**	NOCUOUS
NAIRA	NITID	***NAZIFY**	NONART	***NYMPHO**	NODDIES
NAIVE	NITON	NEARLY	NONEGO	**NAMETAG**	NOISOME
NAKED	NITRE	NEATEN	NONFAN	NANDINA	NOMINAL
NALED	NITRO	NEATLY	NONFAT	NARCOSE	NOMINEE
NAMER	NITTY	NEBULA	**NONGAY**	NARGILE	NONAGON
NANCE	NIVAL	NEBULE	NONMAN	NARRATE	NONCOLA
NANNY	NOBLE	**NECKER**	NONPAR	***NARTHEX**	NONDRUG
NAPPE	NODAL	NECTAR	NONUSE	NASCENT	**NONFACT**
NAPPY	NODUS	NEEDER	NONWAR	NATRIUM	**NONFUEL**
NARCO	NOISE	NEEDLE	NOODGE	NATURAL	**NONHEME**
NARES	NOISY	NEGATE	NOODLE	NECROSE	**NONHOME**
NARIS	NOMAD	NELLIE	NOOSER	NEEDIER	NONIRON
NARKY	NOMEN	NELSON	NORDIC	NEEDLER	***NONJURY**
NASAL	NOMOS	NEREID	NORITE	NEGATON	NONMEAT
NASTY	NONCE	NEREIS	NORMAL	NEGATOR	**NONNEWS**
NATAL	NONET	NEROLI	NORMED	NEGLIGE	**NONOILY**
NATCH	NONYL	NESTER	NOSHER	NEGROID	**NONPAID**
NATES	NOOSE	NESTLE	NOSIER	NEGRONI	NONPAST
NATTY	NOPAL	NESTOR	NOSILY	NEMESIS	**NONPEAK**
NAVAL	NORIA	NETHER	NOSING	NEONATE	**NONPLAY**
NAVAR	NORTH	NETTED	NOSTOC	NERITIC	NONPLUS
NAVEL	NOSED	NETTER	NOTARY	NESTLER	NONPOOR
NEATH	NOSEY	NETTLE	NOTATE	NETLESS	NONPROS
NEEDY	NOTAL	NETTLY	NOTHER	NETTIER	**NONSELF**
NEGRO	NOTED	NEURAL	NOTICE	NETTING	NONSLIP
NEGUS	NOTER	NEURON	NOTING	NETTLER	NONSTOP
NEIGH	NOTUM	NEUTER	NOTION	NEURINE	NONSUIT
NEIST	NOVEL	NEWSIE	NOUGAT	NEUROID	NONUPLE
NELLY	NUBIA	NEWTON	NOVENA	NEUROMA	NONUSER
NERDY	NUDER	NIACIN	NOWISE	NEURONE	**NONWORD**
NEROL	NUDGE	NIDGET	***NOZZLE**	NEURULA	**NONWORK**
NERTS	NUDIE	NIDING	NUANCE	NEUSTON	***NONZERO**
NERVE	***NUDZH**	NIELLO	NUBILE	NEUTRAL	NOONING
NETOP	NUMEN	NIGGLE	NUBLES	NEUTRON	NORLAND
NETTY	NURSE	NILGAI	NUCLEI	***NEWMOWN**	NOSIEST
NEUME	NUTSY	NILGAU	NUDEST	***NEWSBOY**	NOSTRIL
NEVER	NUTTY	NIMROD	NUDGER	***NIBLICK**	NOSTRUM
NEVUS	***NUZAM**	NINETY	NUDISM	NICOTIN	NOTABLE
NEWEL	NYALA	NITERY	NUDIST	NICTATE	**NOTEPAD**
NGWEE	NYLON	NITRIC	NUGGET	NIGGLER	NOTICER

NOUVEAU	NEUROSIS	*NONQUOTA	K N OP	S N OOD	*BU N CHY
NOWNESS	NEUTRINO	NONRATED	K N OT	S N OOK	BU N DLE
NUCLEAL	*NEWCOMER	NONRURAL	K N OW	S N OOL	BU N GEE
NUCLEAR	*NEWFOUND	NONSENSE	K N UR	S N OOP	BU N GLE
NUCLEIN	*NEWLYWED	NONSOLAR	S N AG	S N OOT	BU N ION
NUCLEON	*NEWSHAWK	NONSOLID	S N AP	S N ORE	BU N KER
NUCLEUS	*NEWSPEAK	NONSTORY	S N AW	S N ORT	BU N KUM
NUMERAL	*NEXTDOOR	NONSTYLE	S N ED	S N OUT	BU N TER
NUNATAK	NGULTRUM	NONSUGAR	S N IB	S N OWY	BY N AME
NUPTIAL	*NICKELIC	NONTIDAL	S N IP	S N UCK	CA N APE
NURSING	*NICKNACK	NONTITLE	S N IT	S N UFF	CA N ARD
NURTURE	*NICKNAME	NONTONAL	S N OB	BA N ANA	CA N ARY
NUTCASE	NIELLIST	*NONTOXIC	S N OT	BA N DER	CA N CAN
NUTGALL	*NIGHTCAP	NONUNION	S N OW	BA N DIT	CA N CEL
NUTMEAT	*NIGHTJAR	NONUSING	S N UB	BA N DOG	CA N CER
*NUTPICK	NIGROSIN	NONVALID	S N UG	BA N GER	CA N CHA
NUTTING	NINETEEN	*NONWOODY	S N YE	BA N GLE	CA N DID
*NUZZLER	*NITPICKY	NOONTIDE	G N ARL	BA N IAN	CA N DLE
*NYMPHET	NITRATOR	*NORMALCY	G N ARR	BA N ISH	CA N DOR
NARRATER	NITROGEN	NORMANDE	G N ASH	BA N KER	CA N FUL
NARRATOR	*NIZAMATE	NOSEDIVE	G N AWN	BA N NED	CA N GUE
NASALISE	NOISETTE	NOSELESS	G N OME	BA N NER	CA N INE
*NASCENCY	*NOMARCHY	NOSINESS	J N A N A	BA N NET	CA N ING
NATATION	NONACTOR	NOTARIAL	*K N ACK	BA N TAM	CA N KER
NATIONAL	NONADULT	*NOTARIZE	K N AUR	BA N TER	CA N NED
NATURISM	*NONBLACK	NOTATION	K N EAD	BA N YAN	CA N NEL
NATURIST	NONBRAND	NOTELESS	K N EEL	*BA N ZAI	CA N NER
*NAUMACHY	NONCLING	NOTORNIS	K N ELT	BE N AME	CA N NIE
NAUSEANT	NONCOLOR	NOTTURNO	K N IFE	BE N DAY	CA N NON
NAUSEATE	NONCRIME	NOUVELLE	K N ISH	BE N DEE	CA N NOT
NAUSEOUS	NONDANCE	*NOVELIZE	*K N OCK	BE N DER	CA N OLA
NAUTILUS	NONELITE	*NOWADAYS	K N OLL	BE N IGN	CA N OPY
NAYSAYER	*NONEMPTY	NUCLEOID	K N OSP	BE N NET	CA N TER
NEARNESS	*NONEQUAL	NUDENESS	K N OUT	*BE N ZAL	CA N TIC
NEARSIDE	NONFATTY	*NUMBFISH	K N URL	*BE N ZIN	CA N TLE
NEATNESS	NONFINAL	*NUMERACY	S N ACK	*BE N ZOL	CA N TON
*NEBULIZE	NONGATAL	*NUNCHAKU	S N AFU	*BE N ZYL	CA N TOR
*NECKHAND	NONGLARE	NURSLING	S N AIL	BI N ARY	CA N TUS
*NECKLACE	NONGUEST	NURTURAL	S N AKE	BI N ATE	CA N ULA
*NECKLIKE	NONGUILT	NURTURER	S N AKY	BI N DER	CA N VAS
*NECKWEAR	*NONHARDY	NUTATION	S N ARE	BI N DLE	CA N YON
*NECROPSY	NONIDEAL	NUTGRASS	S N ARK	BI N NED	CE N OTE
NEEDIEST	NONIMAGE	NUTRIENT	S N ARL	BI N OCS	CE N SER
NEEDLESS	NONISSUE	NYSTATIN	S N ASH	BO N ACI	CE N SOR
NEGATION	*NONJUROR		S N ATH	BO N BON	CE N SUS
NEGATRON	NONLABOR		S N EAK	BO N DER	CE N TAL
*NEOMORPH	NONLEAFY		S N EAP	BO N DUC	CE N TER
*NEOMYCIN	NONLEGAL	G N AR	S N ECK	BO N IER	CE N TRA
*NEOPHYTE	*NONMAJOR	G N AT	S N EER	BO N ITA	CE N TRE
*NEPHRISM	NONMETRO	K N AP	S N ELL	BO N ITO	CE N TUM
NESTABLE	NONMUSIC	K N AR	S N ICK	BO N NET	CI N DER
NESTLING	NONNOVEL	K N EE	S N IDE	BO N NIE	CI N EOL
NETTIEST	*NONOHMIC	K N EW	S N IFF	BO N SAI	CI N EMA
*NEURAXON	NONPOINT	K N IT	S N IPE	*BO N ZER	*CI N QUE
NEURITIS	NONPRINT	K N OB			CO N CHA

*CO N CHY	DI N KLY	GA N GLY	HO N KIE	LI N IER	MI N IO N
CO N CUR	DI N KUM	GA N GUE	HO N OUR	LI N ING	MI N IO N
CO N DOM	DIN N ED	*GA N JAH	**HU N GER**	**LI N KER**	MI N TER
CO N DOR	DIN N ER	GA N NET	**HU N GRY**	**LI N KUP**	MI N UET
CO N FAB	DO N ATE	GA N OID	**HU N KER**	LI N NET	MI N UTE
CO N FER	DO N ERD	**GA N TRY**	HU N TER	LI N SEY	**MI N YA N**
CO N FIT	DO N ERT	GE N DER	**JA N GLE**	LI N TEL	MI N GLE
CO N GEE	**DO N JO N**	GE N ERA	*JA N GLY	LI N TER	MO N GER
CO N GER	**DO N KEY**	**GE N EVA**	**JE N N ET**	LI N TOL	MO N GOE
CO N GOU	DON N ED	GE N IAL	**JI N GAL**	LO N ELY	MO N GOL
CO N IES	DON N EE	GE N IUS	*JI N GKO	LO N GA N	MO N GST
CO N INE	DO N SIE	GE N TES	**JI N GLE**	LO N GER	MO N IED
CO N IN G	*DO N ZEL	GE N TIL	*JI N GLY	**LO N GLY**	MO N IES
CO N IUM	DU N ITE	GE N TLE	*JI N KER	**LU N ACY**	MO N IST
CO N KER	DU N LIN	GE N TOO	JIN N EE	LU N ATE	*MO N KEY
CO N N ED	DUN N ED	**GE N TRY**	JU N GLE	LU N GA N	MO N TES
CO N N ER	DUN N ER	GI N GAL	*JU N GLY	LU N GEE	MU N TI N
CO N OID	**DY N AST**	GI N GER	**JU N IOR**	LU N GER	NA N DI N
CO N SOL	**DY N ODE**	**GI N GKO**	*JU N KER	**LU N GYI**	NA N ISM
CO N SUL	**FA N DOM**	**GI N KGO**	*JU N KET	LU N IER	**NA N KI N**
CO N TRA	**FA N EGA**	GIN N ED	*JU N KIE	LU N IES	NAN N IE
*CO N VEX	FA N IO N	GIN N ER	**KA N BA N**	**LU N KER**	NI N ETY
CO N VEY	*FA N JET	**GO N IFF**	**KA N TAR**	LU N ULA	N O N AGE
CO N VOY	FAN N ED	GO N IO N	**KE N N ED**	LU N ULE	N O N ART
CU N DUM	FAN N ER	GO N IUM	**KE N N EL**	MA N AGE	**N O N COM**
CU N EAL	**FA N TOD**	**GO N OPH**	**KI N ASE**	MA N ANA	N O N EGO
CU N N ER	**FA N TOM**	GU N DOG	**KI N DLE**	MA N EGE	N O N FAN
DA N CER	**FE N CER**	GU N MA N	**KI N DLY**	MA N GEL	N O N FAT
DA N DER	**FE N DER**	GU N MA N	**KI N EMA**	MA N GER	**N O N GAY**
DA N DLE	**FE N N EC**	GU N N ED	**KI N GLY**	MA N GLE	N O N MA N
DA N GER	FE N N EL	GU N N EL	LA N ATE	MA N ILA	N O N PAR
DA N GLE	FI N ALE	GU N N EN	LA N CER	MA N ITU	**N O N TAX**
DA N ISH	**FI N DER**	GU N N ER	LA N CET	MAN N AN	N O N USE
DE N ARY	**FI N ELY**	GU N SEL	LA N DAU	MAN N ED	N O N WAR
DE N GUE	**FI N ERY**	**HA N DLE**	LA N DER	MAN N ER	N U N CIO
DE N IAL	FI N EST	**HA N GAR**	LA N ELY	MA N TEL	N U N CLE
DE N IED	**FI N GER**	**HA N GER**	LA N GUE	MA N TES	PA N ADA
DE N IER	FI N IAL	**HA N GUL**	LA N GUR	MA N TID	PA N DER
DE N IES	**FI N IN G**	**HA N GUP**	LA N N ER	MA N TIS	PA N DIT
DE N ME N	**FI N ISH**	**HA N IWA**	LA N OSE	MA N TLE	**PA N FRY**
DE N N ED	FI N ITE	**HA N KER**	LA N UGO	MA N TRA	PA N FUL
DE N OTE	FIN N ED	**HA N KIE**	LE N DER	MA N TUA	PA N GE N
DE N TAL	**FO N DLE**	HA N SEL	**LE N GTH**	MA N UAL	PA N IER
DE N TIL	**FO N DLY**	**HA N SOM**	LE N ITY	MA N URE	PA N N ED
DE N TI N	**FO N DUE**	HA N TLE	LE N TE N	ME N AGE	PA N TIE
DE N UDE	**FU N DUS**	**HE N BIT**	LE N TIC	ME N DER	**PA N TRY**
DI N DLE	**FU N GAL**	**HI N DER**	LE N TIL	ME N HIR	
DI N ERO	**FU N GIC**	**HI N GER**	LI N AGE	ME N IAL	*PA N ZER
DI N GER	**FU N GUS**	**HO N CHO**	LI N DE N	ME N INX	PE N A N G
DI N GEY	**FU N KER**	**HO N DLE**	LI N EAL	*ME N INX	**PE N CEL**
DI N GHY	**FU N KIA**	HO N EST	LI N EAR	ME N TAL	**PE N CIL**
DI N GLE	**FU N N ED**	**HO N IED**	LI N EUP	ME N TOR	PE N MA N
DI N GUS	FUN N EL	**HONIN G**	LI N GAM	MI N DER	PE N N ED
DININ G	GA N DER	**HO N KER**	LI N GER	MINGLE	PE N N ER
DI N KEY	GA N GER	*HO N KEY	LI N GUA	MI N IN G	PE N N O N

PEN SEE	*QIN DAR	SAN TOL	TAN GLE	TUN ICA	WIN NER
PEN SIL	*QIN TAR	SAN TUR	TAN GLY	TUN ING	WIN NOW
PEN TAD	**RAN CHO**	SEN ARY	TAN IST	TUN NED	WIN TER
PEN TYL	RAN CID	SEN ATE	**TAN KER**	TUN NEL	WIN TLE
PEN ULT	RAN COR	SEN DAL	TAN NED	**VAN DAL**	**WIN TRY**
PEN URY	RAN DAN	SEN DER	TAN NER	**VAN ISH**	WON DER
PIN ANG	RAN DOM	SEN DUP	TAN NIC	**VAN ITY**	WON NED
PIN ATA	RAN GER	SEN ECA	TAN NIN	**VAN MAN**	WON NER
PIN CER	**RAN KER**	SEN EGA	TAN REC	**VAN NED**	WON TON
PIN DER	**RAN KLE**	SEN HOR	TAN TRA	VAN NER	*YAN QUI
PIN EAL	**RAN KLY**	SEN ILE	**TAN UKI**	**VEN DEE**	YAN TRA
PINENE	RAN SOM	SEN IOR	TEN ACE	**VEN DER**	YON DER
PIN ERY	RAN TER	SEN ITI	TEN AIL	**VEN DOR**	YON KER
PIN GER	RAN ULA	SEN NET	TENANT	**VEN DUE**	*ZANANA
PiN IER	REN AIL	SEN NIT	TEN DER	**VEN EER**	*ZAN DER
PINING	REN AME	SEN ORA	TEN DON	**VEN ERY**	*ZAN IER
PIN ION	REN DER	SEN SOR	TEN IST	VEN IAL	*ZAN IES
PIN ITE	REN EGE	SEN SUM	TEN NER	VEN INE	*ZEN ANA
PIN KEN	REN EST	SEN TRY	TEN NIS	VEN IRE	*ZEN ITH
PIN KER	REN NET	SHN APS	TEN OUR	VEN OSE	*ZIN CIC
*PIN KEY	REN NIN	SHN OOK	TEN PIN	VEN OUS	*ZIN CKY
PIN KIE	REN OWN	**SIN EWY**	TEN REC	VEN TER	*ZIN GER
*PIN KLY	REN TAL	SIN FUL	TEN SOR	VEN ULE	*ZIN NIA
PIN NAE	REN TER	SIN GER	TEN TER	**VIN EAL**	*ZON ARY
PIN NAL	REN VOI	SIN GLE	TEN TIE	**VIN ERY**	*ZON ATE
PIN NED	RIN GER	**SIN GLY**	TEN UIS	VIN IER	*ZONING
PIN NER	RIN SER	**SIN KER**	TEN URE	*VIN IFY	*ZON KED
PIN OLE	RON DEL	SIN NED	TEN UTO	VIN ING	*ZON ULA
PIN TLE	RON ION	SIN NER	TIN CAL	VIN OUS	*ZON ULE
PIN YIN	RON NEL	SIN TER	TIN DER	WAN DER	BAN DAGE
PIN YON	RON YON	SONANT	TIN FUL	WAN DLE	BAN DANA
PON CHO	**RUN DLE**	SON ATA	TIN GLE	WAN GAN	*BAN DBOX
PON DER	**RUN KLE**	SON DER	**TIN GLY**	WAN GLE	BAN DEAU
PONENT	RUN LET	SON ICS	TIN IER	WAN GUN	BAN DIED
PON GEE	RUN NEL	SON NET	TIN ILY	WAN IER	BAN DIES
PON GID	**RUN NER**	SON SIE	TINING	WANING	BAN DORA
PON IED	**RUN OFF**	SUN BOW	**TIN KER**	WAN ION	BAN DORE
PON IES	RUN OUT	SUN DAE	**TIN KLE**	WAN NED	BAN EFUL
PON TIL	**RUN WAY**	SUN DER	TIN KLY	WAN NER	*BAN GKOK
PON TON	SAN CTA	SUN DEW	TIN MAN	WAN TER	BAN KING
*PUN CHY	SAN DAL	SUN DOG	TIN NED	WAN TON	BAN KSIA
PUN DIT	SAN DER	SUN DRY	TIN NER	WIN CER	BAN NING
PUN GLE	**SAN DHI**	SUN KEN	TIN SEL	WIN CEY	*BAN NOCK
PUN IER	SAN EST	SUN KET	TIN TER	WIN DER	*BAN QUET
PUN ILY	SAN GAR	SUN LIT	TON EME	WIN DLE	BAN SHEE
PUN ISH	SAN GER	SUN NED	TON GER	WIN DOW	BAN SHIE
*PUN KAH	SAN IES	SUN SET	TON GUE	WIN DUP	BEN CHER
PUN KER	SANING	SUN TAN	TON IER	WIN ERY	BEN EATH
*PUN KEY	SAN ITY	SYN COM	TON ISH	WIN GER	BEN EFIC
PUN KIE	*SAN JAK	SYN DET	TON LET	WIN IER	BEN EFIT
PUN KIN	SAN NOP	SYN DIC	TON NER	WINING	BEN EMPT
PUN NED	SAN NUP	SYN GAS	TON NER	WIN ISH	BEN ISON
PUN NER	SAN SAR	*SYN TAX	TON SIL	WIN KER	BEN LIMB
PUN NET	SAN SEI	SYN URA	TUN DRA	WIN KLE	BEN OMYL
PUN TER	SAN TIR	TAN DEM	TUN EUP	WIN NED	BEN THAL

BEN THIC	CEN TARE	CON NECT	DIN NING	FUN GOID	HAN DOUT
BEN THOS	CEN TAUR	CON NING	DON ATOR	FUN GOUS	HAN DSAW
*BEN ZENE	CEN TAVO	CON NIVE	DON GOLA	FUN ICLE	HAN DSEL
*BEN ZINE	CEN TILE	CON NOTE	DON NING	FUN NEST	HAN DSET
*BEN ZOIN	CEN TIME	*CON QUER	DON NISH	FUN NING	HAN GDOG
*BEN ZOLE	CEN TIMO	CON SENT	DUN GEON	GA NACHE	HAN GING
*BEN ZOYL	CEN TNER	CON SIGN	DUN NAGE	GAN GLIA	HAN GMAN
BIN DERY	CEN TRAL	CON SIST	DUN NESS	GAN GREL	HAN GOUT
BIN DING	CEN TRIC	CON SOLE	DUN NEST	*GA NGWAY	HAN GTAG
BIN NING	CEN TRUM	CON SORT	DUN NING	GAN TLET	HAN UMAN
BIN OCLE	CEN TURY	CON SULT	DUN NITE	GE NERAL	HEN BANE
*BO NAN ZA	CIN DERY	CON SUME	*DY NAMIC	GE NERIC	HEN COOP
BON DAGE	CIN EAST	CON TACT	DY NASTY	GE NESIS	HEN LIKE
BON DING	CIN EOLE	CON TAIN	FA NATIC	GE NETIC	HEN NERY
BON DMAN	CIN ERIN	CON TEMN	FAN CIED	GE NETTE	*HEN PECK
BON FIRE	CON ATUS	CON TEND	FAN CIER	GEN IPAP	HIN DGUT
BON KERS	CON CAVE	CON TENT	FAN CIES	GEN ITAL	HON ESTY
*BON NOCK	CON CEAL	CON TEST	FAN FARE	GEN ITOR	HON OREE
BUN DIST	CON CEDE	*CON TEXT	FAN FOLD	GEN SENG	HON ORER
BUN DLER	CON CEIT	CON TORT	FAN LIKE	GEN TEEL	HUN DRED
BUN GLER	CON CENT	CON TOUR	FAN NING	GEN TIAN	HUN NISH
BUN TING	CON CEPT	CON TROL	FAN TAIL	GEN TILE	HUN TING
CAN AKIN	CON CERN	CON TUSE	FAN TASM	GE NUINE	*JAN GLER
CAN ASTA	CON CERT	CON VECT	FAN TAST	GIN GALL	JAN ITOR
CAN DELA	CON CHIE	CON VENE	FAN TASY	GIN GELY	*JIN GALL
CAN DENT	CON CISE	CON VENT	FAN WISE	GIN GERY	*JIN GLER
CAN DIDA	CON COCT	CON VERT	FAN WORT	GIN GHAM	*JON QUIL
CAN DIED	CON CORD	CON VICT	*FA NZINE	GIN GILI	*JU NIPER
CAN DIES	CON CUSS	*CON VOKE	FE NAGLE	GIN GIVA	*JU NKMAN
CAN DLER	CON DEMN	CUN EATE	FEN CING	GIN NING	KAN TELE
CAN DOUR	CON DIGN	CUN NING	FEN LAND	GIN SENG	KEN NING
CAN ELLA	CON DOLE	CY NICAL	FIN ABLE	GIN GELI	KE NOSIS
CAN IKIN	CON DONE	DAN DIER	FIN AGLE	GON DOLA	KIN DLER
CAN NERY	CON DUCE	DAN DIES	FIN ALIS	GUN BOAT	KIN DRED
CAN NIER	CON DUCT	DAN DILY	FIN ALLY	GUN FIRE	KI NESIC
CAN NILY	CON DUIT	DAN DLER	FIN ANCE	GUN LESS	KI NESIS
CAN NING	CON DYLE	DAN GLER	*FIN BACK	GUN LOCK	KI NETIC
CAN NOLI	CON FECT	DAN SEUR	FIN DING	GUN NERY	KI NETIN
CAN NULA	CON FESS	DEN DRON	FIN ESSE	GUN NING	*KIN FOLK
CAN ONRY	CON FIDE	*DE NIZEN	*FIN FISH	GUN PLAY	*KIN GCUP
CAN SFUL	CON FINE	DEN NING	FIN FOOT	GUN ROOM	*KIN GDOM
CAN TALA	CON FIRM	DEN SIFY	FIN ICAL	GUN SHIP	KIN GLET
CAN TATA	*CON FLUX	DEN SITY	*FIN ICKY	GUN SHOT	KIN GPIN
CAN TDOG	CON FORM	DEN TINE	FIN IKIN	GUN WALE	*KIN SHIP
CAN TEEN	CON FUSE	DEN TIST	FIN LESS	GY NECIA	KIN SMAN
CAN TEEN	CON FUTE	DEN TOID	FIN LIKE	*GY NECIC	*KU NZITE
CAN THUS	CON GEAL	DEN TURE	*FIN MARK	HA NAPER	LA NATED
CAN TINA	CON GEST	DEN UDER	FIN NIER	HAND BAG	LAN CING
CAN TRAP	CON GIUS	DIN ERIC	FIN NING	HAND CAR	LAN DING
CAN TRIP	CON ICAL	DIN ETTE	FON DANT	HAND FUL	LAN DLER
CAN VASS	CON IFER	DIN GBAT	FON DLER	HAND GUN	LAN DMAN
*CAN ZONA	CONIINE	DIN GIES	FON TINA	HAN DIER	LAN DMEN
*CAN ZONE	*CON JOIN	DIN GILY	FUN CTOR	HAN DILY	LAN EWAY
CEN ACLE	*CON JURE	DIN KIER	FUN ERAL	HAN DLER	LAN GREL
CEN SURE	CON NATE	DIN KIES	FUN FAIR	*HAN DOFF	LAN GUET

LA N GUID	MA N NITE	NON LIFE	PE N ANCE	*PO N TIFF	SE N MORA
LA N GUOR	MA N NOSE	NON MEAT	PE N ATES	PO N TOO N	SE N OPIA
LA N IARD	*MA N PACK	NON NEWS	PEN DANT	PU N CHER	SE N SATE
LA N IARY	MA N SIO N	NON OILY	PEN DENT	PU N GEN T	SE N SING
LA N ITAL	MA N TEAU	NON PAID	PEN GUIN	PU N IEST	SE N SORY
LA N OLI N	MA N TLET	NON PAST	PE N ICIL	*PU N KISH	SE N SUAL
LAN TA N A	MA N URER	NON PEAK	PE N LITE	PU N NING	SI N CERE
LAN TER N	MA N WARD	NON PLAY	PE N NAME	PU N STER	SI N GLET
LA N YARD	*ME N AZO N	NON PLUS	PE N NANT	RA N CHER	SI N KAGE
LE N GTHY	*ME N FOLK	NON POOR	PE N NATE	RA N COUR	SI N LESS
LE N IENT	ME N TIO N	NON PROS	PE N NIES	RA N DIER	SI N NING
LE N SMA N	MI N ARET	NON SELF	PE N NINE	RA N DIES	SI N OPIA
LE N TIGO	MI N DSET	NON SKED	PE N NING	RA N KING	SI N SYNE
LE N TISK	MI N ERAL	NON SKID	PE N OCHE	RA N KISH	SI N UATE
LE N TOID	MI N ILAB	NON SLIP	PE N SILE	RA N PIKE	SI N UOUS
LI N ABLE	*MI N IMAX	NON STOP	PE N SIVE	RA N SACK	SO N ANCE
LI N ALOL	MI N IVA N	NON SUCH	PE N STER	RE N EGER	SO N GFUL
LI N DANE	MI N STER	NON SUIT	PE N TANE	RE N EWAL	SO N HOOD
LI N EAGE	MI N UTIA	NON UPLE	PE N TODE	RE N EWER	SO N LESS
LI N EATE	MO N ITOR	NON USER	PE N TOSE	RE N NASE	SO N LIKE
LI N ECUT	*MO N KERY	NON WORD	PE N UCHE	RE N TIER	*SO N OVOX
LI N EMA N	*MO N KISH	NON WORK	PE N UCHI	RI N GENT	SO N SHIP
LI N GCOD	MO N SOO N	*NON ZERO	PF N TANE	RI N GLET	*SU N BACK
LI N GIER	MO N STER	NUN LIKE	PI N BALL	RI N GTAW	SU N BATH
LI N GUAL	MO N TANE	NUN NERY	PI N BONE	RI N NING	SU N BEAM
LI N IEST	MO N TERO	NUN NISH	PI N CHER	RI N SING	SU N BELT
LI N KAGE	*MO N THLY	PA N ACEA	PI N ESAP	RO N DEAU	SU N BIRD
*LI N KBOY	MO N URON	PA N ACHE	PI N ETUM	RO N DURE	SU N BURN
LI N KMA N	MU N NIO N	*PA N CAKE	PI N FOLD	RO N TGEN	SU N DECK
LI N OCUT	MU N STER	*PA N CHAX	PI N GUID	RU N AWAY	SU N DIAL
LI N SANG	*MU N TJAC	PA N DECT	PI N HEAD	*RU N BACK	SU N DOWN
LI N SEED	*MU N TJAK	PA N DIED	PI N HOLE	RU N DLET	SU N FAST
LI N TIER	*MY N HEER	PA N DIES	PI N IEST	RU N DOWN	SU N FISH
LI N URO N	NA N DINA	PA N DOOR	*PI N KEYE	RU N LESS	SU N GLOW
LO N GBOW	NA N KEE N	PA N DORA	PI N KIES	RU N NING	SU N LAMP
LO N GIES	NI N EPI N	PA N DORE	PI N KING	RU N OVER	SU N LAND
LO N GING	NI N THLY	PA N DOUR	*PI N KISH	SA N CTUM	SU N LESS
LO N GISH	NO N ACID	PA N DURA	PI N NACE	SA N DBAG	SU N LIKE
LU N ATED	NO N AGO N	*PA N FISH	PI N NATE	SA N DBAR	SU N NING
LU N ATIC	NO N BANK	PA N GENE	PI N NIES	*SA N DBOX	SU N RISE
LU N CHER	NO N BODY	*PA N ICKY	PI N NING	SA N DBUR	SU N ROOF
LU N ETTE	NO N BOOK	PA N ICLE	PI N NULA	SA N DDAB	SU N ROOM
LU N GFUL	NO N CASH	PA N ICUM	PI N NULE	SA N DFLY	SU N SPOT
LU N GING	NO N COLA	PA N NIER	PI N OCLE	SA N DHOG	SU N SUIT
LU N IEST	NO N DRUG	PA N NING	PI N SON	SA N DIER	SU N WARD
LY N CEA N	NO N FACT	PA N OCHA	PI N TADA	SA N DLOT	SU N WISE
*LY N CHER	NO N FARM	PA N OCHE	PI N TADO	SA N DMA N	SYN AGOG
MA N AKI N	NO N FOOD	PA N OPLY	PI N TAIL	SA N DPIT	SYN ANON
MA N ATEE	NO N FUEL	PA N PIPE	PI N TANO	SA N GRIA	SYN APSE
MA N DRIL	NO N GAME	PA N THER	PI N WALE	SA N ICLE	SYN CARP
*MA N GABY	NO N HEME	PA N TIES	PI N WEED	SA N TIMS	*SYN CHRO
MA N ILLA	NO N HERO	PA N TILE	*PI N WORK	SA N TOUR	SYN COPE
MA N ILLE	NO N HOME	PA N TOUM	PI N WORM	SE N ATOR	SYN ERGY
MA N ITOU	NO N IRO N	PE N ALLY	PO N IARD	SE N DOFF	SYN ESIS
MA N LESS	*NO N JURY	PE N ALTY		SE N ECIO	SYN FUEL

*SYN GAMY	TON ETTE	WIN IEST	DON NISH	PRONOUN	BER NICLE
*SYNONYM	TONGMAN	WIN LESS	DRUN KEN	PUN NING	BEUN CLED
SYNOVIA	TON IEST	WIN SOME	DUN NAGE	*QUIN ELA	BIAN NUAL
SYNTONY	TON IGHT	WIN TERY	DUN NESS	*QUIN TAN	BIEN NALE
TANAGER	TON NAGE	WIN DAGE	DUN NEST	*QUIN TIN	BIEN NIAL
TAN BARK	TON NEAU	WIN DIER	DUN NING	REN NASE	BIEN NIUM
TAN GELO	TON NISH	WIN DING	DUN NITE	REU NION	BIGNONIA
TAN GENT	TON SURE	WIN DROW	FIN NIER	RIN NING	BIN NACLE
TAN GIER	TON TINE	WIN ESOP	FIN NING	RUN NING	*BLAN CHER
TAN GLER	TUN ABLE	*WIN GBOW	FLAN KEN	*SCH NOZZ	BLAN DISH
TAN GRAM	TUN DISH	WIN GMAN	FRON TON	SIGNAGE	*BLEN CHER
TAN KAGE	TUN EFUL	WIN NING	FUN NEST	SIN NING	BLIN DAGE
TAN KARD	TUN ICLE	*WIN NOCK	FUN NING	*SPAN DEX	*BLIN KARD
TAN KFUL	TUN NAGE	WON NING	GIN NING	SPON GIN	BLON DISH
TAN NAGE	TUN NING	*XAN THAN	GLAN CER	SPON SON	*BOON DOCK
TAN NATE	*VANDYKE	*XAN THIC	GRAN OLA	STANINE	BOUN DARY
TAN NERY	*XAN THIC	*XAN THIN	GRA NITA	STEN OKY	*BRAN CHIA
TAN NEST	VANILLA	*ZAN YISH	GRA NOLA	SUN NING	BRAN DISH
TAN NING	VAN NING	*ZIN CATE	GRU NION	SWAN PAN	BRAN NING
TAN NISH	VAN POOL	*ZIN CIFY	GUN NERY	*SWIN GBY	BRAN TAIL
TAN TARA	VAN TAGE	*ZIN CITE	GUN NING	TAN NAGE	BRIN DLED
TAN TIVY	VAN WARD	*ZIN COUS	HEN NERY	TAN NATE	BRIN IEST
TAN TRUM	VENATIC	*ZIN GANO	HOR NIST	TAN NERY	*BRON CHIA
TAN YARD	VEN DACE	*ZIN GARA	HUN NISH	TAN NEST	*BRON CHUS
TEN ABLE	VEN ISON	*ZIN GARO	*JOB NAME	TAN NING	*BRON ZING
TENANCY	VEN OMER	*ZIN KIFY	KEN NING	TAN NISH	BRUN ETTE
TEN DRIL	VEN TAGE	*ZIN CKED	MAN NITE	TEE NIER	*BRUN IZEM
TEN FOLD	VEN TAIL	*ZIN COID	MAN NOSE	TEN NIES	BUR NABLE
TEN NIES	VEN TRAL	*ZON ATED	MID NOON	TER NION	BUR NOOSE
TENONER	VEN TURE	BAN NING	MUN NION	TIN NIER	CAN NABIC
TEN SILE	VEN TURI	*BAN NOCK	NON NEWS	TIN NILY	CAN NABIN
TEN SING	VIN ASSE	BIN NING	NOW NESS	TIN NING	CAN NABIS
TEN SION	VINEGAR	*BON NOCK	NUN NERY	TON NAGE	CAN NELON
TEN SITY	VIN IEST	BOUN DEN	NUN NISH	TON NISH	CAN NIFST
TEN SIVE	VIN TAGE	BRINING	PAN NIER	TRAN CHE	CAN NIKIN
TEN TAGE	VINTNER	CAN NERY	PAN NING	TUN NAGE	CAN NONRY
TEN THLY	WAN GLER	CAN NIER	PEN NAME	TUN NING	CAR NAUBA
TEN TIER	WAN IEST	CAN NILY	PEN NANT	*TWIN JET	CAR NIVAL
TEN UITY	WAN IGAN	CAN NING	PEN NATE	TWIN SET	CAT NAPER
TEN UOUS	WAN NESS	CAN NOLI	PEN NIES	VAN NING	CEIN TURE
TINAMOU	WAN NEST	CAN NULA	PEN NINE	WAN NESS	CER NUOUS
TIN FOIL	WAN NING	CHAN SON	PEN NING	WAN NEST	*CHAN CERY
TIN GLER	WAN TAGE	CLAN GER	PHE NATE	WAN NING	*CHAN CIER
TIN HORN	*WEN CHER	CLONING	*PHE NOXY	WEN NISH	*CHAN CILY
TIN IEST	WEN DIGO	CON NATE	PHO NIED	WIN NING	*CHAN DLER
TIN KLER	WEN NISH	CON NECT	PIG NOLI	*WIN NOCK	*CHAN FRON
TIN LIKE	*WIN CHER	CON NING	PIN NACE	WON NING	CHAN TAGE
TIN NIER	WIN CING	CON NIVE	PIN NATE	BAN NERET	CHAN TIES
TIN NILY	WIN DBAG	CON NOTE	PIN NIES	BAN NEROL	CHE NILLE
TIN NING	WIN DIGO	CORN ROW	PIN NING	BAR NACLE	*CHE NOPOD
TIN TING	WIN DILY	CUN NING	PIN NULA	BAR NYARD	*CHIN BONE
TIN TYPE	*WIN DWAY	DEON TIC	PIN NULE	BEAN BALL	CHIN LESS
TIN WARE	WIN GIER	DEN NING	PRE NOON	BEAN LIKE	CHIN NING
TIN WORK	WIN GLET	DIN NING	*BEK NIGHT	BEAN POLE	CIN NABAR
TON EARM	WIN GTIP	DON NING			

CIN NAMON	DAMN DEST	GAUN TLET	LION LIKE	POUN DAGE	REIN DUCE
*CIN NAMYL	DARN DEST	GIA N TESS	LOAN WORD	PRAN DIAL	REIN DUCT
CLAN GOUR	*DAWN LIKE	GIA N TISM	LORN N ESS	*PRAN KISH	REIN FECT
CLAN N ISH	DEAN SHIP	GLAN DERS	MAGN ETON	PRE N ATAL	REIN FORM
CLAN SMAN	DIA N THUS	GLAN DULE	*MAG N IFIC	PRE N OMEN	REIN FUSE
*CLEN CHER	DOG N APER	GOWN SMAN	MAIN TAIN	PRENTICE	*REIN JECT
CLIN ALLY	DON N ERED	GRAN DAME	MAN N ERLY	*PRI N CELY	*REI-N JURE
*CLIN CHER	DON N IKER	GRAN DDAD	MAN N IKIN	PRIN CESS	*REIN JURY
*COAN CHOR	DOWN BEAT	GRAN DDAM	MAN N ITOL	PRIN CIPE	REIN LESS
COEN AMOR	DOWN CAST	GRAN DEUR	MID N IGHT	*PRIN COCK	REIN SERT
COEN DURE	*DOWN COME	*GRA N DKID	MIJN HEER	PRIN TERY	REIN SMAN
COEN URUS	*DOWN FALL	GRAN DSIR	*MOO N CALF	PRIN TING	REIN SURE
*COEN ZYME	*DOWN HAUL	GRAN DSON	MOON DUST	PRIN TOUT	REIN VADE
*COGN IZER	*DOWN HILL	GRAN ULAR	*MOO N FISH	PRO N ATOR	REIN VENT
COGN OMEN	DOWN IEST	GRIN DERY	MOO N PORT	PRO N OTOM	REIN VEST
COGN OVIT	DOWN LAND	GRIN N ING	*MOONWALK	PRUN ELLA	REIN VITE
COIN CIDE	*DOWN LINK	GUAN IDIN	MOUN TAIN	PRUN ELLE	*REIN VOKE
COIN HERE	DOWN LOAD	*GUN NYBAG	N AIN SOOK	PRUN ELLO	REUN ITER
COIN MATE	*DOWN PIPE	GYM N ASIA	NON N AVAL	*PYCN IDIA	RHIN ITIS
COIN SURE	*DOWN PLAY	HERN IATE	NON N OVEL	*PYCN OSIS	*RHO N CHUS
COIN VENT	DOWN POUR	*HORN BEAM	N OO N TIDE	*PYCN OTIC	ROEN TGEN
CON N IVER	DOWN SIDE	HORN BILL	N OO N TIME	*PYKN OSIS	ROUN DISH
COON SKIN	*DOWN SIZE	*HORN BOOK	PAIN LESS	*PYKN OTIC	ROUN DLET
CORN BALL	*DOWN TICK	HORN FELS	PAINTING	QUANDANG	SAIN FOIN
*CORN CAKE	DOWN TROD	HORN IEST	PAN N IKIN	QUAN DARY	SAIN TDOM
CORN CRIB	DOWN TURN	HORN LESS	*PAWN SHOP	QUANDONG	SAN N YASI
CORN EOUS	*DOWN WARD	*HORN LIKE	PEN N ATED	*QUAN TIFY	SCAN DENT
*CORN ETCY	*DOWN WASH	*HORN PIPE	*PHA N TASM	*QUAN TILE	SCAN DIUM
*CORN HUSK	*DOWN WIND	HORN POUT	PHA N TAST	*QUAN TITY	SCAN N ING
*CORN ICHE	DRE N CHER	HORN TAIL	*PHA N TASY	*QUAN TIZE	SCAN SION
CORN ICLE	DRUN KARD	*HORN WORM	*PHEN AZIN	*QUANTONG	SCAN TIER
CORN IEST	FAIN EAN T	*HYMN BOOK	*PHEN ETIC	*QUEN CHER	SCAN TIES
CORN MEAL	FAIN TISH	*HYMN LESS	PHE N ETOL	QUEN ELLE	SCE N ARIO
CORN PONE	FAR N ESOL	HYMN LIKE	*PHEN OLIC	*QUIN CUNX	SCE N ICAL
CORN UTED	*FAWN LIKE	*HYPN OSIS	*PHON ETIC	*QUIN ELLA	*SCH N APPS
COUN TESS	*FIE N DISH	*HYPN OTIC	PHO N IEST	*QUIN IELA	*SCH N ECKE
COUN TIAN	*FIN N ICKY	*JAUN DICE	*PIC N ICKY	*QUIN OLIN	SCIN COID
CRAN IATE	FIN N IEST	*JOHN BOAT	PIG N OLIA	*QUIN TILE	SEN N IGHT
CRAN KIER	FLAN CARD	*JOIN TURE	PIN N ACLE	RAIN BAND	SHAN GRAI
*CRAN KILY	FLAN ERIE	KEEN N ESS	PIN N ATED	RAIN BIRD	SHAN TIES
*CRAN KISH	*FLIN CHER	*KEY N OTER	PIN N IPED	RAIN COAT	SHAN TUNG
CRAN KOUS	*FLIN KITE	*KID N APEE	PLA N ARIA	RAIN DROP	SHIN BONE
*CRAN KPIN	FOUN TAIN	*KID N APER	*PLA N CHET	RAIN FALL	SHIN GLER
CRAN N IED	*FRAN CIUM	LAG N APPE	*PLA N FORM	RAIN IEST	SHIN LEAF
CRAN N IES	*FRAN KEST	LAN N ERET	PLA N GENT	RAIN LESS	SHIN N ERY
CRAN N OGE	*FRAN KLIN	LAUN CHER	*PLANKING	RAIN WASH	SHIN N ING
CRE NATED	FRE N ETIC	LEAN N ESS	PLA N KTER	RAIN WEAR	*SHUN PIKE
CRE N ELLE	FRE N ULUM	LEMN ISCI	PLA N KTON	REAN OINT	SIGN ALER
*CRON YISM	*FRE N ZILY	LIE N ABLE	PLA N LESS	REEN GAGE	SIGN ALLY
*CRUN CHER	FRO N DEUR	LIE N TERY	PLA N N ING	REEN LIST	SIGN IORY
CTEN IDIA	FRO N TAGE	LIGN EOUS	PLA N OSOL	REEN ROLL	SIGN POST
*CYA N AMID	FRO N TIER	LIMN ETIC	PLA N TAIN	REGN AN CY	*SKIN HEAD
CYAN OGEN	FRON TLET	LIO N FISH	PLA N TLET	REIN CITE	SKIN LESS
CYAN OSIS	*FUN NYMAN	*LIO N IZER	POI N TMA N	REIN DEER	*SKIN LIKE
DAM NABLE	GAIN LESS			REIN DICT	SKIN N ING

*SOU N DBOX	SWA N N ERY	TUR N SPIT	CO N N	LOO N	THA N
SOU N DI N G	*SWA N SKI N	TWA N GIER	COO N	LOR N	THE N
SOU N DMA N	SWI N DLER	TWA N GLER	COR N	LOW N	THI N
SPA N DREL	*SWI N EPOX	TWI N BOR N	CUR N	MAI N	TOO N
SPA N DRIL	SWI N GIER	TWI N IEST	CYA N	MAU N	TOR N
*SPA N KI N G	SWI N GI N G	*TWI N IGHT	DAI N	MEA N	TOW N
SPA N LESS	SWI N GMA N	*TWI N KLER	DAM N	MIE N	TUR N
SPA N NI N G	TA N NABLE	TWI N NI N G	DAW N	MOA N	TWI N
*SPA N WORM	TEE N AGED	*TWI N SHIP	DEA N	MOO N	VAI N
SPI N ALLY	TEE N AGER	VAI N N ESS	DOW N	MOR N	VEI N
SPI N DLER	TEE N IEST	*VAR N ISHY	DUR N	MUO N	WAI N
SPI N ELLE	*TEE N YBOP	VAU N TFUL	FAU N	N AA N	WAR N
*SPI N IFEX	THA N ATOS	VEI N IEST	FAW N	N EO N	WEA N
SPI N LESS	*THA N KFUL	VEI N LESS	FER N	N OO N	WEE N
SPI N N ERY	THI N CLAD	*VEI N LIKE	FIR N	N OU N	WHE N
SPI N NI N G	*THI N DOWN	VER N ACLE	FLA N	PAI N	WHI N
SPI N STER	*THI N KI N G	VER N ICLE	FOH N	PAW N	WOR N
SPO N DAIC	THI N N ESS	VIG N ERO N	FOI N	PEA N	WRE N
SPO N GIER	THI N N EST	VIG N ETTE	GAI N	PEE N	WY N N
SPO N GILY	THI N NI N G	*VI N NMARK	GAU N	PEO N	YAR N
SPO N GI N G	THI N N ISH	WAI N SCOT	GIR N	PHO N	YAW N
SPO N SIO N	*THU N DERY	WA N N IGA N	GLE N	PIA N	YEA N
SPO N TOO N	TI N N IEST	WEA N LI N G	GOO N	PIO N	YUA N
STA N CHER	TI N N ITUS	*WHE N EVER	GOW N	PIR N	ZEI N
*STA N CHLY	*TOP N OTCH	*WHI N CHAT	GRA N	PLA N	ZOO N
STA N DARD	TOR N ILLO	WHI N IEST	GRI N	POO N	BACO N
STA N DI N G	*TOW N FOLK	WI N N ABLE	GUA N	POR N	BAIR N
STA N DISH	*TOW N HOME	WI N N OWER	HAE N	PYI N	BARO N
*STA N DOFF	TOW N LESS	WOR N N ESS	HER N	QUI N	BASI N
STA N DOUT	*TOW N SHIP	WRA N GLER	HIS N	RAI N	BATO N
STA N DPAT	TOW N SMA N	YEA N LI N G	HWA N	REI N	BEGA N
STA N HOPE	TOW N WEAR	*WRO N GFUL	HYM N	ROA N	BEGI N
STA N N ARY	*TRA N QUIL	*YOU N GISH	JEA N	RUI N	BEGU N
STA N N ITE	TRA N SACT	*ZOO N OSIS	JEO N	SAI N	BETO N
STA N N OUS	TRA N SECT		JI N N	SAW N	BISO N
STE N OSED	TRA N SEPT		JOH N	SCA N	BLAI N
STE N OSIS	TRA N SFER	BAR N	JOI N	SEE N	BLOW N
STI N GIER	*TRA N SFIX	BEA N	KAI N	SEW N	BOGA N
STI N GILY	TRA N SHIP	BEE N	KAO N	SHI N	BORO N
STI N GRAY	TRA N SMIT	BLI N	KAR N	SHU N	BOSO N
STI N KARD	TRA N SUDE	BOO N	KEE N	SIG N	BOSU N
*STI N KBUG	TRE N CHER	BOR N	KER N	SKI N	BOUR N
STI N KIER	TRI N KUMS	BRA N	KHA N	SOO N	BRAI N
STI N KPOT	TRI N ODAL	BRE N	KIL N	SOR N	BRAW N
STO N EFLY	TRU N CATE	BRI N	KIR N	SOW N	BROW N
STO N IEST	TRU N DLER	BU N N	KOA N	SPA N	BRUI N
STU N NI N G	*TRU N KFUL	BUR N	LAI N	SPI N	BURA N
STU N SAIL	TRU N NIO N	CAI N	LAW N	SPU N	BURI N
STU N TMA N	TU N N ELER	CAR N	LEA N	STU N	CABI N
SUB N ASAL	TUR N COAT	CHI N	LIE N	SU N N	CAIR N
*SUB N ICHE	TUR N DOWN	CHO N	LIM N	SWA N	CAJO N
SUB N ODAL	TUR N HALL	CLA N	LI N N	TAI N	CANO N
SUR N AMER	TUR N OVER	CLO N	LIO N	TAR N	CAPO N
*SWA N HERD	TUR N PIKE	COI N	LOA N	TEE N	CHAI N
*SWA N LIKE	TUR N SOLE	CIO N	LOI N	TER N	CHUR N

CLEA N	GREE N	MUTO N	ROUE N	TITA N	**BEACO N**
CLOW N	GROA N	NI N O N	ROVE N	TOKE N	**BECKO N**
CODE N	GROI N	N ITO N	ROWA N	TOLA N	**BEDAM N**
CODO N	GROW N	N OME N	ROWE N	TOMA N	**BEDPA N**
COGO N	GYRO N	N UME N	RUME N	**TOXI N**	**BEDUI N**
COIG N	*HAZA N	N YLO N	RUTI N	TOYO N	**BEMEA N**
COLI N	**HEMI N**	PAEA N	SABI N	TRAI N	**BEMOA N**
COLO N	HERO N	PAEO N	SARA N	TREE N	BE N IG N
CO N I N	HOGA N	PAGA N	SARI N	TWAI N	*BE N ZI N
COPE N	HO N A N	PATE N	SASI N	TWEE N	BERLI N
COTA N	**HUMA N**	PATI N	SATI N	VEGA N	**BICOR N**
COVE N	**HYME N**	**PAVA N**	SAVI N	VE N I N	**BICRO N**
COVI N	**HYSO N**	**PAVI N**	SCIO N	**VIME N**	**BIDDE N**
*COZE N	**JAPA N**	PECA N	SCOR N	*VIXE N	**BIFFI N**
CROO N	*JAWA N	PEIO N	SEDA N	VODU N	**BIGGI N**
CROW N	**JETO N**	**PEKA N**	SEME N	WAGO N	**BILLO N**
CUMI N	**JUPO N**	**PEKI N**	SERI N	**WAKE N**	**BIOGE N**
CUTI N	KI N I N	PI N O N	SETO N	**WHEE N**	**BIOTI N**
CYTO N	**K N OW N**	PITO N	SEVE N	WIDE N	**BITTE N**
DAMA N	KROO N	PLAI N	SEWA N	WIGA N	*BLAZO N
DAVE N	LADE N	**PRAW N**	SHAR N	WITA N	**BOBBI N**
DAWE N	LAGA N	PREE N	**SHAW N**	WITE N	**BODKI N**
DEIG N	LAPI N	PRIO N	SHEE N	*WIZE N	**BOFFI N**
DEMO N	LATE N	PURI N	SHOO N	**WOKE N**	BOLSO N
DEVO N	LAUA N	PUTO N	SHOR N	**WOMA N**	**BO N BO N**
DEWA N	LEAR N	**PYLO N**	**SHOW N**	**WOME N**	BOREE N
DIVA N	LEBE N	**PYRA N**	SIRE N	**WOVE N**	BOSTO N
DIWA N	LEMA N	**QUEA N**	SKEA N	**XE N O N**	BOUTO N
*DIZE N	LEMO N	**QUEE N**	SKEE N	*XYLA N	**BOWFI N**
DOVE N	LEVI N	**QUER N**	SKEI N	**YAME N**	**BOWMA N**
DOYE N	LIGA N	**QUOI N**	SLAI N	YAMU N	*BRAZE N
*DOZE N	LIKE N	RACO N	SOLA N	YAPO N	BROGA N
DRAI N	LIMA N	RADO N	SOLO N	YEAR N	**BROKE N**
DRAW N	LIME N	RATA N	**SOZI N**	YOGI N	**BROMI N**
DROW N	LI N E N	RAVE N	**SPAW N**	YOUR N	**BRUCI N**
FAGI N	LI N I N	RAWI N	SPEA N	YULA N	**BUMKI N**
FA N O N	LIPI N	RAYO N	SPOO N	**YUPO N**	BU N IO N
FEIG N	LIVE N	RECO N	SPUR N	*ZAYI N	BURDE N
FELO N	LODE N	REDA N	STAI N	*ZAZE N	**BUSKI N**
FICI N	LOGA N	REDO N	STEI N	BABOO N	**BUSMA N**
FLOW N	LORA N	REIG N	STER N	BADMA N	BUTTO N
FOEH N	LUME N	REMA N	SWAI N	BAGMA N	**CABMA N**
FROW N	LUPI N	RE N I N	SWOO N	BALEE N	**CAFTA N**
FURA N	LYSI N	REPI N	SWOR N	BALLO N	**CAIMA N**
FUTO N	MACO N	RERA N	SWOU N	BA N IA N	**CALKI N**
GAMI N	MASO N	RERU N	SYRE N	BA N TA N	CALLA N
GIPO N	MATI N	RESI N	TABU N	BA N YA N	**CAMIO N**
GIRO N	**MAVE N**	REWA N	TAKI N	**BARMA N**	**CA N CA N**
GIVE N	**MAVI N**	REWI N	TALO N	BARRE N	CA N NO N
GLEA N	MELO N	REWO N	**TAXO N**	**BARYO N**	CA N TO N
GLUO N	MESO N	RICI N	TE N O N	BASIO N	**CA N YO N**
G N AW N	*MIZE N	RIPE N	THEG N	**BATMA N**	**CAPLI N**
GOBA N	MORO N	ROBI N	THEI N	BATTE N	**CAPTA N**
GOWA N	MOUR N	ROMA N	THOR N	**BAYMA N**	**CARBO N**
GRAI N	MUCI N	ROSI N	TIGO N		CAREE N

CARLI N	**DARKE N**	GABIO N	**HEMPE N**	LIG NI N	MOREE N
CARMA N	DEACO N	GABOO N	HEREI N	LI N DE N	MORGA N
CARTO N	DEADE N	**GAGMA N**	HEREO N	**LIPPE N**	MORGE N
CARVE N	**DEAFE N**	GALLO N	HEROI N	LISTE N	MORIO N
CASEI N	DECER N	**GAMMO N**	HIDDE N	LITTE N	MOTIO N
CASER N	DEEPE N	GARCO N	**HODDE N**	**LOCHA N**	MOULI N
CATIO N	**DEEWA N**	GARDE N	**HODDI N**	LOGIO N	MOUTO N
CATKI N	**DEHOR N**	GARRO N	**HOIDE N**	LOMEI N	**MUFFI N**
CATLI N	DEMEA N	GASCO N	**HOLDE N**	LO N GA N	MULLE N
CAVER N	DE N TI N	**GASKI N**	**HOLPE N**	LOOSE N	MU N TI N
CAYMA N	DESIG N	**GASMA N**	**HOYDE N**	LOTIO N	MUREI N
*CHAZA N	DETAI N	GERMA N	*HYPHE N	LOUDE N	MUSLI N
CHITI N	**DEVEI N**	GERME N	**JARGO N**	LUCER N	MUTTO N
CHITO N	DIAMI N	**GIBBO N**	*JASMI N	**LUMPE N**	**MYELI N**
CHOPI N	*DIAZI N	GIBSO N	*JERKI N	LU N GA N	**MYOSI N**
CHOSE N	DIOXA N	GITTI N	**JETTO N**	LURDA N	N ANDI N
CITRI N	DIOXI N	GLOBI N	**JORDA N**	LUTEI N	N A N KI N
CITRO N	**DISOW N**	GLUCA N	KAFTA N	**MACRO N**	N APKI N
*CLAXO N	DIURO N	GLUTE N	KALIA N	**MADDE N**	N ASTO N
CLOVE N	**DOBBI N**	**GLYCA N**	KAMSI N	**MADMA N**	N ATIO N
COCAI N	DOBLO N	**GLYCI N**	KA N BA N	MAGIA N	N ATRO N
COCHI N	DOLMA N	G N OMO N	KAOLI N	MAIDE N	N EATE N
COCOO N	DOLME N	GOBLI N	KATIO N	MALIG N	**N EKTO N**
CODEI N	DOMAI N	**GODOW N**	**KELSO N**	**MALKI N**	N ELSO N
CODLI N	**DO N JO N**	GODSO N	**KELVI N**	**MAMMO N**	N EURO N
COFFI N	DORMI N	GOLDE N	**KEPPE N**	MA N NA N	N EWTO N
*COJOI N	**DRIVE N**	GO N IO N	*KHAZE N	MARGI N	N IACI N
COLUM N	DROMO N	GORGO N	**KIPPE N**	MARLI N	N OGGI N
COMMO N	**DUBBI N**	**GORHE N**	**KITTE N**	MAROO N	N O N FA N
CORBA N	DUDEE N	GOSSA N	*KLAXO N	MARRO N	N O N MA N
CORDO N	DU N LI N	GOTTE N	**KRAKE N**	MARTE N	N OTIO N
CORTI N	DURIA N	**GOVER N**	*KUCHE N	MARTI N	**N UBBI N**
COSIG N	DURIO N	GRABE N	KURGA N	**MASCO N**	PAESA N
COTTO N	**DY N EI N**	GRADI N	LAGOO N	MATRO N	PAISA N
COUPO N	FALCO N	GRATI N	LALLA N	MATTI N	PA N GE N
COUSI N	FALLE N	**GRAVE N**	LARDO N	**MAYVI N**	**PAPAI N**
COWMA N	FA N IO N	GRISO N	LATEE N	MEDIA N	PARDO N
CRATO N	FASTE N	GUA NI N	LATTE N	MELTO N	PARIA N
CRAVE N	FATTE N	GUE N O N	LATTI N	MERLI N	PARSO N
CRAYO N	**FIBRI N**	GUIDO N	**LAWMA N**	MERLO N	PARTA N
CREPO N	**FIRKI N**	GULDE N	**LAYMA N**	**MERMA N**	PARTO N
CRETI N	**FIRMA N**	GU N MA N	LEADE N	MESIA N	PATRO N
CROTO N	**FLACO N**	GU N NE N	LEAVE N	MESSA N	PATTE N
CUMMI N	**FLAGO N**	HADRO N	LECTI N	**MICRO N**	PAULI N
CURRA N	**FLAME N**	**HAGDO N**	LEGGI N	**MIDDE N**	**PEAHE N**
CYA NI N	**FLAVI N**	**HAPPE N**	LEGIO N	MIG N O N	**PECHA N**
CYMLI N	*FLAXE N	**HAPTE N**	LEGMA N	**MIKRO N**	**PECTE N**
DAEMO N	**FLYMA N**	**HARDE N**	LE N TE N	MILDE N	**PECTI N**
DAHOO N	**FOEMA N**	**HARMI N**	LEPTO N	MI N IO N	**PE N MA N**
DAIKO N	FOISO N	**HARPI N**	LESIO N	MI N YA N	PE N NO N
DAIME N	**FORBA N**	HASTE N	LESSE N	**MISPE N**	**PEPSI N**
DAIMO N	*FROZE N	**HATPI N**	LESSO N	MITTE N	PEREO N
DALTO N	**FRYPA N**	HAUSE N	LEUCI N	*MIZZE N	PERRO N
DAMPE N	FUSAI N	*HAZZA N	**LEUKO N**	MODER N	PERSO N
DAMSO N	FUSIO N	**HEAVE N**	LICHE N	MOLTE N	**PHO N O N**

PHOTO N	RATTE N	SEXTA N	TARTA N	WITHI N	BOURBO N
PHYLO N	RATTO N	SEXTO N	*TARZA N	WIVER N	BOURDO N
PHYTI N	REAGI N	SHAIR N	TAUTE N	*WIZZE N	*BRACKE N
PHYTO N	REASO N	SHAMA N	TAVER N	WO NTO N	BRADOO N
PIDGI N	REBOR N	SHOGU N	TEGME N	WOODE N	BRECHA N
PIGEO N	RECKO N	SHORA N	TELSO N	WOOLE N	BRIDOO N
PIGGI N	RECOI N	SICCA N	TE N DO N	WORSE N	BROADE N
PIGPE N	REDDE N	SICKE N	TE N PI N	*WYVER N	*BUCKEE N
PI NIO N	REDFI N	SILKE N	TEOPA N	YAUPO N	BUDGOW N
PI N KE N	REEAR N	SILVA N	TESTO N	YEELI N	*BUFFOO N
PI N YI N	REGAI N	SIMIA N	THORO N	YEOMA N	BULLIO N
PI N YO N	REGIO N	SIMLI N	THRAW N	YOUPO N	BULLPE N
PIPKI N	REJOI N	SIMOO N	TIEPI N	*ZEATI N	*BUMPKI N
PIPPI N	RELOA N	SIPHO N	TIFFI N	*ZECHI N	BURGEO N
PISTO N	REMAI N	SISKI N	TIGLO N	*ZIRCO N	BURTHE N
PITMA N	RE N NI N	SITTE N	TI N MA N	BALLOO N	BUSHMA N
PLATA N	RE N OW N	*SKYMA N	TITIA N	BARCHA N	BUTYRI N
PLATE N	REOPE N	SLOGA N	TITMA N	BARGAI N	*CABEZO N
PLUTO N	REPLA N	SLOVE N	TOCSI N	BASEMA N	*CAFFEI N
POISO N	REPUG N	SOCMA N	TOUCA N	BASSOO N	CAISSO N
POLEY N	*REQUI N	SODDE N	TRAPA N	BASTIO N	CALDRO N
POLLE N	RESEE N	SOFTE N	TREPA N	BATSMA N	CAMPIO N
POMPO N	RESIG N	SOLDA N	TRIGO N	BEADMA N	CA N AKI N
PO NTO N	RETAI N	SOLEM N	TRITO N	BECLOW N	CA N IKI N
POPGU N	RETOR N	SOLIO N	TROGO N	BEDEMA N	CA N TEE N
POPLI N	RETUR N	SOUDA N	TROPI N	*BEDIZE N	CAPELA N
POSTI N	RHYTO N	SOVRA N	TUCHU N	BEDOUI N	CAPELI N
POTEE N	RIBBO N	SPAVI N	TURBA N	BEGROA N	CAPSTA N
POTIO N	RICHE N	SPLEE N	TURFE N	BELLMA N	CAPTAI N
POTMA N	RIDDE N	SPOKE N	TYCOO N	BE N ISO N	CAPTIO N
PREMA N	ROBBI N	SPRAI N	TYMPA N	*BE N ZOI N	CARABI N
PREME N	RODMA N	STAME N	TYPHO N	BETHOR N	CARAVA N
PRISO N	RO NIO N	STOLE N	VA N MA N	BETOKE N	CARBAR N
PROLA N	RO N YO N	STOLO N	VERDI N	BETWEE N	CARDOO N
PROTO N	ROTTE N	STRAI N	VERMI N	BIGHOR N	CAROTI N
PTERI N	RURBA N	SUBOR N	VIOLI N	BILLIO N	CARRIO N
PTISA N	RURTO N	SUDDE N	VIRGI N	BIOTRO N	CARRYO N
PUFFI N	RYOKA N	SULDA N	VIRIO N	BIRCHE N	CARTOO N
PU N KI N	SADDE N	SULLE N	VISIO N	BIRDMA N	CATERA N
PURLI N	SALMO N	SULTA N	VODOU N	BITTER N	CAUTIO N
PYTHO N	SALOO N	SUMMO N	WAGGO N	BITUME N	CAVEMA N
*QUI NI N	SAMPA N	SU N KE N	WA N GA N	*BLACKE N	CELADO N
RABBI N	SARSE N	SU N TA N	WA N GU N	BLOUSO N	CERTAI N
RACOO N	SATEE N	SWEVE N	WA N IO N	BLOWGU N	CERUME N
RADIA N	SCREE N	SYLVA N	WA NTO N	BLUEFI N	CESSIO N
RAGLA N	SEAMA N	SYLVI N	WARDE N	BOATMA N	CERATI N
RAGMA N	SEASO N	SYPHO N	WARRE N	BODHRA N	CHAGRI N
RAISI N	SEAWA N	TAIPA N	WEAKE N	BOGBEA N	CHA N SO N
RAMSO N	SECER N	TALIO N	WEAPO N	BOGYMA N	*CHAPMA N
RA N DA N	SEISI N	TAMEI N	WEDEL N	BO N DMA N	CHASTE N
RAPPE N	*SEIZI N	TAMPA N	WELKI N	*BOOKMA N	*CHAZZA N
RATIO N	SELSY N	TAMPO N	WEASO N	*BOOMKI N	*CHAZZE N
RATLI N	*SEQUI N	TA N NI N	WHITE N	*BORAZO N	CHEAPE N
RATOO N	SEREI N	TARPA N	WIGEO N	BOTULI N	*CHEVRO N
RATTA N	SERMO N	TARPO N		BOU N DE N	*CHICKE N

*CHIFFO N	DASHEE N	*FLUXIO N	GUDGEO N	*KITCHE N	MELA N I N
CHIG N O N	DAUPHI N	FOGHOR N	GUERDO N	KLAVER N	*ME N AZO N
CHITLI N	DAYSMA N	FOLACI N	HABITA N	KREMLI N	ME N TIO N
CHLORI N	DEADPA N	FOOTMA N	*HACKMA N	*KRYPTO N	MESSMA N
CHORIO N	DECROW N	FORAME N	HAGBOR N	LACTEA N	METOPO N
CHRO N O N	DECUMA N	FOREIG N	HAIRPI N	*LADYKI N	MIDIRO N
CI N ERI N	DEMETO N	FOREMA N	*HALCYO N	*LAMBKI N	MID N OO N
CIPOLI N	DE N DRO N	FORERU N	HALOGE N	LAMPIO N	MIDTOW N
CISTER N	*DE N IZE N	FORLOR N	HA N DGU N	LAMPOO N	*MILKMA N
CISTRO N	DERAIG N	FORWOR N	HA N GMA N	LA N DMA N	MILLIO N
CITHER N	DERTAI N	FOURGO N	HA N UMA N	LA N DME N	MILLRU N
CITHRE N	DETRAI N	*FOXSKI N	HARDPA N	LA N OLI N	MI N IKI N
*CITIZE N	*DEXTRA N	FREEMA N	*HARIJA N	LA N TER N	MI N IVA N
CITTER N	*DEXTRI N	FRESHE N	HARPOO N	LARDOO N	MISCOI N
CLACHA N	DICTIO N	FRISSO N	HARSHE N	LEADMA N	*MISJOI N
CLARIO N	*DIGOXI N	FROGMA N	HEADMA N	LECTER N	MISLAI N
CLAYPA N	DIP N OA N	FRO N TO N	HEADPI N	LECTIO N	MISPLA N
CLUBMA N	DISCER N	*FUCHSI N	HEARKE N	LEGHOR N	MISSIO N
COALBI N	DISDAI N	FUSTIA N	HEARTE N	LEGUMI N	MITOGE N
COARSE N	DISHPA N	GADROO N	HEATHE N	LE N SMA N	MOISTE N
COITIO N	*DISJOI N	GAGATO N	HECUME N	LESBIA N	*MO N AXO N
COLICI N	DISLIM N	GALLEI N	HELICO N	LETDOW N	MO N ERA N
COLLEE N	DISTAI N	GALLEO N	HEMATI N	LEVULI N	MO N SOO N
COMPLI N	DOESKI N	GALLOO N	HEPARI N	*LEXICO N	MO N URO N
CO N CER N	DOLPHI N	GAMELA N	HERDMA N	LIAISO N	MOORHE N
CO N DEM N	DOORMA N	GASTRI N	HESSTA N	LIFTMA N	MORPHI N
CO N DIG N	DRAGOO N	GATEMA N	*HEXAGO N	LIGHTE N	MORRIO N
*CO N JOI N	DRAYMA N	GELATI N	*HEXOSA N	LIGROI N	MOUFLO N
CO N SIG N	DRUMLI N	GE N TIA N	HIRUDI N	LIMACO N	MUEDDI N
CO N TAI N	DRU N KE N	*GHERKI N	HOARSE N	*LIMPKI N	*MUEZZI N
CO N TEM N	*DUCKPI N	GIAADI N	*HOATZI N	LI N EMA N	MULLEI N
COO N CA N	DUDGEO N	GITTER N	HOEDOW N	LI N KMA N	MULLIO N
COREIG N	DU N GEO N	GLADDE N	HORDEI N	LI N URO N	MU N N IO N
COTHUR N	DURAME N	GLEEMA N	*HORIZO N	LOBEFI N	MURRAI N
COURLA N	DUSTBI N	GLISTE N	*HYPERO N	LORG N O N	MUTAGE N
*COWSKI N	DUSTMA N	GLO N IO N	*JACOBI N	LOWBOR N	NA N KEE N
CRAMPO N	DUSTPA N	GLUTTO N	*JALAPI N	LOWDOW N	N ARCEI N
CREATI N	DUVETY N	GODDAM N	*JARGOO N	LUPULI N	N EGATO N
CREWMA N	FACTIO N	GODROO N	*JAVELI N	LUTHER N	N EPHRO N
CRIMSO N	FASHIO N	GOLDAR N	*JAZZMA N	LY N CEA N	N EUSTO N
CRISPE N	FE N URO N	GOLDUR N	JILLIO N	LYSOGE N	N EUTRO N
CROCEI N	FERMIO N	GOODMA N	*JU N KMA N	*MADZOO N	N EWBOR N
CROUTO N	FESTOO N	GOSSOO N	*JURYMA N	MAILMA N	*N EWMOW N
CRUCIA N	FIBROI N	GRAPLI N	KAMSEE N	MALISO N	N EWSMA N
CRYOGE N	FICTIO N	GREATE N	KEELSO N	MA N AKI N	N ICOTI N
CULLIO N	FIFTEE N	GREISE N	KERATI N	MA N IKI N	N I N EPI N
CUMARI N	FI N IKI N	GREMLI N	KEROGE N	MA N SIO N	N OCTUR N
CURTAI N	FIREMA N	GREYHE N	*KHAMSI N	MARCHE N	NO N AGO N
CUSHIO N	FIREPA N	GRIFFI N	*KIDSKI N	MARTIA N	NO N IRO N
CUTDOW N	FISSIO N	GRIFFO N	KILOTO N	*MATZOO N	N OVATI N
CYCASI N	FLAGMA N	GRIPMA N	KI N ETI N	MAUDLI N	N UCLEI N
CYPRIA N	FLA N KE N	GRISKI N	KI N GPI N	*MAXIMI N	N UCLEO N
CYSTEI N	FLATTE N	GRU N IO N	KI N SMA N	MEATMA N	*PACKMA N
DALAPO N	*FLEXIO N	GRUTTE N	*KIPSKI N	MEDUSA N	PACTIO N
DARSHA N	FLUORI N	*GRYPHO N	*KIRKMA N	MEGATO N	PALADI N

PAMPEA N	*PUMPKI N	SA N DMA N	STIFFE N	TORSIO N	*ZECCHI N
PAPHIA N	PURITA N	SAPO N I N	STOLLE N	TOUGHE N	*ZILLIO N
PARAGO N	PURLOI N	SAURIA N	STOUTE N	TREASO N	*ZITHER N
PASSIO N	PUSHPI N	SAVARI N	STYGIA N	*TRIAZI N	*ZYMOGE N
PASTER N	PUTAME N	*SAXHOR N	SUASIO N	TRICOR N	*ZYMOSA N
PATROO N	PYROGE N	SCULPI N	SUBCLA N	TRODDE N	*BACKSPI N
PATTER N	*QUARTA N	SECTIO N	SUBDEA N	TRUDGE N	BACTERI N
PEEBEE N	*QUASSI N	SEEDMA N	SUBERI N	TRYPSI N	BAILSMA N
PELICA N	*QUICKE N	SERICI N	*SUBJOI N	TUBULI N	BA N DSMA N
PEMICA N	*QUIETE N	SESSIO N	SUBTEL N	TUITIO N	BARBICA N
PE N GUI N	*QUI N TA N	SEXTAI N	SUCTIO N	TURFMA N	BARTISA N
PEREIO N	*QUI N TI N	SHAITA N	SU N BUR N	TWIGGE N	*BARTIZA N
PERIGO N	RACCOO N	SHARPE N	SU N DOW N	TYLOSI N	BASEBOR N
PERTAI N	RAMEKI N	SHEBEA N	SURGEO N	*TYPHOO N	*BAUDEKI N
PHAETO N	RAMPIO N	SHEBEE N	SUSTAI N	VELAME N	BEADSMA N
PICOLI N	RATTEE N	SHEITA N	SWAGMA N	VE N ISO N	BEARSKI N
PIGSKI N	RATTOO N	SHIPMA N	SWA N PA N	VERMIA N	*BEDARKE N
*PIKEMA N	RAVELI N	SHIPPO N	SWEETE N	VERSIO N	BEDEAFE N
PILLIO N	READOR N	SHODDE N	SWIDDE N	VERVAI N	BEDESMA N
PI N SIO N	REALIG N	SHOPMA N	SWOLLE N	VETERA N	BEGOTTE N
PLASMI N	REBEGI N	SHORTE N	SYMBIO N	VIBRIO N	BEHOLDE N
PLASMO N	RECLEA N	SHOTGU N	SY N A N O N	VIDICO N	BEMADDE N
PLATOO N	RECROW N	SHOTTE N	TABORI N	VILLAI N	*BE N JAMI N
PLAYPE N	REDSKI N	*SHOWMA N	*TACHYO N	VILLEI N	*BE N ZIDI N
PLEURO N	REEDMA N	SIDEMA N	TACTIO N	VITAMI N	BERBERI N
PLOSIO N	REFRAI N	SILICO N	TAILFA N	VITRAI N	BESCREE N
PLOWMA N	REGIME N	SILVER N	TAMARI N	VOLUTI N	BETATRO N
PLUMPE N	REGREE N	SIRLOI N	TAMPIO N	WA N IGA N	BEVATRO N
PLUVIA N	RELAXI N	SIXTEE N	TARDYO N	WARISO N	BIATHLO N
POCOSI N	RELEAR N	SLACKE N	*TAXIMA N	WARWOR N	BIGAROO N
POLARO N	RETRAI N	SLEEKE N	TEGUME N	*WAYWOR N	*BILLYCA N
POLYGO N	REU N IO N	SMARTE N	TELAMO N	WESTER N	BIOCLEA N
PO N TOO N	REWAKE N	SMIDGE N	TELEMA N	WHEATE N	*BIOTOXI N
POPCOR N	REWIDE N	SMIDGI N	TELERA N	WHEREI N	*BLACKFI N
PORTIO N	REWOKE N	SMITTE N	TE N SIO N	WHEREO N	BLOODFI N
POSTEE N	REWOVE N	S N OWMA N	TER N IO N	WIDGEO N	*BLOWDOW N
POSTER N	ROCKOO N	*SOCKMA N	TERRAI N	WI N GMA N	BLUDGEO N
POSTMA N	RODSMA N	SOJOUR N	TERREE N	WIREMA N	BLUESMA N
POTHEE N	RO N TGE N	SOKEMA N	TERTIA N	WOODBI N	BOARDMA N
POTTEE N	ROUGHE N	SOLA N I N	TESTOO N	WOODHE N	BOATSMA N
PREDAW N	RUBDOW N	SOLITO N	THEELI N	WOODMA N	*BODEYMA N
PRE N OO N	RUCTIO N	SOUPCO N	THEREI N	WOOLLE N	*BOHEMIA N
PREPLA N	RUFFIA N	SOYBEA N	THEREO N	WOOLMA N	BOMBESI N
PRETEE N	RU N DOW N	SPARTA N	THIAMI N	*WORKMA N	BO N DSMA N
PREWAR N	SABATO N	SPELEA N	*THIAZI N	WRITHE N	*BOOGYMA N
PRO N OU N	SABAYO N	SPO N GI N	*THICKE N	WRITTE N	*BOOMTOW N
PROPMA N	SACATO N	SPO N SO N	THIO N I N	*XA N THA N	BOUGHTE N
PROTEI N	SADIRO N	SPORRA N	TIGHTE N	*XA N THI N	BOUILLO N
PROTEA N	SAFFRO N	STATIO N	TI N HOR N	*XYLIDI N	BOURGEO N
PSAMMO N	SAGAMA N	STEARI N	TOLIDI N	YARDMA N	*BOXTHOR N
PTOMAI N	SALICI N	STEEPE N	TOLIMA N	YATAGA N	BRAI N PA N
PTYALI N	SALPIA N	STEMSO N	TOMPIO N	YEGGMA N	*BRAKEMA N
PUCCOO N	SALTER N	STEPSO N	TO N GMA N	YESTER N	BRASILI N
PULLMA N	SALTPA N	STETSO N	TOPSPI N	*YOYTHE N	*BRAZILI N
PULSIO N	SAMISE N	STEWPA N	TORCHO N	*ZACATO N	BRETHRE N

BRIGHTE N	*COACHMA N	DILATIO N	*FRIGHTE N	HISTAMI N	LOCATIO N
BROMELI N	COACTIO N	DILUTIO N	FRUITIO N	HISTIDI N	*LOCKDOW N
*BRYOZOA N	CODESIG N	DILUVIA N	FUGLEMA N	HISTOGE N	LOCUTIO N
*BUCKBEA N	COERCIO N	DILUVIO N	FU N CTIO N	*HOACTZI N	LOGICIA N
*BUCKSKI N	COG N OME N	DIOBOLO N	*FUN NYMAN	HOLSTEI N	LO N GERO N
BULLETI N	COHESIO N	DIOCESA N	FURFURA N	*HOMESPU N	LO N GHOR N
BULLHOR N	COLISTI N	DIOLEFI N	GAMBESO N	*HOMETOW N	*LOOKDOW N
BUSULFA N	COLLAGE N	DIPTERA N	GAMESMA N	HOMI N IA N	LOVELOR N
*CABOCHO N	*COLOPHO N	DIPTERO N	GA N GLIO N	*HO N EYBU N	LU N ARIA N
*CALFSKI N	COLORMA N	DISCROW N	GARRISO N	HOOLIGA N	LU N ATIO N
CALUTRO N	COMEDIA N	DISTRAI N	GELATIO N	HORSEMA N	LU N CHEO N
*CAMPAIG N	*COMEDOW N	DISU N IO N	GLASSMA N	HOTELMA N	LUTEOLI N
CAN NABI N	COMPIAI N	DIVISIO N	GLOBULI N	HOUSEMA N	*LUXATIO N
CAN NELO N	CO N ATIO N	DOMI N IO N	GLUCAGO N	*HYALOGE N	*LY N CHPI N
CAN N IKI N	*CO N QUIA N	DO N ATIO N	GLUTELI N	*HYDROGE N	MACAROO N
*CAPESKI N	COOLDOW N	DOTATIO N	GLYCERI N	*HYPOGEA N	MACRURA N
CAPSICI N	COO N SKI N	DOUBLOO N	*GLYCOGE N	HYPOPYO N	*MADWOMA N
*CAPUCHI N	COOPTIO N	DOW N TUR N	G N ATHIO N	*JERRICA N	MAGICIA N
CARAGEE N	COPATRO N	*DRAWDOWN	GOATSKI N	*JERRYCA N	MAG N ETO N
CARDAMO N	CORDOVA N	DRIFTPI N	GOMBROO N	*JETTISO N	MAI N TAI N
CARDIGA N	CORDWAI N	DURATIO N	GO N FALO N	*JU N CTIO N	MA N DARI N
CAREWOR N	CORPSMA N	*DUTCHMA N	GO N FANO N	KAISERI N	MA N DOLI N
CARILLO N	COTILLO N	DY N ATRO N	GORGERI N	*KAKIEMO N	MA N N IKI N
CARROTI N	*COTQUEA N	*FACEDOW N	GOW N SMA N	KALLIDI N	MARATHO N
CARYOTI N	COUMARI N	*FALCHIO N	GRA N DSO N	*KARYOTI N	MARGARI N
*CATECHI N	COU N TIA N	FA N FARO N	GRAVAME N	KE N OTRO N	*MARKDOW N
CAULDRO N	*COXSWAI N	FAVO N IA N	GRAVITO N	*KEPHALI N	*MARKSMA N
*CAVICOR N	CRAGSMA N	FE N THIO N	GRIDIRO N	*KHAMSEE N	MAROCAI N
*CEPHALI N	CRAMPOO N	FERRITI N	GROSCHE N	*KLYSTRO N	MARTAGO N
CERULEA N	*CRA N KPI N	*FERRYMA N	GUA N IDI N	*KRUMHOR N	*MARZIPA N
CESAREA N	CREATIO N	FETATIO N	GUARDIA N	*LAMBSKI N	MASTODO N
CESARIA N	*CRUMHOR N	FI N ESPU N	GUERIDO N	LA N DSMA N	MELA N IA N
CETACEA N	CULTIGE N	*FI N ICKI N	GUMPTIO N	LA N GSHA N	MELODEO N
*CHAINMA N	CULVERI N	*FIXATIO N	GYPSEIA N	LA N THOR N	MELTDOW N
*CHAIRMA N	CYA N OGE N	*FLASHGU N	GYRATIO N	LARRIGA N	ME N HADE N
CHALDRO N	*CYCLAME N	FLATIRO N	HAEMATI N	LARRIKI N	MERIDIA N
*CHAMFRO N	*DAKERHE N	FLECTIO N	HALATIO N	LAVATIO N	MESOTRO N
*CHAMPIO N	DALESMA N	*FLEXAGO N	*HA N DSEW N	*LAXATIO N	*METAZOA N
*CHA N FRO N	DECISIO N	FOILSMA N	*HA N DYMA N	*LAYWOMA N	*METAZOO N
*CHAPERO N	DECURIO N	FOOTWOR N	HARRIDA N	LEADSMA N	METHADO N
*CHAPLAI N	DEERSKI N	FORE N OO N	*HAWTHOR N	LEATHER N	*MEZEREO N
*CHARACI N	DELATIO N	*FORESKI N	*HAZELHE N	LECITHI N	MIRLITO N
*CHESSMA N	DELETIO N	FOREWAR N	HEADSMA N	LEGATIO N	MISALIG N
*CHEVERO N	DELUSIO N	FOREWOR N	*HEIGHTE N	LE N GTHE N	MISLEAR N
CHILDRE N	*DEMIJOH N	FORMALI N	*HELMSMA N	LE N ITIO N	MISU N IO N
CHITOSA N	DEMO N IA N	*FOUGHTE N	HEMATEI N	LEWISSO N	MOCCASI N
CHLORDA N	DEMOTIO N	FOU N TAI N	*HE N CHMA N	LIBATIO N	MOLESKI N
*CHOREMA N	DERISIO N	FOURTEE N	*HE N EQUE N	LICHE N I N	MO N ECIA N
*CHRISMO N	DEUTERO N	FRACTIO N	*HE N EQUI N	LIEGEMA N	MO N ELLI N
CHRISTE N	*DEVILKI N	*FRA N KLI N	*HE N IQUE N	LIGATIO N	*MO N EYMA N
CI N NAMO N	DEVOTIO N	FRAULEI N	HEPTAGO N	LIMEKIL N	MO N ITIO N
*CI N QUAI N	DIAPASO N	FREEBOR N	HERDSMA N	*LI N CHPI N	MORTMAI N
CITATIO N	*DIAZI N O N	FREEDMA N	HEREUPO N	LI N ESMA N	MOTORMA N
CIVILIA N	DIELDRI N	*FRESHMA N	*HIGHBOR N	LI N KSMA N	*MOUFFLO N
CLA N SMA N	DIHEDRO N	FRICTIO N	HIMATIO N	LOBATIO N	MOU N TAI N

MULLIGA N	*PHE N AZI N	RAMBUTA N	SECRETI N	STRUCKE N	TRAPPEA N
MULTITO N	*PHOSPHI N	*RAMEQUI N	SEDATIO N	STUBBOR N	TRASHMA N
*MU N CHKI N	*PHTHALI N	RAMSHOR N	SEDITIO N	STU N TMA N	TREELAW N
MU N ITIO N	PICAROO N	*RA N CHMA N	SEEDSMA N	STURGEO N	TRILLIO N
MUSICIA N	*PITCHMA N	RATAPLA N	*SHADCHA N	SUBBASI N	TRIMARA N
MUTATIO N	*PIVOTMA N	REACTIO N	SHAGREE N	*SUBHUMA N	TROPO N I N
*MUTCHKI N	PLACEMA N	REASSIG N	SHALLOO N	*SUBTAXO N	*TRUCKMA N
*MYRMIDO N	PLA N KTO N	REATTAI N	*SHEEPMA N	SUBTILI N	TRUDGEO N
N APOLEO N	PLA N TAI N	*REAWAKE N	SHOEHOR N	SUBURBA N	TRUEBOR N
N ATATIO N	PLASTRO N	REBUTTO N	*SHOPWOR N	SUDATIO N	TRU N N IO N
N EGATIO N	*PLAYDOW N	REDESIG N	*SHOWDOW N	SUPERFA N	TU N GSTE N
N EGATRO N	PLEBEIA N	REFASTE N	*SHRU N KE N	SUPERMA N	TURBOFA N
*N EOMYCI N	PLECTRO N	REHARDE N	*SHUTDOW N	*SUZERAI N	TUR N DOW N
*N EURAXO N	PLEUSTO N	REI N SMA N	*SHWA N PA N	*SWA N SKI N	TWI N BOR N
N IGROSI N	PLIOTRO N	RELATIO N	SIDESPI N	SWI N GMA N	VACATIO N
N I N ETEE N	POI N TMA N	RELIGIO N	SIMOLEO N	SWORDMA N	VALERIA N
N ITROGE N	POLTROO N	REMOTIO N	SIRE N IA N	*SYRPHIA N	VA N ILLI N
N OBLEMA N	*POLYZOA N	REOBTAI N	SKELETO N	TACITUR N	VE N ATIO N
N O N GREE N	POSITIO N	REORDAI N	SLATTER N	TAILSPI N	VE N ETIA N
N O N HUMA N	POSITRO N	REPLEVI N	*SLOWDOW N	*TAKEDOW N	VERATRI N
N O N PAGA N	POSTBUR N	REPLICO N	SMIDGEO N	TALAPOI N	VERBOTE N
N O N U N IO N	POSTTEE N	RESCREE N	SMOOTHE N	TALESMA N	VERSEMA N
N O N URBA N	POTATIO N	RESEASO N	SOLATIO N	TALISMA N	VESUVIA N
N O N WOVE N	*POZZOLA N	RESORCI N	SOLUTIO N	TALLYMA N	*VEXATIO N
N ORTHER N	PRECLEA N	RESPOKE N	*SOMEWHE N	TARLATA N	VIG N ERO N
N OTATIO N	*PREHUMA N	RESTRAI N	SO N ARMA N	TARLETA N	*VIOMYCI N
N OUME N O N	PRE N OME N	REVISIO N	SORPTIO N	TARRAGO N	VIRIDIA N
N UTATIO N	PRESSMA N	RESUMMO N	SOU N DMA N	*TAXATIO N	VITELLI N
N UTBROW N	PRESSRU N	RHODAMI N	SOUTHER N	TEARDOW N	VOCATIO N
N YSTATI N	PRETRAI N	RIFLEMA N	SOUTHRO N	TEASPOO N	VOLITIO N
PAGURIA N	PREU N IO N	RIGADOO N	SPACEMA N	TELETHO N	VOLUTIO N
PALMITI N	PRIAPEA N	RIGAUDO N	SPALPEE N	TERRAPI N	WA N N IGA N
PA N GOLI N	*PROCHAI N	RIPARIA N	SPEARGU N	TETRAGO N	WARFARI N
*PA N HUMA N	*PROCHEI N	ROE N TGE N	SPEARMA N	THEREMI N	*WATCHMA N
PA N N IKI N	PROLAMI N	ROGATIO N	SPECIME N	THERMIO N	WATERMA N
PA N THEO N	*PROPYLO N	ROSARIA N	SPELAEA N	THESPIA N	*WEIGHMA N
PAPILLO N	PROTAMI N	ROTATIO N	SPILIKI N	*THI N DOW N	WELLBOR N
*PARAFFI N	PROU N IO N	ROUTEMA N	SPITTOO N	*THIOPHE N	*WHALEMA N
*PARAZOA N	PSILOCI N	SAFRA N I N	SPO N SIO N	THIRTEE N	*WHEELMA N
PARERGO N	PSORALE N	SAI N FOI N	SPO N TOO N	THOLEPI N	WHORESO N
PARTISA N	PUBLICA N	SALESMA N	*SQUADRO N	THREATE N	WI N DBUR N
*PARTIZA N	*PU N CHEO N	SA N CTIO N	*SQUIREE N	*THROMBI N	*WI N ESKI N
PARVOLI N	PU N ITIO N	SA N TO N I N	STALLIO N	*THUMBKI N	WI N GSPA N
PATHOGE N	PUPATIO N	SAUCEPA N	STASIMO N	*THYMOSI N	WOODSMA N
*PATTYPA N	PURPURI N	SCALEPA N	STEAPSI N	*THYROXI N	*WOOLSKI N
PAULDRO N	*PUSHDOW N	SCALLIO N	STEGODO N	TIMEWOR N	*XA N THEI N
PAVILIO N	*QIOMTAI N	SCA N SIO N	STER N SO N	TOBOGGA N	*YACHTMA N
PAVILLO N	*QUADROO N	*SCARFPI N	*STICKMA N	TOILWOR N	*YATAGHA N
PEARMAI N	*QUARTER N	SCISSIO N	*STICKPI N	TOLUIDI N	YESTREE N
*PEMMICA N	*QUATRAI N	SCORPIO N	STICTIO N	TOW N SMA N	*ZEPPELI N
PE N TAGO N	*QUESTIO N	SCULLIO N	STILLMA N	*TRACKMA N	*ZO N ATIO N
PE N TOSA N	*QUI N OLI N	SEALSKI N	*STOCKMA N	TRACTIO N	
PEREGRI N	RADIOMA N	SEAROBI N	STRAITE N	TRAGOPA N	
PETITIO N	RAFTSMA N	SEATRAI N	STRICKE N	TRAI N MA N	

P

PACA	PELF	PITY	POUF	PYRE	PASEO
PACE	PELT	*PIXY	POUR	PACER	PASHA
PACK	PEND	PLAN	POUT	PACHA	PASSE
PACT	PENT	PLAT	PRAM	PADDY	PASTA
PADI	PEON	PLAY	PRAO	PADLE	PASTE
PAGE	PEPO	PLEA	PRAT	PADRE	PASTY
PAID	PERE	PLEB	PRAU	PAEAN	PATCH
PAIK	PERI	PLED	PRAY	PAEON	PATEN
PAIL	PERK	PLEW	PREE	PAGAN	PATER
PAIN	PERM	PLIE	PREP	PAGED	PATIN
PAIR	PERT	PLOD	PREX	PAGER	PATIO
PALE	PESO	PLOP	PREY	PAGOD	PATLY
PALL	PEST	PLOT	*PREZ	PAINT	PATSY
PALM	PFFT	PLOW	PRIG	PAISA	PATTY
PALP	PFUI	PLOY	PRIM	PAISE	PAUSE
PALY	PHAT	PLUG	PROA	PALEA	PAVAN
PANE	PHEW	PLUM	PROD	PALER	PAVER
PANG	*PHIZ	PLUS	PROF	PALET	PAVID
PANT	PHON	POCK	PROG	PALLY	PAVIN
PAPA	PHOT	POCO	PROM	PALMY	PAVIS
PARA	PHUT	POEM	PROP	PAMPA	PAWER
PARD	PIAL	POET	PROW	PANDA	*PAWKY
PARE	PIAN	POGY	PSST	PANDY	PAYEE
PARK	PICA	POKE	PUCE	PANEL	PAYER
PARR	PICE	POKY	PUCK	PANGA	PAYOR
PART	PICK	POLE	PUFF	PANIC	PEACE
PASE	PIED	POLL	PUGH	PANNE	PEACH
PASH	PIER	POLO	PUJA	PANSY	PEAGE
PASS	PIKA	POLY	PUKE	PANTO	PEAKY
PAST	PIKE	POME	PULA	PANTY	PEARL
PATE	PIKI	POMP	PULE	PAPAL	PEART
PATH	PILE	POND	PULI	PAPAW	PEASE
PATY	PILI	PONE	PULL	PAPER	PEATY
PAVE	PILL	PONG	PULP	PAPPI	PEAVY
PAWL	PILY	PONS	PUMA	PAPPY	PECAN
PAWN	PIMA	PONY	PUMP	PARCH	*PECKY
PEAG	PIMP	POOD	PUNA	PARDI	PEDAL
PEAK	PINA	POOF	PUNG	PARDY	PEDES
PEAL	PINE	POOH	PUNK	PAREO	PEDRO
PEAN	PING	POOL	PUNT	PARER	PEERY
PEAR	PINK	POON	PUNY	PAREU	PEEVE
PEAT	PINT	POOP	PUPA	PARGE	PEISE
PECH	PINY	POOR	PURE	PARGO	PEKAN
PECK	PION	POPE	PURI	PARIS	PEKIN
PEEK	PIPE	PORE	PURL	PARKA	PEKOE
PEEL	PIPY	PORK	PURR	PARLE	PELON
PEEN	PIRN	PORN	PUSH	PAROL	PENAL
PEEP	PISH	PORT	PUSS	PARRY	PENCE
PEER	PISO	POSE	PUTT	PARSE	PENES
PEIN	PISS	POSH	*PUTZ	PARTY	PENGO
PEKE	PITA	POST	PYIC	PARVE	PENIS
PELE	PITH	POSY	PYIN	PARVO	PENNA

PENNE	PILUS	**PLUCK**	PRASE	*PSYCH	PAESAN
PENNI	**PINCH**	**PLUMB**	PRATE	PUBES	**PAGING**
PENNY	PINED	PLUME	**PRAWN**	PUBIC	**PAGODA**
PEONY	**PINEY**	**PLUMP**	PREEN	PUBIS	**PAINCH**
PEPPY	PINGO	PLUMY	PRESA	**PUCKA**	**PAINTY**
PERCH	**PINKO**	**PLUNK**	PRESE	**PUDGY**	PAISAN
PERDU	**PINKY**	**PLUSH**	PRESS	**PUDIC**	*PAJAMA
PERDY	PINNA	**PLYER**	PREST	*PUFFY	*PAKEHA
PERIL	**PINNY**	**POACH**	*PREXY	PUGGY	PALACE
PERKY	PINON	*POCKY	PRICE	**PUJAH**	PALAIS
PERRY	PINOT	**PODGY**	**PRICK**	*PUKKA	PALATE
PERSE	PINTA	PODIA	**PRICY**	PULER	**PALELY**
PESKY	PINTO	**POESY**	PRIDE	PULIK	PALEST
PESTO	PINUP	**POGEY**	PRIED	**PULPY**	PALIER
PESTY	PIOUS	POILU	PRIER	PULSE	PALING
PETAL	PIPAL	**POIND**	PRIES	**PUNCH**	**PALISH**
PETER	PIPER	POINT	PRILL	**PUNKA**	PALLED
PETIT	PIPET	POISE	PRIMA	**PUNKY**	PALLET
PETTI	PIPIT	**POKER**	PRIME	**PUNNY**	PALLIA
PETTO	*PIQUE	**POKEY**	PRIMI	PUNTO	PALLID
PETTY	PIROG	POLAR	PRIMO	**PUNTY**	PALLOR
PEWEE	PISCO	POLED	**PRIMP**	PUPIL	**PALMAR**
PEWIT	PISTE	POLER	**PRINK**	**PUPPY**	**PALMER**
PHAGE	**PITCH**	POLIO	PRINT	PURDA	**PALPAL**
PHASE	**PITHY**	POLIS	PRION	PUREE	**PALPUS**
PHIAL	PITON	**POLKA**	PRIOR	PURER	PALTER
*PHLOX	**PIVOT**	**POLYP**	PRISE	PURGE	**PALTRY**
PHONE	**PIXEL**	PONCE	PRISM	PURIN	**PAMPER**
PHONO	**PIXIE**	**POOCH**	PRISS	PURSE	PANADA
PHONY	*PIZZA	POORI	**PRIVY**	**PURSY**	**PANAMA**
PHOTO	PLACE	**POPPA**	*PRIZE	**PUSHY**	PANDER
*PHPHT	PLAGE	**POPPY**	PROBE	PUSSY	PANDIT
PHYLA	PLAID	**POPSY**	PROEM	**PUTON**	**PANFRY**
PHYLE	PLAIT	**PORCH**	PROLE	PUTTI	**PANFUL**
PIANO	PLANE	**PORGY**	PROMO	PUTTO	**PANGEN**
PIBAL	**PLANK**	**PORKY**	PRONE	**PUTTY**	PANIER
PICAL	PLANT	**PLASH**	PRONG	*PYGMY	PANNED
*PICKY	**PLASH**	POSER	**PROOF**	PYLON	**PANTIE**
PICOT	PLASM	POSIT	PROSE	**PYOID**	**PANTRY**
PICUL	PLATE	POSSE	PROSO	PYRAN	*PANZER
PIECE	**PLATY**	**POTSY**	PROSS	PYRIC	*PAPACY
PIETA	**PLAYA**	POTTO	PROST	*PYXIE	PAPAIN
PIETY	*PLAZA	**POTTY**	**PROSY**	*PYXIS	**PAPAYA**
PIGGY	PLEAD	**POUCH**	PROUD	PABLUM	**PAPERY**
PIGMY	PLEAT	**POUFF**	PROVE	*PACIFY	**PAPIST**
PIING	PLEBE	**POUTY**	**PROWL**	**PACING**	**PAPPUS**
PIKER	**PLENA**	POULT	*PROXY	**PACKER**	**PAPULA**
PILAF	PLICA	POUND	PRUDE	**PACKET**	**PAPULE**
PILAR	PLIED	POWER	PRUNE	*PACKLY	PARADE
PILAU	PLIER	**POYOU**	PRUTA	**PADAUK**	**PARAMO**
PILAW	PLIES	**PRAAM**	**PRYER**	**PADDER**	PARANG
PILEA	**PLINK**	**PRAHU**	PSALM	**PADDLE**	**PARAPH**
PILED	**PLONK**	PRANG	PSEUD	PADNAG	**PARCEL**
PILEI		**PRANK**	**PSHAW**	**PADOUK**	**PARDAH**
PILOT			PSOAS	PAELLA	PARDEE

PARDIE	PATTEN	**PELTRY**	**PHASIS**	PIGNUT	**PIRAYA**
PARDON	PATTER	**PELVIC**	**PHATIC**	PIGOUT	**PIROGI**
PARENT	PATTIE	**PELVIS**	*PHENIX	**PIGPEN**	PISTIL
PAREVE	*PATZER	PENANG	PHENOL	**PIGSTY**	PISTOL
PARGET	PAULIN	**PENCEL**	PHENOM	*PIKAKE	PISTON
PARIAH	**PAUNCH**	**PENCIL**	PHENYL	**PIKING**	*PITCHY
PARIAN	**PAUPER**	**PENMAN**	PHLEGM	**PILAFF**	PITIED
PARIES	PAUSAL	PENNED	PHLOEM	**PILEUM**	PITIER
PARING	PAUSER	PENNER	**PHOBIA**	**PILEUP**	PITIES
PARISH	**PAVANE**	PENNON	*PHOBIC	PILEUS	**PITMAN**
PARITY	**PAVEED**	PENSEE	**PHOEBE**	**PILFER**	**PITSAW**
PARKER	**PAVING**	PENSIL	**PHONAL**	PILING	PITTED
PARLAY	**PAVIOR**	PENTAD	**PHONEY**	PILLAR	*PIZAZZ
PARLEY	**PAVISE**	**PENTYL**	**PHONIC**	**PILLOW**	*PIZZLE
PARLOR	**PAWNEE**	PENULT	**PHONON**	PILOSE	**PLACER**
PARODY	**PAWNER**	**PENURY**	**PHOOEY**	PILOUS	**PLACET**
PAROLE	**PAWNOR**	**PEOPLE**	**PHOTIC**	PILULE	**PLACID**
PAROUS	*PAWPAW	**PEPLOS**	**PHOTOG**	**PIMPLE**	PLAGAL
PARRAL	*PAXWAX	**PEPLUM**	**PHOTON**	*PIMPLY	**PLAGUE**
PARRED	*PAYDAY	**PEPLUS**	**PHRASE**	PINANG	**PLAGUY**
PARREL	**PAYNIM**	**PEPPED**	**PHYLAE**	PINATA	**PLAICE**
PARROT	*PAYOFF	**PEPPER**	**PHYLAR**	**PINCER**	PLAINT
PARSEC	**PAYOLA**	**PEPSIN**	**PHYLLO**	PINDER	PLANAR
PARSER	**PAYOUT**	**PEPTIC**	**PHYLON**	PINEAL	**PLANCH**
PARSON	*PAZAZZ	**PEPTID**	*PHYLUM	PINENE	PLANER
PARTAN	*PEACHY	PERDIE	*PHYSED	**PINERY**	PLANET
PARTLY	**PEAHEN**	PERDUE	**PHYSES**	PINGER	*PLAQUE
PARTON	PEANUT	PEREON	*PHYSIC	PINIER	**PLASHY**
PARURA	**PEARLY**	PERIOD	**PHYSIS**	PINING	**PLASMA**
PARURE	**PEAVEY**	**PERISH**	**PHYTIN**	PINION	PLATAN
PARVIS	**PEBBLE**	**PERMIT**	**PHYTON**	PINITE	PLATED
PASCAL	*PEBBLY	*PEROXY	**PIAFFE**	**PINKEN**	PLATEN
PASSEE	**PECHAN**	PERRON	*PIAZZA	**PINKER**	PLATER
PASSEL	**PECKER**	PERSON	**PICARA**	*PINKEY	**PLAYER**
PASSER	**PECTEN**	**PERUKE**	**PICARO**	**PINKIE**	**PLEACH**
PASSIM	**PECTIN**	PERUSE	*PICKAX	*PINKLY	PLEASE
PASSUS	PEDALO	PESADE	**PICKER**	PINNAE	**PLEDGE**
PASTEL	PEDANT	PESETA	**PICKET**	PINNAL	PLEIAD
PASTER	PEDATE	**PESEWA**	**PICKLE**	PINNED	**PLENCH**
PASTIE	**PEDDLE**	PESTER	*PICKUP	PINNER	**PLENTY**
PASTIL	PEDLER	PESTLE	**PICNIC**	PINOLE	**PLENUM**
PASTIS	PEELER	PETARD	**PICRIC**	PINTLE	PLEURA
PASTOR	**PEEPER**	PETITE	**PIDDLE**	**PINYIN**	*PLEXAL
PASTRY	**PEEPUL**	**PETNAP**	**PIDDLY**	**PINYON**	*PLEXOR
PATACA	PEERIE	PETREL	**PIDGIN**	PIOLET	*PLEXUS
*PATCHY	**PEEWEE**	PETROL	**PIECER**	**PIPAGE**	PLIANT
PATENT	**PEEWIT**	PETSAI	PIEING	**PIPIER**	**PLIGHT**
PATHOS	*PEGBOX	PETTED	**PIERCE**	**PIPING**	**PLINTH**
PATINA	**PEGGED**	PETTER	**PIFFLE**	**PIPKIN**	*PLISKY
PATINE	PELAGE	PETTLE	PIGEON	**PIPPED**	PLISSE
PATOIS	PELITE	**PEWTER**	**PIGGED**	**PIPPIN**	**PLOIDY**
PATROL	PELLET	**PEYOTE**	**PIGGIE**	*PIQUET	**PLOTTY**
PATRON	**PELMET**	**PEYOTL**	**PIGGIN**	**PIRACY**	**PLOUGH**
PATTED	PELOTA	**PHALLI**	PIGLET	PIRANA	**PLOVER**
PATTEE	PELTER	**PHAROS**	PIGNUS	PIRATE	**PLOWER**

*PLUCKY	PONTON	PRATER	PROPYL	*PUNKEY	*PACKAGE
*PLUMMY	POODLE	*PRAXIS	PROSER	PUNKIE	*PACKING
PLUNGE	POORLY	PRAYER	PROSIT	PUNKIN	*PACKMAN
PLURAL	POPERY	PREACH	PROTEA	PUNNED	*PACKWAX
PLUSHY	POPGUN	PREACT	PROTEI	PUNNER	PACTION
PLUTON	POPISH	PREAMP	PROTON	PUNNET	PADDIES
PNEUMA	POPLAR	PREARM	PROTYL	PUNTER	PADDING
*POACHY	POPLIN	PRECIS	PROVER	PUPATE	PADDLER
POCKET	POPPED	PRECUT	PROWAR	PUPPED	*PADDOCK
PODITE	POPPER	PREFAB	PRUNER	PUPPET	*PADLOCK
PODIUM	POPPET	PREFER	PRUNUS	PURANA	PADRONE
PODSOL	POPPLE	*PREFIX	PRUTAH	PURDAH	*PADSHAH
*PODZOL	POPSIE	PRELIM	PSEUDO	PURELY	PAESANO
POETIC	PORISM	PREMAN	PSOCID	PUREST	PAGEANT
POETRY	PORKER	PREMED	*PSYCHE	PURFLE	*PAGEBOY
POGIES	POROSE	PREMEN	*PSYCHO	PURGER	PAGINAL
POGROM	POROUS	PREMIE	PSYLLA	PURIFY	PAGURID
POINTE	PORTAL	*PREMIX	PSYWAR	PURINE	*PAHLAVI
POINTY	PORTER	PREPAY	PTERIN	PURISM	PAILFUL
POISER	PORTLY	*PREPPY	PTISAN	PURIST	PAINFUL
POISON	POSADA	PRESET	PTOSIS	PURITY	PAINTER
POKIER	POSEUR	PRESTO	PUBLIC	PURLIN	PAIRING
POKIES	POSIES	*PRETAX	PUCKER	PURPLE	PAISANA
*POKILY	POSING	PRETOR	PUDDLE	PURPLY	PAISANO
POKING	POSSET	PRETTY	PUDDLY	PURRED	PAISLEY
POLDER	POSSUM	PREVUE	PUEBLO	PURSER	PALABRA
*POLEAX	POSTAL	PREWAR	PUFFER	PURSUE	PALADIN
POLEIS	POSTER	PREYER	PUFFIN	PURVEY	PALATAL
POLEYN	POSTIN	PRIAPI	PUGGED	PUSHER	PALAVER
POLICE	POTAGE	PRICER	PUGGRY	PUSHUP	*PALAZZO
POLICY	POTASH	PRICEY	PUGREE	PUSLEY	PALETOT
POLING	POTATO	*PRICKY	PUISNE	PUSSLY	PALETTE
POLISH	POTBOY	PRIEST	PULING	PUTLOG	*PALFREY
POLITE	POTEEN	PRIMAL	PULLER	PUTOFF	PALIEST
POLITY	POTENT	PRIMER	PULLET	PUTOUT	PALIKAR
POLLEE	POTFUL	PRIMLY	PULLEY	PUTRID	PALLIAL
POLLEN	POTHER	PRIMUS	PULLUP	PUTSCH	PALLIER
POLLER	POTION	PRINCE	PULPAL	PUTTEE	PALLING
*POLLEX	POTMAN	PRIORY	PULPER	PUTTER	PALLIUM
POLYPI	POTPIE	PRISON	PULPIT	*PUZZLE	PALMARY
POMACE	POTSIE	PRISSY	*PULQUE	PYEMIA	PALMATE
POMADE	POTTED	PRIVET	PULSAR	*PYKNIC	PALMIER
POMELO	POTTER	*PRIZEA	PULSER	PYOSIS	PALMIST
POMMEE	POTTLE	PROBER	PUMELO	PYRENE	PALMYRA
POMMEL	*POTZER	PROBIT	PUMICE	PYRITE	PALOOKA
POMPOM	*POUCHY	PROFIT	PUMMEL	PYROLA	PALPATE
POMPON	POUFFE	*PROJET	PUMPER	PYRONE	PALSHIP
PONCHO	POUNCE	PROLAN	*PUNCHY	PYROPE	PALUDAL
PONDER	POURER	PROLEG	PUNDIT	PYRROL	PAMPEAN
PONENT	POUTER	*PROLIX	PUNGLE	PYTHON	PAMPERO
PONGEE	POWDER	PROLOG	PUNIER	PYURIA	PANACEA
PONGID	POWTER	PROMPT	PUNILY	PABULUM	PANACHE
PONIED	*POWWOW	PRONTO	PUNISH	PACHISI	*PANCAKE
PONIES	PRAISE	PROPEL	*PUNKAH	*PACHUCO	*PANCHAX
PONTIL	PRANCE	PROPER	PUNKER	*PACIFIC	PANDECT

PANDIED	PARONYM	PAUCITY	*PEMPHIX	PERIGON	PHONATE
PANDIES	PAROTIC	*PAUGHTY	PENALLY	PERILLA	PHONEME
PANDOOR	PAROTID	*PAUNCHY	PENALTY	*PERIQUE	PHONICS
PANDORA	*PARQUET	PAVIOUR	PENANCE	PERIWIG	PHONIED
PANDORE	PARRIED	PAVISER	PENATES	*PERJURE	PHONIER
PANDOUR	PARRIES	*PAVLOVA	PENDANT	*PERJURY	PHONIES
PANDURA	PARRING	PAWNAGE	PENDENT	*PERKISH	*PHONILY
*PANFISH	PARROTY	PAYABLE	PENGUIN	PERLITE	PHONING
PANGENE	PARSING	*PAYBACK	PENICIL	PERMUTE	PHORATE
*PANICKY	PARSLEY	PAYLOAD	PENLITE	PERORAL	PHOTICS
PANICLE	PARSNIP	PAYMENT	PENNAME	*PEROXID	PHRASAL
PANICUM	PARTAKE	PAYROLL	PENNANT	PERPEND	*PHRATRY
PANNIER	PARTIAL	PEACHER	PENNATE	PERPENT	PHRENIC
PANNING	PARTIED	PEACING	PENNIES	*PERPLEX	*PHRENSY
PANOCHA	PARTIER	PEACOAT	PENNINE	PERSALT	*PHYTANE
PANOCHE	PARTIES	*PEACOCK	PENNING	PERSIST	*PHYTOID
PANOPLY	PARTING	*PEAFOWL	PENOCHE	PERSONA	*PIAFFER
PANPIPE	PARTITA	PEAKIER	PENSILE	PERTAIN	PIANISM
PANTHER	PARTITE	*PEAKISH	PENSION	PERTURB	PIANIST
PANTIES	PARTLET	PEALIKE	PENSIVE	PERUSAL	PIASABA
PANTILE	PARTNER	PEARLER	PENSTER	PERUSER	PIASAVA
PANTOUM	PARTOOK	PEASANT	PENTANE	PERVADE	PIASTER
PAPERER	*PARTWAY	PEASCOD	PENTENE	PERVERT	PIASTRE
PAPHIAN	PARTYER	PECCANT	PENTODE	PESSARY	*PIBROCH
PAPILLA	PARVENU	*PECCARY	PENTOSE	PETASOS	*PICACHO
PAPOOSE	PARVISE	*PECCAVI	PENUCHE	PETASUS	PICADOR
PAPPIER	PASCHAL	*PECKISH	PENUCHI	*PETCOCK	PICCOLO
PAPPIES	*PASQUIL	PECTASE	PEONAGE	PETIOLE	PICEOUS
PAPRICA	PASSADE	PECTATE	PEONISM	*PETRIFY	*PICKAXE
*PAPRIKA	PASSADO	*PECTIZE	PEOPLER	PETROUS	*PICKEER
PAPYRUS	PASSAGE	PEDAGOG	*PEPPERY	PETTIER	*PICKIER
PARABLE	PASSANT	PEDDLER	PEPPING	PETTILY	*PICKING
PARADER	PASSING	PEDICAB	PEPSINE	PETTING	*PICKOFF
PARADOR	PASSION	PEDICEL	PEPTIDE	PETTISH	PICOLIN
PARADOS	PASSIVE	PEDICLE	*PEPTIZE	PETUNIA	PICOTEE
*PARADOX	*PASSKEY	PEDLARY	PEPTONE	PEYTRAL	*PICQUET
PARAGON	PASTERN	PEDLERY	PERACID	PEYTREL	PICRATE
PARAPET	PASTEUP	PEDOCAL	PERCALE	PFENNIG	PICRITE
PARASOL	PASTIER	PEEBEEN	PERCENT	PHAETON	PICTURE
PARBOIL	PASTIES	PEELING	PERCEPT	*PHALANX	PIDDLER
PARDINE	PASTIME	PEERAGE	PERCHER	PHALLIC	*PIDDOCK
PARDNER	PASTINA	PEERESS	PERCOID	PHALLUS	PIEBALD
PAREIRA	PASTING	*PEEVISH	PERCUSS	PHANTOM	PIECING
PARESIS	PASTURE	PEGGING	PERDURE	*PHARAOH	PIEFORT
PARETIC	PATAMAR	PEGLESS	PEREION	*PHARYNX	PIERCER
PARFAIT	PATCHER	PEGLIKE	PERFECT	*PHASMID	PIEROGI
PARGING	PATELLA	PELAGIC	*PERFIDY	PHELLEM	PIERROT
PARKING	PATENCY	PELICAN	PERFORM	PHENATE	PIETIES
*PARKWAY	*PATHWAY	PELISSE	PERFUME	*PHENOXY	PIETISM
PARLING	PATIENT	PELORIA	PERFUSE	PHILTER	PIETIST
PARLOUR	PATNESS	PELORUS	PERGOLA	PHILTRE	PIGBOAT
PARLOUS	PATRIOT	PELTAST	PERHAPS	*PHLEGMY	*PIGFISH
PARODIC	PATROON	PELTATE	PERIAPT	PHOCINE	PIGGERY
PARODOS	PATTERN	PEMBINA	PERIDOT	PHOEBUS	PIGGIER
PAROLEE	PATTING	PEMICAN	PERIGEE	*PHOENIX	PIGGIES

PIGGING	PIPIEST	PLATING	PLUNDER	POPOVER	POULTRY
PIGGISH	PIPPING	PLATOON	PLUNGER	POPPIED	POUNCER
PIGLIKE	*PIQUANT	*PLATTED	PLUNKER	POPPIES	POUNDAL
PIGMENT	PIRAGUA	PLATTER	PLUSSES	POPPING	POUNDER
PIGNOLI	PIRANHA	PLAUDIT	PLUTEUS	POPULAR	POUSSIE
PIGSKIN	PIRATIC	PLAYACT	PLUVIAL	PORCINE	POUTFUL
PIGSNEY	PIROGUE	*PLAYBOY	PLUVIAN	PORCINO	*POVERTY
PIGWEED	*PIROQUE	*PLAYDAY	*PLYWOOD	PORKIER	*POWDERY
*PIKEMAN	PISCARY	*PLAYFUL	POACHER	PORKIES	PRACTIC
PILEATE	PISCINA	PLAYLET	*POCHARD	*PORKPIE	PRAETOR
PILEOUS	PISCINE	*PLAYOFF	POCOSIN	PORRECT	PRAIRIE
PILGRIM	PISHOGE	PLAYPEN	PODAGRA	PORTAGE	PRAISER
PILLAGE	PISMIRE	PLEADER	PODESTA	PORTEND	PRALINE
*PILLBOX	PISSANT	PLEASER	PODLIKE	PORTENT	PRANCER
PILLION	PISSOIR	PLEATER	POETESS	PORTICO	PRATING
PILLORY	PISTOLE	PLEDGEE	POETICS	PORTION	PRATTLE
*PILLOWY	PITAPAT	PLEDGER	*POETIZE	PORTRAY	PRAWNER
PILSNER	PITCHER	PLEDGET	POETISE	POSSESS	*PREACHY
PIMENTO	PITEOUS	PLEDGOR	POGONIA	POSTAGE	PREAGED
PINBALL	PITFALL	PLENARY	POGONIP	POSTBAG	PREANAL
PINBONE	PITHEAD	PLENISH	POINTER	*POSTBOX	PREAVER
PINCHER	PITIFUL	PLENISM	POITREL	POSTBOY	*PREBAKE
PINESAP	PITTING	PLENIST	POKIEST	POSTDOC	PREBEND
PINETUM	PIVOTAL	PLEOPOD	POLARON	POSTEEN	PREBILL
*PINFISH	*PIZAZZY	PLESSOR	*POLEAXE	POSTERN	PREBIND
PINFOLD	PLACARD	PLEURON	POLECAT	*POSTFIX	PREBOIL
PINGUID	PLACATE	PLIABLE	POLEMIC	POSTING	*PREBOOK
PINHEAD	PLACEBO	PLIANCY	POLENTA	POSTMAN	PREBOOM
PINHOLE	PLACING	PLICATE	POLITIC	*POSTTAX	PRECAST
PINIEST	*PLACKET	PLIMSOL	*POLLACK	POSTURE	PRECAVA
PINITOL	PLACOID	PLINKER	POLLARD	POSTWAR	PRECEDE
*PINKEYE	PLAFOND	PLISKIE	POLLIST	POTABLE	PRECENT
PINKIES	PLAGUER	PLODDER	*POLLOCK	POTAMIC	PRECEPT
PINKING	PLAGUEY	PLOSION	POLLUTE	POTBOIL	PRECESS
*PINKISH	PLAITER	PLOSIVE	POLOIST	POTENCE	PRECIPE
PINNACE	PLANATE	PLOTTED	POLYCOT	POTENCY	PRECISE
PINNATE	PLANCHE	PLOTTER	POLYENE	POTHEAD	PRECODE
PINNIES	PLANING	*PLOWBOY	POLYGON	POTHEEN	*PRECOOK
PINNING	PLANISH	PLOWMAN	POLYMER	POTHERB	PRECOOL
PINNULA	PLANNED	*PLUCKER	*POLYNYA	POTHOLE	PRECOUP
PINNULE	PLANNER	PLUGGER	POLYOMA	*POTHOOK	PRECURE
PINOCLE	PLANTAR	PLUGOLA	*POLYPOD	POTICHE	PREDATE
PINTADA	PLANULA	PLUMAGE	POLYPUS	POTLACH	PREDAWN
PINTADO	PLASHER	PLUMATE	POMATUM	POTLIKE	PREDIAL
PINTAIL	PLASMID	PLUMBER	POMFRET	POTLINE	PREDICT
PINTANO	PLASMIN	*PLUMBIC	POMPANO	*POTLUCK	PREDIVE
PINWALE	PLASMON	*PLUMBUM	POMPOUS	POTSHOT	PREDUSK
PINWEED	PLASTER	PLUMIER	PONIARD	POTTAGE	PREEDIT
*PINWORK	PLASTIC	PLUMING	*PONTIFF	POTTEEN	PREEMIE
PINWORM	PLASTID	PLUMMET	PONTINE	POTTERY	PREEMPT
PIONEER	PLATANE	PLUMOSE	PONTOON	POTTIER	PREENER
PIOSITY	PLATEAU	PLUMPEN	POORISH	POTTIES	PREFACE
PIPEAGE	PLATIER	PLUMPER	POPCORN	POTTING	PREFADE
PIPEFUL	PLATIES	*PLUMPLY	POPEDOM	POULARD	PREFECT
PIPETTE	PLATINA	PLUMULE	*POPEYED	POULTER	PREFILE

PREFIRE	PRETRIM	PRODUCT	*PROVOKE	PUNNING	*PACKAGER
PREFORM	PRETYPE	PROETTE	PROVOST	PUNSTER	*PACKNESS
PREGAME	*PRETZEL	PROFANE	PROWESS	*PUPFISH	*PACKSACK
PREHEAT	PREVAIL	PROFESS	PROWLER	PUPILAR	PADDLING
PRELACY	PREVENT	*PROFFER	*PROXIES	PUPPING	*PADISHAH
PRELATE	*PREVIEW	PROFILE	*PROXIMO	PURGING	PADUASOY
PRELECT	PREVISE	PROFUSE	PRUDENT	PURITAN	PAEANISM
PRELIFE	PREWARM	PROGENY	PRUDERY	PURLIEU	PAGANDOM
PRELUDE	PREWARN	PROGGER	PRUDISH	PURLINE	PAGANISE
PREMADE	*PREWASH	PROGRAM	PRUNING	PURLOIN	PAGANISH
PREMEAL	*PREWORK	*PROJECT	PRURIGO	PURPORT	PAGANISM
PREMEET	PREWRAP	PROLATE	PRUSSIC	PURPOSE	PAGANIST
PREMIER	PRIAPIC	PROLINE	*PRYTHEE	PURPURA	*PAGANIZE
PREMISE	PRICIER	PROLONG	PSALMIC	PURPURE	PAGINATE
PREMISS	PRICING	PROMINE	PSALTER	PURRING	PAGURIAN
PREMIUM	*PRICKER	PROMISE	PSALTRY	PURSIER	*PAHOEHOE
PREMOLD	*PRICKET	PROMOTE	PSAMMON	PURSILY	PAILLARD
PREMOLT	*PRICKLE	PRONATE	PSCHENT	PURSING	PAINLESS
PREMUNE	*PRICKLY	PRONOUN	*PSYCHIC	PURSUER	PAINTING
PRENAME	*PRIMACY	PROOFER	PSYLLID	PURSUIT	*PAJAMAED
PRENOON	PRIMAGE	PROPEND	PTERYLA	*PURVIEW	PALATIAL
*PREPACK	PRIMARY	PROPENE	PTOMAIN	*PUSHFUL	PALATINE
PREPAID	PRIMATE	PROPHET	PTYALIN	PUSHIER	*PALAZZOS
PREPARE	PRIMELY	PROPINE	PUBERTY	*PUSHILY	*PALEFACE
PREPILL	PRIMERO	*PROPJET	PUBLISH	PUSHPIN	PALENESS
PREPLAN	PRIMINE	PROPMAN	PUCCOON	PUSSIER	PALEOSOL
PREPPED	PRIMING	PROPONE	*PUCKERY	PUSSIES	PALESTRA
PREPPIE	PRIMMED	PROPOSE	*PUCKISH	PUSSLEY	*PALEWAYS
PREPREG	PRIMMER	PROPPED	PUDDING	PUSTULE	PALEWISE
PREPUCE	PRIMSIE	PRORATE	PUDDLER	PUTAMEN	*PALIMONY
*PREQUEL	PRIMULA	PROSAIC	*PUDENCY	*PUTREFY	PALINODE
PRERACE	*PRINCOX	PROSECT	PUERILE	PUTTIED	PALISADE
PRERIOT	PRINKER	PROSIER	*PUFFERY	PUTTIER	PALLADIA
*PREROCK	PRINTER	PROSILY	PUGAREE	PUTTING	PALLADIC
PRESAGE	PRIORLY	PROSING	PUGGIER	*PUZZLER	PALLETTE
PRESALE	PRISERE	PROSODY	PUGGING	PYAEMIA	PALLIATE
PRESELL	PRITHEE	PROSOMA	PUGGISH	*PYJAMAS	PALLIEST
PRESENT	*PRIVACY	PROSPER	PUGGREE	PYLORUS	PALMATED
PRESHOW	PRIVATE	PROSSIE	*PUGMARK	PYRALID	PALMETTE
PRESIDE	PRIVIER	PROSTIE	PULLMAN	*PYRAMID	PALMETTO
PRESIFT	PRIVIES	PROTEAN	PULLOUT	PYRETIC	PALMIEST
PRESOAK	*PRIVITY	PROTECT	PULPIER	*PYREXIA	PALMITIN
PRESOLD	PROBAND	PROTÉGÉ	PULPILY	PRYOGEN	*PALMLIKE
PRESONG	PROBANG	PROTEID	PULPOUS	PYROSIS	PALOMINO
PRESORT	PROBATE	PROTEIN	PULSANT	*PYRRHIC	PALPABLE
PRESSER	PROBITY	PROTEND	PULSATE	PYRROLE	PALPATOR
PRESSOR	PROBLEM	PROTEST	PULSING	*PACHADOM	PALPEBRA
PRESTER	PROCARP	PROTEUS	PULSION	*PACHALIC	PALTERER
PRESUME	PROCEED	PROTIST	PUMICER	*PACHINKO	PALUDISM
PRETAPE	PROCESS	PROTIUM	PUMMELO	*PACHOULI	PAMPERER
PRETEEN	PROCTOR	PROTYLE	*PUMPKIN	*PACIFIED	*PAMPHLET
PRETEND	PROCURE	PROVERB	PUNCHER	*PACIFIER	PANATELA
PRETERM	PRODDER	PROVIDE	PUNGENT	*PACIFIES	PANBROIL
PRETEST	PRODIGY	PROVING	PUNIEST	*PACIFISM	PANCETTA
PRETEXT	PRODUCE	PROVISO	*PUNKISH	*PACIFIST	PANCREAS

PANDANUS	*PARCHISI	PASTURAL	PEDIGREE	*PERFECTO	*PHANTASM
*PANDEMIC	PARDONER	PASTURER	PEDIMENT	*PERFORCE	PHANTAST
PANDERER	PARECISM	PATAGIAL	*PEDIPALP	*PERFUMER	*PHANTASY
*PANDOWDY	PARENTAL	PATAGIUM	*PEDOLOGY	PERIANTH	PHARISEE
PANELING	PARERGON	PATENTEE	PEDUNCLE	PERIBLEM	*PHARMACY
PANELIST	PARFLESH	PATENTLY	*PEEKABOO	PERICARP	PHASEOUT
PANELLED	*PARFOCAL	PATENTOR	*PEEPHOLE	PERICOPE	PHEASANT
PANETELA	PARHELIA	PATERNAL	*PEEPSHOW	PERIDERM	PHELONIA
PANGOLIN	*PARHELIC	PATHETIC	PEERLESS	PERIDIUM	*PHENAZIN
*PANHUMAN	PARIETAL	PATHLESS	*PEESWEEP	*PERIGYNY	*PHENETIC
*PANMIXIA	*PARKLAND	PATHOGEN	PEETWEET	PERILOUS	PHENETOL
*PANMIXIS	*PARKLIKE	PATIENCE	PEGBOARD	PERILUNE	*PHENOLIC
PANNIKIN	PARLANCE	PATINATE	PEIGNOIR	PERINEUM	*PHILABEG,
PANOPTIC	PARLANDO	*PATINIZE	PELERINE	PERIODIC	*PHILIBEG
PANORAMA	PARLANTE	PATTAMAR	PELLAGRA	PERIODID	*PHILOMEL
*PANSOPHY	PARLEYER	PATTERER	PELLETAL	PERIOTIC	*PHILTRUM
PANTHEON	PARODIED	*PATTYPAN	PELLICLE	*PERIPETY	*PHIMOSIS
PANTOFLE	PARODIES	PATULENT	PELLMELL	PERIPTER	*PHONETIC
PANTSUIT	PARODIST	PATULOUS	PELLUCID	PERISARC	PHONIEST
*PAPERBOY	*PAROQUET	PAULDRON	*PEMMICAN	*PERJURER	PHORONID
PAPILLON	PAROTOID	*PAVEMENT	PEMOLINE	PERLUDER	PHOSGENE
*PAPISTRY	*PAROXYSM	PAVILLON	PENALISE	PERMEANT	*PHOSPHID
PAPPIES	PARRIDGE	PAVONINE	PENALITY	PERMEASE	*PHOSPHIN
PAPPOOSE	*PARRITCH	*PAWNSHOP	PENALIZE	PERMEATE	*PHOSPHOR
PARABOLA	PARROKET	*PAYABLES	*PENCHANT	PERONEAL	*PHOTOMAP
*PARACHOR	PARROTER	*PAYCHECK	PENCILER	PERORATE	*PHOTOPIA
PARADIGM	PARTAKER	*PAYGRADE	*PENDENCY	*PEROXIDE	PHOTOSET
PARADING	PARTERRE	*PEACEFUL	PENDULUM	PERSONAL	PHRASING
PARADISE	PARTIBLE	*PEACENIK	PENITENT	PERSPIRE	*PHREATIC
*PARAFFIN	PARTICLE	*PEACOCKY	*PENKNIFE	PERSUADE	*PHTHALIC
*PARAFORM	PARTISAN	PEAKIEST	PENLIGHT	PERTNESS	*PHTHALIN
PARAGOGE	*PARTIZAN	PEAKLESS	PENNATED	PERVADER	*PHTHISIC
PARAKEET	PARVENUE	*PEAKLIKE	PENOLOGY	PERVERSE	*PHTHISIS
PARAKITE	PARVOLIN	PEARLASH	PENONCEL	PERVIOUS	*PHYLAXIS
*PARALLAX	*PASHADOM	PEARLITE	PENPOINT	PESTERER	*PHYLESIS
PARALLEL	*PASHALIC	PEARMAIN	PENSIONE	PESTHOLE	*PHYLLARY
PARALYSE	*PASHALIK	PEASECOD	*PENSTOCK	PETALINE	*PHYLLITE
*PARALYZE	PASSABLE	*PECCABLE	PENTACLE	PETALODY	*PHYLLODE
PARAMENT	PASSBAND	*PECCANCY	PENTAGON	PETALOID	*PHYLLOID
PARAMOUR	*PASSBOOK	PECORINO	PENTANOL	PETALOUS	*PHYLLOME
PARANOEA	*PASSERBY	PECTORAL	*PENTARCH	*PETECHIA	*PHYSICAL
PARANOIA	PASSIBLE	PECULATE	PENTOMIC	PETIOLAR	*PHYSIQUE
PARANOIC	PASSLESS	PECULIAR	PENTOSAN	PETITION	PIACULAR
PARANOID	PASSOVER	PECULIUM	*PENUCHLE	PETROLIC	PIASSABA
*PARAQUAT	PASSPORT	*PEDAGOGY	*PENUCKLE	PETRONEL	PIASSAVA
*PAREQUET	PASSWORD	PEDALFER	PENUMBRA	PETROSAL	PICAROON
PARASANG	PASTICCI	PEDALIER	PEPERONI	PETTEDLY	*PICAYUNE
*PARASHAH	*PASTICHE	PEDALLED	PEPONIDA	PETTIEST	*PICIFORM
PARASITE	PASTIEST	PEDANTRY	PEPONIUM	PETTIFOG	*PICKADIL
PARAVANE	PASTILLE	*PEDDLERY	PEPPERER	PETULANT	*PICKEREL
PARAWING	PASTLESS	PEDDLING	*PEPTIZER	PETUNTSE	*PICKETER
*PARAZOAN	PASTNESS	PEDERAST	*PERCEIVE	PEWTERER	*PICKIEST
PARCENER	PASTORAL	PEDESTAL	PEREGRIN	PHALANGE	*PICKLOCK
*PARCHESI	PASTRAMI	PEDICURE	PEREOPOD	*PHALLISM	*PICKWICK
	PASTROMI	*PEDIFORM	*PERFECTA	PHALLIST	PICLORAM

*PICNICKY	PIRARUCU	*PLAYBILL	PLUVIOSE	*POLYSEMY	POSTCOUP
*PICOGRAM	*PIRIFORM	*PLAYBOOK	PLUVIOUS	*POLYSOME	POSTDATE
PICOLINE	*PIROZHOK	*PLAYDOWN	POACEOUS	POLYTENE	POSTDIVE
PICOMOLE	PISCATOR	PLAYGIRL	*POCKETER	*POLYTENY	POSTDRUG
PIECRUST	PISHOGUE	PLAYGOER	*POCKMARK	*POLYTYPE	POSTFACE
PIEDFORT	*PISIFORM	PLAYLAND	PODIATRY	POLYURIA	POSTFIRE
PIEDMONT	PISOLITE	PLAYLESS	*PODOCARP	*POLYZOAN	POSTFORM
PIEPLANT	*PISTACHE	*PLAYLIKE	PODOMERE	*POLYZOIC	POSTGAME
PIGGIEST	*PITCHIER	*PLAYMATE	*POECHORE	POMANDER	POSTHEAT
PIGNOLIA	*PITCHILY	*PLAYROOM	POETICAL	*POMOLOGY	POSTHOLE
PIGSTICK	*PITCHMAN	PLAYSUIT	POETISER	PONDERER	*POSTICHE
PILASTER	*PITCHOUT	*PLAYTIME	*POETIZER	*PONDWEED	*POSTIQUE
*PILCHARD	PITHLESS	*PLAYWEAR	POETLESS	*PONTIFEX	POSTLUDE
PILEATED	PITIABLE	PLEADING	POETLIKE	*PONTIFIC	*POSTMARK
PILELESS	PITILESS	PLEASANT	POIGNANT	PONYTAIL	POSTORAL
PILEWORT	PITTANCE	PLEASURE	POINTMAN	POOLHALL	POSTPAID
PILFERER	*PIVOTMAN	PLEBEIAN	POISONER	POOLROOM	POSTPONE
*PILIFORM	*PIXINESS	PLECTRON	POKERGOT	POOLSIDE	POSTRACE
PILLAGER	*PIZZERIA	PLECTRUM	*POKEWEED	POORNESS	POSTRIOT
PILOSITY	PLACABLE	PLEDGEOR	POKINESS	POORTITH	*POSTSHOW
PILOTAGE	PLACATER	PLEDGING	POLARISE	*POPINJAY	*POSTSYNC
PILOTING	PLACEMAN	PLEONASM	POLARITY	POPLITIC	POSTTEEN
PILSENER	PLACENTA	PLETHORA	*POLARIZE	POPULACE	POSTTEST
PIMIENTO	PLAGIARY	PLEURISY	POLELESS	POPULATE	POSTURAL
PINAFORE	PLAGUING	PLEUSTON	POLEMIST	POPULISM	POSTURER
PINASTER	PLAISTER	PLICATED	*POLEMIZE	POPULIST	POTASSIC
*PINCHBUG	PLAITING	PLIGHTER	POLESTAR	POPULOUS	POTATION
*PINCHECK	PLANARIA	PLIMSOLE	POLEWARD	PORKIEST	POTATORY
PINDLING	*PLANCHET	PLIMSOLL	POLISHER	*PORKWOOD	*POTBELLY
PINECONE	*PLANFORM	PLIOTRON	*POLITICK	POROSITY	POTHOUSE
PINELAND	PLANGENT	PLOTLESS	POLITICO	*PORPHYRY	*POTLACHE
PINELIKE	*PLANKING	PLOTLINE	POLITICS	PORPOISE	*POTLATCH
PINEWOOD	PLANKTER	PLOTTAGE	POLLINIA	PORRIDGE	POTSHERD
PINGRASS	PLANKTON	PLOTTIER	POLLINIC	PORTABLE	POTSTONE
PINKNESS	PLANLESS	PLOTTIES	POLLIWOG	*PORTABLY	POTTERER
PINKROOT	PLANNING	PLOTTING	POLLSTER	PORTANCE	POTTIEST
PINNACLE	PLANOSOL	PLOUGHER	POLLUTER	*PORTAPAK	POULARDE
PINNATED	PLANTAIN	*PLOWBACK	*POLLYWOG	PORTHOLE	POULTICE
PINNIPED	PLANTING	*PLOWHEAD	POLONIUM	PORTIERE	POUNDAGE
*PINOCHLE	PLANTLET	PLOWLAND	POLTROON	PORTLESS	POWDERER
PINPOINT	PLASMOID	PLUGLESS	*POLYBIRD	PORTRAIT	*POWERFUL
*PINPRICK	PLASTERY	*PLUGUGLY	POLYGALA	PORTRESS	*POXVIRUS
*PINSCHER	PLASTRON	*PLUMBAGO	*POLYGAMY	POSHNESS	*POZZOLAN
*PINTSIZE	PLASTRUM	*PLUMBERY	POLYGENE	POSINGLY	PRACTICE
*PINWHEEL	PLATEFUL	*PLUMBING	POLYGLOT	POSITION	PRACTISE
*PIPEFISH	PLATELET	*PLUMBISM	*POLYGONY	POSITIVE	PRAECIPE
PIPELESS	*PLATFORM	PLUMBOUS	*POLYGYNY	POSITRON	PRAEDIAL
*PIPELIKE	PLATIEST	PLUMELET	*POLYMATH	POSOLOGY	*PRAEFECT
PIPELINE	PLATINIC	PLUMERIA	*POLYPARY	POSSIBLE	PRAELECT
PIPERINE	PLATINUM	PLUMIEST	*POLYPIDE	POSTALLY	PRANDIAL
PIPESTEM	PLATONIC	*PLUMIPED	*POLYPNEA	POSTANAL	*PRANKISH
PIPINESS	PLATTING	*PLUMLIKE	*POLYPODY	POSTBURN	PRATFALL
*PIPINGLY	*PLATYPUS	*PLUMPISH	*POLYPOID	POSTCARD	*PRATIQUE
*PIQUANCE	PLAUSIVE	PLURALLY	*POLYPORE	POSTCAVA	PRATTLER
*PIQUANCY	*PLAYBACK	PLUSSAGE	*POLYPOUS	POSTCODE	

*PREACHER	*PREPPING	*PRIMMING	PROPIENSE	PSILOSIS	*PURCHASE
PREADAPT	PREPRICE	PRIMNESS	*PROPENYL	PSORALEA	PUREBRED
PREADMIT	PREPRINT	PRIMROSE	*PROPERTY	PSORALEN	PURENESS
PREADOPT	*PREPUNCH	*PRINCELY	*PROPHAGE	*PSYLLIUM	PURFLING
PREADULT	PREPUPAL	PRINCESS	*PROPHASE	PTEROPOD	PURIFIER
PREALLOT	PRERENAL	PRINCIPE	*PROPHECY	PTERYGIA	*PURPLISH
PREAMBLE	PRERINSE	PRINTERY	*PROPHESY	PTOMAINE	PURPURIC
PREAUDIT	PRESAGER	PRINTING	PROPOLIS	*PTYALISM	PURPURIN
*PREAXIAL	PRESCIND	PRINTOUT	PROPOSAL	PUBLICAN	PURSIEST
PREBASAL	PRESCORE	PRIORATE	PROPOSER	*PUBLICLY	PURSLANE
PREBLESS	PRESENCE	PRIORESS	PROPOUND	*PUCKERER	PURSUANT
PREBOUND	PRESERVE	PRIORIES	*PROPPING	PUDDLING	PURSLENT
*PRECHECK	*PRESHAPE	PRIORITY	*PROPYLON	PUDENDUM	*PURVEYOR
*PRECHILL	PRESIDER	PRISMOID	PROROGUE	*PUFFBALL	*PUSHBALL
*PRECIEUX	PRESIDIA	PRISONER	PROSAISM	PUGGAREE	*PUSHCART
PRECINCT	PRESIDIO	PRISTANE	PROSAIST	PUGGIEST	*PUSHDOWN
PRECIOUS	PRESLEEP	PRISTINE	PROSIEST	PUGILISM	PUSHIEST
PRECITED	PRESLICE	PROBABLE	PROSPECT	PUGILIST	*PUSHOVER
PRECLEAN	PRESPLIT	*PROBABLY	PROSTATE	PUISSANT	PUSSIEST
PRECLEAR	PRESSING	PROCAINE	PROSTYLE	PULICENE	PUSSLIKE
PRECLUDE	PRESSMAN	PROTAMIN	PROTAMIN	PULICIDE	*PUSSYCAT
*PRECRASH	PRESSRUN	*PROCHAIN	PROTASIS	PULINGLY	PUTATIVE
PREDATOR	PRESSURE	*PROCHEIN	PROTEASE	*PULLBACK	PUTTERER
PREDRILL	PRESTAMP	PROCLAIM	PROTEGEE	PULLOVER	*PYCNIDIA
PREELECT	PRESTIGE	PROCURAL	PROTEIDE	PULMONIC	*PYCNOSIS
PREENACT	PRESUMER	PROCURER	PROTEOSE	PULMOTOR	*PYCNOTIC
PREERECT	PRETASTE	PRODIGAL	PROTOCOL	PULPIEST	PYELITIS
*PREEXIST	PRETENCE	PRODROME	PROTOPOD	PULPLESS	*PYGIDIUM
*PREFACER	PRETENSE	PRODUCER	*PROTOXID	*PULPWOOD	*PYGMYISM
*PREFIGHT	PRETERIT	PROFANER	*PROTOZOA	PULSATOR	*PYKNOSIS
*PREFIXAL	PRETRAIN	PROFILER	PROTRACT	*PULSEJETR	*PYKNOTIC
*PREFLAME	PRETREAT	PROFITER	PROTRUDE	*PULSOJET	*PYODERMA
*PREFOCUS	PRETRIAL	PROFOUND	PROUDFUL	PULVILLI	*PYOGENIC
*PREFRANK	PRETTIED	PROGERIA	PROUNION	PULVINUS	*PYORRHEA
PREGGERS	PRETTIER	PROGGING	*PROVENLY	PUMICITE	PYRANOSE
PREGNANT	PRETTIES	PROGNOSE	PROVIDER	PUMPLESS	PYRENOID
*PREHUMAN	*PRETTIFY	PROGRADE	*PROVINCE	*PUMPLIKE	PYRIDINE
*PREJUDGE	PREUNION	PROGRESS	PROVIRUS	*PUNCHEON	*PYRIFORM
PRELEGAL	PREUNITE	*PROHIBIT	*PROVOKER	PUNCTATE	*PYROLOGY
PRELIMIT	PREVIOUS	PROLABOR	*PROXEMIC	PUNCTUAL	*PYROLYZE
*PRELUNCH	PREVISOR	PROIAMIN	*PROXIMAL	PUNCTURE	PYRONINE
*PREMEDIC	PRIAPEAN	PROLAPSE	*PRTUNTZE	PUNDITRY	PYROSTAT
PREMIERE	PRIAPISM	*PROLIFIC	PRUDENCE	*PUNGENCY	*PYROXENE
PREMOLAR	PRICIEST	PROLOGUE	PRUINOSE	PUNINESS	*PYRUVATE
PREMORAL	*PRICKIER	PROLONGE	PRUNELLA	PUNISHER	*PYXIDIUM
PREMORSE	*PRICKING	PROMISEE	PRUNELLE	PUNITION	
PRENATAL	PRIDEFUL	PROMISER	PRUNELLO	PUNITIVE	S P AE
PRENOMEN	PRIEDIEU	PROMISOR	PRURIENT	PUNITORY	S P AN
PRENTICE	PRIESTLY	PROMOTER	PRURITUS	PUPARIUM	S P AR
PREORDER	*PRIGGERY	PROMPTER	PSALMIST	PUPATION	S P AT
PREPARER	*PRIGGISH	*PROMPTLY	*PSALMODY	PUPILAGE	S P AY
*PREPASTE	PRIGGISM	PROMULGE	PSALTERY	*PUPILARY	*S P AZ
PREPENSE	PRIMATAL	PRONATOR	PSAMMITE	*PUPPETRY	S P EC
PREPLACE	*PRIMEVAL	PRONOTUM	*PSEPHITE	*PUPPYDOM	S P ED
PREPLANT	PRIMMEST	PROPENOL	PSILOCIN	PURBLIND	S P EW

SP IC	SP ILL	SP OTLIT	CO PIES	GY PSUM	*PA PACY
SP IK	SP ILT	*SP AETZLE	CO PING	HA PPED	PA PAIN
SP IN	SP INE	SP EARGUN	CO PLOT	HA PPEN	PA PAYA
SP IT	SP INY	SP EARMAN	CO PPED	HA PTEN	PA PERY
SP IV	SP IRE	SP IRIEST	CO PPER	HA PTIC	PA PIST
SP OT	SP IRT	SP LURGER	CO PPRA	HE PCAT	PA PPUS
SP RY	SP IRY	*SP OOFERY	CO PRAH	HE PTAD	PA PULA
SP UD	SP ITE	*SP OOKERY	CO PTER	HI PPED	PA PULE
SP UE	*SP ITZ	SP OOLING	CO PULA	HI PPER	PE PLOS
SP UN	SP LAT	*SP OROZOA	CU PFUL	HI PPIE	PE PLUM
SP UR	SP LAY	*SP RITZER	CU POLA	HO PING	PE PLUS
SP ACE	SP LIT	*SP OONSFUL	CU PPED	HO PPLE	PE PPED
SP ACY	SP ODE	CE PE	CU PPER	*HY PHEN	PE PPER
SP ADE	SP OIL	LE PT	CU PRIC	*HY PING	PE PSIN
SP ADO	SP OKE	MO PY	CU PRUM	*HY PNIC	PE PTIC
SP AHI	SP OOF	RE PO	CU PULA	*JA PERY	PE PTID
SP AIL	SP OOK	RE PP	CU PULE	*JA PING	PI PAGE
SP AIT	SP OOL	SY PH	*CY PHER	KA PUTT	PI PIER
SP AKE	SP OON	TY PP	CY PRES	*KE PPED	PI PING
SP ALE	SP OOR	DI PSO	CY PRUS	KE PPEN	PI PKIN
SP ALL	SP ORE	*HO PPY	DA PHNE	KI PPEN	PI PPED
SP ANG	SP ORT	HY PER	DA PPED	KI PPER	PI PPIN
SP ANK	SP OUT	MO PEY	DA PPER	*KO PECK	PO PERY
SP ARE	SP RAG	PO PSY	DA PPLE	KO PPIE	PO PGUN
SP ARK	SP RAT	RE PEG	DE PART	LA PDOG	PO PISH
SP ASM	SP RAY	RE POT	DE PEND	LA PFUL	PO PLAR
SP ATE	SP REE	RO PEY	DE PERM	LA PPED	PO PLIN
SP AWN	SP RIG	TE POY	DE PICT	LA PPER	PO PPED
SP EAK	SP RIT	*ZA PPY	DE PLOY	LA PSER	PO PPER
SP EAN	SP RUE	*BI PACK	DE PONE	LA PSUS	PO PPET
SP EAR	SP RUG	BO PEEP	DE PORT	LA PTOP	PO PPLE
SP ECK	SP UMY	BO PPER	DE POSE	LE PTON	PO PSIE
SP ECS	SP URN	BU PPIE	DE PUTE	LI PASE	PU PATE
SP EED	SP URT	BY PASS	DE PUTY	LI PIDE	PU PPED
SP EEL	SP UTA	BY PAST	*DI PLEX	LI PPED	PU PPET
SP EER	SP ACEY	*BY PATH	DI PLOE	LI PPEN	RA PHIA
SP EIL	SP EEDO	*BY PLAY	DI PNET	LI PPER	RA PHIS
SP EIR	SP ENSE	CA PFUL	DI PODY	LO PPED	RA PIER
SP ELL	*SP IKEY	CA PIAS	DI POLE	LO PPER	RA PINE
SP ELT	SP INTO	CA PITA	DI PPED	LU PINE	RA PING
SP END	SP LIME	CA PLET	DI PPER	LU POUS	RA PINI
SP ENT	SP LINE	CA PLIN	DI PSAS	MO PERY	RA PIST
SP ERM	SP LINK	CA POTE	DO PANT	MO PIER	RA PPED
SP ICA	SP OOFY	CA PPED	DO PIER	NA PALM	RA PPEE
SP ICE	*SP RITZ	CA PPER	DO PING	NA PERY	RA PPEL
SP ICK	*SP ACKLE	CA PRIC	DU PERY	NA PKIN	RA PPEN
SP ICY	*SP ANDEX	CA PRIS	DU PING	NA PPED	RA PPER
SP IED	*SP ARKLY	CA PSID	*DU PLEX	NA PPER	RA PTOR
SP IEL	SP ARTAN	CA PTAN	DU PPED	NA PPIE	RE PACK
SP IER	*SP ATZLE	CA PTOR	FI PPLE	NE PHEW	RE PAID
SP IES	SP EEDUP	CI PHER	GA PING	NI PPER	RE PAIR
SP IFF	SP IRIER	CO PALM	GA PPED	NI PPLE	RE PAND
SP IKE	SP LODGE	CO PIED	GI PPER		RE PARK
SP IKY	SP OOFER	CO PIER	GO PHER		RE PASS
SP ILE	SP ORTIF		GY PPER		RE PAST

RE P AVE	SY P HER	CA P ITOL	DI P LOMA	LE P ROSY	RA P TURE
RE P EAL	SY P HON	CA P LESS	DI P NOAN	LE P ROUS	RE P ANEL
RE P EAT	TA P ALO	CA P ORAL	DI P P ING	LI P LESS	RE P APER
RE P ENT	TA P P ED	*CA P OUCH	DI P TERA	LI P LIKE	RE P ATCH
RE P ERK	TA P P ER	CA P P ING	*DI P TYCA	LI P P ING	RE P INER
RE P INE	TA P P ET	CA P RICE	DO P IEST	LO P P ING	RE P LACE
RE P LAN	TE P EFY	CA P RINE	DU P P ING	LU P ANAR	RE P LANT
RE P LAY	TE P HRA	*CA P ROCK	DU P TRAG	LU P ULIN	RE P LATE
RE P LOT	TI P CAT	*CA P SIZE	*FO P P ERY	*MA P LIKE	RE P LEAD
RE P OLL	TI P OFF	CA P STAN	*FO P P ISH	MO P IEST	RE P LETE
RE P ORT	TI P P ED	CA P SULE	GA P OSIS	*NA P HTHA	*RE P LEVY
RE P OSE	TI P P ER	CA P TAIN	GA P P ING	NA P HTOL	RE P LICA
RE P OUR	TI P P ET	CA P TION	GI P P ING	NA P LESS	RE P LIER
RE P P ED	TI P P LE	CA P TIVE	GY P LURE	NA P P ING	RE P LUMB
RE P UGN	TI P TOE	CA P TURE	GY P STER	NE P HRIC	RE P OSAL
RE P UMP	TI P TOP	*CA P UCHE	HA P LESS	NE P HRON	RE P OSER
RE P UTE	TO P FUL	*CI P HONY	HA P LITE	NI P P IER	RE P OSIT
RI P EST	TO P HUS	CI P OLIN	HA P LOID	NI P P ILY	RE P OWER
RI P ING	TO P ING	CO P AIBA	HA P LONT	NI P P ING	RE P RESS
RI P OFF	TO P P ED	CO P EPOD	*HA P P ING	NU P TIAL	RE P RINT
RI P OST	TO P P ER	CO P IHUE	HA P TENE	PA P ERER	RE P RISE
RI P P ED	TO P P LE	CO P ILOT	HE P ARIN	PA P HIAN	RE P ROBE
RI P P ER	TU P ELO	CO P IOUS	HE P ATIC	PA P ILLA	RE P ROOF
RI P P LE	TU P P ED	*CO P P ERY	HE P TANE	PA P OOSE	RE P ROVE
RI P P LY	TY P HON	*CO P P ICE	HE P TOSE	PA P P IER	RE P TANT
RI P RAP	TY P HUS	CO P P ING	HI P BONE	PA P P IES	RE P TILE
RI P SAW	TY P IER	*CO P YBOY	HI P LESS	PA P RICA	RE P ULSE
RO P ERY	TY P ING	*CO P YCAT	HI P LINE	*PA P RIKA	RI P CORD
RO P IER	TY P IST	CO P YIST	HI P NESS	PA P YRUS	RI P ENER
RO P ILY	VA P ORY	*CU P CAKE	HI P P EST	*PE P P ERY	RI P IENO
RO P ING	VA P OUR	CU P ELER	HI P P IER	PE P P ING	RI P OSTE
RU P IAH	WI P ING	CU P P ING	*HI P P ING	PE P SINE	RI P P ING
SA P OTA	*YA P OCK	CU P RITE	*HI P P ISH	PE P TIDE	RI P P LER
SA P OTE	YA P P ED	CU P ROUS	*HI P SHOT	*PE P TIZE	RI P P LET
SA P OUR	YA P P ER	CU P SFUL	HI P STER	PE P TONE	RI P STOP
SA P P ED	YI P P ED	CU P ULAR	*HO P EFUL	PI P EAGE	RI P TIDE
SA P P ER	YI P P EE	CY P RESS	*HO P HEAD	PI P EFUL	*RO P EWAY
SE P SIS	YI P P IE	CY P RIAN	HO P LITE	PI P ETTE	RO P IEST
SE P TAL	YU P P IE	CY P SELA	*HO P P ING	PI P IEST	RU P TURE
SE P TIC	*ZA P P ER	DA P HNIA	*HO P SACK	PI P P ING	*SA P AJOU
SE P TUM	*ZE P HYR	DA P P ING	HO P TOAD	PO P CORN	SA P HEAD
SI P HON	*ZI P P ER	DA P SONE	*HY P ERON	PO P EDOM	SA P HENA
SI P ING	BA P TISE	DE P LANE	*HY P NOID	*PO P EYED	SA P IENS
SI P P ED	BA P TISM	DE P LETE	*HY P OGEA	PO P OVER	SA P IENT
SI P P ER	BA P TIST	DE P LORE	*HY P ONEA	PO P P IED	SA P LESS
SI P P ET	*BA P TIZE	DE P LUME	*HY P OXIA	PO P P IES	SA P LING
SO P ITE	BI P ARTY	DE P OSAL	*KE P P ING	PO P P ING	SA P ONIN
SO P P ED	BI P LANE	DE P OSER	*KI P P ING	PO P ULAR	*SA P P HIC
SU P ERB	BI P OLAR	DE P OSIT	*KI P SKIN	*PU P FISH	SA P P ING
SU P INE	CA P ABLE	DE P RAVE	LA P IDES	PU P ILAR	SA P P OSE
SU P P ED	CA P ELAN	DE P RESS	LA P P ING	PU P P ING	SA P SAGO
SU P P ER	CA P ELET	DE P RIVE	LA P WING	RA P HIDE	SA P WOOD
SU P P LE	CA P ERER	DE P SIDE	LE P ORID	RA P P ING	*SE P PUKU
SU P P LY	CA P ITAL	DI P HASE	LE P ROSE	RA P P INI	SE P TATE
		DI P LOID		RA P P ORT	

SE P TIME	WI P EOUT	PA P P IER	BES P READ	*CRO P P ING	*FLY P A P ER
SI P P ING	*XI P HOID	PA P P IES	BES P RENT	CUL P ABLE	*FRI P P ERY
SO P HIES	*YA P P ING	*PE P P ERY	BIO P LASM	CUS P IDAL	*GAZ P ACHO
SO P HISM	*YI P P ING	PE P P ING	*CAM P AGNA	CUS P IDOR	GEE P OUND
SO P HIST	*ZA P ATEO	PI P P ING	*CAM P AIGN	CUT P URSE	*GEO P HAGY
SO P P ING	*ZA P TIAH	POP P IED	*CAM P FIRE	DAM P ENER	GEO P HONE
SO P RANO	*ZA P TIEH	POP P IES	*CAM P HENE	DAM P NESS	*GEO P HYTE
SU P P ING	*ZI P LESS	POP P ING	*CAM P HINE	DAU P HINE	GEO P ONIC
SU P PORT	*ZI P P ING	PRE P ILL	CAM P IEST	DEE P ENER	GEO P ROBE
SU P P OSE	BIO P SIC	PRE P REG	CAM P OREE	DEE P NESS	GIM P IEST
SU P REME	BIO P TIC	PU P P ING	CAM P SITE	DEM P STER	GOS P ELER
SU P REMO	CA P P ING	*QUI P P ER	*CHA P BOOK	*DES P ATCH	*GRA P HEME
TA P ERER	CAR P OOL	RA P P ING	*CHA P ERON	DES P ISER	GRA P HITE
TA P ETUM	*CO P P ERY	RA P P INI	*CHA P ITER	DIA P ASON	GRA P LINE
TA P HOLE	*CO P P ICE	RA P P ORT	*CHA P LAIN	DIA P AUSE	GRA P P LER
TA P IOCA	CO P P ING	RES P ACE	*CHA P PATI	DIA P HONE	GRA P TEST
TA P P ING	*COW P LO P	RES P ADE	*CHA P PING	*DIA P HONY	GRI P P IER
TA P ROOM	CRO P PIE	RES P EAK	*CHI P MUCK	DIO P SIDE	GRI P P ING
TA P ROOT	CU P P ING	RES P LIT	*CHI P MUNK	DIO P TASE	*GRI P SACK
TA P STER	DAM P ING	RES P OKE	*CHI P PING	DIO P TRIC	GRI P TEST
TI P CART	DA P P ING	RES P RAY	*CHO P PING	*DI P P ABLE	GUM P TION
TI P LESS	*DEL P HIC	RI P P ING	CIO P PINO	*DIS P ATCH	GUN P A P ER
TI P P IER	DI P P ING	RI P P LER	CLA P TRA P	DIS P ENSE	GUN P OINT
TI P P ING	DU P P ING	RI P P LET	*CLI P PING	DIS P ERSE	*HAM P ERER
TI P P LER	*FO P P ERY	*SA P P HIC	CLU P EOID	DIS P LACE	HEL P LESS
TI P SIER	*FO P P ISH	SA P P ING	COA P P EAR	DIS P LANT	*HEL P MATE
TI P SILY	GA P P ING	*SCY P HUS	*COD P IECE	DIS P LODE	*HEL P MEET
TI P STER	GIM P IER	*SE P P UKU	COL P ITIS	DIS P LUME	*HEM P IEST
TO P COAT	GI P P ING	SHA P E UP	*COM P ADRE	DIS P OSAL	*HEM P WEED
TO P FULL	GRI P MAN	SHI P LA P	COM P ARER	DIS P OSER	*HI P P ARCH
TO P IARY	*HA P P ING	SI P P ING	COM P ILER	DIS P READ	*HI P P IEST
*TO P KICK	HI P P EST	SO P P ING	COM P LAIN	*DIS P RIZE	HOO P LESS
TO P KNOT	HI P P IER	STO P GA P	COM P LEAT	DIS P ROOF	*HOO P LIKE
TO P LESS	*HI P P ING	SU P P ING	*COM P LECT	DIS P ROVE	HOO P STER
TO P LINE	*HI P P ISH	SU P P ORT	COM P LETE	DIS P UTER	HOS P ITAL
TO P MAST	*HO P P ING	SU P P OSE	*COM P LICE	DRI P LESS	HOS P ITIA
TO P MOST	*JEE P NEY	*SYM P HON	*COM P LIED	DRI P P ING	HOS P ODAR
TO P ONYM	*KE P P ING	*SYM P TOM	COM P LIER	*DRO P HEAD	HOT P RESS
TO P P ING	*KI P P ING	TA P P ING	COM P LIES	*DRO P KICK	*HUM P BACK
TO P SAIL	*KOU P REY	TEL P HER	COM P LINE	DRO P P ING	*HUM P LESS
TO P SIDE	LA P P ING	TI P P IER	COM P OSER	DRO P SHOT	*JEO P ARDY
TO P SOIL	LIM P SEY	TI P P ING	*COM P OUND	DRO P WORT	*KEE P SAKE
TO P S P IN	LI P P ING	TI P P LER	COM P RESS	DRU P ELET	*KER P LUNK
*TO P WORK	LO P P ING	TO P P ING	COM P RISE	DRY P OINT	*KEY P UNCH
TU P P ING	MIS P LAN	TU P P ING	*COM P RIZE	*DUM P CART	*KI P P ERER
TY P EBAR	*MUD P ACK	TYM P ANO	COO P TION	DUM P IEST	*KNA P SACK
TY P ESET	NA P P ING	VAN P OOL	*CO P P ERAH	DUM P LING	*KNA P WEED
*TY P HOID	NI P P IER	WA P P ITI	CO P P ERAS	DUO P SONY	*KRE P LACH
*TY P HOON	NI P P ILY	*WIM P ISH	COR P ORAL	*DYS P EPSY	LAM P P OST
*TY P HOSE	NI P P ING	*YA P P ING	COR P SMAN	DYS P NOEA	*LAM P YRID
TY P ICAL	NON P AID	*YI P P ING	COU P LING	*FLA P JACK	LEA P FROG
TY P IEST	NON P AST	*ZI P P ING	*CRA P P ING	FLA P LESS	LIM P NESS
VA P ORER	NON P EAK	*BAG PI P ER	CRI P P LER	*FLA P P ING	LOO P HOLE
*VA P OURY	NON P LAY	BED P LATE	CRO P LAND	*FLI P P ANT	*LUM P FISH
WA P P ITI	NON P OOR	BES P OUSE	CRO P LESS		*LYM P HOMA

*LYO P HILE	PRO P OSER	*SHI P YARD	*STO P BANK	TRA P LINE	BUR P
*MAN P OWER	*PRO P OUND	SHO P GIRL	*STO P COCK	TRA P NEST	CAM P
*MA P PABLE	*PRO P PING	*SHO P LIFT	STO P OVER	TRA P PEAN	CAR P
*MIS P ATCH	*PSE P HITE	*SHO P PING	STO P PAGE	TRA P PING	CHA P
*MIS P RIZE	PUL P IEST	*SHO P TALK	STO P PING	TRA P POSE	CHI P
*MOR P HEME	PUL P LESS	*SHO P WORN	SUB P ANEL	*TRA P ROCK	CHO P
*MOR P HINE	*PUL P WOOD	SIM P ERER	*SUB P HASE	TRA P UNTO	CLA P
*MYO P ATHY	PUM P LESS	SIM P LIFY	*SUB P HYLA	TRE P HINE	CLI P
NAU P LIUS	*PUM P LIKE	SIM P LISM	SUB P OENA	TRI P EDAL	CLO P
*NEO P HYTE	*PUP P ETRY	SIM P LIST	SUB P OLAR	TRI P HASE	COM P
NEO P LASM	*PUP P YDOM	*SIX P ENCE	*SUB P UBIC	TRI P LANE	COO P
NEO P RENE	*PUR P LISH	*SIX P ENNY	SUL P HATE	TRI P LING	COU P
NI P PIEST	PUR P URIC	SKI P JACK	SUL P HIDE	TRI P LITE	CRA P
*NIT P ICKY	PUR P URIN	SKI P LANE	SUL P HITE	TRI P LOID	CRO P
NON P AGAN	*QUI P PISH	*SKI P PING	SUL P HONE	TRI P PING	CUS P
NON P APAL	*QUI P STER	SLA P DASH	*SUL P HURY	TRI P TANE	DAM P
NON P ARTY	RAM P AGER	*SLA P JACK	*SUM P WEED	*TRI P TYCA	DEE P
NON P OINT	*RAM P ANCY	SLA P PING	*SUN P ORCH	*TRI P TYCH	DRI P
NON P OLAR	RAP P AREE	SLI P CASE	SUN P ROOF	TRI P WIRE	DRO P
NON P RINT	*REA P HOOK	SLI P FORM	SU P PLANT	TRO P ONIN	DUM P
PAL P ABLE	REA P P EAR	*SLI P KNOT	SU P PLIER	TUM P LINE	FLA P
PAL P ATOR	REO P P OSE	SLI P LESS	SU P POSAL	TU P PENCE	FLI P
PAL P EBRA	RES P LICE	SLI P OVER	SU P POSER	*TUP P ENNY	FRA P
PAM P ERER	*RES P OKEN	SLI P PAGE	SU P PRESS	*TWO P ENCE	GAM P
*PAM P HLET	RES P ONSA	*SLI P PERY	SUR P LICE	*TWO P ENNY	GAS P
PAP P IEST	RES P ONSE	SLI P PING	SUR P RINT	*TYM P ANAL	GAW P
PAP P OOSE	RES P RANG	SLI P SHOD	SUR P RISE	*TYM P ANIC	GIM P
*PEE P HOLE	RES P READ	SLI P SLOP	*SUR P RIZE	*TYM P ANUM	GLO P
*PEE P SHOW	RES P RING	SLI P SOLE	SUS P ENSE	VES P ERAL	GOO P
PEN P OINT	RES P ROUT	SLI P WARE	*SYM P ATHY	*VES P IARY	GOR P
PEP P ERER	RHA P SODE	SLO P PING	*SYM P ATRY	VOL P LANE	GRI P
PIE P LANT	*RHA P SODY	*SLO P WORK	*SYM P ODIA	WAR P LANE	GUL P
PIN P OINT	RI P PABLE	SNA P BACK	*SYM P OSIA	WAR P OWER	HAS P
*PIN P RICK	RI P P LING	SNA P LESS	*SYR P HIAN	*WAR P WISE	HEA P
*POR P HYRY	*SAM P HIRE	SNA P PIER	TAM P ERER	WAX P LANT	HEL P
POR P OISE	SAM P LING	*SNA P PILY	TAR P APER	*WEA P ONRY	HEM P
PRE P ARER	*SA P P HIRE	SNA P PING	*TAX P AYER	*WET P ROOF	HOL P
PRE P ASTE	*SA P P HISM	SNA P SHOT	TEM P ERER	*WHI P CORD	HUM P
PRE P ENSE	*SA P P HIST	SNA P WEED	TEM P LATE	*WHI P LASH	JAU P
PRE P LACE	*SCA P HOID	*SNI P PETY	TEM P ORAL	*WHI P LIKE	JEE P
PRE P LANT	SCA P ULAR	SNI P PING	TEN P ENCE	*WHI P PIER	*JIM P
*PRE P PING	SCE P TRAL	*SOA P BARK	TEN P ENNY	*WHI P PING	*JUM P
PRE P RICE	*SCU P PAUG	SOA P IEST	TER P INOL	*WHI P TAIL	KEE P
PRE P RINT	SEA P IECE	SOA P LESS	TIM P ANUM	*WHI P WORM	KEL P
*PRE P UNCH	SEA P LANE	SOA P SUDS	TIN P LATE	WIS P IEST	KEM P
PRO P ENOL	SEM P LICE	SOA P WORT	TI P PABLE	*WIS P LIKE	KNA P
PRO P ENSE	*SHE P HERD	SOR P TION	TI P PIEST	*WRA P PING	KNO P
*PRO P ENYL	SHI P LOAD	STA P EDES	*TI P PYTOE	*ZE P PELIN	LAM P
*PRO P ERTY	*SHI P MATE	STA P ELIA	TOE P IECE	*ZOO P HILI	LEA P
*PRO P HAGE	*SHI P MENT	STE P DAME	TOE P LATE	*ZOO P HILY	LIM P
*PRO P HASE	*SHI P PING	STE P LIKE	TOR P IDLY	*ZOO P HOBE	LIS P
*PRO P HECY	SHI P SIDE	STE P PING	TRA P BALL	*ZOO P HYTE	LOO P
*PRO P HESY	*SHI P WORM	STE P WISE	*TRA P DOOR	BEE P	LOU P
PRO P OLIS		STI P PLER	*TRA P EZIA	BLI P	LUM P
PRO P OSAL			TRA P LIKE	BUM P	MAR P

MOO P	WAS P	P RIM P	TWIR P	*MAYHA P	BEDLAM P
MUM P	WEE P	REBO P	WATA P	*MAY P O P	BELLHO P
NEA P	WHA P	RECA P	WHAU P	MEGIL P	*BETHUM P
NEE P	WHI P	REDI P	WHEE P	METUM P	*BIOCHI P
P AL P	WHO P	REMA P	WHEL P	MISHA P	BLUECA P
P EE P	WIM P	SALE P	*WHOM P	MOBCA P	*BREAKU P
P IM P	WIS P	SCAL P	WHOO P	*MOCKU P	BRUSHU P
P LO P	WRA P	SCAM P	*WHUM P	MUDCA P	BUILDU P
P OM P	YAU P	SCAR P	*BACKU P	P ETNA P	CALTRA P
P OO P	YAW P	SCAU P	BARHO P	*P ICKU P	CALTRO P
P RE P	YEL P	SCOO P	BELEA P	P ILEU P	CANTRA P
P RO P	BEBO P	SCRA P	BEWEE P	P REAM P	CANTRI P
P UL P	BECA P	SCRI P	BEWRA P	P ULLU P	*CATCHU P
P UM P	BLEE P	SCUL P	BISHO P	P USHU P	*CHECKU P
*QUI P	BLIM P	SETU P	BLOWU P	RAGTO P	CHIRRU P
RAM P	BLOO P	SHAR P	BO P EE P	RECOU P	CLEANU P
RAS P	CHEA P	SHEE P	BURLA P	REDCA P	*COOKTO P
REA P	CHEE P	SHLE P	CARHO P	REDTO P	COVERU P
RE P P	CHIM P	SIRU P	CARTO P	RE P UM P	*COWFLA P
ROM P	CHIR P	SITU P	CATNA P	RESHI P	*COWFLO P
ROU P	CHOM P	SKEL P	CATNI P	REVAM P	*COW P LO P
RUM P	CHUM P	SKIM P	CATSU P	REWRA P	COWSLI P
SAL P	CLAM P	SLEE P	*COCKU P	RI P RA P	*CRACKU P
SAM P	CLAS P	SLOO P	COLLO P	SALOO P	DEMIRE P
SCO P	CLOM P	SLUM P	DECAM P	SANNO P	DEVELO P
SCU P	CLUM P	SLUR P	DEWLA P	SANNU P	DEWDRO P
SEE P	CRAM P	SNEA P	DOGNA P	SATRA P	FLATCA P
SHI P	CREE P	SNOO P	DOLLO P	SCHLE P	FLATTO P
SHO P	CRIM P	STAM P	DUSTU P	SCRIM P	*FLYTRA P
SIM P	CRIS P	STEE P	FACEU P	SCROO P	FORETO P
SKE P	CROU P	STIR P	FILLI P	SENDU P	GENI P A P
SKI P	CRUM P	STOM P	GALLO P	SHLE P P	*GIDDYA P
SLA P	CUTU P	STOO P	*GAZUM P	SHLUM P	*GIDDYU P
SLI P	DROO P	STOU P	GIDDA P	SHRIM P	GODSHI P
SLO P	FLUM P	STOW P	GOSSI P	*SKYCA P	GROWNU P
SNA P	FRUM P	STRA P	HANGU P	SLI P U P	GUMDRO P
SNI P	GALO P	STRE P	*HICCU P	TAKEU P	GUNSHI P
SOA P	GENI P	STRI P	HOLDU P	TEACU P	HAIRCA P
SOU P	GETU P	STRO P	*HOOKU P	THREA P	HARDTO P
STE P	GRAM P	STUM P	*HUBCA P	THREE P	HARELI P
STO P	GRAS P	SUNU P	HYSSO P	TI P TO P	HENCOO P
SUM P	GROU P	SWAM P	*JOY P O P	TITTU P	HILLTO P
SWA P	GRUM P	SWEE P	*KICKU P	TOECA P	*KETCHU P
SWO P	JALA P	SWOO P	KIDNA P	TOSSU P	*KINGCU P
TAM P	JALO P	SYRU P	LA P TO P	TUNEU P	*KINSHI P
TAR P	JULE P	SYSO P	LARRU P	TURNI P	*KNEECA P
TEM P	KELE P	THRI P	LINEU P	TURNU P	MAINTO P
TRA P	KNOS P	THRO P	LINKU P	*WALKU P	MANTRA P
TRI P	KREE P	THUM P	LOCKU P	WALLO P	*MATCHU P
TRO P	LETU P	TRAM P	LOLLO P	WARMU P	*MIDSHI P
TUM P	*MIXU P	TROM P	LOOKU P	*WIKIU P	*MILKSO P
TY P P	NETO P	TROO P	MADCA P	WINDU P	*MISKEE P
VAM P	P INU P	TRUM P	MAGIL P	*WORKU P	MISSTE P
VEE P	P LUM P	TULI P	MAKEU P	*BARKEE P	MISSTO P
WAR P	P OLY P	TWER P	MARKU P	BECLAS P	*MUGWUM P

NONSLI P	*SHAKEU P	WINESO P	*DRAMSHO P	*LOLLY P O P	*SKULLCA P
NONSTO P	SHALLO P	WINGTI P	DUSTHEA P	LONGSHI P	SLI P SLO P
PALSHI P	SHA P EU P	WIRETA P	*FIREDAM P	LORDSHI P	SNOWDRO P
PARSNI P	SHI P LA P	*WORSHI P	FIRETRA P	MALA P RO P	STARSHI P
PASTEU P	SMASHU P	*BAASKAA P	*FLAGSHI P	*MATESHI P	SUBGROU P
PINESA P	SNOWCA P	*BACKDRO P	*FOOLSCA P	MESOCAR P	SU P ERCO P
POGONI P	SONSHI P	*BACKSLA P	FOOTSTE P	*MINICAM P	SWEETSO P
PRECOU P	SOURSO P	*BACKSTO P	*GROGSHO P	*MOLDWAR P	TABLETO P
PREWRA P	S P EEDU P	*BACKWRA P	GURUSHI P	MONOCAR P	TAILLAM P
PROCAR P	*STACKU P	*BAKESHO P	*HANDGRI P	*NIGHTCA P	*TANKSHI P
RATTRA P	STANDU P	BEAUCOU P	*HANDICA P	NONTRUM P	TEARDRO P
RECLAS P	STARTU P	*BLACKCA P	*HARDSHI P	PARADRO P	*TEENYBO P
*REEQUI P	*STICKU P	*BLACKTO P	*HEADLAM P	*PAWNSHO P	TIECLAS P
REGROU P	STIRRU P	*BOOKSHO P	*HEADSHI P	*P EDI PAL P	*TOWNSHI P
RESTAM P	STO P GA P	*BULLWHI P	*HEDGEHO P	*P EESWEE P	TRANSHI P
RIP STO P	SUNLAM P	*CALTHRO P	*HEIRSHI P	P ERICAR P	*TUCKSHO P
ROLLMO P	SYNCAR P	CANTRAI P	HELISTO P	P HOTOMA P	TWINSHI P
ROLLTO P	TEASHO P	*CHUMSHI P	*HOCKSHO P	*P ODOCAR P	*WARDSHI P
ROOFTO P	TIDERI P	CLA P TRA P	HOUSETO P	P OSTCOU P	*WHITECA P
ROUNDU P	TOUCHU P	*COOKSHO P	*KINGSHI P	P RESLEE P	*WINESHO P
SCALEU P	*TOYSHO P	*CROWSTE P	*LADYSHI P	P RESTAM P	*WORKSHO P
SCALLO P	TREETO P	DEANSHI P	*LANDSKI P	RAINDRO P	*XYLOCAR P
*SCHLE P P	TROLLO P	*DEATHCU P	LANDSLI P	SAND P EE P	
*SCHLUM P	*WARSHI P	*DOGESHI P	LIVETRA P	SANDSOA P	
SCOLLO P	*WICKIU P	DOORSTE P	*LOCKSTE P	SIDESLI P	
SCREWU P	*WICKYU P	DOORSTO P	LOLLI P O P	SIDESTE P	

Q

QAID	*QUARK	QUIRT	*QUARTO	*QUOKKA	*QUASSIN
*QOPH	QUART	QUITE	*QUARTZ	*QUORUM	*QUAVERY
QUAD	*QUASH	QUOIN	*QUASAR	*QUOTER	*QUAYAGE
QUAG	QUASI	QUOIT	*QUATRE	*QUOTHA	*QUEENLY
QUAI	QUASS	QUOTA	*QUAVER	*QURUSH	*QUEERLY
*QUAY	QUATE	QUOTE	*QUEASY	*QWERTY	*QUELLER
*QUEY	QUEAN	*QUOTH	*QUEAZY	*QUADRAT	*QUERIDA
QUID	QUEEN	*QURSH	*QUENCH	*QUADRIC	*QUERIED
QUIN	QUEER	*QINDAR	*QUEUER	*QUAFFER	*QUERIER
*QUIP	QUELL	*QINTAR	*QUEZAL	*QUAHAUG	*QUERIES
QUIT	QUERN	*QIVIUT	*QUICHE	*QUALIFY	*QUERIST
*QUIZ	*QUERY	*QUAERE	*QUINCE	*QUALITY	*QUESTER
QUOD	QUEST	*QUAGGA	*QUINIC	*QUAMASH	*QUESTOR
QANAT	QUEUE	*QUAGGY	*QUININ	*QUANTAL	*QUETZAL
*QUACK	*QUICK	*QUAHOG	*QUINOA	*QUANTIC	*QUIBBLE
*QUAFF	QUIET	*QUAICH	*QUINOL	*QUANTUM	*QUICKEN
QUAIL	*QUIFF	*QUAIGH	*QUINSY	*QUARREL	*QUICKIE
*QUAKE	QUILL	*QUAINT	*QUINTE	*QUARTAN	*QUICKLY
*QUAKY	QUILT	*QUALMY	*QUIPPU	*QUARTER	*QUIETEN
QUALE	QUINT	*QUANTA	*QUIRKY	*QUARTET	*QUIETER
*QUALM	*QUIPU	*QUARRY	*QUITCH	*QUARTIC	*QUIETLY
QUANT	QUIRE	*QUARTE	*QUIVER	*QUASHER	*QUIETUS
QUARE	*QUIRK		*QUOHOG	*QUASSIA	*QUILLAI

*QUILLET	*QIOMTAIN	*QUATRAIN	*QUIPSTER	*PI Q UET	*PRE Q UEL
*QUILTER	*QUAALUDE	*QUAVERER	*QUIRKISH	*RE Q UIN	*BED Q UILT
*QUINARY	*QUACKERY	*QUAYSIDE	*QUISLING	*RO Q UET	*CHA Q UETA
*QUINATE	*QUACKISH	*QUEENDOM	*QUITRENT	*SE Q UEL	*CIN Q UAIN
*QUINELA	*QUACKISM	*QUEERISH	*QUITTING	*SE Q UIN	*CLI Q UISH
*QUININA	*QUADPLEX	*QUENCHER	*QUIVERER	*TO Q UET	*COE Q UATE
*QUININE	*QUADRANS	*QUENELLE	*QUIXOTIC	*BE Q UEST	*CON Q UEST
*QUINNAT	*QUADRANT	*QUERCINE	*QUIXOTRY	*CO Q UINA	*CON Q UIAN
*QUINOID	*QUADRATE	*QUESTION	*QUOTIENT	*CO Q UITO	*COT Q UEAN
*QUINONE	*QUADRIGA	*QUIBBLER		*LI Q UATE	*DAI Q UIRI
*QUINTAL	*QUADROON	*QUICKSET	*S Q UAB	*LI Q UEFY	*DIS Q UIET
*QUINTAN	*QUAGMIRE	*QUIDDITY	*S Q UAD	*LI Q UEUR	*FRE Q UENT
*QUINTAR	*QUAGMIRY	*QUIDNUNC	S Q UAT	*LI Q UIFY	*JAC Q UARD
*QUINTET	*QUALMISH	*QUIETISM	*S Q UAW	*PI Q UANT	*MAR Q UESS
*QUINTIC	*QUANDANG	*QUIETIST	*S Q UEG	*RE Q UEST	*MAR Q UISE
*QUINTIN	*QUANDARY	*QUIETUDE	*S Q UIB	*RE Q UIEM	*MES Q UITE
*QUIPPER	*QUANDONG	*QUILLAIA	*S Q UID	*RE Q UIRE	*MEZ Q UITE
*QUITTED	*QUANTIFY	*QUILLAJA	*S Q UOOSHY	*RE Q UITE	*MIS Q UOTE
*QUITTER	*QUANTILE	*QUILLING	*BU Q SHA	*SE Q UELA	*MOS Q UITO
*QUITTOR	*QUANTITY	*QUILTING	*CO Q UET	*SE Q UENT	*MUS Q UASH
*QUIVERY	*QUANTIZE	*QUINCUNX	*DI Q UAT	*SE Q UOIA	*NON Q UOTA
*QUIXOTE	*QUANTONG	*QUINELLA	*FA Q UIR	*TE Q UILA	*SEA Q UAKE
*QUIZZER	*QUARRIER	*QUINIELA	*LI Q UID	*VA Q UERO	*TOR Q UATE
*QUOMODO	*QUARTERN	*QUINOLIN	*LI Q UOR	*PI Q UANCE	*TOR Q UING
*QUONDAM	*QUARTILE	*QUINTILE	*LO Q UAT	*CLO Q UE	*TUR Q UOIS
*QUOTING	*QUATORZE	*QUIPPISH	*MA Q UIS	*SHE Q EL	*VAN Q UISH

R

RACE	RAPE	REEF	RIFE	RODE	ROUX
RACK	RAPT	REEK	RIFF	ROIL	ROVE
RACY	RARE	REEL	RIFT	ROLE	RUBE
RAFF	RASE	REFT	RILE	ROLF	RUBY
RAFT	RASH	REIF	RILL	ROLL	RUCK
RAGA	RASP	REIN	RIME	ROMP	RUDD
RAGE	RATE	REIS	RIMY	ROOD	RUDE
RAGI	RATH	RELY	RIND	ROOF	RUER
RAIA	RATO	REND	RING	ROOK	RUFF
RAID	RAVE	RENT	RINK	ROOM	RUGA
RAIL	RAYA	REPO	RIOT	ROOT	RUIN
RAIN	RAZE	REPP	RIPE	ROPE	RULE
RAJA	*RAZZ	RESH	RISE	ROPY	RULY
RAKE	READ	REST	RISK	ROSE	RUMP
RAKI	REAL	RETE	RITE	ROSY	RUNE
RALE	REAM	RHEA	RITZ	ROTA	RUNG
RAMI	REAP	RHUS	RIVE	ROTE	RUNT
RAMP	REAR	RIAL	ROAD	ROTI	RUSE
RAND	RECK	RICE	ROAM	ROTL	RUSH
RANG	REDD	RICH	ROAN	ROTO	RUSK
RANI	REDE	RICK	ROAR	ROUE	RUST
RANK	REDO	RIDE	ROBE	ROUP	RUTH
RANT	REED	RIEL	ROCK	ROUT	RYKE

RYND	RAYON	**REHAB**	REWAN	**ROOMY**	**RABBIT**
RYOT	**RAZEE**	**REHEM**	*REWAX	ROOSE	**RABBLE**
RABAT	**RAZER**	**REIFY**	REWED	ROOST	**RABBLE**
RABBI	**RAZOR**	REIGN	REWET	ROOTY	RABIES
RABIC	**REACH**	REINK	REWIN	ROPER	**RACEME**
RABID	REACT	REIVE	REWON	**ROPEY**	**RACHET**
RACER	READD	**REKEY**	**RHEUM**	**ROQUE**	**RACHIS**
RACON	READY	**RELAX**	RHINO	ROSED	RACIAL
RADAR	REALM	RELAY	ROSET	RACIER
RADII	REARM	RELET	**RHOMB**	ROSIN	**RACILY**
RADIO	REATA	RELIC	**RHUMB**	**ROTCH**	RACING
RADIX	REAVE	RELIT	**RHYME**	ROTOR	**RACISM**
RADON	REBAR	REMAN	**RHYTA**	ROUEN	RACIST
RAGEE	REBBE	REMAP	RIANT	ROUGE	**RACKER**
RAGGY	REBEC	REMET	RIATA	ROUGH	**RACKET**
RAINY	REBEL	**REMEX**	**RIBBY**	ROUND	**RACKLE**
RAISE	REBID	REMIT	RIBES	**ROUPY**	RACOON
*RAJAH	REBOP	**REMIX**	RICER	ROUSE	RADDLE
RAKEE	REBUS	RENAL	RICIN	ROUST	RADIAL
RAKER	REBUT	RENEW	RIDER	ROUTE	RADIAN
RALLY	**REBUY**	RENIG	RIDGE	ROUTH	**RADISH**
RALPH	RECAP	RENIN	**RIDGY**	ROVEN	RADIUM
RAMEE	RECCE	RENTE	RIFLE	ROVER	RADIUS
RAMET	RECON	REOIL	RIGHT	ROWAN	RADOME
RAMIE	RECTA	**REPAY**	RIGID	**ROWDY**	RADULA
RAMMY	RECTI	REPEG	RIGOR	ROWEL	**RAFFIA**
RAMUS	RECTO	REPEL	RILEY	ROWEN	**RAFFLE**
RANCE	RECUR	REPIN	RILLE	ROWER	RAFTER
RANCH	RECUT	**REPLY**	RIMER	**ROWTH**	**RAGBAG**
RANDY	REDAN	REPOT	RINSE	ROYAL	RAGGED
RANEE	REDIA	REPRO	**RIOJA**	RUANA	RAGGEE
RANGE	REDID	RERAN	RIPEN	RUBLE	RAGGLE
RANGY	REDIP	RERIG	RIPER	RUBUS	RAGING
RANID	REDLY	RERUN	RISER	**RUCHE**	RAGLAN
RAPER	REDON	RESAW	RISHI	**RUDDY**	RAGMAN
RAPHE	**REDOX**	RESAY	**RISKY**	**RUFFE**	RAGOUT
RAPID	REDRY	RESEE	RISUS	**RUGBY**	RAGTAG
RARER	REDUB	RESET	*RITZY	RUING	RAGTOP
RASER	REDYE	RESEW	RIVAL	RULER	RAIDER
RASPY	**REDUX**	RESID	RIVER	RUMBA	RAILER
RATAL	REEDY	RESIN	RIVET	RUMEN	RAISER
RATAN	**REEFY**	RESOD	RIYAL	**ROACH**	**RUMMY**	RAISIN
RATCH	**REEKY**	RESOW	ROAST	RUMOR	**RAKING**
RATEL	**REEST**	RETAG	ROBIN	RUNIC	**RAKISH**
RATER	REEVE	**RETAX**	ROBLE	RUNNY	RALLYE
RATHE	REFEL	**RETCH**	ROBOT	RUNTY	RAMATE
RATIO	REFER	RETEM	**ROCKY**	RUPEE	**RAMBLE**
RATTY	REFIT	RETIA	RODEO	RURAL	**RAMIFY**
RAVEL	*REFIX	RETIE	ROGER	**RUSHY**	*RAMJET
RAVEN	**REFLY**	RETRO	ROGUE	RUSTY	**RAMMED**
RAVER	**REFRY**	RETRY	ROILY	RUTIN	**RAMMER**
RAVIN	REGAL	REUSE	ROMAN	RUTTY	RAMOSE
RAWIN	REGES	REVEL	ROMEO	RABATO	RAMOUS
RAWLY	REGMA	REVET	RONDO	**RABBET**	RAMROD
RAYAH	REGNA	REVUE	**ROOKY**	**RABBIN**	RAMSON

RAMTIL	RATTLY	**RECOOK**	REFINE	RELINE	**REPLAY**
RANCHO	RATTON	**RECOPY**	REFIRE	**RELINK**	REPLOT
RANCID	**RAUNCH**	RECORD	REFLET	RELISH	REPOLL
RANCOR	**RAVAGE**	**RECORK**	**REFLEW**	RELIST	REPORT
RANDAN	RAVINE	**RECOUP**	*REFLEX	RELIVE	REPOSE
RANDOM	**RAVING**	RECTAL	**REFLOW**	RELOAD	REPOUR
RANGER	**RAVISH**	RECTOR	*REFLUX	RELOAN	**REPPED**
RANKER	**RAWISH**	**RECTUM**	**REFORM**	**RELOOK**	REPUGN
RANKLE	*RAZING	RECTUS	REFUEL	RELUCT	**REPUMP**
RANKLY	READER	RECUSE	**REFUGE**	RELUME	REPUTE
RANSOM	REAGIN	REDACT	REFUSE	REMAIL	*REQUIN
RANTER	REALIA	REDATE	REFUTE	REMAIN	**RERACK**
RANULA	REALLY	**REDBAY**	REGAIN	REMAND	REREAD
RAPHIA	REALTY	**REDBUD**	REGALE	**REMAKE**	RERISE
RAPHIS	REAMER	**REDBUG**	REGARD	REMARK	REROLL
RAPIER	REAPER	**REDCAP**	REGARD	REMATE	REROOF
RAPINE	REARER	REDDED	**REGAVE**	**REMEDY**	REROSE
RAPING	REASON	REDDEN	REGEAR	REMEET	RESAID
RAPINI	REAVER	REDDER	REGENT	REMELT	RESAIL
RAPIST	**REAVOW**	REDDLE	REGGAE	REMEND	RESALE
RAPPED	REBAIT	REDEAR	REGILD	REMIND	RESCUE
RAPPEE	REBATE	REDEEM	REGIME	REMINT	RESEAL
RAPPEL	REBATO	**REDEFY**	REGINA	REMISE	RESEAT
RAPPEN	**REBECK**	**REDENY**	REGION	REMISS	RESEAU
RAPPER	REBILL	**REDEYE**	REGIUS	REMOLD	RESECT
RAPTOR	REBIND	**REDFIN**	**REGIVE**	REMORA	RESEDA
RAREFY	**REBODY**	REDIAL	REGLET	REMOTE	RESEED
RARELY	REBOIL	REDING	**REGLOW**	**REMOVE**	**RESEEK**
RAREST	**REBOOK**	REDLEG	REGLUE	REMUDA	RESEEN
RARIFY	REBOOT	**REDOCK**	REGNAL	RENAIL	RESELL
RARING	REBORE	REDONE	REGNUM	RENAME	RESEND
RARITY	REBORN	REDOUT	REGRET	RENDER	RESENT
RASCAL	*REBOZO	**REDOWA**	**REGREW**	RENEGE	**RESHIP**
RASHER	**REBUFF**	**REDRAW**	**REGROW**	RENEST	RESHOE
RASHLY	**REBUKE**	REDTOP	REHANG	RENNET	**RESHOW**
RASING	**REBURY**	REDUCE	**REHASH**	RENNIN	RESIDE
RASPER	RECALL	REEARN	REHEAR	RENOWN	RESIFT
RASSLE	RECANE	**REECHO**	REHEAT	RENTAL	RESIGN
RASTER	RECANT	**REECHY**	REHEEL	RENTER	RESILE
RASURE	RECAST	REEDIT	REHIRE	RENVOI	RESINY
RATANY	RECEDE	REEFER	**REHUNG**	REOPEN	RESIST
RATBAG	RECENT	**REEKER**	REIVER	**REPACK**	RESITE
RATHER	**RECEPT**	REELER	*REJECT	REPAID	*RESIZE
RATIFY	RECESS	REEMIT	**REJOIN**	REPAIR	**RESOAK**
RATINE	**RECHEW**	**REFACE**	**REKNIT**	REPAND	RESOLD
RATING	**RECIPE**	REFALL	RELACE	**REPARK**	RESOLE
RATION	RECITE	**REFECT**	RELATE	REPASS	RESORB
RATITE	**RECKON**	**REFEED**	RELEND	REPAST	RESORT
RATLIN	RECLAD	REFEEL	RELENT	**REPAVE**	RESPOT
RATOON	RECOAL	REFELL	RELEVE	REPEAL	RESTER
RATTAN	**RECOCK**	**REFFED**	RELICT	REPEAT	RESULT
RATTED	RECODE	REFILE	RELIED	REPENT	RESUME
RATTEN	RECOIL	REFILL	RELIEF	**REPERK**	**RETACK**
RATTER	RECOIN	**REFILM**	RELIER	REPINE	RETAIL
RATTLE	**RECOMB**	**REFIND**	RELIES	REPLAN	RETAIN

RETAKE	REWRAP	RIMPLE	*ROQUET	RUINER	RAILCAR
RETAPE	*REZONE	RINGER	ROSARY	RULING	RAILING
RETARD	RHAPHE	RINSER	ROSCOE	RUMAKI	RAILWAY
RETEAM	*RHEBOK	RIOTER	ROSERY	RUMBLE	RAIMENT
RETEAR	RHESUS	RIPEST	ROSIER	RUMBLY	RAINBOW
RETELL	RHETOR	RIPING	ROSILY	RUMMER	RAINIER
RETENE	RHEUMY	RIPOFF	ROSING	RUMOUR	RAINILY
RETEST	RHINAL	RIPOST	ROSINY	RUMPLE	RAINOUT
RETIAL	RHOMBI	RIPPED	ROSTER	RUMPLY	RAISING
RETILE	RHUMBA	RIPPER	ROSTRA	RUMPUS	*RAKEOFF
RETIME	RHYMER	RIPPLE	ROTARY	RUNDLE	RALLIED
RETINA	RHYTON	RIPPLY	ROTATE	RUNKLE	RALLIER
RETINE	RIALTO	RIPRAP	ROTCHE	RUNLET	RALLINE
RETINT	RIBALD	RIPSAW	ROTGUT	RUNNEL	RAMBLER
RETIRE	RIBAND	RISING	ROTTED	RUNNER	RAMEKIN
RETOLD	RIBBED	RISKER	ROTTEN	RUNOFF	RAMILIE
RETOOK	RIBBER	RITARD	ROTTER	RUNOUT	RAMMIER
RETOOL	RIBBON	RITTER	ROTUND	RUNWAY	RAMMING
RETORE	RIBIER	RITUAL	ROUBLE	RUPIAH	RAMMISH
RETORN	RIBLET	RIVAGE	ROUCHE	RURBAN	RAMPAGE
RETORT	RIBOSE	RIVING	ROUPET	RUSHEE	RAMPANT
RETRAL	RICHEN	ROADEO	ROUSER	RUSHER	RAMPART
RETRIM	RICHES	ROADIE	ROUTER	RUSINE	*RAMPIKE
RETTED	RICHLY	ROAMER	ROVING	RUSSET	RAMPION
RETUNE	RICING	ROARER	ROWING	RUSTIC	RAMPOLE
RETURN	RICKEY	ROBALO	*ROZZER	RUSTLE	RANCHER
RETUSE	*RICKEY	ROBAND	RUBACE	RUTILE	RANCOUR
RETYPE	RICRAC	ROBATO	RUBATO	RUTTED	RANDIER
REVAMP	RICTUS	ROBBED	RUBBED	RYOKAN	RANDIES
REVEAL	RIDDED	ROBBER	RUBBER	RABBLER	RANKING
REVERB	RIDDEN	ROBBIN	RUBBLE	RABBITY	RANKISH
REVERE	RIDDER	ROBUST	RUBBLY	RABBONI	RANPIKE
REVERS	RIDDLE	ROCHET	RUBIED	RACCOON	RANSACK
REVERT	RIDENT	ROCKER	RUBIER	RACEMIC	RAPHIDE
REVERY	RIDGEL	ROCKET	RUBIES	*RACEWAY	RAPPING
REVEST	RIDGIL	ROCOCO	RUBIGO	RACIEST	RAPPINI
REVIEW	RIDING	RODENT	RUBOFF	*RACKETY	RAPPORT
REVILE	RIDLEY	RODMAN	RUBOUT	*RACKFUL	RAPTURE
REVISE	RIEVER	ROLFER	RUBRIC	*RACQUET	RAREBIT
REVIVE	RIFFED	ROLLER	RUCHED	RADIALE	RASBORA
REVOKE	RIFFLE	ROMANO	RUCKLE	RADIANT	RASPISH
REVOLT	RIFLER	ROMPER	RUCKUS	RADIATE	RATABLE
REVOTE	RIGGED	RONDEL	RUDDER	RADICAL	RATAFEE
REVVED	RIGGER	RONION	RUDDLE	RADICEL	RATAFIA
REWAKE	RIGHTO	RONNEL	RUDEST	RADICES	RATATAT
REWARD	RIGHTY	RONYON	RUEFUL	RADICLE	RATCHET
REWARM	RIGOUR	ROOFER	RUFFLE	*RAFFISH	RATFINK
REWASH	RILING	ROOKIE	*RUFFLY	RAFFLER	RATFISH
REWELD	RILLET	ROOMER	RUFOUS	RAGGEDY	RATHOLE
REWIND	RIMIER	ROOSER	RUGGED	RAGGIES	RATLIKE
REWIRE	RIMING	ROOTER	RUGGER	RAGGING	RATLINE
REWOKE	RIMMED	ROPERY	RUGOLA	RAGTIME	RATTAIL
REWORD	RIMMER	ROPILY	RUGOSA	RAGWEED	RATTEEN
REWORK	RIMOSE	ROPIER	RUGOSE	RAGWORT	RATTIER
REWOVE	RIMOUS	ROPING	RUGOUS	RAILBUS	RATTING

RATTISH	**REBUKER**	**REDUCER**	REGRADE	REPANEL	**RESPADE**
RATTLER	**RECARRY**	**REDWARE**	**REGRAFT**	**REPAPER**	**RESPEAK**
RATTOON	**RECEIPT**	**REDWING**	REGRANT	**REPATCH**	**RESPECT**
RATTRAP	**RECEIVE**	**REDWOOD**	REGRATE	REPINER	RESPELL
RAUCITY	**RECENCY**	REEDIER	REGREEN	**REPLACE**	RESPIRE
RAUCOUS	**RECHART**	**REEDIFY**	REGREET	REPLANT	RESPITE
*RAUNCHY	**RECHEAT**	**REEDILY**	REGRESS	REPLATE	RESPLIT
RAVAGER	*RECHECK	REEDING	REGRIND	**REPLEAD**	**RESPOKE**
RAVELER	RECITAL	**REEDMAN**	**REGROOM**	REPLETE	**RESPOND**
RAVELIN	RECITER	*REEJECT	**REGROUP**	*REPLEVY	**RESPRAY**
RAVELLY	**RECLAIM**	REELECT	REGULAR	**REPLICA**	**RESTACK**
RAVENER	**RECLAME**	REENACT	REGULUS	REPLIER	**RESTAFF**
RAVIOLI	**RECLASP**	**REENDOW**	**REHINGE**	**REPLUMB**	RESTAGE
RAWHIDE	RECLEAN	*REENJOY	**REHOUSE**	REPOSAL	**RESTAMP**
RAWNESS	RECLINE	**REENTER**	**REIFIER**	REPOSER	RESTART
RAYLESS	RECLUSE	**REENTRY**	**REIMAGE**	REPOSIT	RESTATE
RAYLIKE	RECOLOR	*REEQUIP	REINCUR	**REPOWER**	**RESTFUL**
REACHER	RECOUNT	REERECT	*REINDEX	REPRESS	**RESTIVE**
REACTOR	**RECOUPE**	**REEVOKE**	REINTER	**REPRICE**	**RESTOCK**
READAPT	**RECOVER**	*REEXPEL	REISSUE	REPRINT	**RESTOKE**
READIED	RECRATE	**REFENCE**	*REITBOX	REPRISE	RESTORE
READIER	RECROSS	**REFEREE**	*REJOICE	**REPROBE**	**RESTUDY**
READIES	**RECROWN**	**REFFING**	*REJUDGE	**REPROOF**	**RESTUFF**
READILY	RECRUIT	**REFIGHT**	RELABEL	**REPROVE**	**RESTYLE**
READING	*RECTIFY	**REFINER**	RELAPSE	REPTANT	RESUMER
READMIT	**RECTORY**	**REFLATE**	RELATER	REPTILE	RESURGE
READOPT	*RECTRIX	**REFLECT**	RELATOR	REPULSE	RETABLE
READORN	**RECURVE**	**REFLIES**	**RELAXER**	*REQUEST	**RETAKER**
READOUT	RECUSAL	**REFLOAT**	**RELAXIN**	*REQUIEM	RETASTE
*REAFFIX	**RECYCLE**	**REFLOOD**	RELEARN	*REQUIRE	**RETEACH**
REAGENT	**REDBAIT**	**REFOCUS**	RELEASE	*REQUITE	**RETHINK**
REALGAR	**REDBIRD**	**REFORGE**	RELIANT	RERAISE	**RETIARY**
REALIGN	**REDBONE**	**REFOUND**	**RELIEVE**	REREDOS	RETICLE
REALISE	**REDCOAT**	**REFRACT**	**RELIEVO**	REROUTE	RETINAL
REALISM	REDDEST	**REFRAIN**	**RELIGHT**	RESCALE	RETINOL
REALIST	**REDDING**	**REFRAME**	*RELIQUE	**RESCIND**	RETINUE
REALITY	**REDDISH**	**REFRESH**	**REMAKER**	RESCORE	RETIREE
*REALIZE	**REDFISH**	**REFRONT**	**REMARRY**	RESCUER	RETIRER
REALLOT	**REDHEAD**	**REFUGEE**	**REMATCH**	*RESEIZE	RETITLE
REALTER	REDLINE	**REFUSAL**	**REMERGE**	**RESERVE**	**RETOUCH**
REANNEX	**REDNECK**	**REFUSER**	REMNANT	**RESHAPE**	RETRACE
REAPPLY	REDNESS	**REFUTAL**	**REMODEL**	**RESHAVE**	RETRACT
REARGUE	**REDOUBT**	**REFUTER**	REMORSE	**RESHINE**	RETRAIN
REAVAIL	REDOUND	REGALER	REMOUNT	**RESHONE**	RETREAD
REAWAKE	**REDPOLL**	REGALIA	**REMOVAL**	**RESHOOT**	RETREAT
REBATER	**REDRAFT**	**REGALLY**	**REMOVER**	RESIDER	RETRIAL
REBEGIN	**REDREAM**	REGATTA	RENEGER	RESIDUA	RETSINA
REBIRTH	REDRESS	REGAUGE	**RENEWAL**	RESIDUE	RETTING
REBLEND	REDRIED	**REGENCY**	**RENEWER**	**RESIGHT**	**RETWIST**
REBLOOM	REDRIES	**REGIMEN**	RENNASE	RESLATE	**RETYING**
REBOANT	REDRILL	*REGLAZE	RENTIER	RESMELT	**REUNIFY**
REBOARD	**REDRIVE**	REGLOSS	**REOCCUR**	**RESOJET**	REUNION
REBOUND	REDROOT	REGNANT	**REOFFER**	**RESOLVE**	REUNITE
REBREED	**REDSKIN**	REGORGE	REORDER	**RESOUND**	REUTTER
REBUILD	REDTAIL	REGOSOL	REPAINT	**RESPACE**	**REVALUE**

REVELER	RIDDING	*ROCKERY	ROULADE	RUSTLER	RAMOSITY
REVELRY	RIDDLER	ROCKIER	ROULEAU	RUTHFUL	RAMPAGER
REVENGE	RIDGIER	ROCKOON	ROUNDEL	RUTTIER	*RAMPANCY
REVENUE	RIDGING	RODLESS	ROUNDER	RUTTILY	RAMSHORN
REVERER	RIDOTTO	RODLIKE	ROUNDLY	RUTTING	RAMULOSE
REVERIE	RIFFING	RODSMAN	ROUNDUP	RUTTISH	RAMULOUS
REVERSE	RIFFLER	*ROEBUCK	ROUSTER	RABBITER	RANCHERO
REVERSO	RIFLERY	ROGUERY	ROUTINE	*RABBITRY	*RANCHMAN
REVILER	RIFLING	ROGUISH	ROUTING	RABIDITY	RANDIEST
REVISAL	RIGGING	ROISTER	ROWBOAT	RACEMATE	RANDOMLY
REVISER	RIGHTER	ROLLICK	*ROWLOCK	RACEMISM	RANKNESS
REVISIT	RIGHTLY	ROLLING	ROYALLY	*RACEMIZE	RANSOMER
REVISOR	RIGIDLY	ROLLMOP	ROYALTY	RACEMOID	*RAPACITY
REVIVAL	RIKISHA	ROLLOUT	ROYSTER	RACEMOSE	RAPESEED
REVIVER	*RIKSHAW	ROLLTOP	RUBABOO	RACEMOUS	RAPIDITY
REVOICE	RILIEVO	ROLLWAY	RUBASSE	RACHILLA	RAPPAREE
REVOKER	RIMFIRE	ROMAINE	RUBBERY	RACHITIS	RAPTNESS
REVOLVE	RIMIEST	ROMANCE	RUBBING	RACINESS	RAREFIER
REVUIST	RIMLAND	ROMAUNT	RUBBISH	*RACKWORK	RARENESS
REVVING	RIMLESS	ROMPISH	RUBDOWN	RACLETTE	RARERIPE
REWAKEN	RIMMING	RONDEAU	RUBELLA	RADIABLE	RASCALLY
REWEAVE	*RIMROCK	RONDURE	RUBEOLA	RADIALLY	RASHNESS
REWEIGH	RINGENT	RONTGEN	RUBIEST	RADIANCE	RASORIAL
REWIDEN	RINGGIT	ROOFING	RUBIOUS	RADIANCY	RATAPLAN
REWOKEN	RINGLET	ROOFTOP	RUCHING	RADIATOR	RATEABLE
REWOUND	RINGTAW	ROOKERY	RUCTION	RADICAND	RATICIDE
REWOVEN	RINNING	ROOMFUL	RUDDIER	RADICATE	RATIFIER
REWRITE	RINSING	ROOSTER	RUDDILY	RADIOMAN	RATIONAL
REYNARD	RIOTOUS	ROOTAGE	*RUDDOCK	RADWASTE	RATOONER
*RHABDOM	RIPCORD	ROOTIER	RUDERAL	RAFTERED	RATSBANE
*RHACHIS	RIPENER	ROOTLET	RUDESBY	RAFTSMAN	RATTENER
RHAMNUS	RIPIENO	*ROPEWAY	RUFFIAN	RAGINGLY	RATTIEST
RHATANY	RIPOSTE	ROPIEST	RUFFLER	RAILBIRD	RATTLING
RHENIUM	RIPPING	*RORQUAL	RUFIYAA	RAILHEAD	RAVELING
*RHIZOID	RIPPLER	ROSARIA	RUGGING	RAILLERY	RAVELLED
*RHIZOMA	RIPPLET	ROSEATE	RUGLIKE	RAILROAD	RAVELLER
*RHIZOME	RIPSTOP	ROSEBAY	RUINATE	RAINBAND	RAVENING
RHODIUM	RIPTIDE	ROSEBUD	RUINOUS	RAINBIRD	RAVENOUS
RHODORA	RISIBLE	ROSELLE	RUMBLER	RAINCOAT	RAVIGOTE
*RHOMBIC	RISOTTO	ROSEOLA	RUMMAGE	RAINDROP	*RAVINGLY
RHOMBUS	RISSOLE	ROSETTE	RUMMEST	RAINFALL	RAVISHER
RHUBARB	RIVALRY	ROSIEST	RUNAWAY	RAINIEST	RAWBONED
RIBBAND	RIVETER	ROSINOL	*RUNBACK	RAINLESS	RAYGRASS
RIBBIER	RIVIERA	ROSOLIO	RUNDLET	RAINWASH	REABSORB
RIBBING	RIVIERE	ROSTRAL	RUNDOWN	RAINWEAR	REACCEDE
RIBBONY	RIVULET	ROSTRUM	RUNLESS	RAISONNE	REACCENT
RIBLESS	ROADBED	ROTATOR	RUNNING	*RAKEHELL	*REACCEPT
RIBLIKE	ROADWAY	ROTIFER	RUNOVER	RALLYING	REACCUSE
RIBWORT	ROARING	ROTTING	RUPTURE	RALLYIST	REACTANT
RICINUS	ROASTER	ROTUNDA	RURALLY	RAMBUTAN	REACTION
RICKETS	ROBBERY	ROUGHEN	RUSHIER	RAMENTUM	REACTIVE
RIBBIER	ROBBING	ROUGHER	RUSHING	*RAMEQUIN	READDICT
*RICKETY	ROBOTRY	ROUGHLY	RUSSIFY	*RAMIFORM	*READERLY
RICOTTA	ROBUSTA	ROUGING	RUSTIER	RAMILLIE	READIEST
RIDABLE	*ROCKABY	ROUILLE	RUSTILY	RAMMIEST	*READJUST

*REAFFIRM	*RECOVERY	REFLOWER	*REJACKET	*REOBJECT	RESELLER
REALISER	RECREANT	REFLUENT	*REJECTEE	REOBTAIN	RESEMBLE
*REALIZER	RECREATE	REFOREST	*REJECTER	*REOCCUPY	RESERVER
REALNESS	RECUSANT	REFORMAT	*REJECTOR	REOPPOSE	RESETTER
REANOINT	*RECYCLER	REFORMER	*REJIGGER	REORDAIN	RESETTLE
*REAPHOOK	REDACTOR	*REFOUGHT	*REJOICER	REORIENT	RESHAPER
REAPPEAR	REDAMAGE	*REFREEZE	*REJUGGLE	REOUTFIT	RESIDENT
REARMICE	REDARGUE	REFUGIUM	REKINDLE	REOVIRUS	RESIDUAL
REARMOST	*REDBRICK	REFUNDER	RELAPSER	*REPACIFY	RESIDUUM
REAROUSE	REDECIDE	*REFUSNIK	RELATION	REPAIRER	RESIGNER
REARREST	REDEEMER	REGAINER	RELATIVE	REPARTEE	RESILVER
REARWARD	REDEFEAT	REGALITY	RELAUNCH	REPEALER	RESINATE
REASCEND	REDEFECT	REGATHER	*RELAXANT	REPEATER	RESINIFY
REASCENT	REDEFINE	REGELATE	RELEASER	REPELLER	RESINOID
REASONER	REDEMAND	REGICIDE	RELEGATE	REPENTER	RESINOUS
REASSAIL	REDEPLOY	REGIMENT	RELETTER	REPEOPLE	RESISTER
REASSERT	REDESIGN	REGIONAL	RELEVANT	REPETEND	RESISTOR
REASSESS	REDHORSE	REGISTER	RELIABLE	REPHRASE	*RESKETCH
REASSIGN	REDIGEST	REGISTRY	RELIABLY	REPLACER	RESMOOTH
REASSORT	REDIRECT	REGNANCY	RELIANCE	REPLEDGE	RESOLDER
REASSUME	REDIVIDE	REGOLITH	RELIEVER	REPLEVIN	RESOLUTE
REASSURE	REDOLENT	REGROOVE	RELIGION	REPLICON	RESOLVER
REATTACH	REDOUBLE	*REGROWTH	RELOADER	REPLUNGE	RESONANT
REATTACK	REDRAWER	REGULATE	RELOCATE	REPOLISH	RESONATE
REATTAIN	*REDSHANK	*REHABBER	RELUCENT	REPORTER	RESORCIN
*REAWAKEN	*REDSHIFT	*REHAMMER	RELUMINE	REPOUSSE	RESORTER
REBELDOM	REDSHIRT	REHANDLE	REMANENT	REPRIEVE	RESOUGHT
REBOTTLE	REDSTART	REHARDEN	REMANNED	REPRISAL	RESOURCE
REBOUGHT	REDUCTOR	REHEARSE	REMARKER	*REPROACH	RESPLICE
*REBRANCH	REDUVIID	REHEATER	REMARKET	REPROVAL	RESPOKEN
REBURIAL	REEDBIRD	*REHOBOAM	*REMARQUE	REPROVER	RESPONSA
REBUTTAL	*REEDBUCK	REIGNITE	REMASTER	REPUBLIC	RESPONSE
REBUTTER	REEDIEST	REIMPORT	REMEDIAL	REPULSER	RESPRANG
REBUTTON	REEDLIKE	REIMPOSE	REMEMBER	*REPURIFY	RESPREAD
RECALLER	REEDLING	REINCITE	REMINDER	REPURSUE	RESPRING
RECAMIER	*REEMBARK	REINDEER	REMITTAL	*REQUIRER	RESPROUT
RECANTER	*REEMBODY	REINDICT	REMITTER	*REQUITAL	RESTITCH
RECEIVER	REEMERGE	REINDUCE	REMITTOR	*REQUITER	RESTLESS
RECEPTOR	*REEMPLOY	REINDUCT	*REMODIFY	RERECORD	RESTORAL
RECHANGE	REENGAGE	REINFECT	REMOLADE	REREMICE	RESTORER
RECHARGE	REENLIST	REINFORM	REMOTION	REREMIND	RESTRAIN
RECHOOSE	REENROLL	REINFUSE	RENATURE	REREPEAT	RESTRESS
RECIRCLE	*REEXPORT	*REINJECT	RENDERER	REREVIEW	RESTRICT
RECISION	*REEXPOSE	*REINJURE	RENDIBLE	REREWARD	RESTRIKE
RECKLESS	REFASTEN	*REINJURY	*RENDZINA	REROLLER	RESTRING
RECKONER	REFERENT	REINLESS	RENEGADE	RESADDLE	RESTRIVE
RECLINER	REFERRAL	REINSERT	RENEGADO	RESALUTE	RESTROOM
RECLOTHE	REFERRED	REINSMAN	RENIFORM	RESAMPLE	RESTRUCK
*RECODIFY	REFERRER	REINSURE	RENITENT	RESCHOOL	RESTRUNG
RECOILER	REFIGURE	REINVADE	RENMINBI	RESCREEN	RESUBMIT
RECOMMIT	REFILTER	REINVENT	RENOGRAM	RESCRIPT	RESUMMON
*RECONVEY	REFINERY	REINVEST	RENOTIFY	RESCULPT	RESUPINE
RECORDER	REFINING	REINVITE	RENOUNCE	RESEARCH	*RESUPPLY
RECOUPLE	REFINISH	*REINVOKE	RENOVATE	RESEASON	RESURVEY
RECOURSE	*REFLEXLY	REISSUER	RENUMBER	RESECURE	RETACKLE

RETAILER	REWARDER	RIGORISM	ROLLAWAY	*ROVINGLY	B R ED
RETAILOR	REWINDER	RIGORIST	*ROLLBACK	*ROWDYISH	B R EE
RETAINER	REWRITER	RIGOROUS	*ROLLICKY	*ROWDYISM	B R EN
RETARDER	*RHABDOME	RIMESTER	ROLLOVER	ROYALISM	B R EW
RETARGET	RHAMNOSE	RIMINESS	ROMANCER	ROYALIST	B R IE
RETEMPER	RHAPSODE	RIMOSITY	ROMANISE	RUBAIYAT	B R IG
RETHREAD	*RHAPSODY	*RINGBARK	*ROMANIZE	RUBBABOO	B R IM
RETIARII	*RHBOBASE	RINGBOLT	ROMANTIC	RUBICUND	B R IN
RETICENT	*RHEMATIC	RINGBONE	RONDELET	RUBIDIUM	B R IO
RETICULA	RHEOBASE	RINGDOVE	RONDELLE	*RUBYLIKE	B R IT
RETICULE	*RHEOLOGY	RINGHALS	ROOFLESS	*RUCKSACK	B R OO
RETIFORM	*RHEOPHIL	RINGLIKE	*ROOFLIKE	RUCTIOUS	B R OS
RETINENE	RHEOSTAT	*RINGNECK	ROOFLINE	RUDDIEST	B R OW
RETINITE	RHETORIC	RINGSIDE	ROOFTREE	RUDENESS	B R R R
RETINOID	RHINITIS	RINGTAIL	ROOMETTE	RUDIMENT	B R UT
RETINULA	*RHIZOBIA	RINGTOSS	ROOMMATE	RUFFLIER	C R AB
RETIRANT	*RHIZOPOD	RINGWORM	*ROORBACK	*RUFFLIKE	C R AG
RETIRING	*RHIZOPUS	RIPARIAN	ROOTHOLD	*RUFFLING	C R AM
RETORTER	RHODAMIN	RIPENESS	ROOTIEST	RUGOSITY	C R AP
RETRENCH	*RHOMBOID	RIPPABLE	ROOTLESS	RUGULOSE	C R AW
RETRIEVE	*RHONCHUS	RIPPLING	ROOTLIKE	RULELESS	C R EW
RETROACT	RHYOLITE	RISIBLES	ROPELIKE	RUMBLING	C R IB
RETROFIT	*RHYTHMIC	RISKLESS	*ROPEWALK	RUMINANT	C R IS
RETRORSE	RIBALDLY	RITUALLY	ROPINESS	RUMINATE	C R OC
RETURNEE	RIBALDRY	RIVERBED	ROSARIAN	RUMMAGER	C R OP
RETURNER	RIBBIEST	RIVERINE	ROSARIUM	RUNABOUT	C R OW
REUNITER	RIBGRASS	RIVULOSE	ROSEBUSH	RUNAGATE	C R UD
REUSABLE	RIBOSOME	ROADKILL	ROSEFISH	RUNROUND	C R US
*REVAMPER	RICEBIRD	ROADLESS	ROSELIKE	RURALISE	C R UX
*REVANCHE	RICERCAR	*ROADSHOW	ROSEMARY	RURALISM	D R AB
REVEALER	RICHNESS	ROADSIDE	ROSEROOT	RURALIST	D R AG
REVEHENT	*RICHWEED	ROADSTER	ROSESLUG	RURALITE	D R AM
REVEILLE	*RICKRACK	*ROADWORK	ROSEWOOD	RURALITY	D R AT
REVELLER	*RICKSHAW	ROBORANT	ROSINESS	*RURALIZE	D R AW
REVENANT	*RICOCHET	ROBOTICS	ROSINOUS	RUSHIEST	D R AY
REVENGER	RIDDANCE	ROBOTISM	ROSTELLA	*RUSHLIKE	D R EE
REVENUER	RIDEABLE	*ROBOTIZE	ROSTRATE	RUSTICAL	D R EG
REVEREND	RIDGIEST	ROCAILLE	ROSULATE	RUSTICLY	D R EK
REVERENT	RIDGLING	*ROCKABYE	ROTATION	RUSTIEST	D R EW
REVERIES	RIDICULE	*ROCKAWAY	ROTATORY	RUSTLESS	D R IB
*REVERIFY	RIESLING	ROCKETER	ROTENONE	RUSTLING	D R IP
REVERING	*RIFAMPIN	*ROCKETRY	ROTIFORM	RUTABAGA	D R OP
REVERSAL	RIFENESS	*ROCKFALL	ROTOTILL	RUTHENIC	D R UB
REVERSER	*RIFFRAFF	*ROCKFISH	ROTURIER	RUTHLESS	D R UM
REVERTER	RIFLEMAN	ROCKIEST	ROUGHAGE	RUTILANT	F R AE
REVIEWAL	RIFTLESS	ROCKLESS	*ROUGHDRY	RUTTIEST	F R AG
REVIEWER	RIGADOON	*ROCKLIKE	*ROUGHHEW	RYEGRASS	F R AP
REVISION	RIGATONI	*ROCKLING	*ROUGHISH		F R AT
REVISORY	RIGAUDON	ROCKROSE	ROUGHLEG	B R AD	F R AY
*REVIVIFY	*RIGHTFUL	*ROCKWEED	ROULETTE	B R AE	F R EE
*REVIVING	RIGHTIES	*ROCKWORK	ROUNDISH	B R AG	F R ET
REVOLTER	RIGHTISM	ROENTGEN	ROUNDLET	B R AN	F R IG
REVOLUTE	RIGHTIST	ROGATION	ROUSSEAU	B R AT	F R IT
REVOLVER	*RIGIDIFY	ROGATORY	ROUTEMAN	B R AW	*F R IZ
REVULSED	RIGIDITY	ROLAMITE	ROUTEWAY	B R AY	F R OE

FR OG	TR IM	BR OAD	CR IPE	DR OOP	GR AIN
FR OM	TR IO	**BR OCK**	CR ISP	DR OPT	**GR AMA**
FR OW	TR IP	BR OIL	**CR OAK**	DR OSS	**GR AMP**
FR UG	TR OD	**BR OKE**	CR OCI	**DR OUK**	GR ANA
GR AB	TR OP	BR OME	**CR OCK**	DR OVE	GR AND
GR AD	TR OT	BR OMO	**CR OFT**	DR OWN	GR ANT
GR AM	TR OW	BR ONC	CR ONE	DR UID	GR APE
GR AN	TR OY	BR OOD	**CR ONY**	**DR UNK**	**GR APH**
GR AT	TR UE	**BR OOK**	**CR OOK**	DR UPE	**GR APY**
GR AY	**VR OW**	BR OOM	CR OON	DR USE	GR ASP
GR EE	WR AP	BR OSE	CR OSS	DR YER	GR ASS
GR EW	WR EN	**BR OSY**	CR OUP	**DR YAD**	GR ATE
GR EY	WR IT	**BR OTH**	**CR OWD**	**DR YLY**	**GR AVY**
GR ID	BR ACE	**BR OWN**	**CR OWN**	FR AIL	*GR AZE
GR IG	**BR ACH**	**BR UGH**	*CR OZE	**FR AME**	GR EAT
GR IM	BR ACT	BR UIN	**CR UCK**	FR ANC	GR EBE
GR IN	BR AID	BR UIT	CR UDE	**FR ANK**	GR EED
GR IP	BR AIL	BR UME	CR UEL	FR ASS	**GR EEK**
GR IT	BR AIN	BR UNT	CR UET	FR AUD	GR EEN
GR OG	BR AKE	**BR USH**	**CR UMB**	FR EAK	GR EET
GR OT	BR AKY	**BR USK**	**CR UMP**	FR EED	GR EGO
GR OW	BR AND	BR UTE	CR UOR	FR EER	GR IDE
GR UB	BR ANK	CR AAL	CR USE	**FR EMD**	GR IEF
GR UE	BR ANT	**CR ACK**	**CR USH**	FR ENA	**GR IFF**
GR UM	BR ASH	**CR AFT**	CR UST	FR ERE	GR IFT
KR IS	BR ASS	**CR AKE**	**CR YPT**	FR ESH	GR IME
PR AM	**BR AVA**	**CR AMP**	**DR AFF**	FR IAR	**GR IMY**
PR AO	**BR AVI**	CR ANE	DR AFT	FR IED	GR IND
PR AT	**BR AVO**	**CR ANK**	DR AIL	FR IER	GR IOT
PR AU	**BR AWL**	CR APE	DR AIN	FR IES	GR IPE
PR AY	**BR AWN**	**CR ASH**	**DR AKE**	FR ILL	GR IPT
PR EE	**BR AWS**	CR ASS	DR AMA	FR ISE	**GR IPY**
PR EP	*BR AXY	CR ATE	**DR ANK**	**FR ISK**	GR IST
PR EX	*BR AZA	**CR AWL**	DR APE	**FR ITH**	GR ITH
PR EY	*BR AZE	*CR AZE	DR AVE	FR ITT	GR OAN
*PR EZ	BR EAD	*CR AZY	DR AWL	*FR ITZ	GR OIN
PR IG	BR EAK	**CR EAK**	DR AWN	*FR IZZ	GR OOM
PR IM	BR EAM	**CR EAM**	DR EAD	**FR OCK**	GR OPE
PR OA	BR EDE	CR EDO	DR EAM	FR OND	GR OSS
PR OD	BR EED	CR EED	DR EAR	FR ONS	*GR OSZ
PR OF	BR ENT	**CR EEK**	DR ESS	FR ONT	GR OUP
PR OG	**BR EVE**	CR EEL	DR EST	FR ORE	GR OUT
PR OM	BR IAR	CR EEP	DR IED	**FR OSH**	GR OVE
PR OP	BR IBE	CR EME	DR IER	FR OST	GR OWL
PR OW	**BR ICK**	CR EPE	DR IES	**FR OTH**	GR OWN
TR AD	BR IDE	CR EPT	DR IFT	**FR OWN**	GR UEL
TR AM	**BR IEF**	**CR EPY**	DR ILL	*FR OZE	**GR UFF**
TR AP	BR IER	CR ESS	DR ILY	FR UIT	GR UME
TR AY	BR ILL	CR EST	**DR INK**	**FR UMP**	**GR UMP**
TR EE	BR INE	**CR ICK**	DR IPT	**FR YER**	GR UNT
TR EF	BR ING	CR IED	DR IVE	GR AAL	KR AAL
TR EK	**BR INK**	CR IER	DR OIT	GR ACE	**KR AFT**
TR ET	**BR INY**	CR IES	DR OLL	GR ADE	KR AIT
TR EY	BR ISK	CR IME	DR ONE	GR AFT	KR AUT
TR IG	BR ITT	**CR IMP**	DR OOL	GR AIL	

K REEP	*PR OXY	TR UCK	BAR REN	BUR ROW	CE RMET
K RILL	PR UDE	TR UED	BAR RET	BUR SAR	CE ROUS
K RONA	PR UNE	TR UER	BAR RIO	BUR TON	CE RTES
K RONE	PR UTA	TR ULL	BAR ROW	BY RNIE	CE RUSE
K ROON	PR YER	TR ULY	BAR TER	BY ROAD	*CE RVIX
K RUBI	TR ACE	TR UMP	BAR YON	CAR ACK	CH RISM
PR AAM	TR ACK	TR UNK	BAR YTA	CAR AFE	CH ROMA
PR AHU	TR ACT	TR USS	BAR YTE	CAR ATE	CH ROME
PR ANG	TR ADE	TR UST	BE RAKE	CAR BON	CH ROMO
PR ANK	TR AGI	TR UTH	BE RIME	CAR BOY	CI RCLE
PR ASE	TR AIK	TR YMA	BE RLIN	CAR CEL	CI RCUS
PR ATE	TR AIL	TR YST	BE RTHA	CAR DIA	*CI RQUE
PR AWN	TR AIN	VR OOM	BIR DER	CAR EEN	CI RRUS
PR EEN	TR AIT	VR OUW	BIR DIE	CAR EER	CO RBAN
PR ESA	TR AMP	WR ACK	BIR KIE	CAR ESS	CO RBEL
PR ESE	TR ANS	WR ANG	BIR LER	CAR FUL	CO RBIE
PR ESS	TR APT	WR APT	BOR AGE	CAR HOP	CO RDER
PR EST	TR ASH	WR ATH	BOR ANE	CAR IBE	CO RDON
*PR EXY	TR ASS	WR EAK	BOR ATE	CAR IES	CO RING
PR ICE	TR AWL	WR ECK	BOR DEL	CAR INA	CO RIUM
PR ICK	TR EAD	WR EST	BOR DER	CAR ING	CO RKER
PR ICY	TR EAT	WR IED	BOR EAL	CAR LIN	CO RMEL
PR IDE	TR END	WR IER	BOR EEN	CAR MAN	CO RNEA
PR IED	TR ESS	WR IES	BOR IDE	CAR NAL	CO RNEL
PR IER	TR EWS	WR ING	BOR ING	CAR NET	CO RNER
PR IES	TR IAD	WR IST	BOR ROW	CAR NEY	CO RNET
PR ILL	TR IAL	WR ITE	BOR SCH	CAR NIE	CO RNUS
PR IMA	TR IBE	WR ONG	BOR SHT	CAR OCH	CO RONA
PR IME	TR ICE	WR OTE	*BOR ZOI	CAR OLI	CO RPSE
PR IMI	TR ICK	WR OTH	BUR BLE	CAR PAL	CO RPUS
PR IMO	TR IED	WR UNG	BUR BLY	CAR PEL	CO RRAL
PR IMP	TR IER	BAR BAL	BUR BOT	CAR PER	CO RRIE
PR INK	TR IES	BAR BEL	BUR DEN	CAR PET	CO RSAC
PR INT	TR IGO	BAR BER	BUR DIE	CAR PUS	*CO RTEX
PR IOR	TR IKE	BAR BET	BUR EAU	CAR REL	CO RTIN
PR ISE	TR ILL	BAR BUT	BUR GEE	CAR ROM	CO RVEE
PR ISM	TR INE	BAR DIC	BUR GER	CAR ROT	CO RVES
PR ISS	TR IOL	BAR EGE	BUR GLE	CAR TEL	CO RVET
PR IVY	TR IPE	BAR ELY	BUR GOO	CAR TER	*CO RYMB
*PR IZE	TR ITE	BAR FLY	BUR IAL	CAR TON	*CO RYZA
PR OBE	TR OAK	BAR HOP	BUR IED	CAR TOP	CU RAGH
PR OEM	TR OCK	BAR ING	BUR IER	CAR VEL	CU RARA
PR OLE	TR ODE	BAR ITE	BUR IES	CAR VEN	CU RARE
PR OMO	TR OKE	BAR IUM	BUR ING	CAR VER	CU RARI
PR ONE	TR OLL	BAR KER	BUR KER	CE RATE	CU RATE
PR ONG	TR OMP	BAR LEY	BUR LAP	CE RCIS	CU RBER
PR OOF	TR ONA	BAR LOW	BUR LER	CE RCUS	CU RDLE
PR OSE	TR ONE	BAR MAN	BUR LEY	CE REAL	CU RFEW
PR OSO	TR OOP	BAR MIE	BUR NER	CE REUS	CU RING
PR OSS	TR OOZ	BAR ONG	BUR NET	CE RING	CU RITE
PR OST	TR OPE	BAR ONY	BUR NIE	CE RIPH	CU RIUM
PR OSY	TR OTH	*BAR QUE	BUR RED	CE RISE	CU RLER
PR OUD	TR OUT	BAR RED	BUR RER	CE RITE	CU RLEW
PR OVE	TR OVE	BAR REL		CE RIUM	CU RRAN
PR OWL	TR UCE				

CUR RIE	**FAR MER**	GA R GET	**HE R EOF**	LA R DON	MU R DER
CUR SED	**FAR ROW**	GA R GLE	HE R EON	LA R IAT	MU R EIN
CUR SER	**FE R HAM**	**GA R ISH**	**HE R ESY**	LA R INE	MU R INE
CUR SOR	FE R INE	GA R LIC	HE R ETO	**LA R KER**	MU R ING
CUR TAL	**FE R ITY**	GA R NER	HE R IOT	LA R RUP	**MU R MUR**
CUR TLY	FE R LIE	GA R NET	**HE R MIT**	*LA R YNX	*MU R PHY
CUR TSY	FE R REL	GA R OTE	HE R NIA	**LO R DLY**	NAR ROW
CUR ULE	FE R RET	GA R RED	**HE R OIC**	LO R EAL	NAR WAL
CUR VEY	**FE R RIC**	GA R RET	HE R OIN	LO R ICA	NE R EID
DAR KEN	**FE R RUM**	GA R RON	**HE R PES**	LO R IES	NE R EIS
DAR KEY	FE R ULE	GA R TER	HI R ING	LU R DAN	NE R OLI
DAR KIE	**FE R VID**	**GA R VEY**	**HI R PLE**	LU R ING	NO R DIC
DAR KLE	**FE R VOR**	GE R BIL	HI R SEL	**LU R KER**	NO R ITE
DAR KLY	**FI R ING**	GE R ENT	HI R SLE	LY R ATE	NO R MAL
DAR NED	**FI R KIN**	GE R MAN	**HO R ARY**	**LY R ISM**	NO R MED
DAR NEL	**FI R MAN**	GE R MEN	HO R NET	LY R IST	NU R SER
DAR NER	**FI R MER**	GE R UND	HO R ROR	MA R AUD	PA R ADE
DAR TER	**FI R MLY**	GI R DER	**HO R SEY**	MA R GIN	**PA R AMO**
DAR TLE	**FO R AGE**	GI R DLE	HO R STE	MA R INA	PA R ANG
DE R ATE	**FO R BAD**	GI R LIE	**HU R DLE**	MA R INE	**PA R APH**
DE R IDE	**FO R BID**	GO R GER	HU R LER	MA R LIN	**PA R CEL**
DE R IVE	**FO R BYE**	GO R GET	HU R LEY	MA R OON	**PA R DAH**
DE R MIS	**FO R CER**	GO R GON	**HU R RAH**	MA R RED	PA R DEE
DE R RIS	**FO R EBY**	**GO R HEN**	**HU R RAY**	MA R RER	PA R DIE
DI R DUM	**FO R EDO**	GO R IER	HU R TER	MA R RON	PA R DON
DI R ECT	**FO R EGO**	**GO R ILY**	HU R TLE	MA R TEN	PA R ENT
DI R ELY	FO R EST	GO R ING	*JA R FUL	MA R TIN	**PA R EVE**
DI R EST	**FO R GAT**	GU R GLE	JA R GON	**MA R TYR**	PA R GET
DI R HAM	**FO R GER**	GU R NET	JA R INA	**ME R CER**	**PA R IAH**
DI R NDL	**FO R GET**	GU R NEY	*JA R RAH	ME R GER	PA R IAN
DO R ADO	FO R INT	GY R ASE	JA R RED	ME R INO	PA R ING
DO R BUG	**FO R KER**	GY R ATE	*JA R VEY	ME R LIN	**PA R ISH**
DO R IES	**FO R MAL**	GY R ENE	*JE R BOA	ME R LON	**PA R ITY**
DO R MER	**FO R MAT**	GY R ING	*JE R KER	ME R LOT	**PA R KER**
DO R MIE	**FO R MER**	GY R OSE	*JE R KIN	MI R AGE	**PA R LAY**
DO R MIN	**FO R MIC**	HAR ASS	JE R RID	MI R IER	**PA R LEY**
DO R PER	**FO R MOL**	HAR BOR	*JE R SEY	MI R ING	PA R LOR
DO R SAD	**FO R MYL**	HA R DEN	JO R DAN	MI R ROR	**PA R ODY**
DO R SAL	*FO R NIX	HA R DLY	JU R ANT	MO R ALE	PA R OLE
DO R SEL	FOR RIT	HA R EEM	JU R IES	MO R ALS	PA R OUS
DO R SER	FO R TES	HA R KER	**JU R IST**	MO R ASS	PAR RAL
DO R SUM	FO R TIS	HAR LOT	KA R ATE	MO R EEN	PAR RED
DUR BAR	*FO R WHY	HA R MER	KA R OSS	MO R GAN	PAR REL
DUR ESS	FU R ANE	HA R MIN	**KA R ROO**	MO R GEN	PAR ROT
DU R IAN	**FU R FUR**	HA R PER	KE R MES	MO R GUE	**PA R SEC**
DU R ING	FU R IES	HA R PIN	KE R MIS	MO R ION	PA R SER
DU R ION	FU R LER	HA R ROW	KE R NEL	MO R OSE	PA R SON
DU R NED	FU R ORE	HA R TAL	**KE R RIA**	MO R RIS	PA R TAN
FA R CER	**FU R RED**	HE R ALD	KE R SEY	MO R SEL	**PA R TLY**
FA R CIE	**FU R ROW**	HE R BAL	*KI R SCH	MO R TAL	PA R TON
FA R DEL	GA R AGE	HE R BED	KI R TLE	MO R TAR	PA R URA
FA R FAL	GA R BLE	HE R DER	KO R UNA	MO R ULA	PA R URE
FA R FEL	GA R CON	HE R DIC	KU R GAN		**PA R VIS**
FA R INA	GA R DEN	HE R EAT	LA R DER		PE R DIE
FA R ING		HE R EIN			PE R DUE

PE R EON	R E R OOF	**SH R UNK**	ST R IPT	TE R ROR	**VE R DIN**
PE R IOD	R E R OSE	SI R DAR	**ST R IPY**	TH R ALL	**VE R GE R**
PE R ISH	R U R BAN	SI R ING	ST R IVE	**TH R ASH**	*VE R IFY
PE R MIT	SÁ R APE	SI R RAH	ST R OBE	**TH R ILL**	VE R ILY
*PE R OXY	SA R DAR	SI R R EE	ST R ODE	**TH R AWN**	VE R ISM
PE R R ON	SA R ODE	SO R BET	**ST R OKE**	TH R EAD	VE R IST
PE R SON	SA R ONG	**SO R BIC**	ST R OLL	**TH R EAP**	VE R ITE
PE R UKE	SA R SAR	SO R DID	ST R OMA	**TH R EEP**	**VE R ITY**
PE R USE	SA R SEN	SO R DO R	ST R ONG	**TH R ESH**	VE R MES
PH R ASE	SA R TO R	SO R ELY	ST R OOK	**TH R ICE**	VE R MIN
PI R ACY	**SC R APE**	SO R EST	ST R OPE	**TH R IFT**	VE R MIS
PI R ANA	**SC R AWL**	**SO R GHO**	ST R OUD	TH R ILL	VE R NAL
PI R ATE	**SC R EAK**	SO R ING	ST R OVE	**TH R IVE**	VE R SAL
PI R AYA	**SC R EAM**	SO R NE R	**ST R UCK**	TH R OAT	VE R SE R
PI R OGI	SC R EED	SO R R EL	ST R UMA	TH R ONE	VE R SET
PO R ISM	SC R EEN	SO R R OW	ST R UNG	**TH R ONG**	VE R STE
PO R KE R	**SC R EWY**	SO R TE R	ST R UNT	**TH R OVE**	VE R SUS
PO R OSE	**SC R IBE**	SO R TIE	SU R ELY	**TH R USH**	*VE R TEX
PO R OUS	SC R IED	SP R AIN	SU R EST	TH R UST	**VE R UCA**
PO R TAL	SC R IES	SP R ANG	SU R ETY	TI R ADE	**VE R VET**
PO R TE R	**SC R IMP**	**SP R AWL**	SU R FE R	TI R ING	**VI R AGO**
PO R TLY	**SC R IPT**	SP R EAD	SU R GE R	TO R E R O	**VI R GIN**
PU R DAH	**SC R IVE**	SP R ENT	SU R R EY	TO R IES	VI R ILE
PU R ELY	SC R OLL	SP R IER	**SU R TAX**	TO R OID	VI R ION
PU R EST	**SC R OOP**	SP R IG	**SU R VEY**	TO R OSE	**VI R OID**
PU R FLE	**SC R UFF**	SP R INT	*SY R INX	TO R OTH	VI R TUE
PU R GE R	SE R AIL	SP R ITE	TA R GET	TO R OUS	*VO R TEX
*PU R IFY	SE R APE	*SP R ITZ	**TA R IFF**	TO R PID	**WA R BLE**
PU R INE	**SE R APH**	SP R OUT	TA R ING	TO R PO R	**WA R DEN**
PU R ISM	SE R ATE	**SP R UCE**	**TA R MAC**	TO R ULA	**WA R DE R**
PU R IST	SE R DAB	**SP R UCY**	TA R NAL	TU R ACO	WA R IE R
PU R ITY	SE R EIN	SP R UNG	TA R PAN	TU R BAN	**WA R ILY**
PU R LIN	SE R ENE	ST R AFE	TA R PON	TU R BID	**WA R ING**
PU R PLE	SE R EST	ST R AIN	TA R R ED	TU R BIT	**WA R ME R**
PU R PLY	SE R IAL	ST R AIT	TA R SAL	TU R BOT	**WA R MLY**
PU R R ED	SE R IES	**ST R AKE**	TA R SIA	TU R EEN	WA R MTH
PU R SE R	SE R INE	ST R AND	TA R SUS	TU R GID	**WA R MUP**
PU R SUE	SE R MON	ST R ANG	TA R TAN	TU R GO R	WA R NE R
PU R VEY	SE R OSA	ST R ASS	TA R TA R	TU R GO R Y	WA R PE R
PY R ENE	SE R OUS	ST R ATA	TA R TLY	TU R KEY	WA R R ED
PY R OLA	SE R VAL	ST R ATH	*TA R ZAN	**TU R KEY**	WA R R EN
PY R ONE	SE R VE R	ST R ATI	**TE R APH**	TU R NE R	**WA R SAW**
PY R OPE	**SH R ANK**	**ST R AWY**	TE R BIA	TU R NIP	WA R SLE
PY R R OL	**SH R EWD**	**ST R EAK**	TE R CEL	TU R NUP	WI R IE R
*QU R USH	**SH R IEK**	ST R EAM	TE R CET	TU R R ET	**WO R KE R**
R A R EFY	**SH R IFT**	**ST R EEK**	TE R EDO	TU R TLE	*WO R KUP
R A R ELY	**SH R IKE**	ST R EET	TE R ETE	TU R VES	**WO R ME R**
R A R EST	SH R ILL	ST R ESS	TE R GAL	TY R ANT	**WO R MIL**
R A R IFY	**SH R IMP**	**ST R ICK**	TE R GUM	**VA R IED**	WO R R IT
R A R ING	SH R INE	ST R ICT	TE R ME R	VA R IE R	WO R SEN
R A R ITY	**SH R INK**	ST R IDE	**TE R MLY**	VA R IES	WO R SE R
R E R ACK	SH R IVE	ST R IFE	TE R MO R	VA R LET	WO R SET
R E R EAD	*SH R OFF	**ST R IKE**	TE R RAS	**VA R OOM**	*WO R THY
R E R ISE	**SH R OUD**	ST R ING	TE R R ET	**VE R BAL**	*WU R ZEL
R E R OLL	**SH R OVE**	ST R IPE	TE R R IT	**VE R BID**	YA R NE R

YA R R OW	BU R GHER	CA R OACH	CO R EIGN	CU R TESY	FE R VENT
*ZA R EBA	BU R GLAR	CA R OCHE	CO R KAGE	CU R TSEY	FE R VOUR
*ZA R IBA	BU R GOUT	CA R OLE R	CO R KIER	DA R BIES	FI R EARM
*ZE R OTH	BU R KITE	CA R OLUS	CO R NCOB	DA R EFUL	*FI R EBOX
*ZI R CON	BU R LESK	CA R OTID	CO R NFED	DA R ESAY	FI R EBUG
BA R BATE	BU R NING	CA R OTIN	CO R NICE	DA R IOLE	FI R EDOG
BA R BELL	BU R NISH	CA R OUSE	CO R NIER	*DA R KIES	*FI R EFLY
BA R BULE	BU R NOUS	CA R PALE	CO R NILY	*DA R KISH	FI R ELIT
BA R CHAN	BU R NOUT	CA R PING	CO RN ROW	DAR NING	FI R EMAN
BA R EFIT	BU R RIER	CA R POOL	CO R NUTE	DAR RING	FI R EPAN
BA R GAIN	BU R RITO	CAR PO R T	CO R NUTO	DA R SHAN	FI R EPOT
BA R GING	BU R SARY	CAR R ELL	CO R OLLA	DE R AIGN	FI R STLY
BA R ILLA	BU R SATE	CA R RIED	CO R ONAL	DE R IDER	FO R AGER
*BA R KEEP	BU R SEED	CA R RIER	CO R ONEL	DE R IVER	FO R AMEN
BA R LESS	BU R STER	CA R RIES	CO R ONER	DE R MOID	FO R AYER
BA R MAID	BU R THEN	CA R RION	CO R ONET	DE R NIER	FO R BADE
BA R ONET	BU R WEED	CA R ROCH	CO R PORA	DE R RICK	FO R BEAR
BA R ONNE	CA R ABAO	CA R ROTY	CO R RADE	DE R VISH	FO R BODE
*BA R OQUE	CA R ABID	CA R RYON	CO R RECT	DI R EFUL	FO R BORE
*BA R RACK	CA R ABIN	*CA R SICK	CO R RIDA	DI R TBAG	FO R CEPS
BA R RAGE	CA R ACAL	CA R TAGE	CO R RODE	*DO R HAWK	FO R CING
BA R RIER	CA R ACOL	CA R TOON	CO R RODY	DO R MANT	FO R EARM
BA R RING	CA R ACUL	CA R VING	CO R RUPT	DO R MICE	*FO R EBAY
BA R ROOM	CA R AMBA	*CA R WASH	CO R SAGE	DO R NECK	*FO R EBYE
BA R TEND	CA R AMEL	CE R AMAL	CO R SAIR	DO R NICK	FO R EGUT
BA R WARE	*CA R APAX	CE R AMIC	CO R SLET	DU R ABLE	FO R EIGN
BE R EAVE	CA R AVAN	CE R ATED	CO R TEGE	DU R AMEN	FO R ELEG
BE R ETTA	CA R AVEL	CE R ATIN	CO R ULER	DU R ANCE	FO R EMAN
BE R GERE	*CA R AWAY	CE R OTIC	CO R VINA	DU R MAST	*FO R EPAW
*BE R HYME	CA R BARN	CE R TAIN	CO R VINE	FA R ADAY	FO R ERUN
BE R LINE	CA R BIDE	*CE R TIFY	CU R ABLE	FA R ADIC	FO R ESEE
BE R OBED	CA R BINE	CE R UMEN	CU R ACAO	*FA R AWAY	FO R ETOP
BE R SEEM	CA R BORA	CE R VINE	CU R ACOA	FA R CEUR	FO R EVER
BE R SERK	CA R CASE	CH R ISOM	CU R ATOR	FA R CING	FO R FEIT
BI R CHEN	CA R CASS	*CH R ISTY	CU R BING	FA R INHA	FO R FEND
BI R DING	CA R DIAC	*CH R OMIC	CU R CUMA	FA R MING	FO R GAVE
BI R DMAN	CA R DING	*CH R OMYL	CU R DIER	FA R NESS	FO R GERY
BI R ETTA	CA R DOON	CH R ONIC	CU R DLER	FA R RAGO	FO R GING
BI R LING	CA R EFUL	CH R ONON	CU R ETTE	FA R RIER	FO R GIVE
BO R ACES	CA R FARE	CIR CLE R	CU R IOSA	FA R SIDE	FO R GOER
BO R ACIC	CA R IBOU	CIR CLET	CU R IOUS	FA R THER	*FO R KFUL
*BO R AZON	CA R ICES	CIR CUIT	CU R LING	FE R MATA	FO R KIER
BO R DURE	CA R IOCA	CIR R ATE	CU R RACH	FE R MENT	FO R LORN
BO R EDOM	CA R IOLE	CIR R OSE	CU R RACY	FE R MION	FO R MANT
BO R NEOL	CA R IOUS	CIR R OUS	CU R RANT	FE R MIUM	FO R MATE
BO R NITE	CA R ITAS	CIR SOID	CU R RENT	FE R NERY	*FO R MFUL
BO R OUGH	CA R LESS	CO R ACLE	CU R RIED	FE R RATE	FO R MULA
BO R SCHT	CA R LINE	CO R ANTO	CU R RIER	FE R RETY	FO R SAKE
BO R STAL	CA R LING	CO R BEIL	CU R RISH	FE R RIED	FO R TIES
BU R BLER	CA R LISH	CO R BINA	CU R SING	FE R RIES	*FO R TIFY
*BU R DOCK	CA R LOAD	CO R DAGE	CU R SIVE	FE R RITE	FO R TUNE
BU R ETTE	CA R MINE	CO R DATE	CU R SORY	FE R ROUS	FO R WARD
BU R GAGE	CA R NAGE	CO R DIAL	CU R TAIL	FE R RULA	FO R WENT
BU R GEON	CA R NIES	CO R DING	CU R TAIN	FE R RULE	FO R WORN
BU R GESS	*CA R NIFY	CO R DOBA	CU R TATE	FE R TILE	*FU R BISH

FU R CATE	HA R ELIP	*JA R LDOM	MA R SUPI	PA R DNER	PE R IGEE
FU R CULA	HA R IANA	*JA R RING	MA R TAGO	PAR EIRA	PE R IGON
FU R IOSO	HA R ICOT	*JA R SFUL	MA R TIAL	PA R ESIS	PE R ILLA
FU R IOUS	*HAR IJAN	*JE R KIES	MA R TIAN	PA R ETIC	*PE R IQUE
FU R LESS	*HA R MFUL	*JE R REED	MA R TINE	PA R FAIT	PE R IWIG
FU R LONG	*HA R MINE	*JU R IDIC	MA R TINI	PA R GING	*PE R JURE
*FU R METY	*HA R MONY	*JU R YMAN	MA R TLET	PA R KING	*PE R JURY
*FU R MITY	HA R NESS	*KA R AKUL	*MAR TYRY	*PA R KWAY	*PE R KISH
FU R NACE	HA R PIES	*KA R AOKE	ME R ISIS	PA R LING	PE R LITE
FU R NISH	HA R PING	KA R TING	MI R ADOR	PAR LOUR	PE R MUTE
FU R RIER	HA R PIST	KE R ATIN	MI R IEST	PAR LOUS	PE R ORAL
FU R RILY	HA R POON	*KE R CHOO	MI R INES	PA R ODIC	*PE R OXID
FU R RING	HA R RIED	KE R MESS	MO R AINE	PA R OLEE	PE R PEND
*FU R ROWY	HA R RIER	KE R NITE	MO R ELLE	PA R ONYM	PE R PENT
FU R THER	HA R RIES	KE R OGEN	MO R ELLO	PA R OTIC	*PE R PLEX
FU R TIVE	HA R RING	*KE R YGMA	*MO R PHIC	PA R OTID	PE R SALT
GA R BAGE	HA R SHEN	*KI R KMAN	MO R RION	*PA R QUET	PE R SIST
GA R BLER	*HA R SHLY	KI R MESS	*MO R TIFY	PA R RIED	PE R SONA
GA R BOIL	HA R SLET	*KU R BASH	MO R TISE	PA R RIES	PE R TAIN
GA R DANT	*HA R UMPH	LA R CENY	MU R IATE	PA R RING	PE R TURB
GA R FISH	HA R VEST	LA R DIER	MU R RAIN	PA R ROTY	PE R USAL
GA R GLER	HE R BAGE	LA R DOON	MU R RINE	PA R SING	PE R USER
GA R LAND	HE R BIER	LA R GESS	MU R THER	PA R SLEY	PE R VADE
GA R MENT	HE R DMAN	LA R GEST	NA R CEIN	PA R SNIP	PE R VERT
GA R NISH	HE R EDES	LA R GISH	NA R CISM	PA R TAKE	PH R ASAL
GA R OTTE	HE R ETIC	LA R KIER	NA R CIST	PA R TIAL	*PH R ATRY
GA R PIKE	HE R ITOR	LA R KISH	NA R COSE	PA R TIED	PH R ENIC
GA R RING	HE R OINE	LO R DING	NA R GILE	PA R TIER	*PH R ENSY
GA R ROTE	HE R OISM	LO R DOMA	NA R RATE	PA R TIES	PI R AGUA
GE R BERA	*HE R OIZE	LO R GNON	*NA R THEX	PA R TING	PI R ANHA
GE R ENUK	HE R ONRY	LO R IMER	NE R ITIC	PA R TITA	PI R ATIC
GE R MANE	HE R RING	LO R INER	NE R VATE	PA R TITE	PI R OGUE
GE R MIER	HE R SELF	LU R CHER	NE R VIER	PA R TLET	*PI R OQUE
GE R MINA	HI R ABLE	LY R ATED	NE R VILY	PAR TNER	PO R CINE
GI R AFFE	HI R CINE	LY R ICAL	NE R VINE	*PA R TWAY	PO R CINO
GI R ASOL	HI R SUTE	MA R ABOU	NE R VING	PA R TYER	PO R KIER
GI R DLER	HI R UDIN	MA R ANTA	NE R VOUS	PA R VENU	PO R KIES
GI R LISH	HO R DEIN	MA R BLER	NE R VULE	PA R VISE	*PO R KPIE
GI R OSOL	*HO R IZON	MA R CATO	NE R VURE	PE R ACID	PO R RECT
*GO R COCK	HO R NIER	MA R CHER	NI R VANA	PE R CALE	PO R TAGE
GO R GING	HO R NILY	MA R ENGO	NO R LAND	PE R CENT	PO R TEND
GO R IEST	HO R NIST	MA R INER	NO R THER	PE R CEPT	PO R TENT
GO R ILLA	HO R NITO	MA R ITAL	NU R SING	PE R CHER	PO R TICO
GO R MAND	HO R RENT	*MAR KHOR	NU R TURE	PE R COID	PO R TION
GU R GLET	*HO R RIFY	MAR LIER	PA R ABLE	PE R CUSS	PO R TRAY
GU R NARD	HO R SIER	MA R LINE	PA R ADER	PE R FECT	PU R GING
GY R ATOR	HO R SILY	MA R LITE	PA R ADOR	*PE R FIDY	PU R ITAN
HA R BOUR	HO R SING	*MA R QUEE	*PA R ADOX	PE R FORM	PU R LIEU
HA R DHAT	HU R DIES	*MA R QUIS	PA R AGON	PE R FUME	PU R LINE
HA R DIER	HU R DLER	MA R RANO	PA R APET	PE R FUSE	PU R LOIN
HA R DIES	HU R LING	MA R RIER	PA R ASOL	PE R GOLA	PU R PORT
HA R DILY	HU R RIER	*MA R ROWY	PA R BOIL	PE R HAPS	PU R POSE
HA R DPAN	HU R TFUL	MA R SALA	PA R CEUR	PE R IAPT	PU R PURA
HA R DSET	*JA R GOON	MA R SHAL	PA R DINE	PE R IDOT	PU R PURE
HA R DTOP	*JA R HEAD				PU R RANA

PU R RING	SE R FAGE	ST R ETTA	TE R EBIC	TU R ISTA	WA R BLER
PU R SIE R	SE R FDOM	ST R ETTO	TE R EFAH	TU R KOIS	WA R FARE
PU R SILY	SE R FISH	ST R EWE R	TE R GITE	TU R MOIL	WA R HEAD
PU R SING	SE R GING	ST R IATE	TE R MITE	**TU R NE R Y**	WA R IEST
PU R SUE R	SE R IATE	ST R IDE R	**TE R NARY**	TU R NING	WA R ISON
PU R SUIT	SE R ICIN	ST R IDO R	TE R NATE	TU R NKEY	WA R LESS
*PU R VIEW	SE R IEMA	ST R IGIL	TE R NION	TU R NOFF	WA R LIKE
PY R ALID	SE R INGA	**ST R IKE R**	TE R PENE	TU R NOUT	*WA R LOCK
*PY R AMID	SE R IOUS	**ST R INGY**	TE R RACE	TU R PETH	WA R LO R D
PY R ETIC	SE R PENT	ST R IPE R	TE R RAIN	TU R TLE R	*WA R MISH
*PY R EXIA	SE R PIGO	ST R IVE R	TE R RANE	**TY R ANNY**	WA R NING
PY R OGEN	SE R R ANO	ST R OBIC	TE R REEN	VA R IANT	WA R PAGE
PY R OSIS	SE R VANT	ST R OBIL	TE R RENE	VA R IATE	*WA R PATH
*PY R R HIC	SE R VICE	**ST R OKE R**	TE R RIE R	VA R ICES	WA R R ANT
PY R R ITE	SE R VILE	ST R OPHE	TE R RIES	VA R IETY	WA R R ING
PY R R OLE	SE R VING	ST R OPPY	**TE R RIFY**	VA R IOLA	WA R R IO R
RARER IT	*SH R IEKY	ST R OYE R	TE R RINE	VA R IOLE	*WA R SHIP
RER AISE	*SH R IMPY	ST R UDEL	TE R TIAL	VA R IOUS	WA R SLE R
RER EDOS	SH R IVEL	SU R BASE	TE R TIAN	VA R MENT	WA R STLE
RER OUTE	SH R IVE R	SU R COAT	**TH R EADY**	VA R MINT	WA R THOG
*RO R QUAL	SH R LINK	SU R FACE	*TH R IFTY	VA R NISH	WA R TIE R
RU R ALLY	*SH R UBBY	SU R FEIT	TH R IVE R	VA R SITY	WA R TIME
SA R CASM	SI R COIN	SU R FIE R	TH R OATY	VE R ANDA	*WA R WO R K
SA R COID	SI R OCCO	SU R GEON	TH R OUGH	VE R BENA	WA R WO R N
SA R COMA	*SK R EEGH	**SU R GE R Y**	TH R OWE R	*VE R BIFY	WE R GELD
SA R COUS	*SK R EIGH	SU R GING	TH R REAT	VE R BILE	WE R GELT
SA R DANA	SO R BATE	SU R MISE	*TH R UMMY	VE R DANT	WE R GILD
SA R DINE	SO R BENT	SU R NAME	TH R UPUT	VE R DICT	*WE R WOLF
SA R DIUS	SO R BOSE	SU R PASS	*TH R UWAY	VE R DU R E	WI R EMAN
SA R MENT	**SO R CE R Y**	SU R PING	TO R CHON	VE R GING	WI R ETAP
SC R AGGY	SO R DINE	SU R PLUS	TO R MENT	VE R GLAS	*WI R EWAY
SC R AIGH	SO R DINO	SU R R EAL	TO R NADO	VE R IDIC	WI R IEST
SC R APE R	SO R GHUM	SU R TOUT	TO R PEDO	VE R IEST	WI R R IE R
SC R APIE	SO R ITES	SU R VEIL	*TO R QUE R	VE R ISMO	WI R R ILY
*SC R APPY	SO R OCHE	SU R VIVE	*TO R QUES	VE R ITAS	WI R R ING
SC R ATCH	SO R O R AL	SY R INGA	TO R R EFY	VE R MEIL	WO R DAGE
*SC R AWLY	SO R OSIS	SY R INGE	TO R R ENT	VE R MIAN	WO R DIE R
*SC R AWNY	SO R R IE R	*SY R PHID	TO R R IFY	*VE R MUTH	WO R DILY
*SC R EAKY	SO R R ILY	TA R BUSH	TO R SADE	VE R NIE R	WO R DING
SC R EECH	*SP R AWLY	TA R DIE R	TO R SION	VE R R IE R	*WO R KBAG
SC R EWE R	SP R AYE R	TA R DIES	TO R TILE	VE R SANT	*WO R KBOX
SC R EWUP	SP R IEST	**TA R DYON**	TO R TONI	*VE R SIFY	*WO R KDAY
SC R IBAL	SP R IGGY	TA R NISH	**TO R T R IX**	VE R SINE	*WO R KING
SC R IBE R	SP R IGHT	TA R R IED	TO R TU R E	VE R SING	*WO R KMAN
SC R IEVE	SP R INGE	TA R R IE R	TU R ACOU	VE R SION	WO R KOUT
*SC R IMPY	SP R INGY	TA R R IES	**TU R BA R Y**	VE R TIGO	WO R LDLY
SC R OGGY	ST R AFE R	TA R R ING	**TU R BETH**	VE R VAIN	WO R MIE R
SC R OOCH	ST R ANGE	TA R SIE R	TU R BINE	VI R ELAI	*WO R MISH
SC R OOGE	ST R ATAL	TA R TANA	**TU R BITH**	VI R ELAY	WO R R IED
SC R OTUM	ST R ATUM	TA R TISH	TU R DINE	VI R EMIA	WO R R IE R
SC R OUGE	ST R ATUS	TA R TLET	**TU R FIE R**	VI R GATE	*WO R SHIP
*SC R UBBY	ST R AYE R	TA R TUFE	TU R FMAN	VI R GULE	WO R STED
*SC R UFFY	ST R EAKY	TA R WEED	TU R FSKI	VI R OSIS	*XE R A R CH
SC R UNCH	ST R EAMY	TE R AOHM	TU R GENT	VI R TUAL	XE R OSIS
SC R UPLE	ST R ETCH	TE R BIUM	TU R GITE	VO R LAGE	YA R DAGE

YA R DA R M	*CHA R ISMA	*DEF R AYER	GA R R OTER	LAB R USCA	MO R IBUND
YA R DMAN	*CHA R LADY	DEG R ADER	GA R R OTTE	LAC R IMAL	MO R ONISM
*ZA R SEBA	*CHA R LOCK	DEG R EASE	GEA R CASE	LAC R OSSE	MO R ONITY
*ZO R ILLA	*CHA R MING	DEP R AVER	GEA R LESS	LA R R IGAN	MO R OSITY
*ZO R ILLE	CHA R R IER	DEP R IVAL	GLO R IOLE	LA R R IKIN	MO R TALLY
*ZO R ILLO	CHA R R ING	DEP R IVER	GLO R IOUS	LA R R UPER	MO R TGAGE
BA R R ABLE	CHA R TEST	DE R R IERE	GNA R R ING	LAU R EATE	MO R TISER
BA R R ANCA	CHA R TIST	DET R ITUS	GOU R MAND	LEA R IEST	MO R TMAIN
BA R R ANCO	CHO R AGUS	DIA R R HEA	GUA R ANTY	LEA R NING	MO R TUARY
BA R R ATER	CHO R DATE	DIC R OTAL	GUA R DANT	LEP R OTIC	MU R AENID
BA R R ATOR	CHO R EGUS	DIC R OTIC	GUA R DIAN	LIB R ETTO	MU R ALIST
BA R R ATRY	*CHO R EMAN	DIE R ESIS	GUE R IDON	LIG R OINE	MU R DEREE
BA R R ETOR	CHO R EOID	DIS R OBER	GUE R ILLA	LOW R IDER	MU R DERER
BA R R ETRY	CHO R IOID	DIU R ESIS	GUE R NSEY	LUB R ICAL	MU R IATED
BA R R ETTE	*CHO R IAMB	DIU R ETIC	HAI R BALL	MA R ASMUS	MU R ICATE
BA R R OWER	CHO R TLER	*DOO R KNOB	HAI R BAND	MA R ATHON	MU R MURER
BEA R LIKE	*CHU R CHLY	DOO R POST	HAI R IEST	MA R AUDER	MUR R ELET
BEA R SKIN	CHU R NING	DOO R BELL	HAI R LESS	MA R AVEDE	NA R RATER
*BED R ENCH	CI R R IPED	*DOO R JAMB	*HAI R LIKE	MA R BLING	NAR R ATOR
BED R IVEL	CIT R EOUS	DOO R LESS	HAI R LINE	MA R GARIN	NEA R NESS
BEF R IEND	CLA R ENCE	DOO R NAIL	*HAI R LOCK	MA R GARIO	NEA R SIDE
BEF R INGE	CLA R INET	DOO R SILL	*HAIR WORK	MA R GINAL	*NEC R OPSY
BEG R UDGE	CLE R ICAL	DOO R STEP	*HAIR WORM	MA R GRAVE	NEC R OSIS
BE R R ETTA	*CLE R KDOM	DOO R STOP	HAR R OWER	MA R IGOLD	*NEU RAXON
BET R AYAL	*CLE R KISH	DOO R YARD	*HAR R UMPH	MA R INADE	NEU R ITIC
BET R AYER	*CLE R IHEW	DOU R NESS	*HEB R AIZE	MA R INARA	NEU R ITIS
*BEW R AYER	COC R EATE	*DWA R FISH	HEI R LESS	MA R INATE	NEU R OSIS
BI R R ETTA	COD R IVER	*DWA R FISM	HEI R LOOM	MA R IPOSA	NEU R OTIC
BOA R DING	COE R CION	FAI R LEAD	*HEI R SHIP	MA R ITIME	NIG R OSIN
BOA R DMAN	*COE R CIVE	FAI R NESS	HID R OSIS	MA R KETER	NIT R ATER
*BOA R FISH	COP R EMIA	*FAI R YISM	HID R OTIC	MA R LIEST	NIT R OGEN
BO R R OWER	CO R R IDOR	FAR R IERY	*HIE R A R CH	MA R MOSET	NIT R OLIC
BOT R YOID	CO R R IVAL	FEA R LESS	HIE R ATIC	MA R R IAGE	NIT R OSYL
BOT R YOSE	COU R ANTE	FEA R SOME	HOA R DING	MER R IEST	NON R ATED
BOU R GEON	COU R ANTO	*FEB R IFIC	HO R R IBLE	ME R CAPTO	NON R IGID
BOU R T REE	COU R SING	FE R R EOUS	*HO R R IBLY	ME R ENGUE	NON R IVAL
BU R R IEST	COU R TESY	FE R R ETER	*HO R R IFIC	ME R GENCE	NON R OYAL
BU R R OWER	COU R TIER	FE R R IAGE	HUA R ACHE	ME R IDIAN	NON R URAL
CAB R ESTA	CUP R EOUS	FE R R ITIN	*HUA R ACHO	ME R INGUE	NUT R IENT
CAB R ESTO	*CU R R ENCY	*FER R YMAN	*HYD R ACID	ME R ISTEM	PA R R IDGE
CAB R ETTA	CU R R ICLE	FIB R ANNE	*HYD R AGOG	ME R ISTIC	*PAR R ITCH
CAB R ILLA	CU R R IERY	FIB R ILLA	*HYD R ANTH	MIC R OBAR	PAR R OKET
CAB R IOLE	CU R R YING	FIB R OSIS	*HYD R ATOR	MIC R ODOT	PA R R OTER
*CAP R ICCI	*CYP R INID	FLO R ALLY	*HYD R OGEL	*MIC R OLUX	PEA R LASH
*CAP R IFIG	*CZA R EVNA	FOR R ADER	*HYD R OGEN	*MIC R OMHO	PEA R LITE
CAP R IOLE	*CZA R ITZA	*FOU R CHEE	*HYD R OMEL	*MIC R URGY	PEA R MAIN
CA R R IAGE	DEA R NESS	*FOU R FOLD	*HYD R ONIC	MIG R ATOR	PEE R LESS
CA R R IOLE	DEB R UISE	*FOU R PLEX	*HYD R OPIC	MIS R EFER	PET R OLIC
*CA R R ITCH	DEC R EASE	*FOU R SOME	*HYD R OPSY	MIS R OUTE	PET R ONEL
CA R R OTIN	DEC R EPIT	FOU R TEEN	*HYD R OSKI	*MOO R COCK	PET R OSAL
CA R R YALL	DEC R ETAL	*FOU R THLY	*HYD R OSOL	*MOO R FOWL	PHA R ISEE
CA R R YOUT	DEC R ETAL	FUR R IERY	*HYD R OXYL	MO R ALISM	*PHA R MACY
*CHA R ACID	DEE R SKIN	FU R R IEST	*JE R R ICAN	MO R ALIST	PHO R ONID
*CHA R ACIN	DEE R WEED	FU R R INER	*JE R R YCAN	MO R ALITY	PLU R ALLY
*CHA R COAL	DEE R YARD	FUR R OWER	*JOY R IDER	MO R ATORY	POO R NESS
CHA R IEST	*DEF R AYAL	GA R R ISON	LAB R ADOR	MO R BILLI	POO R TITH
				MO R EOVER	

PO R R IDGE	SCA R R ING	SPI R ALLY	THE R IACA	CA R R	PU R R
P R E R ENAL	*SCH R IEVE	SPI R ELLA	THE R MION	CHA R	R EAR
P R E R INSE	SCI R OCCO	SPI R IEST	THE R MITE	COI R	R OAR
P R O R OGUE	SCI R R HUS	SPO R ADIC	THE R OPOD	CU R R	R UE R
P R U R IENT	*SCO R CHE R	*SPO R OZOA	THI R STE R	*CZA R	SCA R
P R U R ITUS	SCO R EPAD	SPO R TFUL	THI R TEEN	DEA R	SEA R
PSO R ALEA	SCO R NFUL	SPO R TIVE	*THO R OUGH	DEE R	SEE R
PSO R ALEN	SCO R PION	SPU R GALL	THU R IBLE	DOE R	SLU R
PTE R OPOD	SCU R R IED	SPU R IOUS	THU R IFE R	DOO R	SOA R
PTE R YGIA	SCU R R IES	SPU R R IE R	*THY R EOID	DO R R	SOU R
*PYO R RHEA	SCU R R ILE	SPU R R ING	*THY R OXIN	DOU R	SPA R
*QUAR R IER	SEA R CHE R	STA R DUST	TIT R ABLE	DU R R	SPU R
*QUARTE R N	SEA R OBIN	STA R FISH	TIT R ATO R	DYE R	STA R
*QUA R TILE	SEC R ETIN	*STA R GAZE	TSA R EVNA	FAI R	STI R
*QUE R CINE	SEC R ETLY	STA R KE R S	*TSA R ITZA	FEA R	SUE R
*QUI R KISH	SEC R ETO R	STA R LESS	TU R R ICAL	FIA R	TAH R
R EA R MICE	SE R R ANID	STA R LIKE	*TZA R EVNA	FOU R	TEA R
R EA R MOST	SHE R BE R T	STA R LING	*TZA R ITZA	GAU R	THI R
R EA R OUSE	SHE R TING	STA R NOSE	*VAG R ANCY	GNA R	TIE R
R EAR R EST	SHI R R ING	STA R R ING	*VIB R ANCE	GOE R	TO R R
R EARWARD	SHO R TAGE	STA R SHIP	*VIB R ANCY	GUA R	TOU R
*R EB R ANCH	SHO R TCUT	STA R TLE R	VIB R ATO R	HAA R	TSA R
R EC R EANT	SHO R TIES	STA R WO R T	VIB R ISSA	HAI R	TYE R
R EC R EATE	SHO R TISH	STE R ICAL	*VIB R ONIC	HEA R	TZA R
R ED R AWE R	*SIE R OZEM	STE R IGMA	VIT R EOUS	HEI R	VAI R
*R EF R EEZE	*SKI R IESH	STE R NITE	WA R R AGAL	HOA R	VEE R
R EG R OOVE	SKI R TING	STE R NSON	WA R R ANTY	HOE R	VIE R
*R EG R OWTH	SLU R R ING	STE R NWAY	WA R R ENE R	HOU R	WAI R
R EO R DAIN	SMA R AGDE	STE R R ING	WA R R IGAL	**JEE R**	WAU R
R EO R IENT	SMA R TASS	STO R ABLE	WEA R ABLE	KBA R	WEA R
R EP R IEVE	SOB R IETY	STU R GEON	WEA R IEST	KEI R	WEE R
R EP R ISAL	SO R R IEST	SU R R OUND	WEA R IFUL	KIE R	WEI R
*R EPR OACH	SO R ROWE R	SU R R OYAL	WEI R DIES	KNA R	**WHI R**
R EPR OVAL	SOU R BALL	SWO R DMAN	*WHA R FAGE	KNU R	**WHO R**
R EPR OVE R	SOU R DINE	TA R R AGON	*WHE R EVE R	KYA R	**YEA R**
R ET R ENCH	SOU R NESS	TA R R A R IA	*WHI R R ING	LAI R	YI R R
R ET R IEVE	SOU R PUSS	TEA R AWAY	*WHO R EDOM	LEA R	YOU R
R ET R OACT	SOU R WOOD	TEA R DOWN	WHO R ESON	LEE R	BAKE R
R ET R OFIT	SOV R ANLY	TEA R D R OP	*YEA R BOOK	LEH R	BALE R
R ETR O R SE	SOV R ANTY	TEA R LESS	YEA R LIES	LIA R	BARE R
R EWR ITE R	SPA R ABLE	TE R R APIN	YEA R LING	LIE R	BASE R
R OA R IEST	SPA R E R IB	TE R R ELLA	YEA R LONG	LOU R	***BAZA R**
*R OO R BACK	SPA R KIE R	TE R R IFIC	YEA R NING	MAA R	**BEVO R**
R UN R OUND	*SPA R KILY	TET R ACID	YOU R SELF	MAI R	BIDE R
SAC R A R IA	*SPA R KISH	TET R AGON	BEA R	MOO R	**BIKE R**
SAC R ISTY	SPA R KLE R	TET R AME R	BEE R	MU R R	BITE R
SAF R ANIN	SPA R LIKE	TET R APOD	BIE R	NEA R	BLEA R
SAP R OPEL	SPA R LING	TET R A R CH	BI R R	NOI R	BLUE R
SAU R OPOD	SPA R R IE R	*TET R OXID	BLU R	PAI R	BOLA R
*SCA R CELY	SPA R R ING	THE R EFO R	BOA R	PA R R	BONE R
*SCA R CITY	SPA R SITY	THE R EMIN	BOO R	PEA R	BORE R
*SCA R FPIN	*SPE R MARY		B R R R	PEE R	**BOWE R**
SCA R IEST	SPE R MINE		BUH R	PIE R	BOXE R
SCA R IOSE	SPE R MOUS		BU R R	POO R	**BOYA R**
SCA R IOUS	SPI R ACLE			POU R	B R IA R
SCA R LESS					B R IE R

BUYE R	D R EA R	**HEWE R**	LUGE R	**POWE R**	SHEE R
CABE R	D R IE R	***HEXE R**	LUNA R	P R IE R	SHIE R
CAGE R	D R YE R	HIDE R	LU R E R	P R IO R	SHI R R
CANE R	DUPE R	**HIKE R**	MACE R	**P R YE R**	SHOE R
CAPE R	**FACE R**	HILA R	**MAJO R**	PULE R	**SHYE R**
CA R E R	FADE R	HI R E R	**MAKE R**	PU R E R	SIEU R
CATE R	**FAKE R**	**HOME R**	MALA R	**QUEE R**	SIKE R
CAVE R	FAKI R	HONE R	MANO R	R ACE R	SIMA R
CEDA R	***FAQI R**	HONO R	MASE R	R ADA R	SITA R
CEDE R	FA R E R	**HOPE R**	MATE R	R AKE R	SIVE R
CHAI R	FAVO R	**HOVE R**	**MAYO R**	R APE R	**SIZA R**
CHEE R	FEMU R	HUGE R	***MAZE R**	R A R E R	**SIZE R**
CHI R R	FETO R	**HUMO R**	METE R	R ASE R	SKIE R
CHOI R	FEUA R	**HYPE R**	MILE R	R ATE R	SKI R R
CHU R R	**FEVE R**	**JAGE R**	MIME R	R AVE R	SLIE R
CIDE R	**FIBE R**	**JAPE R**	MINE R	**R AZE R**	SMEA R
CIGA R	**FIFE R**	**JIBE R**	MINO R	**R AZO R**	SNEE R
CITE R	FILA R	***JIVE R**	MISE R	R EBA R	SOBE R
CLEA R	FILE R	***JOKE R**	MITE R	R ECU R	SOFA R
CLOU R	FINE R	**JU R O R**	**MIXE R**	R EFE R	SOLA R
CODE R	FI R E R	**KABA R**	MOLA R	R ICE R	SONA R
COLO R	**FIVE R**	**KAFI R**	MOPE R	R IDE R	SOPO R
COME R	***FIXE R**	**KEBA R**	MOTO R	R IGO R	SOWA R
COOE R	FLAI R	**KEFI R**	**MOVE R**	R IME R	SOWE R
COPE R	FLEE R	KITE R	**MOWE R**	R IPE R	SPEA R
CO R E R	FLIE R	KNAU R	MUCO R	R ISE R	SPEE R
COVE R	FLOU R	LABO R	MUSE R	R IVE R	SPEI R
COWE R	FLUO R	LACE R	MUTE R	R OGE R	SPIE R
C R IE R	**FLYE R**	LADE R	NADI R	R OPE R	SPOO R
C R UO R	**FOYE R**	LAGE R	NAME R	R OTO R	STAI R
CUBE R	F R EE R	LAKE R	NAVA R	R OVE R	STEE R
CU R E R	F R IA R	LAME R	NEVE R	R OWE R	STOU R
CYDE R	F R IE R	LASE R	NITE R	R ULE R	SUBE R
CYMA R	**F R YE R**	LATE R	NOTE R	R UMO R	SUDO R
DAMA R	**FUME R**	LAVE R	NUDE R	SABE R	SUGA R
DA R E R	FU R O R	LAYE R	PACE R	SABI R	SUPE R
DATE R	GAGE R	**LAZA R**	PAGE R	SAFE R	SU R E R
DEAI R	GAME R	LEGE R	PALE R	SAGE R	SWEA R
DEBA R	GAPE R	LEMU R	PAPE R	SAKE R	SWEE R
DEFE R	GATO R	LEPE R	PA R E R	SANE R	TABE R
DEMU R	***GAZA R**	LEVE R	PATE R	SAPO R	TABO R
DETE R	***GAZE R**	LIBE R	**PAVE R**	SATY R	TAKE R
DEWA R	GIBE R	LIDA R	**PAWE R**	SAVE R	TALA R
DICE R	GIVE R	LIFE R	**PAYE R**	SAVO R	TALE R
DIKE R	GLAI R	LIGE R	**PAYO R**	SAWE R	TAME R
DIME R	GLUE R	LIKE R	PETE R	SAYE R	TAPE R
DINA R	GNA R R	LINE R	**PIKE R**	SCAU R	TAPI R
DINE R	GOFE R	LITE R	PILA R	SCOU R	TATA R
DI R E R	GONE R	LIVE R	PIPE R	SEDE R	TATE R
DONO R	GULA R	LOBA R	PLIE R	SENO R	TAWE R
DOPE R	HALE R	LONE R	**PLYE R**	SE R E R	**TAXE R**
DOSE R	HATE R	LOPE R	**POKE R**	SEVE R	TENO R
DOTE R	**HAYE R**	LOSE R	POLA R	SEWA R	THEI R
DOWE R	***HAZE R**	LOVE R	POLE R	SEWE R	TIGE R
***DOZE R**	HEDE R	LOWE R	POSE R	SHEA R	TILE R

TIME R	BAITE R	**BOOKE R**	CANDO R	COLLA R	**DAMPE R**
TITE R	**BALKE R**	**BOOME R**	**CANKE R**	COLOU R	DANCE R
TOKE R	BALLER	*BOOZE R	CANNE R	COLTE R	DANDE R
TONE R	BANDE R	**BOPPE R**	CANTE R	**COMBE R**	DANGE R
TOPE R	BANGE R	BO R DE R	CANTO R	**CONCU R**	**DAPPE R**
TOTE R	**BANKE R**	BOSKE R	**CAPPE R**	CONDO R	DA R NE R
TOWE R	BANNE R	**BOTHE R**	**CAPTO R**	**CONFE R**	DA R TE R
TOYE R	**BA R BE R**	BOWLE R	CA R DE R	CONGE R	**DASHE R**
T R IE R	**BA R KE R**	BOWYE R	CA R EE R	**CONKE R**	DAUBE R
T R UE R	BA R TE R	*BOXCA R	CA R PE R	CONNE R	DEBTO R
TUBE R	**BASHE R**	*BOXIE R	CA R TE R	**COOKE R**	**DECKE R**
TUMO R	BASTE R	**B RACE R**	CA R VE R	COOLE R	**DEFIE R**
TUNE R	**BATHE R**	**B RAVE R**	CASTE R	**COOPE R**	DEICE R
TUTO R	BATTE R	**B RAYE R**	CASTO R	COOTE R	**DELVE R**
TUYE R	**BAWLE R**	*B RAZE R	CAUSE R	**COPIE R**	DENIE R
TWIE R	*BAZAA R	B REWE R	CAVIA R	**COPPE R**	DETOU R
TWYE R	**BEAKE R**	B RIBE R	CEILE R	**COPTE R**	DEVOI R
VALO R	BEA R E R	B RINE R	CELLA R	CO R DE R	**DEWIE R**
VAPO R	BEATE R	B ROKE R	CENSE R	**CO R KE R**	**DEXTE R**
VELA R	**BEAVE R**	**BUCKE R**	CENSO R	CO R NE R	DIALE R
*VEXE R	**BEDDE R**	**BUDDE R**	CENTE R	**COSHE R**	DIAPE R
VICA R	**BEEPE R**	**BUDGE R**	CHADA R	COSIE R	DIAPI R
VIGO R	*BEEZE R	**BUFFE R**	CHADO R	COSTA R	**DIBBE R**
VIPE R	**BEGGA R**	**BUGGE R**	**CHAFE R**	COSTE R	DICIE R
VISO R	BELIE R	BUGLE R	**CHASE R**	COTTA R	**DICKE R**
*VIZI R	BELTE R	BULGE R	**CHAWE R**	COTTE R	DIETE R
*VIZO R	BENDE R	BULGU R	**CHEDE R**	COUGA R	**DIFFE R**
VOLA R	BEST. R	**BUMME R**	**CHEWE R**	COUTE R	DIGGE R
VOME R	BETTE R	**BUMPE R**	**CHIDE R**	**COWIE R**	**DIMME R**
VOTE R	BETTO R	**BUNKE R**	CHIMA R	*COZIE R	DINGE R
VOWE R	*BEZOA R	BUNTE R	CHIME R	C R ATE R	DINNE R
WADE R	**BIBBE R**	BU R GE R	*CHOKE R	C R AVE R	**DIPPE R**
WAFE R	**BICKE R**	BU R IE R	**CHOLE R**	C R OWE R	DISBA R
WAGE R	**BIDDE R**	**BU R KE R**	*CHUKA R	CULLE R	**DITHE R**
WAKE R	**BIGGE R**	BU R LE R	CINDE R	**CULVE R**	**DOBBE R**
WALE R	**BILKE R**	BU R NE R	**CIPHE R**	**CUMBE R**	**DOCKE R**
WATE R	BILLE R	BU R RE R	**CITHE R**	**CUMME R**	DOCTO R
WAVE R	BINDE R	BU R SA R	**CLAMO R**	CUNNE R	DODDE R
*WAXE R	BINGE R	**BUSHE R**	**CLAVE R**	**CUPPE R**	DODGE R
WEBE R	BI R DE R	BUSIE R	**CLAWE R**	**CU R BE R**	**DOFFE R**
WHI R R	BI R LE R	**BUSKE R**	**CLEVE R**	CU R LE R	DOGEA R
WIDE R	BISTE R	BUSTE R	CLONE R	CU R SE R	DOGGE R
WIPE R	BITTE R	BUTLE R	CLOSE R	CU R SO R	DOLLA R
WI R E R	**BLAME R**	BUTTE R	**CLOVE R**	CUSSE R	DOLOU R
WISE R	*BLAZE R	*BUZZE R	COALE R	CUTLE R	*DOOZE R
WIVE R	**BLOWE R**	**CADGE R**	COATE R	CUTTE R	DOPIE R
WOOE R	BOATE R	CAESA R	*COAXE R	**CYCLE R**	DO R ME R
W R IE R	**BOBBE R**	CAGIE R	**COBBE R**	*CYPHE R	DO R PE R
YAGE R	BOILE R	**CAHIE R**	**COCKE R**	**DABBE R**	DO R SE R
ZONE R	BOLTE R	**CALCA R**	**CODDE R**	**DACKE R**	DOSSE R
BACKER	**BOMBE R**	**CALKE R**	**CODGE R**	DAGGE R	DOTIE R
BADGER	BONDE R	CALLE R	**COFFE R**	**DAIKE R**	DOTTE R
BAGGER	BONIE R	**CAMBE R**	**COHEI R**	**DAMMA R**	DOUSE R
BAILE R	*BONZE R	**CAMPE R**	COILE R	**DAMME R**	**DOWNE R**
BAILO R	BOOGE R	**CANCE R**	COINE R	DAMNE R	**DOWSE R**

*DOZIE R	FOAME R	GILDE R	HEALE R	*JAZZE R	LAPPE R
D RAPE R	FODDE R	GILLE R	HEA R E R	JEE R E R	LAPSE R
D RAWE R	FOETE R	GINGE R	HEAVE R	*JE R KE R	LA R DE R
D RIVE R	FOGGE R	GINNE R	HECTO R	JESTE R	LA R KE R
D R ONE R	FOLDE R	GIPPE R	HEDGE R	*JIBBE R	LASCA R
D ROVE R	FOLIA R	GI R DE R	HEEDE R	*JIGGE R	LASHE R
DUBBE R	FOOTE R	GLAMO R	HEELE R	JILTE R	LASTE R
DUCKE R	FO R CE R	*GLAZE R	HEFTE R	*JINKE R	LATHE R
DUELE R	FO R GE R	GLIDE R	HEIFE R	JITTE R	LATTE R
DUFFE R	FO R KE R	GLOVE R	HELLE R	*JOBBE R	LAUDE R
DUIKE R	FO R ME R	GLOWE R	HELPE R	*JOGGE R	LAVEE R
DUMPE R	FOSTE R	GNAWE R	HEMME R	JOINE R	LAWYE R
DUNNE R	FOWLE R	GOBBE R	HE R DE R	*JOKIE R	*LAZIE R
DU R BA R	*FOXIE R	GOFFE R	HILLE R	JOLTE R	LEADE R
DUSTE R	F R AME R	GOITE R	HINDE R	*JOSHE R	LEAKE R
DYVOU R	F R ATE R	GOLFE R	HINGE R	*JUDDE R	LEANE R
FABLE R	F R ILE R	GOOIE R	HIPPE R	*JUDGE R	LEAPE R
FACTO R	*F R IZE R	GOPHE R	HISSE R	*JUICE R	LEASE R
FAKEE R	FUELE R	GO R GE R	HITHE R	*JUMPE R	LEAVE R
FALLE R	FUH R E R	GO R IE R	*HOAXE R	JUNIO R	LECHE R
FALTE R	FULLE R	GOUGE R	HOGGE R	*JUNKE R	LECTO R
FANNE R	FULMA R	G R ATE R	HOMIE R	JUSTE R	LEDGE R
*FAQUI R	FUMIE R	G R AVE R	HONKE R	*KAFFI R	LEKVA R
FA R CE R	FUNKE R	*G R AZE R	HONOU R	KAISE R	LENDE R
FA R ME R	FUNNE R	G R IME R	HOOFE R	KANTA R	LESSE R
FATHE R	FU R FU R	G R OCE R	HOOPE R	KASHE R	LETTE R
FATTE R	FU R LE R	G R OPE R	HOO R O R	KEENE R	LEVIE R
FAVOU R	FUSSE R	G R OWE R	HOOTE R	KEEPE R	LIBBE R
FAWNE R	GABBE R	GUIDE R	HO R R O R	KEGLE R	LICKE R
FEA R E R	GADDE R	GUITA R	HOSIE R	KELTE R	LICTO R
FEEDE R	GAFFE R	GULPE R	HOTTE R	*KICKE R	LIFTE R
FEELE R	GAGGE R	GUMME R	HOWLE R	KIDDE R	LIMBE R
FELLE R	GAINE R	GUNNE R	HUGGE R	KILLE R	LIMIE R
FENCE R	GAITE R	GUSHE R	HULLE R	KILTE R	LIMME R
FENDE R	GAMBI R	GUTTE R	HUMME R	KIPPE R	LIMNE R
FE R VO R	GAMME R	GYPPE R	HUMOU R	KISSE R	LIMPE R
FESTE R	GANDE R	*HACKE R	HUNGE R	KNIFE R	LINEA R
FETTE R	GANGE R	HAFTE R	HUNKE R	KNOWE R	LINGE R
FIBBE R	GAOLE R	HAILE R	HUNTE R	KOSHE R	LINIE R
FILLE R	GA R NE R	HALTE R	HU R LE R	K R ATE R	LINKE R
FILME R	GA R TE R	HAMME R	HU R TE R	K R ONO R	LINTE R
FILTE R	GASPE R	HAMPE R	HUSKE R	K R ONU R	LIPPE R
FINDE R	GASSE R	HANGA R	HUSSA R	KULTU R	*LIQUO R
FINGE R	GASTE R	HANGE R	*JABBE R	LAAGE R	LISPE R
FI R ME R	GATHE R	HANKE R	*JACKE R	LABOU R	LISTE R
FISHE R	GAUGE R	HA R BO R	JAEGE R	LACIE R	LITTE R
FITTE R	GAWKE R	HA R KE R	*JAGGE R	LACKE R	LIVIE R
*FIZZE R	GAWPE R	HA R ME R	JAGUA R	LADDE R	LIVYE R
FLAKE R	*GEEZE R	HA R PE R	JAEGE R	LADLE R	LOADE R
FLAME R	GELDE R	HATTE R	*JAGGE R	LAGGE R	LOAFE R
FLAVO R	GENDE R	HAULE R	JAGUA R	LAMBE R	LOANE R
FLAYE R	GETTE R	HAVIO R	JAILE R	LANCE R	LOBBE R
*FLEXO R	GEYSE R	*HAWKE R	JAILO R	LANDE R	LOCKE R
FLOWE R	GIAOU R	HAWSE R	*JAMME R	LANGU R	LODGE R
FLUTE R	GIBBE R	HEADE R	*JASPE R	LANNE R	LOGGE R

LOGIE R	MIDAI R	**NICKE R**	**PILFE R**	PULSE R	R EPOU R
LOITE R	**MILKE R**	**NIFFE R**	PINDE R	**PUMPE R**	R ESTE R
LOLLE R	MILLE R	**NIPPE R**	PINGE R	PUNIE R	R ETEA R
LONGE R	MILTE R	NOBLE R	PINIE R	**PUNKE R**	R HETO R
LOOKE R	**MIMBA R**	NODDE R	**PINKE R**	PUNNE R	**R HYME R**
LOOPE R	**MINCE R**	NONPA R	PINNE R	PUNTE R	**R IBBE R**
LOOSE R	MINDE R	NONWA R	**PIPIE R**	PU R GE R	R IBIE R
LOOTE R	MINTE R	NOOSE R	PITIE R	PU R SE R	R IDDE R
LOPPE R	MIOLE R	NOSHE R	**PLACE R**	**PUSHE R**	R IEVE R
LOPTE R	MI R IE R	NOSIE R	PLANA R	PUTTE R	R IFLE R
LOUVE R	MI R RO R	NOTHE R	PLANE R	*QINDA R	R IGGE R
LUBBE R	MISTE R	NUDGE R	PLATE R	*QINTA R	R IGOU R
LUGGE R	**MITHE R**	**NUMBE R**	**PLAYE R**	*QUAKE R	R IMIE R
LUMBA R	MITIE R	NU R SE R	*PLEXO R	*QUASA R	**R IMME R**
LUMBE R	MOANE R	NUTTE R	**PLOVE R**	*QUAVE R	R INGE R
LUMPE R	**MOBBE R**	**PACKE R**	**PLOWE R**	*QUEUE R	R INSE R
LUNGE R	**MOCKE R**	**PADDE R**	POISE R	*QUIVE R	R IOTE R
LUNIE R	**MOHAI R**	PALIE R	**POKIE R**	*QUOTE R	**R IPPE R**
LUNKE R	MOLDE R	PALLO R	POLDE R	R ACIE R	**R ISKE R**
LU R KE R	MOLTE R	**PALMA R**	POLLE R	**R ACKE R**	R ITTE R
LUSTE R	**MOMSE R**	**PALME R**	PONDE R	R AFTE R	R OAME R
MAFTI R	*MOMZE R	PALTE R	**POPLA R**	R AIDE R	R OARE R
*MAHZO R	MONGE R	**PAMPE R**	**POPPE R**	R AILE R	**R OBBE R**
MAILE R	MOOTE R	PANDE R	**PO R KE R**	R AISE R	**R OCKE R**
MAIME R	**MOPIE R**	PANIE R	PO R TE R	**R AMME R**	R OLFE R
MAMME R	**MOPPE R**	*PANZE R	POSEU R	R ANCO R	R OLLE R
MANGE R	MO R TA R	**PA R KE R**	POSTE R	R ANGE R	**R OMPE R**
MANNE R	MOSSE R	PA R LO R	**POTHE R**	**R ANKE R**	R OOFE R
MAPPE R	**MOTHE R**	PA R SE R	POTTE R	R ANTE R	R OOME R
MA R KE R	MOUSE R	PASSE R	*POTZE R	R APIE R	R OOSE R
MA R RE R	**MUCKE R**	PASTE R	POU R E R	**R APPE R**	R OOTE R
MA R TY R	**MUDDE R**	PASTO R	POUTE R	R APTO R	R OPIE R
MASHE R	**MUGGA R**	PATTE R	POWDE R	R ASHE R	R OSIE R
MASKE R	**MUGGE R**	*PATZE R	POWTE R	R ASPE R	R OSTE R
MASTE R	**MUGGU R**	**PAUPE R**	P R ATE R	R ASTE R	R OTTE R
MATTE R	MULLE R	PAUSE R	**P R AYE R**	R ATHE R	R OUSE R
MAUGE R	**MUMME R**	**PAVIO R**	P R EFE R	R ATTE R	R OUTE R
MAULE R	**MUMPE R**	PAWNE R	P R ETO R	R EADE R	**R UBBE R**
*MAZIE R	MU R DE R	PAWNO R	**P R EWA R**	R EAME R	R UBIE R
MEAGE R	**MU R MU R**	**PECKE R**	**P R EYE R**	R EAPE R	R UDDE R
MEANE R	**MUSHE R**	PEDLA R	**P R ICE R**	R EARE R	R UGGE R
MEDLA R	MUSTE R	PEDLE R	**P R IME R**	R EAVE R	R UINE R
MEETE R	MUTTE R	PEELE R	*P R IZE R	R ECTO R	**R UMME R**
MELDE R	NAGGE R	**PEEPE R**	**P R OBE R**	R EDDE R	R UMOU R
MELTE R	NAILE R	PELLA R	**P R OPE R**	R EDEA R	R UNNE R
MEMBE R	**NAPPE R**	PELTE R	P R OSE R	R EEFE R	R USHE R
MEMOI R	NATTE R	PENCE R	**P R OVE R**	**R EEKE R**	**SACKE R**
MENDE R	**NECKE R**	PENNE R	**P R OWA R**	R EELE R	SAGGA R
MENHI R	NECTA R	**PEPPE R**	P R UNE R	R EGEA R	SAGGE R
MENTO R	NEEDE R	PESTE R	**PSYWA R**	R EHEA R	SAGIE R
ME R CE R	NESTE R	PETTE R	**PUCKE R**	R EIVE R	SAILE R
ME R GE R	NESTO R	**PEWTE R**	**PUFFE R**	R ELIE R	SAILO R
METEO R	NETHE R	**PHYLA R**	PULLE R	R ENDE R	SALTE R
METIE R	NETTE R	**PICKE R**	**PULPE R**	R ENTE R	SALVE R
MEWLE R	NEUTE R	**PIECE R**	PULSA R	R EPAI R	SALVO R

SAMBA R	SHMEA R	SOWCA R	TEASE R	T R OVE R	WANDE R
SAMBU R	SHOFA R	SPACE R	TEDDE R	TUBBE R	WANIE R
SANDE R	SHOVE R	SPADE R	TEEME R	TUCKE R	WANNE R
SANGA R	SHOWE R	SPA R E R	TEENE R	TUFTE R	WANTE R
SANGE R	SHOWE R	SPEWE R	TEETE R	TUGGE R	WANTE R
SANSA R	SIDDU R	SPICE R	TELFE R	TUMOU R	WA R DE R
SANTI R	SIDLE R	SPIDE R	TELLE R	TU R GO R	WA R IE R
SANTU R	SIFTE R	SPIKE R	TEMPE R	TU R NE R	WA R ME R
SAPOU R	SIGHE R	SPINO R	TENDE R	TUSKE R	WA R NE R
SAPPE R	SIGNE R	SP R IE R	TENNE R	TUSSA R	WA R PE R
SA R DAR	SIGNO R	STAGE R	TENOU R	TUSSE R	WASHE R
SA R SA R	SILLE R	STA R E R	TENSO R	TUSSO R	WASTE R
SA R TO R	SILVE R	STATE R	TENTE R	TUSSU R	WATTE R
SAUCE R	SIMME R	STATO R	TE R ME R	TWINE R	WAVIE R
SAUGE R	SIMPE R	STAYE R	TE R MO R	TWOFE R	*WAXIE R
SAVIO R	SINGE R	STIVE R	TE R RO R	TYPIE R	WEANE R
SAVOU R	SINKE R	STOKE R	TESTE R	*VALKY R	WEA R E R
SAWYE R	SINNE R	STONE R	TETHE R	VALOU R	WEAVE R
SCALA R	SINTE R	STOPE R	TETTE R	VALUE R	WEDDE R
SCALE R	SIPPE R	STOVE R	THALE R	VALVA R	WEEDE R
SCA R E R	SI R DA R	STUPO R	THAWE R	VAMPE R	WEEPE R
SCO R E R	SISTE R	STYLA R	THENA R	VANNE R	WEEVE R
SCOTE R	SITTE R	STYLE R	TICKE R	VAPOU R	WEINE R
SEALE R	*SIZIE R	SUBPA R	TIDIE R	VA R IE R	WELDE R
SEAME R	SKATE R	SUCCO R	TILLE R	VEALE R	WELDO R
SEA R E R	SKEWE R	SUCKE R	TILTE R	VECTO R	WELTE R
SEATE R	SKIVE R	SUDSE R	TIMBE R	VEILE R	WESTE R
SECPA R	SLAKE R	SUFFE R	TINDE R	VEINE R	WETHE R
SECTO R	SLATE R	SUITE R	TINIE R	VELOU R	WETTE R
SEEDE R	SLAVE R	SUITO R	TINKE R	VENDE R	WHALE R
SEEKE R	SLAYE R	SULFU R	TINNE R	VENDO R	WHINE R
SEEME R	SLICE R	SULKE R	TINTE R	VENEE R	WHITE R
SEGGA R	SLIDE R	SUMME R	TIPPE R	VENTE R	*WICKE R
SEINE R	SLIVE R	SUPPE R	TITFE R	VE R GE R	WIDDE R
SEISE R	SLOPE R	SU R FE R	TITHE R	VE R IE R	WIENE R
SEISO R	SMILE R	SU R GE R	TITTE R	VE R SE R	WILDE R
*SEIZE R	SMITE R	SUTLE R	TOCHE R	VESPE R	WILIE R
*SEIZO R	SMOKE R	SWAGE R	TOILE R	VETOE R	WILLE R
SELLE R	SNA R E R	SWAYE R	TOLLE R	VIATO R	WINCE R
SENDE R	SNIPE R	SYPHE R	TONGE R	VICTO R	WINDE R
SENHO R	SNO R E R	TABOU R	TONNE R	VIEWE R	WINGE R
SENIO R	SOAKE R	TACKE R	TOOLE R	VIGOU R	WINIE R
SENSO R	SOA R E R	TAGGE R	TOOTE R	VINIE R	WINKE R
SE R VE R	SOBBE R	TAILE R	TOPPE R	*VIZIE R	WINNE R
SETTE R	SOCCE R	TAILO R	TO R PO R	VOICE R	WINTE R
SEXIE R	SOEVE R	TALKE R	TOSSE R	VOIDE R	WI R IE R
SHADE R	SOLDE R	TAMBU R	TOTHE R	VOYEU R	WISHE R
SHAKE R	SOLVE R	TAMPE R	TOTTE R	VULGA R	WITHE R
SHAPE R	SOMBE R	TANKE R	TOU R E R	WADDE R	WOLFE R
SHA R E R	SONDE R	TANNE R	TOUTE R	WAFTE R	WOLVE R
SHAVE R	SOONE R	TAPPE R	T R ACE R	WAGGE R	WONDE R
SHEWE R	SO R DO R	TA R TA R	T R ADE R	WAILE R	WONNE R
SHIKA R	SO R NE R	TASTE R	T R EMO R	WAITE R	WOOFE R
SHINE R	SO R TE R	TATTE R	T R IME R	WAIVE R	WOOLE R
SHIVE R	SOUTE R	TEA R E R	T R OCA R	WALKE R	WO R ME R

WORSER	BILAYER	*BRAZIER	CAULKER	CLAVIER	COURTER
WOWSER	BIPOLAR	BREAKER	CAVILER	CLEANER	COVERER
WRITER	BITTIER	BREEDER	CENTAUR	CLEARER	COVETER
WUTHER	BLABBER	BREVIER	CENTNER	CLEAVER	*COZENER
*XYSTER	BLADDER	BRIDLER	*CHAFFER	*CLICKER	CRABBER
YABBER	BLASTER	BRIEFER	*CHAMBER	CLIMBER	*CRACKER
*YAKKER	BLATHER	BRIMMER	*CHAMFER	CLINGER	CRADLER
YAMMER	BLATTER	BRINGER	*CHAMPER	CLINKER	CRAMMER
YAPPER	BLEATER	BRINIER	CHANGER	CLIPPER	CRAPPER
YARNER	BLEEDER	BROIDER	CHANTER	CLOBBER	CRASHER
YATTER	BLENDER	BROILER	CHANTOR	*CLOCKER	CRAWLER
YAUPER	BLESSER	*BRONZER	CHAPTER	CLOGGER	CREAMER
YAWNER	BLETHER	BROODER	CHARGER	CLOUTER	CREASER
YAWPER	BLINDER	BROTHER	CHARIER	CLOWDER	CREATOR
YELLER	BLINKER	BROWSER	CHARMER	CLUBBER	CREEPER
YELPER	BLISTER	BRUISER	CHARTER	CLUMBER	CRIBBER
YESTER	BLITHER	BRUITER	CHATTER	CLUNKER	CRIMMER
YODLER	BLOATER	BRUSHER	*CHAUFER	CLYSTER	CRIMPER
YONDER	*BLOCKER	BUBBLER	CHEATER	COACHER	CRINGER
YONKER	BLOOMER	*BUCKLER	*CHECKER	COACTOR	CRISPER
YOWLER	BLOOPER	*BUFFIER	CHEDDAR	COALIER	CRITTER
*ZAFFAR	BLOTTER	BUGBEAR	CHEERER	COASTER	CRITTUR
*ZAFFER	BLOWIER	BUILDER	*CHEQUER	COBBIER	CROAKER
*ZAFFIR	BLUBBER	BULLIER	CHIGGER	COBBLER	CROFTER
*ZANDER	BLUCHER	BUMBLER	CHILLER	COCHAIR	CROONER
*ZANIER	BLUDGER	BUNDLER	*CHIPPER	*COCKIER	CROPPER
*ZAPPER	*BLUFFER	BUNGLER	CHIRPER	CODDLER	CROSIER
*ZEPHYR	BLUNDER	BURBLER	CHITTER	COERCER	CROSSER
*ZESTER	BLUNGER	BURGHER	*CHOMPER	COHERER	CROWBAR
*ZINGER	BLURTER	BURGLAR	CHOOSER	COINFER	CROWDER
*ZIPPER	BLUSHER	BURRIER	*CHOPPER	COINTER	CROWNER
*ZITHER	BLUSTER	BURSTER	CHOUSER	COLLIER	*CROZIER
*ZOSTER	BOARDER	BUSHIER	*CHOWDER	COLORER	CRUISER
BABBLER	BOASTER	BUSTIER	CHUDDAR	*COMAKER	CRULLER
*BAFFLER	BOGGIER	BUTCHER	CHUDDER	COMPEER	CRUMBER
BAHADUR	BOGGLER	BYLINER	CHUGGER	CONIFER	CRUPPER
BARRIER	BOLIVAR	*CACKLER	*CHUKKAR	CONINER	CRUSHER
BASILAR	BOLSTER	CADAVER	CHUNTER	*CONQUER	CUDBEAR
BATCHER	BOODLER	*CAJOLER	CHURNER	CONTOUR	CUDDLER
BATTIER	BOOKIER	CALAMAR	CIRCLER	CORKIER	CUPELER
BATTLER	BOOMIER	CALIBER	CITATOR	CORNIER	CUPULAR
BAWDIER	BOOSTER	CALIPER	CLABBER	CORONER	CURATOR
BEADIER	BOSSIER	CALOYER	*CLACKER	CORSAIR	CURDIER
BEAMIER	BOTCHER	*CAMPHOR	CLAIMER	CORULER	CURDLER
BEEFIER	BOTTLER	CAMPIER	CLAMBER	COTTIER	CURRIER
BEETLER	BOUDOIR	CANDLER	CLAMMER	COUCHER	CUSHIER
*BEHAVER	BOULDER	CANDOUR	CLAMOUR	COUGHER	CUTOVER
BELABOR	BOUNCER	CANNIER	CLAMPER	COULOIR	DABBLER
BELCHER	BOUNDER	CAPERER	CLANGER	COULTER	DABSTER
BENCHER	BOWLDER	CAROLER	CLAPPER	COUNTER	DALLIER
BESCOUR	BRAGGER	CARRIER	*CLAQUER	COUPLER	DAMAGER
BESMEAR	BRANDER	CASHIER	CLASHER	COURIER	DANDIER
BEVELER	BRANNER	CATCHER	CLASPER	COURSER	DANDLER
BICOLOR	BRASIER	CATERER	CLASSER		DANGLER
BIFILAR	BRAWLER	CATTIER	CLATTER		DANSEUR

DASHIE R	DOUCEU R	FLANGE R	GAMBIE R	G ROUPE R	HOODIE R
DAUNDE R	DOWAGE R	FLANKE R	GAMBLE R	G ROUSE R	HO R NIE R
DAUNTE R	DOWNIE R	FLAPPE R	GAMMIE R	G ROUTE R	HO R SIE R
DAYSTA R	D RAFTE R	FLASHE R	GA R BLE R	G ROWLE R	HOSTLE R
*DAZZLE R	D RAGGE R	FLATCA R	GA R GLE R	G RUBBE R	HOTSPU R
DEBATE R	D R AINE R	FLATTE R	GA R OTE R	G RUDGE R	HOUNDE R
DEBONE R	D RAWBA R	FLAVOU R	GAUFFE R	G RUELE R	HOVE R E R
DECAYE R	D RAWLE R	FLEECE R	*GAWKIE R	G RUMME R	*HOWEVE R
DECIDE R	D R EAME R	FLENSE R	GEMMIE R	G RUNTE R	HUDDLE R
DECODE R	D R EDGE R	FLESHE R	GENITO R	GUA R DE R	HUMBLE R
DECOLO R	D R ESSE R	*FLICKE R	GE R MIE R	GUILDE R	HUMIDO R
DECOYE R	D R IFTE R	FLINDE R	GIGGLE R	GULFIE R	HU R DLE R
DEC R EE R	D R ILLE R	FLINGE R	GIMPIE R	GUMMIE R	HU R R IE R
DEC R IE R	D R INKE R	FLIPPE R	GI R DLE R	GUSTIE R	HUSKIE R
DEFACE R	D R IPPE R	FLOUTE R	GLACIE R	GUTTIE R	HUSTLE R
DEFAME R	D R OPPE R	FLUBBE R	GLADDE R	GUTTLE R	*JACAMA R
DEFILE R	D R OWNE R	FLUNKE R	GLADIE R	*GUZZLE R	*JANGLE R
DEFINE R	D R UBBE R	FLUSHE R	GLAMOU R	GYPSTE R	JANITO R
DEIFIE R	D RUDGE R	FLUSTE R	GLANCE R	GY R ATO R	*JEMADA R
DELAYE R	D RUMME R	FLUTIE R	*GLAZIE R	*HACKLE R	*JEMIDA R
DELIVE R	DUCKIE R	FLUTTE R	GLEAME R	HAGGLE R	JETTIE R
DELUDE R	DUELLE R	*FLYOVE R	GLEANE R	HAI R IE R	*JEWELE R
DENUDE R	DUMPIE R	FLYTIE R	GLIMME R	HAMMIE R	*JINGLE R
DEPOSE R	DUSTIE R	FOAMIE R	GLISTE R	HAMSTE R	*JOCULA R
DE R IDE R	DWELLE R	FOCUSE R	GLITTE R	HANAPE R	*JODHPU R
DE R IVE R	FABULA R	FONDLE R	GLOATE R	HANDCA R	*JOGGLE R
DE R NIE R	FADDIE R	FOOTIE R	GLOSSE R	HANDIE R	JOINDE R
DESI R E R	FAGOTE R	FOOTLE R	GOBBLE R	HANDLE R	JOINTE R
DESPAI R	FAINTE R	*FOOZLE R	GODLIE R	HA R BOU R	JOLLIE R
DESUGA R	FAITOU R	FO R AGE R	GOGGLE R	HA R DIE R	JOSTLE R
DEVISE R	FANCIE R	FO R AYE R	G RABBE R	HA R R IE R	JOUSTE R
DEVISO R	FA R CEU R	FO R BEA R	G RAFTE R	*HATCHE R	*JUGGLE R
DEWATE R	FA R R IE R	FO R EVE R	G R AINE R	HAULIE R	*JUGULA R
DIASTE R	FA R THE R	FO R GOE R	G RAMMA R	HAUNTE R	*JUMBLE R
DIBBLE R	FATTIE R	FO R KIE R	G RANGE R	HAUTEU R	*JUNIPE R
DICTIE R	FAVO R E R	FOUNDE R	G RANTE R	HAVIOU R	*KASHMI R
DIDDLE R	FEASTE R	F RACTU R	G RANTO R	HEADIE R	*KAYAKE R
DIESTE R	FEATHE R	F RANKE R	G RAPIE R	HEATHE R	KEESTE R
DIETHE R	FEIGNE R	*F R EEZE R	G RASPE R	HEAVIE R	KEGELE R
DILATE R	FELSPA R	F RETTE R	*G R AZIE R	*HECKLE R	KEISTE R
DILATO R	*FEOFFE R	F RISEU R	G REASE R	HEISTE R	KEYSTE R
DILUTE R	*FEOFFO R	F RISKE R	G REETE R	HEMPIE R	*KHADDA R
DILUTO R	FE R VOU R	F RITTE R	G RIDDE R	HE R BIE R	*KICKIE R
DIMETE R	*FETCHE R	*F R IZZE R	G RIEVE R	HE R ITO R	KIESTE R
DINKIE R	FIDDLE R	F ROWNE R	G RIFTE R	HILLIE R	KILOBA R
DIOPTE R	FIELDE R	F R UITE R	G RILLE R	HIPPIE R	KINDLE R
DISHIE R	FIGHTE R	FUEH R E R	G RIMIE R	HIPSTE R	*KLEZME R
DITCHE R	FIGU R E R	FUMBLE R	G RIMME R	*HITCHE R	KLISTE R
DIVIDE R	*FILCHE R	FUNCTO R	G RINDE R	HOA R DE R	*KNACKE R
DIVINE R	FILMIE R	FUNFAI R	G RINNE R	HOA R IE R	*KNAPPE R
DIVISO R	FINNIE R	FU R R IE R	G RIPPE R	HOBBLE R	KNEADE R
DONATO R	FISHIE R	FU R THE R	G ROANE R	HOISTE R	KNEELE R
DOSSIE R	FLAGGE R	GABBIE R	G ROOME R	HOLSTE R	KNITTE R
DOTTIE R	FLAMIE R	GABBLE R	G ROOVE R	HOMAGE R	*KNOCKE R
DOUBLE R	FLANEU R	GAGSTE R	G ROSSE R	HONO R E R	KNOLLE R

KNOTTE R	*LYNCHE R	MONSTE R	PAPE R E R	*PLUCKE R	*PUZZLE R
KOTOWE R	MACABE R	MOOCHE R	PAPPIE R	PLUGGE R	*QUAFFE R
*K R EUZE R	*MACHZO R	MOONIE R	PA R ADE R	PLUMBE R	*QUA R TE R
*K R IMME R	MADDIE R	MOO R IE R	PA R ADO R	PLUMIE R	*QUASHE R
K R ULLE R	MALODO R	MOSSIE R	PA R CEU R	PLUMPE R	*QUELLE R
LABELE R	MALSTE R	MOTTLE R	PA R DNE R	PLUNDE R	*QUE R IE R
LABO R E R	MANAGE R	MOULDE R	PA R LOU R	PLUNGE R	*QUESTE R
LACUNA R	MANGIE R	MOULTE R	PA R TIE R	PLUNKE R	*QUESTO R
LAMBIE R	MANGLE R	MOUNTE R	PA R TNE R	POACHE R	*QUIETE R
LAMSTE R	MANU R E R	MOU R NE R	PA R TYE R	POINTE R	*QUILTE R
LANDLE R	MA R BLE R	MOUSIE R	PASTIE R	POLYME R	*QUINTA R
LANGUO R	MA R CHE R	MOUTHE R	PATAMA R	POPOVE R	*QUIPPE R
LA R DIE R	MA R INE R	*MUCKIE R	PATCHE R	POPULA R	*QUITTE R
LA R KIE R	*MA R KHO R	MUDDIE R	PAVIOU R	PO R KIE R	*QUITTO R
LASHKA R	MA R LIE R	MUDDLE R	PAVISE R	POSTWA R	*QUIZZE R
LASSOE R	MA R R IE R	*MUFFLE R	PEACHE R	POTTIE R	R ABBLE R
LATHIE R	*MASQUE R	MUGGIE R	PEAKIE R	POULTE R	R AFFLE R
LAUGHE R	MASSEU R	MUMBLE R	PEA R LE R	POUNCE R	R AILCA R
LAUNDE R	MASSIE R	MUNSTE R	PEDDLE R	POUNDE R	R AINIE R
LAYOVE R	MATADO R	MU R THE R	PENSTE R	P R AETO R	R ALLIE R
LEACHE R	MATCHE R	MUSKIE R	PEOPLE R	P R AISE R	R AMBLE R
LEADIE R	MAUNDE R	*MUZZIE R	PE R CHE R	P R ANCE R	R AMMIE R
LEAFIE R	MEALIE R	*MUZZLE R	PE R USE R	P R AWNE R	R ANCHE R
LEAGUE R	MEANDE R	*MYNHEE R	PETTIE R	P R EAVE R	R ANCOU R
LEA R IE R	MEATIE R	NEEDIE R	PHILTE R	P R EENE R	R ANDIE R
LEA R NE R	MEDDLE R	NEEDLE R	PHONIE R	P R EMIE R	R ATTIE R
LEATHE R	MEGABA R	NEGATO R	*PIAFFE R	P R ESSO R	R ATTLE R
LEGATO R	MENACE R	NEITHE R	PIASTE R	P R ESTE R	R AVAGE R
LEGGIE R	MESHIE R	NE R VIE R	PICADO R	P R ICIE R	R AVELE R
LEISTE R	MESSIE R	NESTLE R	*PICKEE R	*P R ICKE R	R AVENE R
LEVATO R	METAME R	NETTIE R	*PICKIE R	P R IMME R	R EACHE R
LEVELE R	MIDDLE R	NETTLE R	PIDDLE R	P R INKE R	R EACTO R
LIBELE R	MIDYEA R	NEWSIE R	PIE R CE R	P R INTE R	R EADIE R
LIGHTE R	MILKIE R	NIBBLE R	PIGGIE R	P R IVIE R	R EALGA R
LIMBIE R	MILLIE R	NIPPIE R	PILSNE R	P R OCTO R	R EALTE R
LIMITE R	MINGIE R	NOBBIE R	PINCHE R	P R ODDE R	R EBATE R
LINGIE R	MINGLE R	NOBBLE R	PIONEE R	*P R OFFE R	R EBUKE R
LINTIE R	MINICA R	NONPOO R	PISSOI R	P R OGGE R	R ECITE R
*LIQUEU R	MINIVE R	NONUSE R	PITCHE R	P R OOFE R	R ECOLO R
LIVENE R	MINSTE R	NO R THE R	PLAGUE R	P R OSIE R	R ECOVE R
LOATHE R	MI R ADO R	NOTCHE R	PLAITE R	P R OSPE R	R EDUCE R
LOBBYE R	MISAVE R	NOTICE R	PLANNE R	P R OWLE R	R EEDIE R
LOBSTE R	MISDOE R	NUBBIE R	PLANTA R	PSALTE R	R EENTE R
LOCATE R	MISHEA R	NUCLEA R	PLASHE R	PUDDLE R	R EFINE R
LOCATO R	MISTIE R	*NUZZLE R	PLASTE R	PUELLE R	R EFUSE R
LOCULA R	MISUSE R	PADDLE R	PLATTE R	PUGGIE R	R EFUTE R
LOFTIE R	MITE R E R	PAINTE R	PLEADE R	PUMICE R	R EGALE R
LO R IME R	MOBSTE R	PALAVE R	PLEASE R	PUNCHE R	R EGULA R
LO R INE R	MODELE R	PALIKA R	PLEATE R	PUNSTE R	R EIFIE R
LUCIFE R	MODULA R	PALLIE R	PLEDGE R	PUPILA R	R EINCU R
LUNCHE R	MOLDIE R	PALMIE R	PLEDGO R	PU R SIE R	R EINTE R
LUPANA R	MONEYE R	PANDOO R	PLESSO R	PU R SUE R	R ELATE R
LU R CHE R	MONIKE R	PANDOU R	PLINKE R	PUSHIE R	R ELATO R
LUSTIE R	MONITO R	PANNIE R	PLODDE R	PUSSIE R	R ELAXE R
LUTHIE R	MONOME R	PANTHE R	PLOTTE R	PUTTIE R	R ELAXO R

R EMAKE R	SAMBHA R	SETTLO R	SLACKE R	SPANNE R	STEPPE R
R EMOVE R	SAMBHU R	SHADIE R	SLAMME R	SPA R GE R	STE R TO R
R ENEWE R	SAMOVA R	SHAKIE R	SLANDE R	SPA R KE R	STICKE R
R ENTIE R	SAMPLE R	SHALIE R	SLAPPE R	SPATTE R	STIFLE R
R EOCCU R	SANDBA R	SHAMME R	SLATIE R	SPAWNE R	STINGE R
R EOFFE R	SANDBU R	SHA R KE R	SLEDDE R	SPEAKE R	STINKE R
R EO R DE R	SANDIE R	SHA R PE R	SLEEPE R	SPEA R E R	STINTE R
R EPAPE R	SANTOU R	SHATTE R	SLENDE R	SPECTE R	STI R R E R
R EPINE R	SASSIE R	SHEA R E R	SLICKE R	SPEEDE R	STOCKE R
R EPLIE R	SAUNTE R	SHEDDE R	SLIMIE R	SPELLE R	STOMPE R
R EPOSE R	SAUTOI R	SHEETE R	SLIMME R	SPELTE R	STONIE R
R EPOWE R	SAVIOU R	SHELLE R	SLINGE R	SPENCE R	STOOKE R
R ESCUE R	SAVO R E R	SHELTE R	SLIPPE R	SPENDE R	STOOPE R
R ESIDE R	SCALIE R	SHELVE R	SLITHE R	SPICIE R	STOPPE R
R ESUME R	SCALPE R	*SHICKE R	SLOBBE R	SPIELE R	ST R AFE R
R ETAKE R	SCAMPE R	SHIFTE R	SLOGGE R	SPILLE R	ST R AYE R
R ETI R E R	SCANNE R	*SHIKKE R	SLUBBE R	SPINIE R	ST R EWE R
R EUTTE R	SCA R IE R	SHIMME R	SLUGGE R	SPINNE R	ST R IDE R
R EVELE R	SCA R PE R	SHINIE R	SLUMBE R	SPI R IE R	ST R IDO R
R EVE R E R	SCATTE R	SHIPPE R	SLUMME R	SPITTE R	ST R IKE R
R EVILE R	SCAUPE R	SHI R KE R	*SMACKE R	SPLICE R	ST R IPE R
R EVISE R	SCEPTE R	*SHOCKE R	SMASHE R	SPOILE R	ST R IVE R
R EVISO R	SCHEME R	SHOOTE R	SMATTE R	SPONGE R	ST R OKE R
R EVIVE R	SCHMEA R	*SHOPHA R	SMEA R E R	SPOOFE R	ST R OYE R
R EVOKE R	SCHMEE R	SHOPPE R	SMELLE R	SPO R TE R	STUDIE R
R IBBIE R	SCHOLA R	SHOUTE R	SMELTE R	SPOUTE R	STUFFE R
R IDDLE R	SCISSO R	SHOWIE R	SMI R KE R	SP R AYE R	STUIVE R
R IDGIE R	*SCOFFE R	SH R IVE R	SMOLDE R	SPUDDE R	STUMPE R
R IFFLE R	SCOLDE R	*SHUCKE R	SMOTHE R	SPUMIE R	STUNNE R
R IGHTE R	SCOOPE R	SHUDDE R	SNAPPE R	SPU R NE R	STUTTE R
R IPPLE R	SCOOTE R	SHUNNE R	SNA R LE R	SPUTTE R	SUBADA R
R IVETE R	SCO R NE R	SHUNTE R	SNEAKE R	*SQUALO R	SUBALA R
R OASTE R	SCOU R E R	SHUTTE R	SNEE R E R	*SQUA R E R	SUBDUE R
R OCKIE R	SCOUTE R	SHYSTE R	*SNEEZE R	STABBE R	SUCCOU R
R OISTE R	SCOWDE R	SIDEBA R	SNICKE R	STABLE R	SUCKLE R
R OOSTE R	SCOWLE R	SIDECA R	SNIFFE R	STACKE R	SULPHU R
R OOTIE R	SC R APE R	SIGHTE R	SNIFTE R	STAFFE R	SUMPTE R
R OTATO R	SC R EWE R	SIGNIO R	SNIGGE R	STAGGE R	SU R FIE R
R OTIFE R	SC R IBE R	SILKIE R	SNIPPE R	STAGIE R	SWABBE R
R OUGHE R	SCULKE R	SIMILA R	SNOOKE R	STAINE R	SWAGGE R
R OUNDE R	SCULLE R	SIMITA R	SNOOPE R	STALKE R	SWAMPE R
R OUSTE R	SCUMME R	SIMULA R	*SNOOZE R	STAMME R	SWAPPE R
R OYSTE R	SCUNNE R	*SIZZLE R	SNO R TE R	STAMPE R	SWA R ME R
R UDDIE R	SCUPPE R	SKEETE R	SNOWIE R	STANDE R	SWASHE R
R UFFLE R	SCUTTE R	SKELTE R	SNUFFE R	STAPLE R	SWATHE R
R UMBLE R	SEAMIE R	SKIDDE R	SOAPIE R	STA R TE R	SWATTE R
R UNOVE R	SECEDE R	*SKIMME R	SOCAGE R	STA R VE R	SWEA R E R
R USHIE R	SECULA R	*SKINKE R	SOLACE R	STEALE R	SWEATE R
R USTIE R	SECU R E R	SKINNE R	SOLDIE R	STEAME R	SWEEPE R
R USTLE R	SEDUCE R	*SKIPPE R	SOOTHE R	STEEPE R	SWELTE R
R UTTIE R	SEEDIE R	SKI R TE R	SO R R IE R	STEE R E R	SWE R VE R
SADDLE R	*SELTZE R	SKITTE R	SOUNDE R	STELLA R	SWIFTE R
SALLIE R	SEMINA R	SKIWEA R	SOUTHE R	STEMME R	SWIGGE R
SALTIE R	SENATO R	*SKULKE R	SPALLE R	STENTO R	SWILLE R
SALUTE R	SETTLE R	SLABBE R	SPANKE R		SWIMME R

SWINGE R	TIPSTE R	VAPO R E R	*WHIPPE R	BAR RATO R	BORDERE R
SWISHE R	TITULA R	VASTIE R	WHI R LE R	BAR RETO R	BOR ROWE R
SWITHE R	TOASTE R	VAULTE R	*WHISKE R	BAR ROWE R	BOTTOME R
SWOBBE R	TODDLE R	VAUNTE R	*WHISPE R	BA R TE R E R	B RABBLE R
SWOONE R	TOGGLE R	VAVASO R	*WHITHE R	BASIFIE R	B R AINIE R
SWOOPE R	TOLLBA R	VEINIE R	WHITTE R	BATTENE R	*B R EACHE R
SWOTTE R	TOOTLE R	VENOME R	*WHIZZE R	BAYADEE R	B R EATHE R
TABO R E R	*TO R QUE R	VE R NIE R	*WHOEVE R	*BEBOPPE R	*B ROACHE R
TABULA R	TOUCHE R	VE R R IE R	*WHOOPE R	*BECKONE R	B ROWNIE R
TACKIE R	T RACKE R	VETIVE R	*WHOPPE R	BECLAMO R	B R USHIE R
TACKLE R	T R ACTO R	VIEWIE R	WIDENE R	*BEDCHAI R	BUDGETE R
TALLIE R	T R AILE R	VILIGE R	WIDOWE R	*BEDCOVE R	BU R DENE R
TAMBOU R	T R AINE R	VINEGA R	WIELDE R	BEDIAPE R	BUR ROWE R
TANAGE R	T R AITO R	VINTNE R	WIGGIE R	*BEDMAKE R	BUSHELE R
TANGIE R	T R AMCA R	VISITE R	WIGGLE R	BEFINGE R	BUTTONE R
TANGLE R	T R AMPE R	VISITO R	*WINCHE R	*BEFLOWE R	CADASTE R
TAPE R E R	T R APPE R	VITAME R	WINDIE R	BEFOULE R	CALCSPA R
TAPSTE R	T R AWLE R	VOCODE R	WINGIE R	BEGETTE R	CALENDA R
TA R DIE R	T R EADE R	VOMITE R	WI R R IE R	BEGINNE R	CALLIPE R
TA R R IE R	T R EATE R	*VOUCHE R	WISPIE R	BEGLAMO R	*CALYPTE R
TA R SIE R	*T R EKKE R	VOYAGE R	WITHIE R	BEGUILE R	CAMELEE R
TATTIE R	T R ICKE R	WABBLE R	WITTIE R	*BEHAVIO R	CANALLE R
TATTLE R	T R IFLE R	WADDLE R	WOBBLE R	BEHOLDE R	CANCELE R
TAUNTE R	T R IGGE R	*WAFFLE R	WOODIE R	BELABOU R	*CANEPHO R
TEACHE R	T R ILLE R	WAGE R E R	WOOLIE R	BELIEVE R	CANISTE R
TEA R IE R	T R IMME R	WAGONE R	WO R DIE R	*BELIQUO R	CANVASE R
TEENIE R	T R IPPE R	WAISTE R	WO R MIE R	BELLOWE R	*CAPMAKE R
TEETHE R	T R OCHA R	WAKENE R	WO R R IE R	BEMU R MU R	CAPONIE R
TEGULA R	T R OFFE R	*WALTZE R	W R APPE R	BE R EAVE R	CAPSOME R
TELPHE R	T R OLLE R	WANGLE R	W R EAKE R	BESETTE R	CAPSULA R
TEMBLO R	T R OOPE R	WA R BLE R	*W R ECKE R	*BESHIVE R	CAPTU R E R
TEMPLA R	T R OTTE R	WA R R IO R	W R ESTE R	BESIEGE R	CA R EENE R
TEMPTE R	T R OUPE R	WA R SLE R	W R INGE R	BETATTE R	CA REFIE R
TENONE R	T R OUSE R	WA R TIE R	W R ITHE R	BET R AYE R	CA R ESSE R
TENTIE R	T R UCKE R	WASHIE R	W R ONGE R	BEVELLE R	*CA RMAKE R
TE R R IE R	T R UDGE R	*WATCHE R	*YACHTE R	BEWAILE R	CA R OUSE R
TESTIE R	T R USSE R	WATE R E R	YEA R NE R	BEWILDE R	CATB R IE R
THANKE R	T R USTE R	WEA R IE R	YIELDE R	*BEW RAYE R	CATHETE R
THEATE R	T R USTO R	WEATHE R	YODELE R	*BICKE R E R	CATNAPE R
THINKE R	T R YSTE R	WEBSTE R	YOUNGE R	BICOLOU R	CAVALIE R
THINNE R	TUBULA R	WEEDIE R	YOUNKE R	*BICYCLE R	CAVEATO R
THITHE R	TUMBLE R	WEIGHE R	*BACHELO R	BILANDE R	CAVILLE R
TH R IVE R	TUMMLE R	*WELCHE R	BACILLA R	BILINEA R	CAVO R TE R
TH R OWE R	TUMULA R	WELSHE R	*BACKDOO R	BIMESTE R	CELLA R E R
THUMPE R	TU R FIE R	*WENCHE R	*BAGPIPE R	BIOVULA R	CELLULA R
THUNDE R	TU R TLE R	*WHACKE R	BALANCE R	BISECTO R	CEMENTE R
*THYMIE R	TUTELA R	*WHAPPE R	BALISAU R	*BLANCHE R	CENSU R E R
TICKLE R	TUTOYE R	*WHECKE R	BALLOTE R	BLASTIE R	*CHANCIE R
TIDDLE R	TWEETE R	WHEELE R	BALUSTE R	*BLAZONE R	CHANDLE R
TINGLE R	*TWEEZE R	*WHEEZE R	BANDAGE R	*BLEACHE R	*CHAPITE R
TINKLE R	TWINIE R	*WHETHE R	BANISHE R	*BLENCHE R	CHA R R IE R
TINNIE R	TWI R LE R	WHETTE R	BANISTE R	BLOODIE R	CHASSEU R
TIPPIE R	TWISTE R	*WHIFFE R	BANTE R E R	BLOTTIE R	*CHAUFFE R
TIPPLE R	TWITTE R	*WHIMPE R	*BAPTIZE R	*BOBROWE R	CHAUNTE R
TIPSIE R	TYPEBA R	WHINIE R	BA R RATE R		

CHEE R IE R	*CONJURE R	DEEPENE R	*DIFFUSE R	FINAGLE R	GLASSIE R
*CHICANE R	*CONJUROR	DEFECTO R	*DIFFUSO R	FINISHE R	GLIMPSE R
CHISELE R	CONNIVE R	DEFENDE R	DIGESTE R	FLAUNTE R	GLOBULA R
CHO R TLE R	CONSIDE R	DEFE R R E R	DIGESTO R	FLAVO R E R	GLOSSIE R
*CHUCKLE R	CONSOLE R	DEFLATE R	DINOSAU R	FLESHIE R	GOSSAME R
CINNABA R	CONSUME R	DEFLATO R	*DIPLEXE R	*FLETCHE R	GOSSIPE R
CI R CULA R	CONVENE R	DEFOAME R	DI R ECTO R	*FLICHTE R	GOVE R NO R
CISLUNA R	CONVENO R	DEFOGGE R	DISA R ME R	*FLINCHE R	G R ABBIE R
CLAMO R E R	*CONVEYE R	DEFO R ME R	DISASTE R	FLOWE R E R	G R ABBLE R
CLANGOU R	*CONVOKE R	*DEF R AYE R	DISCOLO R	*FLYPAPE R	G R ANDEU R
CLASSIE R	COPASTO R	DEGASSE R	DISCOVE R	FOLLOWE R	G R ANDSI R
CLEANSE R	COPLANA R	DEG R ADE R	*DISFAVO R	FOMENTE R	G R ANULA R
*CLENCHE R	CO R RIDO R	DEHO R NE R	DISHONO R	FOOTGEA R	G R APPLE R
*CLINCHE R	COSIGNE R	*DEJEUNE R	DISINTE R	FOOTWEA R	G R EENIE R
CLOISTE R	COSTUME R	DELOUSE R	DISLIKE R	FO R EBEA R	G R IMACE R
CLOTHIE R	COTTAGE R	DELUSTE R	DISO R DE R	FO R EGOE R	G R IPPIE R
*COANCHO R	COU R TIE R	DEMANDE R	DISPOSE R	FO R ESEE R	*G R IZZLE R
COAPPEA R	COWINNE R	DEMEANO R	DISPUTE R	FO R ESTE R	G R OUNDE R
COAUTHO R	*COWORKER	DEME R GE R	DIS R OBE R	*FO R GIVE R	G R OVELE R
*COCKSPU R	C R ANKIE R	DEMPSTE R	DITHE R E R	FO R RADE R	G R UELLE R
CODEBTO R	C R EDITO R	DEMUR RE R	DIVE R TE R	*FO R SAKE R	*G R UFFIE R
CODIFIE R	C R EMATO R	DEPICTE R	DIVO R CE R	FO R SWEA R	G R UMBLE R
COD R IVE R	C R IPPLE R	DEPICTO R	DIVULGE R	FOSTE R E R	GUNPAPE R
COEDITO R	C R OSSBA R	DEPLO R E R	DODDE R E R	*F R EAKIE R	HALLOWE R
COENAMO R	C R OUPIE R	DEP R AVE R	DOGNAPE R	F R ESCOE R	*HAMME R E R
*COFACTO R	*C R UICFE R	DEP R IVE R	DOMINEE R	*F R IBBLE R	*HAMPE R E R
*COGNIZE R	C R UMBIE R	DE R INGE R	DONNIKE R	F R IVOLE R	*HANDOVE R
COHOLDE R	*C R UNCHE R	DESALTE R	DOOMSTE R	*F R IZZIE R	*HANKE R E R
*COIFFEU R	C R USADE R	DESC R IE R	DOPESTE R	*F R IZZLE R	HA R ASSE R
COLANDE R	*CUCUMBE R	DESE R TE R	DOUGHIE R	F R ONDEU R	HA R BO R E R
COLEADE R	CUDGELE R	DESE R VE R	*DOUZEPE R	F R ONTIE R	HA R DENE R
COLESSO R	CULTIVA R	DESIGNE R	DOWNPOU R	F R OTTEU R	*HA R KENE R
COLINEA R	CUMBE R E R	DESILVE R	D R AGGIE R	F R UITIE R	HA R ROWE R
COLLATO R	CUPELLE R	DESPISE R	D R ENCHE R	FU R R INE R	HASTENE R
COLLEGE R	CUSPIDO R	DEST R IE R	D R IBBLE R	FU R ROWE R	*HATMAKE R
COLLIDE R	CUSTOME R	DESULFU R	D R IVELE R	FUSILEE R	*HAVOCKE R
COLLUDE R	CUTWATE R	DETACHE R	D R UMLIE R	FUSILIE R	*HAYMAKE R
COLOU R E R	*CYCLECA R	DETAILE R	DULCIME R	GALLOPE R	HEADGEA R
COMBATE R	CYLINDE R	DETAINE R	*DUPLEXE R	GAMESTE R	*HEMIPTE R
COMBINE R	*CYMBALE R	DETECTE R	FALCONE R	GAMMONE R	*HIJACKE R
*COMEMBE R	DAMPENE R	DETECTO R	FALTE R E R	GANGLIA R	HINDE R E R
*COMETHE R	DA R KENE R	DETE R GE R	FAMILIA R	GANGLIE R	*HIZZONE R
COMMONE R	DAUGHTE R	DETE R R E R	FASTENE R	GANGSTE R	*HOLDOVE R
COMMUTE R	DEADENE R	DETESTE R	FATTENE R	GANISTE R	HONOU R E R
COMPA R E R	DEADLIE R	*DETICKE R	FAVOU R E R	GA R DENE R	HOOPSTE R
COMPILE R	DEBONAI R	DEVIATO R	*FELDSHE R	GA R OTTE R	HO R SECA R
COMPOSE R	DEBUGGE R	DEVOU R E R	FELDSPA R	GA R R OTE R	HOSPODA R
COMPUTE R	*DEBUNKE R	DIALOGE R	FELLATO R	GASALIE R	HOTELIE R
CONCEDE R	DECANTE R	DIALYSE R	FE R R ETE R	GASELIE R	*HOWITZE R
CONDOLE R	DECEIVE R	*DIALYZE R	FETTE R E R	GASIFIE R	*HUCKSTE R
CONDUCE R	DECENTE R	DIAMETE R	FIDGETE R	GASOLIE R	*HUNGOVE R
CONFIDE R	*DECIPHE R	DICTATO R	FIGEATE R	GATHE R E R	*HYD R ATO R
CONFINE R	DECLA R E R	DIDAPPE R	FILISTE R	*GAZUMPE R	*JABBE R E R
CONFUTE R	DECLINE R	*DIEMAKE R	FILMGOE R	GEOLOGE R	*JAPPANE R
CONGENE R	DEEMSTE R		FILTE R E R	GEOMETE R	*JAWBONE R

R ETA R DE R
R ETEMPE R
R ETO R TE R
R ETU R NE R
R EUNITE R
*R EVAMPE R
REVEALE R
R EVELLE R
R EVENGE R
R EVENUE R
R EVER SE R
R EVER TE R
R EVIEWE R
R EVOLTE R
R EVOLVE R
R EWA R DE R
R EWINDE R
R EW R ITE R
R ICE R CA R
R IMESTE R
R OADSTE R
R OCKETE R
R OLLOVE R
R OMANCE R
R OTU R IE R
R UFFLIE R
R UMMAGE R
SABOTEU R
SACCULA R
SALVAGE R
SANDBU R R
SANDSPU R
SAVO R IE R
SAVOU R E R
SCANTIE R
SCAPULA R
*SCHEMEE R
SCHILLE R
*SCHIZIE R
SCHOONE R
SCHUSSE R
SCIMETA R
SCIMITA R
SCIMITE R
*SCLAFFE R
*SCO R CHE R
SCOU R GE R
SCOUTHE R
SC R APPE R
SC R AWLE R
SC R EAME R
SC R EENE R
SC R IMPE R
SC R UBBE R
*SCUFFLE R

SCULPTO R
*SCUTCHE R
SEAFLOO R
SEAMSTE R
SEAFA R ER
SEA R CHE R
SEASONE R
SEAWATE R
SECATEU R
SECONDE R
SEC R ETO R
SEIGNEU R
SEIGNIO R
SELECTO R
SEMESTE R
*SEQUITU R
SE R VICE R
SE R VITO R
*SHACKLE R
*SHADOWE R
SHEATHE R
SHIELDE R
SHINGLE R
SHIVE R E R
SHOULDE R
SHOVELE R
SHOWE R E R
SH R EDDE R
*SH R IMPE R
*SH R INKE R
*SHUFFLE R
SICKENE R
SIFFLEU R
SIGNALE R
SILENCE R
SILVE R E R
SIMPE R E R
SINGULA R
SINISTE R
*SKETCHE R
*SKYDIVE R
SLAVE R E R
SLEEKIE R
SLEIGHE R
SLIPOVE R
SLIVE R E R
SLOUCHE R
SMOOTHE R
SMOULDE R
SMUGGLE R
SNAPPIE R
SNATCHE R
SNIFFIE R
SNIFFLE R
SNIGGLE R

SNITCHE R
SNIVELE R
SNOBBIE R
SNUBBIE R
SNUFFIE R
SNUFFLE R
SOFTENE R
SOLANDE R
SOLDE R E R
SONGSTE R
SO R CE R ER
SO R ROWE R
SOUVENI R
SPA R KIE R
SPA R KLE R
SPEEDIE R
SPHE R IE R
SPINDLE R
SPINSTE R
SPLASHE R
SPLATTE R
SPLENDO R
SPLINTE R
SPLITTE R
SPLU R GE R
SPLUTTE R
SPONGIE R
SPOONIE R
SP R AWLE R
SP R EADE R
SP R IGGE R
SP R INGE R
SP R INTE R
*SP R ITZE R
*SQUALLE R
*SQUANDE R
*SQUASHE R
*SQUATTE R
*SQUAWKE R
*SQUEAKE R
*SQUEALE R
*SQUEEZE R
*SQUINTE R
*SQUI R ME R
*SQUI R TE R
STANCHE R
STARTLE R
STEADIE R
STICKIE R
STICKLE R
STINGIE R
STINKIE R
STIPPLE R

STITCHE R
*STOCKCA R
STOCKIE R
STOPOVE R
ST R AINE R
ST R ANDE R
ST R ANGE R
ST R APPE R
ST R EAKE R
ST R EAME R
ST R EEKE R
ST R ESSO R
ST R INGE R
ST R IPIE R
ST R IPPE R
ST R OLLE R
ST R OPPE R
ST R UMME R
ST R UTTE R
STUBBIE R
STUCCOE R
STUMBLE R
STYLISE R
*STYLIZE R
SUBAHDA R
SUBFLOO R
SUBLIME R
SUBLUNA R
SUBO R DE R
SUBO R NE R
SUBPOLA R
SUBSIDE R
SUBSOLA R
*SUBVICA R
SUCCO R E R
SUFFE R E R
*SUFFICE R
SUMMONE R
SUNDE R E R
SUPE R CA R
SUPE R IO R
SUPPLIE R
SUPPOSE R
SU R FACE R
SU R MISE R
SU R NAME R
SU R VEYO R
SU R VIVE R
SU R VIVO R
*SWIMWEA R
SWINDLE R
SWINGIE R
*SWITCHE R
*SWIZZLE R
TABOU R E R

TAILLEU R
*TAKEOVE R
TAMPE R E R
TA R PAPE R
TATTOOE R
TAUTOME R
TAVE R NE R
*TAXPAYE R
TEAMAKE R
TEAMSTE R
TEASELE R
TEENAGE R
TEMPE R E R
TENDE R E R
TESTATO R
TET R AME R
*THATCHE R
THE R EFO R
THI R STE R
TH R ASHE R
TH R EADE R
TH R EAPE R
TH R ESHE R
TH R ILLE R
*TH R OBBE R
*TH R UMMER
TH R USTE R
TH R USTO R
THU R IFE R
THWA R TE R
TINKE R E R
TISSULA R
TIT R ATO R
TITTE R E R
TOGETHE R
TOPSIDE R
TO R CHIE R
TO R EADO R
TO R TU R ER
TOTTE R E R
TOWNWEA R
T R ADITO R
T R ADUCE R
T R AMPLE R
T R ANSFE R
T R APDOO R
T R AVELE R
T R EADLE R
T R EMBLE R
T R ENCHE R
T R ESSIE R
T R ESSOU R
T R ICKIE R
T R ICOLO R
T R IMETE R

T R IMOTO R
T R IUMVI R
T R OUBLE R
T R OUNCE R
T R OUVEU R
T R OWELE R
T R UCKLE R
T R UNDLE R
TUNNELE R
TU R BOCA R
TU R NOVE R
TWADDLE R
TWANGIE R
TWANGLE R
TWIDDLE R
*TWINKLE R
*TWITCHE R
*TYPIFIE R
VALUATO R
VALVULA R
VANISHE R
VAPOU R E R
VA R ACTO R
VA R ISTO R
VASCULA R
VAVASOU R
VAVASSO R
VENEE R E R
VENTU R E R
VE R DE R E R
VE R DE R OR
VE R DITE R
VE R IFIE R
VIB R ATO R
VILIFIE R
VILLAGE R
VINTAGE R
VIOLATE R
VITIATO R
*VIVIFIE R
VOLLEYE R
VOUSSOI R
*VOYAGEU R
WAGGONE R
*WALKOVE R
WALLOPE R
WALLOWE R
WANDE R E R
WANTONE R
*WA R MAKE R
*WA R POWE R
WA R RENE R
WA R STLE R
WATE R IE R
WATTHOU R

*WAYFARER	WHEATEAR	WHITENER	WINNOWER	WRESTLER	*ZEMINDAR
*WAYLAYER	*WHEEDLER	WHITTLER	WINTERER	WRIGGLER	*ZOOLATER
*WEAKENER	*WHENEVER	*WHOMEVER	WIREHAIR	*YAMMERER	
*WEIGHTER	*WHEREVER	*WHOSEVER	WITHERER	*YAWMETER	
*WELCOMER	*WHIFFLER	*WIGMAKER	WONDERER	YEASAYER	
WELLDOER	*WHIPPIER	WILLOWER	WOOLLIER	YODELLER	
*WHATEVER	WHISTLER	*WINGOVER	WRANGLER	*ZAMINDAR	

S

SABE	SCOP	SHAT	SINK	SLUR	SOPH
SACK	SCOT	SHAW	SIPE	SLUT	SORA
SADE	SCOW	SHAY	SIRE	SMEW	SORB
SADI	SCRY	SHEA	SITE	SMOG	SORD
SAFE	SCUD	SHED	SITH	SMUG	SORE
SAGA	SCUM	SHEW	SITI	SMUT	SORI
SAGE	SCUP	SHIM	SIZE	SNAG	SORN
SAGO	SCUT	SHIN	*SIZY	SNAP	SORT
SAGY	SEAL	SHIP	SKAG	SNAW	SOTH
SAID	SEAM	SHIT	SKAT	SNED	SOUK
SAIL	SEAR	SHIV	SKEE	SNIB	SOUL
SAIN	SEAT	SHMO	SKEG	SNIP	SOUP
SAKE	SECT	SHOD	SKEP	SNIT	SOUR
SAKI	SEED	SHOE	SKEW	SNOB	SOWN
SALE	SEEK	SHOG	SKID	SNOG	SOYA
SALL	SEEL	SHOO	SKIM	SNOT	SPAE
SALP	SEEM	SHOP	SKIN	SNOW	SPAN
SALT	SEEN	SHOT	SKIP	SNUB	SPAR
SAME	SEEP	SHOW	SKIT	SNUG	SPAT
SAMP	SEER	SHRI	SKUA	SNYE	SPAY
SAND	SEGO	SHUL	SLAB	SOAK	*SPAZ
SANE	SEIF	SHUN	SLAG	SOAP	SPEC
SANG	SELF	SHUT	SLAM	SOAR	SPED
SANK	SELL	SIAL	SLAP	SOCK	SPEW
SANS	SEME	SIBB	SLAT	SODA	SPIC
SARD	SEMI	SICE	SLAW	SOFA	SPIK
SARI	SEND	SICK	SLAY	SOFT	SPIN
SARK	SENE	SIDE	SLED	SOIL	SPIT
SASH	SENT	SIFT	SLEW	SOJA	SPIV
SASS	SEPT	SIGH	SLIM	SOKE	SPOT
SATE	SERA	SIGN	SLIP	SOLA	SPRY
SATI	SERE	SIKE	SLIT	SOLD	SPUD
SAUL	SERF	SILD	SLOB	SOLE	SPUE
SAVE	SETA	SILK	SLOE	SOLI	SPUN
SAWN	SETT	SILL	SLOG	SOLO	SPUR
SCAB	SEWN	SILO	SLOP	SOMA	STAB
SCAD	SEXT	SILT	SLOT	SOME	STAG
SCAG	SEXY	SIMA	SLOW	SONE	STAT
SCAM	SHAD	SIMP	SLUB	SONG	STAW
SCAN	SHAG	SINE	SLUE	SOOK	STAY
SCAR	SHAH	SING	SLUG	SOON	STEM
SCAT	SHAM	SINH	SLUM	SOOT	STEP

STET	SABER	SATAY	SCOUT	SERAI	SHERD
STEW	SABIN	SATEM	**SCOWL**	SERAL	SHIED
STEY	SABIR	SATIN	SCRAG	SERER	SHIEL
STIR	SABLE	SATYR	SCRAM	SERGE	SHIER
STOA	SABOT	SAUCE	SCRAP	SERIF	SHIES
STOB	SABRA	SAUCH	SCREE	SERIN	**SHIFT**
STOP	SABRE	**SAUCY**	**SCREW**	SEROW	SHILL
STOW	SACRA	SAUGH	SCRIM	SERRY	**SHILY**
STUB	SADHE	SAULT	SCRIP	SERUM	SHINE
STUD	SADHU	SAUNA	SCROD	SERVE	**SHINY**
STUM	SADLY	SAURY	SCRUB	SERVO	SHIRE
STUN	SAFER	SAUTE	SCRUM	SETON	**SHIRK**
STYE	SAGER	SAVER	SCUBA	SETUP	SHIRR
SUBA	**SAGGY**	SAVIN	SCUDO	SEVEN	SHIRT
SUCH	SAGUM	SAVOR	**SCUFF**	SEVER	SHIST
SUCK	**SAHIB**	**SAVOY**	**SCULK**	SEWAN	**SHIVA**
SUDD	SAICE	**SAVVY**	SCULL	SEWAR	**SHIVE**
SUDS	SAIGA	SAWER	SCULP	SEWER	**SHLEP**
SUER	SAINT	SAYER	**SCURF**	**SEXTO**	SHOAL
SUET	SAITH	SAYID	SCUTA	**SHACK**	SHOAT
SUGH	**SAJOU**	SAYST	SCUTE	SHADE	**SHOCK**
SUIT	SAKER	SCALD	**SEAMY**	**SHADY**	SHOER
SULK	SALAD	SCALE	SEBUM	SHAFT	*SHOJI
SULU	SALAL	SCALL	SECCO	**SHAKE**	SHONE
SUMO	SALEP	SCALP	SEDAN	**SHAKO**	**SHOOK**
SUMP	SALIC	**SCALY**	SEDER	*SHAKY	SHOOL
SUNG	SALLY	**SCAMP**	SEDGE	SHALE	SHOON
SUNK	SALMI	SCANT	**SEDGY**	SHALL	SHOOT
SUNN	SALOL	SCAPE	SEDUM	SHALT	SHORE
SUPE	SALON	SCARE	SEEDY	**SHALY**	SHORL
SURA	SALPA	**SCARF**	SEELY	**SHAME**	SHORN
SURD	SALSA	SCARP	**SEEPY**	**SHANK**	SHORT
SURE	SALTY	SCART	SEGNO	**SHAPE**	SHOTE
SURF	SALVE	**SCARY**	SEGUE	SHARD	SHOUT
SUSS	SALVO	SCATT	SEINE	SHARE	**SHOVE**
SWAB	SAMBA	SCAUP	SEISE	**SHARK**	**SHOWN**
SWAG	SAMBO	SCAUR	SEISM	SHARN	**SHOWY**
SWAM	**SAMEK**	SCENA	**SEIZE**	**SHARP**	**SHOYU**
SWAN	SANDY	SCEND	SELAH	SHAUL	SHRED
SWAP	SANER	SCENE	SELLE	**SHAVE**	**SHREW**
SWAT	SANGA	SCENT	SELVA	**SHAWL**	**SHRUB**
SWAY	SANGH	**SCHAV**	SEMEN	**SHAWM**	SHRUG
SWIG	SANTO	**SCHMO**	SEMIS	**SHAWN**	**SHUCK**
SWIM	SAPID	**SCHUL**	SENGI	**SHEAF**	SHUNT
SWOB	SAPOR	**SCHWA**	SENNA	SHEAL	**SHUSH**
SWOP	**SAPPY**	SCION	SENOR	SHEAR	SHUTE
SWOT	SARAN	**SCOFF**	SENSA	SHEEN	SHUTT
SWUM	SAREE	SCOLD	SENSE	**SHEEP**	**SHYER**
SYBO	SARGE	SCONE	SENTE	SHEER	**SHYLY**
SYCE	SARIN	SCOOP	SENTI	SHEET	**SIBYL**
SYKE	**SARKY**	SCOOT	SEPAL	**SHEIK**	**SICKO**
SYLI	SAROD	SCOPE	SEPIA	**SHELF**	SIDED
SYNC	SAROS	SCORE	**SEPOY**	SHELL	SIDLE
SYNE	SASIN	SCORN	SEPTA	SHEND	SIEGE
SYPH	SASSY	SCOUR	SERAC	SHEOL	SIEUR

SIEVE	SKOAL	SMELL	SOLAR	SPEAN	SPRUE
SIGHT	**SKOSH**	SMELT	SOLDI	SPEAR	SPRUG
SIGIL	**SKULK**	**SMERK**	SOLDO	**SPECK**	SPUME
SIGMA	SKULL	SMILE	SOLED	SPECS	**SPUMY**
SIKER	**SKUNK**	**SMIRK**	SOLEI	SPEED	**SPUNK**
SILEX	*****SKYEY**	SMITE	SOLID	SPEEL	SPURN
SILKY	**SLACK**	**SMITH**	SOLON	SPEER	SPURT
SILLY	SLAIN	**SMOCK**	SOLUM	SPEIL	SPUTA
SILTY	SLAKE	**SMOKE**	SOLUS	SPEIR	*****SQUAB**
SILVA	SLANG	**SMOKY**	SOLVE	SPELL	*****SQUAD**
SIMAR	SLANK	SMOLT	SONAR	SPELT	*****SQUAM**
SINCE	SLANT	SMOTE	SONDE	SPEND	**SQUAT**
SINEW	SLASH	**SNACK**	SONIC	SPENT	*****SQUAW**
SINGE	SLATE	SNAFU	SONLY	SPERM	*****SQUEG**
SINUS	SLATY	SNAIL	SONNY	SPICA	*****SQUIB**
SIREE	SLAVE	SNAKE	SONSY	SPICE	*****SQUID**
SIREN	SLEEK	**SNAKY**	SOOEY	**SPICK**	**STACK**
SIRRA	SLEEP	SNARE	SOOTH	**SPICY**	STADE
SIRUP	SLEET	SNARK	SOOTY	SPIED	**STAFF**
SISAL	SLEPT	SNARL	**SOPHY**	SPIEL	STAGE
SISSY	SLICE	SNASH	SOPOR	SPIER	STAGY
SITAR	**SLICK**	SNATH	**SOPPY**	SPIES	STAID
SITUP	SLIDE	SNEAK	SOREL	SPIFF	STAIG
SITUS	SLIER	SNEAP	SORER	**SPIKE**	STAIN
SIVER	SLILY	**SNECK**	SORGO	**SPIKY**	STAIR
SIXMO	SLIME	SNEER	SORRY	SPILE	STAKE
SIXTE	**SLIMY**	SNELL	SORUS	SPILL	STALE
*****SIXTH**	SLING	**SNICK**	SOTOL	SPILT	STALK
*****SIXTY**	SLINK	SNIDE	SOUGH	SPINE	STALL
SIZAR	SLIPE	SNIPE	SOUND	**SPINY**	STAMP
SIZER	SLIPT	**SNIFF**	SOUPY	SPIRE	STAND
SKALD	SLOID	SNOOD	SOUSE	SPIRT	STANE
SKATE	**SLOJD**	SNOOK	SOUTH	**SPIRY**	STANG
SKEAN	SLOOP	SNOOL	SOWAR	SPITE	STANK
SKEEN	SLOPE	SNOOP	SOWER	*****SPITZ**	**STAPH**
SKEET	SLOSH	SNOOT	*****SOYUZ**	SPLAT	STARE
SKEIN	SLOTH	SNORE	**SOZIN**	**SPLAY**	STARK
SKELM	SLOYD	SNORT	SPACE	SPLIT	START
SKELP	**SLUFF**	SNOUT	**SPACY**	SPODE	STASH
SKENE	SLUMP	**SNOWY**	SPADE	SPOIL	STATE
SKIED	SLUNG	**SNUCK**	SPADO	**SPOKE**	STAVE
SKIER	SLUNK	**SNUFF**	**SPAHI**	**SPOOF**	STEAD
SKIES	SLURB	**SOAPY**	SPAIL	SPOOK	STEAK
SKIEY	SLURP	SOAVE	SPAIT	SPOOL	STEAL
*****SKIFF**	SLUSH	SOBER	**SPAKE**	SPOON	STEAM
SKILL	**SLYPE**	**SOCKO**	SPALE	SPOOR	STEED
SKIMO	**SMACK**	SOCLE	SPALL	SPORE	STEEK
SKIMP	SMALL	**SODDY**	SPANG	SPORT	STEEL
SKINK	SMALT	SODOM	**SPANK**	SPOUT	STEEP
SKINT	SMARM	SOFAR	SPARE	SPRAG	STEER
SKIRL	SMART	SOFTA	**SPARK**	SPRAT	STEIN
SKIRR	**SMASH**	**SOFTY**	SPASM	**SPRAY**	STELA
SKIRT	*****SMAZE**	**SOGGY**	SPATE	SPREE	STELE
SKITE	SMEAR	SOKOL	**SPAWN**	SPRIG	STENO
SKIVE	**SMEEK**	SOLAN	**SPEAK**	SPRIT	STERE

STERN	**STUCK**	**SWANK**	**SADDHU**	SANEST	SCALER
STICH	STUDY	SWARD	SADDLE	SANGAR	**SCAMPI**
STICK	**STUFF**	SWARE	SADISM	SANGER	**SCANTY**
STIED	STULL	**SWARF**	SADIST	SANIES	**SCARAB**
STIFF	STUMP	**SWARM**	SAFARI	SANING	**SCARCE**
STILE	STUNG	SWART	SAFEST	SANITY	SCARER
STILL	STUNK	**SWASH**	**SAFETY**	*SANJAK	**SCAREY**
STILT	STUNT	**SWATH**	SAFROL	SANNOP	**SCARPH**
STIME	STUPA	SWEAR	SAGBUT	SANNUP	**SCARRY**
STIMY	STUPE	SWEAT	SAGEST	SANSAR	**SCATHE**
STING	STURT	SWEDE	SAGGAR	SANSEI	**SCATTY**
STINK	STYLE	**SWEEP**	SAGGED	SANTIR	**SCENIC**
STINT	STYLI	SWEER	SAGGER	SANTOL	**SCHEMA**
STIPE	**STYMY**	SWEET	SAGIER	SANTUR	**SCHEME**
STIRK	SUAVE	SWELL	SAILER	SAPOTA	**SCHISM**
STIRP	SUBER	SWEPT	SAILOR	SAPOTE	**SCHIST**
STOAT	SUCRE	**SWIFT**	SAIMIN	SAPOUR	*SCHIZO
STOCK	SUDOR	SWILL	SAITHE	**SAPPED**	*SCHIZY
STOGY	SUDSY	SWINE	**SAIYID**	**SAPPER**	**SCHLEP**
STOIC	SUEDE	SWING	SALAAM	SARAPE	**SCHMOE**
STOKE	SUGAR	**SWINK**	SALAMI	SARDAR	*SCHNOZ
STOLE	SUING	**SWIPE**	SALARY	SARODE	**SCHOOL**
STOMA	SUINT	**SWISH**	**SALIFY**	SARONG	**SCHORL**
STOMP	SUITE	SWISS	SALINA	SARSAR	*SCHRIK
STONE	SULFA	**SWITH**	SALINE	SARSEN	**SCHROD**
STONY	SULFO	**SWIVE**	SALIVA	SARTOR	*SCHTIK
STOOD	**SULKY**	SWOON	SALLET	**SASHAY**	**SCHUIT**
STOOK	SULLY	**SWOOP**	SALLOW	SATANG	**SCHUSS**
STOOL	SUMAC	SWORD	SALMON	SATARA	SCILLA
STOOP	SUMMA	SWORE	SALOON	SATEEN	**SCLAFF**
STOPE	SUNNA	SWORN	SALOOP	SATING	SCLERA
STOPT	SUNNY	SWOUN	SALPID	SATINY	*SCOLEX
STORE	SUNUP	SWUNG	SALTER	SATIRE	SCONCE
STORK	SUPER	SYCEE	SALTIE	SATORI	**SCORCH**
STORM	SUPRA	**SYLPH**	SALUKI	SATRAP	SCORER
STORY	SURAH	**SYLVA**	SALUTE	SAUCER	SCORIA
STOSS	SURAL	**SYNCH**	SALVER	SAUGER	**SCOTCH**
STOUP	SURER	SYNOD	SALVIA	SAUREL	SCOTER
STOUR	SURGE	**SYNTH**	SALVOR	**SAVAGE**	SCOTIA
STOUT	SURGY	SYREN	SAMARA	SAVANT	**SCOUSE**
STOVE	SURLY	**SYRUP**	**SAMBAR**	SAVATE	**SCOUTH**
STOWP	SURRA	**SYSOP**	**SAMBUR**	SAVINE	**SCRAPE**
STRAP	SUSHI	**SABBAT**	SAMECH	**SAVING**	**SCRAWL**
STRAW	SUTRA	**SABBED**	*SAMEKH	SAVIOR	**SCREAK**
STRAY	SUTTA	SABINE	SAMIEL	SAVOUR	**SCREAM**
STREP	SWAGE	**SACBUT**	SAMITE	**SAVORY**	**SCREED**
STREW	SWAIL	**SACHEM**	SAMLET	*SAWFLY	**SCREEN**
STRIA	SWAIN	**SACHET**	SAMOSA	**SAWLOG**	**SCREWY**
STRIP	SWALE	**SACKER**	**SAMPAN**	**SAWNEY**	**SCRIBE**
STROP	SWALE	*SACQUE	**SAMPLE**	**SAWYER**	SCRIED
STROW	**SWAMI**	SACRAL	**SAMSHU**	*SAXONY	SCRIES
STROY	**SWAMP**	SACRED	SANCTA	**SAYING**	**SCRIMP**
STRUM	**SWAMY**	**SACRUM**	SANDAL	**SAYYID**	**SCRIPT**
STRUT	SWANG	SADDEN	SANDER	*SCABBY	**SCRIVE**
			SANDHI	SCALAR	SCROLL

SCROOP	SELECT	SETTEE	*SHELVY	*SHTICK	SIPPED
SCRUFF	SELLER	SETTER	*SHEQEL	SIALID	SIPPER
SCULPT	SELSYN	SETTLE	SHERIF	SICCAN	SIPPET
*SCUMMY	SELVES	SEVERE	SHERPA	SICKEE	SIRDAR
SCURPY	SEMEME	SEWAGE	SHERRY	SICKEN	SIRING
SCURRY	SEMINA	SEWING	SHEUCH	SICKIE	SIRRAH
SCURVY	SEMPLE	SEXIER	SHEUGH	SICKLE	SIRREE
SCUTCH	SEMPRE	*SEXILY	SHEWER	*SICKLY	SISKIN
SCUTUM	SENARY	*SEXISM	SHIBAH	SIDDUR	SISTER
*SCUZZY	SENATE	SEXIST	SHIELD	SIDING	SISTRA
SCYTHE	SENDAL	*SEXPOT	SHIEST	SIDLER	SITCOM
SEABAG	SENDER	SEXTAN	*SHIFTY	SIENNA	SITING
SEABED	SENDUP	SEXTET	SHIKAR	SIERRA	SITTEN
SEADOG	SENECA	SEXTON	SHIKSA	SIESTA	SITTER
SEALER	SENEGA	SEXUAL	SHIKSE	SIFAKA	*SIZIER
SEAMAN	SENHOR	*SHABBY	*SHIMMY	SIFTER	*SIZING
SEAMER	SENILE	*SHACKO	SHINDY	SIGHER	*SIZZLE
SEANCE	SENIOR	SHADER	SHINER	SIGLOS	SKATER
SEARCH	SENITI	SHADOW	SHINNY	SIGNAL	SKATOL
SEARER	SENNET	SHADUF	SHIRTY	SIGNEE	SKEANE
SEASON	SENNIT	SHAGGY	*SHIVAH	SIGNER	SKEIGH
SEATER	SENORA	SHAIRD	SHIVER	SIGNET	SKERRY
SEAWAN	SENRYU	SHAIRN	SHLEPP	SIGNOR	*SKETCH
SEAWAY	SENSOR	SHAKER	*SHLOCK	SILAGE	SKEWER
SECANT	SENSUM	SHALED	SHLUMP	SILANE	SKIBOB
SECEDE	SENTRY	SHALEY	SHMEAR	SILENI	*SKIDDY
SECERN	SEPSIS	SHALOM	*SHMUCK	SILENT	SKIDOO
SECOND	SEPTAL	SHAMAN	SHNAPS	SILICA	SKIING
SECPAR	SEPTET	SHAMES	SHNOOK	SILKEN	*SKIMPY
SECRET	SEPTIC	*SHAMMY	SHOALY	SILLER	SKINNY
SECTOR	SEPTUM	SHAMOS	SHODDY	SILVAN	SKIVER
SECUND	*SEQUEL	SHAMOY	SHOFAR	SILVER	*SKIVVY
SECURE	*SEQUIN	SHAMUS	SHOGUN	*SILVEX	SKLENT
SEDATE	SERAIL	SHANDY	SHOLOM	SIMIAN	*SKYBOX
SEDILE	SERAPE	SHANNY	SHOPPE	SIMILE	*SKYCAP
SEDUCE	SERAPH	SHANTI	SHORAN	SIMILIN	SKYLIT
SEEDER	SERDAB	SHANTY	SHORTY	SIMMER	*SKYMAN
SEEING	SEREIN	SHAPER	SHOULD	SIMNEL	*SKYWAY
SEEKER	SERENE	SHARER	SHOVEL	SIMONY	SLAGGY
SEEMER	SEREST	SHARIF	SHOVER	SIMOOM	SLAKER
SEEMLY	SERIAL	SHARPY	SHOWER	SIMOON	SLALOM
SEESAW	SERIES	SHAUGH	SHRANK	SIMPER	SLANGY
SEETHE	SERINE	SHAVER	SHREWD	SIMPLE	SLANTY
SEGGAR	SERING	SHAVIE	SHRIEK	SIMPLY	SLATCH
SEICHE	SERMON	SHEATH	SHRIFT	SINEWY	SLATER
SEIDEL	SEROSA	SHEAVE	SHRIKE	SINFUL	SLATEY
SEINER	SEROUS	SHEENY	SHRILL	SINGER	SLAVER
SEISER	SERVAL	SHEEVE	SHRIMP	SINGLE	SLAVEY
SEISIN	SERVER	*SHEIKH	SHRINE	SINGLY	SLAYER
SEISOR	SESAME	SHEILA	SHRINK	SINKER	SLEAVE
*SEIZER	SESTET	SHEKEL	SHRIVE	SINNED	*SLEAZE
*SEIZIN	SETOFF	SHELLY	*SHROFF	SINNER	*SLEAZO
*SEIZOR	SETOSE	SHELTA	SHROUD	SINTER	*SLEAZY
SEJANT	SETOUS	SHELTY	SHROVE	SIPHON	SLEDGE
SELDOM	SETOUT	SHELVE	SHRUNK	SIPING	SLEEKY

SLEEPY	SMUGLY	SOLANO	SPADER	**SPOKEN**	***STANZA**
SLEETY	**SMUTCH**	SOLATE	***SPADIX**	SPONGE	**STARCH**
SLEEVE	SMUTTY	SOLDAN	SPAHEE	**SPONGY**	STARER
SLEIGH	**SNAGGY**	SOLDER	SPARER	**SPOOFY**	STARRY
SLEUTH	**SNAPPY**	SOLELY	SPARGE	***SPOOKY**	STARVE
SLICER	SNARER	SOLEMN	SPARID	SPOONY	STASES
SLIDER	**SNARKY**	SOLEUS	***SPARKY**	SPORAL	STASIS
SLIEST	**SNARLY**	SOLGEL	**SPARRY**	**SPORTY**	STATAL
SLIGHT	**SNATCH**	SOLIDI	SPARSE	**SPOTTY**	STATER
SLIMLY	SNATHE	SOLING	**SPATHE**	SPOUSE	STATIC
SLIMSY	***SNAZZY**	SOLION	SPAVIE	SPRAIN	STATOR
SLINKY	**SNEAKY**	SOLUTE	SPAVIN	SPRANG	STATUE
SLIPPY	SNEESH	SOLVER	**SPECIE**	**SPRAWL**	STATUS
SLIPUP	***SNEEZE**	**SOMBER**	**SPEECH**	SPREAD	STAYER
SLIVER	***SNEEZY**	**SOMBRE**	SPEEDO	SPRENT	**STEADY**
SLOBBY	***SNIFFY**	SOMITE	**SPEEDY**	SPRIER	**STEAMY**
SLOGAN	SNIPER	SONANT	SPEISE	SPRING	STEELY
SLOPER	**SNIPPY**	SONATA	SPEISS	SPRINT	STEEVE
SLOPPY	**SNITCH**	SONDER	***SPELTZ**	SPRITE	STELLA
SLOSHY	SNIVEL	SONICS	**SPENCE**	***SPRITZ**	**STEMMA**
SLOUCH	**SNOBBY**	SONNET	SPENSE	SPROUT	**STEMMY**
SLOUGH	**SNOOPY**	SONSIE	**SPEWER**	**SPRUCE**	**STENCH**
SLOVEN	SNOOTY	SOONER	**SPHENE**	SPRUCY	**STEPPE**
SLOWLY	***SNOOZE**	SOOTHE	**SPHERE**	SPRUNG	STEREO
SLUDGE	***SNOOZY**	SOPITE	**SPHERY**	SPURGE	STERIC
SLUDGY	SNORER	**SOPPED**	***SPHINX**	**SPURRY**	STERNA
SLUICE	SNOTTY	SORBET	**SPICER**	**SPUTUM**	STEROL
SLUICY	SNOUTY	**SORBIC**	**SPICEY**	***SQUALL**	***STICKY**
SLUING	**SNUBBY**	SORDID	SPIDER	***SQUAMA**	STIFLE
SLUMMY	***SNUFFY**	SORDOR	***SPIFFY**	***SQUARE**	STIGMA
SLURRY	**SNUGLY**	SORELY	SPIGOT	***SQUASH**	STILLY
SLUSHY	**SOAKER**	SOREST	**SPIKER**	***SQUAWK**	STINGO
SLUTTY	SOARER	SORGHO	***SPIKEY**	***SQUEAK**	**STINGY**
SMALTI	**SOBBER**	SORING	**SPILTH**	***SQUEAL**	**STINKO**
SMALTO	SOBEIT	SORNER	SPINAL	***SQUILL**	**STINKY**
SMARMY	**SOBFUL**	SORREL	SPINEL	***SQUINT**	STIPEL
SMARTY	SOCAGE	SORROW	SPINET	***SQUIRE**	STIPES
SMEARY	**SOCCER**	SORTER	**SPINNY**	***SQUIRM**	STIRPS
SMEGMA	SOCIAL	SORTIE	SPINOR	***SQUIRT**	**STITCH**
SMELLY	**SOCKET**	SOTTED	SPINTO	***SQUISH**	**STITHY**
SMIDGE	**SOCMAN**	SOUARI	SPIRAL	***SQUUSH**	STIVER
*SMILAX	SODDED	SOUCAR	SPIREA	**SRADHA**	***STOCKY**
SMILER	SODDEN	SOUDAN	SPIREM	STABLE	STODGE
SMILEY	SODIUM	**SOUGHT**	SPIRIT	**STABLY**	**STODGY**
SMIRCH	SODOMY	SOURCE	SPITAL	STACTE	**STOGEY**
*SMIRKY	SOEVER	SOURLY	**SPLAKE**	STADIA	STOGIE
SMITER	**SOFFIT**	SOUTER	**SPLASH**	STAGER	**STOKER**
SMITHY	SOFTEN	SOVIET	SPLEEN	STAGEY	STOLEN
SMOGGY	SOFTIE	SOVRAN	SPLENT	**STAGGY**	STOLID
SMOKER	**SOFTLY**	SOWANS	**SPLICE**	STALAG	STOLON
*SMOKEY	SOGGED	**SOWCAR**	SPLINE	**STALKY**	STOMAL
SMOOCH	SOIGNE	SOWENS	SPLINT	STAMEN	STONER
SMOOTH	SOIREE	***SOZINE**	SPLORE	STANCE	STONEY
SMUDGE	SOLACE	**SPACER**	**SPLOSH**	STANCH	STOOGE
SMUDGY	SOLAND	**SPACEY**	SPOILT	**STANCH**	STOPER

STORAX	STYLAR	SUNDOG	**SWOOSH**	SALTANT	SARDANA
STOREY	STYLER	**SUNDRY**	**SWOUND**	***SALTBOX**	SARDINE
STORMY	STYLET	**SUNKEN**	**SYLVAN**	SALTERN	SARDIUS
STOUND	STYLUS	**SUNKET**	**SYLVIN**	SALTIER	SARMENT
STOURE	**STYMIE**	SUNLIT	**SYMBOL**	**SALTILY**	SASHIMI
STOURY	***STYRAX**	SUNNAH	**SYNCOM**	SALTINE	**SASSABY**
STOVER	SUABLE	SUNNED	**SYNDET**	**SALTING**	SASSIER
STRAFE	**SUBBED**	SUNSET	**SYNDIC**	SALTIRE	SASSIES
STRAIN	**SUBDEB**	SUNTAN	**SYNGAS**	**SALTISH**	**SASSILY**
STRAIT	**SUBDUE**	**SUPERB**	***SYNTAX**	SALTPAN	SATANIC
STRAKE	***SUBFIX**	SUPINE	SYNURA	SALUTER	**SATCHEL**
STRAND	**SUBGUM**	**SUPPED**	**SYPHER**	**SALVAGE**	SATIATE
STRANG	SUBITO	**SUPPER**	**SYPHON**	**SALVING**	**SATIETY**
STRASS	SUBLET	**SUPPLE**	**SYSTEM**	**SAMBHUR**	SATINET
STRATA	SUBLOT	**SUPPLY**	***SYRINX**	**SAMBUAR**	**SATISFY**
STRATH	**SUBMIT**	SURELY	***SYZYGY**	**SAMBUCA**	SATRAPY
STRATI	SUBNET	SUREST	SABATON	***SAMBUKE**	SATSUMA
STRAWY	SUBORN	SURETY	**SABAYON**	SAMISEN	**SATYRID**
STREAK	**SUBPAR**	SURFER	**SABBATH**	**SAMOVAR**	**SAUCING**
STREAM	SUBSEA	SURGER	**SABBING**	**SAMPLER**	SAUNTER
STREEK	SUBSET	SURIMI	SACATON	SAMSARA	SAURIAN
STREET	SUBTLE	SURREY	**SACCADE**	SAMURAI	SAUSAGE
STRESS	**SUBURB**	**SURTAX**	**SACCATE**	**SANCTUM**	SAUTOIR
STRICK	**SUBWAY**	**SURVEY**	**SACCULE**	**SANDBAG**	**SAVABLE**
STRICT	**SUCCAH**	SUSLIK	***SACKBUT**	SANDBAR	**SAVANNA**
STRIDE	**SUCCOR**	SUTLER	***SACKFUL**	***SANDBOX**	**SAVARIN**
STRIFE	**SUCKER**	SUTTEE	**SACKING**	**SANDBUR**	**SAVELOY**
STRIKE	**SUCKLE**	SUTURE	**SACLIKE**	**SANDDAB**	**SAVIOUR**
STRING	**SUDARY**	***SVARAJ**	**SACRING**	**SANDFLY**	**SAVORER**
STRIPE	SUDDEN	SVELTE	SACRIST	**SANDHOG**	**SAVOURY**
STRIPT	SUDSER	***SWABBY**	SADDLER	SANDIER	**SAWBILL**
STRIPY	**SUFFER**	SWAGER	SADIRON	SANDLOT	***SAWBUCK**
STRIVE	***SUFFIX**	***SWAMPY**	SADNESS	**SANDMAN**	**SAWDUST**
STROBE	**SUGARY**	***SWANKY**	**SAFFRON**	**SANDPIT**	***SAWFISH**
STRODE	SUITER	***SWARAJ**	**SAFROLE**	SANGRIA	**SAWLIKE**
STROKE	SUITOR	**SWARTH**	**SAGAMAN**	SANICLE	**SAWMILL**
STROLL	***SUKKAH**	**SWARTY**	**SAGGARD**	SANTIMS	***SAXHORN**
STROMA	SULCUS	**SWATCH**	**SAGGING**	SANTOUR	***SAXTUBA**
STRONG	SULDAN	**SWATHE**	SAGIEST	***SAPAJOU**	**SCABBLE**
STROOK	SULFID	SWAYER	SAGUARO	SAPHEAD	**SCABIES**
STROUD	SULFUR	**SWEATY**	**SAHIWAL**	**SAPHENA**	**SCALADE**
STROVE	**SULKER**	**SWEENY**	**SAHUARO**	SAPIENS	**SCALADO**
STRUCK	SULLEN	**SWEEPY**	SAILING	SAPIENT	**SCALAGE**
STRUMA	**SULPHA**	**SWERVE**	**SAINTLY**	SAPLESS	**SCALARE**
STRUNG	SULTAN	**SWEVEN**	SALABLE	**SAPLING**	**SCALDIC**
STRUNT	SULTRY	***SWIMMY**	***SALCHOW**	SAPONIN	**SCALENE**
STUBBY	SUMACH	SWINGE	SALICIN	***SAPPHIC**	**SCALEUP**
STUCCO	**SUMMED**	SWINGY	SALIENT	**SAPPING**	SCALIER
STUDIO	**SUMMER**	SWIPLE	SALLIED	**SAPROBE**	**SCALING**
STUDLY	SUMMIT	SWIRLY	SALLIER	SAPSAGO	**SCALLOP**
*STUFFY	**SUMMON**	***SWISHY**	SALLIES	**SAPWOOD**	**SCALPEL**
STUMPY	**SUNBOW**	SWITCH	**SALLOWY**	**SARCASM**	SCALPER
STUPID	SUNDAE	**SWITHE**	SALPIAN	**SARCOID**	**SCAMPER**
STUPOR	SUNDER	**SWIVEL**	***SALPINX**	**SARCOMA**	SCANDAL
STURDY	SUNDEW	**SWIVET**	**SALSIFY**	SARCOUS	**SCANDIA**

SCANNED	SCOWDER	SEAPORT	SENATOR	SHADIER	SHERBET
SCANNER	SCOWLER	SEAREST	SENDOFF	SHADILY	SHEREEF
SCANTLY	SCRAGGY	SEASICK	SENECIO	SHADING	*SHERIFF
SCAPOSE	SCRAICH	SEASIDE	SENHORA	SHADOOF	SHEROOT
SCAPULA	SCRAIGH	SEATING	SENOPIA	*SHADOWY	SHERRIS
SCARIER	SCRAPER	SEAWALL	SENSATE	*SHAHDOM	SHIATSU
*SCARIFY	SCRAPIE	SEAWANT	SENSING	SHAITAN	*SHIATZU
SCARILY	*SCRAPPY	SEAWARD	SENSORY	*SHAKEUP	*SHICKER
SCARING	SCRATCH	SEAWARE	SENSUAL	SHAKIER	*SHICKSA
SCARLET	*SCRAWLY	SEAWEED	SENTIMO	*SHAKILY	SHIFTER
SCARPER	*SCRAWNY	SEBACIC	*SEPPUKU	*SHAKING	SHIKARI
SCARRED	*SCREAKY	SEBASIC	SEPTATE	SHALIER	*SHIKKER
SCARVES	SCREECH	SECEDER	SEPTIME	SHALLOP	SHILPIT
SCATTED	SCREWER	SECLUDE	*SEQUELA	SHALLOT	SHIMMER
SCATTER	SCREWUP	SECONDE	*SEQUENT	SHALLOW	SHINDIG
SCAUPER	SCRIBAL	SECONDO	*SEQUOIA	SHAMBLE	SHINGLE
SCENERY	SCRIBER	SECRECY	SERFAGE	SHAMING	SHINGLY
SCEPTER	SCRIEVE	SECRETE	SERFDOM	SHAMMAS	SHINIER
SCEPTIC	*SCRIMPY	SECTARY	SERFISH	*SHAMMED	SHINILY
SCEPTRE	SCROGGY	SECTILE	SERGING	SHAMMER	SHINING
*SCHAPPE	SCROOCH	SECTION	SERIATE	SHAMMES	SHINNED
SCHEMER	SCROOGE	SECULAR	SERICIN	SHAMMOS	SHINNEY
*SCHERZO	SCROTUM	SECURER	SERIEMA	SHAMOIS	SHIPLAP
*SCHIZZY	SCROUGE	SEDARIM	SERINGA	SHAMPOO	SHIPMAN
*SCHLEPP	*SCRUBBY	SEDUCER	SERIOUS	SHANTEY	*SHIPPED
*SCHLOCK	*SCRUFFY	SEEDBED	SERPENT	SHANTIH	SHIPPEN
*SCHLUMP	SCRUNCH	SEEDIER	SERPIGO	*SHAPELY	SHIPPER
*SCHMALZ	SCRUPLE	SEEDILY	SERRANO	SHAPEUP	SHIPPON
SCHMEAR	*SCUFFLE	SEEDMAN	SERRATE	SHAPING	*SHIPWAY
SCHMEER	SCULKER	SEEDPOD	SERVANT	SHARING	SHIRKER
SCHMOOS	SCULLER	SEEMING	SERVICE	SHARKER	SHITAKE
*SCHMUCK	SCULPIN	SEEPAGE	SERVILE	SHARPEN	SHITTAH
SCHNAPS	SCUMBAG	SEERESS	SERVING	SHARPER	SHITTIM
*SCHNOOK	SCUMBLE	SEGETAL	SESSILE	SHARPIE	*SHIVERY
*SCHNOZZ	SCUMMED	SEGMENT	SESSION	*SHARPLY	*SHLUMPY
SCHOLAR	SCUMMER	SEISING	SESTINA	SHASLIK	*SHMALTZ
*SCHTICK	SCUNNER	SEISURE	SESTINE	SHATTER	*SHMOOZE
SCIATIC	SCUPPER	*SEIZING	*SETBACK	SHAVING	*SHOCKER
SCIENCE	SCURRIL	*SEIZURE	SETLINE	SHEARER	SHODDEN
SCISSOR	SCUTAGE	SEJEANT	SETTING	SHEATHE	SHOEPAC
SCIURID	SCUTATE	SELENIC	SETTLER	SHEBANG	*SHOOFLY
*SCOFFER	SCUTTER	SELFDOM	SETTLOR	SHEBEAN	SHOOTER
SCOLDER	SCUTTLE	SELFISH	SEVENTH	SHEBEEN	*SHOPBOY
SCOLLOP	*SCYPHUS	SELLOUT	SEVENTY	SHEDDER	*SHOPHAR
SCOOPER	SEABIRD	*SELTZER	SEVERAL	SHEENEY	SHOPMAN
SCOOTER	SEABOOT	SELVAGE	*SEVICHE	SHEENIE	*SHOPPED
SCOPULA	*SEACOCK	SEMATIC	SEXIEST	SHEETER	SHOPPER
*SCORIFY	SEAFOOD	SEMIDRY	SEXLESS	SHELLAC	SHORING
SCORING	SEAFOWL	SEMIFIT	SEXTAIN	SHELLER	SHORTEN
SCORNER	SEAGIRT	SEMILOG	SEXTANT	SHELTER	SHORTIA
SCOTOMA	SEAGULL	SEMIMAT	SEXTILE	SHELTIE	SHORTIE
SCOTTIE	SEALANT	SEMINAL	SFERICS	SHELVER	SHORTLY
SCOURER	SEALERY	SEMINAR	SFUMATO	SHELVES	SHOTGUN
SCOURGE	SEAMARK	SEMIPRO	*SHACKLE	*SHEGETZ	SHOTTED
SCOUTER	SEAMIER	SEMIRAW	*SHADFLY	SHEITAN	SHOTTEN

SHOUTER	SILENTS	*SKIFFLE	SLIDING	SMUTTED	SOLARIA
SHOVING	SILENUS	SKILFUL	SLIMIER	SNAFFLE	SOLATIA
*SHOWBIZ	SILESIA	SKILLET	SLIMILY	SNAPPED	SOLDIER
*SHOWERY	SILICIC	*SKIMMER	SLIMING	SNAPPER	SOLERET
SHOWIER	SILICLE	SKINFUL	SLIMMED	SNARLER	SOLFEGE
*SHOWILY	SILICON	*SKINKER	SLIMMER	*SNATCHY	SOLICIT
SHOWING	*SILIQUA	SKINNED	SLIMPSY	SNEAKER	SOLIDLY
*SHOWMAN	*SILIQUE	SKINNER	SLINGER	SNEERER	SOLIDUS
*SHOWOFF	SILKIER	*SKIPPED	SLIPOUT	*SNEEZER	SOLITON
*SHRIEKY	SILKILY	*SKIPPER	SLIPPED	SNICKER	SOLOIST
*SHRIMPY	SILURID	*SKIPPET	SLIPPER	SNIFFER	SOLUBLE
SHRIVEL	SILVERN	SKIRRET	*SLIPWAY	SNIFFLE	SOLUBLY
SHRIVER	SILVERY	SKIRTER	SLITHER	SNIFTER	SOLVATE
*SHRUBBY	SILVICS	SKITTER	SLITTED	SNIGGER	SOLVENT
SHTETEL	SIMILAR	SKITTLE	SLOBBER	SNIGGLE	SOLVING
*SHUCKER	SIMIOID	SKIWEAR	SLOGGER	SNIPPED	SOMEDAY
SHUDDER	SIMIOUS	*SKOOKUM	SLOPPED	SNIPPER	*SOMEHOW
*SHUFFLE	SIMITAR	*SKREEGH	SLOTTED	SNIPPET	SOMEONE
SHUNNER	*SIMPLEX	*SKREIGH	*SLOUCHY	SNOOKER	*SOMEWAY
SHUNTER	SIMULAR	*SKULKER	SLOUGHY	SNOOPER	SONANCE
SHUTEYE	SINCERE	*SKYDIVE	SLOWISH	*SNOOZER	SONGFUL
*SHUTOFF	SINGLET	*SKYHOOK	SLUBBER	*SNOOZLE	SONHOOD
SHUTOUT	SINKAGE	*SKYJACK	SLUGGED	SNORKEL	SONLESS
SHUTTER	SINLESS	*SKYLARK	SLUGGER	SNORTER	SONLIKE
SHUTTLE	SINNING	SKYLINE	SLUMBER	SNOWCAP	*SONOVOX
*SHYLOCK	SINOPIA	*SKYPHOS	SLUMISM	SNOWIER	SONSHIP
SHYNESS	SINSYNE	SKYSAIL	SLUMMED	SNOWILY	SOOTHER
SHYSTER	SINUATE	*SKYWALK	SLUMMER	SNOWMAN	SOOTHLY
SIALOID	SINUOUS	*SKYWARD	SLUMGUM	SNUBBER	SOPHIES
SIAMANG	SIPPING	SLABBER	SLURRED	SNUFFER	SOPHISM
SIAMESE	SIRLOIN	SLACKEN	SLYNESS	SNUFFLE	SOPHIST
SIBLING	SIROCCO	SLACKER	*SMACKER	*SNUFFLY	SOPPING
*SICKBAY	SISTRUM	*SLACKLY	SMARTEN	SNUGGLE	SOPRANO
*SICKBED	SITHENS	SLAINTE	SMARTIE	SOAKAGE	SORBATE
*SICKISH	SITTING	SLAMMER	SMARTLY	*SOAPBOX	SORBENT
SICKOUT	SITUATE	SLANDER	SMASHER	SOAPIER	SORBOSE
SIDEARM	*SIXFOLD	SLAPPED	SMASHUP	SOAPILY	SORCERY
SIDEBAR	SIXTEEN	SLAPPER	SMATTER	SOARING	SORDINE
SIDECAR	*SIXTHLY	SLASHER	SMEARER	SOBERLY	SORDINO
SIDEMAN	*SIZABLE	SLATHER	SMECTIC	SOCAGER	SORGHUM
SIDEWAY	*SIZIEST	SLATIER	SMEDDUM	SOCCAGE	SORITES
SIEMENS	*SIZZLER	SLATING	SMELLER	SOCIETY	SOROCHE
SIENITE	*SJAMBOK	SLATTED	SMELTER	*SOCKEYE	SORORAL
SIFTING	SKATING	SLAVERY	SMIDGEN	*SOCKMAN	SOROSIS
SIGANID	SKATOLE	SLAVING	SMIDGIN	SODDING	SORRIER
SIGHTER	SKEETER	SLAVISH	SMIRKER	SOFTIES	SORRILY
SIGHTLY	SKELLUM	SLEDDER	SMITING	SOFTISH	SOTTISH
SIGMOID	SKELTER	SLEEKEN	SMITTEN	SOIGNEE	SOUBISE
SIGNAGE	SKEPSIS	SLEEKIT	SMOKING	SOILAGE	SOUFFLE
SIGNIFY	*SKEPTIC	SLEEKLY	SMOLDER	SOILURE	SOULFUL
SIGNIOR	*SKETCHY	SLEEPER	*SMOOCHY	SOJOURN	SOUNDER
SIGNORA	SKIABLE	SLEIGHT	*SMOOTHY	SOKEMAN	SOUNDLY
SIGNORE	SKIDDER	SLENDER	SMOTHER	SOLACER	SOUPCON
SIGNORY	SKIDDOO	SLICKER	SMUGGLE	SOLANIN	SOURISH
SILENCE	*SKIDWAY	*SLICKLY	*SMUTCHY	SOLANUM	SOURSOP

SOUTANE	SPHERAL	SPONSOR	STABILE	STEELIE	STOMATE
SOUTHER	SPHERIC	SPOOFER	STABLER	STEEPEN	STOMPER
*SOVKHOZ	SPICERY	SPOONEY	STACKER	STEEPER	STONIER
SOYBEAN	SPICIER	SPOROID	*STACKUP	STEEPLE	STONILY
*SOYMILK	SPICILY	SPORRAN	STADDLE	STEEPLY	STONING
*SOZZLED	SPICING	SPORTER	STADIUM	STEERER	STONISH
SPACIAL	SPICULA	SPORTIF	STAFFER	STELLAR	STOOKER
SPACING	SPICULE	SPORULE	STAGGED	STEMMED	STOOLIE
*SPACKLE	SPIDERY	SPOTLIT	STAGGER	STEMMER	STOOPER
SPADING	SPIEGEL	SPOTTER	STAGGIE	STEMSON	STOPGAP
SPAEING	SPIELER	SPOUSAL	STAGIER	STENCIL	STOPING
SPALLER	SPIKING	SPOUTER	STAGILY	STENGAH	STOPPED
SPANCEL	SPILING	*SPRAWLY	STAGING	STENOKY	STOPPER
*SPANDEX	SPILLER	SPRAYER	STAINER	STENTOR	STOPPLE
SPANGLE	SPINACH	SPRIEST	STAITHE	STEPPED	STORAGE
SPANGLY	SPINAGE	SPRIGGY	STALKER	STEPPER	STORIED
SPANIEL	SPINATE	SPRIGHT	STAMINA	STEPSON	STORIES
SPANKER	SPINDLE	SPRINGE	STAMMEL	STERILE	STORING
SPANNED	SPINDLY	SPRINGY	STAMMER	STERLET	STOURIE
SPANNER	SPINIER	SPUDDER	STAMPER	STERNAL	STOUTEN
SPAREST	SPINIES	SPUMIER	STANDBY	STERNUM	STOUTLY
SPARGER	SPINNER	SPUMING	STANDEE	STEROID	STOWAGE
SPARING	SPINNEY	SPUMONE	STANDER	STERTOR	STRAFER
SPARKER	*SPINOFF	SPUMONI	STANDUP	STETSON	STRANGE
SPARKLE	SPINOSE	SPUMOUS	STANINE	STEWARD	STRATAL
*SPARKLY	SPINOUS	SPUNKIE	STANING	STEWBUM	STRATUM
SPAROID	SPINOUT	SPURNER	STANNIC	STEWPAN	STRATUS
SPARRED	SPINULA	SPURRED	STANNUM	STHENIA	STRAYER
SPARROW	SPINULE	SPURRER	STARDOM	STIBIAL	STREAKY
SPARTAN	SPIRAEA	SPURREY	STARETS	STIBINE	STREAMY
SPASTIC	SPIRANT	SPURTLE	STARING	STIBIUM	STRETCH
SPATHIC	SPIREME	SPUTNIK	STARLET	STICKER	STRETTA
SPATIAL	SPIRIER	SPUTTER	STARLIT	STICKIT	STRETTO
SPATTED	SPIRING	*SQUABBY	STARRED	STICKLE	STREWER
SPATTER	SPIROID	*SQUALID	STARTER	*STICKUM	STRIATE
SPATULA	SPIRULA	*SQUALLY	STARTLE	*STICKUP	STRIDER
*SPATZLE	SPITING	*SQUALOR	STARTSY	STIFFEN	STRIDOR
SPAWNER	SPITTED	*SQUARER	STARTUP	*STIFFLY	STRIGIL
SPEAKER	SPITTER	*SQUASHY	STARVER	STIFLER	STRIKER
SPEARER	SPITTLE	*SQUATTE	STATANT	STINGER	STRINGY
SPECIAL	*SPLASHY	*SQUATTY	STATELY	STINKER	STRIPER
*SPECIFY	SPLEENY	*SQUAWKE	STATICE	STINTER	STRIVER
*SPECKLE	SPLENIA	*SQUEAKY	STATING	STIPEND	STROBIC
SPECTER	SPLENIC	*SQUEEZE	STATION	STIPPLE	STROBIL
SPECTRA	SPLICER	*SQUELCH	STATISM	STIPULE	STROKER
SPECTRE	SPLODGE	*SQUIFFY	STATIST	STIRRED	STROPHE
SPEEDER	SPLOTCH	*SQUILLA	STATIVE	STIRRER	STROPPY
SPEEDUP	SPLURGE	*SQUINCH	STATURE	STIRRUP	STROYER
SPELEAN	SPLURGY	*SQUINNY	STATUSY	STOCKER	STRUDEL
SPELLER	SPOILER	*SQUINTY	STATUTE	STOKING	STUBBLE
SPELTER	SPONDEE	*SQUIRMY	STAUNCH	STOLLEN	STUBBLY
SPELUNK	SPONGER	*SQUISHY	STEALER	STOMACH	STUDDIE
SPENCER	SPONGIN	*SQUOOSH	STEALTH	STOMATA	STUDENT
SPENDER	SPONSAL	SRADDHA	STEAMER		STUDIED
SPHENIC	SPONSON	STABBER	STEARIN		STUDIER

STUDIES	SUBLATE	**SULFATE**	SURMISE	**SWIPPLE**	SAGENESS
STUFFER	**SUBLIME**	**SULFIDE**	SURNAME	**SWISHER**	SAGITTAL
STUIVER	SUBLINE	**SULFITE**	SURPASS	**SWITHER**	**SAILBOAT**
STUMBLE	**SUBMENU**	**SULFONE**	SURPLUS	*SWITHLY	**SAILFISH**
STUMMED	SUBMISS	**SULFURY**	SURREAL	**SWIVING**	**SAINFOIN**
STUMPER	SUBORAL	SULLAGE	SURTOUT	*SWIZZLE	**SAINTDOM**
STUNNED	**SUBOVAL**	**SULPHID**	SURVEIL	**SWOBBER**	**SALACITY**
STUNNER	**SUBPART**	**SULPHUR**	SURVIVE	**SWOLLEN**	**SALADANG**
*STUPEFY	**SUBPENA**	SULTANA	SUSPECT	**SWOONER**	SALARIAT
STUTTER	**SUBPLOT**	SUMLESS	SUSPEND	**SWOOPER**	**SALEABLE**
STYGIAN	**SUBRACE**	**SUMMAND**	SUSPIRE	**SWOTTER**	**SALEROOM**
STYLATE	SUBRENT	**SUMMARY**	SUSTAIN	SYCOSIS	**SALESMAN**
STYLING	**SUBRING**	**SUMMATE**	SUTURAL	**SYENITE**	**SALICINE**
STYLISE	**SUBRULE**	**SUMMERY**	SWABBER	**SYLLABI**	**SALIENCE**
STYLISH	**SUBSALE**	**SUMMING**	SWABBIE	*SYLPHID	**SALIENCY**
STYLIST	**SUBSECT**	**SUMMONS**	SWADDLE	**SYLVINE**	**SALINITY**
STYLITE	SUBSERE	**SUMPTER**	SWAGGED	**SYLVITE**	*SALINIZE
*STYLIZE	**SUBSIDE**	*SUNBACK	**SWAGGER**	**SYMBION**	**SALIVATE**
STYLOID	**SUBSIDY**	**SUNBATH**	SWAGGIE	**SYMBIOT**	**SALMONID**
STYPSIS	**SUBSIST**	**SUNBEAM**	**SWAGING**	*SYMPTOM	SALSILLA
STYPTIC	**SUBSITE**	**SUNBELT**	SWAGMAN	SYNAGOG	**SALTBUSH**
STYRENE	**SUBSOIL**	**SUNBIRD**	**SWALLOW**	SYNANON	SALTIEST
SUASION	**SUBSUME**	**SUNBURN**	SWAMIES	**SYNAPSE**	SALTLESS
SUAVITY	**SUBTASK**	**SUNDECK**	SWAMPER	**SYNCARP**	**SALTLIKE**
SUBACID	**SUBTEEN**	**SUNDIAL**	SWANNED	*SYNCHRO	SALTNESS
SUBADAR	**SUBTEND**	**SUNDOWN**	SWANPAN	**SYNCOPE**	*SALTWORK
SUBALAR	**SUBTEST**	**SUNFAST**	SWAPPER	**SYNERGY**	**SALTWORT**
SUBAREA	*SUBTEXT	**SUNFISH**	SWARMER	**SYNESIS**	**SALUTARY**
SUBARID	**SUBTILE**	**SUNGLOW**	*SWARTHY	**SYNFUEL**	**SALVABLE**
SUBATOM	**SUBTONE**	**SUNLAMP**	SWASHER	*SYNGAMY	**SALVAGEE**
SUBBASE	**SUBTYPE**	**SUNLAND**	SWATHER	*SYNONYM	**SALVAGER**
SUBBASS	**SUBUNIT**	SUNLESS	SWATTED	**SYNOVIA**	*SALVIFIC
SUBBING	**SUBVENE**	**SUNLIKE**	SWATTER	**SYNTONY**	**SAMARIUM**
SUBCELL	**SUBVERT**	SUNNING	*SWAYFUL	**SYRINGA**	**SAMENESS**
SUBCLAN	*SUBZERO	SUNRISE	SWEARER	**SYRINGE**	*SAMIZDAT
SUBCODE	*SUBZONE	**SUNROOF**	SWEATER	*SYRPHID	*SAMPHIRE
SUBCOOL	**SUCCEED**	**SUNROOM**	SWEEPER	**SYSTOLE**	**SAMPLING**
SUBCULT	**SUCCESS**	SUNSPOT	**SWEETEN**	SABBATIC	SANATIVE
SUBDEAN	**SUCCORY**	**SUNSUIT**	**SWEETIE**	**SABOTAGE**	*SANCTIFY
SUBDUAL	**SUCCOTH**	**SUNWARD**	**SWEETLY**	**SABOTEUR**	**SANCTION**
SUBDUCE	**SUCCOUR**	**SUNWISE**	**SWELTER**	**SABULOSE**	**SANCTITY**
SUBDUCT	**SUCCUBA**	SUPPING	**SWELTRY**	**SABULOUS**	SANDARAC
SUBDUER	*SUCCUMB	**SUPPORT**	SWERVER	**SACCULAR**	*SANDBANK
SUBECHO	**SUCCUSS**	**SUPPOSE**	SWIDDEN	**SACCULUS**	**SANDBURR**
SUBEDIT	**SUCKLER**	**SUPREME**	**SWIFTER**	*SACKLIKE	*SANDFISH
SUBERIC	**SUCRASE**	**SUPREMO**	*SWIFTLY	*SACKSFUL	SANDIEST
SUBERIN	**SUCROSE**	**SURBASE**	**SWIGGER**	**SACRARIA**	**SANDLIKE**
SUBFILE	**SUCTION**	SURCOAT	**SWILLER**	**SACRISTY**	**SANDLING**
SUBFUSC	**SUFFARI**	**SURFACE**	**SWIMMER**	**SADDLERY**	**SANDPEEP**
SUBGOAL	*SUFFICE	**SURFEIT**	**SWINDLE**	**SADDLING**	**SANDPILE**
SUBHEAD	**SUFFUSE**	**SURFIER**	*SWINGBY	**SAFENESS**	**SANDSHOE**
SUBIDEA	**SUGGEST**	**SURFING**	**SWINGER**	**SAFRANIN**	**SANDSOAP**
SUBITEM	**SUICIDE**	SURGEON	**SWINGLE**	**SAGACITY**	**SANDSPUR**
*SUBJECT	**SUITING**	**SURGERY**	**SWINISH**	**SAGAMORE**	*SANDWICH
*SUBJOIN	**SULCATE**	**SURGING**	SWINNEY	SAGANASH	**SANDWORM**

SANDWORT	SAVAGISM	*SCHLOCKY	*SCRAPPED	SEASHELL	*SELFHOOD
SANENESS	SAVANNAH	*SCHMALTZ	SCRAPPER	SEASHORE	SELFLESS
SANGAREE	*SAVINGLY	*SCHMALZY	SCRAPPLE	SEASONAL	SELFNESS
SANGUINE	SAVORIER	*SCHMELZE	*SCRATCHY	SEASONER	SELFSAME
SANITARY	SAVORIES	*SCHMOOSE	SCRAWLER	SEATLESS	*SELFWARD
SANITATE	SAVOROUS	*SCHMOOZE	SCREAMER	SEATMATE	SELVEDGE
SANITIES	SAVOURER	*SCHNAPPS	*SCREECHY	SEATRAIN	SEMANTIC
SANITISE	SAWBONES	*SCHNECKE	SCREENER	*SEATWORK	SEMESTER
*SANITIZE	SAWHORSE	*SCHOLIUM	SCRIBBLE	SEAWATER	SEMIARID
SANNYASI	SAWTOOTH	SCHOONER	SCRIMPER	SECALOSE	SEMIBALD
SANSERIF	*SAXATILE	*SCHRIEVE	SCRIMPIT	SECANTLY	SEMICOMA
SANTALIC	SAYONARA	SCHUSSER	*SCRIPTER	SECATEUR	SEMIDEAF
SANTALOL	*SCABBARD	SCIAENID	SCROFULA	SECONDER	SEMIDOME
SANTONIN	SCABIOSA	SCIATICA	*SCROOTCH	SECONDLY	SEMIGALA
SAPIDITY	SCABIOUS	SCILICET	SCROUNGE	SECRETIN	SEMIHARD
SAPIENCE	SCABLAND	SCIMETAR	SCROUNGY	SECRETLY	*SEMIHIGH
*SAPIENCY	*SCABLIKE	SCIMITAR	SCRUBBER	SECRETOR	*SEMIHOBO
*SAPONIFY	SCABROUS	SCIMITER	SCRUTINY	SECTORAL	SEMIMATT
SAPONINE	*SCAFFOLD	SCINCOID	*SCUFFLER	SECUNDUM	SEMIMUTE
SAPONITE	SCALABLE	SCIOLISM	SCULLERY	SECUREST	SEMINARY
*SAPPHIRE	SCALAWAG	SCIOLIST	SCULLION	SECURING	SEMINUDE
*SAPPHISM	SCALENUS	SCIROCCO	SCULPTOR	SECURITY	SEMIOSTS
*SAPPHIST	SCALEPAN	SCIRRHUS	*SCUMLIKE	SEDATION	SEMIOTIC
SAPREMIA	SCALIEST	SCISSILE	*SCUMMING	SEDATIVE	SEMISOFT
SAPROPEL	SCALLION	SCISSION	*SCUPPAUG	SEDERUNT	SEMITIST
SARABAND	*SCAMMONY	SCISSURE	SCURRIED	SEDILIUM	SEMITONE
SARCENET	*SCAMPISH	SCIURINE	SCURRIES	SEDIMENT	SEMIWILD
SARDONIC	SCANDENT	SCIUROID	SCURRILE	SEDITION	SEMOLINA
*SARDONYX	SCANDIUM	*SCLAFFER	*SCUTCHER	SEDULITY	SEMPLICE
SARGASSO	SCANNING	SCLEREID	SCUTELLA	SEDULOUS	SENARIUS
SARMENTA	SCANSION	SCLERITE	*SCYPHATE	*SEECATCH	SENILELY
SARODIST	SCANTIER	SCLEROID	*SEABEACH	*SEEDCAKE	SENILITY
SARSENET	SCANTIES	SCLEROMA	SEABOARD	SEEDCASE	SENNIGHT
SARTORII	*SCAPHOID	SCLEROSE	SEABORNE	SEEDIEST	SENORITA
SASSIEST	SCAPULAR	SCLEROUS	SEACOAST	SEEDLESS	SENSEFUL
SASSWOOD	*SCARCELY	*SCOFFLAW	SEACRAFT	SEEDLIKE	SENSIBLE
SASTRUGA	*SCARCITY	SCOLDING	SEADROME	SEEDLING	SENSILLA
SATANISM	*SCARFPIN	SCOLIOMA	SEAFARER	SEEDSMAN	SENSORIA
SATANIST	SCARIEST	*SCOOPFUL	SEAFLOOR	SEEDTIME	SENSUOUS
SATIABLE	SCARIOSE	*SCORCHER	SEAFRONT	SEICENTO	SENTENCE
SATINPOD	SCARIOUS	SCOREPAD	SEAGOING	SEIGNEUR	SENTIENT
SATIRISE	SCARLESS	SCORNFUL	SEALLIKE	SEIGNIOR	SENTINEL
SATIRIST	SCARRING	SCORPION	SEALSKIN	SEIGNORY	SEPARATE
*SATIRIZE	*SCATBACK	SCOTOPIA	SEAMIEST	SEISMISM	SEPTARIA
SATIRTSE	SCATTING	SCOURGER	SEAMLESS	SELADANG	SEPTETTE
SATURANT	SCAVENGE	SCOURING	SEAMLIKE	SELAMLIK	SEPTUPLE
SATURATE	SCENARIO	SCOUTHER	SEAMOUNT	SELCOUTH	*SEQUENCE
*SAUCEBOX	SCENICAL	SCOUTING	SEAMSTER	SELECTEE	*SEQUENCY
SAUCEPAN	SCEPTRAL	SCRABBLE	SEAPIECE	SELECTLY	*SEQUITUR
SAUROPOD	SCHEDULE	*SCRABBLY	SEAPLANE	SELECTOR	SERAGLIO
SAUTERNE	SCHILLER	*SCRAGGLY	*SEAQUAKE	SELENATE	*SERAPHIM
SAUTOIRE	*SCHIZIER	SCRAMBLE	SEAROBIN	SELENIDE	SERENADE
*SAVAGERY	*SCHIZOID	*SCRAMJET	SEASCAPE	SELENITE	SERENATA
SAVAGEST	*SCHIZONT	SCRANNEL	SEASCOUT	SELENIUM	SERENITY
SAVAGING	SCHLIERE	SCRAPING	SEASHELL	SELFHEAL	*SERFHOOD

*SERFLIKE	SHANTIES	*SHMALTZY	SIDEHILL	SIMULANT	*SKYDIVER
SERGEANT	SHANTUNG	SHOEBILL	*SIDEKICK	SIMULATE	*SKYLIGHT
SERIALLY	*SHASHLIK	SHOEHORN	SIDELINE	SINAPISM	*SKYWARDS
SERIATIM	SHEALING	SHOELACE	SIDELING	SINCIPUT	*SKYWRITE
*SERJEANT	SHEARING	SHOELESS	SIDELONG	SINECURE	*SLABBERY
SEROLOGY	SHEATHER	*SHOEPACK	SIDEREAL	SINFONIA	SLABBING
SEROSITY	SHEDABLE	SHOETREE	SIDERITE	SINGSONG	SLABLIKE
SEROTINE	SHEDDING	SHOOTING	*SIDESHOW	SINGULAR	SLAPDASH
SEROTYPE	*SHEDLIKE	SHOOTOUT	SIDESLIP	*SINICIZE	*SLAPJACK
SERRANID	SHEENFUL	SHOPGIRL	SIDESPIN	SINISTER	SLAPPING
SERVABLE	*SHEEPCOT	*SHOPLIFT	SIDESTEP	*SINKHOLE	SLASHING
SERVICER	*SHEEPDOG	*SHOPPING	*SIDEWALK	SINOLOGY	SLATIEST
SERVITOR	*SHEEPISH	*SHOPTALK	SIDEWALL	SINUSOID	SLATTERN
SESAMOID	*SHEEPMAN	*SHOPWORN	SIDEWARD	SIPHONAL	SLATTING
SESSPOOL	*SHEETFED	SHORTAGE	*SIDEWAYS	*SIPHONIC	SLAVERER
SESTERCE	SHEETING	SHORTCUT	SIDEWISE	SIRENIAN	SLEDDING
SETENANT	*SHEIKDOM	SHORTIES	*SIEROZEM	SIRVENTE	SLEEKIER
SETIFORM	*SHELDUCK	SHORTISH	SIFFLEUR	SISSYISH	SLEEPING
SETSCREW	*SHELFFUL	SHOTTING	SIGHLESS	SISTERLY	SLEIGHER
SETTLING	*SHELLACK	SHOULDER	*SIGHLIKE	SISTROID	*SLIDEWAY
SETULOSE	*SHELVING	SHOULDST	SIGHTING	SITARIST	SLIMIEST
SETULOUS	*SHEPHERD	SHOVELER	SIGHTSEE	SITHENCE	SLIMMEST
SEVERITY	SHERBERT	*SHOWBOAT	SIGNALER	SITOLOGY	SLIMMING
SEWERAGE	*SHERLOCK	*SHOWCASE	SIGNALLY	*SITZMARK	SLIMNESS
*SEXINESS	SHETLAND	*SHOWDOWN	SIGNIORY	*SIXPENCE	SLIPCASE
*SEXOLOGY	SHIELDER	SHOWERER	SIGNPOST	*SIXPENNY	*SLIPFORM
*SEXTARII	SHIELING	*SHOWGIRL	SILENCER	*SIXTIETH	SLIPKNOT
*SEXTETTE	SHIGELLA	SHOWIEST	SILICATE	*SIXTYISH	SLIPLESS
*SEXTUPLE	*SHIITAKE	*SHOWRING	SILICIDE	*SIZEABLE	SLIPOVER
*SEXTUPLY	*SHIKAREE	*SHOWROOM	*SILICIFY	*SIZINESS	SLIPPAGE
*SFORZATO	SHILINGI	SHRAPNEL	SILICIUM	SKELETON	*SLIPPERY
*SHACKLER	SHILLALA	SHREDDER	SILICONE	*SKETCHER	SLIPPING
*SHADBLOW	SHILLING	*SHREWDIE	SILICULA	*SKEWBACK	SLIPSHOD
*SHADBUSH	*SHIMMERY	*SHREWISH	SILKIEST	*SKEWBALD	SLIPSLOP
*SHADCHAN	*SHIMMING	*SHRIEKER	*SILKLIKE	*SKEWNESS	SLIPSOLE
*SHADDOCK	SHINBONE	SHRIEVAL	*SILKWEED	*SKIAGRAM	SLIPWARE
SHADIEST	SHINGLER	*SHRIMPER	*SILKWORM	*SKIJORER	SLITHERY
*SHADOWER	SHINIEST	*SHRINKER	SILLABUB	SKILLESS	SLITLESS
*SHADRACH	SHINLEAF	*SHRIVING	SILLIBUB	*SKILLFUL	SLITTING
*SHAFTING	SHINNERY	*SHRUNKEN	*SILOXANE	SKILLING	SLIVERER
*SHAGBARK	SHINNING	*SHUCKING	SILUROID	*SKIMMING	*SLIVOVIC
SHAGREEN	SHIPLOAD	*SHUDDERY	SILVERER	*SKINHEAD	*SLOBBERY
*SHAKEOUT	*SHIPMATE	*SHUFFLER	SILVERLY	SKINLESS	*SLOBBISH
*SHAKIEST	*SHIPMENT	*SHUNPIKE	SILVICAL	*SKINLIKE	SLOGGING
SHALIEST	*SHIPPING	*SHUTDOWN	SIMARUBA	SKINNING	SLOPPING
SHALLOON	SHIPSIDE	SHUTTING	*SIMAZINE	SKIORING	*SLOPWORK
*SHAMABLE	*SHIPWORM	*SHWANPAN	SIMOLEON	*SKIPJACK	*SLOTBACK
*SHAMEFUL	*SHIPYARD	SIALIDAN	SIMONIAC	SKIPLANE	SLOTHFUL
*SHAMMASH	SHIRRING	SIBILANT	SIMONIES	*SKIPPING	SLOTTING
*SHAMMIED	SHIRTING	SIBILATE	SIMONIST	*SKIRMISH	SLOUCHER
*SHAMMIES	SHITTING	SICKENER	*SIMONIZE	SKIRTING	SLOVENLY
*SHAMMING	SHIVAREE	*SICKERLY	SIMPERER	*SKITTERY	*SLOWDOWN
*SHAMOSIM	SHIVERER	SICKNESS	*SIMPLIFY	*SKITTISH	SLOWNESS
*SHAMROCK	*SHKOTZIM	*SICKROOM	SIMPLISM	*SKULLCAP	*SLOWPOKE
*SHANGHAI	SHLEMIEL	SIDEBAND	SIMPLIST	*SKYBORNE	*SLOWWORM

SLUBBING	SNITCHER	*SODOMIZE	SONGFEST	*SPANKING	SPINALLY
SLUGABED	SNIVELER	*SOFTBACK	SONGLESS	SPANLESS	SPINDLER
SLUGFEST	*SNOBBERY	SOFTBALL	SONGLIKE	SPANNING	SPINELLE
SLUGGARD	SNOBBIER	SOFTENER	SONGSTER	*SPANWORM	*SPINIFEX
SLUGGING	*SNOBBILY	*SOFTHEAD	SONICATE	SPARABLE	SPINLESS
SLUGGISH	*SNOBBISH	SOFTNESS	SONOBUOY	SPARERIB	SPINNERY
SLUGPEST	SNOBBISM	SOFTWARE	SONOGRAM	SPARKIER	SPINNING
*SLUMBERY	SNOUTISH	*SOFTWOOD	SONORANT	*SPARKILY	SPINSTER
SLUMLORD	SNOWBALL	SOILLESS	SONORITY	*SPARKISH	SPIRACLE
SLUMMING	*SNOWBANK	SOLANDER	SONOROUS	SPARKLER	SPIRALLY
SLURRING	SNOWBELL	SOLANINE	SOOCHONG	SPARLING	SPIRIEST
SLYBOOTS	SNOWBELT	SOLARISE	SOOTHEST	SPARRIER	SPIRILLA
SMALLAGE	SNOWBIRD	SOLARISM	SOOTHING	SPARRING	SPITBALL
SMALLISH	*SNOWBUSH	SOLARIUM	SOOTHSAY	SPARSITY	SPITEFUL
*SMALLPOX	SNOWDROP	*SOLARIZE	SORBITOL	SPATTING	SPITFIRE
SMALTINE	SNOWFALL	SOLATION	SORCERER	*SPEAKING	SPITTING
SMALTITE	SNOWIEST	SOLATIUM	SOREHEAD	SPEARGUN	SPITTOON
SMARAGDE	SNOWLAND	SOLDERER	SORENESS	SPEARMAN	SPLASHER
SMARTASS	SNOWLESS	SOLDIERY	SORICINE	SPECIATE	SPLATTER
SMECTITE	*SNOWLIKE	SOLECISE	SORORATE	*SPECIFIC	SPLENDID
SMELTERY	SNOWMELT	SOLECISM	SORORITY	SPECIMEN	SPLENDOR
SMIDGEON	SNOWMOLD	SOLECIST	SORPTION	SPECIOUS	SPLENIAL
SMITHERS	*SNOWPACK	*SOLECIZE	SORRIEST	SPECTATE	SPLENIUM
*SMITHERY	*SNOWPLOW	SOLELESS	SORROWER	SPECTRAL	SPLENIUS
*SMOCKING	*SNOWSHED	SOLENESS	SOUCHONG	SPECTRUM	SPLINTER
*SMOKEPOT	SNOWSHOE	SOLENOID	SOUGHING	SPECULUM	SPLITTER
SMOOTHEN	SNOWSUIT	SOLFEGGI	*SOUFFLED	SPEEDIER	*SPLOTCHY
SMOOTHER	SNUBNESS	SOLIDAGO	*SOUNDBOX	SPEEDILY	SPLURGER
SMOOTHIE	*SNUFFBOX	SOLIDARY	SOUNDING	SPEEDING	SPLUTTER
*SMOOTHLY	SNUFFIER	*SOLIDIFY	SOUNDMAN	*SPEEDWAY	SPOILAGE
*SMOTHERY	*SNUFFILY	SOLIDITY	SOURBALL	SPEERING	SPOLIATE
SMOULDER	SNUFFLER	*SOLIQUID	SOURDINE	SPELAEAN	SPONDAIC
SMUGGLER	SNUGGERY	SOLITARY	SOURNESS	SPELLING	SPONGIER
SMUGNESS	SNUGGEST	SOLITUDE	SOURPUSS	*SPERMARY	SPONGILY
SMUTTING	SNUGGIES	SOLLERET	SOURWOOD	SPERMINE	SPONGING
SNAGLIKE	SNUGGING	SOLONETS	SOUTACHE	SPERMOUS	SPONSION
SNAKEBIT	SNUGNESS	*SOLONETZ	SOUTHERN	*SPHAGNUM	SPONTOON
*SNAPBACK	*SOAPBARK	SOLSTICE	SOUTHING	SPHENOID	*SPOOFERY
SNAPLESS	SOAPIEST	SOLUTION	*SOUTHPAW	*SPHERICS	*SPOOKERY
SNAPPIER	SOAPLESS	SOLVABLE	SOUTHRON	SPHERIER	*SPOOKISH
*SNAPPILY	SOAPSUDS	*SOLVENCY	SOUVENIR	SPHERING	SPOOLING
SNAPPING	SOAPWORT	SOMBRERO	*SOUVLAKI	SPHEROID	SPOONFUL
*SNAPPISH	*SOBERIZE	SOMBROUS	SOVRANLY	SPHERULE	SPOONIER
SNAPSHOT	SOBRIETY	*SOMEBODY	SOVRANTY	SPHINGES	SPOONIES
SNAPWEED	SOCIABLE	SOMEDEAL	*SOWBELLY	*SPHINGID	SPOONING
SNATCHER	*SOCIABLY	SOMERSET	SOWBREAD	*SPHYGMUS	SPORADIC
SNEERFUL	SOCIALLY	SOMETIME	SPACEMAN	SPICCATO	*SPOROZOA
*SNICKERY	SOCKLESS	*SOMEWAYS	SPACIOUS	SPICIEST	SPORTFUL
SNIFFIER	SODALIST	*SOMEWHAT	SPADEFUL	SPICULUM	SPORTIVE
*SNIFFILY	SODALITE	*SOMEWHEN	SPADICES	*SPIFFING	SPOTLESS
*SNIFFISH	SODALITY	SOMEWISE	SPADILLE	SPIKELET	SPOTTING
SNIFFLER	SODAMIDE	SONARMAN	*SPAETZLE	SPILIKIN	SPRADDLE
SNIGGLER	SODDENLY	SONATINA	*SPAGYRIC	SPILLAGE	SPRATTLE
*SNIPPETY	SODOMIST	SONGBIRD	SPALPEEN	*SPILLWAY	SPRAWLER
SNIPPING	SODOMITE	*SONGBOOK	SPANDREL		SPREADER

SPRIGGER	STAKEOUT	STELLIFY	STOKESIA	STROLLER	*SUBERIZE
SPRINGAL	STALLION	STEMLESS	STOLPORT	STRONGYL	SUBEROSE
SPRINGER	STALWART	STEMLIKE	*STOMACHY	STRONTIA	SUBEROUS
SPRINKLE	STAMPEDE	*STEMMERY	STOMATAL	STROPPER	SUBFIELD
SPRINTER	STANCHER	STEMMING	STOMATIC	STRUCKEN	SUBFLOOR
*SPRITZER	*STANCHLY	STEMWARE	STOMODEA	STRUGGLE	SUBFLUID
*SPROCKET	STANDARD	STENOSED	STONEFLY	STRUMMER	*SUBFRAME
SPRYNESS	STANDING	STENOSIS	STONIEST	STRUMOSE	SUBGENRE
SPUMIEST	STANDISH	STEPDAME	*STOPBANK	STRUMOUS	SUBGENUS
SPURGALL	*STANDOFF	STEPLIKE	*STOPCOCK	STRUMPET	SUBGRADE
SPURIOUS	STANDOUT	STEPPING	STOPOVER	STRUTTER	*SUBGRAPH
SPURRIER	STANDPAT	STEPWISE	STOPPAGE	STUBBIER	SUBGROUP
SPURRING	STANHOPE	STERICAL	STOPPING	*STUBBILY	*SUBHUMAN
SPYGLASS	STANNARY	STERIGMA	STORABLE	STUBBING	*SUBHUMID
*SQUABBLE	STANNITE	STERLING	STOTINKA	STUBBORN	*SUBINDEX
*SQUADRON	STANNOUS	STERNITE	STOUTISH	STUCCOER	SUBLEASE
*SQUALENE	STANNOUS	STERNSON	*STOWAWAY	*STUDBOOK	SUBLEVEL
*SQUALLER	STAPEDES	STERNWAY	STRADDLE	STUDDING	SUBLIMER
*SQUANDER	STAPELIA	STIBNITE	STRAGGLE	*STUDFISH	SUBLUNAR
*SQUARELY	*STARGAZE	*STICKFUL	STRAGGLY	STUDIOUS	SUBMERGE
*SQUAREST	STARKERS	STICKIER	STRAIGHT	*STUDWORK	SUBMERSE
*SQUARING	STARLESS	*STICKILY	STRAINER	STUFFIER	SUBNASAL
*SQUARISH	STARLIKE	STICKLER	STRAITEN	*STUFFING	*SUBNICHE
*SQUASHER	STARLING	*STICKMAN	STRAMASH	STULTIFY	SUBNODAL
*SQUATTER	STARNOSE	STICKOUT	STRAMONY	STUMBLER	SUBOPTIC
*SQUAWKER	STARRING	*STICKPIN	STRANDER	STUMMING	SUBORDER
*SQUEAKER	STARSHIP	STICTION	STRANGER	STUMPAGE	SUBORNER
*SQUEALER	STARTLER	*STIFFISH	STRANGLE	STUNNING	SUBOVATE
*SQUEEGEE	STARWORT	STILBENE	STRAPPER	STUNSAIL	*SUBOXIDE
*SQUEEZER	STASIMON	STILBITE	STRATEGY	STUNTMAN	SUBPANEL
*SQUELCHY	STATABLE	STILETTO	STRATIFY	STURGEON	*SUBPHASE
*SQUIFFED	STATEDLY	STILLMAN	STRATOUS	STYLISER	*SUBPHYLA
*SQUIGGLE	*STATICKY	STIMULUS	STRAVAGE	*STYLIZER	SUBPOENA
*SQUIGGLY	STATUARY	STINGIER	STRAVAIG	SUBABBOT	SUBPOLAR
*SQUILGEE	STAUMREL	STINGILY	STRAWHAT	SUBACRID	*SUBPUBIC
*SQUINTER	STAYSAIL	STINGRAY	STREAKER	SUBACUTE	SUBSCALE
*SQUIREEN	STEADIED	STINKARD	STREAMER	SUBADULT	SUBSENSE
*SQUIRISH	STEADIER	*STINKBUG	STREEKER	SUBAGENT	SUBSERVE
*SQUIRMER	STEADIES	STINKIER	STRENGTH	SUBANHAR	*SUBSHAFT
*SQUIRREL	STEADING	STINKPOT	STRESSOR	*SUBAXIAL	SUBSHELL
*SQUIRTER	STEALAGE	STIPPLER	*STRETCHY	SUBBASIN	*SUBSHRUB
*SQUOOSHY	STEALING	STIRRING	STREUSEL	*SUBBLOCK	SUBSIDER
STABLEST	STEALTHY	STITCHER	STRICKEN	SUBBREED	SUBSKILL
STABLING	STEAPSIN	STOCCADO	STRICKLE	SUBCASTE	SUBSOLAR
STABLISH	STEARATE	STOCCATA	STRIDENT	SUBCAUSE	SUBSONIC
STACCATO	STEARINE	*STOCKADE	STRIDING	*SUBCHIEF	SUBSPACE
STAGEFUL	STEATITE	*STOCKCAR	STRIGOSE	SUBCLASS	SUBSTAGE
STAGGARD	STEDFAST	STOCKIER	STRINGER	*SUBCLERK	SUBSTATE
STAGGART	STEENBOK	*STOCKILY	STRIPIER	SUBCUTIS	*SUBTAXON
STAGGERY	STEEPISH	*STOCKING	STRIPING	SUBDEPOT	*SUBTHEME
STAGGING	STEERAGE	*STOCKISH	STRIPPED	SUBDURAL	SUBTILIN
STAGIEST	STEEVING	STOCKIST	STRIPPER	SUBENTRY	SUBTILTY
STAGNANT	STEGODON	*STOCKMAN	STROBILA	*SUBEPOCH	SUBTITLE
STAGNATE	STEINBOK	*STOCKPOT	STROBILE	SUBERECT	SUBTLETY
STAIRWAY	STELLATE	STOICISM	STROBILI	SUBERISE	SUBTONIC

SUBTOPIA	SUMMONER	SURGICAL	SYLLABLE	PE S TO	BU S TIC
SUBTOPIC	*SUMPWEED	SURICATE	*SYLLABUB	PE S TY	BU S TLE
SUBTOTAL	*SUNBAKED	SURMISER	SYLLABUS	PI S CO	BY S S US
SUBTRACT	SUNBATHE	SURMOUNT	*SYLVATIC	PI S TE	CA S ABA
SUBTREND	*SUNBLOCK	SURNAMER	RE S OD	CA S AVA
SUBTRIBE	SUNBURST	SURPLICE	*SYMBIONT	RE S OD	CA S AVA
SUBTUNIC	*SUNCHOKE	SURPRINT	*SYMBIOTE	RI S US	CA S BAH
SUBULATE	SUNDERER	SURPRISE	*SYMBOLIC	S U S HI	CA S EFY
SUBURBAN	SUNDRESS	*SURPRIZE	*SYMMETRY	S Y S OP	CA S EIN
SUBURBIA	SUNDRIES	SURROUND	*SYMPATHY	WA S HY	CA S ERN
*SUBVICAR	SUNDROPS	SURROYAL	*SYMPATRY	WU S S Y	CA S HEW
SUBVIRAL	SUNGLASS	SURVEYOR	*SYMPHONY	BA S ALT	CA S ING
*SUBVOCAL	SUNLIGHT	SURVIVAL	*SYMPODIA	BA S ELY	CA S INO
SUBWORLD	*SUNPORCH	SURVIVER	*SYMPOSIA	BA S EST	CA S ITA
SUCCINCT	SUNPROOF	SURVIVOR	SYNAPSID	BA S HAW	CA S KET
SUCCINIC	SUNSCALD	SUSPENSE	SYNAPSIS	BA S HER	*CA S QUE
*SUCCINYL	SUNSHADE	SUSURRUS	*SYNCARPY	BA S IFY	CA S RAW
SUCCORER	SUNSHINE	*SUZERAIN	SYNCLINE	BA S ING	CA S ROD
SUCCUBUS	SUNSTONE	*SVEDBERG	*SYNCYTIA	BA S ION	CA S SIA
*SUCHLIKE	SUNWARDS	*SWABBING	SYNDESIS	BA S KET	CA S SIS
SUCHNESS	SUPERADD	SWAGGING	SYNDETIC	*BA S QUE	CA S TER
*SUCKFISH	SUPERBAD	*SWAMPISH	SYNDROME	BA S SET	CA S TLE
SUCKLESS	SUPERCAR	*SWANHERD	*SYNECTIC	BA S SLY	CA S TOR
*SUCKLING	SUPERCOP	*SWANLIKE	SYNERGIA	BA S TER	CA S UAL
SUDARIUM	SUPEREGO	SWANNERY	SYNERGID	BE S EEM	CE S IUM
SUDATION	SUPERFAN	SWANNING	*SYNONYME	BE S IDE	CE S S US
SUDATORY	*SUPERFIX	*SWANSKIN	*SYNONYMY	BE S MUT	CE S TO S
SUDSLESS	SUPERHIT	SWASTICA	SYNOPSIS	BE S NOW	CE S TU S
SUFFERER	SUPERHOT	*SWASTIKA	SYNTAGMA	BE S TIR	CE S URA
*SUFFICER	SUPERIOR	SWATTING	*SYPHILIS	BE S TOW	CI S TU S
*SUFFIXAL	*SUPERJET	*SWAYBACK	*SYRPHIAN	BE S TUD	CO S HER
SUFFLATE	SUPERLIE	*SWEATBOX	*SYSTEMIC	BI S ECT	CO S IED
*SUFFRAGE	SUPERMAN	SWEEPING	P S ST	BI S HOP	CO S IER
SUICIDAL	SUPERMOM	SWEETING	T S AR	*BI S QUE	CO S IE S
SUITABLE	SUPERNAL	SWEETISH	P S ALM	BI S TER	CO S ILY
SUITCASE	SUPERPRO	SWEETSOP	P S EUD	BI S TRE	CO S INE
SUITLIKE	*SUPERSEX	SWELLING	P S HAW	BI S TRO	CO S MIC
*SUKIYAKI	*SUPERSPY	SWIFTLET	P S OA S	BO S KER	CO S MO S
SULCATED	*SUPERTAX	*SWIMMING	*P S YCH	BO S KET	CO S SET
SULFINYL	SUPINATE	SWIMSUIT	T S ADE	BO S OMY	CO S TAR
SULFONAL	SUPINELY	*SWIMWEAR	T S ADI	*BO S QUE	CO S TER
SULFONIC	SUPPLANT	SWINDLER	T S UBA	BO S TON	CO S TLY
SULFONYL	SUPPLIER	*SWINEPOX	BA S ES	BU S BOY	CU S CU S
SULFURET	SUPPOSAL	SWINGIER	BA S IS	BU S HEL	CU S HAT
SULFURIC	SUPPOSER	SWINGING	CA S US	BU S HER	CU S HAW
SULFURYL	SUPPRESS	SWINGMAN	CI S SY	BU S HWA	CU S PID
SULPHATE	SURCEASE	*SWITCHER	DA S HI	BU S IER	CU S PIS
SULPHIDE	SUREFIRE	*SWIZZLER	GU S S Y	BU S IE S	CU S S ER
SULPHITE	SURENESS	SWORDMAN	HI S S Y	BU S ILY	CU S TOM
*SULPHONE	SURFACER	SYBARITE	HO S TA	BU S ING	CU S TO S
*SULPHURY	SURFBIRD	*SYCAMINE	KI S S Y	BU S KER	CY S TIC
SUMMABLE	SURFBOAT	*SYCAMORE	LU S US	BU S KIN	DA S HER
*SUMMERLY	*SURFFISH	*SYCOMORE	LY S I S	BU S MAN	DA S SIE
SUMMITAL	SURFIEST	*SYCONIUM	MY S ID	BU S SED	DE S ALT
*SUMMITRY	*SURFLIKE	*SYLLABIC	NI S US	BU S SES	DE S AND
				BU S TER	DE S CRY

DE S ERT	GA S TER	LI S TEL	PA S TI S	RE S IST	TU S S EH
DE S IRE	GE S TIC	LI S TEN	PA S TOR	RE S ITE	TU S S ER
DE S IST	GO S PEL	LI S TER	**PA S TRY**	***RE S IZE**	TU S S IS
DE S MID	GO S S AN	LO S ING	PE S ADE	**RE S OAK**	TU S S LE
DE S ORB	GO S S IP	LU S TER	PE S ETA	RE S OLD	TU S S OR
***DE S OXY**	**GU S HER**	LU S TRA	**PE S EWA**	RE S OLE	TU S S UR
DE S POT	GU S S ET	LU S TRE	PE S TER	RE S ORB	VA S S AL
DI S ARM	GU S S IE	LY S ATE	PE S TLE	RE S ORT	**VA S TLY**
DI S BAR	HA S LET	LY S INE	PI S TIL	RE S POT	**VE S ICA**
DI S BUD	HA S S EL	**LY S ING**	PI S TOL	RE S TER	**VE S PER**
DI S CU S	HA S S LE	***MA S JID**	PI S TON	RE S ULT	**VE S PID**
DI S MAL	HA S TEN	***MA S QUE**	PO S ADA	RE S UME	VE S S EL
DI S MAY	**HI S PID**	MA S TER	PO S EE S	RI S ING	VE S TAL
DI S OWN	HI S S ER	***MA S TIX**	PO S EUR	**RI S KER**	VE S TEE
DI S PEL	**HO S ING**	ME S IAL	PO S IE S	***RI S QUE**	**VE S TRY**
DI S S ED	HO S TEL	ME S IAN	PO S ING	RO S ARY	**VI S AGE**
DI S S ES	**HO S TLY**	ME S S AN	PO S S ET	RO S COE	**VI S ARD**
DI S TAL	**HU S KER**	ME S TEE	**PO S SUM**	RO S ERY	**VI S CID**
DI S TIL	HU S S AR	MI S EAT	PO S TAL	RO S IER	**VI S CUS**
DI S U S E	HU S TLE	MI S LIE	PO S TER	RO S ILY	**VI S ING**
DO S AGE	**HY S S OP**	MI S LIT	PO S TIN	RO S ING	VI S ION
DO S S AL	***JA S MIN**	MI S S EL	**PU S HER**	RO S INY	**VI S IVE**
DO S S EL	***JA S PER**	MI S S ET	**PU S HUP**	RO S TER	VI S UAL
DO S S ER	JA S S ID	MI S S IS	**PU S LEY**	RO S TRA	WA S ABI
DO S S IL	JE S TER	MI S SUS	**PU S S LY**	RU S HEE	**WA S HER**
DU S TER	JE S UIT	MI S TER	RA S CAL	RU S HER	WA S TER
DU S TUP	JO S TLE	MI S U S E	RA S HER	RU S INE	**WA S TRY**
FA S CE S	JU S TER	***MO S QUE**	**RA S HLY**	RU S S ET	WE S KIT
FA S CIA	JU S TLE	MO S S ER	RA S ING	RU S TIC	WE S TER
FA S TEN	***JU S TLY**	***MU S JID**	RA S PER	RU S TLE	**WI S DOM**
FE S CUE	***KA S BAH**	MU S LIN	RA S S LE	SA S HAY	**WI S ELY**
FE S TAL	KA S HER	MU S S EL	RA S TER	SE S AME	WI S ENT
FE S TER	***KI S HKA**	MU S TEE	RA S URE	SE S TET	WI S EST
FI S CAL	***KI S HKE**	MU S TER	RE S AID	**SI S KIN**	WI S HER
***FI S HLY**	KI S MAT	**MY S TER**	RE S ALE	SI S TER	***XY S TER**
FI S TIC	KI S MET	NA S ION	RE S CUE	SI S TRA	***XY S TO S**
FI S HER	KI S S ER	NA S TIC	RE S EAL	**SU S LIK**	***XY S TU S**
FO S SIL	KO S HER	NE S TER	RE S EAT	**SY S TEM**	***YA S MAK**
FO S TER	LA S CAR	NE S TLE	RE S EAU	TA S S EL	YE S S ED
FU S AIN	LA S HER	NE S TOR	RE S ECT	TA S S ET	YE S S ES
FU S ILE	LA S ING	NO S HER	RE S EDA	TA S S IE	YE S TER
FU S ION	LA S S IE	NO S IER	RE S EED	TA S TER	***ZE S TER**
FU S S ER	LA S TER	NO S ILY	**RE S EEK**	TE S TEE	***ZO S TER**
FU S TIC	LA S TLY	NO S ING	RE S EEN	TE S TER	**BA S CULE**
GA S BAG	LE S ION	NO S TOC	RE S ELL	TE S TE S	**BA S EMAN**
GA S CON	LE S S EE	PA S CAL	RE S END	TE S TI S	***BA S ENJI**
GA S IFY	LE S S EN	PA S S EE	RE S ENT	TE S TON	***BA S HFUL**
GA S KET	LE S S ER	PA S S EL	**RE S HIP**	TI S ANE	***BA S HLYK**
GA S KIN	LE S S ON	PA S S ER	RE S HOE	TI S S UE	BA S ILAR
GA S LIT	LI S PER	PA S S IN	**RE S HOW**	TO S S ER	**BA S ILIC**
GA S MAN	LI S S OM	PA S SUS	RE S IDE	TO S S UP	BA S INET
GA S PER	LI S TEE	PA S TEL	RE S IFT	**TU S KER**	**BA S MATI**
GA S S ED		PA S TER	RE S IGN	TU S S AH	BA S SIST
GA S S ER		PA S TIE	RE S ILE	TU S S AL	BA S S OON
GA S S ES		PA S TIL	RE S INY	TU S S AR	**BA S TARD**

BA S TILE	CA S S ATA	**DI S ABLE**	DO S S IER	GO S S OON	**LU S TILY**
BA S TING	CA S S AVA	**DI S AVOW**	*DU S KI S H	GU S TIER	LU S TRAL
BA S TION	CA S S INO	**DI S BAND**	DU S THIN	**GU S TILY**	LU S TRUM
BE S COUR	*CA S S OCK	**DI S CANT**	DU S TIER	*HA S HI S H	LY S OGEN
BE S EECH	CA S TING	**DI S CARD**	DU S TILY	*HA S S OCK	*MA S QUER
BE S HAME	*CA S TOFF	**DI S CA SE**	DU S TMAN	HA S TATE	*MA S SAGE
*BE S HREW	CAS UI S T	**DI S CEPT**	DU S TOFF	HE S S IAN	MA S S EUR
BE S IDE S	CE S S ION	**DI S CERN**	DU S TPAN	HE S S ITE	MA S S IER
BE S IEGE	CE S S PIT	**DI S COID**	DY S PNEA	HI S S ELF	*MA S TIFF
BE S LIME	CE S TODE	**DI S CORD**	DY S URIA	HI S S ING	ME S EEM S
BE S MEAR	CE S TOID	**DI S CU S S**	FA S CINE	HI S TOID	ME S HIER
BE S MILE	CIS S OID	**DI S DAIN**	FA S CI S M	HI S TONE	ME S HUGA
*BE S MOKE	CI S TERN	DI SEA SE	FA S CI S T	HI S TORY	ME S TE S O
*BE S PEAK	CI S TRON	DI SEU S E	FA S HION	HO S ANNA	ME S TINO
BE S TEAD	CO SIE S T	DI S GU S T	FA S TING	HO S IERY	*ME S TIZA
BE S TIAL	CO S MI S M	**DI S HELM**	FE S TIVE	HO S PICE	*ME S TIZO
BE S TREW	CO S MI S T	**DI S HFUL**	FE S TOON	HO S TAGE	MI S BIA S
BE S TROW	*CO S SACK	**DI S HIER**	*FI S HERY	HO S TE S S	MI S CODE
BE S WARM	CO S TARD	**DI S HPAN**	*FI S HEYE	HO S TILE	*MI S COOK
BI S CUIT	CO S TATE	DI S HRAG	*FI S HGIG	HO S TLER	MI S COPY
BI S MUTH	CO S TIVE	*DI S JECT	FI S HIER	HU S BAND	MI S DIAL
BI S NAGA	CO S TREL	*DI S JOIN	FI S HING	*HU S HFUL	MI SEA S E
BI S TORT	CO S TUME	**DI S LIKE**	FI S HNET	HU S KIER	*MI S JOIN
BI S TATE	CU S HIER	**DI S LIMN**	*FI S HWAY	HU S KIE S	*MI S KEEP
BO S CAGE	*CU S HILY	DI S MA S T	FI S S ATE	*HU S KILY	*MI S KICK
BO S KAGE	CU S HION	DI S MI S S	FI S S ILE	*HU S KING	*MI S KNOW
*BO S QUET	CU S S CU S	DI S OBEY	FI S S ION	HU S RIE S	MI S LAIN
BO S S DOM	CU S TARD	DI S OMIC	FI S S URE	HU S TLER	MI S LIKE
BO S S IER	CU S TODY	DI S PART	FI S TFUL	*HU S WIFE	*MI S MAKE
BO S S IES	CY S TEIN	DI S PEND	FI S TULA	*JA S MINE	*MI S MARK
BO S S ISM	CY S TINE	DI S PLAY	*FO S S ICK	JE S S ANT	MI S PLAN
BU S HIDO	CY S TOID	DI S PORT	FU S COU S	*JE S TFUL	MI S RATE
BU S HIER	DA S HEEN	DI S PUTE	FU S IBLE	*JE S TING	MI S RULE
*BU S HILY	DA S HIER	DI S RATE	FU S ILLI	JO S TLER	MI S S EAT
BU S HING	*DA S HIKI	DI S ROBE	FU S S ING	*JU S S IVE	MI S S IE S
BU S HMAN	DA S HPOT	DI S ROOT	FU S S POT	*JU S TICE	MI S S ILE
*BU S HPIG	DA S TARD	DI S RUPT	FU S TIAN	*JU S TIFY	MI S S ION
BU S HTIT	DA S YURE	DI S S AVE	GA SEOU S	*KA S HMIR	MI S S ORT
*BU S HWAH	DE S CANT	DI S S EAT	GA S KING	KA S HRUT	MI S S OUT
BU S IE S T	DE S CEND	DI S S ECT	GA S LES S	KE S TREL	MI S S UIT
BU S LOAD	DE S CENT	DI S S ENT	GA S OHOL	KI S TFUL	MI S TIER
BU S S ING	DE S ERVE	DI S S ERT	GA S S ING	**LA S AGNA**	MI S TIE S
BU S TARD	DE S IRER	DI S S ING	GA S TRAL	LA S AGNE	MI S TRAL
BU S TIER	DE S MOID	**DI S TAFF**	GA S TREA	**LA S HING**	MI S TUNE
CA S CADE	DE S PAIR	DI S TAIN	GA S TRIC	LA S HIN S	MI S U S ER
CA S CARA	DE S PI SE	DI S TANT	GA S TRIN	*LA S HKAR	*MI S YOKE
CA SEA SE	DE S PITE	DI S TEND	GE S TALT	LA S S OER	MO S S IER
CA S EATE	DE S POIL	DI S TENT	GE S TAPO	LA S TING	MO S TE S T
CA S EOU S	DE S POND	**DI S TICH**	GE S TATE	LE S BIAN	MU S ETTE
CA S ERNE	DE S S ERT	DI S TILL	GE S TURE	LI S ENTE	MU S ICAL
CA S ETTE	DE S TAIN	**DI S TOME**	**GI S ARME**	LI S S OME	*MU S KILY
*CA S HBOX	DE S TINE	DI S TORT	*GO S HAWK	LI S TING	*MU S PIKE
CA S HIER	DE S TROY	**DI S TURB**	GO S LING	LU S TFUL	MU S S ING
CAS S ABA	DE S UGAR	*DI S YOKE	GO S PORT	LU S TIER	

*MY S TIFY	PU S S IE S	RO S ARIA	VE S TIGE	BLA S TEMA	CLA S S ILY
NA S ALLY	PU S S LEY	RO S EATE	VE S TING	BLA S TIER	CLA S S I S M
NA S CENT	PU S TULE	RO S EBAY	VE S TUBE	BLA S TING	CLA S S I S T
NE S TLER	RA S BORA	RO S EBUD	VI S CERA	*BLA S TOFF	CLO S EOUT
NO S EBAG	RA S PI S H	RO S ELLE	VI S COID	BLA S TOMA	CLU S TERY
NO S EGAY	RE S CALE	RO S EOLA	VI S CO S E	BLA S TULA	COA S S I S T
NO S IE S T	RE S CIND	RO S ETTE	VI S COU S	*BLE S BUCK	COA S S UME
NO S TRIL	RE S CORE	RO S IE S T	VI S IBLE	BLE S S ING	COA S TING
NO S TRUM	RE S CUER	RO S INOL	VI S ITER	BLI S TERN	COI S TREL
PA S CHAL	*RE S EIZE	RO S OLIO	VI S ITOR	BLO S S ONY	COI S TRIL
*PA S QUIL	RE S ERVE	RO S TRAL	*WA S HDAY	*BLU S HFUL	CON S ERVE
PA S S ADE	RE S HAPE	RO S TRUM	WA S HIER	BLU S TERY	CON S IDER
PA S S ADO	RE S HAVE	RU S HIER	WA S HING	BOA S TFUL	CON S OLER
PA S S AGE	RE S HINE	RU S HING	WA S HOUT	BOI S ERIE	CON S OMME
PA S S ANT	RE S HONE	RU S S IFY	*WA S HTUB	BON S PELL	CON S PIRE
PA S S ING	RE S HOOT	RU S TIER	WA S HRAG	BON S PIEL	CON S TANT
PA S S ION	RE S IDER	RU S TILY	WA S S AIL	BOU S OUKI	CON S TRUE
PA S S IVE	RE S IDUA	RU S TLER	WA S TAGE	*BOW S PRIT	CON S UMER
*PA S S KEY	RE S IDUE	S A S HIMI	WA S TERY	BRA S ILIN	COR S ELET
PA S TERN	RE S IGHT	S A S S ABY	WA S TING	BRA S S AGE	COR S ETRY
PA S TEUP	RE S LATE	S A S S IER	WA S TREL	BRA S S ARD	COU S COU S
PA S TIER	RE S MELT	S A S S IE S	WA S TRUE	BRA S S ART	COU S INRY
PA S TIE S	RE S OJET	S A S S ILY	WE S S AND	BRA S S ICA	*COX S WAIN
PA S TIME	RE S OLVE	S E S S ILE	WE S TERN	BRA S S I S H	CRE S CENT
PA S TINA	RE S OUND	S E S S ION	WE S TING	BRI S ANCE	*CRE S CIVE
PA S TING	RE S PACE	S E S TINA	WI S EA S S	BRI S LING	CRE S TING
PA S TURE	RE S PADE	S E S TINE	*WI S HFUL	BRU S HIER	*CRE S YLIC
PE S S ARY	RE S PEAK	S I S TRUM	WI S PIER	*BRU S HOFF	CRI S PATE
PI S CARY	RE S PECT	S U S PECT	*WI S PILY	BUR S ITI S	CRI S TATE
PI S CINA	RE S PELL	S U S PEND	*WI S PI S H	BUR S TONE	CRO S S ARM
PI S CINE	RE S PIRE	S U S TAIN	WI S S ING	CAB S TAND	CRO S S BAR
PI S HOGE	RE S PITE	S Y S TOLE	WI S TFUL	*CAN S HAFT	*CRO S S BOW
PI S MIRE	RE S PLIT	TA S TING	*YA S HMAC	CAP S ICIN	CRO S S CUT
PI S S ANT	RE S POKE	TE S S ERA	*YA S HMAK	*CAP S ICUM	CRO S S ING
PI S S OIR	RE S POND	TE S TACY	*YE S HIVA	CAP S OMER	CRO S S LET
PI S TOLE	RE S PRAY	TE S TATE	YE S S ING	CAP S TONE	CRO S S TIE
PO S S E S S	RE S TACK	TE S TIER	YE S TERN	CAP S ULAR	*CRO S SWAY
PO S TAGE	RE S TAFF	TE S TIFY	*ZE S TFUL	CA S S ETTE	CRU S ADER
PO S TBAG	RE S TAGE	TE S TILY	*BAA S KAAP	CAU S ABLE	CRU S TO S E
*PO S TBOX	RE S TAMP	TE S TOON	*BAK S HI S H	CAU S ALLY	CU S S EDLY
PO S TBOY	RE S TART	TE S TUDO	BAL S AMIC	CAU S ERIE	CU S S WORD
PO S TDOC	RE S TATE	TU S S CHE	BAR S TOOL	*CAU S EWAY	*DAI S HIKI
PO S TEEN	RE S TFUL	TU S S OCK	BA S S INET	CEN S URER	DAN S EU S E
PO S TERN	RE S TIVE	TU S S ORE	BA S S NE S S	CE S S POOL	DIA S PORA
*PO S TFIX	RE S TOCK	TU S S UCK	BA S S WOOD	CHA S S EUR	DIA S PORE
PO S TING	RE S TOKE	VA S TIER	BED S HEET	CHA S TI S E	DIA S TA S E
PO S TMAN	RE S TORE	VA S TITY	BED S ONIA	*CHA S TITY	DIA S TEMA
*PO S TTAX	RE S TUDY	VE S ICLE	BED S TAND	*CHA S UBLE	DIA S TOLE
PO S TURE	RE S TUFF	VE S PINE	BED S TEAD	CHE S S MAN	*DIE S TOCK
PO S TWAR	RE S TYLE		BED S TRAW	*CHE S TFUL	DIE S TRUM
*PU S HFUL	RE S UMER		BEE S WING	CHE S TNUT	DIE S TRU S
PU S HIER	RE S URGE		BIA S NE S S	CHE S WING	*DIP S TICK
PU S HILT	RI S IBLE		BIO S COPE	CHI S ELER	DI S S EI S E
PU S HPIN	RI S OTTO		*BIO S COPY	CLA S S IFY	*DI S S EIZE
PU S S IER	RI S S OLE		*BIT S TOCK	CLA S S ICO	DI S S ERVE
				CLA S S IER	

DIS SUADE	GRI SEOUS	MIS SILRY	*PEE SWEEP	PRO STATE	SEN SUOUS
*DOG SBODY	GRI SETTE	MIS SOUND	PEN SIONE	PRO STYLE	SES SPOOL
DOR SALLY	*GRO SBEAK	MIS SPACE	*PEN STOCK	PUI SSANT	SET SCREW
DOS SERET	GRO SCHEN	*MIS SPEAK	PER SONAL	PUL SATOR	*SHA SHLIK
DOW SABEL	*GUN SMITH	MIS SPELL	PER SPIRE	*PUL SEJET	SIS SYISH
DRES SAGE	*GUN STOCK	MIS SPEND	PER SUADE	*PUL SOJET	SLA SHING
DRES SING	GYP SEOUS	*MIS SPOKE	PHA SEOUT	PUR SIEST	SOL STICE
DRY STONE	*GYP SYDOM	MIS START	*PHO SGENE	PUR SLANE	STA SIMON
*DYE STUFF	*GYP SYISH	MIS STATE	*PHO SPHID	PUR SUANT	SUB SCALE
FALS ETTO	HAU SFRAU	MIS STEER	*PHO SPHIN	PUS SIEST	SUB SENSE
*FAT STOCK	*HAY STACK	MIS STYLE	*PHO SPHOR	PUS SLIKE	SUB SERVE
FEA SANCE	HER STORY	MON STERA	*PHY SICAL	*PUS SYCAT	*SUB SHAFT
FEA SIBLE	*HOG SHEAD	*MOS SBACK	*PHY SIQUE	*QUE STION	SUB SHELL
FEA STFUL	*HOO SEGOW	MOS SIEST	PIA SABA	*QUI SLING	*SUB SHRUB
FEL STONE	HOR SECAR	MOS SLIKE	PIA SAVA	RAI SONNE	SUB SIDER
FES SWISE	*HOR SEFLY	MUD SLIDE	*PIG STICK	RAM SHORN	SUB SKILL
FIS SIPED	HOR SEMAN	*MYO SCOPE	PIL SENER	RAN SOMER	SUB SOLAR
*FLA SHGUN	HOR SIEST	MYO SITIS	*PIN SCHER	RAT SBANE	SUB SONIC
*FLA SHING	*HOU SEBOY	MYO SOTIS	PLA SMOID	REA SCEND	SUB SPACE
FLE SHIER	*HOU SEFLY	NAU SEANT	PLA STERY	REA SCENT	SUB STAGE
*FLE SHING	HOU SEFUL	NAU SEATE	PLA STRON	REA SONER	SUB STATE
*FLE SHPOT	HOU SEMAN	NAU SEOUS	PLA STRUM	REA SSAIL	SUD SLESS
*FLY SPECK	HOU SETOP	NAY SAYER	PLU SSAGE	REA SSERT	SUN SCALD
*FOR SAKER	*HYO SCINE	NEW SCAST	POI SONER	REA SSESS	SUN SHADE
FOR SOOTH	*JOY STICK	*NEW SHAWK	POS SIBLE	REA SSORT	SUN SHINE
FOR SPENT	KAI SERIN	NEW SIEST	POT SHARD	REA SSUME	SUN STONE
FOR SWEAR	*KEE SHOND	NEW SLESS	POT SHERD	REA SSURE	SWA STICA
FOS SETTE	*KEY STONE	*NEW SPEAK	POT STONE	*RED SHANK	*SWA STIKA
FRE SCOER	*KIN SFOLK	NEW SREEL	PRE SAGER	*RED SHIFT	TEA SELER
*FRE SHMAN	*KLY STRON	NEW SROOM	PRE SCIND	RED SHIRT	TEA SPOON
FRI SETTE	LIN STOCK	NOI SETTE	PRE SCORE	RED START	TEN SIBLE
FRO STBIT	*LIP STICK	NON SENSE	PRE SENCE	REI SSUER	TEO SINTE
FRO STING	*LOB STICK	NON SKIER	PRE SERVE	REU SABLE	THE SAURI
FRU STULE	LOO SENER	NON SOLAR	PRE SIDER	RIE SLING	THE SPIAN
GEL SEMIA	LOP SIDED	NON SOLID	PRE SIDIA	ROL STEIN	TIN SELLY
*GEM SBUCK	*LOP STICK	NON STICK	PRE SIDIO	ROU SSEAU	TIN SMITH
GEM STONE	MA SSACRE	NON STORY	PRE SLEEP	SAL SILLA	TIN STONE
*GHA STFUL	MAS SCULT	NON STYLE	PRE SLICE	SAN SERIF	TIP SIEST
GHO STING	MAS SEDLY	NUI SANCE	PRE SPLIT	SAR SENET	*TIP STAFF
GLA SNOST	MAS SETER	NUM SKULL	PRE SRAPE	SAS SIEST	*TIP STOCK
GLA SSFUL	MAS SEUSE	NUR SLING	PRE SSING	SAS SWOOD	TIS SULAR
GLA SSIER	MAS SICOT	NUT SEDGE	PRE SSMAN	SCI SSILE	TOP SIDER
GLA SSILY	MAS SIEST	NUT SHELL	PRE SSRUN	SCI SSION	TOP STONE
GLA SSINE	MAS SLESS	*PAN SOPHY	PRE SSURE	SCI SSURE	TRA SHMAN
GLA SSMAN	*MEM SAHIB	PAS SABLE	PRE STAMP	SEA SCAPE	TRE SPASS
GLI SSADE	MES SIEST	PAS SBAND	PRE STIGE	SEA SCOUT	TRE SSIER
GLO SSARY	MES SMATE	*PAS SBOOK	PRE SUMER	SEA SDORE	TRE SSOUR
GLO SSEME	MES SUAGE	*PAS SERBY	PRI SMOID	SEA SHELL	TRE SSURE
GLO SSIER	*MID SHIPS	PAS SIBLE	PRI SONER	SEA SONAL	TRI SCELE
GLO SSIES	*MID SIZED	PAS SLESS	PRI STANE	SEA SONER	TRI SKELE
GLO SSINA	*MID SPACE	PAS SOVER	PRI STINE	SEI SMISM	TRI SOMIC
GO SSAMER	MIS SABLE	PAS SWORD	PRO SAISM	SEN SEFUL	TRI STATE
GO SSIPER	MIS SENSE	PEA SECOD	PRO SAIST	SEN SIDLE	*TRI STEZA
GO SSIPRY	*MIS SHAPE		PRO SIEST	SEN SILLA	TRI STFUL
GO SSYPOL			PRO SPECT	SEN SORIA	TRI STICH

TRUS SING	MIS S	DEMO S	LUPU S	SOLU S	**BUS SES**
TRUS TFUL	MON S	DRES S	LUSU S	SORU S	**BYPAS S**
TWIS TING	MOS S	DRIE S	LYSI S	SPEC S	**BYS SUS**
VERS EMAN	MUS S	DROS S	MABI S	SPIE S	**CACTU S**
VERS ICLE	NAO S	**FAVU S**	MAGU S	STOS S	**CADDI S**
VOUS SOIR	NES S	FECE S	MANU S	SWIS S	**CALCE S**
*WAES UCKS	NEW S	FETU S	**MAVI S**	TABE S	CALLU S
WAIS TING	NOE S	**FICU S**	METI S	TALU S	**CALVE S**
WARS TLER	NOU S	FINI S	MINU S	TAMI S	**CAMAS S**
WEAS ELLY	PAS S	FLIE S	MITI S	TAPI S	**CAMPU S**
*WHIS PERY	PIS S	**FOCU S**	MODU S	**TAXU S**	CANTU S
WHIS TLER	PLU S	FRAS S	MOMU S	TELO S	**CANVA S**
*WHOS EVER	PON S	FRIE S	MONA S	**TEXA S**	**CAPIA S**
WRES TLER	PUS S	FRON S	MUCU S	TONU S	**CAPRI S**
WRIS TLET	REI S	**FUCU S**	NARE S	TOOT S	CARES S
YEAS AYER	RHU S	GAUS S	NARI S	TOPO S	CARIE S
*ZOOS PERM	SAN S	GENU S	NATE S	TORU S	**CARPU S**
*ZOOS PORE	SAS S	GIGA S	NEGU S	TRAN S	**CAS SIS**
	SUD S	GLAN S	NERT S	TRAS S	**CAUCU S**
BAA S	SUS S	GLAS S	NEVU S	TRES S	CAULE S
BAS S	TAS S	GLOS S	NIDU S	TREW S	CAULI S
BIA S	THI S	GRAS S	NISU S	TRIE S	**CAVIE S**
BOS S	THU S	GROS S	NODU S	TROI S	**CENS US**
BUS S	TOS S	GUES S	NOMO S	TRUS S	**CERCI S**
CES S	WIS S	GULE S	PARI S	TURP S	**CERCU S**
CRI S	WUS S	GYRU S	**PAVI S**	VAGU S	CEREU S
CRU S	YWI S	HARD S	PEDE S	VARU S	CEROU S
CUS S	BALA S	HERE S	PENE S	**VIBE S**	CERTE S
DAI S	BANN S	HILU S	PENI S	VIRE S	**CES SUS**
DIE S	BASE S	**HOCU S**	PILU S	VIRU S	CESTO S
DIS S	BASI S	**HUMU S**	PIOU S	**VOCE S**	**CES TUS**
DOE S	BLES S	HURD S	PLIE S	**WAMU S**	**CHARA S**
DOS S	BLIS S	***JAKE S**	POLI S	**WIVE S**	CHIAU S
FES S	BOGU S	JONE S	PRES S	**WOOP S**	**CHINT S**
FOS S	BOLA S	JUDA S	PRIE S	WRIE S	**CHORU S**
FUS S	BOLU S	**KUMY S**	PRIS S	**XERU S**	**CIRCU S**
GEN S	BONU S	**KVAS S**	PROS S	**YIKE S**	CIRRU S
HER S	BRAS S	LAPI S	PSOA S	**YIPE S**	CISTU S
HIS S	**BRAW S**	LARE S	PUBE S	YOUR S	CITIE S
HOL S	BURB S	LEGE S	PUBI S	***ZOOK S**	CITRU S
JES S	CAMA S	LENE S	***PYXI S**	**BABIE S**	CIVIC S
JOS S	CASU S	LENI S	QUAS S	BAGA S	CLAVU S
KAA S	**CHAO S**	LEWI S	RAMU S	**BATHO S**	CLEVI S
KIS S	**CHES S**	**LEXI S**	REBU S	**BEEVE S**	CLONU S
KOS S	CLAS S	LIME S	REGE S	**BEKIS S**	COCCU S
KRI S	CONU S	LITA S	RIBE S	**BEVIE S**	COITU S
KVA S	CORP S	LIVE S	RISU S	**BICEP S**	COLEU S
LAS S	CRAS S	LOCU S	RUBU S	**BINOC S**	COLIE S
LEN S	CRES S	LOES S	SARO S	BLINI S	COMOU S
LES S	CRIE S	LOGO S	SEMI S	BODIE S	CONIE S
LOS S	CROS S	LORI S	SHIE S	BOGIE S	**COPIE S**
LUE S	CUTE S	LOTO S	SINU S	**BREEK S**	CORNU S
MAS S	CUTI S	LOTU S	SITU S	BREWI S	**CORPU S**
MES S	**CYCA S**	LOUI S	SKIE S	BURIE S	**CORVE S**
	DEGA S	LUCE S		BUSIE S	**COSIE S**

CO S MO S	FUNGU S	MATRE S	***PRAXI S**	TABER S	***ZOUND S**
*COZIE S	FURIE S	MEATU S	**PRECI S**	TALLI S	**BADNE S S**
*COZZE S	GABIE S	MEGA S S	**PRIMU S**	TAR S U S	***BAFFIE S**
CRA S E S	GALLU S	MIO S L S	PRUNU S	TENNI S	**BALDIE S**
CRA S I S	GA S SE S	MI S SI S	PTO S I S	TENUI S	**BALLIE S**
CRIPE S	GENIU S	MI S SU S	**PYO S I S**	TERRA S	**BANDIE S**
CRI S I S	GENTE S	MOLIE S	RABIE S	TE S TE S	**BARLE S S**
CROCU S	GLACI S	MONIE S	**RACHI S**	TE S TI S	**BAWDIE S**
CRUCE S	GLOMU S	MONTE S	RADIU S	THEIR S	**BEDLE S S**
CULLI S	GNEI S S	MORAL S	RAMOU S	THE S I S	***BEJE S U S**
CULTU S	GNO S I S	MORA S S	**RAPHI S**	THOLO S	BELLIE S
CU S CU S	GOBIE S	MORRI S	RECE S S	**THYMU S**	**BENTHO S**
CU S PI S	GRADU S	**MUCOU S**	RECTU S	TIDIE S	**BE S IDE S**
CU S TO S	GRATI S	**MYA S I S**	REGIU S	**TIGHT S**	**BETIME S**
CUTLA S	HAERE S	**MYO S I S**	RELIE S	TME S I S	**BIBLE S S**
CYE S I S	**HAGGI S**	**MYTHO S**	REMI S S	**TOPHU S**	**BIGNE S S**
CYMOU S	**HALVE S**	**NACHA S**	REPA S S	TORIE S	**BILIOU S**
CYPRE S	HARA S S	**NACHE S**	REVER S	TOROU S	**BILLIE S**
CYPRU S	**HERPE S**	NAEVU S	RHE S U S	TRAGU S	**BIOMA S S**
DALLE S	HIATU S	NAVIE S	RICUE S	TRAPE S	**BIONIC S**
DEBRI S	HOLIE S	NEREI S	RIMOU S	TRIEN S	**BIOTIC S**
DEDAN S	**HOMMO S**	**NIMBU S**	RUBIE S	TRIPO S	**BOBBIE S**
DEFIE S	**HOOVE S**	NODOU S	**RUCKU S**	T S ORE S	BOLETU S
DEIXI S	**HUBRI S**	NOE S I S	RUFOU S	T S ORI S	**BONKER S**
DEMIE S	**HUMMU S**	**NOWAY S**	RUGOU S	T S URI S	**BOONIE S**
DENIE S	**HYBRI S**	NUBLE S	**RUMPU S**	TURVE S	**BOOTIE S**
DERMI S	***JOYOU S**	PALAI S	S ANIE S	TU S SI S	**BORACE S**
DERRI S	**JURIE S**	PALPU S	**S CHU S S**	**TYPHO S**	BO S SIE S
DEXIE S	**KARO S S**	PAPPU S	S CRIE S	***TZURI S**	**BOWLE S S**
DIDIE S	**KAVA S S**	PARIE S	S ELVE S	**VALGU S**	BRALE S S
DINGU S	**KAYLE S**	PAROU S	SEP S I S	VARIE S	BRINIE S
DIP S A S	**KERME S**	**PARVI S**	S ERIE S	VENOU S	BRI S SE S
DI S CU S	**KERMI S**	PA S SU S	S EROU S	**VERME S**	**BUBALI S**
DI S SE S	**KNIVE S**	PA S TI S	S ETOU S	**VERMI S**	**BUBBIE S**
DOBIE S	**KOUMI S**	**PATHO S**	S HAME S	VER S U S	**BUDDIE S**
DOGIE S	***KOUMY S**	PATOI S	S HAMO S	VILLU S	**BUDLE S S**
DOOFU S	**KOURO S**	**PELVI S**	S HAMU S	VINOU S	**BUGLO S S**
DORIE S	**KUMI S S**	**PEPLO S**	S HNAP S	VI S CU S	**BULBOU S**
DURE S S	**LACHE S**	**PEPLU S**	S IGLO S	VITAL S	**BULLIE S**
FACIE S	LADIE S	**PHARO S**	S OLEU S	VIVER S	BULLOU S
FAECE S	LAMPA S	**PHA S I S**	S ONIC S	**VULGU S**	**BURGE S S**
FALCE S	LAP S U S	**PHY S E S**	S OWAN S	**WADIE S**	BURNOU S
FAMOU S	***LAZIE S**	**PHY S I S**	S OWEN S	**WALIE S**	**BUTTAL S**
FA S CE S	LEAVE S	PIGNU S	S PEI S S	WALRU S	**BUTTIE S**
FAUCE S	LEVIE S	PILEU S	S TAPE S	**WAMMU S**	**CABROU S**
*FIZZE S	LIMBU S	PILOU S	S TA SE S	**WAMPU S**	CAE S TU S
FLATU S	LITMU S	PITIE S	S TA S I S	**WAVIE S**	**CALAMU S**
FOETU S	LOAVE S	***PLEXU S**	S TATU S	**WHENA S**	**CALEND S**
FOLLE S	LORIE S	POGIE S	S TIPE S	**WHO S I S**	**CALICE S**
FOLLI S	LUNIE S	**POKIE S**	S TIRP S	**WOLVE S**	CALLOU S
FORTE S	LUPOU S	POLEI S	S TRA S S	***XY S TO S**	**CALYCE S**
FORTI S	MADRA S	PONIE S	S TRE S S	***XY S TU S**	**CANDIE S**
FRACA S	MANTE S	**PORCU S**	STYLU S	YES SE S	**CANTHU S**
FUCOU S	MANTI S	PO S EE S	S ULCU S	***YOICK S**	**CANVA S S**
FUNDU S	***MAQUI S**	PO S IE S	S YNGA S	***ZANIE S**	**CAPLE S S**

CARCA S S	DEARIE S	FORTRE S	HIPNE S S	LIMULU S	NONPRO S
CARICE S	DECLA S S	FOULNE S	HITLE S S	LIONE S S	NOWNE S S
CARIOU S	DEFOCU S	*FOXINE S	HOBBIE S	LIPLE S S	NOXIOU S
CARITA S	DEGAU S S	*FOZINE S	HOLLIE S	LITOTE S	NUCLEU S
CARLE S S	DEPRE S S	FRACTU S	HOMINE S	LOCULU S	PADDIE S
CARNIE S	DEVIOU S	FREENE S	HOOKIE S	LOGGAT S	PANDIE S
CAROLU S	DEWLE S S	FRONTE S	HO S TE S S	LOGGET S	PANTIE S
CARRIE S	DIARIE S	FULNE S S	HOTNE S S	LOLLIE S	PAPPIE S
CA S EOU S	DICKEN S	FULVOU S	HUGEOU S	LONGIE S	PAPYRU S
CHABLI S	DIGRE S S	FUMULU S	HUMERU S	LOWNE S S	PARADO S
CHALLI S	DIMNE S S	FUNGOU S	HURDIE S	LUTEOU S	PARE S I S
CHAMOI S	DINGIE S	FURIOU S	HU S KIE S	*LYCHNI S	PARLOU S
CHA S SIS	DINKIE S	FURLE S S	HU S RIE S	MADNE S S	PARODO S
*CHEVIE S	DI S CU S S	FU S COU S	*HYDROP S	MALLEU S	PARRIE S
*CHLAMY S	DI S MI S S	GALLOU S	HYDROU S	MAMMIE S	PARTIE S
*CHYMOU S	DOGGIE S	GALLOW S	*JACKA S S	MANLE S S	PA S TIE S
CIRROU S	DOLLIE S	GAPO S I S	*JACKIE S	*MARQUI S	PATNE S S
CITROU S	DRYNE S S	GA S EOU S	*JACOBU S	MARRIE S	PEERE S S
CLARIE S	DUBIOU S	GA S LE S S	*JAGLE S S	MATLE S S	PEGLE S S
CLA S SE S	DUCHE S S	*GAWKIE S	*JAMMIE S	MATRA S S	PELORU S
CLA S SIS	DUCKIE S	GAYNE S S	JEALOU S	MEANIE S	PENATE S
CLIVER S	DUENE S S	GENE S I S	*JEEPER S	MEIO S I S	PENNIE S
CLYPEU S	DULNE S S	GIBBOU S	*JERKIE S	MERCIE S	PERCU S S
CODICE S	DUNNE S S	GLOBOU S	JETTIE S	MERI S I S	PERHAP S
COLITI S	DUTEOU S	GLORIE S	*JIMJAM S	ME S EEM S	PETA S O S
COLLIE S	DWARVE S	GLOTTI S	*JIVEA S S	MIDDIE S	PETA S U S
COLLIN S	FAIRIE S	GLUTEU S	JOANNE S	MILREI S	PETROU S
COLOBU S	FAMULU S	GODDE S S	*JOBLE S S	MIME S I S	PHALLU S
COLONU S	FANCIE S	GODLE S S	JOLLIE S	MINIBU S	PHOEBU S
COMMIE S	FARNE S S	GOODIE S	*JOYLE S S	MI S BIA S	PHONIC S
COMPA S S	FATLE S S	GRAMPU S	KALEND S	MI S SIE S	PHONIE S
CONATU S	FATNE S S	GRAVIE S	KENO S I S	MI S TIE S	PHOTIC S
CONCU S S	FATTIE S	GRUMOU S	KERME S S	MITO S I S	PICEOU S
CONFE S S	FATUOU S	GUMLE S S	KETO S I S	MODULU S	PIETIE S
CONGIU S	FEELE S S	GUMMOU S	KEYLE S S	MOLLIE S	PIGGIE S
COOKIE S	FELLIE S	GUNLE S S	KIDDIE S	MONADE S	PILEOU S
COOLIE S	FERRIE S	GUTLE S S	KINE S I S	MUDDIE S	PINKIE S
COPIOU S	FERROU S	HABITU S	KIRME S S	MUGGIN S	PINNIE S
COYNE S S	FEWNE S S	HALITU S	KITTIE S	MUMMIE S	PITEOU S
*CROQUI S	FEYNE S S	HALVER S	*KOLKHO S	MURICE S	PLATIE S
CUDDIE S	FIBROU S	HAMULU S	KOUMI S S	MYCO S I S	PLU S SE S
CUIRA S S	FILLIE S	HAPLE S S	*KOUMY S S	MYIA S I S	PLUTEU S
CULLIE S	FINALI S	HARDIE S	LAMPER S	NAPLE S S	POETE S S
CUMULU S	FINLE S S	HARNE S S	LAPIDE S	NEME S I S	POETIC S
CUPROU S	FITNE S S	HARPIE S	LARGE S S	NERVOU S	POLYPU S
CURIOU S	*FIXING S	HARRIE S	LA S HIN S	NETLE S S	POMPOU S
CU S SCU S	FLYLE S S	HATLE S S	LATICE S	NEWNE S S	POPPIE S
CUTLA S S	FOGLE S S	HEAVIE S	LAWLE S S	NEW S IE S	PORKIE S
CUTTIE S	FOLIOU S	HEINOU S	LAXNE S S	NITROU S	PO S SE S S
*CYCLOP S	FOLLIE S	HEIRE S S	LEFTIE S	NIVEOU S	POTTIE S
CYPRE S S	FORCEP S	HELICE S	LEGLE S S	NOCUOU S	PRECE S S
*CZARDA S	FORDLE S	HEREDE S	LEMURE S	NODDIE S	PREMI S S
DANDIE S	FORKLE S	HIDEOU S	LEPROU S	NOMBLE S	PRIAPU S
DARBIE S	FORMLE S	*HIJINK S	LIDLE S S	NONNEW S	PRIVIE S
DARKIE S	FORTIE S	HIPLE S S	LIMITE S	NONPLU S	PROCE S S

PROFESS	*SCYPHUS	TEARGAS	WEARIES	BIMANOUS	*CHROMOUS
PROTEUS	SEERESS	TEDIOUS	WEBLESS	BLOODIES	*CHUCKIES
PROWESS	SERIOUS	TELESIS	WELLIES	BLOTLESS	CITREOUS
*PROXIES	SEXLESS	TELLIES	WETNESS	BLUENESS	CLAWLESS
PULPOUS	SFERICS	TENNIES	WHATSIS	BODILESS	CLEMATIS
PUSSIES	SHAMMAS	TENUOUS	WHEREAS	BOLDNESS	CLITORIS
*PYJAMAS	SHAMMES	TERRIES	WHITIES	*BOLLOCKS	CLUELESS
PYLORUS	SHAMMOS	TETANUS	*WHIZZES	BONELESS	COALLESS
PYROSIS	SHAMOIS	THALLUS	WHOOSIS	BONINESS	COATLESS
*PYXIDES	SHELVES	THERMOS	WIGLESS	BOOTLESS	CODELESS
*QUERIES	SHERRIS	THIEVES	WILLIES	BOTANIES	COENURUS
*QUIETUS	SHYNESS	THYRSUS	WINLESS	BOTRYTIS	COLDNESS
RADICES	SIEMENS	TIELESS	WISEASS	*BOXINESS	COLINIES
RAGGIES	SILENTS	TIGRESS	WITHIES	BRIMLESS	COLOSSUS
RAILBUS	SILENUS	TIMEOUS	WITLESS	*BRITCHES	COLPITIS
RANDIES	SILVICS	TIPLESS	WITNESS	*BRONCHUS	*COMBINGS
RAUCOUS	SIMLOUS	TITTIES	WOENESS	BROWLESS	COMEDIES
RAWNESS	SINLESS	TOADIES	WOODIES	BURSITIS	COMPLIES
RAYLESS	SINUOUS	TODDIES	WOOLIES	BUSHLESS	COMPRESS
READIES	SITHENS	TOELESS	WRYNESS	BUSINESS	CONGRATS
RECROSS	SKEPSIS	TOPLESS	XEROSIS	BUSYNESS	CONGRESS
REDNESS	*SKYPHOS	*TORQUES	*ZEALOUS	BUTTRESS	COOKLESS
REDRESS	SLYNESS	TOWARDS	*ZEBRASS	BUTYROUS	COOLNESS
REDRIES	SOFTIES	TOWNIES	*ZINCOUS	CADUCEUS	COPPERAS
REFLIES	SOLIDUS	TOYLESS	*ZIPLESS	CADUCOUS	CORDLESS
REFOCUS	SONLESS	TRAVOIS	*ZYGOSIS	CAGINESS	CORELESS
REGLOSS	SOPHIES	TRELLIS	*ZYMOSTS	CALATHOS	CORNEOUS
REGRESS	SORITES	TRICEPS	*BACCHIUS	CALATHUS	COSINESS
REGULUS	SOROSIS	TRISMUS	BACILLUS	CALCULUS	COSTLESS
REPRESS	SPINIES	TROILUS	*BACKLESS	CALMNESS	COUNTESS
REREDOS	SPINOUS	TSIMMES	BALDNESS	CALVADOS	COUSCOUS
*RHACHIS	SPUMOUS	TSOORIS	BARBLESS	CANITIES	COVETOUS
RHAMNUS	STARETS	TUGLESS	BARENESS	CANNABIS	*COZINESS
RHOMBUS	STORIES	TUMULUS	BARKLESS	CANONESS	CRANKOUS
RIBLESS	STRATUS	TURKOIS	BARONESS	CANOROUS	CRANNIES
RICINUS	STUDIES	*TZIMMES	BASALTES	CAPTIOUS	CREMAINS
RICKETS	STYPSIS	*TZITZIS	BASELESS	CARDITIS	CREWLESS
RIMLESS	SUBBASS	VACUOUS	BASENESS	CARELESS	CRIBROUS
RIOTOUS	SUBMISS	VARICES	BATHLESS	CASHLESS	CROPLESS
RODLESS	SUCCESS	VARIOUS	BAUDRONS	CATERESS	CROUPOUS
RUBIOUS	SUCCUSS	VELITES	BEAMLESS	*CATHEXIS	CRUDITES
RUINOUS	SUMLESS	VERGLAS	BEATLESS	CAUTIOUS	*CRYONICS
RUNLESS	SUMMONS	VERITAS	*BEDWARDS	CENTESIS	*CUFFLESS
SADNESS	SUNLESS	VICIOUS	BEEFLESS	CERASTES	CUMBROUS
SALLIES	SURPASS	VIROSIS	*BEJABERS	CERNUOUS	CUPREOUS
SANTIMS	SURPLUS	VISCOUS	*BEJEEZUS	CERVELAS	CURELESS
SAPIENS	SWAMIES	VOMITUS	BELTLESS	CHALLIES	CURTNESS
SAPLESS	SYCOSIS	VOTRESS	*BENDWAYS	CHANTIES	CUSTODES
SARCOUS	SYNESIS	VOWLESS	BERBERIS	CHAUSSES	CUTENESS
SARDIUS	TABBIES	WADDIES	BERMUDAS	*CHIASMUS	CUTGRASS
SASSIES	TALIPES	WAENESS	BIASNESS	*CHICNESS	CYANOSIS
SCABIES	TALLIES	WALLIES	BIBULOUS	CHINLESS	CYSTITIS
SCARVES	TARDIES	WANNESS	BIGAMOUS	CHLOROUS	DACTYLUS
SCHMOOS	TARRIES	WARLESS	*BIJUGOUS	CHORAGUS	DAFTNESS
SCHNAPS	TAXLESS	WAYLESS		CHOREGUS	DAMPNESS

DANKNESS	FAMELESS	GLADNESS	HOLINESS	LIFELESS	MESDAMES
DARKNESS	FASHIOUS	GLANDERS	HOMELESS	LIGNEOUS	*METHINKS
DATELESS	FASTNESS	GLAUCOUS	HOMINESS	LIKENESS	METRITIS
DEADNESS	FASTUOUS	GLEGNESS	HOMINIES	LIMELESS	MICROBUS
DEAFNESS	FEARLESS	GLIBNESS	HOODLESS	LIMINESS	*MIDSHIPS
DEARNESS	*FECKLESS	GLORIOUS	HOOFLESS	LIMPNESS	MILDNESS
DECOROUS	FELLNESS	GLOSSIES	*HOOKLESS	LINELESS	MINDLESS
DECURIES	FERREOUS	GLUMNESS	HOOPLESS	LINTLESS	MIRINESS
DEEDLESS	FETIALIS	GOALLESS	HOPELESS	LISTLESS	MISCLASS
DEEPNESS	FEVEROUS	GONENESS	HORNFELS	LIVENESS	*MISFOCUS
DEFTNESS	FIBROSIS	GOODNESS	HORNLESS	LOAMLESS	MISGUESS
DEMONESS	FINENESS	GORGEOUS	HOTPRESS	LOFTLESS	MISTRESS
DEMOTICS	FIRELESS	GORINESS	HUGENESS	LOGINESS	MITTIMUS
DENARIUS	FIRMNESS	GORMLESS	HUMOROUS	LONENESS	MODIOLUS
DESIROUS	FISHLESS	GRACILIS	*HUMPLESS	LONGNESS	MOLASSES
DETRITUS	*FIVEPINS	GRACIOUS	HURTLESS	*LONGWAYS	MOONLESS
*DEXTROUS	FLAGLESS	GRAVITAS	HUSTINGS	LORDLESS	MOTORBUS
DIABETES	FLAMINES	*GRAVLAKS	*HYMNLESS	LORDOSIS	MOVELESS
DIALYSIS	FLAPLESS	GRAYNESS	*HYPNOSIS	LORNNESS	*MUCHNESS
DIANTHUS	FLATNESS	GREYNESS	*JOHANNES	LOSTNESS	*MUNCHIES
*DIDYMOUS	*FLATWAYS	GRIEVOUS	*JOKINESS	LOUDNESS	MUTENESS
DIECIOUS	FLAWLESS	GRIMNESS	*JUSTNESS	LOVELESS	MUTICOUS
DIERESIS	*FLEXUOUS	GRISEOUS	KEELLESS	LOVELIES	MUTINIES
DIESTRUS	FLUERICS	GUMMOSIS	KEENNESS	LUCKLESS	MUTINOUS
DIGAMIES	FLUIDICS	GUSTLESS	KINDLESS	LUMINOUS	MYELITIS
DIGGINGS	FOAMLESS	GYPSEOUS	KINDNESS	LUSCIOUS	MYOSITIS
DIMEROUS	FONDNESS	HAIRLESS	KINESICS	LUSHNESS	MYOSOTIS
DIOICOUS	*FOODWAYS	HALENESS	KINETICS	LUSTROUS	NABOBESS
DIPLOSIS	FOOTLESS	HALFNESS	*KINFOLKS	MAILLESS	NAMELESS
DIRENESS	*FORCIPES	HARDNESS	KINGLESS	MALENESS	NARCOSIS
DISTAVES	*FRABJOUS	HARMLESS	*KNICKERS	MAMMATUS	NATHLESS
DISTRESS	FREMITUS	HAUTBOIS	KNOTLESS	MAMMITIS	NAUPLIUS
DIURESIS	FRETLESS	*HAZINESS	KURTOSIS	MANDAMUS	NAUSEOUS
*DIZYGOUS	FULLNESS	HEADLESS	*KYPHOSIS	MANWARDS	NAUTILUS
DOLDRUMS	FUMELESS	HEATLESS	LACELESS	MARASMUS	NEARNESS
DOLOROUS	FUSELESS	HEDONICS	LACINESS	*MARQUESS	NEATNESS
DONENESS	*GADZOOKS	HEEDLESS	LACTEOUS	MASSLESS	NEBULOUS
DOORLESS	GAINLESS	HEELLESS	LAMENESS	MASTITIS	NECKLESS
DOPINESS	GALLEASS	HEIRLESS	LAMINOUS	MASTLESS	NECROSIS
DOURNESS	GAMASHES	HELMLESS	LANCIERS	MATELESS	NEEDLESS
*DOZINESS	GAMENESS	HELPLESS	LANDLESS	MATINESS	NEURITIS
DRABNESS	GAMINESS	HERBLESS	LANDMASS	MATTRASS	NEUROSIS
DRIPLESS	GARBLESS	HERCULES	LANKNESS	MATTRESS	NEWSLESS
DRUIDESS	GASTNESS	*HIBISCUS	LAPILLUS	MAYORESS	NICENESS
DRUTHERS	*GASWORKS	HIDELESS	LATENESS	*MAZINESS	NIGHNESS
DUCTLESS	GATELESS	HIDROSIS	*LAZINESS	MEANNESS	NIGHTIES
DULLNESS	*GAYWINGS	HIGAMIES	LEADLESS	MEATLESS	NORMLESS
DUMBNESS	GEARLESS	*HIGHNESS	LEAFLESS	MEEKNESS	NOSELESS
DURABLES	GENEROUS	HILTLESS	LEAKLESS	MEETNESS	NOSINESS
DUSTLESS	GENETICS	HIOLYSIS	LEANNESS	MEGALOPS	NOTELESS
FABULOUS	GENITALS	HIPAROUS	*LECYTHIS	MELANOUS	NOTORNIS
FACELESS	*GEOTAXIS	HIRAMOUS	*LECYTHUS	MELODIES	*NOWADAYS
FACTIOUS	GIANTESS	HIVELESS	*LEKYTHOS	*MENFOLKS	NUBILOUS
FADELESS	GIFTLESS	*HOKINESS	*LEKYTHUS	MENISCUS	NUCELLUS
FAIRNESS	GLABROUS	HOLELESS	LIBELOUS	*MEPHITIS	NUDENESS

NUMBNESS	PORTRESS	RIGOROUS	SIGHLESS	STEMLESS	TIDELESS
NUMEROUS	POSHNESS	RIMINESS	SIMONIES	STENOSIS	TIDINESS
NUMINOUS	*POXVIRUS	RINGHALS	*SIZINESS	STIMULUS	TIDYTIPS
NUTGRASS	PREBLESS	RINGTOSS	*SKEWNESS	STRATOUS	TIMELESS
*PACIFIES	PRECIOUS	RISIBLES	SKILLESS	STRUMOUS	TIMOROUS
*PACKNESS	*PREFOCUS	RISKLESS	SKINLESS	STUDIOUS	TININESS
PAINLESS	PREGGERS	ROADLESS	*SKYWARDS	SUBCLASS	TINNITUS
*PALAZZOS	PRETTIES	ROBOTICS	SLIMNESS	SUBCUTIS	TINTLESS
PALENESS	PREVIOUS	ROCKLESS	SLIPLESS	SUBEROUS	TIRELESS
*PALEWAYS	PRIMNESS	ROOFLESS	SLITLESS	SUBGENUS	TITANESS
PANCREAS	PRINCESS	ROOTLESS	SLOWNESS	SUCCUBUS	TITANOUS
PANDANUS	PRIORESS	ROPINESS	SLYBOOTS	SUCHNESS	TOADLESS
*PANMIXIS	PRIORIES	ROSINESS	SMARTASS	SUCKLESS	TONELESS
PARODIES	PROGRESS	ROSINOUS	SMITHERS	SUDSLESS	TONETICS
PASSLESS	PROPOLIS	RUCTIOUS	SMUGNESS	SUNDRESS	TOOLLESS
PASTLESS	PROTASIS	RUDENESS	SNAPLESS	SUNDRIES	TOPCROSS
PASTNESS	PROVIRUS	RULELESS	SNOWLESS	SUNDROPS	TORTIOUS
PATHLESS	PRURITUS	RUSTLESS	SNUBNESS	SUNGLASS	TORTUOUS
PATULOUS	PSILOSIS	RUTHLESS	SNUGNESS	SUNWARDS	TOUGHIES
*PAYABLES	PULPLESS	RYEGRASS	SOAPLESS	SUPPRESS	TOWNLESS
PEAKLESS	PULVINUS	SABULOUS	SOAPSUDS	SURENESS	TRAMLESS
PEERLESS	PUMPLESS	SACCULUS	SOCKLESS	SUSURRUS	TRAPPOUS
PERILOUS	PUNINESS	SAFENESS	SOFTNESS	SYLLABUS	TREELESS
PERTNESS	PURENESS	SAGENESS	SOILLESS	SYNAPSIS	TRESPASS
PERVIOUS	*PYCNOSIS	SALTLESS	SOLELESS	SYNDESIS	TRIGNESS
PETALOUS	PYELITIS	SALTNESS	SOLENESS	SYNOPSIS	TRIMNESS
*PHIMOSIS	*PYKNOSIS	SAMENESS	SOLONETS	*SYPHILIS	TRINKUMS
*PHTHISIS	*QUADRANS	SANENESS	SOMBROUS	TACKLESS	TROLLIES
*PHYLAXIS	RACEMOUS	SCABIOUS	*SOMEWAYS	TACTLESS	TROUSERS
*PHYLESIS	RACHITIS	SCALENUS	SONGLESS	TAILLESS	TROWSERS
PILELESS	RACINESS	SCANTIES	SONOROUS	TALLNESS	TRUENESS
PINGRASS	RAINLESS	SCARIOUS	SORENESS	TAMELESS	*TRYWORKS
PINKNESS	RAMULOUS	SCARLESS	SOURNESS	TAMENESS	TSORRIS
PIPELESS	RANKNESS	*SCHNAPPS	SOURPUSS	TANTALUS	TUBELESS
PIPINESS	RAPTNESS	SCIRRHUS	SPACIOUS	TAPELESS	TUBEROUS
PITHLESS	RARENESS	SCLEROUS	SPADICES	TARANTAS	TUBULOUS
PITILESS	RASHNESS	SCURRIES	SPANLESS	TARTNESS	TUMULOUS
*PIXINESS	RAVENOUS	SEAMLESS	SPECIOUS	TAUTNESS	TUNELESS
PLANLESS	RAYGRASS	SEATLESS	SPERMOUS	TEARLESS	TURFLESS
*PLATYPUS	REALNESS	SEDULOUS	*SPHERICS	TENESMUS	*TURQUOIS
PLAYLESS	REASSESS	SEEDLESS	SPHINGES	TENIASIS	TUSKLESS
PLOTLESS	RECKLESS	SELFLESS	*SPHYGMUS	TENTLESS	TUTORESS
PLOTTIES	REINLESS	SELFNESS	SPINLESS	TERMINUS	TWIGLESS
PLUGLESS	RESINOUS	SEMIOSIS	SPLENIUS	TERMLESS	VAINNESS
PLUMBOUS	RESTLESS	SENARIUS	SPOONIES	TETANIES	VALOROUS
PLUVIOUS	RESTRESS	SENSUOUS	SPOTLESS	*TEXTLESS	VAPOROUS
POACEOUS	REVERIES	SETULOUS	SPRYNESS	THALAMUS	VASTNESS
POETLESS	RHINITIS	*SEXINESS	SPURIOUS	THANATOS	VEINLESS
POKINESS	*RHIZOPUS	*SHAMMIES	SPYGLASS	THAWLESS	VENOMOUS
POLELESS	*RHONCHUS	SHANTIES	STANNOUS	THELITIS	VENTLESS
POLITICS	RIBGRASS	SHOELESS	STAPEDES	THEORIES	VERBLESS
*POLYPOUS	RICHNESS	SHORTIES	STARKERS	THEWLESS	VESTLESS
POORNESS	RIFENESS	SICKNESS	STARLESS	THINNESS	VICELESS
POPULOUS	RIFTLESS	*SIDEWAYS	STEADIES	THOWLESS	VICTRESS
PORTLESS	RIGHTIES			*THROMBUS	

VIEWLESS VOTELESS WATTLESS WIDENESS WISENESS *YOKELESS
VIGOROUS VULVITIS WAVELESS WIFELESS WISHLESS *ZANINESS
VILENESS *WAESUCKS WAVINESS WILDNESS WONDROUS *ZESTLESS
VIRTUOUS WAGELESS *WAXINESS WILINESS WOODLESS *ZONELESS
VITELLUS WAITRESS *WEAKNESS WINDLASS WOOLLIES *ZOONOSIS
VITREOUS *WAKELESS WEEDLESS WINDLESS WORDLESS
VOIDNESS WARDRESS WEIRDIES WINELESS *WORKLESS
VOLVULUS WARINESS WELDLESS WINGLESS WORNNESS
VOMITOUS WARMNESS WELLNESS WIRELESS *XANTHOUS
VOTARESS WARTLESS WHATNESS WIRINESS YEARLIES

T

TABU	TEAT	TIDY	TONG	TRIO	**TYPP**
TACE	TEEL	TIED	TONY	TRIP	**TYPY**
TACH	TEEM	TIER	TOOK	TROD	TYRE
TACK	TEEN	**TIFF**	TOOL	TROP	TYRO
TACO	**TEFF**	TIKE	TOOM	TROT	**TZAR**
TACT	TELA	TIKI	TOON	TROW	**TABBY**
TAEL	TELE	TILE	TOOT	TROY	TABER
TAHR	TELL	TILL	TOPE	TRUE	TABES
TAIL	TEMP	TILT	TOPH	TSAR	TABID
TAIN	TEND	TIME	TOPI	TUBA	TABLA
TAKA	TENT	TINE	TORA	TUBE	TABLE
TAKE	TEPA	TING	TORC	**TUCK**	TABOO
TALA	TEPF	TINT	TORE	TUFA	TABOR
TALC	TERM	TINY	TORI	**TUFF**	TABUN
TALE	TERN	TIPI	TORN	TUFT	TACET
TALI	TEST	TIRE	TORO	TULE	**TACHE**
TALK	TETH	TIRL	TORR	TUMP	TACIT
TALL	**TEXT**	TIRO	TORT	TUNA	**TACKY**
TAME	THAE	TITI	TORY	TUNE	**TAFFY**
TAMP	THAN	**TIVY**	TOSH	TUNG	TAFIA
TANG	THAT	TOAD	TOSS	TURD	TAIGA
TANK	**THAW**	TOBY	TOST	TURF	TAINT
TAPA	THEE	TODY	TOTE	TURK	TAKER
TAPE	THEM	TOEA	TOUR	TURN	TAKIN
TARE	THEN	**TOFF**	TOUT	TUSH	TALAR
TARN	**THEW**	TOFT	TOWN	TUSK	TALER
TARO	**THEY**	TOFU	**TOWY**	TUTU	**TALKY**
TARP	THIN	TOGA	TOYO	TWAE	TALLY
TART	THIO	TOIL	TRAD	TWAT	TALON
TASK	THIR	TOIT	TRAM	TWEE	TALUK
TASS	THIS	TOKE	TRAP	TWIG	TALUS
TATE	THOU	TOLA	TRAY	TWIN	TAMAL
TAUT	THRO	TOLD	TREE	TWIT	TAMER
TAXA	THRU	TOLE	TREF	TYEE	TAMIS
TAXI	THUD	TOLL	TREK	TYER	**TAMMY**
TEAK	THUG	TOLU	TRET	**TYKE**	TANGO
TEAL	THUS	TOMB	TREY	TYNE	TANGY
TEAM	**TICK**	TOME	TRIG	TYPE	TANKA
TEAR	TIDE	TONE	TRIM	TYPO	TANSY

TANTO	TENTH	**THRIP**	TONDO	TRAPT	TSADE
TAPER	TENTY	**THROB**	TONER	TRASH	TSADI
TAPIR	TEPAL	THROE	TONEY	TRASS	TSUBA
TAPIS	TEPEE	**THROW**	TONGA	TRAVE	TUBAL
TARDO	TEPID	**THRUM**	TONIC	TRAWL	**TUBBY**
TARDY	**TEPOY**	*THUJA	TONNE	TREAD	TUBER
TARGE	TERAI	**THUMB**	TONUS	TREAT	**TUFTY**
TAROC	TERCE	**THUMP**	TOOTH	TREEN	TULIP
TAROK	TERGA	**THUNK**	TOOTS	TREND	TULLE
TAROT	TERNE	THURL	*TOPAZ	TRESS	TUMID
TARRE	TERRA	**THUYA**	TOPEE	TREWS	**TUMMY**
TARRY	TERRY	**THYME**	TOPER	TRIAC	TUMOR
TARSI	TERSE	**THYMI**	**TOPHE**	TRIAD	TUNER
TARTY	TESLA	TIARA	TOPIC	TRIAL	TUNIC
TASSE	TESTA	TIBIA	TOPOI	TRIBE	**TUNNY**
TASTE	TESTY	TICAL	TOPOS	TRICE	**TUPIK**
TASTY	TETRA	TIDAL	**TOQUE**	**TRICK**	**YUQUE**
TATAR	**TEUCH**	TIGER	TORAH	TRIED	TURBO
TATER	TEUGH	TIGHT	**TORCH**	TRIER	**TURFY**
TATTY	**TEXAS**	TIGON	TORIC	TRIES	TURPS
TAUNT	**THACK**	TILAK	TORII	TRIGO	TUTEE
TAUPE	THANE	TILDE	TOROT	TRIKE	TUTOR
TAWER	**THANK**	TILER	TORSE	TRILL	TUTTI
TAWIE	**THARM**	TILTH	TORSI	TRINE	TUTTY
TAWNY	**THEBE**	TIMER	TORSK	TRIOL	TUYER
TAWSE	**THECA**	TIMID	TORSO	TRIPE	TWAIN
TAXER	**THEFT**	TINCT	TORTE	TRITE	TWANG
TAXON	THEGN	TINEA	TORUS	TROAK	**TWEAK**
TAXUS	THEIN	TINGE	TOTAL	**TROCK**	TWEED
*TAZZA	THEIR	TINNY	TOTEM	TRODE	TWEEN
TEACH	**THEME**	**TIPPY**	TOTER	TROIS	TWEET
TEARY	THERE	**TIPSY**	**TOUCH**	TROKE	**TWERP**
TEASE	**THERM**	TIRED	TOUGH	TROLL	**TWICE**
TECHY	THESE	TITAN	TOUSE	TROMP	TWIER
TECTA	THEfA	TITER	TOWEL	TRONA	TWILL
TEDDY	**THEWY**	TITHE	TOWER	TRONE	TWINE
TEENY	**THICK**	TITLE	TOWIE	TROOP	**TWINY**
TEETH	**THIEF**	TITRE	**TOWNY**	**TROOZ**	TWIRL
TEGUA	**THIGH**	TITTY	**TOXIC**	TROPE	**TWIRP**
TEIID	THILL	*TIZZY	**TOXIN**	TROTH	TWIST
TEIND	THINE	TOADY	TOYER	TROUT	*TWIXT
TELEX	THING	TOAST	TOYON	TROVE	**TWYER**
TELIA	**THINK**	TODAY	TRACE	TRUCE	TYING
TELIC	THIOL	**TODDY**	**TRACK**	**TRUCK**	**TYPAL**
TELLY	THIRD	**TOFFY**	TRACT	TRUED	**TYPED**
TELOS	THIRL	TOGUE	TRADE	TRUER	**TYPEY**
TEMPI	THOLE	TOILE	TRAGI	TRULL	**TYPIC**
TEMPO	THONG	**TOKAY**	TRAIK	TRULY	**TYTHE**
TEMPT	THORN	TOKEN	TRAIL	TRUMP	TABARD
TENCH	THORO	TOKER	TRAIN	TRUNK	**TABBED**
TENET	**THORP**	TOLAN	TRAIT	TRUSS	**TABBIS**
TENIA	THOSE	TOLYL	TRAMP	TRUST	TABLET
TENON	**THRAW**	TOMAN	TRANK	TRUTH	TABOUR
TENOR	THREE	**TOMMY**	**TRANQ**	**TRYMA**	TABULI
TENSE	**THREW**	TONAL	TRANS	TRYST	**TACKER**

TACKET	TAPPED	TEEMER	TESTIS	THRUST	**TIPPER**
*TACKEY	**TAPPER**	TEENER	TESTON	THULIA	**TIPPET**
TACKLE	**TAPPET**	TEENSY	TETANY	**THUSLY**	**TIPPLE**
TACTIC	TARAMA	TEEPEE	**TETCHY**	*THWACK	TIPTOE
TAENIA	TARGET	TEETER	THETHER	THWART	**TIPTOP**
TAFFIA	**TARIFF**	TEETHE	TETRAD	*THYMEY	TIRADE
TAGGED	TARING	TEGMEN	TETRYL	*THYMIC	TIRING
TAGGER	**TARMAC**	TELEDU	TETTER	**THYMOL**	TISANE
TAGRAG	TARNAL	TELEGA	**THAIRM**	**THYMUS**	TISSUE
TAHINI	TARPAN	TELFER	THALER	**THYRSE**	TITBIT
TAHSIL	TARPON	TELIAL	**THATCH**	**TICKER**	TITFER
TAILER	TARRED	TELIUM	**THAWER**	**TICKET**	TITIAN
TAILLE	TARSAL	TELLER	THEINE	**TICKLE**	TITMAN
TAILOR	TARSIA	TELOME	THEIRS	**TICTAC**	TITTER
TAIPAN	TARSUS	TELSON	**THEISM**	**TICTOC**	TITTIE
TAKAHE	TARTAN	**TEMPEH**	THEIST	TIDBIT	TITTLE
TAKEUP	TARTAR	**TEMPER**	THENAL	**TIDDLY**	TITTUP
TAKING	TARTLY	**TEMPLE**	THENAR	TIDIED	TMESIS
TALCUM	*TARZAN	TENACE	**THENCE**	TIDIER	TOASTY
TALENT	TASSEL	TENAIL	**THEORY**	TIDIES	**TOCHER**
TALION	TASSET	TENANT	**THERBY**	**TIDILY**	TOCSIN
TALKER	TASSIE	TENDER	**THERME**	TIDING	TODDLE
TALKIE	TASTER	TENDON	THESIS	TIEPIN	**TOECAP**
TALLIS	TATAMI	TENNER	**THETIC**	TIERCE	**TOFFEE**
TALLIT	TATTED	TENNIS	**THIEVE**	**TIFFIN**	TOGATE
TALLOL	TATTER	TENOUR	**THINLY**	**TIGHTS**	TOGGED
TALLOW	TATTIE	TENPIN	**THIRAM**	TIGLON	TOGGLE
TALUKA	TATTLE	TENREC	THIRST	TILING	TOILER
TAMALE	TATTOO	TENSOR	**THIRTY**	TILLER	TOILET
TAMARI	**TAUGHT**	TENTER	THOLOS	TILTER	**TOKING**
TAMBAC	TAUTEN	TENTIE	*THORAX	**TIMBAL**	TOLANE
TAMBAK	TAUTLY	TENUIS	THORIA	**TIMBER**	TOLEDO
TAMBUR	TAUTOG	TENURE	**THORIC**	**TIMBRE**	TOLING
TAMEIN	TAVERN	TENUTO	**THORNY**	**TIMELY**	TOLLER
TAMELY	**TAWDRY**	TEOPAN	THORON	TIMING	TOLUIC
TAMEST	**TAWNEY**	**TEPEFY**	**THORPE**	TINCAL	TOLUID
TAMING	**TAWPIE**	**TEPHRA**	**THOUGH**	TINDER	TOLUOL
TAMMIE	*TAXEME	**TERAPH**	THRALL	TINEID	TOLUYL
TAMPAN	**TAXITE**	TERBIA	**THRASH**	TINFUL	TOMATO
TAMPER	*TAXMAN	TERCEL	**THRAVE**	TINGLE	**TOMBAC**
TAMPON	*TEABOX	TERCET	**THRAWN**	**TINGLY**	**TOMBAK**
TANDEM	**TEACUP**	TEREDO	**THREAD**	TINIER	**TOMBAL**
TANGLE	TEAPOT	TERETE	**THREAP**	TINILY	**TOMBOY**
TANGLY	**TEAPOY**	TERGAL	THREAT	TINING	**TOMCAT**
TANIST	TEARER	TERGUM	**THREEP**	**TINKER**	**TOMCOD**
TANKER	TEASEL	TERMER	**THRESH**	**TINKLE**	**TOMMED**
TANNED	TEASER	**TERMLY**	**THRICE**	**TINKLY**	TOMTIT
TANNER	*TEAZEL	TERMOR	**THRIFT**	TINMAN	TONEME
TANNIC	*TEAZLE	TERRAS	THRILL	TINNED	TONGER
TANNIN	**TECHED**	TERRET	**THRIVE**	TINNER	TONGUE
TANREC	**TECHIE**	TERRIT	THROAT	TINSEL	TONIER
TANTRA	TECTAL	TERROR	THRONE	TINTER	TONING
TANUKI	**TECTUM**	TESTEE	**THRONG**	**TIPCAT**	TONISH
TAPALO	TEDDER	TESTER	**THROVE**	**TIPOFF**	TONLET
TAPING	TEDIUM	TESTES	**THRUSH**	**TIPPED**	TONNER

TONSIL	TRAPES	TROVER	**TURKEY**	**TABETIC**	TANAGER
TOOLER	**TRASHY**	TROWEL	TURNER	TABLEAU	**TANBARK**
TOOTER	TRAUMA	**TROWTH**	TURNIP	**TABLING**	TANGELO
TOOTHY	TRAVEL	TRUANT	TURNUP	**TABLOID**	TANGENT
TOOTLE	TREATY	TRUDGE	TURRET	TABORER	TANGIER
TOOTSY	TREBLE	TRUEST	TURTLE	TABORET	TANGLER
TOPFUL	**TREBLY**	**TRUFFE**	TURVES	TABORIN	**TANGRAM**
TOPHUS	**TREFAH**	TRUING	**TUSCHE**	TABOULI	**TANKAGE**
TOPING	TREMOR	TRUISM	**TUSKER**	TABULAR	**TANKARD**
TOPPED	**TRENCH**	TRUSTY	TUSSAH	**TACHISM**	**TANKFUL**
TOPPER	**TRENDY**	TRYOUT	TUSSAL	**TACHIST**	TANNAGE
TOPPLE	TREPAN	TRYSTE	TUSSAR	***TACHYON**	TANNATE
*TOQUET	TREPID	TSETSE	TUSSEH	**TACKIER**	**TANNERY**
TORERO	TRESSY	**TSKTSK**	TUSSER	***TACKIFY**	TANNEST
TORIES	TREVET	TSORES	TUSSIS	***TACKILY**	TANNING
TOROID	TRIAGE	TSORIS	TUSSLE	**TACKLER**	**TANNISH**
TOROSE	TRIBAL	TSURIS	TUSSOR	**TACNODE**	TANTARA
TOROTH	***TRICKY**	TUBATE	TUSSUR	**TACTFUL**	**TANTIVY**
TOROUS	TRICOT	**TUBBED**	TUTTED	TACTILE	TANTRUM
TORPID	TRIENE	**TUBBER**	**TUXEDO**	TACTION	**TANYARD**
TORPOR	TRIENS	**TUBFUL**	TUYERE	**TADPOLE**	TAPERER
*TORQUE	**TRIFID**	TUBING	**TWANGY**	**TAFFETA**	**TAPETUM**
TORRID	TRIFLE	TUBIST	***TWANKY**	**TAGGING**	**TAPHOLE**
TORULA	**TRIGLY**	TUBULE	***TWEAKY**	**TAGLIKE**	**TAPIOCA**
TOSSER	TRIGON	**TUCHUN**	TWEEDY	**TAGMEME**	**TAPPING**
TOSSUP	**TRIJET**	**TUCKER**	TWEENY	**TAILFAN**	**TAPROOM**
TOTHER	**TRILBY**	**TUCKET**	***TWEEZE**	TAILING	TAPROOT
TOTING	TRIMER	**TUFFET**	**TWELVE**	***TAKEOFF**	TAPSTER
TOTTED	**TRIMLY**	TUFOLI	**TWENTY**	**TAKEOUT**	**TARBUSH**
TOTTER	TRINAL	TUFTER	**TWIBIL**	TALARIA	TARDIER
TOUCAN	TRIODE	TUGGER	**TWIGGY**	**TALIPED**	TARDIES
TOUCHE	TRIOSE	**TUGRIK**	TWILIT	TALIPES	**TARDYON**
TOUCHY	TRIPLE	TUILLE	TWINER	TALIPOT	**TARNISH**
TOUGHY	**TRIPLY**	TULADI	**TWINGE**	**TALKING**	TARRIED
TOUPEE	TRIPOD	**TUMBLE**	**TWIRLY**	TALLAGE	TARRIER
TOURER	TRIPOS	**TUMEFY**	TWISTY	**TALLBOY**	TARRIES
TOUSLE	**TRIPPY**	TUMOUR	**TWITCH**	TALLIED	TARRING
TOUTER	TRISTE	TUMULI	**TWOFER**	TALLIER	TARSIER
*TOUZLE	TRITON	TUMULT	**TYCOON**	TALLIES	TARTANA
TOWAGE	TRIUNE	**TYMBAL**	**TYMBAL**	**TALLISH**	**TARTISH**
TOWARD	TRIVET	TUNEUP	**TYMPAN**	**TALLITH**	TARTLET
TOWERY	TRIVIA	TUNICA	**TYPHON**	**TALLOWY**	**TARTUFE**
TOWHEE	TROCAR	TUNING	**TYPHUS**	**TALLYHO**	**TARWEED**
TOWNEE	**TROCHE**	TUNNED	**TYPIER**	**TALOOKA**	TASTING
TOWNIE	TROGON	TUNNEL	***TYPIFY**	**TAMABLE**	TATOUAY
TOXINE	**TROIKA**	TUPELO	**TYPING**	TAMANDU	TATTIER
TOXOID	TROLLY	**TUPPED**	**TYPIST**	TAMARAO	**TATTILY**
TOYISH	**TROMPE**	TURACO	TYRANT	TAMARAU	TATTING
TRACER	**TROPHY**	TURBAN	***TZETZE**	**TAMARIN**	TATTLER
TRADER	**TROPIC**	TURBID	***TZURIS**	**TAMASHA**	TAUNTER
TRAGIC	TROPIN	TURBIT	**TABANID**	TAMARAU	TAURINE
TRAGUS	TROTYL	TURBOT	TABARET	**TAMBALA**	TAUTAUG
TRAMEL	**TROUGH**	TUREEN	**TABBIED**	**TAMBOUR**	TAVERNA
TRANCE	TROUPE	TURGID	**TABBIES**	TAMBURA	***TAXABLE**
TRAPAN	TROUTY	TURGOR	**TABBING**	TAMPION	***TAXICAB**

*TAXIMAN	TENSING	THEELIN	THUNDER	TISSUEY	TOOLING
*TAXIWAY	TENSION	THEELOL	*THYMIER	TITANIA	TOOTLER
TAXLESS	TENSITY	THENAGE	*THYMINE	TITANIC	TOOTSIE
*TAXPAID	TENSIVE	THEOLOG	THYROID	TITHING	TOPCOAT
*TAXWISE	TENTAGE	THEORBO	THYRSUS	TITLARK	TOPFULL
*TAXYING	TENTHLY	THEOREM	*THYSELF	TITLIST	TOPIARY
TEABOWL	TENTIER	*THERAPY	TICKING	TITRANT	*TOPKICK
TEACAKE	TENUITY	THEREAT	TICKLER	TITRATE	TOPKNOT
TEACART	TENUOUS	THEREIN	TIDDLER	TITTIES	TOPLESS
TEACHER	*TEQUILA	THEREOF	TIDERIP	TITULAR	TOPLINE
TEALIKE	TERAOHM	THEREON	TIDEWAY	TOADIED	TOPMAST
TEARFUL	TERBIUM	THERETO	TIDIEST	TOADIES	TOPMOST
TEARGAS	TEREBIC	THERIAC	*TIEBACK	TOADISH	TOPONYM
TEARIER	TEREFAH	THERMAE	TIELESS	TOASTER	TOPPING
TEARILY	TERGITE	THERMAL	TIERCED	TOBACCO	TOPSAIL
TEAROOM	TERMITE	THERMEL	TIERCEL	TOCCATA	TOPSIDE
TEASHOP	TERNARY	THERMIC	*TIFFANY	TODDIES	TOPSOIL
TEASING	TERNATE	THERMIT	TIGHTEN	TODDLER	TOPSPIN
TEATIME	TERNION	THERMOS	TIGRESS	TOEHOLD	*TOPWORK
TEAWARE	TERPENE	THEROID	TIGRISH	TOELESS	TORCHON
TECHNIC	TERRACE	THEURGY	TILAPIA	TOELIKE	TORMENT
TECTITE	TERRAIN	THIAMIN	TILBURY	TOENAIL	TORNADO
*TECTRIX	TERRANE	*THIAZIN	TILLAGE	TOESHOE	TORPEDO
TEDIOUS	TERREEN	*THIAZOL	TILLITE	TOGATED	*TORQUER
TEENAGE	TERRENE	*THICKEN	TIMARAU	TOGGERY	*TORQUES
TEENFUL	TERRIER	*THICKET	TIMBALE	TOGGING	TORREFY
TEENIER	TERRIES	*THICKLY	TIMBREL	TOGGLER	TORRENT
TEENTSY	TERRIFY	THIEVES	TIMEOUS	TOILFUL	TORRIFY
TEETHER	TERRINE	THIMBLE	TIMEOUT	*TOKAMAK	TORSADE
TEGULAR	TERTIAL	THINKER	TIMOLOL	*TOKOMAK	TORSION
TEGUMEN	TERTIAN	THINNED	TIMOTHY	TOLIDIN	TORTILE
TEKTITE	TESSERA	THINNER	TIMPANO	TOLLAGE	TORTONI
TELAMON	TESTACY	THIONIC	TINAMOU	TOLLBAR	TORTRIX
TELEMAN	TESTATE	THIONIN	TINFOIL	TOLLMAN	TORTURE
TELEOST	TESTIER	THIONYL	TINGLER	TOLLWAY	TOSSPOT
TELERAN	TESTIFY	THIRDLY	TINHORN	TOLUATE	TOSTADA
TELESIS	TESTILY	THIRSTY	TINIEST	TOLUENE	TOSTADO
TELFORD	TESTING	THISTLE	TINKLER	TOLUIDE	TOTABLE
TELLIES	TESTOON	THISTLY	TINLIKE	TOLUOLE	TOTALLY
TELPHER	TESTUDO	THITHER	TINNIER	*TOMBACK	TOTTERY
TEMBLOR	TETANAL	THORITE	TINNILY	TOMBOLO	TOTTING
TEMPERA	TETANIC	THORIUM	TINNING	TOMFOOL	TOUCHER
TEMPEST	TETANUS	THOUGHT	TINTING	TOMMING	TOUCHUP
TEMPLAR	TETCHED	THREADY	TINTYPE	TOMPION	TOUGHEN
TEMPLET	TETOTUM	THREAVE	TINWARE	TONEARM	TOUGHIE
TEMPTER	TETRODE	THRIVER	TINWORK	TONETTE	TOUGHLY
TEMPURA	TEXTILE	THROATY	TIPCART	TONGMAN	TOURACO
TENABLE	TEXTUAL	THROUGH	TIPLESS	TONIEST	TOURING
TENANCY	TEXTURE	THROWER	TIPPIER	TONIGHT	TOURISM
TENDRIL	THALLUS	*THRUMMY	TIPPING	TONNAGE	TOURIST
TENFOLD	THANAGE	THRUPUT	TIPPLER	TONNEAU	TOURNEY
TENNIES	THANKER	*THRUWAY	TIPSIER	TONNISH	TOWARDS
TENNIST	*THATCHY	THUGGEE	TIPSILY	TONSURE	*TOWAWAY
TENONER	THEATER	THULIUM	TIPSTER	TONTINE	TOWBOAT
TENSILE	THEATRE	THUMPER	TISSUAL	*TOOLBOX	TOWHEAD

TOWLINE	TREHALA	TRISHAW	TSUNAMI	TWANGLE	*TACHISME
TOWMOND	*TREKKER	TRISMUS	TUATARA	TWASOME	TACHISTE
TOWMONT	TRELLIS	TRISOME	TUATERA	TWATTLE	TACITURN
TOWNIES	TREMBLE	TRISOMY	TUBAIST	TWEEDLE	TACKIEST
TOWNISH	TREMBLY	TRITIUM	TUBBING	TWEETER	TACKLESS
*TOWPATH	TRENAIL	TRITOMA	TUBLIKE	*TWEEZER	*TACKLING
TOWROPE	TREPANG	TRITONE	TUBULAR	*TWELFTH	TACONITE
*TOXEMIA	TRESSEL	TRIUMPH	TUBULIN	TWIBILL	TACTLESS
*TOXICAL	TRESTLE	TRIVIAL	TUGBOAT	TWIDDLE	TAFFAREL
TOYLESS	TRIABLE	TRIVIUM	TUGGING	*TWIDDLY	TAFFEREL
TOYLIKE	TRIACID	TROCHAL	*TUGHRIK	TWIGGEN	TAFFRAIL
*TOYSHOP	TRIADIC	TROCHAR	TUGLESS	TWINIER	TAFFRAIL
TRACERY	*TRIAZIN	TROCHEE	TUITION	TWINING	TAGALONG
TRACHEA	TRIBADE	TROCHIL	TUMBLER	*TWINJET	TAGBOARD
TRACHLE	TRIBUNE	TRODDEN	TUMBREL	TWINKLE	*TAGMEMIC
TRACING	TRIBUTE	TROFFER	TUMBRIL	*TWINKLY	TAIGLACH
TRACKER	TRICEPS	TROILUS	TUMMLER	TWINNED	*TAILBACK
TRACTOR	TRICING	TROLAND	TUMULAR	TWINSET	TAILBONE
TRADUCE	TRICKER	TROLLER	TUMULUS	TWIRLER	TAILCOAT
*TRAFFIC	TRICKIE	TROLLEY	TUNABLE	TWISTER	TAILGATE
TRAGEDY	*TRICKLY	TROLLOP	TUNDISH	*TWITCHY	TAILLAMP
TRAILER	*TRICKSY	TROOPER	TUNEFUL	TWITTED	TAILLESS
TRAINEE	TRICLAD	TROPHIC	TUNICLE	TWITTER	TAILLEUR
TRAINER	TRICORN	TROPINE	TUNNAGE	TWOFOLD	TAILLIKE
TRAIPSE	TRIDENT	TROPISM	TUNNING	TWOSOME	TAILPIPE
TRAITOR	TRIDUUM	TROTTED	TUPPING	TYLOSIN	TAILRACE
*TRAJECT	TRIFLER	TROTTER	TURACOU	TYMPANA	TAILSKID
TRAMCAR	TRIFOLD	TROUBLE	TURBARY	TYMPANI	TAILSPIN
TRAMELL	TRIFORM	TROUNCE	TURBETH	TYMPANO	TAILWIND
TRAMMED	TRIGGER	TROUPER	TURBINE	*TYMPANY	*TAKEAWAY
TRAMMEL	TRIGRAM	TROUSER	TURBITH	TYPEBAR	*TAKEDOWN
TRAMPER	TRILLER	TRUANCY	TURDINE	TYPESET	*TAKEOVER
TRAMPLE	TRILOGY	TRUCKER	TURFIER	*TYPHOID	*TAKINGLY
*TRAMWAY	TRIMMED	TRUCKLE	TURFMAN	*TYPHOON	TALAPOIN
TRANCHE	TRIMMER	TRUDGEN	TURFSKI	*TYPHOSE	TALESMAN
TRANGAM	TRINARY	TRUDGER	TURGENT	TYPICAL	TALEYSIM
TRANSIT	TRINDLE	TRUFFLE	TURGITE	TYPIEST	TALISMAN
TRANSOM	TRINITY	TRUMEAU	TURISTA	TYRANNY	TALKABLE
*TRAPEZE	TRINKET	TRUMPET	TURKOIS	*TZADDIK	TALLNESS
TRAPPED	TRIOLET	TRUNDLE	TURMOIL	*TZARDOM	TALLYMAN
TRAPPER	*TRIOXID	TRUNNEL	TURNERY	*TZARINA	TALMUDIC
TRAVAIL	*TRIPACK	TRUSSER	TURNING	*TZARISM	TAMANDUA
TRAVOIS	TRIPART	TRUSTEE	TURNKEY	*TZARIST	*TAMARACK
TRAWLER	TRIPLET	TRUSTER	TURNOFF	*TZIGANE	TAMARIND
TRAWLEY	*TRIPLEX	TRUSTOR	TURNOUT	*TZIMMES	TAMARISK
TRAYFUL	TRIPODY	TRYPSIN	TURPETH	*TZITZIS	TAMBOURA
TREACLE	TRIPOLI	TRYSAIL	TURTLER	*TZITZIT	TAMEABLE
TREADER	TRIPPED	TRYSTER	TUSSOCK	TABLEFUL	TAMELESS
TREADLE	TRIPPER	TSARDOM	TUSSORE	TABLETOP	TAMENESS
TREASON	TRIPPET	TSARINA	TUSSUCK	TABOOLEY	TAMPERER
TREATER	TRIREME	TSARISM	TUTELAR	TABORINE	TANGENCE
TREDDLE	TRISECT	TSARIST	TUTOYER	TABOURER	TANGENCY
TREETOP	TRISEME	TSIMMES	TUTTING	TABOURET	TANGIBLE
TREFOIL	TRISEME	TSOORIS	TWADDLE	TABULATE	TANGIBLY
		TSIMMES		TACHINID	TANGIEST

TANISTRY	TEENIEST	TEPIDITY	THEREFOR	THRUSTOR	*TIPSTAFF
*TANKLIKE	*TEENYBOP	TERATISM	THEREMIN	*THUGGERY	*TIPSTOCK
*TANKSHIP	TEETHING	TERATOMA	THERIACA	*THUGGISH	TIRAMISU
TANNABLE	TEETOTAL	TERAWATT	THERMION	*THUMBKIN	TIRELESS
TANTALUM	TEETOTUM	TERCELET	THERMITE	*THUMBNUT	TIRESOME
TANTALUS	TEFILLIN	TEREBENE	THEROPOD	*THUNDERY	TIRRIVEE
TAPADERA	TEGMENTA	*TERIYAKI	THESAURI	THURIBLE	TISSULAR
TAPADERO	TEGMINAL	TERMINAL	THESPIAN	THURIFER	TITANATE
TAPELESS	TEGUMENT	TERMINUS	THETICAL	*THWACKER	TITANESS
TAPELIKE	TEIGLACH	TERMLESS	THEWLESS	THWARTER	TITANISM
TAPELINE	TELECAST	TERMTIME	THIAMINE	*THWARTLY	TITANITE
TAPESTRY	TELEFILM	TERPINOL	*THIAZIDE	*THYMIEST	TITANIUM
*TAPEWORM	TELEGONY	TERRAPIN	*THIAZINE	*THYMOSIN	TITANOUS
TAPHOUSE	TELEGRAM	TERRARIA	*THIAZOLE	*THYREOID	TITHABLE
TARANTAS	TELEMARK	*TERRAZZO	*THICKISH	*THYROXIN	TITHONIA
TARBOOSH	TELEPATH	TERRELLA	*THICKSET	TIDELAND	TITIVATE
TARLATAN	TELEPLAY	TERRIBLE	*THIEVERY	TIDELESS	TITMOUSE
TARLETAN	TELEPORT	TERRIFIC	*THIEVING	TIDELIKE	TITRABLE
TARPAPER	TELESTIC	TERTIARY	*THIEVISH	*TIDEMARK	TITRATOR
TARRAGON	*TELETEXT	TESTATOR	THINCLAD	TIDINESS	TITTERER
TARRIEST	TELETHON	TESTICLE	*THINDOWN	TIDYTIPS	*TITTUPPY
TARTNESS	TELEVIEW	TESTIEST	*THINKING	TIECLASP	TITULARY
TARTRATE	TELEVISE	TETANIES	THINNESS	TIGEREYE	*TOADFLAX
TARTUFFE	TELLTALE	TETANISE	THINNEST	TIGERISH	*TOADFISH
*TASKWORK	TELLURIC	*TETANIZE	THINNING	*TIGHTWAD	TOADLESS
TASTEFUL	TELOMERE	TETRACID	THINNISH	TILEFISH	TOADLIKE
TATTIEST	TEMERITY	TETRAGON	THIONATE	TILELIKE	*TOADYISH
TATTOOER	TEMPERER	TETRAMER	THIONINE	TILTYARD	TOADYISM
TAUTNESS	TEMPLATE	TETRAPOD	*THIOPHEN	TIMECARD	TOBOGGAN
TAUTOMER	TEMPORAL	TETRARCH	THIOTEPA	TIMELESS	TOCOLOGY
TAUTONYM	TENACITY	*TETROXID	THIOUREA	TIMELINE	TOEPIECE
TAVERNER	TENACULA	*TEXTBOOK	THIRLAGE	*TIMEWORK	TOEPLATE
*TAXATION	TENAILLE	*TEXTLESS	THIRSTER	TIMEWORN	TOGETHER
*TAXINGLY	TENANTRY	*TEXTUARY	THIRTEEN	TIMIDITY	TOILETRY
*TAXONOMY	TENDANCE	*TEXTURAL	THOLEPIN	TIMOROUS	TOILETTE
*TAXPAYER	TENDENCE	THALAMUS	*THOROUGH	TIMPANUM	TOILSOME
TEABERRY	TENDENCY	THALLIUM	THOUSAND	TINCTURE	TOILWORN
TEABOARD	TENDERER	THANATOS	THOWLESS	TININESS	TOKENISM
TEACHING	TENDERLY	*THANKFUL	THRALDOM	TINKERER	*TOKOLOGY
TEAHOUSE	TENEBRAE	*THATAWAY	THRASHER	TINKLING	TOKONOMA
*TEAKWOOD	TENEMENT	*THATCHER	THRAWART	TINNIEST	TOLBOOTH
TEAMAKER	TENESMUS	THAWLESS	THREADER	TINNITUS	TOLERANT
TEAMMATE	TENIASIS	*THEARCHY	THREAPER	TINPLATE	TOLERATE
TEAMSTER	TENORITE	THEBAINE	THREATEN	TINSELLY	TOLIDINE
*TEAMWORK	TENOTOMY	THELITIS	THRENODE	TINSMITH	TOLLGATE
TEARAWAY	TENPENCE	*THEMATIC	*THRENODY	TINSTONE	TOLUIDIN
TEARDOWN	TENPENNY	THEOCRAT	THRESHER	TINTLESS	*TOMAHAWK
TEARDROP	TENSIBLE	*THEODICY	THRILLER	TIPPABLE	TOMALLEY
TEARIEST	TENTACLE	*THEOGONY	*THROBBER	TIPPIEST	TOMBLESS
TEARLESS	TENTIEST	*THEOLOGY	*THROMBIN	*TIPPYTOE	*TOMBLIKE
TEASELER	TENTLESS	*THEONOMY	*THROMBUS	TIPSIEST	TOMENTUM
TEASPOON	TENTLIKE	THEORIES	THROSTLE		*TOMMYROT
TECTONIC	TEOCALLI	THEORISE	THROTTLE		TOMOGRAM
TEENAGED	TEOSINTE	THEORIST	*THRUMMER		TOMORROW
TEENAGER	TEPHRITE	*THEORIZE	THRUSTER		TONALITY

TONELESS	TRABEATE	TREADLER	TRIMETER	TRUANTRY	TURBINAL
TONETICS	TRACHEID	TREASURE	TRIMMEST	*TRUCKAGE	TURBOCAR
TONGUING	*TRACHOMA	TREASURY	TRIMMING	*TRUCKFUL	TURBOFAN
TONICITY	*TRACHYTE	TREATISE	TRIMNESS	*TRUCKING	*TURBOJET
TOOLHEAD	*TRACKAGE	TRECENTO	*TRIMORPH	TRUCKLER	TURFIEST
TOOLLESS	*TRACKING	TREELAWN	TRIMOTOR	*TRUCKMAN	TURFLESS
TOOLROOM	*TRACKMAN	TREELESS	TRINKUMS	TRUDGEON	*TURFLIKE
TOOLSHED	*TRACKWAY	TREELIKE	TRINODAL	TRUDGING	TURGENCY
TOPCROSS	TRACTATE	TREENAIL	*TRIOXIDE	TRUEBLUE	TURMERIC
*TOPLOFTY	TRACTILE	TREMBLER	TRIPEDAL	TRUEBORN	TURNCOAT
*TOPNOTCH	TRACTION	TRENCHER	TRIPHASE	TRUEBRED	TURNDOWN
TOPOLOGY	*TRADEOFF	TREPHINE	TRIPLANE	TRUELOVE	TURNHALL
*TOPONYMY	TRADITOR	TRESPASS	TRIPLING	TRUENESS	TURNOVER
*TOPOTYPE	TRADUCER	TRESSIER	TRIPLITE	*TRUMPERY	TURNPIKE
TOPSIDER	TRAGICAL	TRESSOUR	TRIPLOID	TRUNCATE	TURNSOLE
TOPSTONE	TRAGOPAN	TRESSURE	TRIPPING	TRUNDLER	TURNSPIT
TORCHERE	TRAINFUL	TRIADISM	TRIPTANE	*TRUNKFUL	*TURQUOIS
TORCHIER	TRAINING	TRIANGLE	*TRIPTYCA	TRUNNION	TURRICAL
TOREADOR	TRAINMAN	*TRIARCHY	*TRIPTYCH	TRUSSING	TURTLING
TOREUTIC	TRAINWAY	*TRIAXIAL	TRIPWIRE	TRUSTFUL	TUSKLESS
TORNILLO	TRAMLESS	*TRIAZINE	TRISCELE	TRUTHFUL	*TUSKLIKE
TOROSITY	TRAMLINE	*TRIAZOLE	TRISKELE	*TRYINGLY	TUTELAGE
TORPIDLY	TRAMMING	TRIBASIC	TRISOMIC	*TRYWORKS	TUTELARY
*TORQUATE	*TRAMPISH	*TRIBRACH	TRISTATE	TSAREVNA	TUTORAGE
*TORQUING	TRAMPLER	TRIBUNAL	*TRISTEZA	*TSARITZA	TUTORESS
TORTILLA	TRAMROAD	TRICHINA	TRISTFUL	TSORRISS	TUTORIAL
TORTIOUS	*TRANQUIL	TRICHITE	TRISTICH	TUBBABLE	TWADDLER
TORTOISE	TRANSACT	TRICHOID	TRITHING	TUBELESS	TWANGIER
TORTUOUS	TRANSECT	*TRICHOME	TRITICUM	TUBELIKE	TWANGLER
TORTURER	TRANSEPT	*TRICKERY	TRIUMVIR	TUBENOSE	*TWELVEMO
TOTALISE	TRANSFER	TRICKIER	TRIUNITY	TUBERCLE	TWIDDLER
TOTALISM	*TRANSFIX	*TRICKILY	TRIVALVE	TUBEROID	TWIGLESS
TOTALIST	TRANSHIP	*TRICKISH	*TROCHAIC	TUBEROSE	*TWIGLIKE
TOTALITY	TRANSMIT	TRICOLOR	TROCHILI	TUBEROUS	*TWILIGHT
*TOTALIZE	TRANSUDE	TRICORNE	TROCHLEA	*TUBEWORK	TWILLING
TOTALLED	TRAPBALL	TRICTRAC	TROCHOID	*TUBIFORM	TWINBORN
TOTEMISM	TRAPDOOR	*TRICYCLE	TROILISM	TUBULATE	TWINIEST
TOTEMIST	TRAPEZIA	TRIENNIA	TROILITE	TUBULOSE	*TWINIGHT
TOTEMITE	TRAPLIKE	TRIETHYL	TROLLIED	TUBULOUS	*TWINKLER
TOTTERER	TRAPLINE	TRIFECTA	TROLLIES	TUBULURE	TWINNING
TOUGHIES	TRAPNEST	TRIFLING	TROLLING	*TUCKAHOE	*TWINSHIP
*TOUGHISH	TRAPPEAN	TRIFOCAL	TROMBONE	*TUCKSHOP	TWISTING
*TOVARICH	TRAPPING	TRIFORIA	TROOPIAL	TULLIBEE	*TWITCHER
TOVARISH	TRAPPOSE	TRIGGEST	TROPONIN	TUMBLING	TWITTERY
*TOWARDLY	TRAPPOUS	TRIGGING	TROTLINE	TUMIDITY	TWITTING
TOWELING	*TRAPROCK	*TRIGLYPH	TROTTING	TUMPLINE	*TWOPENCE
*TOWNFOLK	TRAPUNTO	TRIGNESS	TROUBLER	TUMULOSE	*TWOPENNY
*TOWNHOME	TRASHMAN	TRIGONAL	TROUNCER	TUMULOUS	*TYMPANAL
TOWNLESS	TRAUCHLE	TRIGRAPH	TROUPIAL	TUNEABLE	*TYMPANIC
*TOWNSHIP	TRAVELER	TRIHEDRA	TROUPING	TUNELESS	*TYMPANUM
TOWNSMAN	TRAVELOG	TRILLION	TROUSERS	TUNGSTEN	*TYPECASE
TOWNWEAR	TRAVERSE	TRILLIUM	TROUVERE	TUNICATE	*TYPECAST
*TOXAEMIA	TRAVESTY	TRILOBAL	TROUVEUR	TUNNELER	*TYPEFACE
*TOXICANT	TRAVOISE	TRILOBED	TROWELER	TUPPENCE	*TYPIFIER
*TOXICITY	TRAWLNET	TRIMARAN	TROWSERS	*TUPPENNY	*TYPOLOGY

TYRAMINE
TYRANNIC
TYROSINE
*TZAREVNA
*TZARITZA
*TZITZITH

STAB
STAG
STAR
STAT
STAW
STAY
STEL
STEM
STEP
STET
STEW
STEY
STIR
STOA
STOB
STOP
STOW
STUB
STUD
STUM
STUN
STYE
STACK
STADE
STAFF
STAGE
STAGY
STAID
STAIG
STAIN
STAIR
STAKE
STALE
STALK
STALL
STAMP
STAND
STANE
STANG
STANK
STAPH
STARE
STARK
START
STASH
STATE
STAVE
STEAD

STEAK
STEAL
STEAM
STEED
STEEK
STEEL
STEEP
STEER
STEIN
STELA
STELE
STENO
STERE
STERN
STICH
STICK
STIED
STIES
STIFF
STILE
STILL
STILT
STIME
STIMY
STING
STINK
STINT
STIPE
STIRK
STIRP
STOAT
STOCK
STOGY
STOIC
STOKE
STOLE
STOMA
STOMP
STONE
STONY
STOOD
STOOK
STOOL
STOOP
STOPE
STOPT
STORE
STORK
STORM
STORY
STOSS
STOUP
STOUR
STOUT
STOVE

STOWP
STRAP
STRAW
STRAY
STREP
STREW
STRIA
STRIP
STROP
STROW
STROY
STRUM
STRUT
STUDY
STUFF
STULL
STUNT
STUPA
STUPE
STURT
STYLE
STYLI
STYMY
BATBOY
BATEAU
BATHER
BATHOS
BATING
BATMAN
BATTED
BATTEN
BATTER
BATTIK
BATTLE
BATTUE
BETAKE
BETHEL
BETIDE
BETIME
BETISE
BETONY
BETOOK
BETRAY
BETTED
BETTER
BETTOR
*BITCHY
BITTED
BITTEN
BITTER
BOTANY
*BOTCHY
BOTFLY
BOTHER
BOTTLE

BOTTOM
BUTANE
BUTENE
BUTLER
BUTTER
BUTTON
*BYTALK
*CATCHY
CATENA
CATGUT
CATION
CATISH
CATKIN
CATLIN
CATNAP
CATNIP
CATSUP
CATTED
CATTIE
CATTLE
CETANE
CITRIN
CITHER
CITIED
CITIES
CITIFY
CITING
CITOLA
CITOLE
CITRAL
CITRIC
CITRON
CITRUS
COTEAU
COTING
COTTAR
COTTER
COTTON
COTYPE
CUTEST
CUTESY
CUTLAS
CUTLER
CUTLET
CUTOFF
CUTOUT
CUTTER
CUTTLE
DATARY
DATCHA
DATING
DATIVE
DATURA
DETACH
DETAIL

DETAIN
DETECT
DETENT
DETEST
DETICK
DETOUR
DITHER
DOTAGE
DOTARD
DOTIER
DOTING
DOTTEL
DOTTER
DOTTLE
FATHER
FATHOM
FATING
FATTED
FATTEN
FATTER
FETICH
FETING
FETISH
FETTED
FETTER
FETTLE
*FITCHY
FITFUL
FITTED
FITTER
FUTILE
FUTURE
GATEAU
GATHER
GATING
GETTER
GITANO
GOTTEN
GUTTED
GUTTER
GUTTLE
*HATBOX
HATFUL
HATING
HATPIN
HATRED
HATTED
HATTER
HETERO
HITHER
HOTBED
*HOTBOX
HOTDOG
HOTROD

HOTTED
HOTTER
HUTTED
*HUTZPA
*JETSAM
*JETSOM
JETTED
JETTON
*JITNEY
JITTER
KATION
KETENE
KETONE
KETOSE
KETTLE
KITIES
KITING
*KITSCH
KITTED
KITTEL
KITTEN
KITTLE
LATEEN
LATELY
LATENT
LATEST
LATHER
LATIGO
LATINO
LATISH
LATRIA
LATTEN
LATTER
LATTIN
LETHAL
LETTED
LETTER
LITANY
LITCHI
LITERY
LITHIA
LITHIC
LITMUS
LITTEN
LITTER
LITTLE
LOTION
LOTTED
LOTTLE
LUTEAL
LUTEIN
LUTEST
LUTEUM
LUTING
LUTIST
MATRES

*MATRIX	NOTING	PUTLOG	**RETYPE**	TITTER	*BETHINK
MATRON	NOTION	PUTOFF	RITARD	TITTIE	BETHORN
MATSAH	NUTANT	**PUTOUT**	RITTER	TITTLE	*BETHUMP
MATTED	NUTATE	PUTRID	RITUAL	TITTUP	BETIMES
MATTER	NUTING	**PUTSCH**	ROTARY	TOTHER	BETOKEN
MATTIN	NUTLET	PUTTEE	ROTATE	TOTING	BETROTH
MATURE	NUTMEG	PUTTER	**ROTCHE**	TOTTED	BETTING
*MATZAH	NUTRIA	**PYTHON**	ROTGUT	TOTTER	BETWEEN
*MATZOH	NUTTED	RATANY	ROTTED	TUTTED	*BETWIXT
*MATZOT	NUTTER	RATBAG	ROTTEN	VATFUL	BITABLE
METAGE	**PATACA**	RATHER	ROTTER	VATTED	BITTERN
METATE	*PATCHY	**PATHOS**	ROTUND	VETOER	BITTIER
METEOR	PATENT	RATIFY	RUTILE	VITALS	BITTING
METIER	PATHOS	RATINE	RUTTED	VITRIC	*BITTOCK
METING	PATINA	RATING	SATANG	VITTAE	BITUMEN
METTLE	PATINE	RATION	SATARA	VITTLE	BOTANIC
MITIER	PATOIS	RATITE	SATEEN	VOTARY	BOTCHER
MITRAL	PATROL	RATLIN	SATING	VOTING	BOTONEE
MITTEN	PATRON	RATOON	SATINY	VOTIVE	BOTTLER
MOTILE	PATTED	RATTAN	SATORI	WATAPE	BOTULIN
MOTION	PATTEE	RATTED	SATRAP	WATERY	BUTANOL
MOTTLE	PATTEN	RATTEN	**SETOFF**	WATSIT	BUTCHER
MUTANT	PATTER	RATTER	SETOSE	WATTER	BUTLERY
MUTASE	PATTIE	RATTLE	SETOUS	WATTLE	BUTTALS
MUTATE	PETARD	RATTLY	SETOUT	WETHER	BUTTERY
MUTEST	PETITE	RATTON	SETTEE	WETTED	BUTTIES
MUTINE	**PETNAP**	**RETACK**	SETTER	WETTER	*BUTTOCK
MUTING	PETREL	RETAIL	SETTLE	*WITCHY	BUTTONY
MUTTER	PETROL	RETAIN	SHTETL	WITHAL	BUTYRAL
MUTTON	PETTED	**RETAKE**	SITCOM	WITHER	BUTYRIC
MUTUAL	PETTER	RETAPE	SITING	WITHIN	BUTYRIN
MUTUEL	PETTLE	RETARD	SITTEN	WITING	*BUTYRYL
MUTULE	*PITCHY	RETEAM	SITTER	WITTED	CATALOG
*MYTHIC	PITIED	RETEAR	SOTTED	WUTHER	CATALPA
NATANT	PITIER	RETELL	SUTLER	YATTER	CATARRH
NATION	PITIES	RETENE	SUTTEE	YTTRIA	CATAWBA
NATIVE	**PITMAN**	RETEST	SUTURE	*ZITHER	CATBIRD
NATRON	**PITSAW**	RETIAL	TATAMI	BATCHER	CATBOAT
NATTER	PITTED	RETILE	TATTED	*BATFISH	CATCALL
NATURE	POTAGE	RETIME	TATTER	*BATFOWL	CATCHER
NETHER	**POTASH**	RETINA	TATTIE	BATHING	*CATCHUP
NETTED	POTATO	RETINE	TATTLE	BATHMAT	CATCLAW
NETTER	**POTBOY**	RETINT	TATTOO	BATHTUB	CATECHU
NETTLE	POTEEN	RETIRE	TETANY	*BATHYAL	CATERAN
NETTLY	POTENT	RETOLD	TETCHY	BATISTE	CATERER
NITERY	**POTFUL**	**RETOOK**	TETHER	BATLIKE	CATFACE
NITRIC	**POTHER**	RETOOL	TETRAD	BATSMAN	CATFALL
NITRID	POTION	RETORE	TETRYL	BATTEAU	*CATFISH
NITRIL	**POTMAN**	RETORN	TETTER	**BATTERY**	CATHEAD
NITWIT	**POTPIE**	RETORT	TITBIT	BATTIER	CATHECT
NOTARY	POTSIE	RETRAL	TITFER	BATTING	CATHODE
NOTATE	POTTED	RETRIM	TITHER	BATTLER	CATLIKE
NOTHER	POTTER	RETTED	TITIAN	**BATWING**	CATLING
NOTICE	POTTLE	RETUNE	TITMAN	BETAINE	CATMINT
NOTIFY	*POTZER	RETUSE	TITMAN	*BETAXED	CATSPAW

CAT TAIL	DOT TREL	*HAT CHEL	LAT TICE	NIT ROSO	PO TLIKE
CAT TALO	DUT EOUS	*HAT CHER	LET DOWN	NIT ROUS	PO TLINE
CAT TERY	DUT IFUL	*HAT CHET	LET TING	NOT ABLE	*PO TLUCK
CAT TIER	FAT ALLY	HAT EFUL	LET TUCE	NOT ABLY	PO TSHOT
CAT TILY	*FAT BACK	HAT LESS	LIT ERAL	NOT CHER	PO TTEEN
CAT TING	FAT BIRD	HAT LIKE	*LIT HIFY	NOT EDLY	PO TTENT
*CAT WALK	FAT EFUL	*HAT RACK	LIT HIUM	NOT EPAD	PO TTERY
CIT ABLE	FAT HEAD	HAT SFUL	LIT HOID	NOT HING	PO TTIER
CIT ADEL	FAT IDIC	HET AERA	LIT ORAL	NOT ICER	PO TTIES
CIT ATOR	FAT IGUE	HET AIRA	LIT OTES	NUT CASE	PO TTING
CIT HARA	FAT LESS	*HIT CHER	LIT URGY	NUT GALL	PU TAMEN
CIT HERN	FAT LIKE	HIT LESS	LOT TERY	NUT LIKE	*PU TREFY
CIT HREN	FAT NESS	*HOT CAKE	LOT TING	NUT MEAT	PU TTIED
*CIT IZEN	FAT TEST'	HOT FOOT	LUT EOUS	*NUT PICK	PU TTIER
CIT RATE	FAT TIER	HOT HEAD	LUT HERN	NUT WOOD	PU TTING
CIT RINE	FAT TIES	HOT LINE	LUT HIER	PAT AMAR	RA TAFEE
CIT ROUS	FAT TILY	HOT NESS	*MAT CHUP	PAT CHER	RA TAFIA
CIT TERN	FAT TING	HOT SHOT	MAT ELOT	PAT ELLA	RATATAT
CO TERIE	FAT TISH	HOT SPUR	MAT INAL	PAT ENCY	RAT CHET
CO THURN	FAT UITY	HOT TEST	MAT INEE	*PAT HWAY	RAT FINK
CO TIDAL	FAT UOUS	HOT TING	MAT LESS	PAT IENT	RAT FISH
CO TTAGE	FAT WOOD	HOT TISH	MAT RASS	PAT NESS	RAT HOLE
CO TTIER	*FET CHER	HUT LIKE	MAT TING	PAT RIOT	RAT LIKE
CO TTONY	*FET LOCK	HUT MENT	*MAT TOCK	PAT ROON	RAT LINE
*CUT AWAY	FET TING	HUT TING	*MAT ZOON	PAT TERN	RAT TAIL
*CUT BACK	*FIT CHEE	*HUT ZPAH	*MAT ZOTH	PAT TING	RAT TEEN
*CUT BANK	*FIT CHET	*JET BEAD	MET AMER	PE TASOS	RAT TIER
CUT DOWN	*FIT CHEW	*JET LIKE	MET HOXY	PE TASUS	RAT TING
CUT ESIE	FIT MENT	*JET PORT	MET ICAL	PE TIOLE	RAT TISH
CUT ICLE	FIT NESS	*JET TIED	MET ISSE	*PET COCK	RAT TLER
CUT LASS	FIT TEST	JET TIER	*MET RIFY	*PET RIFY	RAT TOON
CUT LERY	FIT TING	JET TIES	MET RIST	PET ROUS	RAT TRAP
CUT LINE	*FU THARC	*JET TING	MIT ERER	PET TIER	RET ABLE
CUT OVER	*FU THARC	*JIT TERY	MIT ICID	PE TTING	RET AKER
CUT TAGE	*FU THORC	*JOT TING	MIT IEST	PE TTISH	RET ASTE
CUT TIES	*FU THORK	KAT CINA	*MIT ZVAH	PET UNIA	RET EACH
CUT TING	*FU TTOCK	*KAT HODE	*MO THERY	PI TAPAT	RET HINK
*CUT WORK	GAT EMAN	*KAT YDID	MOT TLER	PIT CHER	RET IARY
CUT WORM	GAT EWAY	KE TOSIS	NA TRIUM	PIT EOUS	RET ICLE
DAT ABLE	GET AWAY	*KIT CHEN	NAT URAL	PIT FALL	RET INAL
DAT EDLY	GET TING	KIT HARA	NET LESS	PIT HEAD	RET INOL
DET ENTE	GIT TERN	KIT LING	NET LIKE	PIT IFUL	RET INUE
DET ERGE	GO THITE	KIT TING	NET SUKE	PIT TING	RET IREE
DET INUE	GO THITE	KO TOWER	NET TIER	PO TABLE	RET IRER
DET RACT	GUT LESS	LA TAKIA	NET TING	PO TAMIC	RET ITLE
DET RAIN	GUT LIKE	LAT CHET	NET TLER	PO TBOIL	RET OUCH
DET RUDE	GUT SILY	LAT ENCY	NET WORK	PO TENCE	RET RACE
DIT CHER	GUT TATE	LAT ERAD	NIT CHIE	PO TENCY	RET RACK
DIT HERY	GUT TERY	LAT ERAL	NIT INOL	PO THEAD	RET RACT
DIT HIOL	GUT TIER	LAT HERY	NIT RATE	PO THEEN	RET RAIN
DIT TANY	GUT TING	LAT HIER	NIT RIDE	PO THERB	RET READ
DOT IEST	GUT TLER	LAT ICES	NIT RILE	PO THOLE	RET REAT
DOT TIER	HAT ABLE	LAT OSOL	*NIT RIFY	*PO THOOK	RET RIAL
DOT TILY	HAT BAND	LAT RINE	NIT RITE	PO TICHE	RET SINA
DOT TING		LAT RING		PO TLACH	

RETTING	TOTTING	BISTORT	FATTIES	PARTIER	RUTTISH
RETWIST	TUTELAR	BITTERN	FATTILY	PARTLET	SALTANT
RETYING	TUTOYER	BITTIER	FATTING	PARTYER	SALTING
ROTATOR	TUTTING	BITTING	FATTISH	PASTEUP	SENTIMO
ROTIFER	VATICAL	*BITTOCK	FETTING	PATTERN	SETTING
ROTTING	VATTING	BLATANT	FITTEST	PATTING	SETTLER
ROTUNDA	VETERAN	BOATFUL	FITTING	PELTAST	SETTLOR
RUTHFUL	VETIVER	BRITTLY	FLATLET	PENTENE	SEXTANT
RUTTIER	VETTING	BUSTIER	FLUTIST	PENTODE	SHITAKE
RUTTILY	VITALLY	BUTTALS	*FOXTROT	PETTING	SHUTOUT
RUTTING	VITAMER	BUTTERY	FRETTER	PETTISH	SITTING
RUTTISH	VITAMIN	BUTTIES	*FUTTOCK	PIETIST	SMOTHER
SATANIC	VITESSE	*BUTTOCK	GANTLET	PITTING	SOFTBAC
SATCHEL	VITIATE	BUTTONY	GESTALT	PLUTEUS	SOFTISH
SATIATE	VITRAIN	CATTAIL	GETTING	PORTENT	SOTTISH
SATIETY	*VITRIFY	CATTALO	GITTERN	POSTDOC	SOUTANE
SATINET	VITRINE	CATTERY	*GLITCHY	*POSTTAX	*SPATZLE
SATISFY	VITRIOL	CATTIER	GOTHIC	POTTEEN	SPOTLIT
SATRAPY	VOTABLE	CATTILY	GUTTATE	POTTENT	STATANT
SATSUMA	VOTRESS	CATTING	GUTTERY	POTTERY	STATIST
SATYRID	WATERER	CHATTED	GUTTIER	POTTIER	STATUSY
*SETBACK	WATTAGE	CHETRUM	GUTTING	POTTIES	SUBTASK
SETLINE	WATTAPE	CHUTIST	GUTTLER	POTTING	SUBTEST
SETTING	*WETBACK	CITTERN	HASTING	PRETAPE	*SUBTEXT
SETTLER	WETLAND	CONTACT	HOTTEST	PRETERM	SURTOUT
SETTLOR	WETNESS	CONTENT	HOTTING	PRETEST	TARTLET
SHTETEL	WETTEST	CONTEST	HOTTISH	*PRETEXT	TATTIER
SITHENS	WETTING	*CONTEXT	HUTTING	PRETRIM	TATTILY
SITTING	WETTISH	CONTORT	*JETTIED	PRETYPE	TATTING
SITUATE	WITHIER	COTTAGE	JETTIER	PROTECT	TATTLER
SOTTISH	WITHIES	COTTIER	JETTIES	PROTEST	TECTITE
SUTURAL	WITHING	COTTIES	*JETTING	PROTEUS	TITTIES
TATOUAY	WITHOUT	COTTONY	*JITTERY	PROTIST	TOSTADA
TATTIER	WITLESS	CULTISH	*JOTTING	PUTTIED	TOSTADO
TATTILY	WITLING	CULTIST	KITTING	PUTTIER	TOTTERY
TATTING	WITLOOP	CUTTAGE	KNOTTED	PUTTING	TOTTING
TATTLER	WITNESS	CUTTIES	*KVETCHY	RATTAIL	TUTTING
TETANAL	WITTIER	CUTTING	LATTICE	RATTEEN	TWATTLE
TETANIC	WITTILY	DENTIST	LEFTIES	RATTIER	*TZITZIT
TETANUS	WITTING	DICTIER	LEFTISH	RATTING	VATTING
TETCHED	WOTTETH	DIETHER	LEFTIST	RATTISH	VETTING
TETOTUM	YATAGAN	DIRTBAG	LETTING	RATTLER	WATTAGE
TETRODE	YTTRIUM	DISTANT	LETTUCE	RATTOON	WATTAPE
TITANIA	*ZITHERN	DISTENT	LOFTIER	RATTRAP	WATTEST
TITANIC	BANTENG	DISTORT	LOTTERY	REDTAIL	WETTEST
TITHING	BAPTIST	DITTANY	LOTTING	REPTANT	WETTING
TITLARK	BARTMAN	DOGTROT	MANTLET	RESTART	WETTISH
TITLIST	BATTEAU	DOTTIER	MARTLET	RESTOKE	WHATNOT
TITRANT	BATTERY	DOTTILY	*MATTOCK	RETTING	WHATSIS
TITRATE	BATTIER	DOTTING	MOSTEST	ROOTLET	WHITEST
TITTIES	BATTING	DOTTREL	MOTTLER	ROTTING	WITTIER
TITULAR	BATTLER	DUSTOFF	NETTIER		WITTILY
TOTABLE	BEETLER	FACTOID	NETTING		WITTING
TOTALLY	BETTING	FANTAST	NETTLER		*XANTHAN
TOTTERY		FATTEST			BACTERIA
		FATTIER			

BACTERIN	BUSTINGS	CONTRACT	DISTASTE	FLATLAND	GESTICAL
BANTERER	BUSTLINE	CONTRAIL	DISTAVES	FLATLING	GESTURAL
BANTLING	BUTTONER	CONTRARY	DISTINCT	FLATLONG	*GIFTEDLY
*BAPTIZER	BUTTRESS	CONTRAST	DISTRACT	FLATMATE	GIFTLESS
BARTERER	BYSTREET	CONTRITE	DISTRAIN	FLATNESS	*GIFTWARE
BARTISAN	*CALTHROP	CONTRIVE	DISTRAIT	FLATTERY	GILTHEAD
BASTILLE	CANTICLE	CORTISOL	DISTRESS	FLATTEST	GLITTERY
BATTALIA	CANTONAL	COSTLESS	DISTRICT	FLATTING	GLUTELIN
BATTENER	CANTRAIP	COSTUMER	DISTRUST	FLATTISH	GLUTTING
BATTERIE	CAPTIOUS	*COSTUMEY	DOCTORAL	FLATWARE	GLUTTONY
BATTIEST	CAPTURER	COTTAGER	DOCTRINE	*FLATWASH	GNATHION
*BEATIFIC	CARTLOAD	CRETONNE	DOGTOOTH	*FLATWAYS	GNATHITE
BEATLESS	CARTOONY	CRITERIA	DOTTEREL	FLATWISE	GNATLIKE
BEETROOT	*CARTOUCH	*CRITIQUE	DOTTIEST	*FLATWORK	*GOATFISH
BELTLESS	CASTANET	*CROTCHET	DRUTHERS	*FLATWORM	GOATHERD
BELTLINE	*CASTAWAY	CULTIGEN	DUCTLESS	*FLETCHER	GOATLIKE
BENTWOOD	CASTEISM	CULTIVAR	*DUCTWORK	FLUTIEST	GOATSKIN
BESTIARY	CASTRATE	CULTRATE	DUETTIST	FLUTTERY	GOETHITE
BESTOWAL	CASTRATO	CULTURAL	DUSTHEAP	*FOOTBALL	GRATEFUL
BESTRIDE	CATTIEST	*CURTALAX	DUSTIEST	*FOOTBATH	GRATINEE
BIATHLON	CATTLEYA	CURTNESS	DUSTLESS	*FOOTFALL	GRATUITY
BIOTICAL	CAUTIOUS	CUSTODES	DUSTLIKE	*FOOTGEAR	GUSTABLE
*BIOTOXIN	CENTAURY	CUSTOMER	*DYSTAXIA	*FOOTHILL	GUSTIEST
*BIRTHDAY	CENTESIS	CUSTUMAL	DYSTONIA	*FOOTHOLD	GUSTLESS
BISTOURY	CENTIARE	CUTTABLE	DYSTOPIA	FOOTIEST	GUTTATED
BITTIEST	CENTRING	CYSTEINE	FACTIOUS	*FOOTLESS	GUTTIEST
*BLATANCY	CENTRISM	CYSTITIS	*FACTOTUM	*FOOTLIKE	GUTTURAL
BLATTING	CENTRIST	*DACTYLIC	*FAITHFUL	*FOOTMARK	*HAFTARAH
BLOTLESS	CENTROID	DACTYLUS	FALTBOAT	*FOOTNOTE	*HAFTORAH
BLOTTIER	CENTUPLE	DAFTNESS	FALTERER	*FOOTPACE	*HAPTICAL
BLOTTING	*CHATCHKA	DALTONIC	FANTASIA	*FOOTPATH	HASTEFUL
BOATBILL	*CHATCHKE	*DEATHBED	FANTASIE	*FOOTRACE	HASTENER
*BOATHOOK	CHATTING	*DEATHCUP	FARTHEST	FOOTREST	HATTERIA
BOATLIKE	*CHITCHAT	*DEATHFUL	*FARTHING	*FOOTSORE	*HAWTHORN
BOATLOAD	CHITLING	DEFTNESS	*FASTBACK	*FOOTWEAR	*HEATEDLY
BOATSMAN	CHITOSAN	DENTALIA	FASTBALL	*FOOTWORK	HEATLESS
BOATYARD	*CHUTZPAH	DENTATED	FASTENER	FORTBESS	*HECTICAL
BOLTHEAD	CISTERNA	DENTICLE	FASTNESS	FORTIETH	HEPTAGON
BOLTHOLE	CLATTERY	DESTRIER	FASTUOUS	FORTUITY	*HEPTARCH
BOLTONIA	CLITELLA	DESTRUCT	FATTENER	*FORTYISH	HILTLESS
BOLTROPE	CLITORIS	DEUTERIC	FATTIEST	FOSTERER	HISTAMIN
*BONTEBOK	CLOTHIER	*DEXTRINE	*FEATHERY	*FRETWORK	HISTIDIN
*BOOTJACK	CLOTHING	*DEXTROSE	*FELTLIKE	FRITTING	HISTOGEN
BOOTLACE	CLOTTING	*DEXTROUS	FESTIVAL	FROTTAGE	HISTORIC
BOOTLESS	CLUTTERY	DIATOMIC	FETTERER	FROTTEUR	HURTLESS
*BOOTLICK	COATLESS	DIATONIC	FETTLING	FURTHEST	HYSTERIA
BOTTOMER	*COATRACK	DIATRIBE	*FIFTYISH	GANTLINE	*HYSTERIC
*BOTTOMRY	COATROOM	DICTATOR	FILTERER	GANTLOPE	*JETTIEST
*BOUTIQUE	COATTAIL	DICTIEST	FILTRATE	GASTIGHT	*JETTISON
*BOXTHORN	COATTEND	DIETETIC	FISTNOTE	GASTNESS	*JUSTNESS
BRATTICE	COATTEST	DIPTERAL	FITTABLE	GASTRAEA	KNITTING
BRETHREN	CONTAGIA	DIPTERAN	FLATBOAT	GASTRULA	*KNITWEAR
*BRITCHES	CONTEMPT	DIPTERON	FLATFOOT	GENTRICE	KNOTLESS
*BRITZSKA	CONTINUA	DISTANCE	*FLATHEAD	*GENTRIFY	*KNOTLIKE
BUNTLINE	CONTINUE		FLATIRON	*GEOTAXIS	KNOTTING

*KNO T WEED	*MOU T HFUL	PAS T NESS	*POR T ABLY	PRO T AMIN	RUS T LESS
*KOW T OWER	MUL T IAGE	PAS T ORAL	POR T ANCE	PRO T ASIS	RUS T LING
KUR T OSIS	MUL T ICAR	PAS T RAMI	*POR T APAK	PRO T EASE	RUT T IES T
LAC T EOUS	*MUL T IJE T	PAS T ROMI	POR T HOLE	PRO T EGEE	SAL T BUSH
LAE T RILE	*MUL T IPLY	PAS T URAL	POR T IERE	PRO T EIDE	SAL T IES T
LAI T ANCE	MUL T I T ON	PAS T URER	POR T LESS	PRO T EOSE	SAL T LESS
LAN T HORN	MUL T IUSE	PA T T AMAR	POR T RAI T	PRO T OCOL	SAL T LIKE
LA T T ERLY	*MUS T ACHE	PA T T ERER	POR T RESS	PRO T OPOD	SAL T NESS
LEA T HERN	MUS T ARDY	*PA T TYPAN	POS T ALLY	*PRO T OXID	*SAL T WORK
LEA T HERY	MU T T ERER	PEC T ORAL	POS T ANAL	*PRO T OZOA	SAL T WOR T
LEC T URER	*MYS T AGOG	PEE T WEE T	POS T BURN	PRO T RAC T	SAN T ALIC
LEF T OVER	*MYS T ICAL	PEN T ACLE	POS T CARD	PRO T RUDE	SAN T ALOL
*LEF T WARD	*MYS T ICLY	PEN T AGON	*POS T CAVA	PU T T ERER	SAN T ONIN
*LEF T WING	*MYS T IQUE	PEN T ANOL	POS T CODE	*QUA T ORZE	SAR T ORII
LE T T ERER	NAE T HING	*PEN T ARCH	POS T COUP	*QUA T RAIN	SAS T RUGA
LIF T GATE	NAU T ICAL	PEN T OMIC	POS T DA T E	*QUI T REN T	SAU T ERNE
LIN T IES T	NAU T ILUS	PEN T OSAN	POS T DIVE	*QUI T T ING	SAU T OIRE
LIN T LESS	NEA T HERD	*PEP T IZER	POS T DRUG	*QUO T IEN T	SAW T OO T H
LIS T ENER	NEA T NESS	PER T NESS	*POS T FACE	RAF T ERED	*SCA T BACK
LIS T LESS	NEO T ERIC	PES T ERER	POS T FIRE	RAF T SMAN	SCA T T ING
LI T T ERER	NES T ABLE	PES T HOLE	*POS T FORM	RAP T NESS	SCO T OPIA
LI T T LISH	NES T LIKE	PE T T EDLY	POS T GAME	RA T T ENER	*SCU T CHER
LI T T ORAL	NES T LING	PE T T IES T	POS T HEA T	RA T T IES T	SCU T ELLA
LOA T HFUL	NE T T ABLE	PE T T IFOG	POS T HOLE	RA T T LING	SEA T LESS
LOA T HING	NE T T IES T	PEW T ERER	*POS T ICHE	REA T T ACH	SEA T MA T E
LOF T IES T	NEU T RINO	*PHO T OMAP	*POS T IQUE	REA T T ACK	SEA T RAIN
LOF T LESS	*NEX T DOOR	*PHO T OPIA	POS T LUDE	REA T T AIN	*SEA T WORK
LOI T ERER	NOC T URNE	PHO T OSE T	*POS T MARK	RES T I T CH	SEC T ORAL
LOS T NESS	NON T IDAL	*PIN T SIZE	POS T ORAL	RES T LESS	SEN T ENCE
LUS T IES T	NON T I T LE	*PIS T ACHE	POS T PAID	RES T ORAL	SEN T IEN T
LUS T RA T E	NON T ONAL	PI T T ANCE	POS T PONE	RES T ORER	SEN T INEL
LUS T RING	*NON T OXIC	PLA T EFUL	POS T RACE	RES T RAIN	SEP T ARIA
LUS T ROUS	NON T RUMP	PLA T ELE T	POS T RIO T	RES T RESS	SEP T E T T E
MAL T IES T	NON T RU T H	*PLA T FORM	*POS T SHOW	RES T RIC T	SEP T UPLE
MAL T REA T	NOR T HING	PLA T IES T	*POS T SYNC	RES T RIKE	SES T ERCE
MAN T ELE T	NOR T HERN	PLA T INIC	POS T T EEN	RES T RING	SE T T LING
MAR T INE T	NO T T URNO	PLA T INUM	POS T T ES T	RES T RIVE	*SEX T ARII
*MAR T YRLY	NUR T URAL	PLA T T ING	POS T URAL	RES T ROOM	*SEX T E T T E
*MAS T ABAH	NUR T URER	*PLA T YPUS	POS T URER	RES T RUCK	*SEX T UPLE
*MAS T ICHE	NYS T A T IN	PLE T HORA	PO T T ERER	RES T RUNG	*SEX T UPLY
MA T T EDLY	PAL T ERER	PLO T LESS	PO T T IES T	RHE T ORIC	SHE T LAND
MA T T RASS	PAN T HEON	PLO T LINE	PRA T FALL	*RHY T HMIC	SHI T T ING
MA T T RESS	PAN T OFLE	PLO T T AGE	*PRA T IQUE	RIF T LESS	SHO T T ING
MEA T IES T	PAN T SUI T	PLO T T IER	PRA T T LER	ROO T HOLD	*SHU T DOWN
MEA T LOAF	PAR T AKER	PLO T T IES	PRE T AS T E	ROO T IES T	SHU T T ING
MEL T DOWN	PAR T ERRE	PLO T T ING	PRE T ENCE	ROO T LESS	SIS T ERLY
*MIS T EACH	PAR T IBLE	POE T ICAL	PRE T ENSE	ROO T LIKE	SIS T ROID
*MIS T HROW	PAR T ICLE	POE T ISER	PRE T ERI T	ROS T ELLA	*SIX T IE T H
MIS T IES T	PAR T ISAN	*POE T IZER	PRE T RAIN	ROS T RA T E	*SIX T YISH
*MIS T OUCH	*PAR T IZAN	POE T LESS	PRE T REA T	ROU T EMAN	*SKE T CHER
MIS T REA T	PAS T ICCI	POE T LIKE	PRE T RIAL	ROU T EWAY	*SKI T T ERY
MIS T HINK	*PAS T ICHE	POL T ROON	PRE T IED	RUC T IOUS	*SKI T T ISH
MIS T RUS T	PAS T IES T	*PON T IFEX	PRE T T IER	RUS T ICAL	SLA T IES T
MIS T RYS T	PAS T ILLE	*PON T IFIC	PRE T T IES	RUS T ICLY	SLA T T ERN
MON T EDLY	PAS T LESS	POR T ABLE	*PRE T T IFY	RUS T IES T	SLA T T ING

SLI T HERY	SWA T T ING	VAS T IES T	WIS T ERIA	CLO T	GLU T
SLI T LESS	*SWI T CHER	VAS T NESS	WI T T IES T	COA T	GNA T
SLI T T ING	SYN T AGMA	VEN T LESS	*WOR T HFUL	COF T	GOA T
*SLO T BACK	*SYS T EMIC	VEN T URER	WOS T TE TH	COL T	GOU T
SLO T HFUL	T AN T ALUM	VER T ICAL	*WRA T HFUL	COO T	GRA T
SLO T T ING	T AN T ALUS	VER T ICIL	*WRE T CHED	CUL T	GRI T
SMI T HERS	T AR T NESS	VES T ALLY	WRI T RING	CUR T	GRO T
*SMI T HERY	T AR T RATE	VES T IARY	*WRO T HFUL	CYS T	GUS T
*SMO T HERY	T AR T UFFE	VES T IGIA	*XAN T HEIN	DAF T	HAE T
SMU T T ING	T AS T EFUL	VES T LESS	*XAN T HENE	DAR T	**HAF T**
SNA T CHER	T A T T IES T	*VES T LIKE	*XAN T HINE	DAU T	HAL T
SNI T CHER	T A T T OOER	VES T MEN T	*XAN T HOMA	DAW T	HAR T
SOF T BALL	T AU T NESS	VES T URAL	*XAN T HONE	DEB T	HAS T
SOF T ENER	T AU T OMER	VIA T ICAL	*XAN T HOUS	DEE T	HAU T
*SOF T HEAD	T AU T ONYM	*VIA T ICUM	YES T REEN	DEF T	HEA T
SOF T NESS	T EC T ONIC	VIC T ORIA	*YOU T HFUL	DEN T	**HEF T**
SOF T WARE	T EE T O T AL	VIC T RESS	*ZAS T RUGA	DIE T	HEN T
*SOF T WOOD	T EE T O T UM	VIN T AGER	*ZES T LESS	DIN T	HES T
SOO T HEST	T EE T HING	VIR T UOSA		DIP T	HIL T
SOO T HSAY	T EN T ACLE	VIR T UOSO	BAH T	DIR T	HIS T
SOU T ACHE	T EN T IES T	VIR T UOUS	BAI T	DOA T	HOL T
SOU T HERN	T EN T LESS	VOL T AISM	BAN T	DOI T	HOO T
*SOU T HPAW	T EN T LIKE	WAI T RESS	BAS T	DOL T	HOS T
SOU T HRON	T ER T IARY	WAN T ONER	BA T T	DOS T	HUN T
SOU T RING	T ES T A T OR	WAN T ONLY	BEA T	DRA T	HUR T
SPA T T ING	T ES T ICLE	WAR T IES T	BEE T	DUC T	JES T
SPI T BALL	T ES T IES T	WAR T LESS	BEL T	DUE T	JIL T
SPI T EFUL	*T EX T BOOK	*WAR T LIKE	BEN T	DUI T	JOL T
SPI T FIRE	*T EX T LESS	WAS T EFUL	BES T	DUN T	JUS T
SPI T T ING	*T EX T UARY	WAS T ELO T	BHU T	FAC T	KAR T
SPI T T OON	*T EX T URAL	WAS T ERIE	BIN T	FAR T	KEE T
SPO T LESS	*T HA T AWAY	*WAS T EWAY	BI T T	FAS T	KEN T
SPO T T ING	T HA T CHER	WAT T HOUR	BLA T	FEA T	**KEP T**
S T A T ABLE	T HE T ICAL	WAT T LESS	BLE T	FEE T	**KHA T**
S T A T EDLY	T IL T YARD	*WEF T WISE	BLO T	FEL T	KHE T
*S T A T ICKY	T IN T LESS	WES T ERLY	BOA T	FIA T	KIL T
S T A T UARY	T I T T ERER	WES T MOS T	BOL T	FIS T	KIS T
S T I T CHER	*T I T T UPPY	*WES T WARD	BOO T	FIX T	KNI T
S T O T INKA	T OR T ILLA	WE T T ABLE	BOR T	FLA T	KNO T
*SUB T AXON	T OR T IOUS	*WHA T EVER	BO T T	FON T	**KYA T**
*SUB T HEME	T OR T OISE	WHA T NESS	BOU T	FOO T	LAS T
SUB T IL T Y	T OR T UOUS	*WHE T T ING	BRA T	FOR T	LEE T
SUB T I T LE	T OR T URER	*WHI T ECAP	BRI T	FRA T	LEF T
SUB T LE T Y	T O T T ERER	*WHI T EFLY	BRU T	FRE T	LEN T
SUB T ONIC	T RI T HING	WHI T ENER	BUN T	FRI T	LEP T
SUB T OPIA	T RI T ICUM	WHI T EOU T	BUS T	GAI T	LES T
SUB T OPIC	T RO T LINE	WHI T IES T	BU T T	GAS T	LIF T
SUB T O T AL	T RO T T ING	*WHI T RACK	CAN T	GEL T	LIL T
SUB T RAC T	T RU T HFUL	WHI T T LER	CAR T	GEN T	LIN T
SUB T REND	T UR T LING	WHI T T RE T	CAS T	GES T	LIS T
SUB T RIBE	*T WI T CHER	*WID T HWAY	CEL T	GHA T	LOF T
SUB T UNIC	T WI T T ERY	WIN T ERER	CEN T	GIF T	LOO T
SUI T ABLE	T WI T T ING	WIN T ERLY	CHA T	GIL T	LOS T
SUI T CASE	*T ZI T ZI T H	WIS T ARIA	CHI T	GIR T	LOU T
SUI T LIKE			CIS T	GIS T	LUN T

LUS T	REF T	TIN T	BIGO T	CRAP T	FROS T
MAL T	REN T	T OF T	BINI T	CREP T	FRUI T
MAR T	RES T	T OI T	BION T	CRES T	**FUME T**
MAS T	RIF T	T OO T	BLAS T	**CROF T**	GAMU T
MAT T	RIO T	T OR T	BLEA T	CRUE T	GAUL T
MAU T	ROO T	T OS T	BLEN T	CRUS T	GAUN T
MEA T	ROU T	T OU T	BLES T	**CRYP T**	GAVO T
MEL T	RUN T	TRE T	BLOA T	CUBI T	GEES T
MIL T	RUS T	TRO T	BLUE T	CULE T	GEMO T
MIN T	RYO T	TUF T	BLUN T	CURE T	GENE T
MIS T	SAL T	TWA T	BLUR T	CURS T	GHAS T
MI T T	SCA T	TWI T	BOAR T	DAUN T	GHAU T
MIX T	SCO T	VAS T	BOAS T	DAVI T	GHOS T
MOA T	SCU T	VEN T	BOOS T	DEAL T	GIAN T
MOL T	SEA T	VER T	BRAC T	DEBI T	GIGO T
MOO T	SEC T	VES T	BRAN T	DEBU T	GLEE T
MOR T	SEN T	**VEX T**	BREN T	DEFA T	GLIN T
MOS T	SEP T	VOL T	BRI T T	DEIS T	GLOA T
MOT T	SE T T	**WAF T**	BRUI T	DEMI T	GLOS T
MUS T	**SEX T**	WAI T	BRUN T	DEPO T	GLOU T
MUT T	SHA T	WAN T	BUIL T	DERA T	GODE T
NEA T	SHI T	WAR T	BUND T	DICO T	GRAF T
NES T	SHO T	WAS T	BURE T	DIDS T	GRAN T
NE T T	SHU T	WA T T	BURN T	**DIGH T**	GREA T
NEW T	SIF T	WEE T	BURS T	DIGI T	GREE T
NEX T	SIL T	**WEF T**	BUTU T	DIVO T	GRIF T
NOW T	SKA T	WEL T	CADE T	DOES T	GRIO T
PAC T	SKI T	WEN T	CANS T	DONU T	GRIP T
PAN T	SLA T	WEP T	CAPU T	DRAF T	GRIS T
PAR T	SLI T	WER T	CARA T	DRES T	GROU T
PAS T	SLO T	WES T	CARE T	DRIF T	GRUN T
PEA T	SLU T	**WHA T**	CHAN T	DRIP T	GUES T
PEL T	SMU T	**WHE T**	**CHAP T**	DROI T	GUIL T
PEN T	SNI T	**WHI T**	**CHEA T**	DROP T	GUYO T
PER T	SNO T	WIL T	**CHER T**	DUVE T	**HABI T**
PES T	SOF T	WIS T	**CHES T**	DWEL T	HADS T
PFF T	SOO T	WON T	**CHO T T**	**FACE T**	HAUN T
PHA T	SOR T	WOR T	**CIVE T**	FAGO T	HEAR T
PHO T	SPA T	WOS T	CLAS T	FAIN T	HEIS T
PHU T	SPI T	WRI T	CLEA T	FAUL T	HELO T
PIN T	SPO T	**XYS T**	**CLEF T**	FEAS T	**HIGH T**
PLA T	STA T	YE T T	**CLIF T**	FEIN T	HOIS T
PLO T	STE T	YUR T	CLIP T	FEIS T	HORS T
POE T	SUE T	**ZES T**	CLOO T	**FIGH T**	HURS T
POR T	SUI T	BEAS T	CLOU T	FILE T	**JABO T**
POS T	SWA T	BEAU T	COAC T	FIRS T	JAUN T
POU T	SWO T	**BEFI T**	COAP T	*FIXI T	JOIN T
PRA T	TAC T	BEGE T	COAS T	FLEE T	JOIS T
PSS T	TAR T	BEGO T	COME T	FLIN T	JOUS T
PUN T	TAU T	BERE T	**COMP T**	FLOU T	JURA T
PUT T	TEA T	BESE T	COOP T	**FLUY T**	KAPU T
QUI T	TEN T	BESO T	COSE T	FOIS T	KARA T
RAF T	TES T	**BHOO T**	COUN T	FOUN T	KARS T
RAN T	**TEX T**	BIDE T	COUR T	FRI T T	**KEMP T**
RAP T	TIL T	**BIGH T**	COVE T	FRON T	KNEL T

KNOU T	**QUIE T**	SLEE T	T RYS T	**BOMLE T**	CORNE T
KORA T	**QUIL T**	SLEP T	T WEE T	BONNE T	CORSE T
KRAF T	**QUIN T**	SLIP T	T WIS T	**BORSH T**	**CORVE T**
KRAI T	**QUIR T**	SMAL T	*T WIX T	**BOSKE T**	COSSE T
KRAU T	**QUOI T**	SMAR T	VALE T	**BOUGH T**	**COVER T**
LEAN T	RABA T	SMEL T	VAUL T	**BOWPO T**	**COWPA T**
LEAP T	RAME T	SMOL T	VAUN T	BREAS T	CRAUN T
LEAS T	REAC T	SNOO T	VELD T	**BREVE T**	**CRAVA T**
LEGI T	REBU T	SNOR T	VERS T	**BRIGH T**	CREDI T
LICH T	RECU T	SNOU T	VISI T	BRULO T	CRUSE T
LICI T	REES T	SPAI T	**VOMI T**	BRUNE T	**CUBIS T**
LIGH T	REFI T	SPEL T	WAIS T	**BUCKE T**	CULLE T
LIMI T	RELE T	SPEN T	**WECH T**	**BUDGE T**	CUSRA T
LUNE T	RELI T	SPIL T	WEES T	**BUFFE T**	CUT ES T
LYAR T	REME T	SPIR T	**WHEA T**	BULLE T	CUT LE T
MAGO T	REMI T	SPLA T	**WHIP T**	BURBO T	CUT OU T
MAIS T	REPO T	SPLI T	**WHIS T**	**BURKE T**	**CYGNE T**
MAYS T	RESE T	SPOR T	**WHOR T**	BUYOU T	DACOI T
MEAN T	REVE T	SPOU T	**WIGH T**	**BYPAS T**	DECAN T
MERI T	REWE T	SPRA T	WORS T	*BYZAN T	DECEI T
MIDS T	RIAN T	SPRI T	**WRAP T**	**CABLE T**	DECEN T
MIGH T	**RIGH T**	SPUR T	WRES T	**CACHE T**	**DECOC T**
MOIS T	RIVE T	**SQUA T**	WRIS T	CADEN T	**DEDUC T**
MOTE T	ROAS T	S TAR T	WURS T	**CAHOO T**	**DEFEA T**
MOUL T	ROBO T	S TIL T	YACH T	CALLE T	**DEFEC T**
MOUN T	ROOS T	S TIN T	YEAS T	**CAMLE T**	DEGUS T
MULC T	ROSE T	S TOA T	*ZIBE T	CANNO T	**DEHOR T**
NEIS T	ROUS T	S TOP T	*ZIZI T	**CAPLE T**	*DEJEC T
NIGH T	SABO T	S TOU T	BAGUE T	CARNE T	DELIC T
NONE T	SAIN T	S TRU T	BALES T	**CARPE T**	DELIS T
PAIN T	SAUL T	S TUN T	BALLE T	CARRO T	DEMAS T
PALE T	SAYS T	S TUR T	BALLO T	CASKE T	DEMEN T
PEAR T	SCAN T	SUIN T	BANDI T	CA T GU T	DEPAR T
PE TI T	SCAR T	SWAR T	BANNE T	**CAUGH T**	DEPIC T
PEWI T	SCA T T	SWEA T	**BARBE T**	**CAVEA T**	DEPOR T
*PHPH T	SCEN T	SWEE T	BARBU T	**CAVOR T**	DESAL T
PICO T	SCOO T	**SWEP T**	BARES T	**CEMEN T**	DESER T
PILO T	SCOU T	**SWIF T**	BARRE T	**CERME T**	DESIS T
PINO T	**SHAF T**	T ACE T	BASAL T	**CHALE T**	DESPO T
PIPE T	SHAL T	T ACI T	BASES T	**CHALO T**	DE TEC T
PIPI T	SHEE T	T AIN T	**BASKE T**	CLARE T	DE TEN T
PIVO T	**SHIF T**	T ARO T	BASSE T	CLIEN T	DE TES T
PLAI T	SHIR T	T AUN T	BECKE T	CLOSE T	**DEVES T**
PLAN T	SHIS T	T EMP T	BEDSI T	**COBAL T**	**DEVOU T**
PLEA T	SHOA T	T ENE T	**BEFRE T**	COBNU T	DICAS T
POIN T	SHOO T	**T HEF T**	**BEHES T**	**COEMP T**	DIDAC T
POSI T	SHOR T	T IGH T	BEKNO T	COGEN T	DIGES T
POUL T	SHO T T	T INC T	**BEMIS T**	**COHOR T**	DIGLO T
PRES T	SHOU T	T OAS T	BENNE T	**COHOS T**	DIK TA T
PRIN T	SHUN T	T RAC T	**BESMU T**	COLLE T	DIMOU T
PROS T	SIGH T	T RAI T	*BEZAN T	**COMBA T**	**DIMWI T**
QANA T	SKEE T	T RAP T	BILLE T	**COMFI T**	DIPNE T
QUAN T	SKIN T	T REA T	BISEC T	**COMMI T**	*DIQUA T
QUAR T	SKIR T	T ROU T	BLUES T	COPLO T	DIREC T
QUES T	SLAN T	T RUS T	**BOBCA T**	*COQUE T	DIRES T

DIVER T	**GOBBE T**	**LIMPE T**	NONAR T	PUNDI T	RESPO T
DIVES T	GOBLE T	LINNE T	NONFA T	PUNNE T	RESUL T
DOCEN T	**GODWI T**	LIVES T	NOUGA T	**PUPPE T**	RE TES T
DOCKE T	GOGLE T	**LOCKE T**	**NOUGH T**	PURES T	RE TIN T
DOPAN T	GORGE T	LOCUS T	NUDES T	PURIS T	RE TOR T
DOUGH T	**GRIVE T**	LOMEN T	NUDIS T	PU TOU T	REVER T
DREAM T	GUGLE T	LUCEN T	NUGGE T	*QIVIU T	REVES T
DRIES T	GULLE T	LU TES T	NU TAN T	*QUAIN T	REVOL T
DRYLO T	GURNE T	LU TIS T	NU TLE T	**RABBE T**	RIBLE T
DULCE T	GUSSE T	LYRIS T	**PACKE T**	**RABBI T**	RIDEN T
DYNAS T	**HAGBU T**	**MAGGO T**	PALES T	**RACHE T**	RILLE T
FAGGO T	HALES T	MAGNE T	PALLE T	RACIS T	RIPES T
*FANJE T	HALLO T	MAHOU T	PANDI T	**RACKE T**	RIPOS T
FERRE T	HARLO T	MALLE T	**PAPIS T**	RAGOU T	ROBUS T
FIDGE T	HASLE T	MAMME T	PAREN T	*RAMJE T	**ROCHE T**
FILLE T	**HEIGH T**	MARKE T	PARGE T	RAPIS T	**ROCKE T**
FINES T	**HELME T**	MARMO T	PARRO T	RARES T	RODEN T
FLAUN T	**HENBI T**	MASCO T	PA TEN T	REBAI T	*ROQUE T
FLIES T	**HEPCA T**	*MA TZO T	PAYOU T	REBOO T	RO TGU T
FLIGH T	HEREA T	MAUME T	PEANU T	RECAN T	ROUPE T
FLUEN T	HERIO T	MAYES T	PEDAN T	RECAS T	RUBOU T
FOMEN T	**HERMI T**	MERLO T	PELLE T	RECEN T	RUDES T
FORES T	**HOBBI T**	**MIDGE T**	**PELME T**	**RECEP T**	RUNLE T
FORGA T	**HOGNU T**	**MIDGU T**	PENUL T	REDAC T	RUNOU T
FORGE T	HOLIS T	MILLE T	**PERMI T**	REDOU T	RUSSE T
FORGO T	HONES T	MINUE T	**PICKE T**	REEDI T	**SABBA T**
FORIN T	HORNE T	MISAC T	PIGLE T	REEMI T	**SACBU T**
FORMA T	**HOWLE T**	MISCU T	PIGNU T	**REFEC T**	**SACHE T**
FORRI T	**HUGES T**	MISEA T	PIGOU T	REFLE T	SADIS T
FOUGH T	*JACKE T	MISFI T	PIOLE T	REGEN T	SAFES T
FREES T	**JENNE T**	MISHI T	*PIQUE T	REGLE T	SAGBU T
FRIGH T	**JESUI T**	MISLI T	**PLACE T**	REGRE T	SAGES T
FROWS T	*JUNKE T	MISSE T	PLAIN T	REHEA T	SALLE T
FUNES T	**JURAN T**	MODES T	PLANE T	**REKNI T**	SAMLE T
FYLPO T	**JURIS T**	MODIS T	PLIAN T	RELEN T	SANES T
GADGE T	**KAINI T**	MOLES T	**PLIGH T**	RELIC T	SAVAN T
GAINS T	**KAPUT T**	MONGS T	**POCKE T**	RELIS T	**SCHIS T**
GALIO T	**KEYSE T**	MONIS T	PONEN T	RELUC T	**SCHUI T**
GALLE T	**KISMA T**	MOPPE T	**POPPE T**	REMEE T	**SCRIP T**
GALOO T	**KISME T**	MO TMO T	POSSE T	REMEL T	**SCULP T**
GAMBI T	*KLEPH T	MUDCA T	PO TEN T	REMIN T	SECAN T
GAMES T	**KNIGH T**	MULLE T	**PREAC T**	RENES T	SECRE T
GANNE T	**KRUBU T**	MUSCA T	**PRECU T**	RENNE T	**SEJAN T**
GARGE T	LABRE T	**MUSKE T**	PRESE T	REPAS T	SELEC T
GARNE T	LAMEN T	**MUSKI T**	PRIES T	REPEA T	SENNE T
GARRE T	LAMES T	MU TAN T	**PRIVE T**	REPEN T	SENNI T
GASKE T	LANCE T	MU TES T	**PROBI T**	REPLO T	SEPTE T
GASLI T	**LAPPE T**	MYSOS T	**PROFI T**	REPOR T	SERES T
GELAN T	LARIA T	NA TAN T	*PROJE T	RESEA T	SESTE T
GEREN T	LA TEN T	**NAUGH T**	**PROMP T**	RESEC T	SE TOU T
GIBBE T	LA TES T	NIDGE T	PROSI T	RESEN T	**SEXIS T**
GIBLE T	LEARN T	NI TWI T	PULLE T	RESIF T	*SEXPO T
GIGLE T	LEGIS T	NOCEN T	**PULPI T**	RESIS T	SEX TE T
GIGLO T	LEVAN T			RESOR T	SHIES T
GIMLE T	**LIKES T**				**SHRIF T**

SIGNE T	T EAPO T	WEIGH T	BLANKE T	CHU TIS T	COOKOU T
SILEN T	T ENAN T	WESKI T	BLA T AN T	*CHYMIS T	COOLAN T
SIPPE T	T ERCE T	WHILS T	BLOWOU T	CIGARE T	COPILO T
SKLEN T	T ERRE T	*WHISH T	BOMBAS T	CINEAS T	*COPYCA T
SKYLI T	T ERRI T	*WICKE T	BONESE T	CIRCLE T	COPYIS T
SLIES T	T HEIS T	WIDES T	BONIES T	CIRCUI T	CORONE T
SLIGH T	T HIRS T	WIDGE T	BOOKLE T	CLADIS T	CORREC T
SOBEI T	T HREA T	WIGLE T	BORSCH T	CLAMAN T	CORRUP T
SOCKE T	T HRIF T	WILLE T	*BOSQUE T	CLAUCH T	CORSLE T
SOFFI T	T HROA T	WISEN T	*BOUQUE T	CLAUGH T	COSIES T
SONAN T	T HRUS T	WISES T	*BOWKNO T	CLEMEN T	COSMIS T
SONNE T	T HWAR T	WOMBA T	*BOWSHO T	CLOSES T	COULDS T
SORBE T	T ICKE T	WORRI T	*BOXIES T	COADMI T	COUPLE T
SORES T	T IDBI T	WORSE T	BOYCO T T	COAGEN T	COURAN T
SOUGH T	T IPCA T	WRIES T	BRACHE T	COALPI T	COWIES T
SOVIE T	T IPPE T	WRIGH T	*BRACKE T	COCOMA T	*COZIES T
SPIGO T	T ITBI T	YCLEP T	BRAVES T	COCONU T	CRAMPI T
SPINE T	T OILE T	YOGUR T	*BRIQUE T	COENAC T	CREDEN T
SPIRI T	T OMCA T	*ZEALO T	BRISKE T	COEREC T	CRESSE T
SPLEN T	T OM TIT	BABBI T	*BROCKE T	*COEXER T	*CRICKE T
SPLIN T	T ONLE T	*BACKFI T	BROUGH T	*COEXIS T	CROCHE T
SPOIL T	*T OQUE T	*BACKLI T	BULBLE T	*COFFRE T	*CROCKE T
SPREN T	T REVE T	*BACKOU T	BULLBA T	COHABI T	*CROQUE T
SPRIN T	T RICO T	*BACKSE T	BUMBOA T	COLLEC T	CROWNE T
SPROU T	T RIJE T	BAILOU T	BUMMES T	COMBUS T	CRUMPE T
*SQUIN T	T RIVE T	BALLAS T	BUNDIS T	COMFOR T	CULPRI T
*SQUIR T	T RUAN T	*BANQUE T	BUOYAN T	COMMEN T	CUL TIS T
S TRAI T	T RUES T	BAP TIS T	BURGOU T	*COMPAC T	CULVER T
S TREE T	T RYOU T	BAREFI T	BURNOU T	COMPAR T	*CUMQUA T
S TRIC T	T UBIS T	BARONE T	BUSH TIT	COMPLO T	CURRAN T
S TRIP T	T UCKE T	BASINE T	BUSIES T	COMPOR T	CURREN T
S TRUN T	T UFFE T	BASSIS T	CABARE T	COMPOS T	CYCLIS T
S TYLE T	T UMUL T	BA T HMA T	CABINE T	CONCEI T	*CZARIS T
SUBLE T	T URBI T	BAWSUN T	CAGIES T	CONCEN T	DADAIS T
SUBLO T	T URBO T	BAYONE T	*CAJAPU T	CONCEP T	DASHPO T
SUBMI T	T URRE T	BEARCA T	*CAJUPU T	CONCER T	*DECRYP T
SUBNE T	T WILI T	BECRUS T	CALLAN T	CONDUC T	DEFAUL T
SUBSE T	T YPIS T	BEDFAS T	CALUME T	CONDUI T	DEFIAN T
SUFLI T	T YRAN T	BEDIGH T	CAMBIS T	CONFEC T	DEFICI T
SUMMI T	VACAN T	BEDPOS T	CANDEN T	CONGES T	DEFLEC T
SUNKE T	VARLE T	BEIGNE T	CAPELE T	CONNEC T	DEFROS T
SUNSE T	VELVE T	BENEFI T	CARPOR T	CONSEN T	DEFUNC T
SURES T	VERIS T	BENEMP T	CASUIS T	CONSIS T	DELIGH T
SWIVE T	VERSE T	BEPAIN T	CA T BOA T	CONSOR T	DELIMI T
SYNDE T	VERVE T	*BEQUES T	CA T HEC T	CONSUL T	DEMERI T
T ABLE T	VIBIS T	BESHOU T	CA T MIN T	CON TAC T	DEMOUN T
TACKE T	VIOLE T	*BE T WIX T	CELLIS T	CON TEN T	DEN TIS T
T ALEN T	VOLAN T	BEVOMI T	CESSPI T	CON TES T	DEORBI T
T ALLI T	VOLOS T	*BEZZAN T	CHALLO T	*CON TEX T	DEPAIN T
T AMES T	WADSE T	BIBELO T	CHAPLE T	CON TOR T	DEPOSI T
T ANIS T	WALLE T	BIBLIS T	CHARIO T	CONVEC T	DESCAN T
T APPE T	WALNU T	BIGFOO T	CHEMIS T	CONVEN T	DESCEN T
T ARGE T	WA T SIT	BIGGES T	CHEROO T	CONVER T	DESSER T
T ASSE T	WAUCH T	BISCUI T	*CHEVIO T	CONVIC T	DE TRAC T
T AUGH T	WAUGH T	BIS T OR T	CHOLEN T		DEVIAN T

DEWIES T	FERMEN T	GILBER T	HO T SHO T	*MAZIES T	*PARQUE T
DIALEC T	FERVEN T	GILLNE T	HO T T ES T	MEANES T	PAR T LE T
DIALIS T	FEUDIS T	*GJE T OS T	*HOWBEI T	MEDIAN T	PASSAN T
DIARIS T	FIDEIS T	GLAIKE T	HU T MEN T	MEERKA T	PA T IEN T
DICIES T	FIGMEN T	GLAIKI T	HYDRAN T	MEGABI T	PA T RIO T
DILUEN T	FIGWOR T	GLUEPO T	HYGEIS T	MEGAHI T	PAYMEN T
DIMMES T	FILBER T	GNOMIS T	*HYMNIS T	MELILO T	PEACOA T
DINGBA T	FILEMO T	GOOIES T	*JACKPO T	*MESQUI T	PEASAN T
DISCAN T	FILMSE T	GORIES T	*JACONE T	ME T RIS T	PECCAN T
DISCEP T	FINFOO T	GOSPOR T	JESSAN T	*MEZQUI T	PEL T AS T
DISGUS T	FIRELI T	GOURME T	*JE T POR T	MIDCUL T	PENDAN T
*DISJEC T	FIREPO T	GRAVES T	*JOKIES T	MIDMOS T	PENDEN T
DISMAS T	FISHNE T	GRAYOU T	*JUDOIS T	MIGRAN T	PENNAN T
DISPAR T	*FI T CHE T	GROMME T	*JUJUIS T	MINARE T	PERCEN T
DISPOR T	FI T MEN T	GRUMME T	*KAJEPU T	MINDSE T	PERCEP T
DISROO T	FI T TES T	GUMBOO T	KASHRU T	MIRIES T	PERFEC T
DISRUP T	FLASKE T	GUNBOA T	KILOBI T	MISCAS T	PERIAP T
DISSEA T	FLA T LE T	GUNSHO T	KINGLE T	MISEDI T	PERIDO T
DISSEC T	FLEAPI T	GURGLE T	KNESSE T	MISMEE T	PERPEN T
DISSEN T	FLU T IS T	GYMNAS T	*KUMQUA T	MISPAR T	PERSAL T
DISSER T	*FLYBEL T	HABI TA T	LACIES T	MISSEA T	PERSIS T
DIS T AN T	*FLYBOA T	*HACKBU T	LAMBAS T	MISSOR T	PERVER T
DIS T EN T	*FLYPAS T	HADDES T	LAMBEN T	MISSOU T	PIANIS T
DIS T OR T	FOLDOU T	HAIRCU T	LAMBER T	MISSUI T	*PICQUE T
DOGCAR T	*FOLKMO T	HAIRNE T	LANGUE T	MI T IES T	PIEFOR T
DOG T RO T	FONDAN T	HALBER T	LARGES T	MONOCO T	PIERRO T
DONNER T	FOREGU T	HALIBU T	LA T CHE T	MOONLE T	PIE T IS T
DOORMA T	FORFEI T	HANDOU T	LAWSUI T	MOONLI T	PIGBOA T
DOPIES T	FORMAN T	HANDSE T	*LAZARE T	MOONSE T	PIGMEN T
DORMAN T	FORWEN T	HANGOU T	*LAZIES T	MOPIES T	PINIES T
DO T IES T	*FOXHUN T	HAPLON T	LEAFLE T	MORDAN T	PIPIES T
DOUBLE T	*FOXIES T	HARDHA T	LEF T IS T	MORDEN T	*PIQUAN T
DOVECO T	*FOX T RO T	HARDSE T	LENIEN T	MOS T ES T	PISSAN T
*DOZIES T	FRAUGH T	HARICO T	LEVERE T	MUDFLA T	PI T APA T
DRABBE T	FREIGH T	HARPIS T	LIMIES T	MUGWOR T	*PLACKE T
DRAGNE T	FRESHE T	HARSLE T	LINECU T	MUSKRA T	PLAUDI T
DRAUGH T	FRISKE T	HARVES T	LINOCU T	NARCIS T	PLAYAC T
DRIBLE T	FUGUIS T	*HA T CHE T	LOCKNU T	NASCEN T	PLAYLE T
DROPLE T	FULGEN T	*HAYLOF T	LOCKOU T	NEGLEC T	PLEDGE T
DROPOU T	FUMIES T	*HAZIES T	LOOKOU T	NOBLES T	PLENIS T
DROUGH T	FUNNES T	HEADSE T	LOOSES T	NONFAC T	PLUMME T
DRUGGE T	FUSSPO T	HELIAS T	LUNIES T	NONMEA T	POKIES T
DUALIS T	GABBAR T	HELLCA T	MADDES T	NONPAS T	POLECA T
DUELIS T	GABFES T	HIDEOU T	MADWOR T	NONSUI T	POLLIS T
DUNNES T	GALIPO T	HINDGU T	MAILLO T	NOSIES T	POLOIS T
DURMAS T	GALLAN T	HIPPES T	MANCHE T	NU T MEA T	POLYCO T
FADDIS T	GALLNU T	*HIPSHO T	MANHUN T	*NYMPHE T	POMFRE T
FALLOU T	GALLOO T	HOLDOU T	MANIHO T	PAGEAN T	PORREC T
FAN T AS T	GAMIES T	HOLIBU T	MAN T LE T	PALE T O T	POR T EN T
FANWOR T	GAN T LE T	HOLIES T	MANUMI T	PALIES T	PO T SHO T
FASCIS T	GARDAN T	HOMIES T	MARGEN T	PALMIS T	PO T T EN T
FA T T ES T	GARMEN T	HOOKLE T	MARPLO T	PANDEC T	PRECAS T
FAUVIS T	GELLAN T	HORNIS T	MAR T LE T	PARAPE T	PRECEN T
FEEDLO T	GES T AL T	HORREN T	MA T ELO T	PARFA T T	PRECEP T
FELWOR T	GIGABI T	HO T FOO T			PREDIC T

PREEDI T	REALIS T	ROLLOU T	**SOLVEN T**	**T HEREA T**	VIADUC T
PREEMP T	REALLO T	ROMAUN T	**SOPHIS T**	**T HERMI T**	VIBRAN T
PREFEC T	REBOAN T	ROO T LE T	SORBEN T	*T HICKE T	VILAYE T
PREHEA T	**RECEIP T**	ROPIES T	SPARES T	**T HOUGH T**	VINIES T
PRELEC T	**RECHAR T**	ROSIES T	SPINOU T	**T HRUPU T**	VIOLEN T
PREMEE T	**RECHEA T**	**ROWBOA T**	SPIRAN T	T IDIES T	VIOLIS T
PREMOL T	RECOUN T	RUBIES T	SPO T LI T	T IMEOU T	WALKOU T
PRERIO T	RECRUI T	**RUMMES T**	SPRIES T	T INIES T	WANIES T
PRESEN T	**REDBAI T**	RUNDLE T	**SPRIGH T**	T IPCAR T	WANNES T
PRESIF T	**REDCOA T**	SACRIS T	S T ARLE T	T IT LIS T	WARIES T
PRESOR T	REDDES T	S T ARLI T	**REDDES T**	T IT RAN T	WARRAN T
PRE T ES T	**REDOUB T**	SAGIES T	S T ATAN T	T ONIES T	WASHOU T
*PRE T EX T	**REDRAF T**	SALIEN T	S T AT IS T	T ONIGH T	WA T T ES T
PREVEN T	REDROO T	SAL T AN T	S T ERLE T	T OPCOA T	WAVELE T
*PRICKE T	*REEJEC T	SANDLO T	**S T ICKI T**	T OPKNO T	WAVIES T
PRODUC T	REELEC T	SANDPI T	S T UDEN T	T OPMAS T	*WAXIES T
*PROJEC T	REENAC T	SAPIEN T	**S T YLIS T**	T OPMOS T	*WEBFOO T
PROPHE T	REEREC T	SARMEN T	**SUBCUL T**	T ORMEN T	WERGEL T
*PROPJE T	REFIGH T	SA T INE T	**SUBDUC T**	T ORREN T	WE T T ES T
PROSEC T	**REFLEC T**	SAWDUS T	**SUBEDI T**	T OSSPO T	WHA T NO T
PRO T EC T	**REFLOA T**	SCARLE T	*SUBJEC T	T OURIS T	WHEREA T
PRO T ES T	**REFRAC T**	SEABOO T	**SUBPAR T**	T OWBOA T	*WHIFFE T
PRO T IS T	**REFRON T**	SEAGIR T	**SUBPLO T**	T OWMON T	*WHIPPE T
PROVOS T	REGNAN T	SEALAN T	**SUBSEC T**	T OWNLE T	WHI T ES T
PRUDEN T	**REGRAF T**	SEAPOR T	SUBSIS T	T RANSI T	WIDEOU T
PSCHEN T	REGRAN T	SEARES T	SUB T ES T	T RIDEN T	WILDCA T
PULLOU T	REGREE T	SEAWAN T	*SUB T EX T	T RINKE T	WILIES T
PULSAN T	RELIAN T	**SEGMEN T**	SUBUNI T	T RIOLE T	WINGLE T
PUNGEN T	**RELIGH T**	SEJEAN T	**SUBVER T**	T RIPAR T	WINIES T
PUNIES T	REMNAN T	SELLOU T	SUGGES T	T RIPLE T	WIPEOU T
PURPOR T	REMOUN T	**SEMIFI T**	SUNBEL T	T RIPPE T	WIRIES T
PURSUI T	REPAIN T	SEMIMA T	SUNFAS T	T RISEC T	WI T HOU T
*QUADRA T	REPLAN T	*SEQUEN T	SUNSPO T	T RUMPE T	WOODCU T
*QUAR T E T	REPOSI T	SERPEN T	SUNSUI T	T SARIS T	WOODLO T
*QUERIS T	REPRIN T	**SERVAN T**	SURCOA T	T UBAIS T	WOOLHA T
*QUILLE T	REP T AN T	SEXIES T	**SURFEI T**	T UGBOA T	WORKOU T
*QUINNA T	*REQUES T	SEX T AN T	SUR T OU T	T URGEN T	WOULDS T
*QUIN T E T	**RESHOO T**	**SHALLO T**	SUSPEC T	T URNOU T	WROUGH T
RACIES T	**RESIGH T**	**SHERBE T**	**SYMBIO T**	*T WINJE T	YOGHUR T
*RACQUE T	RESMEL T	SHEROO T	T ABARE T	T WINSE T	*ZIKURA T
RADIAN T	**RESOJE T**	SHILPI T	T ABORE T	T YPESE T	BACCARA T
RAGWOR T	**RESPEC T**	SHU T OU T	T ABORE T	T YPIES T	*BACCHAN T
RAIMEN T	RESPLI T	SICKOU T	T ACHIS T	*T ZARIS T	*BACKBEA T
RAINOU T	RES T AR T	SINGLE T	**T AKEOU T**	*T ZI T ZI T	*BACKCAS T
RAMPAN T	RE T RAC T	*SIZIES T	T ALIPO T	VAGRAN T	*BACKCHA T
RAMPAR T	RE T REA T	SKILLE T	T ANGEN T	VALIAN T	*BACKLIS T
RAPPOR T	RE T WIS T	*SKIPPE T	T ANNES T	VARIAN T	*BACKMOS T
RAREBI T	**REVISI T**	SKIRRE T	T APROO T	VARMEN T	*BACKRES T
RA T A T A T	**REVUIS T**	SLEEKI T	T AR T LE T	VARMIN T	*BACKSEA T
RA T CHE T	**RIBWOR T**	SLEIGH T	T EACAR T	VEINLE T	BAILMEN T
READAP T	RIMIES T	SLIPOU T	T ELEOS T	VERDAN T	*BAKEMEA T
READMI T	RINGEN T	**SNIPPE T**	T EMPES T	VERDIC T	BALLONE T
READOP T	RINGLE T	SOLERE T	**T EMPLE T**	VERIES T	*BANJOIS T
READOU T	**RIPPLE T**	SOLICI T	T ENNIS T	VERSAN T	*BANKRUP T
REAGEN T	**RIVULE T**	SOLOIS T	T HEREA T	VERSAN T	BANNERE T

BAREBOAT	*BUFFIEST	*COCKIEST	DASHIEST	DOWNBEAT	FOOTREST
BAREFOOT	BULLIEST	*COCKLOFT	*DAYLIGHT	DOWNCAST	FORECAST
BARGHEST	BULLPOUT	*COCKSHUT	DEADBEAT	DOWNIEST	FOREFOOT
BARGUEST	BULLSHIT	CODIRECT	DEADBOLT	DRAGONET	FOREMAST
BASEMENT	BULLSHOT	*COEFFECT	DEADLIFT	DRIBBLET	FOREMOST
BASSINET	BURGONET	COGNOVIT	DEBUTANT	DROPSHOT	FOREPART
BATTIEST	BURRIEST	COHERENT	DECADENT	DROPWORT	FOREPAST
BAWDIEST	BUSHGOAT	COINVENT	DECEDENT	DRUGGIST	FOREWENT
BEADIEST	BUSHIEST	COLEWORT	DECREPIT	DRUMBEAT	*FORKIEST
BEAMIEST	BYSTREET	COLLARET	DEFERENT	DRUPELET	*FORKLIFT
BECARPET	CABALIST	COLONIST	DEFOREST	DRYPOINT	FORSPENT
*BEDQUILT	CABERNET	COLORANT	DEMIVOLT	DUBONNET	FOVEOLET
BEDSHEET	*CACHALOT	COLORIST	DEMONIST	*DUCKIEST	FRAGMENT
*BEECHNUT	*CACHEPOT	*COMFIEST	DEMOTIST	DUELLIST	FRAGRANT
BEEFIEST	CALAMINT	COMPLEAT	DEPONENT	DUETTIST	*FRANKEST
BEETROOT	CAMPIEST	*COMPLECT	DERELICT	*DUMPCART	*FREAKOUT
*BEKNIGHT	*CAMSHAFT	*CONFLICT	DESELECT	DUMPIEST	FREEBOOT
BELLWORT	CANNIEST	CONFRONT	DESINENT	DUSTIEST	*FREQUENT
BENEDICT	CANOEIST	*CONJUNCT	DESTRUCT	DYNAMIST	FRONTLET
BERGAMOT	CANONIST	CONODONT	DIALLIST	FABULIST	FROSTBIT
BESOUGHT	*CANZONET	*CONQUEST	DICTIEST	FADDIEST	FRUITLET
BESPRENT	CARBURET	CONSTANT	*DIFFRACT	FAINEANT	FUMIGANT
BETELNUT	CARCANET	CONTEMPT	DIGAMIST	FALCONET	FURRIEST
BIGAMIST	CARRYOUT	CONTRACT	DILATANT	FALTBOAT	FURTHEST
BIRDSHOT	CASEMENT	CONTRAST	DILIGENT	*FANLIGHT	FUTURIST
BITTIEST	CASTANET	COPARENT	DINKIEST	FARTHEST	GABBIEST
BIVALENT	CATALYST	*COPYEDIT	DIPLOMAT	FATALIST	GADABOUT
*BLACKOUT	CATAPULT	CORKIEST	DIRIMENT	FATTIEST	GALAVANT
BLOWIEST	CATARACT	CORNIEST	DISCOUNT	FECULENT	GALIVANT
BLUECOAT	*CATFIGHT	CORSELET	DISHERIT	FEMINIST	GAMMIEST
BOBBINET	CATTIEST	*CORYBANT	DISHIEST	FIGURANT	GASLIGHT
BODEMENT	CELLARET	COSCRIPT	*DISJOINT	FILAMENT	GASTIGHT
BODYSUIT	CENTRIST	COSECANT	*DISJUNCT	FILMIEST	GATEPOST
BOGGIEST	CERAMIST	COTENANT	DISMOUNT	FINALIST	GAUNTLET
BONGOIST	CEREMENT	*COUCHANT	DISPIRIT	FINNIEST	GEMMIEST
BOOKREST	CERVELAT	COULDEST	DISPLANT	FIREBOAT	GERMIEST
BOOMIEST	CHARIEST	COVALENT	*DISQUIET	FIREBRAT	GIGAWATT
BOTANIST	CHARTIST	COVENANT	DISTINCT	*FISHBOLT	GIMPIEST
*BOUFFANT	*CHECKOUT	COVERLET	DISTRACT	FISHIEST	GLADDEST
*BOUGHPOT	CHESTNUT	CRABMEAT	DISTRAIT	FLAGRANT	GLADIEST
*BOWFRONT	*CHEVALET	*CRACKPOT	DISTRICT	FLAMEOUT	GLASNOST
*BOWSPRIT	CHILIAST	CREODONT	DISTRUST	FLAMIEST	GOALPOST
BRACELET	*CHITCHAT	CRESCENT	DITHEIST	FLATBOAT	GODLIEST
BRACTLET	CLAIMANT	CROSSCUT	DIVALENT	FLATFOOT	GRADIENT
BRAGGART	CLARINET	CROSSLET	DOCUMENT	FLATTEST	GRAPIEST
BRAGGEST	CLASSIST	*CROTCHET	*DOGFIGHT	FLEAWORT	GREENLET
BRASSART	CLOSEOUT	*CROWFOOT	*DOGGIEST	*FLESHPOT	GRIEVANT
BREADNUT	CLOUDLET	CRYOSTAT	DOMINANT	*FLIPPANT	GRIMIEST
BREAKOUT	*CLUBFOOT	CUCURBIT	DOORPOST	FLOWERET	GRIMMEST
*BRICKBAT	CLUBROOT	CURDIEST	DORMIENT	FLUTIEST	GRIPIEST
BRINIEST	COALIEST	CUSHIEST	DOSSERET	FOAMIEST	GRUMMEST
BROOKLET	COASSIST	DAMEWORT	DOTTIEST	*FOGFRUIT	GUARDANT
*BROWBEAT	COATTEST	DAMNDEST	DOUGHNUT	FOLDBOAT	*GUITQUIT
BROWNOUT	COBBIEST	DANEWORT		*FOLKMOOT	GULFIEST
*BUCKSHOT	*COCKBOAT	DARNDEST		FOOTIEST	GUMMIEST

*GUNFIGH T	*JAILBAI T	LU T ENIS T	MIS T RYS T	NO T ORIS T	PLAYSUI T
GUNFLIN T	*JE T T IES T	LYRICIS T	MI T LIAN T	NOVELIS T	PLEASAN T
GUNPOIN T	*JINGOIS T	MAINMAS T	MOBOCRA T	NUBBIES T	PLUMELE T
GUS T IES T	*JOHNBOA T	*MAKEFAS T	MODELIS T	NU T RIEN T	PLUMIES T
GU T T IES T	*JOLLIES T	MALAPER T	MOLDIES T	*PACIFIS T	POIGNAN T
GYROS TA T	*JUBILAN T	MALEDIC T	MONOCRA T	PAGANIS T	POKEROO T
HABI T AN T	*JUDGMEN T	MALEMIU T	MONODIS T	PALLIES T	POLYGLO T
HAGADIS T	KEELBOA T	MAL T IES T	MONOGLO T	PALMIES T	POO T IES T
HAIRIES T	*KICKIES T	MAL T REA T	MONO T IN T	*PAMPHLE T	POO T RES T
*HALAKIS T	*KILOVOL T	MANGIES T	MONUMEN T	PANELIS T	POPULIS T
*HAMMIES T	*KILOWA T T	MANIFES T	MOONDUS T	PAN T SUI T	PORKIES T
HANDCAR T	*KINGBOL T	MAN T ELE T	MOONIES T	PAPPIES T	POR T RAI T
*HANDFAS T	*KINGPOS T	MARABOU T	MOONPOR T	PARAKEE T	POS T HEA T
HANDIES T	*KNOCKOU T	MARLIES T	MOONSHO T	PARAMEN T	POS T RIO T
HANDLIS T	LAKEPOR T	MARMOSE T	MOONWOR T	*PARAQUA T	POS T T ES T
HANGNES T	LAMBIES T	MAR T INE T	MORALIS T	*PARAQUE T	PO T T IES T
HARDBOO T	LAMPPOS T	MASSCUL T	MOSSIES T	PARODIS T	*PRAEFEC T
HARDIES T	LANCELE T	MASSICO T	MO T ORIS T	*PAROQUE T	PRAELEC T
*HAZELNU T	LANNERE T	MASSIES T	MOUSIES T	PARROKE T	PREADAP T
HEADIES T	LAPIDIS T	*MAXICOA T	*MOVEMEN T	PASSPOR T	PREADMI T
HEADMOS T	LARDIES T	MEALIES T	*MUCKIES T	PAS T IES T	PREADOP T
HEADRES T	LARKIES T	MEA T IES T	MUDDIES T	PA T ULEN T	PREADUL T
HEDONIS T	LA T HIES T	MEDALIS T	MUGGIES T	PAVEMEN T	PREALLO T
*HELICOP T	LAYABOU T	MEGAVOL T	*MUL T IJE T	PEAKIES T	PREAUDI T
HELILIF T	LEADIES T	MEGAWA T T	MUNIMEN T	PEDERAS T	PRECINC T
HELIPOR T	LEADWOR T	MELANIS T	MURALIS T	PEDIMEN T	PREELEC T
HELLBEN T	LEAFIES T	MELODIS T	MURRELE T	PEE T WEE T	PREENAC T
*HELPMEE T	LEARIES T	*MERCHAN T	MUSCADE T	*PENCHAN T	PREEREC T
HEMOS TA T	LEGALIS T	MESHIES T	MUSKIES T	PENI T EN T	*PREEXIS T
*HEMPIES T	LEGGIES T	MESSIES T	*MUZZIES T	PENLIGH T	*PREFIGH T
HERBIES T	LIBELAN T	ME T ALIS T	*MYOBLAS T	PENPOIN T	PREGNAN T
HESI T AN T	LIBELIS T	MICRODO T	NANOWA T T	PERMEAN T	PRELIMI T
*HIGHSPO T	*LICKSPI T	*MIDNIGH T	NA T IVIS T	PE T T IES T	PREPLAN T
HILLIES T	LIFEBOA T	MIDPOIN T	NA T URIS T	PE T ULAN T	PREPRIN T
HINDMOS T	LIGAMEN T	MILEPOS T	NAUSEAN T	PHALLIS T	PRESPLI T
*HIPPIES T	LILLIPU T	MILKIES T	NAVICER T	PHAN T AS T	PRE T ERI T
HOARIES T	LIMBIES T	*MILKWOR T	NEEDIES T	PHASEOU T	PRE T REA T
*HOBBYIS T	LINGIES T	MINGIES T	NEPO T IS T	PHEASAN T	PRICIES T
*HOLDFAS T	LINGUIS T	*MIQUELE T	NERVIES T	PHONIES T	PRIMMES T
*HOMEPOR T	LINIMEN T	MISADAP T	NESCIEN T	PHO T OSE T	PRIN T OU T
HOMILIS T	LIN T IES T	MISAGEN T	NE T T IES T	*PICKIES T	*PROHIBI T
HONEWOR T	LI T IGAN T	MISBEGO T	NEWSCAS T	PIECRUS T	PROSAIS T
HOODIES T	*LOBBYIS T	MISCOUN T	NEWSIES T	PIEDFOR T	PROSPEC T
*HOOFBEA T	LOCALIS T	MISDOUB T	NIELLIS T	PIEDMON T	PROS T ES T
*HOOKIES T	LODGMEN T	MISEVEN T	NIHILIS T	PIEPLAN T	PRO T RAC T
HORNIES T	LOF T IES T	MISGRAF T	NIPPIES T	PIGGIES T	PSALMIS T
HORNPOU T	LONGBOA T	MISLIGH T	NOBBIES T	PILEWOR T	PUGGIES T
HORNWOR T	LORIKEE T	MISPAIN T	NONADUL T	PINKROO T	PUGILIS T
HORSIES T	*LOWLIGH T	MISPLAN T	NONELEC T	PINPOIN T	PUISSAN T
*HO T CHPOT	LOYALIS T	MISPOIN T	NONEVEN T	*PI T CHOU T	PULPIES T
*HUMBLES T	LUCULEN T	MISPRIN T	NONGUIL T	*PLANCHE T	*PULSEJE T
HUMORIS T	LUMINIS T	MISS T AR T	NONPOIN T	PLANGEN T	*PULSOJE T
*HUSKIES T	LUNGWOR T	MIS T IES T	NONPRIN T	PLAN T LE T	PURSIES T
*HYGIEIS T	LUS T IES T	MIS T REA T	NONUPLE T	PLA T ELE T	PURSUAN T
*JACKBOO T	LU T ANIS T	MIS T RUS T	NO T ARIS T	PLA T IES T	PURULEN T

*PUSHCAR T	REINVES T	SANDIES T	SIMPLIS T	S T RAWHA T	TO T EMIS T
PUSHIES T	*REJACKE T	SANDWOR T	SIMULAN T	S T RIDEN T	*T OXICAN T
PUSSIES T	*RELAXAN T	*SAPPHIS T	SINCIPU T	S T RUMPE T	T RANSAC T
*PUSSYCA T	RELEVAN T	SARCENE T	SI T ARIS T	SUBABBO T	T RANSEC T
PYROS T A T	RELUCEN T	SARODIS T	*SKYLIGH T	SUBADUL T	T RANSEP T
*QUADRAN T	REMANEN T	SARSENE T	SLA T IES T	SUBAGEN T	T RANSMI T
*QUICKSE T	REMARKE T	SARSENE T	SLIMIES T	SUBDEPO T	T RAPNES T
*QUIE T IS T	RENI T EN T	SASSIES T	SLIMMES T	SUBEREC T	T RAWLNE T
*QUIT REN T	*REOBJEC T	SCALIES T	SLIPKNO T	*SUBSHAF T	T RIGGES T
*QUO T IEN T	REORIEN T	SCANDEN T	SLUGFES T	SUB T RAC T	T RIMMES T
RAINCOA T	REOU T FIT	SCARIES T	*SMOKEPO T	SUCCINC T	*T URBOJE T
RAINIES T	REREPEA T	*SCHIZON T	SNAKEBI T	SULFURE T	T URFIES T
RALLYIS T	RESCRIP T	SCILICE T	SNAPSHO T	SUNBURS T	T URNCOA T
RAMMIES T	RESCULP T	SCIOLIS T	SNOWBEL T	SUNLIGH T	T URNSPI T
RANDIES T	RESIDEN T	*SCRAMJE T	SNOWIES T	SUPERHI T	*T WILIGH T
RA T T IES T	RESONAN T	SCRIMPI T	SNOWMEL T	SUPERHO T	T WINIES T
REACCEN T	RESPROU T	SEACOAS T	SNOWSUI T	*SUPERJE T	*T WINIGH T
REACCEP T	RES T RIC T	SEACRAF T	SNUGGES T	SUPPLAN T	*T YPECAS T
REAC TAN T	RESUBMI T	SEAFRON T	SOAPIES T	SURFBOA T	VALVELE T
READDIC T	RE T ARGE T	SEAMIES T	SOAPWOR T	SURFIES T	VAR T IES T
READIES T	RE T ICEN T	SEAMOUN T	SODALIS T	SURMOUN T	VAS T ELO T
*READJUS T	RE T IRAN T	SEASCOU T	SODOMIS T	SURPRIN T	VAS T IES T
REANOIN T	RE T ROAC T	SECURES T	SOLECIS T	SWIF T LE T	VEGE T AN T
REARMOS T	RE T ROFI T	SEDERUN T	SOLLERE T	SWIMSUI T	VEGE T IS T
REARRES T	REVEHEN T	SEDIMEN T	SOMERSE T	*SYMBION T	*VEHEMEN T
REASCEN T	REVENAN T	SEEDIES T	*SOMEWHA T	T ABOURE T	VEINIES T
REASSER T	REVEREN T	SEMIMA T T	SONGFES T	TACKIES T	VEINULE T
REASSOR T	RHEOS T A T	SEMISOF T	SONORAN T	T AILCOA T	VELVERE T
REBOUGH T	RIBBIES T	SEMI T IS T	SOO T HES T	T ANGIES T	VESICAN T
RECOMMI T	*RICOCHE T	SENNIGH T	SOO T RES T	T ARRIES T	VES T MEN T
RECREAN T	RIDGIES T	SEN T IEN T	SORRIES T	TAT T IES T	VE T IVER T
RECUSAN T	RIGH T IS T	SERGEAN T	SPICIES T	T EARIES T	VIEWIES T
REDEFEA T	RIGORIS T	*SERJEAN T	SPIKELE T	T EENIES T	VIGILAN T
REDEFEC T	RINGBOL T	SE T ENAN T	SPIRIES T	T EGUMEN T	VIRULEN T
REDIGES T	SEN T IEN T	SHADIES T	*SPROCKE T	T ELECAS T	VISCOUN T
REDIREC T	ROBORAN T	*SHAKEOU T	SPUMIES T	T ELEPOR T	VISI T AN T
REDOLEN T	ROCKIES T	*SHAKIES T	*SQUARES T	*TELE TEX T	VI T ALIS T
*REDSHIF T	RONDELE T	SHALIES T	S T ABLES T	T ENEMEN T	*VIVISEC T
REDSHIR T	ROO T IES T	*SHEEPCO T	S T AGGAR T	T EN T IES T	VOCALIS T
REDS T AR T	ROSEROO T	SHERBER T	S T AGIES T	T ERAWA T T	VOLI T AN T
REEDIES T	ROUNDLE T	SHINIES T	S T AGNAN T	T ERCELE T	VO T ARIS T
REENLIS T	ROYALIS T	*SHIPMEN T	S T AKEOU T	TES T IES T	WAINSCO T
*REEXPOR T	RUBAIYA T	SHOO T OU T	S T ALWAR T	T HEOCRA T	*WARCRAF T
REFEREN T	RUDDIES T	*SHOPLIF T	S T ANDOU T	T HEORIS T	WAR T IES T
REFLUEN T	RUDIMEN T	SHOR T CU T	S T ANDPA T	*T HICKSE T	WASHIES T
REFORES T	RUMINAN T	SHOO T OU T	S T ARDUS T	T HINNES T	WAS T ELO T
REFORMA T	RUNABOU T	*SHOPLIF T	S T ARWOR T	T HRAWAR T	*WA T CHOU T
*REFOUGH T	RURALIS T	SHOR T CU T	S T EDFAS T	*T HUMBNU T	*WAXPLAN T
REGIMEN T	RUSHIES T	SHOULDS T	S T ICKOU T	*T HYMIES T	WEARIES T
REIMPOR T	RUS T IES T	*SHOWBOA T	S T INKPO T	T INNIES T	WEEDIES T
REINDIC T	RU T ILAN T	SHOWIES T	S T OCKIS T	T IPPIES T	WELDMEN T
REINDUC T	RU T T IES T	SIBILAN T	*S T OCKPO T	T IPSIES T	WES T MOS T
REINFEC T	SAILBOA T	SIGNPOS T	S T OLPOR T	T OLERAN T	*WHINCHA T
*REINJEC T	SALARIA T	SILKIES T	S T ONIES T	*TOMMYRO T	WHINIES T
REINSER T	SAL T IES T	SIMONIS T	S T RAIGH T	TO T ALIS T	WHI T EOU T

WHIT IES T	WILLYAR T	WI T HIES T	WOOLIES T	WORMROO T	*YOGHOUR T
WHIT TRE T	WINDIES T	WI T T IES T	WORDIES T	WOULDES T	*ZIGGURA T
*WHODUNI T	WINGIES T	*WOODCHA T	*WORKBOA T	WRIS T LE T	*ZIKKURA T
WIGGIES T	WISPIES T	WOODIES T	WORMIES T	*YAHRZEI T	

V

VAGI	VIRL	VENAL	*VIXEN	VALOUR	VENDOR
VAIL	VISA	VENGE	*VIZIR	VALUER	VENDUE
VAIN	VISE	VENIN	*VIZOR	VALUTA	VENEER
VAIR	VITA	VENOM	VOCAL	VALVAL	VENERY
VALE	VIVA	VENUE	VOCES	VALVAR	VENIAL
VAMP	VIVE	VERGE	VODKA	VAMOSE	VENINE
VANE	VOID	VERSE	VODUN	VAMPER	VENIRE
VANG	VOLE	VERSO	VOGIE	VANDAL	VENOSE
VARA	VOLT	VERST	VOGUE	VANISH	VENOUS
VARY	VOTE	VERTU	VOICE	VANITY	VENTER
VASE	VROW	VERVE	VOILA	VANMAN	VENULE
VAST	VUGG	VESTA	VOILE	VANNED	VERBAL
VATU	VUGH	VETCH	VOLAR	VANNER	VERBID
VEAL	VACUA	*VEXER	VOLTA	VAPORY	VERDIN
VEEP	VAGAL	*VEXIL	VOLTE	VAPOUR	VERGER
VEER	VAGUE	VIAND	VOLTI	VARIED	VERIER
VEIL	VAGUS	VIBES	VOLVA	VARIER	*VERIFY
VEIN	VAKIL	VICAR	VOMER	VARIES	VERILY
VELA	VALET	*VICHY	VOMIT	VARLET	VERISM
VELD	VALID	VIDEO	VOTER	VAROOM	VERIST
VENA	VALOR	VIEWY	VOUCH	VASSAL	VERITE
VEND	VALSE	VIGIL	VOWEL	VASTLY	VERITY
VENT	VALUE	VIGOR	VOWER	VATFUL	VERMES
VERA	VANDA	VILLA	VROOK	VATTED	VERMIN
VERB	VAPID	VIMEN	VROUW	VAULTY	VERMIS
VERT	VAPOR	VINAL	VUGGY	VAUNTY	VERNAL
VERY	VARIA	VINCA	VULGO	VAWARD	*VERNIX
VEST	*VARIX	VINIC	VULVA	VEALER	VERSAL
VETO	VARNA	VINYL	VYING	VECTOR	VERSER
VEXT	VARUS	VIOLA	VACANT	*VEEJAY	VERSET
VIAL	VARVE	VIPER	VACATE	VEEPEE	VERSTE
VIBE	VASTY	VIRAL	VACUUM	VEGETE	VERSUS
VICE	VATIC	VIREO	VADOSE	VEGGIE	*VERTEX
VIDE	VAULT	VIRES	VAGARY	VEILER	VERVET
VIER	VAUNT	VIRGA	VAGILE	VEINAL	VESICA
VIEW	VEALY	VIRID	VAGINA	VEINER	VESPER
VIGA	VEENA	VIRTU	VAGROM	VELATE	VESPID
VILE	VEERY	VIRUS	VAHINE	VELLUM	VESSEL
VILL	VEGAN	VISIT	VAKEEL	VELOCE	VESTAL
VINA	VEINY	VISOR	VALGUS	VELOUR	VESTEE
VINE	VELAR	VISTA	VALINE	VELURE	VESTRY
VINO	VELDT	VITAL	VALISE	VELVET	VETOER
VINY	VELUM	VITTA	*VALKYR	VENDEE	VETTED
VIOL		VIVID	VALLEY	VENDER	VIABLE

VIATIC	VOMICA	VATTING	VESPINE	VITAMIN	*VALUABLY
VIATOR	VOMITO	VAULTER	VESTIGE	VITESSE	VALUATOR
VIBIST	VOODOO	VAUNTER	VESTING	VITIATE	VALVELET
VIBRIO	*VORTEX	VAUNTIE	VESTURE	VITRAIN	VALVULAR
VICING	VOTARY	VAVASOR	VETERAN	*VITRIFY	*VAMBRACE
VICTIM	VOTING	VAWNTIE	VETIVER	VITRINE	VANADATE
VICTOR	VOTIVE	VEBROSE	VETTING	VITRIOL	VANADIUM
VICUNA	VOYAGE	VEDALIA	*VEXEDLY	*VIVIFIC	VANGUARD
VIEWER	VOYEUR	VEDETTE	VIADUCT	VOCABLE	VANILLIN
VIGOUR	VULGAR	VEGETAL	VIBRANT	*VOCABLY	VANISHER
VIKING	VULGUS	*VEHICLE	VIBRATE	VOCALIC	VANITORY
*VILIFY	*VACANCY	VEILING	VIBRATO	*VOCALLY	*VANQUISH
VILLUS	VACCINA	VEINIER	VIBRION	VOCODER	*VAPIDITY
VINEAL	VACCINE	VEINING	*VICARLY	VOGUISH	VAPORING
VINERY	*VACUITY	VEINLET	*VICEROY	VOICING	VAPORISE
VINIER	VACUOLE	VEINULE	VICINAL	VOLANTE	*VAPORISH
*VINIFY	VACUOUS	VELAMEN	VICIOUS	VOLCANO	*VAPORIZE
VINING	VAGRANT	VELIGER	VICOMTE	VOLTAGE	VAPOROUS
VINOUS	VALANCE	VELITES	*VICTORY	VOLUBLE	VAPOURER
VIOLET	VALENCE	VELOUTE	VICTUAL	VOLUTIN	VARACTOR
VIOLIN	*VALENCY	VENATIC	VICUGNA	VOMITER	VARIABLE
VIRAGO	VALIANT	VENDACE	VIDETTE	VOMITUS	*VARIABLY
VIRGIN	VALIDLY	VENISON	VIDICON	VORLAGE	VARIANCE
VIRILE	VALLATE	VENOMER	VIDUITY	VOTABLE	VARICOSE
VIRION	VALONIA	VENTAGE	VIEWIER	VOTRESS	*VARIEDLY
VIROID	VALUATE	VENTAIL	VIEWING	*VOUCHEE	VARIETAL
VIRTUE	VALVATE	VENTRAL	VILAYET	*VOUCHER	*VARIFORM
VISAGE	VALVULA	VENTURE	VILLAGE	*VOUVRAY	VARIORUM
VISARD	VALVULE	VENTURI	VILLAIN	VOWLESS	VARISTOR
VISCID	VAMOOSE	VERANDA	VILLEIN	VOYAGER	VARLETRY
VISCUS	VAMPIRE	VERBENA	VINASSE	VULGATE	*VARNISHY
VISING	*VAMPISH	*VERBIFY	VINEGAR	VULPINE	VASCULAR
VISION	*VANDYKE	VERBILE	VINIEST	VULTURE	*VASCULUM
VISIVE	VANILLA	VERDANT	VINTAGE	*VYINGLY	*VASIFORM
VISUAL	VANNING	VERDICT	VINTNER	VACATION	*VASOTOMY
VITALS	VANPOOL	VERDURE	VIOLATE	*VACCINEE	VASTIEST
VITRIC	VANTAGE	VERGING	VIOLENT	*VACCINIA	VASTNESS
VITTLE	VANWARD	VERGLAS	VIOLIST	*VAGABOND	VATICIDE
VIVACE	VAPORER	VERIDIC	VIOLONE	*VAGILITY	VAULTING
*VIVARY	*VAPOURY	VERIEST	VIRELAI	VAGINATE	VAUNTFUL
VIVERS	*VAQUERO	VERISMO	VIRELAY	*VAGOTOMY	VAVASOUR
*VIVIFY	VARIANT	VERITAS	VIREMIA	*VAGRANCY	VAVASSOR
*VIZARD	VARIATE	VERMEIL	VIRGATE	VAINNESS	VEGANISM
*VIZIER	VARICES	VERMIAN	VIRGULE	VALENCIA	VEGETANT
*VIZSLA	VARIETY	*VERMUTH	VIROSIS	VALERATE	VEGETATE
VODOUN	VARIOLA	VERNIER	VIRTUAL	VALERIAN	VEGETIST
VOICER	VARIOLE	VERRUCA	VISCERA	VALIANCE	*VEGETIVE
VOIDER	VARIOUS	VERSANT	VISCOID	*VALIANCY	*VEHEMENT
VOLANT	VARMENT	*VERSIFY	VISCOSE	VALIDATE	*VEILEDLY
VOLERY	VARMINT	VERSINE	VISCOUS	*VALIDITY	*VEILLIKE
VOLLEY	VARNISH	VERSING	VISIBLE	*VALKYRIE	VEINIEST
VOLOST	VARSITY	VERSION	VISITER	VALORISE	VEINLESS
VOLUME	VASTIER	VERTIGO	VISITOR	*VALORIZE	*VEINLIKE
VOLUTE	VASTITY	VERVAIN	VITALLY	VALOROUS	VEINULET
*VOLVOX	VATICAL	VESICLE	VITAMER	VALUABLE	VELARIUM

*VELARIZE	VESTIARY	VIOLENCE	VOLITIVE	DY V OUR	RE V I V E
VELLEITY	VESTIGIA	*VIOMYCIN	VOLLEYER	FA V ELA	RE V OKE
*VELOCITY	VESTLESS	VIRGINAL	VOLPLANE	FA V ISM	RE V OLT
VELVERET	*VESTLIKE	VIRICIDE	VOLTAISM	FA V OUR	RE V OTE
VENALITY	VESTMENT	VIRIDIAN	VOLUTION	GA V AGE	REV V ED
VENATION	VESTURAL	*VIRIDITY	VOLVULUS	GA V IAL	RI V AGE
VENDETTA	VESUVIAN	VIRILISM	*VOMITIVE	GI V ING	RI V ING
VENDEUSE	VETIVERT	VIRILITY	*VOMITORY	GO V ERN	SA V AGE
VENDIBLE	*VEXATION	*VIROLOGY	VOMITOUS	HA V ING	SA V ANT
*VENDIBLY	*VEXILLUM	VIRTUOSA	*VORACITY	HA V IOR	SA V ATE
VENEERER	*VEXINGLY	VIRTUOSO	VOTARESS	*JO V IAL	SA V INE
VENENATE	VIATICAL	VIRTUOUS	VOTARIST	KA V ASS	SA V ING
VENENOSE	*VIATICUM	VIRUCIDE	VOTEABLE	LA V ABO	SA V IOR
VENERATE	*VIBRANCE	VIRULENT	VOTELESS	LA V AGE	SA V ORY
VENEREAL	*VIBRANCY	*VISCACHA	VOUSSOIR	LA V EER	SA V OUR
VENETIAN	VIBRATOR	VISCERAL	*VOWELIZE	LA V ING	SO V IET
*VENGEFUL	VIBRISSA	VISCOUNT	*VOYAGEUR	LA V ISH	SO V RAN
VENOGRAM	*VIBRONIC	*VISELIKE	*VULCANIC	LE V ANT	TA V ERN
VENOMOUS	*VIBURNUM	VISIONAL	VULVITIS	LE V IED	VI V ACE
VENOSITY	VICARAGE	VISITANT		LE V IER	*VI V ARY
VENTLESS	VICARATE	VISUALLY	K V AS	LE V IES	*VI V ERS
VENTURER	VICARIAL	VITALISE	K V ASS	LE V ITY	*VI V IFY
*VERACITY	*VICENARY	VITALISM	CO V IN	LI V ELY	*WA V ERY
*VERANDAH	VICINAGE	VITALIST	DU V ET	LI V ERY	WA V IER
VERATRIA	*VICINITY	VITALITY	*JI V ER	LI V EST	WA V IES
VERATRIN	VICTORIA	*VITALIZE	*JI V EY	LI V IER	*WA V ILY
VERATRUM	VIC RESS	VITAMINE	SA V VY	LI V ING	WA V ING
*VERBALLY	*VIDEOTEX	VITELLIN	BE V IES	LI V YER	WI V ERN
*VERBATIM	*VIDEODATA	VITELLUS	BO V INE	LO V AGE	WI V ING
VERBIAGE	*VIEWDATA	VITIATOR	CA V EAT	LO V ELY	*WY V ERN
VERBLESS	VIEWIEST	VITILIGO	CA V ERN	LO V ING	BE V ELER
VERBOTEN	VIEWLESS	VITREOUS	CA V IAR	NA V AID	BE V OMIT
*VERDANCY	VIGILANT	VITULINE	CA V IES	NO V ENA	*BI V ALVE
VERDERER	VIGNERON	*VIVACITY	CA V ING	NO V ICE	*BI V INYL
VERDEROR	VIGNETTE	*VIVARIUM	CA V ITY	PA V ANE	BI V OUAC
VERDITER	*VIGORISH	*VIVERRID	CA V ORT	PA V EED	CA V ALLA
VERECUND	VIGOROSO	*VIVIFIER	CI V ICS	PA V ING	*CA V ALLY
VERGENCE	VIGOROUS	*VIVIPARA	CI V ISM	PA V IOR	*CA V ALRY
VERIFIER	VILENESS	*VIVISECT	CO V ERT	PA V ISE	CA V EMAN
*VERJUICE	VILIFIER	*VIZCACHA	CO V ING	*QI V IUT	CA V ETTO
VERMOULU	VILIPEND	*VIZIRATE	DE V EIN	RA V AGE	CA V ILER
*VERMOUTH	VILLADOM	VOCALISE	DE V EST	RA V INE	CA V TARE
VERNACLE	VILLAGER	*VOCALISM	DE V ICE	RA V ING	*CE V ICHE
VERNICLE	VILLAINY	VOCALIST	DE V ISE	RA V ISH	*CI V ILLY
VERONICA	VILLATIC	*VOCALITY	DE V OID	RE V AMP	CO V ERER
VERSEMAN	*VINCIBLE	*VOCALIZE	DE V OIR	RE V EAL	CO V ERUP
VERSICLE	*VINCULUM	VOCATION	DE V OTE	RE V ERB	CO V ETER
VERTEBRA	VINDALOO	*VOCATIVE	DE V OUR	RE V ERE	CU V ETTE
VERTICAL	*VINEYARD	*VOICEFUL	DE V OUT	RE V ERS	DE V ALUE
VESICANT	VINIFERA	VOIDANCE	DI V ERT	RE V ERT	DE V ELOP
VESICATE	VINOSITY	VOIDNESS	DI V EST	RE V ERY	DE V IATE
VESICULA	VINTAGER	VOLATILE	DI V IDE	RE V EST	DE V ILRY
VESPERAL	VIOLABLE	*VOLCANIC	DI V INE	RE V IEW	DE V IOUS
*VESPIARY	VIOLATER	VOLITANT	DI V ING	RE V ILE	DE V ISAL
VESTALLY	VIOLATOR	VOLITION	DO V ISH	RE V ISE	DE V ISEE

DE V ISER	MO V IOLA	RE V UIST	CLE V EITE	NON V IRAL	SIL V ICAL
DE V ISOR	NA V ETTE	RE V VING	*COE V ALLY	NON V OCAL	SIR V ENTE
DE V OICE	NA V VIES	RI V ALRY	*COE V OLVE	NON V OTER	SLA V ERER
DE V OLVE	NI V EOUS	RI V ETER	CON V ENER	NOU V ELLE	SLI V ERER
DE V OTEE	NO V ATIN	RI V IERA	CON V ENOR	PAR V ENUE	*SLI V OVIC
DI V ERSE	NO V ELLA	RI V IERE	CON V ERGE	PAR V OLIN	SLO V ENLY
DI V IDER	NO V ELLY	RI V ULET	CON V ERSE	PER V ADER	SNI V ELER
DI V INER	NO V ELTY	RO V VING	*CON V EXLY	PER V ERSE	SOL V ABLE
DI V ISOR	PA V IOUR	SA V ABLE	*CON V EYER	PER V IOUS	*SOL V ENCY
DI V ORCE	PA V ISER	SA V ANNA	*CON V EYOR	PLU V IOSE	SOU V ENIR
DI V ULGE	*PA V LOVA	SA V ARIN	*CON V INCE	PLU V IOUS	*SOU V LAKI
DO V ECOT	PI V OTAL	SA V ELOY	*CON V OKER	*POX V IRUS	*SUB V ICAR
*DO V EKEY	*PO V ERTY	SA V IOUR	*CON V OLVE	PRE V IOUS	SUB V IRAL
*DO V EKIE	RA V AGER	SA V ORER	CON V ULSE	PRE V ISOR	*SUB V OCAL
DU V ETYN	RA V ELER	SA V OURY	COR V ETTE	*PRO V ENLY	SUR V EYOR
FA V ELLA	RA V ELIN	SE V ENTH	*CRA V ENLY	PRO V IDER	SUR V IVAL
FA V ORER	RA V ELLY	SE V ENTY	CRE V ALLE	PRO V IRUS	SUR V IVOR
FO V EOLA	RA V ENER	SE V ERAL	CRE V ASSE	*PRO V OKER	*SYL V ATIC
FO V EOLE	RA V IOLI	*SE V ICHE	CUL V ERIN	PUL V ILLI	TRA V ELER
GA V OTTE	RE V ALUE	SE V VERE	DIS V ALUE	PUL V INUS	TRA V ELOG
HA V EREL	RE V ELER	*SO V KHOZ	DRI V ELER	*PUR V EYOR	TRA V ERSE
HA V IOUR	RE V ELRY	TA V ERNA	*DRI V EWAY	*QUA V ERER	TRA V ESTY
HO V ERER	RE V ENGE	VA V ASOR	*FER V ENCY	*QUI V ERER	TRA V OISE
*JA V ELIN	RE V ENUE	*V I V IFIC	FLA V ONOL	REO V IRUS	TRI V ALVE
*JI V EASS	RE V ERER	WA V ELET	FLA V ORER	SAL V ABLE	VAL V ELET
*JU V ENAL	RE V ERIE	*WA V EOFF	*FLA V OURY	SAL V AGEE	VAL V ERET
*LA V ROCK	RE V ERSE	WA V ERER	FRI V OLER	SAL V AGER	VAL V ULAR
LE V ATOR	RE V ERSO	WA V IEST	GAL V ANIC	*SAL V IFIC	VEL V ERET
LE V ELER	RE V ILER	BIO V ULAR	GRA V AMEN	SCA V ENGE	VOL V ULUS
LE V ELLY	RE V ISAL	BLO V IATE	GRA V ITAS	SEL V EDGE	VUL V ITIS
LE V ERET	RE V ISER	*BRE V ETCY	GRA V ITON	SER V ABLE	
LE V ULIN	RE V ISIT	*BRE V IARY	*GRA V LAKS	SER V ICER	SHI V
LI V ABLE	RE V ISOR	CAL V ADOS	GRO V ELER	SER V ITOR	SPI V
LI V ENER	RE V IVAL	CAL V ARIA	*HEA V ENLY	SHI V AREE	GANE V
LO V ABLE	RE V IVER	CAN V ASER	*HEA V YSET	SHI V ERER	SCHA V
LO V EBUG	RE V OICE	CER V ELAS	SHO V ELER	SIL V ERER	MAGLE V
*MO V ABLY	RE V OKER	CER V ELAT	NER V IEST	SIL V ERLY	MOSHA V
MO V ELES	RE V OLVE	*CHE V ALET	NON V ALID		

W

WACK	WAIT	WARD	WATT	WEAR	WELD
WADE	WAKE	WARE	WAUK	WEED	WELL
WADI	WALE	WARK	WAUL	WEEK	WELT
WADY	WALK	WARM	WAUR	WEEL	WEND
WAFF	WALL	WARN	WAVE	WEEN	WENT
WAFT	WALY	WARP	WAVY	WEEP	WEPT
WAGE	WAME	WART	WAWL	WEER	WERE
WAIF	WAND	WARY	*WAXY	WEET	WERT
WAIL	WANE	WASH	WEAK	WEFT	WEST
WAIN	WANT	WASP	WEAL	WEIR	WHAM
WAIR	WANY	WAST	WEAN	WEKA	WHAP

WHAT	WORE	WEDEL	WIDEN	WOULD	*WALKUP
WHEE	**WORK**	**WEDGE**	WIDER	WOUND	**WALLAH**
WHEN	WORM	**WEDGY**	**WIDOW**	**WOVEN**	WALLET
WHET	WORN	**WEEDY**	**WIDTH**	**WRACK**	WALLIE
WHEW	WORT	**WEENY**	WIELD	WRANG	**WALLOP**
WHEY	WOST	**WEEPY**	**WIFTY**	**WRAPT**	**WALLOW**
WHID	**WOVE**	WEEST	WIGAN	**WRATH**	WALNUT
WHIG	WRAP	**WEIGH**	**WIGGY**	**WREAK**	WALRUS
WHIM	WREN	WEIRD	**WIGHT**	**WRECK**	**WAMBLE**
WHIN	WRIT	**WELCH**	**WILCO**	WREST	*WAMBLY
WHIP	WUSS	**WELLY**	**WILLY**	**WRICK**	**WAMMUS**
WHIR	*WYCH	**WELSH**	*WIMPY	WRIED	*WAMPUM
WHIT	WYLE	WENCH	**WINCE**	WRIER	**WAMPUS**
*WHIZ	WYND	**WENNY**	**WINCH**	WRIES	**WANDER**
WHOA	WYNN	**WETLY**	**WINDY**	WRING	**WANDLE**
WHOM	WYTE	*WHACK	**WINEY**	WRIST	**WANGAN**
WHOP	**WACKE**	**WHALE**	**WINGY**	WRITE	**WANGLE**
WICH	**WACKO**	**WHAMO**	*WINZE	WRONG	**WANGUN**
WICK	*WACKY	**WHANG**	**WIPER**	WROTE	WANIER
WIDE	**WADDY**	**WHARF**	WIRER	**WROTH**	**WANING**
WIFE	WADER	**WHAUP**	WIRRA	WRUNG	WANION
WILD	**WAEFU**	**WHEAL**	WISED	WURST	**WANNED**
WILE	**WAFER**	**WHEAT**	WISER	**WUSSY**	**WANNER**
WILL	WAGER	**WHEEL**	WISHA	**WABBLE**	**WANTER**
WILT	WAGON	**WHEEN**	**WISPY**	*WABBLY	**WANTON**
WILY	**WAHOO**	**WHEEP**	WITAN	**WADDER**	**WAPITI**
WIMP	WAIST	*WHELK	**WITCH**	**WADDIE**	**WARBLE**
WIND	**WAIVE**	**WHELM**	WITEN	**WADDLE**	**WARDEN**
WINE	**WAKEN**	**WHELP**	**WITHE**	**WADDLY**	**WARDER**
WING	**WAKER**	**WHERE**	**WITHY**	**WADIES**	WARIER
WINK	WALER	*WHICH	**WITTY**	**WADING**	**WARILY**
WINO	WALLA	*WHIFF	**WIVER**	**WADMAL**	**WARING**
WINY	**WALLY**	**WHILE**	**WIVES**	**WADMEL**	**WARMER**
WIPE	*WALTZ	**WHINE**	*WIZEN	**WADMOL**	**WARMLY**
WIRE	**WAMUS**	**WHINY**	WOALD	**WADSET**	**WARMTH**
WIRY	**WANEY**	**WHIPT**	**WODGE**	**WAEFUL**	**WARMUP**
WISE	**WANLY**	**WHIRL**	**WOFUL**	*WAFERY	**WARNER**
WISH	**WARTY**	**WHIRR**	**WOKEN**	*WAFFIE	**WARPER**
WISP	**WASHY**	**WHISH**	**WOMAN**	*WAFFLE	**WARRED**
WISS	**WASPY**	*WHISK	*WOMBY	**WAFTER**	**WARREN**
WIST	**WASTE**	**WHIST**	**WOMEN**	**WAGGED**	**WARSAW**
WITE	**WATAP**	**WHITE**	*WONKY	**WAGGER**	WARSLE
WITH	**WATCH**	**WHITY**	**WOODY**	**WAGGLE**	WASABI
WIVE	WATER	*WHIZZ	**WOOER**	**WAGGLY**	**WASHER**
WOAD	**WAUGH**	**WHOLE**	**WOOLY**	**WAGGON**	WASTER
WOKE	**WAVER**	*WHOMP	**WOOPS**	**WAGING**	**WASTRY**
WOLD	**WAVEY**	**WHOOF**	**WOOSH**	**WAHINE**	**WATAPE**
WOLF	*WAXEN	**WHOOP**	*WOOZY	WAILER	**WATERY**
WOMB	*WAXER	**WHORE**	**WORDY**	WAITER	**WATTER**
WONK	WEALD	**WHORL**	WORLD	**WAIVER**	**WATTLE**
WONT	**WEARY**	**WHORT**	**WORMY**	WALIES	**WAUCHT**
WOOD	**WEAVE**	**WHOSE**	**WORRY**	**WALING**	**WAUGHT**
WOOF	*WEBBY	**WHOSO**	WORSE	**WALKER**	*WAVERY
WOOL	WEBER	*WHUMP	WORST		**WAVIER**
WORD	**WECHT**	**WIDDY**	**WORTH**		**WAVIES**

*WAVILY	WHILOM	WINCEY	WOOFER	WAKENER	WATERER
WAVING	WHILST	WINDER	WOOLED	*WALKING	WATTAGE
*WAXIER	*WHIMSY	WINDLE	WOOLEN	WALKOUT	WATTAPE
*WAXILY	WHINER	WINDOW	WOOLER	*WALKWAY	WATTEST
*WAXING	*WHINEY	WINDUP	WOOLIE	*WALLABY	WAVELET
*WAYLAY	WHINGE	WINERY	WOOLLY	WALLEYE	*WAVEOFF
WEAKEN	*WHINNY	WINGER	WORKER	WALLIES	WAVERER
*WEAKLY	*WHIPPY	WINIER	*WORKUP	*WALTZER	WAVIEST
WEALTH	*WHIRLY	WINING	WORMER	*WAMEFOU	*WAXBILL
WEANER	*WHIRRY	WINISH	WORMIL	*WAMEFUL	*WAXIEST
WEAPON	*WHISHT	WINKER	WORRIT	*WAMPISH	*WAXLIKE
WEARER	*WHISKY	WINKLE	WORSEN	WANGLER	*WAXWEED
WEASEL	WHITEN	WINNED	WORSER	WANIEST	*WAXWING
WEASON	WHITER	WINNER	WORSET	WANIGAN	*WAXWORK
WEAVER	*WHITEY	WINNOW	*WORTHY	WANNESS	*WAXWORM
*WEBFED	*WHOLLY	WINTER	WOWSER	WANNEST	*WAYBILL
WEDDER	WHOMSO	WINTLE	WRAITH	WANNING	WAYLESS
WEDELN	*WHOOSH	WINTRY	WRASSE	WANTAGE	WAYSIDE
WEDGIE	WHOSIS	WIPING	*WRATHY	WARBLER	*WAYWARD
WEEDER	*WHYDAH	WIRIER	WREATH	WARFARE	*WAYWORN
*WEEKLY	*WICKED	WIRILY	WRENCH	WARHEAD	*WEAKISH
WEENIE	*WICKER	WIRING	WRETCH	WARIEST	*WEALTHY
WEENSY	*WICKET	WISDOM	WRIEST	WARISON	WEARIED
WEEPER	*WICOPY	WISELY	WRIGHT	WARLESS	WEARIER
WEEVER	WIDDER	WISENT	WRISTY	WARLIKE	WEARIES
WEEVIL	WIDDIE	WISEST	WRITER	*WARLOCK	WEARISH
WEEWEE	WIDDLE	WISHER	WRITHE	WARLORD	WEASAND
WEIGHT	WIDEST	WISING	*WURZEL	*WARMISH	WEASELY
WEINER	WIDGET	*WITCHY	WUTHER	WARNING	WEATHER
WEIRDO	WIDISH	WITHAL	*WYVERN	WARPAGE	*WEAZAND
WEIRDY	WIELDY	WITHER	WABBLER	*WARPATH	*WEBBING
WELDER	WIENER	WITHIN	WADABLE	WARRANT	*WEBFOOT
WELDOR	WIENIE	WITING	WADDIED	WARRING	WEBLESS
WELKIN	*WIFELY	WITNEY	WADDIES	WARRIOR	*WEBLIKE
WELLIE	WIFING	WITTED	WADDING	*WARSHIP	WEBSTER
WELTER	WIGEON	WITTOL	WADDLER	WARSLER	*WEBWORM
WESKIT	WIGGED	WIVERN	WADMAAL	WARSTLE	WEDDING
WESTER	WIGGLE	WIVING	WADMOLL	WARTHOG	*WEDLOCK
WETHER	WIGGLY	*WIZARD	WAENESS	WARTIER	WEEDIER
WETTED	WIGLET	*WIZZEN	*WAESUCK	WARTIME	WEEDILY
WETTER	WIGWAG	WOBBLE	*WAFFLER	*WARWORK	*WEEKDAY
*WHACKO	*WIGWAM	*WOBBLY	WAFTAGE	WARWORN	*WEEKEND
*WHACKY	*WIKIUP	WOEFUL	WAFTURE	*WASHDAY	WEIGELA
WHALER	WILDER	WOLFER	WAGERER	WASHIER	WEIGHER
*WHAMMO	WILDLY	WOLVER	*WAGGERY	WASHING	*WEIGHTY
*WHAMMY	WILFUL	WOLVES	WAGGING	WASHOUT	WEIRDIE
*WHARVE	WILIER	WOMBAT	*WAGGISH	WASHRAG	WEIRDLY
*WHEEZE	WILILY	WOMERA	WAGONER	*WASHTUB	*WELCHER
*WHEEZY	WILING	WONDER	WAGSOME	WASSAIL	WELCOME
*WHELKY	WILLER	WONNED	WAGTAIL	WASTAGE	WELFARE
WHENAS	WILLET	WONNER	WAILFUL	WASTERY	WELLIES
WHENCE	WILLOW	WONTON	WAISTER	WASTING	WELSHER
*WHERRY	WIMBLE	WOODEN	WAITING	WASTREL	WELTING
*WHERVE	WIMPLE	WOODIE	*WAKANDA	WASTRIE	*WENCHER
*WHIDAH	WINCER	WOODSY	*WAKEFUL	*WATCHER	WENDIGO

WENNISH	WHITEST	WINDROW	WOOLHAT	WAGGONER	*WATCHCRY
WERGELD	*WHITHER	*WINDWAY	WOOLIER	WAGONAGE	*WATCHDOG
WERGELT	WHITIES	WINESOP	WOOLIES	*WAHCONDA	*WATCHEYE
WERGILD	WHITING	*WINGBOW	WOOLLED	*WAIFLIKE	*WATCHFUL
*WERWOLF	*WHITISH	WINGIER	WOOLLEN	WAILSOME	*WATCHMAN
WESSAND	*WHITLOW	WINGLET	WOOLMAN	WAINSCOT	*WATCHOUT
WESTERN	WHITTER	WINGMAN	WOOMERA	WAISTING	WATERAGE
WESTING	WHITTLE	WINGTIP	WOORALI	WAITRESS	WATERBED
*WETBACK	*WHIZZED	WINIEST	WOORARI	*WAKELESS	WATERDOG
WETLAND	*WHIZZER	WINLESS	WORDAGE	*WAKENING	WATERIER
WETNESS	*WHIZZES	WINNING	WORDIER	*WAKERIFE	WATERILY
WETTEST	*WHOEVER	*WINNOCK	WORDILY	*WALKAWAY	WATERING
WETTING	*WHOLISM	WINSOME	WORDING	*WALKOVER	WATERISH
WETTISH	*WHOOPEE	WINTERY	*WORKBAG	*WALKYRIE	WATERLOG
*WHACKER	*WHOOPER	WIPEOUT	*WORKBOX	WALLAROO	WATERLOO
WHALING	*WHOOPLA	WIREMAN	*WORKDAY	WALLOPER	WATERMAN
WHANGEE	WHOOSIS	WIRETAP	*WORKING	WALLOWER	*WATERWAY
*WHAPPER	*WHOPPER	*WIREWAY	*WORKMAN	WANDERER	WATTHOUR
WHATNOT	WHORING	WIRIEST	WORKOUT	WANDEROO	WATTLESS
WHATSIS	*WHORISH	WISEASS	WORLDLY	WANNIGAN	*WAVEBAND
WHEATEN	WHORTLE	*WISHFUL	WORMIER	WANTONER	*WAVEFORM
WHEEDLE	*WICKAPE	WISPIER	*WORMISH	WANTONLY	WAVELESS
WHEELER	*WICKING	*WISPILY	WORRIED	*WARCRAFT	*WAVELIKE
WHEELIE	*WICKIUP	*WISPISH	WORRIER	*WARDENRY	WAVINESS
*WHEEPLE	*WICKYUP	WISTFUL	*WORSHIP	WARDRESS	*WAXBERRY
*WHEEZER	WIDENER	WITHIER	WORSTED	WARDROBE	*WAXINESS
WHEREAS	WIDEOUT	WITHIES	WOTTETH	WARDROOM	*WAXPLANT
WHEREAT	WIDGEON	WITHING	WOULDST	*WARDSHIP	*WAYFARER
*WHEREBY	WIDOWER	WITHOUT	WRANGLE	WAREROOM	*WAYGOING
WHEREIN	WIELDER	WITLESS	WRAPPER	WARFARIN	*WAYLAYER
*WHEREOF	*WIFEDOM	WITLING	WRASSLE	WARHORSE	*WEAKENER
WHEREON	*WIGGERY	WITLOOF	WRASTLE	WARINESS	*WEAKFISH
WHERETO	WIGGIER	WITNESS	WREAKER	*WARMAKER	*WEAKLING
*WHETHER	WIGGING	WITTIER	WREATHE	WARMNESS	*WEAKNESS
WHETTER	WIGGLER	WITTILY	*WRECKER	*WARMOUTH	*WEAKSIDE
*WHICKER	WIGLESS	WITTING	WRESTER	WARPLANE	WEANLING
*WHIFFER	*WIGLIKE	*WOADWAX	WRESTLE	*WARPOWER	*WEAPONRY
*WHIFFET	WILDCAT	WOBBLER	WRIGGLE	*WARPWISE	WEARABLE
*WHIFFLE	WILDING	WOENESS	*WRIGGLY	WARRAGAL	WEARIEST
*WHIMPER	WILDISH	WOESOME	WRINGER	WARRANTY	WEARIFUL
*WHIMSEY	WILIEST	*WOLFISH	WRINKLE	WARRENER	WEASELLY
WHINIER	WILLFUL	*WOLFRAM	*WRINKLY	WARRIGAL	WEEDIEST
WHINING	WILLIED	*WOMANLY	WRITHEN	*WARSTLER	WEEDLESS
*WHIPPED	WILLIES	WOMMERA	WRITHER	WARTIEST	*WEEDLIKE
*WHIPPER	WILLING	WONNING	WRITING	WARTLESS	WEEKLONG
*WHIPPET	*WILLOWY	WOODBIN	WRITTEN	*WARTLIKE	*WEFTWISE
*WHIPRAY	*WIMPISH	*WOODBOX	WRONGER	*WASHABLE	WEIGELIA
*WHIPSAW	*WINCHER	WOODCUT	WRONGLY	*WASHBOWL	*WEIGHMAN
WHIRLER	WINCING	WOODHEN	WROUGHT	WASHIEST	*WEIGHTER
WHIRRED	WINDAGE	WOODIER	*WRYNECK	*WASHROOM	WEIRDIES
*WHISKER	WINDBAG	WOODIES	WRYNESS	WASTABLE	*WELCOMER
*WHISKEY	WINDIER	WOODLOT	WADEABLE	WASTEFUL	WELDLESS
*WHISPER	WINDIGO	WOODMAN	*WAESUCKS	WASTELOT	WELDMENT
WHISTLE	WINDILY	WOODSIA	*WAFFLING	WASTERIE	*WELLADAY
*WHITELY	WINDING	*WOODWAX	WAGELESS	*WASTEWAY	*WELLAWAY

WELLBORN	*WHOSEVER	*WIREWORK	*WOOLWORK	S W OP	S W OUN
*WELLCURB	*WIDEBAND	*WIREWORM	*WORDBOOK	S W OT	S W UNG
WELLDOER	WIDENESS	WIRINESS	WORDIEST	S W UM	T W AIN
*WELLHEAD	*WIDTHWAY	WISEACRE	WORDLESS	T W AE	T W ANG
WELLHOLE	WIFELESS	WISENESS	*WORDPLAY	T W AT	T W EAK
WELLNESS	*WIFEHOOD	*WISHBONE	*WORKABLE	T W EE	T W EED
WELLSITE	*WIFELIKE	WISHLESS	*WORKADAY	T W IG	T W EEN
WEREGILD	WIGGIEST	WISPIEST	*WORKBOAT	T W IN	T W EET
*WEREWOLF	*WIGMAKER	*WISPLIKE	*WORKBOOK	T W IT	T W ERP
WESTERLY	*WILDFIRE	WISTARIA	*WORKFARE	Y W IS	T W ICE
WESTMOST	*WILDFOWL	WISTERIA	*WORKFOLK	B W ANA	T W IER
*WESTWARD	WILDLAND	*WITCHERY	*WORKLESS	D W ARF	T W ILL
*WETPROOF	*WILDLIFE	*WITCHING	*WORKLOAD	D W ELL	T W INE
WETTABLE	WILDLING	*WITHDRAW	*WORKMATE	D W ELT	T W INY
*WHALEMAN	WILDNESS	WITHERER	*WORKROOM	D W INE	T W IRL
*WHARFAGE	WILINESS	*WITHHOLD	*WORKSHOP	S W AGE	T W IRP
*WHATEVER	WILLIWAU	WITHIEST	*WORKWEEK	S W AIL	T W IST
WHATNESS	*WILLIWAW	WITTIEST	*WORMHOLE	S W AIN	*T W IXT
WHEATEAR	WILLOWER	*WIZARDRY	WORMIEST	S W ALE	T W YER
*WHEEDLER	*WILLYARD	WOBEGONE	*WORMLIKE	S W AMI	*K W ANZA
*WHEELING	WILLYART	*WOLFFISH	WORMROOT	S W AMP	*Q W ERTY
*WHEELMAN	*WILLYWAW	*WOLFLIKE	WORMSEED	S W AMY	T W EENY
*WHENEVER	WINDBURN	WOMANISE	*WORMWOOD	S W ANG	T W ISTY
*WHEREVER	*WINDFALL	*WOMANISH	WORNNESS	S W ANK	S W AGGIE
*WHETTING	WINDFLAW	*WOMANIZE	*WORTHFUL	S W ARD	S W ALLOW
*WHEYFACE	WINDGALL	WONDERER	WOSTTETH	S W ARE	S W IDDEN
*WHEYLIKE	WINDIEST	WONDROUS	WOULDEST	S W ARF	*S W INGBY
*WHIFFLER	WINDLASS	*WONTEDLY	*WRACKFUL	S W ARM	T W ATTLE
*WHIMBREL	WINDLESS	*WOODBIND	WRANGLER	S W ART	*T W IDDLY
*WHINCHAT	WINDLING	WOODBINE	*WRAPPING	S W ASH	*T W INJET
WHINIEST	WINDMILL	*WOODCHAT	*WRATHFUL	S W ATH	T W INSET
*WHIPCORD	*WINDPIPE	*WOODCOCK	*WRECKAGE	S W EAR	S W IFTLET
*WHIPLASH	*WINDSOCK	WOODIEST	*WRECKFUL	S W EAT	*SWIMWEAR
*WHIPLIKE	*WINDSURF	WOODLAND	*WRECKING	S W EDE	S W INGIER
*WHIPPIER	*WINDWARD	*WOODLARK	WRESTLER	S W EEP	S W INGING
*WHIPPING	WINELESS	WOODLESS	*WRETCHED	S W EER	S W INGMAN
*WHIPTAIL	*WINESHOP	WOODLORE	WRIGGLER	S W EET	*S W INGIES
*WHIPWORM	*WINESKIN	WOODNOTE	WRISTLET	S W ELL	DE W AR
*WHIRRING	*WINGBACK	WOODPILE	*WRITHING	S W EPT	*JO W AR
*WHISPERY	WINGDING	*WOODRUFF	*WRONGFUL	S W IFT	RA W IN
WHISTLER	*WINGEDLY	*WOODSHED	*WROTHFUL	S W ILL	RE W ED
*WHITECAP	*WINGIEST	WOODSMAN	WRITERLY	S W INE	RE W ET
*WHITEFLY	WINGLESS	*WOODWIND		S W ING	BA W BEE
WHITENER	*WINGLIKE	*WOODWORK	H W AN	S W INK	*BA W DRY
WHITEOUT	*WINGOVER	*WOODWORM	L W EI	S W IPE	BA W LER
WHITIEST	WINGSPAN	*WOOINGLY	S W AB	S W IRL	BA W TIE
*WHITRACK	WINNABLE	WOOLFELL	S W AG	S W ISH	BE W AIL
WHITTLER	WINNOWER	WOOLIEST	S W AM	S W ISS	BE W ARE
WHITTRET	WINTERER	WOOLLIER	S W AN	S W ITH	BE W EEP
*WHIZBANG	WINTERLY	WOOLLIES	S W AP	S W IVE	BE W ORM
*WHIZZING	*WIREDRAW	*WOOLLIKE	S W AT	S W OON	BE W RAP
*WHODUNIT	WIREHAIR	*WOOLPACK	S W AY	S W OOP	BE W RAY
*WHOMEVER	WIRELESS	*WOOLSACK	S W IG	S W ORD	BO W ERY
*WHOREDOM	*WIRELIKE	*WOOLSHED	S W IM	S W ORE	BO W FIN
WHORESON		*WOOLSKIN	S W OB	S W ORN	BO W ING

BO W LEG	PA W NEE	*BE W ORRY	*JA W LINE	*DRA W BACK
BO W LER	PA W NER	*BO W HEAD	*JE W ELER	DRA W BORE
BO W MAN	PA W NOR	*BO W KNOT	*JE W ELRY	*DRAWDOWN
BO W POT	*PA W PA W	BO W LDER	*JE W FISH	DRA W TUBE
*BO W WO W	PE W TER	BO W LESS	*LA W BOOK	FLA W LESS
BO W YER	PO W DER	*BO W LFUL	LA W LESS	FLO W ERER
*BY W ORD	PO W TER	*BO W LIKE	LA W LIKE	FLO W ERET
*BY W ORK	*PO W WO W	BO W LINE	LA W SUIT	*FLY W HEEL
CO W AGE	RA W ISH	BO W LING	LO W BALL	*GAS W ORKS
CO W ARD	RE W AKE	*BO W SHOT	LO W BORN	*GAY W INGS
*CO W BOY	RE W ARD	CO W BANE	LO W BRED	*GLOW WORM
CO W IER	RE W ARM	CO W BELL	*LO W BRO W	GRE W SOME
CO W MAN	RE W ASH	*CO W BIND	LO W DO W N	*LAY W OMAN
CO W PAT	RE W ELD	*CO W BIRD	LO W LAND	*MAD W OMAN
CO W PEA	RE W IND	*CO W EDLY	LO W LIFE	*MID W ATCH
CO W PIE	RE W IRE	*CO W FISH	LO W NESS	NAR W HALE
*CO W POX	RE W OKE	*CO W FLAP	*MA W KISH	NON W HITE
CO W RIE	RE W ORD	*CO W FLOP	NE W BORN	*NON WOODY
DA W TIE	RE W ORK	CO W GIRL	*NE W MOWN	NON W OVEN
DE W IER	RE W OVE	*CO W HERB	NE W NESS	*PIN W HEEL
DE W ILY	RE W RAP	*CO W HERD	NE W SIER	*PLO W BACK
DE W LAP	RO W ING	*CO W HIDE	NE W SIES	*PLO W HEAD
DE W OOL	*SA W FLY	CO W IEST	NE W SMAN	PLO W LAND
DE W ORM	SA W LOG	*CO W LICK	NO W HERE	RAD W ASTE
DO W ERY	SA W NEY	CO W LING	NO W NESS	*REA W AKEN
DO W NER	SA W YER	*CO W PLOP	PA W NAGE	SEA W ATER
DO W SER	SE W AGE	*CO W POKE	*PO W DERY	*SHO W BOAT
FA W NER	SE W ING	CO W RAGE	RA W HIDE	*SHO W CASE
FO W LER	SO W ANS	CO W RAND	RA W NESS	*SHOWDOWN
GA W KER	SO W CAR	CO W RITE	RE W AKEN	SHO W ERER
GA W PER	SO W ENS	*CO W SHED	RE W EAVE	*SHO W GIRL
GA W SIE	TA W DRY	*CO W SKIN	RE W EIGH	SHO W IEST
GE W GA W	TA W NEY	CO W SLIP	RE W IDEN	*SHO W RING
*HA W KER	TA W PIE	DE W ATER	RE W OKEN	*SHO WROOM
*HA W KEY	*TH W ACK	*DE W CLA W	RE W OUND	*SKE W BACK
*HA W KIE	TH W ART	DE W DROP	RE W OVEN	*SKE W BALD
HA W SER	TO W AGE	DE W FALL	RE W RITE	*SKE W NESS
HO W LER	TO W ARD	DE W IEST	RO W BOAT	*SKY W ARDS
HO W LET	TO W ERY	DE W LESS	*RO W LOCK	*SKY W RITE
*KO W TO W	TO W HEE	DO W ABLE	SA W BILL	*SLOWDOWN
LA W FUL	TO W NEE	DO W AGER	*SA W BUCK	SLO W NESS
LA W INE	TO W NIE	DO W NIER	SA W DUST	*SLO W POKE
LA W ING	VA W ARD	FE W NESS	*SA W FISH	*SLOW WORM
LA W MAN	W O W SER	FO W LING	SA W LIKE	SNO W BALL
LA W YER	YA W NER	*FO W LPOX	SA W MILL	SNO W BANK
LO W BOY	YA W PER	*GA W KIER	TO W ARDS	SNO W BELL
LO W BRO	YO W LER	*GA W KIES	*TO W A WAY	SNO W BELT
LO W ERY	*BA W COCK	*GA W KISH	TO W BOAT	SNO W BIRD
LO W ING	BA W DIER	*HA W KING	TO W HEAD	*SNO W BUSH
LO W ISH	BA W DIES	*HA W KISH	TO W LINE	SNO W DROP
NE W ISH	*BA W DILY	*HO W BEIT	TO W MOND	SNO W FALL
NE W SIE	*BA W DRIC	*HO W EVER	TO W MONT	SNO W IEST
NE W TON	BA W SUNT	*HO W DWDAH	TO W NIES	SNO W LAND
NO W AYS	*BE W EARY	*JA W BONE	TO W NISH	SNO W LESS
NO W ISE	*BE W ITCH	*JA W LIKE		*SNO W LIKE

SNO W MELT	GRO W	SHRE W	MARRO W	*CUMSHA W	*CHECKRO W
SNO W MOLD	KNE W	SINE W	MEADO W	*DAYGLO W	*CHOW CHOW
*SNO W PACK	KNO W	*SQUA W	MELLO W	*DE W CLA W	*CLERIHE W
*SNO W PLO W	MEO W	STRA W	MILDE W	DISAVO W	*COCKCRO W
*SNO W SHED	PHE W	STRE W	MINNO W	*FLYBLO W	COLESLA W
SNO W SHOE	PLE W	STRO W	MORRO W	*FOREPA W	*CROSSBO W
SNO W SUIT	PLO W	THRA W	NARRO W	FRETSA W	CURASSO W
*STO W A WAY	PRO W	THRE W	NEPHE W	*HACKSA W	DISALLO W
SUB W ORLD	SCO W	THRO W	*PA W PA W	HANDSA W	DISENDO W
SUN W ARDS	SHA W	VROU W	PILLO W	HOOSGO W	*FENCERO W
THA W LESS	SHE W	W IDO W	PITSA W	*JACKDA W	*FEVERFE W
THE W LESS	SKE W	BARLO W	*PO W WO W	*LOCKJA W	*FOOFARA W
THO W LESS	SLA W	BARRO W	REAVO W	LONGBO W	*FOREKNO W
TRA W LNET	SLE W	BASHA W	RECHE W	*LO W BRO W	*FORESHO W
TRO W ELER	SLO W	BELLO W	REDRA W	MISDRA W	*FURBELO W
TRO W SERS	SME W	BESNO W	REFLE W	MISGRO W	*GANGPLO W
*TRY W ORKS	SNA W	BESTO W	REFLO W	*MISKNO W	*HA W KSHA W
*VIE W DATA	SNO W	BILLO W	REGLO W	MISTBO W	*HEDGERO W
VIE W IEST	SPE W	BORRO W	REGRE W	MOONBO W	*HIGHBRO W
VIE W LESS	STA W	BURRO W	RESHO W	*PRESHO W	*HONEYDE W
*CLA W LIKE	STE W	BYELA W	REVIE W	*PREVIE W	*HOOSEGO W
	STO W	CALLO W	RIPSA W	*PURVIE W	*KICKSHA W
BLA W	THA W	CASHA W	SALLO W	RAINBO W	*LOBBYGO W
BLO W	THE W	CASHE W	SEESA W	REENDO W	*MACCABA W
BRA W	TRO W	CURFE W	SHADO W	*RIKSHA W	*MACKINA W
BRE W	VIE W	CURLE W	SORRO W	RINGTA W	*MISTHRO W
BRO W	VRO W	CUSHA W	SUNBO W	*SALCHO W	*PEEPSHO W
CHA W	W HE W	FALLO W	SUNDE W	SEMIRA W	*POSTSHO W
CHE W	BEDE W	FARRO W	TALLO W	SHALLO W	REREVIE W
CHO W	BELO W	FELLO W	W ALLO W	SPARRO W	*RICKSHA W
CLA W	BYLA W	*FOGBO W	W ARSA W	SUNGLO W	*ROADSHO W
CLE W	CAHO W	FOLLO W	W ILLO W	S WALLO W	*ROUGHHE W
CRA W	KOTO W	FURRO W	W INDO W	TRISHA W	*SCOFFLA W
CRE W	MACA W	GEEGA W	W INNO W	*VITCHE W	*SETSCRE W
CRO W	MIAO W	GE W GA W	YARRO W	*W HIPSA W	*SHADBLO W
DHO W	NOHO W	*GUFFA W	YELLO W	*W HITLO W	*SIDESHO W
DRA W	PAPA W	HALLO W	*BACKSA W	W INDRO W	*SNO W PLO W
DRE W	PILA W	HARRO W	*BESHRE W	*W INGBO W	*SOUTHPA W
FLA W	PSHA W	*HAYMO W	BESTRE W	*BACKFLO W	TELEVIE W
FLE W	RENE W	*HEEHA W	BESTRO W	BEDSTRA W	TOMORRO W
FLO W	RESA W	HOLLO W	*BUCKSA W	BUNGALO W	*WILLIWA W
FRO W	RESE W	*JIGSA W	CATCLA W	CARASSO W	*WILLY WA W
GLO W	RESO W	*KO W TO W	CATSPA W	*CHAINSA W	*W INDFLA W
GNA W	SCRE W	MALLO W	CORNRO W		*W IREDRA W
GRE W	SERO W				*W ITHDRA W

X

XYST	XENON	*XYLAN	*XYLENE	*XYSTOS	*XANTHIN
*XEBEC	XERIC	*XYLEM	*XYLOID	*XYSTUS	*XERARCH
XENIA	*XEROX	*XYLOL	*XYLOSE	*XANTHAN	XEROSIS
XENIC	XERUS	*XYLYL	*XYSTER	*XANTHIC	*XIPHOID

*XYLIDIN	SE X TET	SE X TILE	FAU X	*COCCY X	*COANNE X
*XANTHATE	SE X TON	*SI X FOLD	FLA X	*COMMI X	*COMPLE X
*XANTHEIN	SE X UAL	SI X TEEN	FLE X	*CONVE X	*CONFLU X
*XANTHENE	*TA X EME	*SI X THLY	FLU X	*CORTE X	*FEEDBO X
*XANTHINE	TA X ITE	*TA X ABLE	HOA X	*COWPO X	*FIREBO X
*XANTHOMA	*TA X MAN	*TA X ICAB	*JIN X	*DIPLE X	*FLUMMO X
*XANTHONE	TO X INE	*TA X IMAN	LYN X	*DUPLE X	*FOWLPO X
*XANTHOUS	TO X OID	*TA X IWAY	MIN X	*FORNI X	*GEARBO X
*XENOGAMY	TU X EDO	TA X LESS	PRE X	*HALLU X	*GRAVLA X
*XENOGENY	*WA X IER	*TA X PAID	ROU X	*HATBO X	*HELLBO X
*XENOLITH	*WA X ILY	*TA X WISE	BEAU X	*HOTBO X	*HOMOSE X
*XEROSERB	*WA X ING	*TA X YING	*BEMI X	*LARYN X	*JUKEBO X
*XYLIDINE	*BO X FISH	TE X TILE	BORA X	*LUMMO X	*LOCKBO X
*XYLOCARP	*BO X HAUL	TE X TUAL	CALI X	*MASTI X	*MAILBO X
*XYLOTOMY	*BO X IEST	TE X TURE	*CALY X	*MATRI X	*MINIMA X
	*BO X LIKE	*TO X EMIA	CARE X	*MENIN X	*NARTHE X
*DE X Y	*BO X WOOD	*TO X ICAL	*CIME X	NONTA X	*PACKWA X
*PI X Y	*CO X ALGY	*VE X EDLY	*CODE X	*PA X WA X	*PANCHA X
DE X IE	*CO X COMB	*WA X BILL	*COMI X	*PEGBO X	*PARADO X
*FI X IT	*DE X TRAL	*WA X IEST	CULE X	*PHENI X	*PEMPHI X
LE X IS	*DE X TRIN	*WA X LIKE	*CYLI X	*PICKA X	*PERPLE X
PI X EL	*DE X TRAN	*WA X WEED	DESE X	*POLEA X	*PHALAN X
*BO X CAR	*FI X EDLY	*WA X WING	DETO X	*POLLE X	*PHARYN X
*BO X FUL	*FI X INGS	*WA X WORK	*DEWA X	*PREFI X	*PHOENI X
*BO X IER	*FI X TUTE	*WA X WORM	GALA X	*PREMI X	*PILLBO X
*BO X ING	*FO X FIRE	*BO X BOARD	*HAPA X	*PRETA X	*POSTBO X
DE X IES	*FO X FISH	*PI X INESS	*HELI X	*PROLI X	*POSTFI X
DE X TER	*FO X HOLE	*SI X TYISH	*HYRA X	*REFLE X	*POSTTA X
DE X TRO	*FO X HUNT	*DEO X Y	*KYLI X	*REFLU X	*PRINCO X
*FI X ATE	*FO X IEST	DEI X IS	LATE X	*SCOLE X	*REAFFI X
*FI X ITY	*FO X LIKE	DIO X AN	MIRE X	*SILVE X	*REANNE X
*FI X URE	*FO X SKIN	DIO X IN	MURE X	*SKYBO X	*RECTRI X
*FO X ILY	*FO X TAIL	*PLE X AL	*PHLO X	*SMILA X	*REINDE X
*FO X ING	*FO X TROT	*COE X TEND	RADI X	*SPADI X	*SALPIN X
*FO X TER	*HE X AGON	*FLA X SEED	REDO X	*SPHIN X	*SALTBO X
*HE X ADE	*HE X APLA	*FLE X AGON	REDU X	STORA X	*SANDBO X
*HE X ANE	*HE X APOD	*FLE X IBLE	*REFI X	*STYRA X	*SIMPLE X
*HE X ONE	*HE X EREI	*FLE X TIME	RELA X	*SUBFI X	*SOAPBO X
*HE X OSE	*HE X OSAN	*FLE X UOSE	REME X	*SUFFI X	*SONOVO X
*LA X ITY	LA X NESS	*FLE X UOUS	REMI X	SURTA X	*SPANDE X
*LE X EME	*LE X ICAL	*FLU X GATE	RETA X	*SYNTA X	*TECTRI X
LU XATE	*LE X ICON	*GLO X INIA	*REWA X	*SYRIN X	*TOOLBO X
*LU X URY	*MA X ILLA	*PRO X EMIC	SILE X	*TEABO X	*TORTRI X
*MA X IMA	*MA X IMAL	*PRO X IMAL	TELE X	*THORA X	*TRIPLE X
*MA X IXE	*MA X IMUM	*QUI X OTIC	*VARI X	*VERNI X	*TUBIFE X
*MY X OID	*MA X WELL	*QUI X OTRY	*X ERO X	*VERTE X	*WOADWA X
*MY X OMA	*MI X TURE	*REE X PORT	*BANJA X	*VERTE X	*WOODBO X
*PA X WA X	NO X IOUS	*REE X POSE	*BIFLE X	*VOLVO X	*WOODWA X
*SA X ONY	*PY X IDES		*BOLLI X	*VORTE X	*WORKBO X
SE X IER	*SA X HORN	BOA X	*BOLLO X	*BANDBO X	*BICONVE X
*SE X ILY	*SA X TUBA	CAL X	*BOMBA X	*BEESWA X	*BORDEAU X
*SE X ISM	SE X IEST	COA X	*BOMBY X	*BOOMBO X	*BREADBO X
SE X IST	SE X LESS	CRU X	*CAUDE X	*BROADA X	*CICATRI X
*SE X POT	SE X TAIN	DOU X	*CERVI X	*CARAPA X	*CRUCIPI X
SE X TAN	SE X TANT	FAL X	*CLIMA X	*CASHBO X	*CURTALA X
				*COALBO X	

*FOURPLE X	*MICROLU X	*QUADPLE X	*SNUFFBO X	*SUPERSE X	*TRANSFI X
*HARUSPE X	*MILLILU X	*QUINCUN X	*SOUNDBO X	*SUPERTA X	*VIDEOTE X
*HERETRI X	*PARALLA X	*SARDONY X	*SPINIFE X	*SWEATBO X	
*HERITRI X	*PONTIFE X	*SAUCEBO X	*SUBINDE X	*SWINEPO X	
*MATCHBO X	*PRECIEU X	*SMALLPO X	*SUPERFI X	*TOADFLA X	

Y

YACK	YOWL	YOWIE	YONKER	*YARMELKE	G Y VE
YAFF	YUAN	YUCCA	YOUPON	*YARMULKE	H Y LA
YAGI	YUCA	*YUCCH	YOWLER	*YATAGHAN	H Y MN
YALD	YUCH	*YUCKY	YTTRIA	*YAWMETER	H Y PO
YANG	YUCK	YULAN	YUPPIE	YEANLING	H Y TE
YANK	YUGA	*YUMMY	*YACHTER	*YEARBOOK	*K Y AK
YARD	YULE	YUPON	*YAMALKA	YEARLIES	K Y AR
YARE	YURT	YABBER	*YAMULKA	YEARLING	K Y AT
YARN	YWIS	*YAKKER	*YAPPING	YEARLONG	K Y TE
YAUD	YACHT	YAMMER	YARDAGE	YEARNING	L Y NX
YAUP	YAGER	*YANQUI	YARDARM	YEASAYER	L Y RE
YAWL	YAHOO	YANTRA	YARDMAN	*YEOMANRY	L Y SE
YAWN	YAIRD	*YAPOCK	*YASHMAC	*YESHIVAH	M Y NA
YAWP	YAMEN	YAPPED	*YASHMAK	YESTREEN	P Y IC
YEAH	YAMUN	YAPPER	YATAGAN	YODELLER	P Y IN
YEAN	YAPOK	YARNER	*YAWPING	*YOGHOURT	P Y RE
YEAR	YAPON	YARROW	*YCLEPED	*YOKELESS	R Y KE
YECH	YAULD	*YASMAK	YEALING	*YOKELISH	R Y ND
YEGG	YEARN	YATTER	YEAREND	*YOKEMATE	R Y OT
YELD	YEAST	YAUPER	YEARNER	*YOKOZUNA	S Y BO
YELK	*YECCH	YAUPON	YEGGMAN	*YOUNGISH	S Y CE
YELL	*YECHY	YAUTIA	*YELLOWY	YOURSELF	S Y KE
YELP	YENTA	YAWNER	*YESHIVA	*YOUTHFUL	S Y LI
YERK	YENTE	YAWPER	YESSING	YTTERBIA	S Y NC
YETI	YERBA	YCLEPT	YESTERN	YULETIDE	S Y NE
YETT	*YEUKY	YEARLY	YIELDER	YODELLING	S Y PH
YEUK	YIELD	YEASTY	*YIPPING		T Y EE
YILL	YIKES	YEELIN	YODELER	B Y RE	T Y ER
YIPE	YINCE	YELLER	YOGHURT	B Y RL	T Y KE
YIRD	YIPES	YELLOW	YOUNGER	B Y TE	T Y NE
YIRR	YIRTH	YELPER	YOUNKER	C Y AN	T Y PE
YLEM	YOBBO	YEOMAN	*YOYTHEN	C Y MA	T Y PO
YOCK	YODEL	YESSED	YPERITE	C Y ME	T Y PP
YODH	YOGEE	YESSES	YTTRIUM	C Y ST	T Y PY
YOGA	YOGIC	YESTER	*YACHTING	D Y AD	T Y RE
YOGH	YOGIN	YIPPED	*YACHTMAN	D Y ER	T Y RO
YOGI	YOKEL	YIPPEE	*YAHOOISM	D Y KE	*W Y CH
YOKE	*YOLKY	YIPPIE	*YAHRZEIT	D Y NE	W Y LE
YOLK	YOUNG	YODLER	*YAKITORI	F Y CE	W Y ND
YOND	YOURN	YOGINI	*YAMMERER	F Y KE	W Y NN
YONI	YOURS	YOGURT	*YARDBIRD	G Y BE	W Y TE
YORE	YOUSE	*YOICKS	YARDLAND	G Y RE	X Y ST
YOUR	YOUTH	YOKING	*YARDWAND	G Y RI	*Z Y ME
YOWE		YONDER	*YARDWORK	G Y RO	B Y LAW

*B Y WA Y	P Y RAN	GL Y COL	*SK Y HOO	FE Y NESS	*PH Y TANE
C Y ANO	P Y RTC	*GL Y CYL	SK Y LIT	*FL Y ABLE	*PH Y TOID
C Y CAD	*P Y XIS	HA Y ING	*SK Y MAN	*FL Y AWA Y	*PL Y WOOD
C Y CAS	S Y CEE	*HA Y MOW	*SK Y WA Y	*FL Y BELT	*PR Y THEE
C Y CLE	S Y LPH	*HE Y DA Y	ST Y LAR	*FL Y BLOW	PS Y CHIC
C Y CLO	S Y LVA	*HE Y DE Y	ST Y LER	*FL Y BOAT	PS Y LLID
C Y DER	S Y NCH	HO Y DEN	ST Y LET	*FL Y LEAF	PT Y ALIN
*C Y LIX	S Y NOD	*JA Y GEE	ST Y LUS	FL Y LESS	*RA Y COCK
C Y MAR	S Y NTH	*JA Y VEE	ST Y MIE	*FL Y OVER	RA Y LESS
C Y MOL	S Y REN	*JO Y FUL	*ST Y RAX	*FL Y PAST	RA Y LIKE
C Y NIC	S Y RUP	*JO Y OUS	*TH Y ME Y	FL Y TIER	RA Y WIRE
C Y TON	S Y SOP	*JO Y POP	*TH Y MIC	FL Y TING	RE Y NARD
D Y ING	T Y PED	KA Y LES	TH Y MOL	*FL Y TRAP	RO Y ALL Y
D Y NEL	T Y ING	*KE Y PAD	TH Y MUS	GA Y NESS	RO Y ALT Y
F Y TTE	T Y PAL	KE Y SET	TH Y RSE	GL Y CINE	RO Y STER
G Y PS Y	T Y PEY	*KE Y WA Y	TO Y ISH	*GL Y PTIC	*SC Y PHUS
G Y RAL	T Y PIC	LA Y MAN	TR Y OUT	*GR Y PHON	*SH Y LOCK
G Y RON	T Y THE	*LA Y OFF	TR Y STE	GU Y LINE	SH Y NESS
G Y RUS	V Y ING	*MA Y DA Y	TU Y ERE	*HA Y COCK	SH Y STER
H Y DRA	*X Y LAN	*MA Y FL Y	VO Y AGE	*HA Y FORK	*SK Y DIVE
H Y DRO	*X Y LEM	*MA Y HAP	VO Y EUR	HA Y LAGE	*SK Y JACK
H Y ENA	*X Y LOL	*MA Y HEM	*WH Y DAH	*HA Y LOFT	*SK Y LARK
H Y ING	*X Y LYL	*MA Y POP	*WA Y LA Y	*HA Y RACK	SK Y LINE
H Y MEN	BA Y AMO	NO Y ADE	*ZO Y SIA	HA Y RICK	*SK Y PHOS
H Y PER	BA Y ARD	*PA Y DA Y	BA Y ONET	HA Y RIDE	SK Y SAIL
*H Y PHA	*BE Y LIK	PA Y NIM	*BA Y WOOD	HA Y SEED	*SK Y WALK
*H Y RAX	BE Y OND	*PA Y OFF	*BO Y CHIK	*HA Y WARD	*SK Y WARD
H Y SON	BO Y ARD	PA Y OLA	BO Y COTT	*JA Y BIRD	SL Y NESS
*K Y ACK	BO Y ISH	PA Y OUT	*BO Y HOOD	*JA Y WALK	SO Y BEAN
*K Y LIX	BR Y ON Y	PE Y OTE	*BU Y BACK	*JO Y ANCE	*SO Y MILK
K Y RIE	BU Y OUT	PE Y OTL	CA Y ENNE	*JO Y LESS	ST Y GIAN
*K Y THE	CA Y MAN	PH Y LAE	*CH Y MIST	*JO Y RIDE	ST Y LATE
L Y ARD	CA Y USE	PH Y LAR	*CH Y MOUS	*KA Y AKER	ST Y LING
L Y ART	*CH Y MIC	PH Y LLO	CL Y PEUS	*KE Y CARD	ST Y LISE
L Y ASE	CO Y DOG	PH Y LON	CL Y STER	*KE Y HOLE	ST Y LISH
L Y CEA	CO Y ISH	*PH Y LUM	CO Y NESS	KE Y LESS	ST Y LIST
L Y CEE	CO Y OTE	*PH Y SED	*CR Y BAB Y	KE Y NOTE	ST Y LITE
L Y ING	CO Y POU	PH Y SES	CR Y OGEN	KE Y STER	*ST Y LIZE
*L Y MPH	CR Y PTO	*PH Y SIC	*CR Y PTIC	*KE Y WORD	ST Y LOID
L Y NCH	DA Y BED	PH Y SIS	CR Y STAL	*KR Y PTON	ST Y PSIS
L Y RIC	*DA Y FL Y	PH Y TIN	*DA Y BOOK	*LA Y AWA Y	ST Y PTIC
L Y SIN	DO Y LE Y	PH Y TON	*DA Y GLOW	LA Y ETTE	ST Y RENE
L Y SIS	DR Y ISH	PR Y PAN	DA Y LIL Y	LA Y OVER	*TH Y MIER
L Y SSA	DR Y LOT	*PS Y CHE	DA Y LONG	LO Y ALL Y	*TH Y MINE
L Y TIC	*FL Y BO Y	*PS Y CHO	DA Y MARE	LO Y ALT Y	TH Y ROID
L Y TTA	FL Y ING	PS Y LLA	DA Y ROOM	*MA Y BUSH	TH Y RSUS
*M Y OP Y	FL Y MAN	PS Y WAR	DA Y SIDE	MA Y ORES	*TH Y SELF
M Y SID	*FL Y OFF	RH Y MER	DA Y SMAN	*MA Y WEED	TO Y LESS
*M Y TH Y	*FL Y SCH	*RH Y THM	DA Y STAR	PA Y ABLE	TO Y LIKE
N Y ALA	*FL Y WA Y	RH Y TON	DA Y TIME	*PA Y BACK	*TO Y SHOP
N Y LON	GA Y ET Y	SA Y ING	*DA Y WORK	PA Y LOAD	TR Y PSIN
*N Y MPH	GE Y SER	SA Y YID	DO Y ENNE	PA Y MENT	TR Y SAIL
*P Y GM Y	GL Y CAN	SC Y THE	DR Y LAND	PA Y ROLL	TR Y STER
P Y LON	GL Y CIN	*SK Y BOX	DR Y NESS	PE Y TRAL	VO Y AGER
P Y OID		*SK Y CAP	DR Y WALL	PE Y TREL	*WA Y BILL

WA Y LESS	*GAN Y MEDE	*POL Y TENE	DUL Y	PLO Y	*ZAN Y
WA Y SIDE	*GRAY BACK	*POL Y TENY	DUT Y	POG Y	BADD Y
*WA Y WARD	*GRA Y FISH	*POL Y TYPE	FLA Y	POK Y	BADL Y
*WA Y WORN	GRA Y LING	POL Y URIA	FLE Y	POL Y	*BAFF Y
*WR Y NECK	GRA Y MAIL	*POL Y ZOAN	FOG Y	PON Y	BAGG Y
WR Y NESS	GRA Y NESS	*POL Y ZOIC	*FOX Y	POS Y	BALD Y
*Y O Y THEN	GRE Y NESS	PON Y TAIL	*FOZ Y	PRA Y	BALK Y
*BAB Y HOOD	*HOKY POKY	*QUA Y SIDE	FRA Y	PRE Y	BALL Y
BAR Y TONE	*HOL Y TIDE	*REC Y CLER	FUM Y	PUN Y	BALM Y
*BIC Y CLER	*KAL Y PTRA	*RUB Y LIKE	FUR Y	*QUA Y	BAND Y
*BIC Y CLIC	*KAR Y OTIN	*SPH Y GMUS	GAB Y	*Q UEY	BANT Y
BOD Y SUIT	*LAD Y BIRD	SPR Y NESS	GAM Y	RAC Y	BARK Y
*BOD Y SURF	*LAD Y FISH	STA Y SAIL	GAP Y	REL Y	BARM Y
*BODY WORK	*LAD Y HOOD	*SWAY BACK	GLE Y	RIM Y	BARN Y
*BUO Y ANCE	*LAD Y LIKE	TID Y TIPS	GOB Y	ROP Y	BASS Y
*BUO Y ANCY	*LAD Y LOVE	*WHE Y FACE	GOR Y	ROS Y	BATT Y
*BUS Y BODY	*LAD Y PALM	*WHE Y LIKE	GRA Y	RUB Y	BAWD Y
BUS Y NESS	*LAD Y SHIP		GRE Y	RUL Y	BAWT Y
*BUS Y WORK	*LEC Y THIS	BAB Y	*HAZ Y	SAG Y	BEAD Y
BUT Y LATE	*LEC Y THUS	BEV Y	HOL Y	SCR Y	BEAK Y
BUT Y LENE	*LEK Y THOS	BOD Y	HOM Y	SEX Y	BEAM Y
BUT Y RATE	*LEK Y THUS	BOG Y	JOE Y	SHA Y	BEEF Y
BUT Y ROUS	*MAN Y FOLD	BON Y	*JOK Y	*SIZ Y	BEER Y
*CAL Y CATE	*MAR Y JANE	*BOX Y	JUR Y	SLA Y	BEIG Y
*CAL Y CINE	*MOL Y BDIC	BRA Y	LAC Y	SPA Y	BELA Y
*CAL Y CULI	*PLA Y TIME	BUO Y	LAD Y	SPR Y	BELL Y
*CAL Y PTER	*PLA Y BACK	BUR Y	LAK Y	STA Y	BEND Y
*CAL Y PTRA	*PLA Y BILL	BUS Y	*LAZ Y	STE Y	BENN Y
*CAP Y BARA	*PLA Y BOOK	CAG Y	LEV Y	SWA Y	BERR Y
*CAR Y ATIC	*PLA Y DOWN	CAK Y	LIL Y	THE Y	BIAL Y
CAR Y ATID	PLA Y GIRL	CAV Y	LIM Y	TID Y	BIDD Y
CAR Y OTIN	PLA Y GOER	CHA Y	LIN Y	TIN Y	*BIFF Y
*CIT Y FIED	PLA Y LAND	CIT Y	LOG Y	TIV Y	BIGL Y
*CIT Y WARD	PLA Y LESS	CLA Y	LOR Y	TOB Y	BILG Y
*CIT Y WIDE	*PLA Y LIKE	CLO Y	LUN Y	TOD Y	BILL Y
*CLA Y BANK	*PLA Y MATE	COL Y	MAN Y	TON Y	BITS Y
*CLA Y LIKE	*PLA Y ROOM	CON Y	*MAZ Y	TOR Y	BITT Y
*CLA Y MORE	PLA Y SUIT	COP Y	MIR Y	TOW Y	BLIM Y
*CLA Y WARE	*PLA Y WEAR	COR Y	MIT Y	TRA Y	BLOW Y
*COPY BOOK	*POL Y BIRD	COW Y	MOL Y	TRE Y	BLUE Y
*COP Y DESK	POL Y GALA	*COZ Y	MON Y	TRO Y	BOBB Y
*COP Y EDIT	*POLY GAMY	DAV Y	MOP Y	T Y P Y	BOGE Y
*COP Y HOLD	POL Y GENE	DEF Y	NAN Y	VAR Y	BOGG Y
*COP Y READ	POL Y GLOT	DEM Y	NAR Y	VER Y	BONE Y
*COR Y BANT	*POL Y GONY	DEN Y	NAV Y	VIN Y	BONN Y
*COR Y PHEE	*POLY GYNY	DEW Y	NIX Y	WAD Y	BOOB Y
COT Y LOID	*POL Y MATH	*DEX Y	NOS Y	WAL Y	BOOG Y
*CRA Y FISH	*POL Y PARY	DID Y	PAL Y	WAN Y	BOOM Y
*DIC Y CLIC	*POL Y PIDE	DOG Y	PAT Y	WAR Y	BOOT Y
*DID Y MIUM	*POL Y PNEA	DOP Y	PIL Y	WAV Y	*BOOZ Y
*DID Y MOUS	*POL Y POD Y	DOR Y	PIN Y	*WAX Y	BOSK Y
*DID Y NAMY	*POL Y POID	DOT Y	PIP Y	WHE Y	BOSS Y
*DIH Y BRID	*POL Y PORE	*DOX Y	PIT Y	WIL Y	BOTH Y
*DIH Y DRIC	*POL Y SEM Y	*DOZ Y	*PIX Y	WIN Y	BOUS Y
*DIZ Y GOUS	*POL Y SOME	DRA Y	PLA Y	WIR Y	BRAK Y

*BRAX Y	*COZE Y	DOBB Y	FLAW Y	GOOE Y	HOOL Y
BRIN Y	*CRAZ Y	DOGE Y	*FLAX Y	GOOF Y	*HOPP Y
BROS Y	CREP Y	DOGG Y	*FLUK Y	GOON Y	HORN Y
BUBB Y	CRON Y	DOIL Y	FLUT Y	GOOP Y	HORS Y
BUDD Y	CUBB Y	DOLL Y	*FL Y B Y	GOOS Y	HOTL Y
*BUFF Y	CUDD Y	DONS Y	FOAM Y	GORS Y	*HUBB Y
BUGG Y	CULL Y	DOOL Y	FOGE Y	GOUT Y	*HUFF Y
BULG Y	CUMM Y	DOOM Y	FOGG Y	GRAP Y	*HULK Y
BULL Y	CUPP Y	*DOOZ Y	*FOLK Y	GRAV Y	*HUMP Y
BUMP Y	CURD Y	DOPE Y	FOLL Y	GRIM Y	*HUNK Y
BUNN Y	CURL Y	DORK Y	FOOT Y	GRIP Y	HURL Y
BURL Y	CURR Y	DORM Y	FORA Y	GULF Y	*HUSK Y
BURR Y	CURV Y	DORT Y	FORB Y	GULL Y	HUSS Y
BUSB Y	CUSH Y	DOTT Y	*FORK Y	GULP Y	*JACK Y
BUSH Y	CUTE Y	DOUG Y	FORT Y	GUMM Y	*JAGG Y
BUST Y	CUTT Y	DOWD Y	FUBS Y	GUNN Y	*JAMM Y
BUTT Y	DADD Y	DOWN Y	FUGG Y	GUPP Y	*JANT Y
*B Y WA Y	*DAFF Y	DOWR Y	FULL Y	GURR Y	*JAZZ Y
CABB Y	DAIL Y	DO Y L Y	*FUNK Y	GUSH Y	*JELL Y
CADD Y	DAIR Y	DRIL Y	FUNN Y	GUSS Y	*JEMM Y
CADG Y	DAIS Y	DR Y L Y	FURR Y	GUST Y,	*JENN Y
CAGE Y	DALL Y	DUCH Y	*FURZ Y	GUTS Y	*JERK Y
CAKE Y	DAND Y	*DUCK Y	FUSS Y	GUTT Y	*JERR Y
CAMP Y	DARK Y	DUDD Y	FUST Y	G Y PS Y	*JETT Y
CAND Y	DASH Y	DULL Y	*FUZZ Y	HAIR Y	*JIFF Y
CANN Y	DAUB Y	DUMM Y	GABB Y	*HAMM Y	*JIMM Y
CANT Y	DEAR Y	DUMP Y	GAIL Y	HAND Y	*JIMP Y
CARN Y	DECA Y	DUNG Y	GALL Y	*HANK Y	*JIVE Y
CARR Y	DECO Y	DUST Y	GAMA Y	HAPL Y	*JOLL Y
CASK Y	DECR Y	FADD Y	GAME Y	*HAPP Y	*JOLT Y
CATT Y	DEED Y	FAER Y	GAMM Y	HARD Y	*JOTT Y
*CHEV Y	DEIF Y	FAIR Y	GAPP Y	HARP Y	*JOWL Y
*CHEW Y	DEIT Y	*FAKE Y	GASS Y	HARR Y	*JUIC Y
*CHIV Y	DELA Y	FANC Y	GAUD Y	HEAV Y	*JUMP Y
*CHOK Y	DELL Y	FANN Y	*GAUZ Y	HEDG Y	*JUNK Y
CISS Y	*DEOX Y	FARC Y	*GAWK Y	HEFT Y	*JUTT Y
*CIVV Y	DERA Y	FATL Y	GAWS Y	*HEMP Y	KAUR Y
CLAR Y	DERB Y	FATT Y	GA Y L Y	HENR Y	KELL Y
COAL Y	DERR Y	FAWN Y	GEEK Y	HERB Y	KELP Y
COBB Y	DIAR Y	FELL Y	GEMM Y	HERR Y	KERR Y
*COCK Y	DICE Y	FENN Y	GERM Y	HILL Y	*KICK Y
COLL Y	*DICK Y	FERL Y	GIDD Y	HINN Y	KIDD Y
*COMF Y	DICT Y	FERN Y	GILL Y	*HIPP Y	KILT Y
CONE Y	DILL Y	FERR Y	GIMP Y	HISS Y	*KINK Y
CONK Y	DIML Y	FIER Y	GINN Y	HOAG Y	KISS Y
COOE Y	DING Y	FIFT Y	GIPS Y	HOAR Y	KITT Y
COOK Y	DINK Y	FILL Y	GIRL Y	*HOBB Y	*KOOK Y
COOL Y	DIPP Y	FILM Y	GLAD Y	*HOKE Y	LACE Y
CORB Y	DIRT Y	FINN Y	GLAR Y	HOLE Y	LAIT Y
CORK Y	DISH Y	FIRR Y	*GLAZ Y	HOME Y	LAMB Y
CORN Y	DITS Y	FISH Y	GLOR Y	HONE Y	LANK Y
COSE Y	DITT Y	FITL Y	GLUE Y	*HONK Y	LARD Y
COVE Y	*DITZ Y	*FIZZ Y	GODL Y	HOOD Y	LARK Y
COWR Y	*DIVV Y	*FLAK Y	GOLL Y	HOOE Y	LATH Y
CO Y LY	*DIZZ Y	FLAM Y	GOOD Y	*HOOK Y	*LAXL Y

LEAD Y	MIDD Y	NINN Y	*POCK Y	RESA Y	SISS Y
LEAF Y	***MIFF Y**	**NIPP Y**	**PODG Y**	RETR Y	***SIXT Y**
LEAK Y	**MILK Y**	**NITT Y**	POES Y	**RIBB Y**	SKIE Y
LEAR Y	**MILT Y**	**NOBB Y**	POGE Y	**RIDG Y**	***SK Y E Y**
LEAV Y	**MING Y**	**NOBL Y**	POKE Y	RILE Y	SLAT Y
LEDG Y	**MINN Y**	**NODD Y**	**POPP Y**	RISK Y	SLIL Y
LEER Y	**MINT Y**	NOIS Y	POPS Y	***RITZ Y**	**SLIM Y**
LEFT Y	**MIRK Y**	**NOOK Y**	PORG Y	**ROCK Y**	**SMOK Y**
LEGG Y	**MISS Y**	NOSE Y	**PORK Y**	ROIL Y	SNAK Y
LIMB Y	**MIST Y**	NOWA Y	PORN Y	**ROOK Y**	**SNOW Y**
LIND Y	**MOGG Y**	**NUBB Y**	POTS Y	**ROOM Y**	**SOAP Y**
LINE Y	**MOLD Y**	NUTS Y	**POTT Y**	ROOT Y	**SODD Y**
LING Y	**MOLL Y**	**NUTT Y**	**POUT Y**	ROPE Y	**SOFT Y**
LINK Y	**MOMM Y**	**PADD Y**	***PREX Y**	**ROUP Y**	**SOGG Y**
LINT Y	**MONE Y**	**PALL Y**	PRIC Y	**ROWD Y**	SONL Y
LIPP Y	**MOOD Y**	**PALM Y**	PRIV Y	**RUDD Y**	**SONN Y**
LOAN Y	**MOON Y**	PALS Y	PROS Y	**RUGB Y**	SONS Y
LOBB Y	**MOOR Y**	PAND Y	***PROX Y**	**RUMM Y**	SOOE Y
LOFT Y	**MOPE Y**	PANS Y	***PUFF Y**	**RUNN Y**	SOOT Y
LOGG Y	**MORA Y**	**PANT Y**	**PUGG Y**	**RUNT Y**	**SOPH Y**
LOLL Y	**MOSE Y**	**PAPP Y**	**PULP Y**	**RUSH Y**	**SOPP Y**
LOOB Y	**MOSS Y**	**PARD Y**	**PUNK Y**	**RUST Y**	SORR Y
LOOE Y	**MOTE Y**	**PARR Y**	**PUNN Y**	**RUTT Y**	**SOUP Y**
LOON Y	**MOTH Y**	**PART Y**	**PUNT Y**	SADL Y	SPAC Y
LOOP Y	**MOUS Y**	**PAST Y**	**PUPP Y**	**SAGG Y**	SPIC Y
LOPP Y	***MUCK Y**	PATL Y	PURS Y	SALL Y	SPIK Y
LORR Y	**MUDD Y**	PATS Y	PUSH Y	**SALT Y**	**SPIN Y**
LOSS Y	**MUGG Y**	**PATT Y**	PUSS Y	SAND Y	SPIR Y
LOUR Y	**MUHL Y**	***PAWK Y**	**PUTT Y**	**SAPP Y**	SPLA Y
LOUS Y	**MULE Y**	**PEAK Y**	***P Y GM Y**	**SARK Y**	SPRA Y
LOWL Y	**MUMM Y**	**PEAT Y**	***QUAK Y**	SASS Y	**SPUM Y**
LUCK Y	**MURK Y**	**PEAV Y**	***QUER Y**	SATA Y	STAG Y
LUMP Y	**MURR Y**	***PECK Y**	**RAGG Y**	SAUC Y	**STIM Y**
LUST Y	**MUSH Y**	PEER Y	RAIN Y	SAUR Y	STOG Y
MADL Y	**MUSK Y**	**PENN Y**	RALL Y	SAVO Y	STON Y
MALM Y	**MUSS Y**	PEON Y	**RAMM Y**	**SAVV Y**	STOR Y
MALT Y	**MUST Y**	**PEPP Y**	RAND Y	SCAL Y	STRA Y
MAME Y	***MUZZ Y**	**PERD Y**	RANG Y	SCAR Y	STRO Y
MAMM Y	***M Y OP Y**	**PERK Y**	RASP Y	**SEAM Y**	STUD Y
MANG Y	***M Y TH Y**	**PERR Y**	**RATT Y**	**SEDG Y**	**ST Y M Y**
MANL Y	**NAGG Y**	**PESK Y**	RAWL Y	SEED Y	SUDS Y
MARL Y	**NANN Y**	**PEST Y**	READ Y	SEEL Y	**SULK Y**
MARR Y	**NAPP Y**	**PETT Y**	REBU Y	**SEEP Y**	SULL Y
MARV Y	**NARK Y**	**PHON Y**	REDL Y	SEPO Y	**SUNN Y**
MASH Y	**NAST Y**	***PICK Y**	REDR Y	SERR Y	**SURF Y**
MASS Y	**NATT Y**	PIET Y	REED Y	**SHAD Y**	SURG Y
MATE Y	**NAVV Y**	**PIGG Y**	**REEF Y**	***SHAK Y**	SURL Y
MEAL Y	**NEED Y**	**PIGM Y**	**REEK Y**	SHAL Y	**SWAM Y**
MEAN Y	**NELL Y**	PINE Y	REFL Y	SHIL Y	**TABB Y**
MEAT Y	**NERB Y**	**PINK Y**	REFR Y	**SHIN Y**	**TACK Y**
MEIN Y	**NERD Y**	**PINN Y**	**REIF Y**	**SHOW Y**	**TAFF Y**
MERC Y	**NETT Y**	**PITH Y**	REKE Y	**SH Y LY**	**TALK Y**
MERR Y	**NEWL Y**	**PLAT Y**	RELA Y	**SILK Y**	TALL Y
MESH Y	**NEWS Y**	**PLOW Y**	REPA Y	SILL Y	**TAMM Y**
MESS Y	**NIFT Y**	**PLUM Y**	REPL Y	**SILT Y**	TANG Y

TANS Y	*WEBB Y	*BAWDR Y	*BRONZ Y	*CHUNK Y	CRUDD Y
TARD Y	WEDG Y	*BEACH Y	BROOD Y	CICEL Y	*CRUMB Y
TARR Y	WEED Y	BEAUT Y	BROOM Y	CITIF Y	*CRUMM Y
TART Y	WEEN Y	*BEECH Y	BROTH Y	*CLAMM Y	CRUST Y
TAST Y	WEEP Y	BELAD Y	BROWN Y	CLASS Y	CUDDL Y
TATT Y	WELL Y	BELFR Y	*BRUMB Y	CLA Y E Y	CULLA Y
TAWN Y	WENN Y	BENDA Y	BRUSH Y	CLERG Y	CURAC Y
TEAR Y	WETL Y	BETON Y	BR Y ON Y	*CLIFF Y	CURTL Y
TECH Y	WHIN Y	BETRA Y	*BUBBL Y	CLING Y	CURTS Y
TEDD Y	WHIT Y	BEWRA Y	*BUNCH Y	*CLIQU Y	CURVE Y
TEEN Y	WIDD Y	BIGAM Y	BURBL Y	CLODD Y	CUTES Y
TELL Y	WIFT Y	BINAR Y	BURLE Y	CLOGG Y	DAINT Y
TENT Y	WIGG Y	BIOPS Y	BUSBO Y	CLOTT Y	DAMPL Y
TERR Y	WILL Y	*BITCH Y	BUSIL Y	CLOUD Y	DARKE Y
TEST Y	*WIMP Y	*BLABB Y	*B Y PLA Y	*CLUBB Y	DARKL Y
THEW Y	WIND Y	BLAST Y	CAGIL Y	*CLUMP Y	DATAR Y
*TH Y M Y	WINE Y	BLEAR Y	CALOR Y	CLUMS Y	DAUBR Y
TINN Y	WING Y	BLENN Y	CANAR Y	*CLUNK Y	*DA Y FL Y
TIPP Y	WISP Y	BLIME Y	CANOP Y	*CODIF Y	DEADL Y
TIPS Y	WITH Y	*BLOCK Y	CARBO Y	*COGWA Y	DEAFL Y
TITT Y	WITT Y	BLOOD Y	CARNE Y	COLDL Y	DEARL Y
*TIZZ Y	*WOMB Y	BLOOE Y	CASEF Y	COLON Y	DEATH Y
TOAD Y	*WONK Y	BLOOM Y	*CATCH Y	COMED Y	DECUR Y
TODA Y	WOOD Y	BLOTT Y	CAUSE Y	COMEL Y	*DEEJA Y
TODD Y	WOOL Y	BLOUS Y	CAVIT Y	COMIT Y	DEEPL Y
TOFF Y	*WOOZ Y	*BLOWB Y	CELER Y	*COMPL Y	DEFRA Y
TOKA Y	WORD Y	BLOWS Y	*CHAFF Y	*CONCH Y	DENAR Y
TOMM Y	WORM Y	*BLOWZ Y	*CHALK Y	CONVE Y	DEPLO Y
TONE Y	WORR Y	BLUEL Y	CHALL Y	CONVO Y	DEPUT Y
TOWN Y	WUSS Y	BLUES Y	*CHAMM Y	*COOKE Y	DESCR Y
TRUL Y	*Y ECH Y	BLURR Y	*CHAMP Y	COOLL Y	*DESOX Y
TUBB Y	*Y EUK Y	BODIL Y	*CHANC Y	COROD Y	DHOOL Y
TUFT Y	*Y OLK Y	BOLSH Y	CHANT Y	COSIL Y	*DICKE Y
TUMM Y	*Y UCK Y	BOOGE Y	CHARR Y	COSTL Y	DIDDL Y
TUNN Y	*Y UMM Y	BOSOM Y	CHATT Y	COUNT Y	DIGAM Y
TURF Y	*ZAPP Y	BOTAN Y	*CHEEK Y	*COWBO Y	DIMIT Y
TUTT Y	*ZEST Y	*BOTCH Y	CHEER Y	*CRABB Y	DIMPL Y
TWIN Y	*ZINC Y	BOTFL Y	CHEES Y	*CRACK Y	DINGE Y
T Y PE Y	*ZING Y	BOUNC Y	CHERR Y	CRAFT Y	DINGH Y
VAST Y	*ZINK Y	BOUNT Y	CHERT Y	CRAGG Y	DINKE Y
VEAL Y	*ZIPP Y	BOWER Y	CHEST Y	*CRANK Y	DINKL Y
VEER Y	*ZLOT Y	BRAGG Y	*CHICL Y	CRANN Y	DIOEC Y
VEIN Y	*ZOOT Y	BRAIN Y	CHILL Y	*CRAPP Y	DIPOD Y
*VICH Y	BAILE Y	BRAND Y	*CHINK Y	CRAWL Y	DIREL Y
VIEW Y	*BAKER Y	BRANN Y	*CHIPP Y	*CREAK Y	DISMA Y
*WACK Y	BALDL Y	BRASH Y	*CHIRP Y	CREAM Y	*DJINN Y
WADD Y	BAREL Y	BRASS Y	CHITT Y	CREAS Y	DONKE Y
WALL Y	BARFL Y	BRATT Y	*CHIVV Y	CREEP Y	DOUBL Y
WANE Y	BARLE Y	BRAWL Y	*CHOKE Y	CREPE Y	DOUGH Y
WANL Y	BARON Y	BRAWN Y	CHOOS Y	*CRIKE Y	DOURL Y
WART Y	BASEL Y	BREAD Y	*CHOPP Y	*CRIMP Y	DOWER Y
WASH Y	BASIF Y	*BREEZ Y	*CHUBB Y	CRISP Y	DO Y LE Y
WASP Y	BASSL Y	*BRICK Y	*CHUCK Y	*CROAK Y	*DOZIL Y
WAVE Y	BATBO Y	BRION Y	*CHUFF Y	CROUP Y	DRABL Y
WEAR Y	*BAULK Y	BROLL Y	*CHUMM Y	*CROWD Y	*DRAFF Y

DRAFT Y	*FOLKS Y	GOODL Y	*HUBBL Y	LONGL Y	MUTIN Y
DRAGG Y	FONDL Y	GOOGL Y	*HUMBL Y	LOONE Y	NAMEL Y
DRAPE Y	FOOTS Y	GOONE Y	HUNGR Y	LORDL Y	NAPER Y
DRAWL Y	FOREB Y	GOOSE Y	HURLE Y	LOUDL Y	*NAZIF Y
DREAM Y	*FORWH Y	GORIL Y	HURRA Y	LOUNG Y	NEARB Y
DREGG Y	FOULL Y	GRABB Y	*JALOP Y	LOVEL Y	NEARL Y
DRESS Y	*FOXIL Y	GRAIN Y	*JANGL Y	LOWBO Y	NEATL Y
DRIFT Y	*FREAK Y	GRANN Y	*JAPER Y	LOWER Y	NEBUL Y
DRIPP Y	FREEL Y	GRASS Y	*JARVE Y	LUNAC Y	NETTL Y
DROLL Y	*FRENZ Y	GRA Y L Y	*JAUNT Y	*LUXUR Y	NICET Y
DROOP Y	FRETT Y	GREAS Y	*JERSE Y	MAGUE Y	NIDIF Y
DROPS Y	FRIAR Y	GREED Y	*JIGGL Y	MAINL Y	NIGHT Y
DROSK Y	FRILL Y	GREEN Y	*JIMIN Y	MALAD Y	NINET Y
DROSS Y	FRING Y	GREMM Y	*JINGL Y	*MAMME Y	NITER Y
DROWS Y	*FRISK Y	GRE Y L Y	*JITNE Y	MANGE Y	NOBOD Y
DRUGG Y	*FRIZZ Y	GRIPE Y	*JOCKE Y	MARBL Y	NONGA Y
DRUML Y	FROGG Y	GRIPP Y	*JOHNN Y	MARGA Y	NOSIL Y
DUALL Y	FROST Y	GRISL Y	*JOUNC Y	MARSH Y	NOTAR Y
DUMBL Y	*FROTH Y	GRITT Y	*JUNGL Y	MAUND Y	NOTIF Y
DUPER Y	*FROUZ Y	GROGG Y	*JUSTL Y	*MA Y DA Y	NUBBL Y
FAIRL Y	*FROWS Y	GROOV Y	KEENL Y	*MA Y FL Y	NUDIT Y
*FAKER Y	*FROWZ Y	GROUT Y	KERSE Y	*MAZIL Y	NUMBL Y
FEALT Y	FRUIT Y	GROWL Y	*KE Y WA Y	MEANL Y	*PACIF Y
*FECKL Y	*FRUMP Y	GRUBB Y	KIDNE Y	MEASL Y	*PACKL Y
FEIST Y	GADFL Y	*GRUFF Y	KINDL Y	*MEDFL Y	PAINT Y
FELON Y	GAIET Y	GRUMP Y	KINGL Y	MEDLE Y	PALEL Y
FERIT Y	GAINL Y	GRUNG Y	*KLUTZ Y	MEETL Y	PALTR Y
FIDDL Y	*GALAX Y	GUANA Y	*KNOBB Y	MELOD Y	PANFR Y
*FILTH Y	GALLE Y	GUILT Y	KNOLL Y	MEMOR Y	PANTR Y
FIRML Y	GAMEL Y	GULLE Y	KNOTT Y	*MICKE Y	*PAPAC Y
*FISHL Y	GAMIL Y	GURNE Y	KNURL Y	MIDDA Y	PAPER Y
*FITCH Y	GANGL Y	*HACKL Y	LACIL Y	*MIDWA Y	PARIT Y
*FIXIT Y	GANTR Y	HARDL Y	*LACKE Y	*MIGHT Y	PARLA Y
*FLABB Y	GARVE Y	HAULM Y	LAMEL Y	MILAD Y	PARLE Y
FLAGG Y	GASIF Y	*HAWKE Y	LANEL Y	MINIF Y	PAROD Y
*FLAKE Y	GA Y ET Y	*HAZIL Y	LASTL Y	MISER Y	PARTI Y
*FLAPP Y	GENTR Y	HEART Y	LATEL Y	MISLA Y	PASTR Y
*FLASH Y	GHOST Y	*HEATH Y	*LAXIT Y	MISSA Y	*PATCH Y
FLATL Y	GIGGL Y	HERES Y	*LAZIL Y	*MIZZL Y	*PA Y DA Y
*FLECK Y	GLADL Y	*HE Y DA Y	LEACH Y	*MODIF Y	*PEACH Y
FLEDG Y	GLAIR Y	*HE Y DE Y	LEALT Y	MOIET Y	PEARL Y
FLEEC Y	GLASS Y	*HICKE Y	LEEWA Y	*MONKE Y	PEAVE Y
*FLESH Y	GLEAM Y	*HIGHL Y	LEGAC Y	MONOD Y	*PEBBL Y
FLEUR Y	GLEET Y	*HOCKE Y	LENIT Y	MOOLE Y	PELTR Y
FLIMS Y	*GLITZ Y	HOLIL Y	LEVIT Y	MOPER Y	PENUR Y
FLINT Y	GLOBB Y	HOMEL Y	LIKEL Y	MOSTL Y	*PEROX Y
*FLIPP Y	GLOOM Y	HOMIL Y	LIMPL Y	MOTLE Y	PHONE Y
FLOUR Y	GLOPP Y	HOMIN Y	LIMPS Y	MOULD Y	PHOOE Y
*FLUFF Y	GLOSS Y	LINSE Y	MOUSE Y	PIDDL Y
*FLUKE Y	GLUMP Y	*HONKE Y	LINSE Y	MOUSE Y	PIDDL Y
*FLUNK Y	GNARL Y	*HOOKE Y	LITAN Y	MOUTH Y	PIGST Y
FLURR Y	GNATT Y	HOORA Y	LIVEL Y	MULLE Y	*PIMPL Y
FLUTE Y	GOBON Y	HORAR Y	LIVER Y	*MUMBL Y	PINER Y
*FLY BO Y	GOGGL Y	HORSE Y	LOGIL Y	*MURPH Y	*PINKE Y
*FL Y WA Y	GOODB Y	HOSTL Y	LOGWA Y	MURRE Y	*PINKL Y
		HOURL Y	LONEL Y	MUSCL Y	PIRAC Y

*PITCH Y	RASHL Y	*SCUZZ Y	SLOWL Y	SPORT Y	*TACKE Y
PLAGU Y	RATAN Y	SEAWA Y	SLUDG Y	SPOTT Y	TAMEL Y
PLASH Y	RATIF Y	SEEML Y	SLUIC Y	SPRUC Y	TANGL Y
PLENT Y	RATTL Y	SENAR Y	SLUMM Y	*SPUNK Y	TARTL Y
*PLISK Y	REALL Y	SENTR Y	SLURR Y	SPURR Y	TAUTL Y
PLOID Y	REALT Y	*SEXIL Y	SLUSH Y	STAGE Y	TAWDR Y
*PLUCK Y	REBOD Y	*SHABB Y	SLUTT Y	STAGG Y	TAWNE Y
*PLUMM Y	REBUR Y	SHAGG Y	SMARM Y	STAHL Y	TEAPO Y
PLUSH Y	RECOP Y	SHALE Y	SMART Y	STALK Y	TEENS Y
*POACH Y	REDBA Y	*SHAMM Y	SMEAR Y	STARR Y	TEPEF Y
POETR Y	REDEF Y	SHAMO Y	SMELL Y	STEAD Y	TERML Y
POINT Y	REDEN Y	SHAND Y	SMILE Y	STEAM Y	TETAN Y
*POKIL Y	REECH Y	SHANN Y	*SMIRK Y	STEEL Y	TETCH Y
POLIC Y	REMED Y	SHANT Y	SMITH Y	STEMM Y	THEOR Y
POLIT Y	REPLA Y	SHARP Y	SMOGG Y	*STICK Y	THERB Y
POORL Y	RESIN Y	SHEEN Y	*SMOKE Y	STILL Y	THINL Y
POPER Y	REVER Y	SHELL Y	SMUDG Y	STING Y	THIRT Y
PORTL Y	RHEUM Y	SHELT Y	SMUGL Y	STINK Y	THORN Y
POTBO Y	RICHL Y	*SHELV Y	SMUTT Y	STITH Y	THUSL Y
*POUCH Y	RIDLE Y	SHERR Y	SNAGG Y	*STOCK Y	*TH Y ME Y
PREPA Y	RIGHT Y	*SHIFT Y	SNAPP Y	STODG Y	TIDDL Y
*PREPP Y	RIPPL Y	*SHIMM Y	SNARK Y	STOGE Y	TIDIL Y
PRETT Y	ROPER Y	SHIND Y	SNARL Y	STONE Y	TIMEL Y
PRICE Y	ROPIL Y	SHINN Y	*SNAZZ Y	STORE Y	TINGL Y
*PRICK Y	ROSAR Y	SHIRT Y	SNEAK Y	STORM Y	TINIL Y
PRIML Y	ROSER Y	SHOAL Y	*SNEEZ Y	STOUR Y	TINKL Y
PRIOR Y	ROSIL Y	SHODD Y	*SNIFF Y	STRAW Y	TOAST Y
PRISS Y	ROSIN Y	SHORT Y	SNIPP Y	STRIP Y	TOMBO Y
PUDDL Y	ROTAR Y	*SICKL Y	SNOBB Y	STUBB Y	TOOTH Y
PUGGR Y	RUBBL Y	SIMON Y	SNOOP Y	STUDL Y	TOOTS Y
PULLE Y	*RUFFL Y	SIMPL Y	SNOOT Y	*STUFF Y	TOUCH Y
*PUNCH Y	RUMBL Y	SINEW Y	*SNOOZ Y	STUMP Y	TOUGH Y
PUNIL Y	RUMPL Y	SINGL Y	SNOTT Y	STURD Y	TOWER Y
*PUNKE Y	RUNWA Y	SKERR Y	SNOUT Y	SUBWA Y	TRASH Y
PUREL Y	SAFET Y	*SKIDD Y	SNUBB Y	SUDAR Y	TREAT Y
PURIF Y	SALAR Y	*SKIMP Y	*SNUFF Y	SUGAR Y	TREBL Y
PURIT Y	SALIF Y	SKINN Y	SNUGL Y	SULTR Y	TREND Y
PURPL Y	SANIT Y	*SKIVV Y	SODOM Y	SUNDR Y	TRESS Y
PURVE Y	SASHA Y	*SK Y WA Y	SOFTL Y	SUPPL Y	*TRICK Y
PUSLE Y	SATIN Y	SLAGG Y	SOLEL Y	SUREL Y	TRIGL Y
PUSSL Y	SAVOR Y	SLANG Y	SOREL Y	SURET Y	TRILB Y
*QUAGG Y	*SAWFL Y	SLANT Y	SOURL Y	SURRE Y	TRIML Y
*QUALM Y	SAWNE Y	SLATE Y	SPACE Y	SURVE Y	TRIPL Y
*QUARR Y	*SAXON Y	SLAVE Y	*SPARK Y	*SWABB Y	TRIPP Y
*QUEAS Y	*SCABB Y	*SLEAZ Y	SPARR Y	*SWAMP Y	TROLL Y
*QUEAZ Y	SCANT Y	SLEEK Y	SPEED Y	*SWANK Y	TROPH Y
*QUINS Y	SCARE Y	SLEEP Y	SPHER Y	SWART Y	TROUT Y
*QUIRK Y	SCARR Y	SLEET Y	SPICE Y	SWEAT Y	TRUST Y
RACIL Y	SCATT Y	SLIML Y	*SPIFF Y	SWEEN Y	TUMEF Y
RAMIF Y	*SCHIZ Y	SLIMS Y	*SPIKE Y	SWEEP Y	TURKE Y
RANKL Y	SCREW Y	SLINK Y	SPINN Y	*SWIMM Y	TWANG Y
RAREF Y	*SCUMM Y	SLIPP Y	SPONG Y	SWING Y	*TWANK Y
RAREL Y	SCURF Y	SLOBB Y	SPOOF Y	SWIRL Y	*TWEAK Y
RARIF Y	SCURR Y	SLOPP Y	*SPOOK Y	*SWISH Y	TWEED Y
RARIT Y	SCURV Y	SLOSH Y	SPOON Y	*S Y Z Y G Y	TWEEN Y

TWENT Y	*WHITE Y	*BLACKL Y	*CHANTR Y	*CRUCIF Y	*DRIBBL Y
TWIGG Y	*WHOLL Y	*BLANKL Y	*CHARIL Y	CRUDIT Y	*DRIZZL Y
TWIRL Y	*WICOP Y	BLARNE Y	*CHARIT Y	CRUELT Y	*DROSHK Y
TWIST Y	WIELD Y	*BLEAKL Y	*CHARLE Y	*CRUMBL Y	DROUTH Y
*T Y PIF Y	*WIFEL Y	*BLIGHT Y	*CHARPO Y	*CRUMPL Y	DUALIT Y
VAGAR Y	WIGGL Y	BLINDL Y	*CHEAPL Y	*CRUNCH Y	DUBIET Y
VALLE Y	WILDL Y	*BLOTCH Y	*CHEERL Y	CRUSIL Y	*DULCIF Y
VANIT Y	WILIL Y	*BLOWFL Y	*CHICOR Y	*CR Y BAB Y	*DUMPIL Y
VAPOR Y	WINCE Y	*BLUEJA Y	*CHIEFL Y	*CUBICL Y	DUOPOL Y
VASTL Y	WINER Y	*BOBBER Y	*CHILDL Y	CURSOR Y	DUSTIL Y
VAULT Y	WINTR Y	BOBSTA Y	*CHIMBL Y	CURTES Y	*D Y ARCH Y
VAUNT Y	WIRIL Y	BOLONE Y	*CHIMLE Y	CURTSE Y	D Y NAST Y
*VEEJA Y	WISEL Y	BOOTER Y	*CHIMNE Y	*CUSHIL Y	*FACTOR Y
VENER Y	*WITCH Y	*BRAMBL Y	*CHINCH Y	CUSTOD Y	*FACULT Y
*VERIF Y	WITNE Y	*BRANCH Y	*CHINTZ Y	*CUTAWA Y	FAINTL Y
VERIL Y	*WOBBL Y	*BRAVER Y	*CHOOSE Y	CUTLER Y	*FAIRWA Y
VERIT Y	WOODS Y	*BREATH Y	*CHRIST Y	*C Y CLER Y	*FALLAC Y
VESTR Y	WOOLL Y	*BREVIT Y	*CHURCH Y	DACOIT Y	*FALSIF Y
*VILIF Y	*WORTH Y	*BREWER Y	*CHUTNE Y	*DAKOIT Y	FALSIT Y
VINER Y	*WRATH Y	BRIBER Y	CILIAR Y	*DAMNIF Y	FANTAS Y
*VINIF Y	WRIST Y	*BRIEFL Y	CINDER Y	DANDIL Y	FARADA Y
*VIVAR Y	Y EARL Y	*BRISKL Y	*CIPHON Y	DARESA Y	*FARAWA Y
*VIVIF Y	Y EAST Y	BRISTL Y	*CIVILL Y	DATEDL Y	FATALL Y
VOLER Y	*ZINCK Y	BRITTL Y	*CLARIF Y	DAUBER Y	FATTIL Y
VOLLE Y	*ZONAR Y	BROADL Y	CLARIT Y	DA Y LIL Y	FATUIT Y
VOTAR Y	BAIRNL Y	BRUTEL Y	CLEANL Y	DEANER Y	FELONR Y
*WABBL Y	BALCON Y	*BRUTIF Y	CLEARL Y	DEATHL Y	FEODAR Y
WADDL Y	BALONE Y	BUGGER Y	CLERIS Y	*DECENC Y	FERNER Y
*WAFER Y	BATTER Y	BUIRDL Y	*CLERKL Y	DEERFL Y	FERRET Y
WAGGL Y	*BAWDIL Y	BURSAR Y	*CLIQUE Y	DENSIF Y	FEUDAR Y
*WAMBL Y	BEADIL Y	*BUSHIL Y	*CLUTCH Y	DENSIT Y	*FIDGET Y
WARIL Y	BEAMIL Y	BUTLER Y	*COALIF Y	DESTIN Y	*FIFTHL Y
WARML Y	BEANER Y	BUTTER Y	*COCKIL Y	DESTRO Y	*FILMIL Y
WASTR Y	BEASTL Y	BUTTON Y	*COCKNE Y	DEVILR Y	FINALL Y
WATER Y	*BEATIF Y	*CACHEX Y	*COCKSH Y	*DIARCH Y	*FINICK Y
*WAVER Y	BEDIRT Y	*CADENC Y	*COGENC Y	DICLIN Y	*FIREFL Y
*WAVIL Y	*BEEFIL Y	*CALCIF Y	*COLICK Y	*DIC Y CL Y	FIRSTL Y
*WAXIL Y	BEGGAR Y	CALLBO Y	*COMFRE Y	DIDDLE Y	*FISHER Y
*WA Y LA Y	BELLBO Y	CALUMN Y	*COMPAN Y	DIETAR Y	*FISHWA Y
*WEAKL Y	*BELTWA Y	*CALVAR Y	*COMPON Y	*DIGNIF Y	*FIXEDL Y
*WEEKL Y	*BEWEAR Y	*CAMPIL Y	*COOKER Y	DIGNIT Y	FLAUNT Y
WEENS Y	*BEWORR Y	CANNER Y	COOPER Y	DINGIL Y	*FLAVOR Y
WEIRD Y	*BHEEST Y	CANNIL Y	*COP Y BO Y	DISOBE Y	*FLESHL Y
*WHACK Y	*BIBBER Y	CANONR Y	CORNIL Y	DISPLA Y	*FLIGHT Y
*WHAMM Y	BIGGET Y	*CARAWA Y	CORROD Y	DITHER Y	*FLOWER Y
*WHEEZ Y	BIGGIT Y	*CARNIF Y	COTTON Y	DITTAN Y	*FLUENC Y
*WHELK Y	BIGOTR Y	CARROT Y	COUNTR Y	DODDER Y	FLUIDL Y
*WHERR Y	*BIKEWA Y	CATTER Y	COURTL Y	DODGER Y	*FLUNKE Y
*WHIMS Y	BILIAR Y	CATTIL Y	*COWEDL Y	DOGGER Y	*FL Y AWA Y
*WHINE Y	*BILLOW Y	CAUTER Y	*COXALG Y	DOORWA Y	*FOAMIL Y
*WHINN Y	BINDER Y	*CAVALL Y	*CRANKL Y	DOTTIL Y	*FOCALL Y
*WHIPP Y	BIOGEN Y	*CAVALR Y	*CRICKE Y	*DOUGHT Y	*FOLKWA Y
*WHIRL Y	BIOLOG Y	CENTUR Y	*CRINKL Y	*DOVEKE Y	FOOLER Y
*WHIRR Y	BIONOM Y	*CERTIF Y	CRISPL Y	DRAMED Y	*FOOTBO Y
*WHISK Y	BIPART Y	*CHANTE Y	CROSSL Y	DRAPER Y	*FOOTWA Y

*FOPPER Y	*GRUMPH Y	*JOBBER Y	*MALARK Y	NAUGHT Y	PETTIL Y
*FOREBA Y	GUNNER Y	*JOINER Y	MALMSE Y	NECTAR Y	*PHENOX Y
FORGER Y	GUNPLA Y	*JOINTL Y	*MAMMAR Y	NEEDIL Y	*PHLEGM Y
*FORTIF Y	GUSTIL Y	*JOLLIF Y	*MANGAB Y	NEOLOG Y	*PHONIL Y
FOUNDR Y	GUTSIL Y	*JOLLIT Y	MANGIL Y	NEOTEN Y	*PHRATR Y
FRAILT Y	GUTTER Y	*JOURNE Y	MANUAR Y	NERVIL Y	*PHRENS Y
*FRANKL Y	*HACKNE Y	*JUSTIF Y	*MARROW Y	*NEWSBO Y	PIGGER Y
*FRECKL Y	*HALFWA Y	*KILLJO Y	*MART Y R Y	NIGHTL Y	PIGSNE Y
*FREEWA Y	*HALLWA Y	*KNAVER Y	MASONR Y	NIGRIF Y	PILLOR Y
*FRESHL Y	*HAMMIL Y	*KNOBBL Y	MASTER Y	NIMIET Y	*PILLOW Y
*FRIZZL Y	HANDIL Y	*KNUCKL Y	MATTER Y	NINTHL Y	PIOSIT Y
*FROWSTY	HARDIL Y	*KOLACK Y	MEATIL Y	NIPPIL Y	PISCAR Y
*FULFIL Y	*HARMON Y	*KOUPRE Y	*MEDIAC Y	NITRIF Y	*PIZAZZ Y
FULLER Y	*HARSHL Y	*KVETCH Y	MERCER Y	NOBBIL Y	PLAGUE Y
*FURMET Y	*HAUGHT Y	*LACQUE Y	MERCUR Y	NONBOD Y	*PLA Y BO Y
*FURMIT Y	*HAUTBO Y	LACTAR Y	MESALL Y	*NONJUR Y	*PLA Y DA Y
FURRIL Y	*HAZELL Y	LAMPRE Y	MESSIL Y	NONOIL Y	PLENAR Y
*FURROW Y	HEADIL Y	LANEWA Y	*METHOX Y	NONPLA Y	PLIANC Y
GAINSA Y	*HEADWA Y	LANIAR Y	*METRIF Y	NOONDA Y	*PLOWBO Y
GALLER Y	*HEALTH Y	LARCEN Y	*MICRIF Y	NOSEGA Y	*PLUMPL Y
GALLFL Y	HEARSA Y	LATENC Y	*MILDEW Y	NOTABL Y	PORTRA Y
*GANGWA Y	HELLER Y	LATHER Y	MILIAR Y	NOTEDL Y	POSTBO Y
GATEWA Y	HELOTR Y	LAUNDR Y	*MILKIL Y	NOVELL Y	POTENC Y
GAUDER Y	HENNER Y	*LA Y AWA Y	*MIMICR Y	NOVELT Y	POTTER Y
GAUNTR Y	HERONR Y	*LECHER Y	MISALL Y	NULLIF Y	POULTR Y
*GEMMIL Y	*HICKOR Y	LEGALL Y	*MISCOP Y	NULLIT Y	*POVERT Y
GEODES Y	*HIGHBO Y	LENGTH Y	MISERL Y	NUMMAR Y	*POWDER Y
GEOLOG Y	*HIGHWA Y	LEPROS Y	MISPLA Y	NUNNER Y	*PREACH Y
GETAWA Y	HISTOR Y	LEVELL Y	MISREL Y	NURSER Y	PRELAC Y
GHASTL Y	HOARIL Y	LIBERT Y	MISTIL Y	*PAGEBO Y	*PRICKL Y
GHOSTL Y	*HODADD Y	LIBRAR Y	*MOCKER Y	PAISLE Y	*PRIMAC Y
GINGEL Y	HOLIDA Y	*LICHTL Y	MODEST Y	*PALFRE Y	PRIMAR Y
GINGER Y	*HOL Y DA Y	LIFEWA Y	MOISTL Y	PALMAR Y	PRIMEL Y
*GLITCH Y	*HOMEBO Y	LIGHTL Y	*MOLLIF Y	*PANICK Y	PRIORL Y
GLORIF Y	HONEST Y	LIGNIF Y	*MONKER Y	PANOPL Y	*PRIVAC Y
*GLOWFL Y	HOOTER Y	LIMPSE Y	MONOEC Y	*PARKWA Y	*PRIVIT Y
*GOOMBA Y	HORNIL Y	*LINKBO Y	*MONTHL Y	PARROT Y	PROBIT Y
GOSSIP Y	*HORRIF Y	*LIQUEF Y	MOONIL Y	PARSLE Y	PRODIG Y
GRAMAR Y	HORSIL Y	*LIQUIF Y	MORTAR Y	*PARTWA Y	PROGEN Y
GRANAR Y	HOSIER Y	*LITHIF Y	*MORTIF Y	*PASSKE Y	PROSIL Y
GRANDL Y	*HUMANL Y	LITTER Y	*MOTHER Y	PATENC Y	PROSOD Y
GRAPER Y	*HUMIDL Y	LITURG Y	MOUSIL Y	*PATHWA Y	PRUDER Y
GRATIF Y	*HUSHAB Y	LOATHL Y	*MOVABL Y	PAUCIT Y	PSALTR Y
GRAVEL Y	*HUSKIL Y	LOCALL Y	*MUCKIL Y	*PAUGHT Y	PUBERT Y
GRAVIT Y	*H Y DROX Y	LOFTIL Y	MUDDIL Y	*PAUNCH Y	*PUCKER Y
GREATL Y	*H Y MNAR Y	LOTTER Y	MUGGIL Y	*PECCAR Y	*PUDENC Y
GREENL Y	*H Y MNOD Y	LO Y ALL Y	*MUMMER Y	PEDIAR Y	*PUFFER Y
*GRIML Y	*JAGGAR Y	LO Y ALT Y	*MUMMIF Y	PEDLER Y	PURSIL Y
GRISTL Y	*JAGGER Y	LUCENC Y	*MUSKIL Y	PENALL Y	*PUSHIL Y
*GRIZZL Y	*JALOPP Y	LULLAB Y	*MUZZIL Y	PENALT Y	PUSSLE Y
GROCER Y	*JEEPNE Y	LUSTIL Y	*M Y OLOG Y	PEPPER Y	*PUTREF Y
GROSSL Y	*JELLIF Y	L Y INGL Y	*M Y STER Y	*PERFID Y	*QUALIFY
*GROUCH Y	*JEWELR Y	*MAGNIF Y	*M Y STIF Y	*PERJUR Y	*QUALITY
*GROWTH Y	*JIMMIN Y	*MAJEST Y	NAIVET Y	PESSAR Y	*QUAVER Y
*GRUFFL Y	*JITTER Y	*MAJORL Y	NASALL Y	*PETRIF Y	*QUEENL Y

*QUEERL Y	RUBBER Y	*SHLUMP Y	SPLEEN Y	TANNER Y	TROLLE Y
*QUICKL Y	RUDDIL Y	*SHOOFL Y	SPLURG Y	TANTIV Y	TRUANC Y
*QUIETL Y	RUDESB Y	*SHOPBO Y	SPOONE Y	TATOUA Y	TUGGER Y
*QUINAR Y	RUNAWA Y	*SHOWER Y	*SPRAWL Y	TATTIL Y	TURBAR Y
*QUIVER Y	RURALL Y	*SHOWIL Y	SPRIGG Y	*TAXIWA Y	TURNER Y
RABBIT Y	RUSSIF Y	*SHRIEK Y	SPRING Y	TEARIL Y	TURNKE Y
*RACEWA Y	RUSTIL Y	*SHRIMP Y	SPURRE Y	TEENTS Y	*TWIDDL Y
*RACKET Y	RUTTIL Y	*SHRUBB Y	*SQUABB Y	TENANC Y	*TWINKL Y
RAGGED Y	SAINTL Y	*SICKBA Y	*SQUALL Y	TENSIT Y	*TWITCH Y
RAILWA Y	SALLOW Y	SIDEWA Y	*SQUASH Y	TENTHL Y	*T Y MPAN Y
RAINIL Y	SALSIF Y	SIGHTL Y	*SQUATT Y	TENUIT Y	T Y RANN Y
RAUCIT Y	SALTIL Y	SIGNIF Y	*SQUEAK Y	TERNAR Y	*VACANC Y
*RAUNCH Y	SANDFL Y	SIGNOR Y	*SQUIFF Y	TERRIF Y	*VACUIT Y
RAVELL Y	SASSAB Y	SILKIL Y	*SQUINN Y	TESTAC Y	*VALENC Y
READIL Y	SASSIL Y	SILVER Y	*SQUINT Y	TESTIF Y	VALIDL Y
REALIT Y	SATIET Y	*SIXTHL Y	*SQUIRM Y	TESTIL Y	*VAPOUR Y
REAPPL Y	SATISF Y	*SKETCH Y	*SQUISH Y	*THATCH Y	VARIET Y
RECARR Y	SATRAP Y	*SKIDWA Y	STAGIL Y	*THERAP Y	VARSIT Y
RECENC Y	SAVELO Y	*SLACKL Y	STANDB Y	THEURG Y	VASTIT Y
*RECTIF Y	SAVOUR Y	SLAVER Y	*STARCH Y	*THICKL Y	*VERBIF Y
RECTOR Y	SCANTL Y	SLEEKL Y	STARTS Y	THIRDL Y	*VERSIF Y
REEDIF Y	*SCARIF Y	*SLICKL Y	STATEL Y	THIRST Y	*VEXEDL Y
REEDIL Y	SCARIL Y	SLIMIL Y	STEEPL Y	THISTL Y	*VICARL Y
*REENJO Y	SCENER Y	SLIMPS Y	*STENCH Y	THREAD Y	*VICERO Y
REENTR Y	*SCHIZZ Y	*SLIPWA Y	STERNL Y	*THRIFT Y	*VICTOR Y
REGALL Y	*SCORIF Y	*SLOUCH Y	*STIFFL Y	THROAT Y	VIDUIT Y
REGENC Y	SCRAGG Y	SLOUGH Y	STONIL Y	*THRUMM Y	VIRELA Y
REMARR Y	*SCRAPP Y	SMARTL Y	STOUTL Y	TIDEWA Y	VITALL Y
*REPLEV Y	*SCRAWL Y	*SMOOCH Y	STREAK Y	*TIFFAN Y	*VITRIF Y
RESPRA Y	*SCRAWN Y	*SMOOTH Y	STREAM Y	TILBUR Y	*VOCABL Y
RESTUD Y	*SCREAK Y	*SMUTCH Y	STRING Y	*TIMOTH Y	*VOCALL Y
RETIAR Y	*SCRIMP Y	*SNATCH Y	STROPP Y	TINNIL Y	*VOUVRA Y
REUNIF Y	SCROGG Y	SNOWIL Y	STUBBL Y	TIPSIL Y	*WAGGER Y
REVELR Y	*SCRUBB Y	*SNUFFL Y	*STUPEF Y	TISSUE Y	*WALKWA Y
RHATAN Y	*SCRUFF Y	SOAPIL Y	SUAVIT Y	TOLLWA Y	*WALLAB Y
RIBBON Y	SEALER Y	SOBERL Y	SUBSID Y	TOPIAR Y	*WASHDA Y
*RICKET Y	SECREC Y	SOCIET Y	SUCCOR Y	TORREF Y	WASTER Y
RIFLER Y	SECTAR Y	SOLIDL Y	SULFUR Y	TORRIF Y	*WEALTH Y
RIGHTL Y	SEEDIL Y	SOLUBL Y	SUMMAR Y	TOTALL Y	WEASEL Y
RIGIDL Y	SEMIDR Y	SOMEDA Y	SUMMER Y	TOTTER Y	WEEDIL Y
RIVALR Y	SENSOR Y	*SOMEWA Y	SURGER Y	TOUGHL Y	*WEEKDA Y
ROADWA Y	SEVENT Y	SOOTHL Y	*SWARTH Y	TOURNE Y	*WEIGHT Y
ROBBER Y	*SHADFL Y	SORCER Y	SWEETL Y	*TOWAWA Y	WEIRDL Y
ROBOTR Y	SHADIL Y	SORRIL Y	SWELTR Y	TRACER Y	*WHEREB Y
*ROCKAB Y	*SHADOW Y	SOUNDL Y	*SWIFTL Y	TRAGED Y	*WHIMSE Y
*ROCKER Y	*SHAKIL Y	SPANGL Y	*SWINGB Y	*TRAMWA Y	*WHIPRA Y
ROGUER Y	SHANTE Y	*SPARKL Y	SWINNE Y	TRAWLE Y	*WHISKE Y
ROLLWA Y	*SHAPEL Y	*SPECIF Y	*SWITHL Y	TREMBL Y	WHITEL Y
ROOKER Y	*SHARPL Y	SPICER Y	S Y NERG Y	*TRICKL Y	*WIGGER Y
*ROPEWA Y	SHEENE Y	SPICIL Y	*S Y NGAM Y	*TRICKS Y	*WILLOW Y
ROSEBA Y	SHINGL Y	SPIDER Y	S Y NTON Y	TRILOG Y	WINDIL Y
ROUGHL Y	SHINIL Y	SPINDL Y	*TACKIF Y	TRINAR Y	*WINDWA Y
ROUNDL Y	SHINNE Y	SPINNE Y	*TACKIL Y	TRINIT Y	WINTER Y
RO Y ALL Y	*SHIPWA Y	*SPLASH Y	TALLBO Y	TRIPOD Y	*WIREWA Y
RO Y ALT Y	*SHIVER Y		TALLOW Y	TRISOM Y	*WISPIL Y

WITTIL Y	BORINGL Y	*CHICKOR Y	*CUPIDIT Y	*FALLAWA Y	GADGETR Y
*WOMANL Y	*BOTCHER Y	*CHIMBLE Y	*CURRENC Y	FARRIER Y	*GAPINGL Y
WORDIL Y	*BOTTOMR Y	*CHIVALR Y	CURRIER Y	FATALIT Y	GARGANE Y
*WORKDA Y	BOUNDAR Y	*CHOIRBO Y	*CUSHION Y	*FATHERL Y	GELIDIT Y
WORLDL Y	*BOVINEL Y	*CHORALL Y	CUSSEDL Y	*FEATHER Y	*GEMOLOG Y
*WRIGGL Y	*BOVINIT Y	*CHRONAX Y	*CUTCHER Y	*FEDERAC Y	*GENTRIF Y
*WRINKL Y	*BOWINGL Y	*CHURCHL Y	*C Y TOGEN Y	*FELICIT Y	GEOGNOS Y
WRONGL Y	*BOXBERR Y	CINERAR Y	*C Y TOLOG Y	FELINEL Y	*GEOMANC Y
*Y ELLOW Y	BRAINIL Y	*CIRCUIT Y	DARINGL Y	FELINIT Y	GEOMETR Y
*ZEDOAR Y	*BRAZENL Y	*CIVILIT Y	DEACONR Y	*FELLOWL Y	*GEOPHAG Y
*ZINCIF Y	*BREVETC Y	*CLASSIF Y	DEBILIT Y	*FEMINAC Y	*GIFTEDL Y
*ZINKIF Y	*BREVIAR Y	CLASSIL Y	DECENAR Y	*FEMINIT Y	*GIMMICK Y
*ZOMBIF Y	BRIDALL Y	CLATTER Y	*DELEGAC Y	*FERACIT Y	GINGELE Y
*ZOOLOG Y	BROGUER Y	*CLEMENC Y	*DELICAC Y	FERETOR Y	GINGELL Y
*ZOOTOM Y	BROIDER Y	CLINALL Y	*DELIVER Y	*FEROCIT Y	GINGERL Y
*Z Y MURG Y	*BR Y OLOG Y	*CLOWNER Y	DELUSOR Y	FERVENC Y	*GIVEAWA Y
*BACKSTA Y	*BULL Y BO Y	CLUSTER Y	*DEMAGOG Y	*FETOLOG Y	GLASSIL Y
*BADGERL Y	*BUO Y ANC Y	CLUTTER Y	*DENAZIF Y	*FIDELIT Y	*GLAZIER Y
BANALIT Y	BURGLAR Y	*COAGENC Y	DERISOR Y	FINALIT Y	GLITTER Y
BANDITR Y	*BURGUND Y	*COBWEBB Y	*DETOXIF Y	FINITEL Y	GLOSSAR Y
*BARBERR Y	*BUS Y BOD Y	*COEMBOD Y	*DEVILTR Y	*FINNICK Y	GLUTTON Y
BARRETR Y	*BUTCHER Y	*COEMPLO Y	*DEWBERR Y	*FIRECLA Y	GORBELL Y
*BASICIT Y	*CABLEWA Y	*COEVALL Y	DIABLER Y	*FLACKER Y	*GORBLIM Y
BASILAR Y	*CADUCIT Y	COLLIER Y	*DIAPHON Y	FLATTER Y	GOSSIPR Y
*BASKETR Y	*CAJOLER Y	*COLLOQU Y	*DID Y NAM Y	*FLICKER Y	*GRAMERC Y
BASTARD Y	*CALAMAR Y	*COLOTOM Y	DILATOR Y	FLORALL Y	GRATUIT Y
*BA Y BERR Y	*CALAMIT Y	*COMMONL Y	*DIPLOID Y	*FLUIDIT Y	*GRAVELL Y
*BEACHBO Y	*CANDIDL Y	CONICIT Y	DISARRA Y	*FLUMMER Y	GREENER Y
*BEAUTIF Y	CANINIT Y	CONTRAR Y	DISUNIT Y	FLUTTER Y	*GREENFL Y
*BEGGARL Y	CANNONR Y	*CONVEXL Y	*DIVINIT Y	*FOLDAWA Y	*GREENWA Y
BESTIAR Y	*CAPACIT Y	COOINGL Y	DOCILIT Y	*FOREBOD Y	GRINDER Y
*BIFIDIT Y	CARTOON Y	*COPURIF Y	*DOGBERR Y	*FORELAD Y	GROGGER Y
*BIGEMIN Y	*CASTAWA Y	*COQUETR Y	*DOGGEDL Y	*FOREPLA Y	*GRUFFIL Y
*BIHOURL Y	CASUALL Y	CORDURO Y	*DOGSBOD Y	FORESTA Y	GUARANT Y
*BILBERR Y	CASUALT Y	*CORNETC Y	*DOMESDA Y	FORESTR Y	GUERNSE Y
BIOASSA Y	*CATCHFL Y	CORONAR Y	*DOOMSDA Y	*FORMALL Y	*GUIDEWA Y
*BIOMETR Y	CATEGOR Y	CORSETR Y	*DORMANC Y	*FORMERL Y	GULOSIT Y
*BIOSCOP Y	CATENAR Y	*COSTMAR Y	DORSALL Y	FORTUIT Y	*G Y NANDR Y
*BIRTHDA Y	CAUSALL Y	*COSTUME Y	DOTINGL Y	*FOURTHL Y	*G Y NARCH Y
BISTOUR Y	*CAUSEWA Y	COURTES Y	*DOUGHBO Y	*FREAKIL Y	*G Y NIATR Y
*BITCHER Y	*CAVITAR Y	COUSINR Y	*DOWNPLA Y	*FRENZIL Y	*G Y RATOR Y
BITINGL Y	CELERIT Y	*COVERTL Y	DOXOLOG Y	FRIENDL Y	HAGBERR Y
*BIWEEKL Y	*CELIBAC Y	*COWARDL Y	*DRAUGHT Y	*FRIPPER Y	*HAPLOID Y
*BI Y EARL Y	*CEMETER Y	*COWBERR Y	*DRIVEWA Y	*FRIZZIL Y	HARLOTR Y
*BLACKBO Y	CENTAUR Y	*CRAMOIS Y	DROLLER Y	FROMENT Y	*HATCHER Y
*BLACKFL Y	*CEREMON Y	*CRANKIL Y	*DROUGHT Y	*FRUCTIF Y	*HATCHWA Y
*BLATANC Y	CETOLOG Y	*CRAVENL Y	DRUDGER Y	*FRUMENT Y	*HEADACH Y
*BLAZONR Y	*CHAMBRA Y	*CRAWLWA Y	*DUDISHL Y	*FUGACIT Y	*HEADSTA Y
BLISTER Y	*CHANCER Y	*CREAMER Y	DULCETL Y	*FUMATOR Y	*HEATEDL Y
BLOODIL Y	*CHANCIL Y	*CROCKER Y	DUOPSON Y	*FUMITOR Y	*HEAVENL Y
*BLOOMER Y	*CHARLAD Y	*CROOKER Y	*D Y SPEPS Y	FUNERAR Y	*HEGEMON Y
*BLOSSOM Y	*CHASTIT Y	*CROSSWA Y	*FACIALL Y	*FURMENT Y	*HEGUMEN Y
*BLUBBER Y	*CHEERIL Y	*CR Y OGEN Y	*FACILIT Y	FURRIER Y	*HELICIT Y
BLUSTER Y	*CHEMURG Y	*CUBICIT Y	*FADEAWA Y	FUTILIT Y	*HERALDR Y
*BODINGL Y	*CHICCOR Y	CULINAR Y	*FALCONR Y	FUTURIT Y	*HEREDIT Y

*HERMITRY	LATENTLY	MILLIARY	*MYSTICLY	*PHANTASY	*QUACKERY
HERSTORY	LATINITY	*MINACITY	*NABOBERY	*PHARMACY	*QUAGMIRY
*HEXAPODY	LATTERLY	*MINATORY	NASALITY	*PHYLLARY	*QUANDARY
*HEXARCHY	LAVATORY	MINISTRY	*NASCENCY	*PICNICKY	*QUANTIFY
*HIDEAWAY	LEATHERY	MINORITY	NATALITY	PILOSITY	*QUANTITY
*HILAPITY	LEGALITY	MISANDRY	NATATORY	*PIPINGLY	*QUIDDITY
*HOGMANAY	LEGENDRY	*MISAPPLY	NATIVELY	*PIQUANCY	*QUIXOTRY
*HOGMENAY	LEGERITY	MISASSAY	NATIVITY	*PITCHILY	*RABBITRY
*HOKYPOKY	LENIENCY	*MISCARRY	*NAUMACHY	PLAGIARY	RABIDITY
*HOLOGAMY	LETHALLY	MISENTRY	*NECROPSY	PLASTERY	RADIALLY
*HOLOGYNY	*LETHARGY	*MISOGAMY	NIHILITY	PLEURISY	RADIANCY
*HOMEBODY	LIENTERY	MISOLOGY	*NITPICKY	*PLUGUGLY	RAGINGLY
*HOMESTAY	LIMITARY	MISSILRY	NOBILITY	*PLUMBERY	RAILLERY
*HOMOGONY	*LIQUIDLY	*MIXOLOGY	NODALITY	PLURALLY	RAMOSITY
*HOMOLOGY	LITERACY	MODALITY	NODOSITY	PODIATRY	*RAMPANCY
*HOMONYMY	LITERARY	MOLALITY	NOGATORY	POLARITY	RANDOMLY
HONORARY	*LIVIDITY	MOLARITY	*NOMARCHY	*POLYGAMY	*RAPACITY
*HOROLOGY	*LIVINGLY	*MOMENTLY	NOMOLOGY	*POLYGONY	RAPIDITY
*HORRIBLY	LOBLOLLY	MONANDRY	NONDAIRY	*POLYGYNY	RASCALLY
*HORSEFLY	*LOBOTOMY	*MONARCHY	*NONEMPTY	*POLYPARY	*RAVINGLY
*HOUSEBOY	LOCALITY	MONETARY	NONENTRY	*POLYPODY	*RECONVEY
*HOUSEFLY	LOCUTORY	*MONITORY	NONFATTY	*POLYSEMY	*RECOVERY
*HUMIDIFY	*LOGOTYPY	*MONOGAMY	*NONHARDY	*POLYTENY	REDEPLOY
*HUMILITY	LOSINGLY	MONOGENY	NONLEAFY	*POMOLOGY	*REEMBODY
*HUMIVITY	LOVELILY	*MONOGYNY	NONMONEY	*POPINJAY	*REEMPLOY
*HYDROPSY	*LOVINGLY	MONOLOGY	NONPARTY	POROSITY	REFINERY
*HYPOGYNY	LUCIDITY	*MONOPODY	NONSTORY	*PORPHYRY	*REFLEXLY
*JACKSTAY	LUMINARY	*MONOPOLY	*NONWOODY	*PORTABLY	REGALITY
*JAGGHERY	*LYSOGENY	*MONOSOMY	*NORMALCY	POSINGLY	REGISTRY
*JANISARY	*MACCABOY	MONOTONY	NORMALLY	POSOLOGY	REGNANCY
*JANIZARY	*MACCOBOY	*MOPINGLY	NOSOLOGY	POSTALLY	*REINJURY
*JAPINGLY	*MAHOGANY	MORALITY	NUBILITY	POTATORY	RELIABLY
*JEALOUSY	MAINSTAY	MORATORY	*NUMERACY	*POTBELLY	*REMODIFY
*JEJUNITY	MAJORITY	*MORDANCY	NUMERARY	*PRETTIFY	RENOTIFY
*JEOPARDY	*MALARKEY	MORONITY	PADUASOY	PRIESTLY	*REOCCUPY
*JESUITRY	MALIGNLY	MOROSITY	*PALIMONY	*PRIGGERY	*REPACIFY
*JOCOSITY	*MANGABEY	MORTALLY	*PANDOWDY	*PRINCELY	*REPURIFY
*JOKINGLY	MANNERLY	MORTUARY	*PANSOPHY	PRINTERY	RESINIFY
*JOVIALTY	MANUALLY	*MOTHERLY	*PAPERBOY	PRIORITY	*RESUPPLY
*JUGGLERY	*MARKEDLY	MOTILITY	*PAPISTRY	*PROBABLY	RESURVEY
*JURATORY	*MARTYRLY	*MOTIVITY	*PASSERBY	*PROMPTLY	*REVERIFY
*KAZATSKY	MASSEDLY	*MOTORWAY	PATENTLY	*PROPERTY	REVISORY
*KNACKERY	MASTERLY	*MOVEABLY	*PEACOCKY	*PROPHECY	*REVIVIFY
*KNIGHTLY	MATTEDLY	*MOVINGLY	*PECCANCY	*PROPHESY	*RHAPSODY
*KOLINSKY	MATURITY	*MUCIDITY	*PEDAGOGY	*PROVENLY	*RHEOLOGY
LABIALLY	*MAUMETRY	*MUCOSITY	PEDANTRY	*PSALMODY	RIBALDLY
LABILITY	MEDIALLY	*MUDPUPPY	*PEDDLERY	PSALTERY	RIBALDRY
*LACKADAY	*MEGACITY	*MULBERRY	*PEDOLOGY	*PUBLICLY	*RIGIDIFY
LAMASERY	MENIALLY	*MULTIPLY	PENALITY	PULINGLY	RIGIDITY
*LAMBENCY	MENOLOGY	MUSINGLY	*PENDENCY	PUNDITRY	RIMOSITY
LANDLADY	MESNALTY	*MUSKETRY	PENOLOGY	*PUNGENCY	RITUALLY
LANOSITY	*METONYMY	MUSTARDY	*PERIGYNY	PUNITORY	*ROCKAWAY
LAPIDARY	*MICRURGY	*MYCOLOGY	*PERIPETY	*PUPILARY	*ROCKETRY
*LAPIDIFY	MIDSTORY	*MYOPATHY	PETALODY	*PUPPETRY	ROGATORY
*LATCHKEY	MILITARY		PETTEDLY	*PYROLOGY	ROLLAWAY

*ROLLICK Y	*SEXOLOG Y	SOVRANL Y	*SUPERSP Y	TONICIT Y	*VEXINGL Y
ROSEMAR Y	*SEXTUPL Y	SOVRANT Y	SUPINEL Y	*TOPLOFT Y	*VIBRANC Y
ROTATOR Y	*SHIMMER Y	*SOWBELL Y	SWANNER Y	TOPOLOG Y	*VICENAR Y
*ROUGHDR Y	SHINNER Y	*SPARKIL Y	*S Y MMETR Y	*TOPONYM Y	*VICINIT Y
ROUTEWA Y	*SHMALTZ Y	SPARSIT Y	*S Y MPATH Y	TOROSIT Y	VILLAIN Y
*ROVINGL Y	*SHUDDER Y	SPEEDIL Y	*S Y MPATR Y	TORPIDL Y	VINOSIT Y
RUGOSIT Y	*SICKERL Y	*SPEEDWA Y	*S YMPHON Y	TOTALIT Y	*VIRIDIT Y
RURALIT Y	SIGNALL Y	*SPERMAR Y	*S Y NCARP Y	*TOWARDL Y	VIRILIT Y
RUSTICL Y	SIGNIOR Y	*SPILLWA Y	*SYNONYMY	*TOXICIT Y	*VIROLOG Y
SACRIST Y	*SILICIF Y	SPINALL Y	TABOOLE Y	*TRACKWA Y	*VISCALL Y
SADDLER Y	SILVERL Y	SPINNER Y	*TAKEAWA Y	TRAINWA Y	VISUALL Y
SAGACIT Y	*SIMPLIF Y	SPIRALL Y	*TAKINGL Y	TRAVEST Y	VITALIT Y
SALACIT Y	SINOLOG Y	*SPLOTCH Y	TANGENC Y	TREASUR Y	*VIVACIT Y
SALIENC Y	SISTERL Y	SPONGIL Y	TANGIBL Y	*TRIARCH Y	*VOCALIT Y
SALINIT Y	SITOLOG Y	*SPOOFER Y	TANISTR Y	*TRICKER Y	*VOMITOR Y
SALUTAR Y	*SIXPENN Y	*SPOOKER Y	TAPESTR Y	*TRICKIL Y	*VORACIT Y
*SANCTIF Y	*SKITTER Y	*SQUAREL Y	*TAXINGL Y	TRIUNIT Y	*WALKAWA Y
SANCTIT Y	*SLABBER Y	*SQUELCH Y	*TAXONOM Y	TRUANTR Y	WANTONL Y
SANITAR Y	*SLIDEWA Y	*SQUIGGL Y	TEABERR Y	*TRUMPER Y	*WARDENR Y
SAPIDIT Y	*SLIPPER Y	*SQUOOSH Y	TEARAWA Y	*TR Y INGL Y	WARRANT Y
*SAPIENC Y	SLITHER Y	STAGGER Y	TELEGON Y	TUMIDIT Y	*WASTEWA Y
*SAPONIF Y	*SLOBBER Y	STAIRWA Y	TELEPLA Y	*TUPPENN Y	*WATCHCR Y
*SAVAGER Y	SLOVENL Y	*STANCHL Y	TEMERIT Y	TURGENC Y	WATERIL Y
*SAVINGL Y	*SLUMBER Y	STANNAR Y	TENACIT Y	TUTELAR Y	*WATERWA Y
*SCAMMON Y	SMELTER Y	STATEDL Y	TENANTR Y	TWITTER Y	*WAXBERR Y
*SCARCEL Y	*SMITHER Y	*STATICK Y	TENDENC Y	*TWOPENN Y	*WEAPONR Y
*SCARCIT Y	*SMOOTHL Y	STATUAR Y	TENDERL Y	*TYPOLOG Y	WEASELL Y
*SCHLOCK Y	*SMOTHER Y	STEALTH Y	TENOTOM Y	*VAGILIT Y	*WELLADA Y
*SCHMALZ Y	*SNAPPIL Y	STELLIF Y	TENPENN Y	*VAGOTOM Y	*WELLAWA Y
*SCRABBL Y	*SNICKER Y	*STEMMER Y	TEPIDIT Y	*VAGRANC Y	WESTERL Y
*SCRAGGL Y	*SNIFFIL Y	STERNWA Y	TERTIAR Y	*VALIANC Y	*WHISPER Y
*SCRATCH Y	*SNIPPET Y	*STICKIL Y	*TEXTUAR Y	*VALIDIT Y	*WHITEFL Y
*SCREECH Y	*SNOBBER Y	STINGIL Y	*THATAWA Y	*VALUABL Y	WIDTHWA Y
SCROUNG Y	*SNOBBIL Y	STINGRA Y	*THEARCH Y	VANITOR Y	*WINGEDL Y
SCRUTIN Y	*SNUFFIL Y	*STOCKIL Y	*THEODIC Y	*VAPIDIT Y	WINTERL Y
SCULLER Y	SNUGGER Y	*STOMACH Y	*THEOGON Y	*VARIABL Y	*WITCHER Y
SECANTL Y	SOBRIET Y	STONEFL Y	*THEOLOG Y	*VARIEDL Y	*WIZARDR Y
SECONDL Y	*SOCIABL Y	*STOWAWA Y	*THEONOM Y	VARLETR Y	*WONTEDL Y
SECRETL Y	SOCIALL Y	STRAGGL Y	*THIEVER Y	*VARNISH Y	*WOOINGL Y
SECURIT Y	SODALIT Y	STRAMON Y	*THRENOD Y	*VASOTOM Y	*WORDPLA Y
SEDULIT Y	SODDENL Y	STRATEG Y	*THUGGER Y	*VEILEDL Y	*WORKADA Y
SEIGNOR Y	SOLDIER Y	STRATIF Y	*THUNDER Y	VELLEIT Y	*XENOGAM Y
SELECTL Y	SOLIDAR Y	*STRETCH Y	*THWARTL Y	*VELOCIT Y	*XENOGEN Y
SEMINAR Y	*SOLIDIF Y	*STUBBIL Y	TIMIDIT Y	VENALIT Y	*X Y LOTOM Y
SENILEL Y	SOLIDIT Y	STULTIF Y	TINSELL Y	*VENDIBL Y	*YEOMANR Y
SENILIT Y	SOLITAR Y	SUBENTR Y	*TITTUPP Y	VENOSIT Y	*ZEALOTR Y
*SEQUENC Y	*SOLVENC Y	SUBTILT Y	TITULAR Y	*VERACIT Y	*ZOOLATR Y
SERENIT Y	*SOMEBOD Y	SUBTLET Y	TOCOLOG Y	*VERBALL Y	*ZOOMETR Y
SERIALL Y	SONOBUO Y	SUDATOR Y	TOILETR Y	*VERDANC Y	*ZOOPHIL Y
SEROLOG Y	SONORIT Y	*SULPHUR Y	*TOKOLOG Y	*VESPIAR Y	*Z Y GOSIT Y
SEROSIT Y	SOOTHSA Y	*SUMMERL Y	TOMALLE Y	VESTALL Y	*Z Y MOLOG Y
SEVERIT Y	SORORIT Y	*SUMMITR Y	TONALIT Y	VESTIAR Y	

Z

*ZANY	*ZAFFRE	*ZAMARRA	*ZAIBATSU	*BA Z OO	*MI Z ZLY
*ZARF	*ZAFTIG	*ZAMARRO	*ZAMINDAR	*GA Z AR	*MU Z HIK
ZEAL	*ZAIKAI	*ZANYISH	*ZANINESS	*Z A Z EN	*MU Z JIK
*ZEBU	*ZANANA	*ZAPATEO	*ZARATITE	*Z I Z IT	*MU Z ZLE
ZEIN	*ZANDER	*ZAPTIAH	*ZARZUELA	*BA Z AAR	*NA Z IFY
*ZERK	*ZANIER	*ZAPTIEH	*ZASTRUGA	*BE Z ANT	*NO Z ZLE
ZERO	*ZANIES	*ZAREEBA	*ZEALOTRY	*BE Z OAR	*PA ZA Z Z
ZEST	*ZAPPER	*ZEALOUS	*ZECCHINO	*BI Z ONE	*PI ZA Z Z
ZETA	*ZAREBA	*ZEBRASS	*ZEMINDAR	*BU Z UKI	*PI Z ZLE
ZILL	*ZARIBA	*ZEBRINE	*ZEPPELIN	*BU Z ZER	*PU Z ZLE
*ZINC	*ZEALOT	*ZEBROID	*ZESTLESS	*BY Z ANT	*PU Z LER
ZING	*ZEATIN	*ZECCHIN	*ZIBELINE	*CO Z IED	*RE Z ONE
ZITI	*ZEBECK	*ZEDOARY	*ZIGGURAT	*CO Z IER	*RO Z ZER
ZOEA	*ZECHIN	*ZELKOVA	*ZIKKURAT	*CO Z IES	*SI Z IER
*ZOIC	*ZENANA	*ZEMSTVO	*ZINCKING	*CO Z ZES	*SI Z ING
ZONE	*ZENITH	*ZENAIDA	*ZIRCONIA	*DA Z ZLE	*SI Z ZLE
*ZONK	*ZEPHYR	*ZEOLITE	*ZIRCONIC	*DE Z INC	*SO Z INE
*ZOOM	*ZEROTH	*ZESTFUL	*ZOMBIISM	*DO Z IER	*SY Z YGY
ZOON	*ZESTER	*ZIKURAT	*ZONATION	*DO Z ILY	*VI Z ARD
ZORI	*ZEUGMA	*ZILLION	*ZONELESS	*DO Z ING	*VI Z IER
*ZYME	*ZIBETH	*ZINCATE	*ZONETIME	*FI Z GIG	*VI Z SLA
ZAIRE	*ZIGZAG	*ZINCIFY	*ZOOCHORE	*FI Z ZER	*WI Z ARD
*ZAMIA	*ZILLAH	*ZINCITE	*ZOOGENIC	*FI Z ZES	*WI Z ZEN
*ZANZA	*ZINCIC	*ZINCKED	*ZOOGLOEA	*FI Z ZLE	*Z I Z ZLE
*ZAPPY	*ZINCKY	*ZINCOID	*ZOOLATER	*GA Z ABO	*Z I Z ITH
*ZAYIN	*ZINGER	*ZINCOUS	*ZOOLATRY	*GA Z EBO	*BA Z OOKA
*ZAZEN	*ZINNIA	*ZINGANO	*ZOOMANIA	*GA Z ING	*BE Z IQUE
*ZEBEC	*ZIPPER	*ZINGARA	*ZOOMETRY	*GA Z UMP	*BE Z ZANT
*ZEBRA	*ZIRCON	*ZINGARO	*ZOOMORPH	*GU Z ZLE	*BI Z ARRE
*ZESTY	*ZITHER	*ZINKIFY	*ZOONOSIS	*HA Z ARD	*BI Z NAGA
*ZIBET	*ZIZITH	*ZIPLESS	*ZOOPHILE	*HA Z IER	*BU Z ZARD
*ZILCH	*ZIZZLE	*ZIPPING	*ZOOPHILY	*HA Z ILY	*BU Z ZWIG
*ZINCY	*ZODIAC	*ZITHERN	*ZOOPHOBE	*HA Z ING	*CA Z IQUE
*ZINEB	*ZOFTIG	*ZOARIUM	*ZOOPHYTE	*HA Z ZAN	*CO Z ENER
*ZINGY	*ZOMBIE	*ZOECIUM	*ZOOSPERM	*HU Z ZAH	*CO Z IEST
*ZINKY	*ZONARY	*ZOISITE	*ZOOSPORE	*JA Z ZER	*DA Z ZLER
*ZIPPY	*ZONATE	*ZOMBIFY	*ZUCCHINI	*JE Z AIL	*DO Z ENTH
*ZIRAM	*ZONING	*ZONATED	*ZWIEBACK	*LA Z IED	*DO Z IEST
*ZIZIT	*ZONKED	*ZOOGLEA	*ZYGOSITY	*LA Z IER	*FA Z ENDA
*ZLOTY	*ZONULA	*ZOOLOGY	*ZYGOTENE	*LA Z IES	*FU Z ZING
*ZOMBI	*ZONULE	*ZOOTOMY	*ZYMOGENE	*LA Z ILY	*GA Z ANIA
ZONAL	*ZOSTER	*ZORILLA	*ZYMOGRAM	*LA Z ING	*GA Z ELLE
ZONER	*ZOUAVE	*ZORILLE	*ZYMOLOGY	*LA Z ULI	*GA Z ETTE
*ZOOID	*ZOUNDS	*ZORILLO		*LI Z ARD	*GI Z ZARD
*ZOOKS	*ZOYSIA	*ZYGOSIS	*C Z AR	*MA Z ARD	*GU Z ZLER
*ZOOTY	*ZYDECO	*ZYMOGEN	T ZAR	*MA Z IER	*HA Z ELLY
ZORIL	*ZYGOID	*ZYMOSAN	*T Z IT Z IT	*MA Z ING	*HA Z IEST
*ZOWIE	*ZYGOMA	*ZYMOSIS	*FI Z Z	*MA Z UMA	*JA Z ZMAN
*ZADDIK	*ZYGOTE	*ZYMURGY	*FU Z Z	*ME Z CAL	*JE Z EBEL
*ZAFFAR	*ZYMASE	*ZYZZYVA	*JA Z Z	*ME Z UZA	*LA Z ARET
*ZAFFER	*ZACATON	*ZABAIONE	*ME Z E	*MI Z ZEN	*LA Z IEST
*ZAFFIR	*ZADDICK	*ZABAJONE	*RA Z Z	*MI Z ZLE	*LA Z YISH

*LO Z ENGE	*BEN Z OATE	*GRA Z IOSO	DIT Z	*GLIT Z	*SC
*MA Z IEST	*BLA Z ONER	*GRI Z Z LER	*FI Z Z	*GROS Z	*SPEL'T
*MA Z URKA	*BLA Z ONRY	*HI Z Z ONER	*FRI Z	*HAFI Z	*SPRIT Z
*MA Z ZARD	*BLI Z Z ARD	*JA Z Z LIKE	*FU Z Z	*KLUT Z	*CHALUT Z
*MA Z ILY	*BOU Z OUKI	*MAR Z IPAN	GEE Z	*HERT Z	*KIBBIT Z
*ME Z QUIT	*BRA Z ENLY	*MO Z ETTA	*JA Z Z	*SPIT Z	*KIBBUT Z
*ME Z U Z AH	*BRA Z ILIN	*MU Z Z IEST	*JEE Z	*TOPA Z	*KOLKHO Z
*MO Z ETTA	*BUZ Z WORD	*PI Z Z ERIA	LUT Z	*TROO Z	*SCHMAL Z
*MU Z Z IER	*CAN Z ONET	*POZ ZOLAN	*PHI Z	*WALT Z	*SCHNO Z Z
*MU Z Z ILY	*CRU Z EIRO	*RHI Z OBIA	*PRE Z	*WHI Z Z	*SHEGET Z
*MU Z Z LER	*DIA Z EPAM	*RHI Z OPOD	*PUT Z	*BLINT Z	*SHMALT Z
*NU Z Z LER	*DIA Z INON	*RHI Z OPUS	*QUI Z	*CHINT Z	*SHOWBI Z
*PI Z A Z Z Y	*DOU Z EPER	*SIT Z MARK	*RA Z Z	*HALUT Z	*SOVKHO Z
*RA Z Z ING	*FOR Z ANDO	*SWI Z Z LER	RIT Z	*KIBIT Z	*SOLONET Z
*SI Z ABLE	*FRI Z ETTE	*WHI Z BANG	*SPA Z	*KOLHO Z	
*SI Z IEST	*FRI Z Z IER	*WHI Z Z ING	*BLI T Z	*KOLKO Z	
*SI Z Z LER	*FRI Z Z ILY	*ZAR Z UELA	*BORT Z	*KUVAS Z	
*SO Z Z LED	*FRI Z Z LER		*FRIT Z	*PA Z A Z Z	
*Z Y Z Z YVA	*GAD Z OOKS	*BU Z Z	*FRI Z Z	*PI Z A Z Z	
*BEN Z IDIN	*GLA Z IERY	*CHE Z			

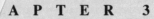

C H A P T E R   3

Two-Letter Words

If there's one list in this book that you should memorize, this is it.

AA	BE	ET	LI	OP	TO
AB	BI	FA	LO	OR	UN
AD	BO	GO	MA	OS	UP
AE	BY	HA	ME	OW	US
AH	DA	HE	MI	OX	UT
AI	DE	HI	MY	OY	WE
AM	DO	HO	NA	PA	XI
AN	ED	ID	NO	PE	YA
AR	EF	IF	NU	PI	YE
AS	EH	IN	OD	RE	YO
AT	EL	IS	OE	SH	
AW	EM	IT	OF	SI	
AX	EN	JO	OH	SO	
AY	ER	KA	OM	TA	
BA	ES	LA	ON	TI	

CHAPTER 4

3-Letter Words Formed from 2-Letter Words

B AA	G AR	T AW	A EF	S ET	S IN
C AD	J AR	W AW	R EF	V ET	T IN
D AD	L AR	Y AW	Y EH	W ET	V IN
F AD	M AR	F AX	B EL	Y ER	W IN
H AD	O AR	L AX	D EL		Y IN
L AD	P AR	P AX	G EL	A GO	B IS
M AD	T AR	R AX	M EL	E GO	S IS
P AD	W AR	S AX	S EL		V IS
R AD	Y AR	T AX	G EM	A HA	W IS
S AD	G AS	W AX	H EM	S EH	A IT
T AD	H AS	Z AX	R EM	T HE	B IT
W AD	P AS	B AY	B EN	C HI	F IT
H AE	V AS	C AY	F EN	G HI	G IT
K AE	W AS	D AY	H EN	K HI	K IT
M AE	B AT	F AY	M EN	P HI	L IT
N AE	C AT	G AY	P EN	M HO	N IT
S AE	E AT	H AY	S EN	O HO	P IT
W AE	F AT	J AY	T EN	R HO	S IT
A AH	G AT	L AY	W EN	T HO	T IT
H AH	H AT	M AY	Y EN		U IT
P AH	L AT	N AY	F ER	D ID	W IT
R AH	M AT	P AY	H ER	F ID	
Y AH	O AT	R AY	P ER	G ID	O KA
B AN	P AT	S AY	S ER	L ID	
C AN	S AT	W AY	P ES	M ID	A LA
F AN	T AR	Y AY	R ES	R ID	
G AN	V AT		Y ES	K IF	A MA
M AN	W AT	A BA	F ET	D IN	E ME
P AN	D AW	O BE	G ET	F IN	A MI
R AN	H AW	O BI	J ET	G IN	
T AN	J AW	O BO	L ET	J IN	A NA
W AN	M AW	A BY	M ET	K IN	
B AR	P AW		N ET	L IN	B OD
E AR	R AW	O DE	P ET	P IN	C OD
F AR	S AW	A DO	R ET	R IN	G OD

H OD	C OX	T UT	BA T	EL L	HO B
N OD	F OX	A WE	BA Y	EL M	HO D
P OD	G OX	E WE	BE D	EM E	HO E
R OD	L OX	O WE	BE E	EN D	HO G
S OD	O OX		BE G	EN G	HO P
T OD	S OX	P YA	BE L	EN S	HO T
Y OD	B OY	R YA	BE N	ER A	HO W
H OE	F OY	A YE	BE T	ER E	HO Y
J OE	G OY	D YE	BI B	ER G	
R OE	H OY	E YE	BI D	ER N	IN K
W OE	S OY	L YE	BI G	ER R	IN N
N OH	T OY	P YE	BI N	ER S	IS M
O OH		R YE	BI O	ES S	IT S
P OH	A PE	T YE	BI S	ET A	
D OM	O PE	W YE	BI T	ET H	JO B
C ON			BO A		JO E
D ON	A RE	AA H	BO B	FA D	JO G
E ON	I RE	AA L	BO D	FA G	
F ON		ADD	BO G	FA N	
I ON	A SH	AD O	BO P	FA R	KA B
M ON	P SI	AD Z	BO T	FA T	KA E
S ON		AH A	BO W	FA X	KA X
T ON	E TA	AI L	BO X	FA Y	KA Y
V ON	U TA	AI M	BO Y		
W ON		AI R		GO A	LA B
Y ON	B UN	AI T	DA B	GO B	LA C
B OP	D UN	AM A	DA D	GO D	LA D
C OP	F UN	AM I	DA G	GO O	LA G
F OP	G UN	AM P	DA K	GO R	LA M
L OP	H UN	AM U	DA M	GO X	LA P
M OP	J UN	AN A	DA W	GO Y	LA R
O OP	M UN	AN D	DA Y		LA T
S OP	N UN	AN E	DE I		LIB
T OP	P UN	AN I	DE L	HA D	LID
W OP	S UN	AN T	DE N	HA E	LIE
D OR	T UN	AN Y	DE S	HA G	LIN
G OR	C UP	AR C	DE V	HA H	LIP
M OR	D UP	AS H	DE W	HA J	LIT
N OR	H UP	AS K	DE X	HA M	LO B
T OR	P UP	AS P	DE Y	HA P	LOG
C OS	S UP	AS S	DO C	HA S	LO O
K OS	T UP	AT E	DO E	HA T	LOP
B OW	Y UP	AW A	DO G	HA W	LOT
C OW	B US	AW E	DO L	HA Y	LOW
D OW	J US	AW L	DO M	HE M	LOX
H OW	P US	AW N	DO N	HE N	
L OW	B UT	AX E	DO R	HE P	MA C
M OW	C UT	AY E	DO T	HE R	MA D
N OW	G UT		DO R	HE X	MA E
O OW	H UT	BA A	DO W	HE Y	MA G
S OW	J UT	BA D		HI C	MAN
T OW	M UT	BA G	EFF	HI E	MA P
V OW	N UT	BA H	EFT	HI M	MA R
W OW	O UT	BA L	EL D	HI N	MA T
Y OW	P UT	BA N	EL F	HI P	MA W
B OX	R UT	BA R	EL K	HI S	MAY
				HI T	ME L

MEN	NUB	PAN	REP	TAD	TOR
MET	NUN	PAP	RES	TAE	TOT
MEW	NUT	PAR	RET	TAG	TOW
MIB		PAS	REV	TAJ	TOY
MID	ODD	PAT	REX	TAM	
MIG	ODE	PAW		TAN	
MIL	OFF	PAX		TAO	UPO
MIM	OFT	PAY	SHH	TAP	USE
MIR	OHM	PEA	SHY	TAR	UTA
MIX	OHO	PED	SIB	TAT	
	ONE	PEE	SIM	TAU	
	OPT	PEG	SIN	TAV	WEB
NAB	ORA	PEN	SIP	TAW	WED
NAE	ORB	PEP	SIS	TAX	WEE
NAG	ORC	PER	SIT		WEN
NAP	ORE	PES	SIX	TIC	WET
NAY	ORT	PET	SOL	TIE	
NOB	OSE	PEW	SON	TIL	
NOD	OWE		SOP	TIN	YAY
NOG	OWL		SOT	TIP	YEA
NOH		REB	SOU	TIT	YEH
NOM		RED	SOW	TOD	YEN
NOO	PAD	REE	SOX	TOG	YEP
NOR	PAH	REF	SOY	TOM	YES
NOT	PAL	REI		TON	YET
NOW	PAM	REM	TAB	TOP	

Prefixes, Suffixes, and Plurals

PREFIXES

The criteria for an acceptable Scrabble® prefix is:

1. The word cannot contain a hyphen.
2. The root or base word must be able to stand alone.

The following are acceptable prefixes:

A	COL	FORE	ORTHO	SUPER
AB	COM	HAY	OVER	TRANS
ABS	CON	IL	PAR	TRI
AD	DE	IM	PARA	ULTRA
ANTE	DI	IN	POST	UN
ANTI	DIA	INTER	PRE	UNI
AUTO	DIS	MAL	PRO	UP
BE	EM	MICRO	RE	
BI	EN	MIS	SEMI	
CO	EX	NON	SUB	

A-	BIDE	BOUT	AB-	SENT
BASE	BLOOM	BREAST	BE	SOLVE
BASH	BOARD	BRIDGE	BEY	USE
BEAM	BODE	BUT	DUCE	USER
BED	BOIL	BUTTED	NORMAL	VOLT
BET	BOON	BUTTER	OUT	YE
BETTER	BOUGHT	BUZZ	REACT	
BETTING	BOUND			

ABS-	AD-	JOIN	MIX	VERSE	ANTE-
TRACT	APT	JOINT	OPTION	VICE	DATE
	AXIAL	JUDGE	RIFT	VISOR	LOPE
	DRESS	JUROR	SCRIPT		TYPE
	DOCT	MAN	VENT		
	HERE	MIRE	VERB		

ANTI-	HERO	NODE	SKID	AUTO-	GYRO
BODY	KING	POLE	SMOG	BUS	MATE
DOTE	LOG	POPE		CADE	SOME
FAT	MASK	RUST		GIRO	TYPE

BE-	DAZZLE	GET	LACED	RATE	STOW
BLOOD	DECK	GIRDLE	LADY	RINGED	STREW
BOP	DELL	GLAD	LAY	ROBED	STRIDE
BOPPER	DEVIL	GLOOM	LEAP	ROUGED	STUD
CALM	DEW	GONE	LIKE	SCORCH	SWARM
CAME	DIAPER	GOT	LIQUOR	SCREEN	TAKE
CAP	DIM	GOTTEN	LITTLE	SEEM	TAXED
CARPET	DOTTED	GRIM	LIVE	SET	THANK
CAUSE	DRAPE	GRIME	LONG	SETTER	THINK
CHALK	DRENCH	GROAN	LOW	SHADOW	THORN
CHANCE	DROLL	GRUDGE'	LYING	SHAME	THUMP
CHARM	DUMB	GUILE	MADAM	SHIVER	TIDE
CLAMOR	DUNCE	GULF	MEAN	SHOUT	TIME
CLASP	FALL	GUM	MINGLE	SHREW	TIMES
CLOAK	FINGER	GUN	MIRE	SHROUD	TOKEN
CLOG	FLAG	HALF	MIST	SIEGE	TOOK
CLOTHE	FLEA	HAVE	MIX	SLIME	TRAY
CLOUD	FLECK	HEAD	MOAN	SMEAR	TROTH
CLOWN	FLOWER	HIND	MOCK	SMIRCH	VOMIT
COME	FOG	HOLD	MUDDLE	SMOKE	WAIL
COMING	FOOL	HOLDER	MURMUR	SMOOTH	WARE
COWARD	FORE	HOOF	MUSE	SMUDGE	WEARY
CRAWL	FOUL	HOWL	MUZZLE	SMUT	WEEP
CRIME	FOULER	JEWEL	NAME	SNOW	WIG
CROWD	FRET	JUMBLE	PAINT	SOOTHE	WINGED
CRUST	FRIEND	KISS	PIMPLE	SOUGHT	WORM
CUDGEL	FRINGE	KNIGHT	QUEST	SPEAK	WORRY
CURSE	GALL	KNOT	RASCAL	SPOUSE	WRAP
DABBLE	GAZE	LABOR	RAKE	SPREAD	

BI-	CONVEX	FOLD	CO-	APPEAR	CHIN
ANNUAL	CORN	FORKED	ACT	ASSIST	COON
AXAL	CUSPID	GOT	ACTION	ASSUME	CREATE
AXIAL	DENTAL	LINEAR	ACTIVE	ATTEND	DEBTOR
CHROME	FACIAL	MANUAL	ADMIRE	ATTEST	DERIVE
COLOR	FOCAL	METAL	ADMIT	AUTHOR	EDITOR
			AGENCY	AXAL	EFFECT
			AGENT	CAIN	EMBODY
			ANNEX	CHAIR	EMPLOY

CO-	EXTEND	MATE	PECK	RING	WAGE
ENACT	FACTOR	MEDIAN	PIED	ROTATE	WARD
ENURE	HABIT	MEDIC	PIER	SET	WINNER
ENZYME	HOG	MET	PIES	STAR	WORKER
EQUAL	LESSEE	NATION	PILOT	TENANT	
EQUATE	LESSOR	PALM	PIOUS	TIDAL	
ERECT	LOCATE	PARENT	PLOT	TING	
EXERT	LOG	PASTOR	REDEEM	TYPE	
EXIST	MAKER	PATRON	REIGN	UPON	

COL-	LIES	**COM-**	MIX	PART	POSE
DISH	LOP	ATIC	MOVE	PEER	POST
LAPSE	ON	BAT	MUTE	PLAIN	POUND
LARD		BUST	PACT	PLIER	PRESS
LATE		FIT	PADRE	PLIES	PRIZE
LET		FORT	PARE	PLOT	

CON-	FINE	GLOBE	SOLE	TEXT	VERGE
CAVE	FIRM	JOIN	SORT	TORT	VERSE
DENSE	FLUX	JUROR	TACT	TOUR	VEX
DOLE	FOCAL	QUEST	TEMPT	TRACT	
DONE	FOUND	SENT	TEND	TRAIL	
DUCE	FRONT	SERVE	TENT	TRITE	
DUCT	FUSE	SIGN	TEST	VENT	

DE-	CARE	LOUSE	PORT	SIRE	VICE
AIR	CAY	MARK	POSE	SPITE	VISE
ASH	CEASE	MAST	POT	SPOIL	VISOR
BARK	CENT	MEAN	PRESS	SUGAR	VOICE
BASE	CIDER	MERIT	RAIL	SULFUR	VOID
BIT	CLAIM	MOB	RANGE	TAIL	VOTE
BONE	CLASS	MODE	RAT	TENT	WAN
BRIEF	CODE	MOUNT	RAY	TEST	WATER
BRUISE	COLOR	NATURE	RIDE	TESTER	WAX
BUG	COY	NOTE	SALT	TICK	WOOL
BUNK	LAY	PAINT	SAND	TOUR	WORM
BUT	LEAD	PART	SELECT	TRACT	
BYE	LEGACY	PEND	SERVE	TRAIN	
CAMP	LIGHT	PLOY	SEX	VALUE	
CANE	LIME	PLUME	SIGN	VEIN	
CANTER	LIST	POLISH	SILVER	VEST	

DI-	ATOM	COT	PHASE	VAN	VINE
ACID	BASIC	DAPPER	POLE	VERSE	VISOR
ARIES	CAST	OXIDE	REST	VEST	

DIA-	LOGIC	MINE	PHONE		
GRAM	METER	PAUSE	SPORE		
LIST					

DIS-	BUD	FAVOR	MISS	PROOF	TRACT
ABLE	CASE	FROCK	MOUNT	PROVE	TRAIN
ABUSE	CLAIM	GORGE	OBEY	QUIET	TRAIT
AGREE	CLOSE	GRACE	ORDER	ROBE	TRUST
ALLOW	COLOR	GUST	OWN	ROOT	UNION
ARM	CORD	HELM	PATCH	SAVE	UNITE
ARRAY	COUNT	JOIN	PLACE	SEIZE	UNITY
AVOW	COVER	LIKE	PLAY	SERVE	USE
BAND	CROWN	LODGE	PLUME	SOLVE	VALUE
BAR	CUSS	LOYAL	PORT	TASTE	YOKE
BOUND	EASE	MAST	POSE	TILL	
BOWEL	ENDOW	MAY	PRIZE	TORT	

EM-	BLAZE	BRACE	PLOY		
BANK	BODY	IRATE	POISON		
BARK	BORDER	MET	POWER		
BARRED	BOSOM	PALE	PRESS		
BATTLE	BOSS	PANEL	PRIZE		
BED	BOW	PLACE			
BITTER	BOWEL	PLANE			

EN-	CORE	GRAFT	NOBLER	SKY	TREAT
ABLE	CRUST	GRAIL	OUNCE	SLAVE	TREATY
ABLER	CRYPT	GRAIN	PLANE	SLAVER	TREE
ACT	CYST	GRAM	RAGE	SNARE	TRENCH
ACTIVE	DAMAGE	GRAVE	RAPT	SNARL	TRIES
ACTOR	DANGER	GRAVER	RAVISH	SOUL	TRUST
AMOUR	DIVE	GROSS	RICH	SPHERE	TRY
ATE	DOWER	GULF	RICHER	SUE	TWINE
CAGE	DUE	HALO	ROBE	SURE	TWIST
CAMP	FETTER	ISLE	ROLL	SURER	VENOM
CASE	FEVER	JAMBED	ROLLER	SWATHE	VIABLE
CASH	FIN	JOIN	ROLLING	TAIL	VISON
CHAIN	FLAME	JOY	ROOT	THRONE	WHEEL
CHANT	FOLD	KINDLE	SAMPLE	TIRE	WIND
CHASER	FOLDER	LACE	SCONCE	TITLE	WOMB
CIPHER	FORCE	LARGE	SCROLL	TOIL	WRAP
CIRCLE	FRAME	LARGER	SERF	TOMB	
CLASP	GENDER	LIST	SHEATH	TOPIC	
CLOSE	GIRDLE	LIVEN	SHRINE	TRAILS	
CLOSER	GLUT	MESH	SHROUD	TRANCE	
CODE	GORGE	NOBLE	SIGN	TRAP	

EX-	AMPLE	PLAIN	PULSE	TORT
ACT	ARCH	PLANT	SECT	TRACT
ACTION	CHANGE	PORT	TEND	
ACTOR	CITE	POSE	TENT	
ALTER	CLAIM	POUND	TOLL	
AMEN	HALE	PRESS	TOLLING	

FORE-	DATE	HAND	MILK	RUN	TIME
ARM	DECK	HEAD	MOST	SAID	TOP
BAY	DO	HOOF	NAME	SAIL	WARN
BEAR	DOOM	KNOW	NOON	SEE	WENT
BODE	FACE	LADY	PART	SEER	WORD
BODY	FEEL	LEG	PAST	SHOW	WORN
BOOM	FEND	LIMB	PAW	SIDE	YARD
BY	FOOT	LOCK	PEAK	SKIN	
BYE	GO	MAN	PLAY	STAY	
CAST	GUT	MAST	RANK	TELL	

HAY-	RACK	IL-
COCK	RIDE	LEGAL
FORK	SEED	LIQUID
LOFT	STACK	LOGIC
MAKER	WARD	
MOW	WIRE	

IM-	BOSOM	MODEST	PLANT	PORTER	PROPER
AGE	BROWN	MORAL	PLEAD	POSE	PROVE
AGING	BRUTE	PACT	PLEDGE	POSTER	PULSE
BALM	MANE	PAIN	PLIED	POTENT	PURE
BARK	MATURE	PAIR	PLIES	POUND	PURITY
BED	MERGE	PALE	PLY	POWER	
BITTER	MESH	PANEL	POLICY	PRESS	
BLAZE	MIX	PARITY	POLITE	PRINT	
BODY	MOBILE	PEACH	PORT	PRISON	

IN-	CAGE	CROSS	DOW	FARE	FORMER
ACTION	CASE	CRUST	DRAFT	FIELD	FRINGE
ACTIVE	CITE	CULT	DRAWN	FIRM'	FRUGAL
ARCH	CIVIL	CUR	DUCE	FIRMLY	FUSE
ARM	CLASP	CURVE	DUCT	FLAME	FUSION
BEING	CLIP	CUS	DUE	FLEXED	GATE
BOARD	CLOSE	DEED	EARTH	FLIGHT	GATHER
BORN	CLOSER	DENT	EDIBLE	FLOW	GOING
BOUND	COG	DEVOUT	EDITED	FLUENT	GOT
BOUNDS	COME	DIRECT	EQUITY	FLUX	GRAFT
BREED	COMING	DOCILE	EXACT	FOLD	GRAIN
BUILT	CORPSE	DOLE	EXPERT	FOLDER	GROUP
BURST	CREASE	DOOR	FAMOUS	FORM	GROWN
BYE	CREATE	DOORS	FANCY	FORMAL	GROWTH

GULF	MESH	SET	STALL	TENSE	VALID
HABIT	MOST	SETTER	STANCE	TENT	VENT
HALE	NERVE	SHEATH	STAR	THRONE	VEST
HAUL	POUR	SHORE	STATE	TIME	VIABLE
HUMAN	PUT	SHRINE	STEAD	TITLE	VITAL
HUMANE	QUEST	SIDE	STEP	TOMB	VOICE
JURY	QUIET	SIGHT	STILL	TONE	WALL
LACE	ROAD	SISTER	STROKE	TONER	WARD
LAID	RUSH	SNARE	SURE	TORT	WARDS
LAND	SANE	SOLE	SWATHE	TOWN	WEAVE
LAY	SANITY	SOLD	TACT	TREAT	WIND
LAYER	SCRIBE	SPAN	TAKE	TRENCH	WRAP
LET	SCROLL	SPHERE	TEND	TRUST	
LIER	SEAM	SPIRIT	TENDED	TWINE	
MATE	SECT	STABLE	TENDER	URBANE	

INTER-	MAL-	MICRO-
ACT	LARD	BAR
CUT	LOW	BUS
LAP	MY	
MIX	ODOR	
RING	POSED	
SEX	TIER	
TIE	TREAT	
WAR		

MIS-	COOK	FIT	LIVE	SAY	THROW
ADD	COPY	FORM	LODGE	SEAT	TIER
AGENT	COUNT	FRAME	LYING	SEND	TIME
AIM	CUE	GAUGE	MARK	SENSE	TITLE
ALLY	CUT	GIVE	MATCH	SHAPE	TOOK
ALTER	DATE	GRAFT	MATE	SHOD	TOUCH
APPLY	DEAL	GROW	MEET	SORT	TRACE
ASSAY	DEED	GUESS	MOVE	SOUND	TREAT
ATE	DEEM	GUIDE	NAME	SPACE	TRIAL
ATONE	DO	HEAR	PAGE	SPEAK	TRUST
AVER	DOER	HIT	PAINT	SPELL	TRYST
AWARD	DOING	INFER	PART	SPEND	TUNE
BEGIN	DONE	JOIN	PATCH	SPOKE	TUTOR
BEGOT	DOUBT	JUDGE	PEN	SPOKEN	TYPE
BIAS	DRAW	KEEP	PLACE	START	UNION
BILL	DRIVE	KNOW	PLEAD	STATE	USAGE
BIND	EASE	LABEL	POINT	STEER	USE
BRAND	EAT	LABOR	POISE	STEP	USER
BUILD	EDIT	LAIN	PRINT	STOP	VALUE
CALL	ENROLL	LAY	PRIZE	STYLE	WORD
CARRY	ENTER	LAYER	QUOTE	SUIT	WRITE
CAST	ENTRY	LEAD	RAISE	TAKE	YOKE
CHIEF	EVENT	LEARN	RATE	TAKER	
CLAIM	FAITH	LIE	READ	TEACH	
CLASS	FIELD	LIGHT	REFER	TEND	
COIN	FILE	LIKE	RELY	TERM	
COLOR	FIRE	LIT	RULE	THINK	

NON-	EQUAL	IDEAL	PAPAL	SLIP	TRUTH
ACID	EVENT	JUROR	PARTY	SOLAR	UNION
ADULT	FARM	LEGAL	PLUS	SOLID	URBAN
AGE	FAT	LIFE	POLAR	STICK	USE
BANK	FATAL	LOCAL	QUOTA	STOP	USER
BASIC	FLUID	MAN	RATED	SUCH	USING
BEING	FOCAL	METAL	RIGID	SUGAR	VIRAL
BOOK	FOOD	MONEY	RIVAL	SUIT	VOCAL
CASH	GAME	MORAL	ROYAL	TAX	VOTER
DAIRY	GREEN	NAVAL	RURAL	TIDAL	WHITE
ELECT	GUILT	OBESE	SENSE	TITLE	WOODY
EMPTY	HERO	OWNER	SKID	TOXIC	WOVEN
ENTRY	HUMAN	PAGAN	SKIER	TRUMP	ZERO

ORTHO-	COOL	HANG	LONG	RUN	TASK
TIC	COY	HARD	LOOK	SAD	TAX
	CRAM	HATE	LORD	SALE	THIN
OVER-	CROP	HAUL	LOUD	SALT	TIME
ABLE	DARE	HEAD	LOVE	SAVE	TIRE
ACT	DEAR	HEAP	LYING	SAW	TOIL
AGE	DECK	HEAR	MAN	SEA	TONE
ALL	DO	HEAT	MANY	SEAS	TOOK
APT	DOER	HIGH	MEEK	SEE	TOP
ARCH	DOSE	HOLD	MELT	SEED	TRIM
ARM	DRAW	HOLY	MEN	SEER	TURN
ATE	DRY	HOPE	MILD	SELL	URGE
AWE	DUE	HOT	MIX	SET	USE
BAKE	DYE	HUNG	MUCH	SEW	VIEW
BEAR	EASY	HUNT	NEAR	SHOE	VOTE
BET	EAT	IDLE	NEAT	SHOT	WARM
BID	FAR	JOY	NEW	SICK	WARY
BIG	FAST	JUST	NICE	SIDE	WEAK
BITE	FAT	KEEN	PASS	SIZE	WEAR
BLOW	FEAR	KILL	PAY	SLIP	WEEN
BOLD	FEED	KIND	PERT	SLOW	WET
BOOK	FILL	LAID	PLAY	SOAK	WIDE
BORE	FISH	LAIN	PLUS	SOFT	WILY
BORN	FLOW	LAND	PLY	SOLD	WIND
BORNE	FLY	LAP	RAN	SOON	WISE
BOUGHT	FOND	LATE	RANK	SOUL	WORD
BRED	FOUL	LAX	RASH	SPIN	WORE
BUSY	FREE	LAY	RATE	STAY	WORK
BUY	FULL	LEAF	RICH	STEP	WORN
CALL	GILD	LEAP	RIDE	STIR	WOUND
CAME	GIRD	LET	RIFE	SUP	WROUGHT
CAST	GLAD	LEWD	RIPE	SURE	ZEAL
COAT	GOAD	LIE	RODE	TAKE	
COLD	GROW	LIVE	RUDE	TAME	
COME	HAND	LOAD	RULE	TART	
COOK					

PAR-	LANCE	TIED	PARA	POST-	FACE
BOIL	LAY	TIES	DROP	AGE	FIX
DINE	RED	TON	FORM	ALLY	FORM
DONER	RIDGE	TOOK	PET	ANAL	HOLE
EVE	SING	VENUE	SANG	BAG	MAN
FLESH	SNIP	VISE	SHAH	BOX	MARK
FOCAL	SON		SITE	BOY	PAID
GET	TAKE		SOL	CARD	PONE
GO	TAKER		VANE	DATE	WAR
KING	TAN				

PRE-	BIND	DUSK	MEDIC	SCORE	TENSE
ACT	BLESS	ELECT	MEN	SELL	TEST
ADAPT	BOIL	ENACT	MIX	SENT	TEXT
ADMIT	BOUND	EXIST	MOLAR	SERVE	TREAT
ADOPT	CAST	FACE	NAME	SET	UNION
ADULT	CENT	FIX	NATAL	SHAPE	UNITE
AGED	CHECK	FOCUS	PACK	SHOW	VENT
ALLOT	CHILL	FORM	PAID	SIDE	VIEW
AMBLE	CITED	FRANK	PARE	SIFT	VISE
AMP	CLEAN	GAME	PAY	SOAK	VISOR
ANAL	COOK	HEAT	PLACE	SOLD	WAR
ARM	COOL	HUMAN	PLAN	STAMP	WARM
AVER	CURE	JUDGE	PLANT	TASTE	WARN
AXIAL	DATE	LEGAL	PRINT	TAX	WASH
BEND	DAWN	LIMIT	PUNCH	TEEN	WRAP
BILL	DIAL	MAN	SAGE	TEND	

PRO-	GRADE	PANE	STYLE
BAND	GRAM	PHASE	TEASE
CARP	JET	PONE	TEND
CLAIM	LABOR	POSE	TEST
CURE	LAPSE	PYLON	TRACT
DUCE	LATE	RATE	UNION
FILE	LEG	ROGUE	VIRUS
FIT	LONG	SECT	WAR
FOUND	MOTE	SING	
FUSE	NOUN	STATE	

RE-	ADORN	ASSAIL	BIRTH	BUTTON	CLASP
ACTIVE	AFFIX	ASSORT	BLOOM	CALL	CLEAN
ACTOR	AGENT	ASSUME	BOIL	CANE	CLOTHE
ABSORB	ALLOT	ATTACH	BOP	CAP	COAL
ACCEDE	ALTER	ATTACK	BRANCH	CARRY	COCK
ACCENT	ANNEX	ATTAIN	BUFF	CAST	CODIFY
ACCEPT	ANOINT	AWAKE	BURIAL	CHANGE	COIL
ACCUSE	ARGUE	AWAKEN	BURY	CHART	COIN
ADAPT	AROUSE	BAIT	BUS	CHOOSE	COLOR
ADD	ASCEND	BID	BUT	CLAD	COMMIT
ADDICT	ASCENT	BIND	BUTTING	CLAIM	CONVEY

RE- (cont.)

COOK	EVOKE	GROOVE	LEND	PURIFY	STACK
CORD	EXPEL	GORGE	LETTER	PURSUE	STRIKE
CROWN	EXPORT	HAMMER	LINE	QUITE	STRUCK
CURVE	FALL	HANDLE	LIST	RISE	STRUNG
DATE	FEED	HANG	LIT	ROLL	STUDY
DEAR	FELL	HARDEN	LOAN	ROLLER	STUFF
DEEM	FLEX	HEAR	MAIL	SAID	SUMMON
DEFEAT	FIGHT	HEARSE	MANNED	SAIL	SUPPLY
DEFY	FILTER	HEEL	MAP	SALUTE	TAILOR
DEMAND	FIND	HEM	MARQUE	SAW	TASTE
DIRECT	FIRE	HINGE	MEMBER	SAY	TIME
DIVIDE	FLEW	HOUSE	MEET	SCREEN	TINT
DOCK	FLIES	HUNG	MEND	SCRIPT	TITLE
DRAW	FLOW	IMAGE	MERGE	SEAT	TRIM
DRIED	FLOWER	IMPORT	MET	SEE	TUNE
DRIES	FLY	IMPOSE	MOLD	SEEK	TWIST
DRILL	FORGE	INCITE	MOTION	SEEN	TYING
DRIVE	FOUGHT	INDEX	NATURE	SEIZE	UTTER
DRY	FOUND	INDUCE	OBJECT	SEND	VEST
DYE	FRONT	INFORM	OIL	SEW	VOICE
EARN	FUSE	INJURE	OPPOSE	SHIP	WAKE
ECHO	GAUGE	INSERT	PACIFY	SHOW	WAN
EDIT	GAVE	INTER	PASS	SIFT	WEIGH
EJECT	GEAR	INVENT	PEOPLE	SILVER	WELD
EMBARK	GILD	INVITE	PERK	SIZE	WIN
EMBODY	GIVE	INVOKE	PIN	SMELT	WOKE
EMERGE	GLAZE	JUDGE	PLAN	SMOOTH	WOKEN
EMIT	GLOSS	KEY	PLATE	SOLD	WON
ENDOW	GLOW	KNIT	PLEDGE	SOLDER	WROUGHT
ENJOY	GRADE	LABEL	PLUNGE	SOUGHT	ZONE
EQUIP	GRAFT	LACE	POWER	SPELL	
ERECT	GREW	LAPSE	PRICE	SPREAD	
	GRIND	LEARN	PROBE	SPRING	

SEMI-

ARID	DEAF	HOBO	RAW
BALD	DOME	LOG	SOFT
COMA	GALA	MUTE	TONE
	HIGH	NUDE	WILD

SUB-

ABBOT	BASS	DUCT	GUM	ORDER	SOLAR
ACID	BED	DUE	HEAD	OVAL	SONIC
ACRID	BREED	ECHO	HUMAN	OXIDE	STAGE
ACUTE	CAUSE	EDIT	HUMID	PAR	TEND
ADULT	CELL	ENTRY	IDEA	POLAR	TONIC
AGENT	CLAN	ERECT	INDEX	RACE	TOPIC
AREA	CLASS	FIELD	JOIN	RING	TRIBE
ARID	CLERK	FIX	LEVEL	RULE	TUNIC
ATOM	DEAN	FLOOR	LIME	SECT	URBAN
AXIAL	DEPOT	FLUID	NASAL	SHAFT	VOCAL
BASE	DUAL	GRADE	OPTIC	SHRUB	ZONE
	DUCE	GROUP	ORAL	SOIL	

SUPER-	TRANS-	TRI-	PART	SOME	ULTRA-
ADD	ACT	METER	PHASE	STATE	RED
JET	SECT	MOTOR	PLANE	UNITY	
LIE	FIX	OXIDE	POD	VALVE	
SEX		PACK	SECT		

UN-			PART	SOME	
ABATED	BROKE	EARTH	HEROIC	NOISY	ROUGH
ABUSED	BUILD	EDIBLE	HEWN	NOTED	ROUND
ACTED	BUNDLE	ENVIED	HIP	OILED	ROVE
AGED	BURIED	ERASED	HIRED	ORNATE	ROVEN
AGEING	BURNT	EVADED	HOOD	OWNED	RUSHED
AGILE	CAKE	EXOTIC	HOPED	PAGED	SALTED
AGING	CANDID	EXPERT	HOUSE	PAIRED	SAVED
AIMED	CASE	FADED	HUNG	PARTED	SAY
AIRED	CAUGHT	FADING	HUSK	PAYING	SEAM
ALLIED	CAUSED	FAITH	IDEAL	PEG	SEIZED
ANCHOR	CHANCY	FALLEN	JOYFUL	PEOPLE	SEW
ANELED	CHARGE	FANCY	KENNEL	PILE	SEXUAL
APT	CHARY	FEARED	KINGLY	PITIED	SHADED
APTLY	CHASTE	FED	KNIT	PLACED	SHARED
ARGUED	CHIC	FELT	LEAD	PLIANT	SHARP
ARTFUL	CHOKE	FILIAL	LEASED	PLOWED	SHED
ATONED	CHURCH	FILMED	LED	POETIC	SHELL
AVOWED	CLENCH	FIRED	LETHAL	POISED	SHIFT
AWARE	CLINCH	FITLY	LET	POLLED	SHIP
AWED	CLOAK	FIX	LETTED	POSED	SHRUNK
BACKED	CLOSE	FLEXED	LEVEL	POSTED	SHUT
BAKED	CLOUD	FOLDER	LEVIED	PRETTY	SICKER
BAR	CLOYED	FORCED	LIMBER	PRICED	SIGHT
BARBED	COATED	FORGOT	LIVE	PRIMED	SILENT
BASED	COCK	FORKED	LIVELY	PRIZED	SINFUL
BATED	COFFIN	FREE	LOBED	PROBED	SLAKED
BEAR	COIL	FROCK	MAKER	PRUNED	SLING
BELIEF	COMELY	FUNNY	MAN	PUCKER	SOAKED
BELT	COMIC	FUSED	MAPPED	PURGED	SOBER
BEND	CREATE	GALLED	MARRED	PUZZLE	SOLID
BID	CROWN	GENIAL	MASKER	QUIET	SORTED
BIDDEN	CURED	GIFTED	MATED	RAISED	SOUGHT
BIND	CURSED	GLAZED	MATTED	RANKED	SOURED
BITTED	DAMPED	GOT	MEANT	RAZED	SOWN
BLAMED	DARING	GOTTEN	MEET	READY	SPEAK
BLEST	DECKED	GOWNED	MELLOW	REASON	SPHERE
BLOODY	DENIED	GRACED	MENDED	REELER	SPOILT
BODIED	DEVOUT	GRADED	MET	REEVE	SPRUNG
BONED	DIMMED	GREEDY	MEW	RENT	SPUN
BONNET	DOCK	HAILED	MILLED	REPAIR	STABLY
BOSOM	DOER	HAIR	MIXT	RESTED	STEEL
BOWED	DOUBLE	HALLOW	MODISH	RHYMED	STEP
BOX	DREAMT	HALVED	MOLTEN	RIFLED	STICK
BRACE	DRIED	HASTY	MORAL	RIG	STOP
BRED	DRUNK	HEALED	MOVING	RIMED	STRESS
BREECH	DYED	HELM	MOWN	RISEN	STUNG
			NEEDED	ROOF	SUBTLE

UN- *(cont.)*	THINK	VEXED	WARMED	WILLED	WORKED
SUNK	TILLED	VIABLE	WARNED	WINDER	WORN
SWATHE	TILTED	VOCAL	WARPED	WISDOM	WRUNG
SWEAR	TRUSTY	VOICE	WEANED	WISH	
SWAYED	TUNE	WALLED	WEIGHT	WIT	
TAGGED	TUFTED	WARIER	WEPT	WON	
TAKEN	VARIED	WARIEST	WETTED	WOODED	
TEACH	VEINED	WARILY	WIFELY	WOOED	

UNI-	FACE	VERSE
AXIAL	FORM	VOCAL
COLOR	SEX	
CORN	SON	
CYCLE	VALVE	

UP-	DIVE	LAND	SEND	THROW
BEAR	DRY	LANDER	SETTER	TILT
BEARER	FIELD	LEAP	SHIFT	TIME
BIND	FLOW	LIGHT	SOAR	TOWNER
BOIL	FOLD	PILE	SPRING	TREND
BORE	GATHER	PITY	STAIR	WAFT
BUILD	GAZE	PROP	STARE	WELL
BYE	GOING	RAISE	STATER	
CAST	GROWTH	RAISER	STEP	
CHUCK	HEAP	ROOTER	STIR	
CLIMB	HEAVER	ROSE	STOOD	
CURL	HOARD	ROUSE	SWEEP	
DATER	HOLDER	RUSH	TEAR	

SUFFIXES

The criteria for an acceptable Scrabble® suffix is:

1. No letter can be dropped when adding the suffix.

2. The suffix, in most cases, does not have a meaning of its own.

3. The use of the suffix changes the meaning of the base or root word or converts it to another part of speech.

The following are acceptable suffixes:

ABLE	EER	IBLE	KIN	RY
AGE	EN	IE/Y	LER	SHIP
AL	ER	IER	LESS	SOME
AN	ERY	ING	LET	STER
ANCE	ESE	ISH	LIKE	TH
ATION	ESS	ISM	LING	ULE
CLE	ETTE	IST	LY	WARD
CY	FOLD	ITIS	MENT	WAYS
DOM	FUL	ITY	NESS	WISE
ED	GRAPHER	IVE	OCK	Y
EE	HOOD	IZE	OUS	

-ABLE	IMPRESSION	-AGE	PEER	-AL	FICTION
AGREE	PREFER	ACRE	STOP	BESTOW	MUSIC
BREAK	READ	CART	VICAR	BETROTH	OCCASION
DETECT	TREASON	CELLAR		COAST	PROVISION
EAT	UNDER-	HERMIT		EDUCATION	RENEW
EXCHANGE	STAND	ORPHAN			WITHDRAW
		PACK			

-AN	-ATION	-CLE	-CY	-DOM	-ED
REPUBLIC	BOTHER	MONO	BANKRUPT	BORE	BOOT
	FLIRT	UN	CAPTAIN	DUKE	LAND
-ANCE	SEDIMENT		CHAPLAIN	EARL	MONEY
FORBEAR			COLONEL	FILM	TALENT
FURTHER			NORMAL	HEATHEN	ROOT
UTTER				MARTYR	UMBRELLA
				OFFICIAL	WOOD
				SAVAGE	
				VILLA	

-EE	-EER	-EN	GOLD	-ER	-ERY
BIOGRAPH	AUCTION	BLACK	HARD	FOREIGN	BREW
MURDER	PAMPHLET	DARK	LENGTH	HEAD	COOK
TEST	SLOGAN	DEEP	MOIST	HUNT	DEAN
TOWN	SONNET	EARTH	SHORT	PAINT	FISH
STAND		FAST	SILK	TROT	FOOL
		FRIGHT	WOOD		ROOK

-ESE	-ETTE	-FOLD	-FUL	-GRAPHER	-HOOD
JOURNAL	CELLAR	TWO	FORGET	PHOTO	BACHELOR
TRANSLA-	FLANNEL	TEN	HAND	TELE	FALSE
TION	KITCHEN	THOUSAND			FATHER
	LEADER				NEIGHBOR
	SERMON				PRIEST
-ESS					
AUTHOR					
COUNT					
MURDER					

-IBLE	-IER	-ISH		-ISM	-IST
CONVERT	HOTEL	AMATEUR	GIRL	ALCOHOL	BALLOON
DISCERN		BOOK	GREEN	BARBAR	COLON
	-ING	BOY	HELL	DESPOT	COPY
-IE/Y	INN	CHILD	POP	HERO	NOVEL
DEAR	OFF	FEVER	SELF	IMPERIAL	ROYAL
HANK	OUT	DEVIL		PARALLEL	SAD
NIGHT	SACK	FOOL		PATRIOT	VIOLIN
	SHIRT			IMPERIAL	
	SKIRT				

-ITY	-IVE	-IZE	-KIN	-LESS	
COMICAL	ATTRACT	CIVIL	LAMB	CEASE	DOUBT
HISTORIC	POSSESS	FAMILIAR	MUNCH	COUNT	NUMBER
SENTI-	PRODUCT	LEGAL		FEAR	TAME
MENTAL	INSTINCT	MATERIAL	-LER	LIFE	TIRE
		NATIONAL	CUT		
		PATRON			
		SOBER			

-LET	IS	-LIKE	-LING	-LY	KING
ARM	KING	CHILD	CAT	COWARD	LEISURE
BOOK	LEAF	GENTLE-	NURSE	DEAD	LIVE
CAB	NECK	MAN	PRINCE	EARTH	LOVE
EYE	OWE	GOD	SAP	GENTLE-	MAN
FLAT	RING	LADY	SEED	MAN	MASTER
		SPORTS-	UNDER	GREAT	MONTH
		MAN		HEAVEN	SCHOLAR
				KIND	USUAL

-MENT	-NESS	-OCK	-RY	-SHIP	-SOME
ARRANGE	DIVINE	BULL	CHEMIST	AUTHOR	BURDEN
BEWILDER	DRUNKEN	HILL	DRUDGE	CENSOR	FEAR
EMPLOY	GOOD		NURSE	FELLOW	LONE
ENDOW	HARSH	-OUS	PEASANT	FRIEND	QUARREL
EN-	KIND	DANGER	RIVAL	HARD	TIRE
LIGHTEN	PREPARED	MOUNTAIN	YEOMAN	LADY	TROUBLE
REFRESH	SWEET	MURDER		MEMBER	
SHIP	WICKED	THUNDER		SCHOLAR	
TREAT				TOWN	

-STER	-TH	-ULE	-WARD	HOME
GAME	FOUR	NOD	BACK	LAND
PUNT	HUNDRED		DOWN	ON
SPEED	SIX		EAST	UP
SPIN	THIRTEEN		FOR	
TAP	THOUSAND		HEAVEN	
TRICK				

-WAYS	-WISE	-Y
LENGTH	CLOCK	EARTH
NO	LENGTH	CHOOSE
SIDE	CRAB	CRAFT
	LIKE	FISH
	NO	SLANG
	OTHER	WOODS
	POKER	

PLURALS

Pluralization can create some of the most spirited disagreements in a Scrabble® game. Keep in mind that a plural may sound new and unusual to you and may even be omitted from some dictionaries, but if the rules are followed you should have little difficulty claiming the rights to use the plural.

1. Most nouns become plural with the addition of "s" or "es."

2. If pluralization requires the removal of a letter or letters or the addition of an apostrophe, under Scrabble® rules the plural cannot be made.

3. Most exceptions to the rules are listed in the dictionary. Here are a few:

OX-	EN
CHILD-	REN
LARVA-	E
TABLEAU-	X
MORCEAU-	X
CHERUB-	IM
ANTENNA-	E
FORMULA-	E
NEBULA-	E
ALGA-	E
ALUMNA-	E
PLATEAU-	X
BUREAU-	X
ADIEU-	X
KIBBUTZ-	IM

CHAPTER 6

Quick-Check Usage Guide

This section lists all the official Scrabble® words that fall into one of eight major categories of special knowledge:

Animal

Computer

Legal

Medical

Military

Nautical

Performing Arts

Sports

Players using an unusual word in one of these categories need only provide the subject or category (very often a precise definition is not known even by the individual playing the word) and in a very few seconds, using the Quick-Check Usage Guide, the authenticity of the word can be verified. The Quick-Check Usage Guide can also be used to review your knowledge of the specific terms in the specific fields provided.

ANIMALS

AARDVARK	ANT	BASENJI	BLUEFIN	BRIT	CALVES
AARDWOLF	ANTBEAR	BASILISK	BLUEFISH	BROCK	CAMEL
AASVOGEL	ANTEATER	BASS	BLUEGILL	BROCKET	CANARY
ABALONE	ANTELOPE	BASSET	BLUEHEAD	BRONC	CANID
ABOMA	ANTLION	BATFISH	BLUEJAY	BRONCHO	CANINE
ACALEPH	ANURAN	BAUDRONS	BLUETICK	BRONCO	CAPELAN
ACALEPHE	AOUDAD	BAWTIE	BOA	BROOKIE	CAPELIN
ACARID	APHID	BAWTY	BOAR	BRUIN	CAPLIN
ACARIDAN	APHIDIAN	BAY	BOARFISH	BRULOT	CAPON
ACARINE	APHIS	BAYARD	BOATBILL	BRUMBY	CAPUCHIN
ACARUS	APOD	BEAGLE	BOBCAT	BRYOZOAN	CAPYBARA
ACCENTOR	APTERYX	BEARCAT	BOBOLINK	BUBAL	CARABAO
ACRODONT	ARACHNID	BEAST	BOBWHITE	BUBALE	CARABID
ACTINIA	ARANEID	BEASTIE	BOCACCIO	BUCK	CARACAL
ACTINIAN	ARAPAIMA	BEAVER	BOLLWORM	BUDGIE	CARACARA
ADDAX	ARGALA	BEDBUG	BOMBYCID	BUDWORM	CARACUL
ADDER	ARGALI	BEE	BOMBYX	BUFFALO	CARANGID
AEDES	ARGONAUT	BEEF	BONACI	BULBUL	CARASSOW
AGAMA	ARGUS	BEEFALO	BONEFISH	BULL	CARBORA
AGOUTI	ARIEL	BEETLE	BONGO	BULLBAT	CARCAJOU
AGOUTY	ARMYWORM	BEHEMOTH	BONITA	BULLDOG	CARCASE
AI	ASCARID	BELLBIRD	BONITO	BULLFROG	CARCASS
AIVER	ASCARIS	BELUGA	BONTEBOK	BULLHEAD	CARDINAL
ALAN	ASCIDIAN	BENTHOS	BOOBY	BULLOCK	CARIBE
ALAND	ASP	BERNICLE	BOOKLICE	BUNNY	CARIBOU
ALANT	ASPIC	BETTA	BOOKWORM	BUNTING	CARP
ALATE	ASPIS	BEVY	BORZOI	BURBOT	CARRION
ALBACORE	ASS	BHARAL	BOSCHBOK	BURRO	CASEWORM
ALBICORE	AUDAD	BIDDY	BOSHBOK	BUSHBUCK	CATALO
ALCID	AUK	BIGEYE	BOSHVARK	BUSHGOAT	CATBIRD
ALDERFLY	AUKLET	BIGFOOT	BOSSY	BUSHPIG	CATFISH
ALEC	AUROCHS	BIGHORN	BOTFLY	BUSHTIT	CATTALO
ALEVIN	AVADAVAT	BILLBUG	BOUQUET	BUSTARD	CATTLE
ALEWIFE	AVIAN	BILLFISH	BOUVIER	BUT	CAVALLA
ALIPED	AVIFAUNA	BIPAROUS	BOVID	BUTEO	CAVALLY
ALPACA	AVOCET	BIPED	BOVINE	BUZZARD	CAVEFISH
AMADAVAT	AVOSET	BISON	BOWFIN		CAVIES
AMEBA	AXIS	BITTERN	BOWHEAD	CABEZON	CAVY
AMIA	AXOLOTL	BIVALVE	BOXER	CABEZONE	CAYMAN
AMMOCETE		BLACKCAP	BOXFISH	CABRILLA	CAYUSE
AMMONITE	BABIRUSA	BLACKFIN	BRACH	CACHALOT	CAZIQUE
AMPHIBIA	BABOON	BLACKFLY	BRACHET	CACIQUE	CEBID
AMPHIPOD	BACALAO	BLAUBOK	BRACONID	CACOMIXL	CEBOID
ANABAS	BALE	BLEAK	BRAHMA	CADELLE	CERASTES
ANABLEPS	BALISAUR	BLENNY	BRAIZE	CAGELING	CERCARIA
ANACONDA	BANDOG	BLESBOK	BRANT	CAHOW	CERO
ANCHOVY	BANGTAIL	BLESBUCK	BRANTAIL	CAIMAN	CETACEAN
ANHINGA	BANTAM	BLOODFIN	BREAM	CALAMAR	CETE
ANI	BANTENG	BLOWFISH	BRENT	CALAMARI	CETOLOGY
ANNELID	BANTY	BLOWFLY	BRIARD	CALAMARY	CHACMA
ANOA	BARBET	BLUEBILL	BRILL	CALF	CHAFER
ANOLE	BARNACLE	BLUEBIRD	BRISLING	CALICO	CHALCID

CHAMOIS	COCKATOO	CRAWFISH	DESMAN	DUROC	EWE
CHARACID	COCKEREL	CRAYFISH	DESTRIER		EYAS
CHARACIN	COCKLE	CREEPER	DEVON	EAGLE	EYRA
CHARGER	COD	CREODONT	DHOLE	EAGLET	
CHARR	CODFISH	CREVALLE	DIDAPPER	EARWIG	FALCON
CHAT	COHO	CRICETID	DIKDIK	EARWORM	FALCONET
CHEBEC	COHOG	CRICKET	DINGO	EBBET	FALLFISH
CHEETAH	COLIES	CRINITE	DINOSAUR	ECHIDNA	FATBACK
CHEGOE	COLIN	CRINOID	DIPLOPOD	ECHINOID	FATBIRD
CHETAH	COLLIE	CRITTER	DIPNOAN	ECHINUS	FATLING
CHEWINK	COLOBUS	CRITTUR	DIPPER	ECOTYPE	FATSTOCK
CHICK	COLONY	CROAKER	DIPTERA	ECTOZOAN	FAUNA
CHIGETAI	COLT	CROC	DIPTERAN	ECTOZOON	FAWN
CHIGGER	COLUBRID	CROPPIE	DIPTERON	EDENTATE	FEIST
CHIGOE	COLUGO	CROW	DISCUS	EEL	FELID
CHILOPOD	COLY	CRUCIAN	DISTOME	EELPOUT	FELINE
CHIMAERA	COMATULA	CRUMMIE	DOBBIN	EELWORM	FENNEC
CHIMP	CONCH	CUB	DOBSON	EFT	FERRET
CHINCH	CONDOR	CUCKOO	DODO	EGGER	FIGEATER
CHIPMUCK	CONENOSE	CUDDY	DOE	EGRET	FILARIA
CHIPMUNK	CONEPATE	CULCH	DOGEY	EIDER	FILARIID
CHIRO	CONEPATL	CULEX	DOGFISH	ELAND	FILEFISH
CHITAL	CONEY	CULICID	DOGGY	ELAPHINE	FILLIES
CHOOK	CONGER	CULICINE	DOGIE	ELAPID	FILLY
CHORDATE	CONGO	CULVER	DOGIES	ELAPINE	FINBACK
CHOUGH	CONY	CUNNER	DOGY	ELATER	FINCH
CHROMIDE	COON	CUR	DOLPHIN	ELATERID	FINFISH
CHUB	COOT	CURASSOW	DOMINICK	ELEPHANT	FINFOOT
CHUCKY	COOTER	CURCULIO	DONKEY	ELK	FIREBIRD
CHUKAR	COOTIE	CURLEW	DOR	ELKHOUND	FIREBRAT
CICADA	COPEPOD	CURTAL	DORADO	ELVER	FIREFLY
CICALA	COQUINA	CUSCUS	DORBUG	EMEU	FIREWORM
CICHLID	CORAL	CUSHAT	DORHAWK	EMMET	FISHER
CIMEX	CORBIE	CUSK	DORMICE	EMU	FISHWORM
CIRRIPED	CORBINA	CUTWORM	DORMOUSE	EMYD	FISSIPED
CISCO	CORBY	CYCLOPS	DORPER	EMYDE	FITCH
CIVET	CORGI	CYGNET	DOTTEREL	ENDAMEBA	FITCHET
CLAM	CORSAC	CYPRINID	DOTTREL	ENTAMEBA	FITCHEW
CLAMWORM	CORVINA		DOVE	ENTELLUS	FLAMINGO
CLERID	COUGAR	DABCHICK	DOVEKEY	EOHIPPUS	FLATFISH
CLOWDER	COURLAN	DACE	DOVEKIE	EPIFAUNA	FLATHEAD
CLUMBER	COVERT	DAKERHEN	DRAGON	EQUID	FLATWORM
CLUPEID	COVEY	DAMAN	DRAGONET	EQUINE	FLEA
CLUPEOID	COW	DANIO	DRAKE	ERGATE	FLICKER
COALA	COWBIRD	DAPHNIA	DRILL	ERMINE	FLIGHT
COALFISH	COWFISH	DARTER	DRONE	ERN	FLOCK
COATI	COYDOG	DASSIE	DRONGO	ERNE	FLOUNDER
COB	COYOTE	DASYURE	DROVE	ESCARGOT	FLUKE
COBB	COYPOU	DAYFLY	DRUMFISH	ESCOLAR	FOAL
COBIA	COYPU	DEALATE	DUCK	ETHOLOGY	FOOLFISH
COBRA	CRAB	DEALFISH	DUCKBILL	EUGLENA	FORAM
COCCID	CRAKE	DECAPOD	DUCKLING	EULACHAN	FOSSA
COCHIN	CRANE	DEER	DUGONG	EULACHON	FOSSETTE
COCK	CRAPPIE	DEERFLY	DUIKER	EURO	FOWL
COCKAPOO	CRAWDAD	DENTALIA	DUNLIN	EURYBATH	FOXFISH

FOXHOUND	GLOWWORM	GUACHARO	HEXAPOD	JABIRU	KITE
FROGFISH	GNAT	GUAN	HIND	JACAMAR	KITLING
FUGU	GNU	GUANACO	HINNY	JACANA	KITTEN
FULMAR	GOA	GUANAY	HIPPO	JACK	KITTY
	GOANNA	GUENON	HIVE	JACKAL	KIWI
GADFLY	GOAT	GUITGUIT	HOATZIN	JACKAROO	KNOT
GADID	GOATFISH	GULL	HOG	JACKASS	KOALA
GADOID	GOBBLER	GUNDOG	HOGFISH	JACKDAW	KOB
GADWALL	GOBIES	GUNNEL	HOGG	JACKEROO	KOEL
GAGGLE	GOBIOID	GUPPY	HOGGET	JACKFISH	KOI
GALAGO	GOBY	GURNARD	HOGNOSE	JACOBIN	KOKANEE
GALAH	GODWIT	GURNET	HOLIBUT	JAEGER	KOLINSKI
GALLFLY	GOLDBUG	GWEDUC	HOLSTEIN	JAGUAR	KOLINSKY
GAM	GOLDEYE	GWEDUCK	HOMINOID	JAVELINA	KOMONDOR
GAMBUSIA	GOLDFISH		HONEYBEE	JAY	KOODOO
GAMECOCK	GOONEY	HABU	HOODIE	JAYBIRD	KORAT
GAMODEME	GOOSE	HACKEE	HOOKWORM	JENNET	KOUPREY
GANDER	GOPHER	HADDOCK	HOOPOE	JENNY	KRAIT
GANG	GORAL	HAGDON	HOPTOAD	JERBOA	KRILL
GANNET	GORCOCK	HAGFISH	HORNBILL	JEWFISH	KUDU
GANOID	GORHEN	HAGGARD	HORNET	JOCKO	KUVASZ
GAPEWORM	GORILLA	HAIRWORM	HORNPOUT	JOEY	
GAR	GOSHAWK	HAKE	HORNTAIL	JUMBUCK	LABRADOR
GARFISH	GOSLING	HALFBEAK	HORNWORM	JUNCO	LABROID
GARGANEY	GOURAMI	HALIBUT	HORSEFLY	JUREL	LACERTID
GARPIKE	GRACKLE	HAMLET	HOST		LACEWING
GARRON	GRAMPUS	HAMSTER	HOTBLOOD	KABELJOU	LADYBIRD
GATOR	GRANDDAM	HANGBIRD	HOUND	KAE	LADYBUG
GAUR	GRAYBACK	HANGNEST	HOUSEFLY	KAGU	LADYFISH
GAVIAL	GRAYFISH	HANUMAN	HOWLER	KAKA	LAKER
GAYAL	GRAYLAG	HARE	HOWLET	KAKAPO	LAMB
GAZELLE	GRAYLING	HARIANA	HUSK	KALONG	LAMBER
GECKO	GREBE	HARRIER	HUSKY	KANGAROO	LAMBIE
GED	GREENBUG	HART	HYDRA	KARAKUL	LAMBKIN
GEESE	GREENFLY	HATTERIA	HYENA	KATYDID	LAMPREY
GELADA	GREENLET	HAUSEN	HYLA	KEA	LAMPYRID
GELDING	GREYHEN	HAWFINCH	HYRACOID	KEESHOND	LANCELET
GEMSBOK	GREYLAG	HAWK	HYRAX	KEET	LANGSHAN
GEMSBUCK	GRIBBLE	HAWKBILL		KEITLOA	LANGUR
GENET	GRIFFIN	HAWKEY	IBEX	KELEP	LANNER
GENTOO	GRIFFON	HAWKIE	IBIS	KELPFISH	LANNERET
GEODUCK	GRILSE	HAWKMOTH	IGUANA	KELPIE	LAPDOG
GERBIL	GRISON	HAZELHEN	IGUANIAN	KENNEL	LAPIN
GERBILLE	GRIVET	HEADFISH	IMAGO	KERRY	LAPWING
GERENUK	GRIZZLY	HEDGEHOG	IMPALA	KESTREL	LARK
GHARIAL	GROSBEAK	HEDGEPIG	INCHWORM	KIANG	LARVA
GIBBON	GROUPER	HEIFER	INCONNU	KID	LAUNCE
GILT	GROUSE	HELLERI	INDRI	KILLDEE	LAVEROCK
GILTHEAD	GRUB	HELMINTH	INFAUNA	KILLDEER	LAVROCK
GIRAFFE	GRUBWORM	HEMIPTER	INFAUNAL	KILLIE	LEAFWORM
GLED	GRUIFORM	HEN	INSECT	KINE	LEAP
GLEDE	GRUMPHIE	HERD	ISOPOD	KINGBIRD	LECHWE
GLIDER	GRUMPHY	HERN	ISOPODAN	KINGFISH	LEECH
GLOSSINA	GRUNION	HERON	IXODID	KINGLET	LEMMING
GLOWFLY	GRUNT	HERRING		KINKAJOU	LEMUR

LEMUROID	MALEMIUT	METAZOON	MUDFISH	NILGHAI	OUSEL
LEOPARD	MALEMUTE	MEW	MUDPUPPY	NILGHAU	OUZEL
LEPORID	MALLARD	MICE	MUGGER	NOCTUID	OVENBIRD
LEVERET	MAMBA	MIDGE	MULE	NOCTULE	OVIBOS
LIGER	MAMMAL	MILKFISH	MULEY	NOTORNIS	OVINE
LIMPET	MAMMOTH	MILLIPED	MULLET	NUMBAT	OVIPARA
LIMPKIN	MANAKIN	MILTER	MULTIPED	NUMBFISH	OWL
LIMULOID	MANATEE	MINK	MUNGOOSE	NUTHATCH	OWLET
LIMULUS	MANDRILL	MINKE	MUNTJAC	NUTRIA	OWSE
LINGCOD	MANGABEY	MINNOW	MUNTJAK	NYALA	OWSEN
LINNET	MANGABY	MINNY	MURAENID	NYLGHAI	OX
LINSANG	MANTA	MINORCA	MUREX	NYLGHAU	OXEN
LION	MANTES	MISSEL	MURICES		OXPECKER
LIONESS	MANTID	MITE	MURID	OARFISH	OYSTER
LIONFISH	MANTIS	MOA	MURINE	OBELIA	
LIZARD	MARABOU	MOGGIE	MURR	OCELOT	PACA
LLAMA	MARABOUT	MOGGY	MURRE	OCELOID	PACER
LOACH	MARE	MOJARRA	MURRELET	OCTOPI	PACK
LOBEFIN	MARGAY	MOKE	MURRY	OCTOPOD	PADNAG
LOBO	MARKHOOR	MOL	MUSCA	OCTOPUS	PAGURIAN
LOBSTER	MARKHOR	MOLA	MUSCOVY	ODONATE	PAGURID
LOCUST	MARLIN	MOLDWARP	MUSKIE	OILBIRD	PALFREY
LONGHORN	MARMOSET	MOLE	MUSKRAT	OKAPI	PALOMINO
LONGSPUR	MARMOT	MOLLIE	MUSPIKE	OLDSQUAW	PANCHAX
LOOKDOWN	MARTEN	MOLLIES	MUSQUASH	OLDWIFE	PANDA
LOON	MARTIN	MOLLUSC	MUSSEL	OLDWIVES	PANFISH
LORICATE	MARTLET	MOLLUSK	MUSTANG	OMNIVORA	PANGOLIN
LORIES	MASTIFF	MOLLY	MUSTER	OMNIVORE	PANTHER
LORIKEET	MASTODON	MOLOCH	MUTT	ONAGER	PAPILLON
LORIS	MAVERICK	MONGEESE	MYNA	ONAGRI	PARAKEET
LORY	MAVIE	MONGOOSE	MYNAH	OOLACHAN	PARAQUET
LOTTE	MAVIS	MONGREL	MYRIAPOD	OPAH	PARAZOAN
LOUSE	MAYFLY	MONITOR	MYRIOPOD	OPHIDIAN	PARD
LOVEBIRD	MEALWORM	MONKFISH	MYSID	OPOSSUM	PARGO
LOVEBUG	MEALYBUG	MONOPODE		OPPOSSUM	PAROQUET
LUCE	MEASLE	MOONEYE	NAG	OQUASSA	PARR
LUGWORM	MEDAKA	MOONFISH	NARWAL	ORANG	PARROKET
LUMPFISH	MEDFLY	MOORCOCK	NARWHAL	ORC	PARROT
LUNGFISH	MEDUSA	MOORFOWL	NARWHALE	ORCA	PARTAN
LUNGWORM	MEDUSAN	MOORHEN	NAUPLIUS	ORIBATID	PEACOCK
LUNKER	MEDUSOID	MOOSE	NAUPLIAL	ORIBI	PEAFOWL
LYNX	MEERKAT	MOPOKE	NAUTILUS	ORIOLE	PEAHEN
LYREBIRD	MEGALOPS	MORAY	NEAT	ORMER	PECCARY
	MEGAPOD	MORPHO	NEKTON	ORNIS	PEEPER
MACACO	MEGAPODE	MOSASAUR	NEKTONIC	ORTOLAN	PEESWEEP
MACAQUE	MELOID	MOSQUITO	NEMA	ORYX	PEETWEET
MACAW	MENDIGO	MOSSBACK	NEMATODE	OSCINE	PEEWIT
MACKEREL	MENHADEN	MOTH	NENE	OSCININE	PEKAN
MACRURAN	MERL	MOTMOT	NEREIS	OSPREY	PEKE
MAGGOT	MERLE	MOUFFLON	NEST	OSTRACOD	PELICAN
MAGOT	MERLIN	MOUFLON	NESTLING	OSTRICH	PEN
MAGPIE	MESSAN	MOUSE	NEWT	OTTER	PENGUIN
MAHIMAHI	METAZOAN	MUCKWORM	NIGHTJAR	OUISTITI	PERCH
MAKO	METAZOAL	MUDCAT	NILGAI	OURANG	PERCOID
MALAMUTE	METAZOIC	MUDDER	NILGAU	OUREBI	PEREGRIN

PERMIT	POLECAT	QUOKKA	RINGHALS	SANDLING	SHEEPDOG
PETRALE	POLLACK		RINGNECK	SANDPEEP	SHELDUCK
PETREL	POLLIWOG	RACCOON	RINGTAIL	SANDWORM	SHELTIE
PEWEE	POLLOCK	RACOON	ROACH	SAPAJOU	SHELTY
PEWIT	POLLYWOG	RAIL	ROADKILL	SARDINE	SHEPHERD
PHASMID	POMFRET	RAINBIRD	ROAN	SASIN	SHIER
PHEASANT	POMPANO	RAM	ROBALO	SASSABY	SHINER
PHILOMEL	PONGID	RAMSHORN	ROBIN	SATYRID	SHIPWORM
PHOEBE	PONY	RANID	ROCKFISH	SAUGER	SHOAL
PHORONID	POOCH	RAPTOR	ROCKLING	SAUREL	SHOAT
PICKEREL	POODLE	RASBORA	RODENT	SAURIAN	SHOEBILL
PIDDOCK	PORGY	RATEL	ROEBUCK	SAUROPOD	SHOTE
PIEBALD	PORKER	RATFISH	RONION	SAURY	SHOVELER
PIG	PORKY	RATITE	RONYON	SAWBILL	SHREW
PIGEON	PORPOISE	RATTAIL	ROOK	SAWFISH	SHRIKE
PIGFISH	POSSUM	RATTER	ROOKERY	SAWFLY	SHRIMP
PIGGY	POTTO	RATTON	ROOSTER	SCAD	SIALID
PIGLET	POULARD	RAVEN	RORQUAL	SCALARE	SIALIDAN
PIKA	POULARDE	REARMICE	ROSEFISH	SCALLOP	SIAMANG
PIKE	POULT	REDBIRD	ROSESLUG	SCARAB	SIFAKA
PILCHARD	POULTRY	REDBONE	ROTCH	SCAT	SIFFLEUR
PINCHBUG	POWTER	REDBUG	ROTCHE	SCAUP	SIGANID
PINFISH	POYOU	REDEAR	ROTIFER	SCHOOL	SILD
PINNIPED	PRAWN	REDFIN	ROUEN	SCHROD	SILKWORM
PINSCHER	PREDATOR	REDFISH	ROUGHLEG	SCIAENID	SILKY
PINTADA	PREY	REDHORSE	RUDD	SCINCOID	SILURID
PINTADO	PRIDE	REDIA	RUDDOCK	SCIURINE	SILUROID
PINTAIL	PRIMATE	REDIAL	RUFFE	SCORPION	SIMIAN
PINTANO	PSOCID	REDLEG	RUMINANT	SCOTER	SIRE
PINTO	PTEROPOD	REDPOLL	RUNT	SCOTTIE	SIRENIAN
PINWORM	PUFFER	REDSHANK		SCROD	SISKIN
PIPEFISH	PUFFIN	REDSTART	SABLE	SCULPIN	SKATE
PIPIT	PUG	REDTAIL	SAHIWAL	SCUP	SKEIN
PIRANA	PULI	REDUVIID	SAIGA	SCUPPAUG	SKEWBALD
PIRANHA	PULLET	REDWING	SAILFISH	SCIURID	SKIMMER
PIRARUCU	PUMA	REE	SAITHE	SEAFOWL	SKINK
PIRAYA	PUNKIE	REEDBIRD	SAJOU	SEAGULL	SKIPJACK
PISMIRE	PUP	REEDBUCK	SAKER	SEAPERCH	SKUA
PLACOID	PUPFISH	REEDLING	SAKI	SEAROBIN	SKUNK
PLAGUE	PUPPY	REINDEER	SALADANG	SEECATCH	SLIDER
PLAICE	PUREBRED	REITBOK	SALMON	SEI	SLOTH
PLANARIA	PUSS	REMORA	SALMONID	SELADANG	SLOWWORM
PLANKTER	PUSSYCAT	REMUDA	SALP	SERIEMA	SLUG
PLANKTON	PYRALID	REPTILE	SALPA	SERIN	SMELT
PLANULA	PYTHON	REQUIN	SALPIAN	SEROTINE	SMEW
PLATY		REREMICE	SALPID	SEROW	SMOLT
PLATYPUS	QUAGGA	REX	SALUKI	SERPENT	SNAIL
PLOVER	QUAHAUG	REYNARD	SAMBAR	SERRANID	SNAKE
PLUMPED	QUAHOG	RHEA	SAMBHAR	SERVAL	SNAPPER
PLUTEI	QUAIL	RHEBOK	SAMBHUR	SETTER	SNARK
PLUTEUS	QUETZAL	RHESUS	SAMBUR	SHAD	SNIPE
POCHARD	QUEY	RICEBIRD	SAMLET	SHADFLY	SNOOK
POD	QUEZAL	RIDGLING	SANDDAB	SHANNY	SNOWBIRD
POGY	QUINNAT	RIDLEY	SANDFISH	SHARK	SOCKEYE
POINTER	QUOHOG	RINGDOVE	SANDFLY	SHEEP	SOLAN

SOLE	SUNBIRD	TERRIER	TUATERA	VIVIPARA	WIGEON
SONGBIRD	SUNFISH	TETRA	TUBENOSE	VIXEN	WILDCAT
SORA	SURFBIRD	TETRAPOD	TUBIFEX	VIZCACHA	WILDFOWL
SORD	SURFFISH	THEROPOD	TUI	VIZSLA	WILDING
SORICINE	SURICATE	THRASHER	TULADI	VOLE	WILDLIFE
SOW	SUSLIK	THROSTLE	TULLIBEE	VOLVOX	WILDLING
SPANIEL	SWALLOW	THRUSH	TUNA	VULTURE	WILLET
SPANWORM	SWARM	TICK	TUNICATE		WIREHAIR
SPARID	SWIFT	TIDDLER	TUNNY	WAGTAIL	WISENT
SPARLING	SWIFTLET	TIGER	TURACO	WAHOO	WOLF
SPARROW	SWINE	TIGLON	TURACOU	WALER	WOLFFISH
SPHINGID	SYNAPSID	TIGON	TURBIT	WALLABY	WOLVES
SPIDER	SYRPHIAN	TIGRESS	TURBOT	WALLAROO	WOMBAT
SPIRULA	SYRPHID	TILAPIA	TURDINE	WALRUS	WOODCHAT
SPITZ		TILEFISH	TURKEY	WANDEROO	WOODCOCK
SPLAKE	TABANID	TIMARAU	TURTLE	WAPITI	WOODHEN
SPOROZOA	TABBY	TINAMOU	TUSKER	WARBLER	WOODLARK
SPRAT	TACHINID	TINEID	TUSSAH	WARMOUTH	WOODWORM
SPRUG	TADPOLE	TIT	TUSSAR	WARRAGAL	WOOLER
SQUAB	TAHR	TITLARK	TUSSEH	WARRIGAL	WRASSE
SQUID	TAIPAN	TITMAN	TUSSER	WARSAW	WREN
SQUILLA	TAKAHE	TITMOUSE	TUSSOR	WARTHOG	WRYNECK
SQUIRREL	TAKIN	TOAD	TUSSORE	WASP	
STAG	TALAPOIN	TOADFISH	TUSSUR	WAT	XERUS
STAGGARD	TAMANDU	TODY	TYEE	WATCH	
STAGGART	TAMANDUA	TOGUE	TZETZE	WATERDOG	YAGER
STAGGIE	TAMARAO	TOKAY		WAVEY	YAK
STAIG	TAMARAU	TOM	UMBRETTE	WAXBILL	YAPOCK
STALLION	TAMARIN	TOMCOD	UNAI	WAXWING	YAPOK
STARFISH	TAMPAN	TOMTIT	UNAU	WAXWORM	YAUD
STARLING	TANAGER	TOPCROSS	UNGULATE	WEAKFISH	YEANLING
STARNOSE	TANUKI	TOPLINE	UNIVALVE	WEASEL	YEARLING
STEED	TAPEWORM	TORO	URIAL	WEAVER	YEELIN
STEENBOK	TAPIR	TORSK	URODELE	WEBWORM	YETI
STEER	TARPAN	TORTOISE	URSA	WEEVER	YOWE
STEGODON	TARPON	TORTRIX	URUS	WEEVIL	YOWIE
STEINBOK	TARSIER	TOUCAN	UTA	WEKA	
STERLET	TATOUAY	TOURACO		WETHER	ZANDER
STILT	TAUTAUG	TOWHEE	VARMINT	WHAUP	ZEBRA
STINGRAY	TAUTOG	TRAGOPAN	VEALER	WHEATEAR	ZEBRASS
STINKBUG	TEAL	TREPANG	VEDALIA	WHELK	ZEBU
STIRK	TEAM	TRICHINA	VEERY	WHELP	ZENAIDA
STOAT	TEG	TRICLAD	VELIGER	WHIDAH	ZIBET
STOCKER	TEIID	TRITON	VENDACE	WHIMBREL	ZIBETH
STONEFLY	TELEDU	TROCHIL	VERDIN	WHINCHAT	ZOEA
STORK	TELEOST	TROGON	VERMIN	WHIPPET	ZOEAE
STRIPER	TENCH	TROILUS	VERVET	WHIPRAY	ZOEAL
STROBILA	TENIA	TROOP	VESPID	WHIPTAIL	ZOIC
STRONGYL	TENREC	TROOPIAL	VICEROY	WHIPWORM	ZOOID
STUD	TERCEL	TROTTER	VICUGNA	WHITEFLY	ZOOIDAL
STUDFISH	TERCELET	TROUPIAL	VICUNA	WHITING	ZOOLATRY
STURGEON	TEREDO	TROUT	VIPER	WHITRACK	ZOOLOGY
SUCKFISH	TERMITE	TRUEBRED	VIREO	WHITTRET	ZOOMANIA
SUCKLING	TERN	TSETSE	VISCACHA	WHYDAH	ZOOMETRY
SUMPTER	TERRAPIN	TUATARA	VIVERRID	WIDGEON	ZOOMORPH

ZOONOSIS	ZOOPHILY	ZOOPHYTE	ZOOTOMY	ZORILLA	ZORILLO
ZOOPHILE	ZOOPHOBE	ZOOSPERM	ZORIL	ZORILLE	ZYZZYVA

COMPUTER

ABORT	CABLE	DAEMON	DUPLEX	FORK	INPUT
ACCESS	CACHE	DAISY	DUPLEXER	FORMAT	INSERT
ACOUSTIC	CAPTURE	DAMPING	DYADIC	FORMULA	INTEGER
ACTUATOR	CARD	DATA	DYNAMIC	FORUM	INVALID
ADAPTER	CARRIAGE	DATABANK		FRY	INVOKE
ADDRESS	CASSETTE	DATABASE	ECHO	FUNCTION	
ALIGN	CATALOG	DATUM	EDIT	FUZZY	JACK
ALLOCATE	CATHODE	DEADLOCK	ELITE		JITTER
ANALOG	CHAD	DEBUG	ELLIPSIS	GARBAGE	JOB
ANALYSIS	CHANNEL	DECIMAL	EMBEDDED	GATE	JOBNAME
ANALYST	CHAT	DECODER	EMULATE	GENDER	JUMP
APPEND	CHILD	DEFAULT	EMULATOR	GIGABIT	JUMPER
ARCHIVE	CHIP	DEGAUSS	ENABLE	GIGABYTE	JUSTIFY
AVATAR	CHUNK	DELETE	ENCIPHER	GLITCH	
	CIPHER	DELIMIT	ENCODE	GLOBAL	KERN
BACKBONE	CIRCUIT	DENSITY	ENGINE	GOPHER	KERNEL
BACKUP	CLEAR	DESKTOP	ENTER	GRABBER	KEY
BANK	CLICK	DEVICE	ENTITY	GRAPHIC	KEYPAD
BASIC	CLIENT	DIALECT	ENTRY	GRID	KEYWORD
BATCH	CLOBBER	DIALOG	ESCAPE	GULP	KILOBAUD
BAUD	CLOCK	DIGIT	EXECUTE	GUTTER	KILOBIT
BETA	CLONE	DIGITAL	EXIT		KILOBYTE
BINARY	CLOSE	DIGITIZE	EXPORT	HACK	KLUDGE
BINIT	CLUSTER	DINGBAT	EXTRACT	HACKER	KLUGE
BIOCHIP	COAXIAL	DISABLE		HALFTONE	
BIT	CODE	DISC	FALLOUT	HANG	LABEL
BLOCK	CODEC	DISCRETE	FANFOLD	HARDWARE	LAPTOP
BLOWUP	CODER	DISK	FATHER	HARDWIRE	LASER
BOARD	COLLATE	DISKETTE	FAULT	HASH	LAYOUT
BOMB	COMMAND	DISPLAY	FAX	HASHING	LEADING
BOOT	COMPILE	DOCUMENT	FEEDBACK	HAT	LEAPFROG
BRANCH	COMPILER	DOMAIN	FETCH	HEAD	LEXICON
BREAKOUT	COMPUTE	DOT	FICHE	HELP	LINEAR
BROWNOUT	COMPUTER	DOWN	FIELD	HERTZ	LITERAL
BUBBLE	CONNECT	DOWNLOAD	FILE	HIT	LOAD
BUCKET	CONSOLE	DOWNTIME	FIRMWARE	HOME	LOCAL
BUFFER	CONSTANT	DRAFT	FLAG	HOOK	LOCKOUT
BUG	CONTROL	DRAG	FLAME	HOST	LOCKUP
BULLET	COPY	DRIVE	FLAMER	HOT	LOG
BUNDLE	CORE	DRIVER	FLASH	HYBRID	LOGGED
BUNDLING	COUNTER	DROP	FLICKER		LOGIC
BURN	CRASH	DRUM	FLIPPY	ICON	LOGICAL
BURST	CRUNCH	DUMB	FLOPPY	IMAGE	LOGO
BURSTER	CRYSTAL	DUMMY	FLOW	IMAGING	LOOP
BUS	CURSOR	DUMP	FOLDER	IMPACT	LOOPHOLE
BYTE	CYCLE	DUPE	FONT	INDEX	

MACRO	PALETTE	QUAD	SCALE	SOUND	THERMAL
MAGNETIC	PARALLEL	QUANTIZE	SCAN	SOURCE	THIMBLE
MAILBOX	PARENT	QUANTUM	SCANNER	SPACE	THREAD
MANAGER	PARITY	QUERY	SCHEMA	SPATIAL	TICK
MANUAL	PARK	QUEUE	SCRAP	SPEC	TILE
MASTER	PARSE	QUIT	SCRATCH	SPIKE	TILING
MATRIX	PASCAL	QWERTY	SCREEN	SPIKES	TOGGLE
MEDIA	PASS		SCRIPT	SPLAT	TOKEN
MEGABIT	PASSWORD	RANDOM	SCROLL	SPLINE	TONER
MEGABYTE	PASTE	RASTER	SCROLLING	SPOILER	TOOLBOX
MEMORY	PATCH	READ	SEAMLESS	SPOOL	TOUCH
MENU	PATH	READER	SEARCH	SPOOLING	TRACK
MERGE	PAUSE	READOUT	SECTOR	SPRITE	TRACTOR
MICRO	PERIOD	REAL	SECURITY	SPROCKET	TRAFFIC
MINI	PERSONAL	REALITY	SEED	STACK	TRAILER
MIRROR	PHASE	REBOOT	SEEK	STAR	TRAIN
MNEMONIC	PHYSICAL	RECORD	SEGMENT	STARTUP	TRANSFER
MODE	PICA	RECOVER	SELECT	STATIC	TRAVERSE
MODEM	PIN	REFORMAT	SEMANTIC	STATION	TREE
MODULATE	PIPE	REFRESH	SENSOR	STATUS	TRUNCATE
MODULE	PIRACY	REGISTER	SENTINEL	STEPPER	TUBE
MONITOR	PITCH	RELATION	SERIAL	STORAGE	TURNKEY
MOUNT	PIXEL	RELATIVE	SERVER	STREAMER	TURNPIKE
MOUSE	PLANAR	RELAY	SERVICE	STRING	TURTLE
	PLATEN	RELEASE	SERVO	STROBE	TUTORIAL
NESTING	PLATFORM	RELOCATE	SESSION	STROKE	TWEAK
NETWORK	PLATTER	REMARK	SETUP	STUB	TYPE
NEURAL	PLOT	REMOTE	SHELL	STYLI	
NIBBLE	PLOTTER	REPORT	SHIFT	STYLUS	UNDO
NODE	POKE	RESET	SHOUTING	SUBMENU	UNIPOLAR
NOISE	POLARITY	RESOURCE	SILICA	SUPPORT	UNPACK
NOTATION	POLLING	RESPONSE	SILICON	SURF	UNSET
NOTEBOOK	PORT	RESTART	SIMPLEX	SURGE	UNZIP
NULL	PORTABLE	RESTORE	SINE	SUSPEND	UP
NUMERIC	PORTRAIT	RETRACE	SINK	SWAP	UPDATE
	POST	RETRIEVE	SITE	SWITCH	UPGRADE
OBJECT	POWER	RETROFIT	SKEW	SWITCHED	UPLOAD
OCTAL	PRIMARY	RETURN	SLARE	SYMBOL	UPTIME
ODD	PRINT	REVERSE	SLASH	SYMBOLIC	UPWARD
OFFSET	PRINTER	REVERT	SLEEP	SYNC	USER
OPERAND	PRINTOUT	REWIND	SLEEVE	SYSOP	UTILITY
OPERATOR	PRIORITY	REWRITE	SLOT	SYSTEM	
OPTICAL	PROCESS	ROBOT	SMART		VALUE
ORPHAN	PROGRAM	ROBOTICS	SMILEY	TAB	VARIABLE
OUTPUT	PROJECT	ROLLBACK	SMOKE	TABLE	VECTOR
OVERFLOW	PROMPT	ROLLOVER	SMOOTH	TABLET	VERIFY
OVERLAY	PROTECT	ROOT	SNAIL	TAG	VERSION
OVERRIDE	PROTOCOL	ROTATE	SNAPSHOT	TAPE	VERTICAL
OVERRUN	PULL	ROUTER	SNOW	TARGET	VIDEO
	PULSE	ROUTINE	SOFT	TASK	VIEW
PACKET	PUNCH	RULER	SOFTWARE	TEMPLATE	VIRTUAL
PADDLE	PURGE	RUN	SOLAR	TERMINAL	VIRUS
PAGE	PUSH		SOLENOID	TERNARY	VOICE
PAGING	PUSHDOWN	SAVE	SORT	TEST	VOLATILE
PAINT	PUT	SCALAR	SORTER	TEXT	VOLUME

WAFER	WEB	WINDOW	WORM	YOKE	ZIP
WAIT	WHEEL	WIZARD	WRAP		ZONE
WAND	WIDEBAND	WORD	WRITE	ZAP	ZOOM
WARM	WIDOW	WORK		ZERO	ZOOMING

LEGAL

ABATOR	ATTESTER	CHARGE	DELATOR	EDICT	FINDING
ABEYANCE	ATTESTOR	CHATTEL	DELICT	EDILE	FINE
ABEYANY	AWARD	CITABLE	DEMESNE	ELEGIT	FINEABLE
ABEYANT		CITATION	DEMIURGE	EMPOWER	FIRMAN
ABJURE	BAIL	CITATOR	DEMPSTER	ENACT	FISCAL
ABJURER	BAILEE	CITE	DEODAND	ENACTIVE	FORGER
ACQUIT	BAILER	CITER	DEPONE	ENACTOR	FORGERY
ADDUCE	BAILIE	CLEMENCY	DEPONENT	ENACTORY	FORJUDGE
ADJUDGE	BAILIFF	COATTEST	DEPOSAL	ENDORSE	FRAUD
ADJURE	BAILMENT	CODICIL	DEPOSE	ENDORSEE	
ADOPT	BAILOR	COGNOVIT	DEPOSER	ENDORSER	GAVEL
ADOPTEE	BAILSMAN	COHEIR	DERAIGN	ENDORSOR	GET
ADULTERY	BATTERY	COLESSEE	DETAINER	ENFEOFF	GRAFT
AEDILE	BENCHER	COLESSOR	DETINUE	ENTAIL	GRANT
AFFIANT	BENEFICE	COMAKER	DEVISEE	ENTAILER	GRAVAMEN
ALDERMAN	BEQUEATH	CONVICT	DEVISER	EPHOR	GUILT
ALIAS	BEQUEST	COPYHOLD	DEVISOR	EPHORAL	GUILTY
ALIBI	BIGAMIST	COSIGN	DHARMA	EPHORATE	
ALIENEE	BIGAMOUS	COSIGNER	DHARMIC	ESCHEAT	HALACHA
ALIENER	BIGAMY	COTENANT	DICAST	ESCROW	HALACHOT
ALIENOR	BINDER	COUNSEL	DICASTIC	ESTATE	HALAKAH
ALIMONY	BREACH	COVENANT	DICTUM	ESTOP	HALAKHA
AMERCE	BRIBEE	CREDITOR	DIGAMIES	ESTOPPEL	HALAKHOT
AMICUS	BRIBERY	CRIME	DIGAMIST	ESTOVERS	HALAKIC
ANNUL	BRIEF	CRIMINAL	DIGAMY	ESTREAT	HALAKIST
APPELLEE	BURGLAR	CULPA	DISBAR	EVICT	HALAKOTH
APPELLOR	BURGLARY	CURIA	DISENDOW	EVICTEE	HEARING
ARBITER	BURGLE	CURTESY	DISHERIT	EVICTION	HEARSAY
ARCHON		CUSTODY	DISMISS	EVICTOR	HEIR
ARRAIGN	CADASTER	CUSTUMAL	DISSENT	EXECUTER	HEIRDOM
ARREST	CADASTRE	CUTCHERY	DISTRAIN	EXECUTOR	HEIRESS
ARRESTEE	CADI	CYPRES	DIVORCE	EXHIBIT	HEIRLESS
ARRESTER	CALENDAR		DOCKET		HEIRLOOM
ARRESTOR	CAMERA	DEBTOR	DOGE	FALSIFY	HEIRSHIP
ARROGATE	CAMERAL	DECEMVIR	DOGEDOM	FATWA	HELIAST
ARSON	CANON	DECERN	DOGESHIP	FEASANCE	HEREIN
ARSONIST	CANONIST	DECREE	DOMICILE	FELON	HEREINTO
ARTICLE	CAPIAS	DECREER	DOOMSTER	FELONRY	HEREOF
ASSAULT	CASEBOOK	DEED	DOTATION	FELONY	HEREON
ASSIGNEE	CASELOAD	DEEMSTER	DRAWEE	FEU	HERES
ASSIGNER	CASUS	DEFAULT	DROIT	FEUAR	HERETO
ASSIGNOR	CAVEAT	DEFENSE	DURESS	FIAR	HERETRIX
ASSIZE	CAVEATOR	DELATE	DUTY	FIAT	HEREUNTO
ATTEST	CHANCERY	DELATION	DUUMVIR	FINABLE	HEREUPON

HEREWITH	KADI	LIEN	PANDECT	REPLEVY	TIPSTAFF
HERITAGE		LIENABLE	PARCENER	REPRIEVE	TIPSTAVES
HERITOR	LACHES	LITIGANT	PARDON	RESCIND	TORA
HERITRIX	LARCENER	LITIGATE	PAROLE	RETAINER	TORAH
HOMICIDE	LARCENY		PAROLEE	REVERSAL	TORT
HORNBOOK	LAW	MAJORITY	PATENT	REVOKE	TORTIOUS
HOTCHPOT	LAWBOOK	MANDAMUS	PATENTEE	ROGATION	TRESPASS
HUSTINGS	LAWFUL	MAYHEM	PATENTOR		TRIABLE
HYPOTHEC	LAWGIVER	MEDIACY	PERJURE	SCILICET	TRIAL
	LAWMAKER	MISPLEAD	PERJURER	SEIZIN	TRIBUNAL
IMMUNITY	LAWSUIT	MISTRIAL	PERJURY	SEIZOR	TROVER
IMMURE	LAWYER	MITTIMUS	PIGNUS	SENTENCE	TRUST
IMPANEL	LAWYERLY	MITZVAH	PIGNORA	SERVICE	TRUSTEE
IMPLEAD	LEASE	MITZVOTH	PLEA	SETTLOR	TRUSTOR
IMPOUND	LEET	MORTMAIN	PLEAD	SHRIEVAL	
INDICT	LEGACY	MOTION	PLEADING	SHYSTER	USUFRUCT
INDICTEE	LEGAL	MOTIVE	PODESTA	SIGNEE	USURER
INDICTER	LEGALESE	MUFTI	POIND	SLAMMER	USURIES
INDICTOR	LEGALISE	MURDER	PRAECIPE	SLANDER	USURIOUS
INFEOFF	LEGALISM		PRAETOR	SOKE	USURP
INFRACT	LEGALIST	NOLO	PRECIPE	SOLATIUM	USURPER
INFRINGE	LEGALITY	NOMISM	PRELEGAL	SOLON	USURY
INHERIT	LEGALIZE	NOMISTIC	PRETRIAL	STATUTE	
INQUEST	LEGALLY	NONJUROR	PROBATE	STAY	VAKEEL
INSOMUCH	LEGATE	NONJURY	PROVISO	STRIKE	VAKIL
INTENT	LEGATEE	NONLEGAL	PROXY	SUABLE	VALIDATE
	LEGATING	NONPROS	PUNITION	SUABLY	VENIRE
JEOPARDY	LEGATOR	NONSUIT	PUNITIVE	SUBORN	VERDICT
JOINDER	LEGES	NOTARIAL	PUNITORY	SUBORNER	VOID
JOINTURE	LEGIST	NOTARIZE	PURVIEW	SUBPENA	VOIDANCE
JUDGE	LESSEE	NOTARY		SUBPOENA	
JUDGMENT	LESSOR	NOTICE	QUAESTOR	SUE	WAIVER
JUDICIAL	LEVY	NOVATION	QUASH	SUER	WARRANT
JURA	LEX	NUISANCE	QUESTOR	SUIT	WEREGILD
JURAL	LIBEL	NULLITY		SUMMONS	WERGELD
JURANT	LIBELANT		REBUTTAL	SUNNA	WERGELT
JURAT	LIBELEE	OATH	RECESS	SUNNAH	WERGILD
JURATORY	LIBELER	OBLIGOR	RECOVERY		WHEREAS
JURIDIC	LIBELIST	OFFENSE	RECUSAL	TALESMAN	WHEREAT
JURIST	LIBELLED	OPINION	RECUSANT	TALMUDIC	WHEREBY
JURISTIC	LIBELLEE	OPTIONEE	RECUSE	TEMPLAR	WHEREIN
JUROR	LIBELLER	ORDER	REDRESS	TENDER	WHEREOF
JURY	LIBELLING	OVERRULE	RELEASE	TERMOR	WHEREON
JURYMAN	LIBELOUS	OYER	REMAND	TERMTIME	WHERETO
JUS	LIBER	OYES	REMEDY	TESTACY	WILL
JUSTICE	LICENSE	OYEZ	REMISE	TESTATE	WRIT
	LICTOR		REPLEVIN	TESTATOR	

MEDICAL

ABASIA	ALLOPATH	APHASIA	AUXETIC	BUBOED	CHALAZIA
ABLATION	ALLOTYPE	APHASIAC	AXENIC	BUBONIC	CHANCRE
ABNORMAL	ALLOTYPY	APHASIC	AZOTEMIA	BULIMIA	CHARNEL
ABORNING	ALOIN	APHONIA	AZOTIZE	BULIMIAC	CHILDING
ABORT	ALOPECIA	APHONIC	AZOTURIA	BULKAGE	CHLOASMA
ABORTION	ALOPECIC	APHTHA		BULLA	CHOKE
ABREACT	ALPHOSIS	APLASIA	BACTERIN	BUNION	CHOLERA
ABROSIA	AMAH	APNEA	BANDAGE	BURSITIS	CHOREA
ABSCESS	AMENT	APNEAL	BANDAGER	BUTE	CHOREOID
ABSCISE	AMENTIA	APNEIC	BANE		CHRONAXY
ABSTERGE	AMNESIA	APNOEA	BANEFUL	CACHEXIA	CHRONIC
ACAPNIA	AMNESIAC	APNOEAL	BARBITAL	CACHEXY	CICATRIX
ACCIDIA	AMNESIC	APNOEIC	BARF	CADAVER	CITRININ
ACCIDIE	AMNESTIC	APOPLEXY	BEDSONIA	CAFFEINE	CLAVUS
ACEDIA	AMPUTATE	APRAXIA	BEDSORE	CALAMINE	CLINIC
ACHOLIA	AMPUTEE	APYRETIC	BERIBERI	CALISAYA	CLONE
ACIDEMIA	AMUSIA	ARYTHMIA	BEVOMIT	CALOMEL	CLONIC
ACIDOSIS	AMYLOID	ARYTHMIC	BIOLOGIC	CAMOMILE	CLONING
ACIDOTIC	ANAEMIA	ASCITES	BIOLYSIS	CANCER	CLONISM
ACIDURIA	ANAEMIC	ASCITIC	BIOLYTIC	CANCROID	CLONUS
ACNE	ANALGIA	ASCORBIC	BIOMETRY	CANELLA	CLUBFOOT
ACROTIC	ANALITY	ASEPSIS	BIONICS	CANITIES	CLUBHAND
ACROTISM	ANASARCA	ASEPTIC	BIOPLASM	CANKER	CLYSTER
ADENITIS	ANEMIA	ASPHYXIA	BIOPSIC	CANNULA	COELIAC
ADENOID	ANERGIA	ASPHYXY	BIOPSY	CANNULAE	COENURE
ADENOMA	ANERGY	ASPIRIN	BIOPTIC	CANULA	COENURUS
ADENOSIS	ANESTRUS	ASTASIA	BIOSCOPY	CANULAE	COHOSH
ADIPOSIS	ANEURISM	ASTATIC	BIOTOXIN	CANULATE	COLIC
ADIPOUS	ANEURYSM	ASTHENIA	BIOTYPE	CAPSID	COLICIN
ADNEXA	ANGINA	ASTHENIC	BIOVULAR	CAPSIDAL	COLICINE
ADYNAMIA	ANGINAL	ASTHENY	BISTOURY	CARATE	COLICKY
ADYNAMIC	ANGINOSE	ASTHMA	BLAIN	CARDIAC	COLIFORM
AFEBRILE	ANGINOUS	ASTIGMIA	BLASTOMA	CARDITIC	COLISTIN
AGENESIA	ANGIOMA	ATARAXIC	BLASTULA	CARDITIS	COLITIS
AGENESIS	ANKYLOSE	ATARAXY	BLEB	CARIES	COLLYRIA
AGNAIL	ANODYNE	ATAVISM	BLEEDER	CARSICK	COLOBOMA
AGNOSIA	ANOOPSIA	ATAVIST	BLIND	CARUNCLE	COLONIC
AGRAPHIA	ANOPIA	ATAXIA	BLISTER	CASCARA	COLOTOMY
AGRIA	ANOPSIA	ATAXIC	BLISTERY	CASTRATE	COLPITIS
AGRYPNIA	ANORETIC	ATAXY	BLOOD	CATARRH	COMA
AGUE	ANOREXIA	ATHEROMA	BLOODY	CATHETER	COMATIC
AILMENT	ANOREXIC	ATHETOID	BLUEBALL	CATLIN	COMATOSE
AIRSICK	ANOREXY	ATONY	BOLUS	CATLING	COMEDO
ALEXIA	ANOSMIA	ATOPY	BORAGE	CAUTERY	CONCUSS
ALEXIN	ANOXEMIA	ATRESIA	BOTULIN	CELIAC	CONDYLAR
ALEXINE	ANOXIA	ATROPHIA	BOTULISM	CENTAURY	CONDYLE
ALIENIST	ANTHRAX	ATROPHY	BRANK	CENTESIS	CONIOSIS
ALLELISM	ANTIPYIC	ATROPISM	BROMISM	CERATE	CONTAGIA
ALLERGEN	ANTISERA	AURIST	BROMIZE	CESAREAN	CONTUSE
ALLERGIC	ANURESIS	AUTOPSIC	BROMO	CESARIAN	CONVULSE
ALLERGIN	ANURIA	AUTOPSY	BRUXISM	CESTODE	COPREMIA
ALLERGY	APHAGIA	AUXESIS	BUBO	CESTOID	CORONER

CORPORA	DEADNESS	DIGOXIN	EARACHE	EXANTHEM	GOITRE
CORPSE	DEAF	DIHYBRID	ECBOLIC	EXCIDE	GOITROUS
CORPSMAN	DEAFEN	DILATANT	ECCRINE	EXCISE	GOUT
CORPUS	DEAFISH	DILATATE	ECDYSIS	EXCISION	GOUTIER
CORSE	DEAFLY	DILATE	ECRASEUR	EXCITANT	GOUTILY
CORYZA	DEAFNESS	DILATER	ECTHYMA	EXOCRINE	GOUTY
CORYZAL	DEATH	DILATION	ECTOPIA	EXOTOXIN	GRAVIDA
COSTIVE	DEATHBED	DILATIVE	ECZEMA	EXTUBATE	GRAYOUT
COUGH	DEATHCUP	DILATOR	EDEMA	EYECUP	GRIPPE
COUGHER	DEATHFUL	DILDO	EDUCABLE	EYEDNESS	GRIPPY
COXALGIA	DEATHLY	DILDOE	ELIXIR	EYEDROPS	GRIPY
COXALGY	DEATHY	DIOPTRIC	EMBALMER	EYESTONE	GUAIACUM
COXITIS	DEAVE	DIPLEGIA	EMBOLI	EYEWASH	GUAIOCUM
CREMAINS	DEBRIDE	DIPLOPIA	EMBOLISM	EYEWATER	GULOSITY
CREMATE	DECAY	DIPLOPIC	EMBOLUS	EYEWEAR	GUMBOIL
CREMATOR	DECAYER	DISBOWEL	EMBOWEL		GUMMA
CRICK	DECEASE	DISGORGE	EMEROD		GURNEY
CROUP	DECEDENT	DISINTER	EMEROID	FASTING	GYNANDRY
CROUPILY	DEGERM	DISOMIC	EMESIS	FATAL	GYNIATRY
CROUPOUS	DEMENT	DIURESES	EMETIC	FATALITY	
CROUPY	DEMENTIA	DIURESIS	EMPYEMA	FATALLY	
CROWNER	DENGUE	DIURETIC	ENATION	FAVISM	HABITUS
CRUOR	DENTIST	DIZYGOUS	ENCYST	FAVUS	HAKIM
CRYONICS	DERMOID	DOC	ENDEMIC	FEBRIFIC	HANGNAIL
CRYPT	DESEX	DOCTOR	ENDEMISM	FEBRILE	HANGOVER
CUPPING	DESMOID	DOCTORAL	ENEMA	FEEBLE	HAPLOPIA
CURARA	DETOX	DOOLEE	ENFEVER	FELDSHER	HARELIP
CURARE	DETOXIFY	DOOLIE	ENTASIA	FETICIDE	HEADACHE
CURARI	DEX	DOOLY	ENURESES	FETOLOGY	HEADACHY
CURARINE	DEXIE	DOPA	ENURESIS	FIBROMA	HEALTH
CURARIZE	DEXIES	DOPAMINE	ENURETIC	FIBROSIS	HEALTHY
CURATIVE	DEXTRAN	DOSAGE	EPHEDRIN	FISTULA	HEMAGOG
CURE	DEXTRIN	DOSE	EPIDEMIC	FLACCID	HEMATIC
CURELESS	DEXTRINE	DOSER	EPILEPSY	FLEAM	HEMATOMA
CURER	DEXTROSE	DOWNER	EPISTASY	FLU	HEMOLYZE
CURET	DEXY	DRESSING	ERETHISM	FOOTSORE	HEMOSTAT
CURETTE	DIABETES	DROPSY	ERGOTISM	FOOTWORN	HEPATIC
CURING	DIABETIC	DROWN	ERRHINE	FORCEPS	HEPATIZE
CYANOSED	DIAGNOSE	DROWND	ERYNGO	FORCIPES	HEPATOMA
CYANOSIS	DIALLEL	DROWNER	ERYTHEMA	FROSTBIT	HERNIA
CYANOTIC	DIALYSE	DRUG	ESCHAR	FURUNCLE	HERNIATE
CYESES	DIALYSER	DUMB	ESTHESES		HEROIN
CYESIS	DIALYSIS	DWARFISM	ESTHESIA	GALANGAL	HERPES
CYSTIC	DIALYTIC	DYING	ESTHESIS	GANGRENE	HERPETIC
CYSTITIS	DIALYZE	DYSEGENIC	ETHER	GASSING	HIC
CYSTOID	DIALYZER	DYSLEXIA	ETHICAL	GAVAGE	HICCOUGH
CYTASTER	DIARRHEA	DYSLEXIC	ETIOLOGY	GELSEMIA	HICCUP
CYTOLOGY	DICHOTIC	DYSPEPSY	EUCAINE	GENERIC	HIDROSIS
	DICROTIC	DYSPNEA	EUPEPSIA	GERMFREE	HIDROTIC
DALTONIC	DIE	DYSPNOEA	EUPEPSY	GERMY	HIRUDIN
DANDRIFF	DIED	DYSTAXIA	EUPNEA	GIANTISM	HOSPITAL
DANDRUFF	DIET	DYSTOCIA	EUPNOEA	GLAUCOMA	HOWDIE
DAPSONE	DIETARY	DYSTONIA	EUTROPHY	GLEET	HUNGOVER
DEAD	DIETER	DYSURIA	EVACUANT	GLIOMA	HYDATID
DEADLY	DIETETIC		EVERTOR	GLUTTONY	HYDRAGOG
				GOITER	HYDROPS

HYDROPSY	IRITIS	LIVID	MENARCHE	MYOTONIA	OEDEMA
HYGEIST	ISCHEMIA	LIVIDITY	MEROPIA	MYOTONIC	OINTMENT
HYGIEIST	ISCHEMIC	LIVIDLY	MEROPIC	MYRICA	OLIGURIA
HYGIENE		LOBOTOMY	METH	MYXEDEMA	ONCOGENE
HYGIENIC	JALAPIN	LOCHIA	METHADON	MYXOID	ONCOLOGY
HYOSCINE	JIMJAMS	LOCHIAL	METOPON	MYXOMA	OPIOD
HYP	JOHNNY	LOCKJAW	METRITIS		OPIUM
HYPHEMIA	JONES	LOCO	MIDWIFE	NAEVOID	OPSONIC
HYPNOSIS	JOYPOP	LORDOMA	MIGRAINE	NAEVUS	OPSONIFY
HYPNOTIC	JUGULATE	LORDOSIS	MILIARIA	NARCOSE	OPSONIN
HYPO		LORDOTIC	MILIUM	NARCOSIS	OPSONIZE
HYPOACID	KAHUNA	LOZENGE	MIOSIS	NARCOTIC	OPTICIST
HYPOGYNY	KELOID	LUES	MIOTIC	NAUSEA	ORCHITIC
HYPONOIA	KELOIDAL	LUETIC	MISSENSE	NAUSEANT	ORCHITIS
HYPOPNEA	KERATOMA	LUMBAGO	MONECIAN	NAUSEATE	ORTHOSIS
HYPOPYON	KERATOSE	LUPOUS	MONGOL	NAUSEOUS	ORTHOTIC
HYPOXIA	KETOSIS	LUPUS	MONO	NECROPSY	OSMICS
HYSTERIA	KETOTIC	LYMPHOMA	MONOSOMY	NECROSE	OSTEITIC
HYSTERIC	KIBE	LYSE	MORBIFIC	NECROSIS	OSTEITIS
HYTE	KINESIC	LYSIN	MORBILLI	NEOMYCIN	OSTEOID
	KINESICS	LYSING	MORIBUND	NEONATAL	OSTEOMA
IATRIC	KURU	LYSIS	MORON	NEONATE	OSTOMY
IATRICAL	KYPHOSIS	LYSSA	MORONIC	NEOPLASM	OTALGIA
IBOGAINE	KYPHOTIC	LYTIC	MORONISM	NEPENTHE	OTALGIC
ICHOR			MORONITY	NEPHRISM	OTITIC
ICTERIC	LAKING	MAGNESIA	MORPHIA	NERVINE	OTITIS
ICTERUS	LAKY	MAIM	MORPHIN	NEURINE	OTOLITH
IGNATIA	LAXATIVE	MAINLINE	MORPHINE	NEURITIC	OTOLOGY
ILEITIS	LAZAR	MALADY	MORTUARY	NEURITIS	OTOSCOPE
ILEUS	LAZARET	MALAISE	MOTHER	NEUROMA	OTOSCOPY
IMMUNE	LENITIVE	MALARIA	MUTE	NEUROSAL	OTOTOXIC
IMMUNISE	LEPER	MALARIAL	MUTENESS	NEUROSIS	OUABAIN
IMMUNITY	LEPROSE	MALARIAN	MUTISM	NEUROTIC	OVARITIS
IMMUNIZE	LEPROSY	MALINGER	MYALGIA	NEVOID	OXAZEPAM
IMPETIGO	LEPROTIC	MAMMITIS	MYALGIC	NEVUS	OXYTOCIC
IMPREGN	LEPROUS	MARASMIC	MYASIS	NICOTIN	
INBRED	LESION	MARASMUS	MYCETOMA	NICOTINE	PAIN
INBREED	LETHAL	MASSAGE	MYCOSIS	NODE	PAINFUL
INCISION	LETHALLY	MASSAGER	MYCOTIC	NODOSE	PAINLESS
INCUBATE	LEUCEMIA	MASSEUR	MYELITIS	NODOSITY	PALSY
INFARCT	LEUCEMIC	MASSEUSE	MYELOMA	NODOUS	PALUDISM
INFECT	LEUCOMA	MASTITIC	MYIASIS	NODULAR	PANACEA
INFECTER	LEUKEMIA	MASTITIS	MYOGRAPH	NODULE	PANACEAN
INFECTOR	LEUKEMIC	MATTERY	MYOLOGY	NODULOSE	PANDEMIC
INJECT	LEUKOMA	MATTOID	MYOMA	NODULOUS	PARAFORM
INJECTOR	LEUKOSIS	MAUNDER	MYOPATHY	NOMA	PAREIRA
INOCULUM	LEUKOTIC	MEDIC	MYOPE	NONA	PARESIS
INSOMNIA	LIMP	MEDICAL	MYOPIA	NONUNION	PARETIC
INTERN	LIMPSY	MEDICATE	MYOPY	NONVIRAL	PATHOGEN
INTERNE	LINIMENT	MEDICINE	MYOSCOPE	NOSTRUM	PATIENT
INTERSEX	LIPOMA	MEDICO	MYOSIS	NYSTATIN	PELLAGRA
INTUBATE	LIPOMATA	MELANIC	MYOSITES		PEMOLINE
IODISM	LITHEMIA	MELANISM	MYOSITIS	OBESITY	PEMPHIX
IODIZE	LITHEMIC	MELANIST	MYOSOTE	OCTAN	PEPTIC
IODIZER	LIVERISH	MELANOMA	MYOTIC	OCULIST	PETECHIA

PHTHISIC	PRURIGO	QUINSY	SCROGGY	SPLENT	TABID
PHTHISIS	PRURITUS	QUINTAN	SCURF	SPLINT	TALIPED
PHYLAXIS	PSILOCIN		SCURVY	SPRAIN	TALIPES
PHYSIC	PSILOSIS	RABIC	SEDATE	SPRUE	TENACULA
PHYSICAL	PSORALEN	RABID	SEDATION	SQUELA	TENESMIC
PIAN	PTERYGIA	RABIDITY	SEDATIVE	STANCH	TENESMUS
PILLBOX	PTOMAIN	RABIES	SEMICOMA	STANCHER	TENIASIS
PILULAR	PTOMAINE	RACHITIC	SEMIDEAF	STAPH	TENOTOMY
PILULE	PTOSIS	RACHITIS	SEMIMUTE	STARVE	TERATISM
PIMPLE	PTOTIC	RALE	SENEGA	STASES	TERATOID
PIMPLY	PTYALISM	RALPH	SENILE	STASIS	TERATOMA
PINKEYE	PUKE	RANULA	SENILELY	STENOSED	TERTIAN
PINTA	PULMOTOR	RASH	SENILITY	STENOSIS	TESTIS
PITH	PURBLIND	REAGIN	SENNA	STENOTIC	TETANAL
PLACEBO	PURPURA	REAGINIC	SENOPIA	STERILE	TETANIC
PLEURA	PURPURIC	REGORGE	SEPSES	STOUND	TETANIES
PLEURISY	PURULENT	REINJURY	SEPSIS	STREP	TETANISE
PLEXOR	PUS	RELAXANT	SEPTIC	STRESSOR	TETANIZE
POCK	PUSTULAR	RENOGRAM	SEPTICAL	STRUMA	TETANUS
POCKILY	PUSTULE	REOVIRUS	SEQUELA	STRUMOSE	TETANY
POCKMARK	PYAEMIA	RESECT	SERA	STRUMOUS	TETTER
POCKY	PYAEMIC	RHEUM	SEROLOGY	STUN	THEBAINE
PODAGRA	PYCNOSIS	RHEUMIC	SERPIGO	STUNT	THELITIS
PODAGRAL	PYCNOTIC	RHEUMY	SERUM	STUPE	THERAPY
PODAGRIC	PYELITIC	RHINITIS	SERUMAL	STUTTER	THIAZIDE
PODIATRY	PYELITIS	RHONCHAL	SETON	STYE	THROE
POISON	PYEMIA	RHONCHUS	SEXOLOGY	STYPSIS	THROMBUS
POLIO	PYEMIC	RICKETS	SEXTAN	STYPTIC	TIC
POLYOMA	PYGIDIUM	RIFAMPIN	SHAMAN	SUBTILIN	TIMOLOL
POLYPUS	PYIC	RINGWORM	SHAMANIC	SUBVIRAL	TINEA
POLYURIA	PYKNOSES	ROENTGEN	SICK	SUDATION	TINEAL
POLYURIC	PYKNOSIS	ROSEOLA	SICKBED	SUDATORY	TINNITUS
POSOLOGY	PYKNOTIC	ROSEOLAR	SICKEE	SUDOR	TISSULAR
POTION	PYODERMA	RUBELLA	SICKEN	SUDORAL	TOCOLOGY
POX	PYOGENIC	RUBEOLA	SICKIE	SULFA	TOMOGRAM
POXVIRUS	PYOID		SICKLY	SULFATE	TONICITY
PREEMIE	PYORRHEA	SANATIVE	SICKNESS	SULFUR	TOXAEMIA
PREGNANT	PYOSIS	SANICLE	SICKO	SULFURET	TOXAEMIC
PREMED	PYRETIC	SANIES	SICKOUT	SUNBURN	TOXEMIA
PREMEDIC	PYREXIA	SANIOUS	SICKROOM	SUNTAN	TOXEMIC
PREMIE	PYREXIAL	SANITISE	SINAPISM	SUPERFIX	TOXIC
PREMUNE	PYREXIC	SANITIZE	SMALLPOX	SURGERY	TOXICAL
PRENATAL	PYROGEN	SAPREMIA	SORE	SURGICAL	TOXICANT
PRESSOR	PYROSIS	SAPREMIC	SORENESS	SWAYBACK	TOXIN
PRETERM	PYURIA	SARCOMA	SPASM	SWEATBOX	TOXINE
PRIAPISM		SCABIES	SPASTIC	SYCOSES	TOXOID
PROBANG	QUAALUDE	SCALL	SPECIFIC	SYCOSIS	TRACHOMA
PROCAINE	QUARTAN	SCALPEL	SPECULAR	SYNDROME	TRANK
PRODROME	QUASSIN	SCAR	SPECULUM	SYPH	TRANQ
PROGERIA	QUEASY	SCIATICA	SPEW	SYPHILIS	TRAUMA
PROGNOSE	QUEAZY	SCIRRHUS	SPEWER	SYRINGE	TREPAN
PROPHAGE	QUININ	SCLEROMA	SPINAL		TREPHINE
PROVIRAL	QUININA	SCOLIOMA	SPLENIA	TABES	TRIAGE
PROVIRUS	QUININE	SCROFULA	SPLENIUM	TABETIC	TRISMIC

TRISMUS	TURPETH	URINEMIA	VARIX	VIRULENT	WEN
TROCAR	TUSSIS	URINEMIC	VARUS	VIRUS	WENNISH
TROCHAR	TUSSIVE	UROLITH	VASOTOMY	VITILIGO	WENNY
TROCHE	TWINBORN	UROLOGIC	VENIN	VITRIOL	WHITLOW
TROPHIC	TWINGE	UROLOGY	VENINE	VOLVULUS	WINDBURN
TROPIN	TWINNING	UROSCOPY	VENOGRAM	VOMICA	WOOPS
TROPINE	TYLOSIN	UVEITIC	VENOM	VOMIT	WORKUP
TUMEFY	TYMPANY	UVEITIS	VERATRIN	VOMITER	
TUMID	TYPHOID	UVULITIS	VERRUCA	VOMITIVE	XANTHOMA
TUMIDITY	TYPHOSE		VIOMYCIN	VOMITO	XEROSIS
TUMIDLY	TYPHOUS	VACCINA	VIRAL	VOMITORY	XEROTIC
TUMOR	TYPHUS	VACCINAL	VIRALLY	VOMITOUS	XYSTER
TUMORAL		VACCINE	VIREMIA	VOMITUS	
TUMOROUS	ULCER	VACCINEE	VIREMIC	VULVITIS	ZEDOARY
TUMOUR	ULCERATE	VACCINIA	VIRICIDE		ZOOGLEA
TURGENCY	ULCEROUS	VAGOTOMY	VIRILISM	WALLEYE	ZOOGLEAL
TURGENT	URAEMIA	VALGOID	VIRION	WART	ZOOGLOEA
TURGID	URAEMIC	VALGUS	VIROID	WARTLIKE	ZOSTER
TURGIDLY	UREDO	VARICOSE	VIROLOGY	WARTY	
TURGOR	UREMIA	VARIOLA	VIROSIS	WEBFEET	
TURISTA	UREMIC	VARIOLAR	VIRUCIDE	WEBFOOT	

MILITARY

ABRI	ARBALIST	BAILOUT	BORDURE	CAPTOR	CHOPPER
ACELDAMA	ARBELEST	BALLISTA	BOWMAN	CAPTURE	CIPHONY
ADMIRAL	ARCHER	BANZAI	BOWYER	CARABIN	CITADEL
AGA	ARM	BARBICAN	BREN	CARABINE	CIVIE
AGGER	ARMADA	BARBUT	BRISANCE	CARBINE	CIVILIAN
AGGRESS	ARMAMENT	BARD	BRISANT	CARNAGE	CIVVY
AGHA	ARMATURE	BARESARK	BULWARK	CASCABEL	CLAXON
AIDMAN	ARMET	BARRAGE	BURGONET	CASCABLE	CLAYMORE
AIRBURST	ARMIES	BASINET	BUSHIDO	CASEMATE	CODE
AIRPOWER	ARMIGER	BASTION	BYRNIE	CASERN	CODEBOOK
ALCAIDE	ARMIGERO	BATTALIA		CASERNE	COLONEL
ALCAYDE	ARMOR	BATTLE	CADET	CASHIER	COMBAT
ALCAZAR	ARMORER	BAZOOKA	CAISSON	CASQUE	COMMANDO
AMBUSH	ARMORY	BEVOR	CALIBER	CASUALTY	CONELRAD
AMTRAC	ARMOUR	BILLET	CALIBRE	CATAPULT	CONQUER
AMTRACK	ARMOURER	BILLETER	CALIBRED	CAUDILLO	CONQUEST
ANABASIS	ARMOURY	BINNACLE	CAMAIL	CAVALRY	CONVOY
ANGARIA	ARMY	BIRDFARM	CAMION	CHAMFRON	COPTER
ANGARY	ARQUEBUS	BLAM	CAMISADE	CHANFRON	CORDON
ANLACE	ARSENAL	BLOWGUN	CAMISADO	CHAPE	CORNETCY
ANLAS	ASSAGAI	BLOWPIPE	CAMPAIGN	CHASSEUR	CORPORAL
ANTIAIR	ASSAIL	BLOWTUBE	CANNON	CHAUSSES	CORPS
ANTINUKE	ASSAULT	BLOWUP	CANNONRY	CHEDDITE	CORPSMAN
ANTITANK	ASSEGAI	BOLA	CAPONIER	CHEDITE	CORSELET
ANTIWAR	ATLATL	BOLAS	CAPTAIN	CHEVERON	CORVET
ARBALEST	AZON	BOMBLOAD	CAPTIVE	CHEVRON	CORVETTE

COSSACK	ENCRYPT	FOIN	HELIO	MAILLESS	PENTOMIC
COUTER	ENFILADE	FOOTSLOG	HILT	MANCIPLE	PERDU
CROSSBOW	ENLIST	FORT	HIPPARCH	MANGONEL	PETARD
CUIRASS	ENLISTEE	FORTRESS	HOLSTER	MANTELET	PETRONEL
CUISH	ENLISTER	FOXHOLE	HOPLITE	MANTLET	PEYTRAL
CUISSE	ENSIFORM	FRAG	HOTLINE	MARCH	PEYTREL
CULET	ENSIGN	FRAGGING	HOWITZER	MARCHER	PHALANX
CULVERIN	ENSIGNCY	FROGMAN	HUMVEE	MARTELLO	PICKEER
CUTLAS	EQUERRY	FUSIL	HUP	MARTIAL	PIKE
CUTLASS	EQUITES	FUSILEER	HUSSAR	MEDEVAC	PIKEMAN
	ESCUAGE	FUSILIER		MESSMAN	PLATOON
DAH	EVZONE		IMPI	MESSMATE	PLEBE
DEADEYE	ECHELON	GANTLOPE	INDUCT	MILITARY	POILU
DEBOUCH	ELINT	GARRISON	INDUCTEE	MILITIA	POMPOM
DEBOUCHE	EMBATTLE	GARROTE	INDUCTOR	MIQUELET	PRIVATE
DEBRIEF	ENCAMP	GARROTTE	INFANTRY	MORION	PROLONGE
DECIPHER	ENCEINTE	GENERAL	INROAD	MORSE	PSYWAR
DECODE	ENCODE	GHAZI	INSIGNEE	MUDCAP	
DECURIES	ENCODER	GISARME	INSIGNIA	MUNIMENT	RADAR
DECURION	ENCRYPT	GLAIVE	INTERN	MUNITION	RADIOMAN
DECURY	ENFILADE	GORGET	INTERNEE	MUSKET	RADOME
DEFENCE	ENLIST	GREAVE	INTERWAR	MUSKETRY	RADWASTE
DEFILADE	ENLISTEE	GRENADE	IRONCLAD		RAINOUT
DEMOB	ENLISTER	GUERILLA		NAPALM	RANKER
DEPLOY	ENSIFORM	GUN	JAMBE	NAUMACHY	RAPIER
DESTRIER	ENSIGN	GUNBOAT	JAMBEAU	NAVIES	RATO
DETENTE	ENSIGNCY	GUNFIGHT	JANISARY	NAVY	RAVELIN
DETONATE	EPAULET	GUNFIRE	JANIZARY	NONCOM	REARWARD
DISARM	EQUERRY	GUNFLINT	JARHEAD	NONWAR	REB
DISHELM	EQUITES	GUNFOUGHT	JAWAN	NUKE	REBELDOM
DISTAFF	ESCUAGE	GUNLOCK	JAYGEE		RECCE
DISTAVES	EVZONE	GUNNER	JEMADAR	ORDNANCE	RECRUIT
DIT		GUNNERY	JEMIDAR	OUTFLANK	REDAN
DIVEBOMB	FALCHION	GUNPLAY	JERRICAN	OUTGUN	REDCOAT
DOGFACE	FALLBACK	GUNPOINT	JERRY	OUTPOST	REDEPLOY
DOGFIGHT	FALLOUT	GUNROOM	JERRYCAN	OUTWAR	REDOUBT
DOGTROT	FASCINE	GUNSHIP	JEZAIL	OVERKILL	REG
DOT	FAULD	GUNSHOT	JINGAL		REGIMENT
DOUGHBOY	FEDAYEE	GUNSMITH	JINGALL	PACIFISM	RETIARII
DOVISH	FENCIBLE	GUNSTOCK		PACIFIST	REVEILLE
DRAFT	FIRE	GYRENE	KAMIKAZE	PALIKAR	REVOLVER
DRAFTEE	FIREARM		KERNE	PALLETTE	RIFLEMAN
DRAGOON	FIREBASE	HACKBUT	KLEPHT	PANDOOR	RIFLERY
DRUMFIRE	FIREBOMB	HAGBUT	KNIGHTLY	PANDOUR	RIFLING
DUD	FIRELOCK	HALBERD	KRIS	PANOPLY	RITTER
DUSTOFF	FLAK	HALBERT		PANZER	
	FLAMEOUT	HANDGUN	LAAGER	PAULDRON	SABATON
ECHELON	FLANCARD	HANGFIRE	LANCER	PAVIS	SABER
ENCODER	FLATTOP	HAUBERK	LANGRAGE	PAVISE	SAGUM
ENCODE	FLYBOY	HAWKISH	LANGREL	PAVISER	SALIENT
EPAULET	FLYBY	HAYWARD	LEAGUER	PAYGRADE	SALLET
ELINT	FLYOVER	HEADHUNT	LEGION	PEACENIK	SALVO
EMBATTLE	FLYPAST	HEAUME	LONGBOW	PELE	SANGA
ENCAMP	FOEMAN	HELICOPT	LOOIE	PELTAST	SANGAR
ENCEINTE	FOILSMAN	HELILIFT		PELTATE	SAPPER

SARGE	SOLDIERY	SWORD	TOPKICK	VIGIL	WARWORN
SCALADE	SOLLERET	SWORDMAN	TORPEDO		WATERLOO
SCALADO	SORTIE		TRIPWIRE	WAR	WEAPONRY
SCIMETAR	SOWAR	TACE	TROOPER	WARCRAFT	WHIZBANG
SCIMITAR	SPAHEE	TAMPION	TRUCE	WARDROOM	WILCO
SCIMITER	SPAHI	TARGE	TSUBA	WARFARE	WINGMAN
SCRAMJET	SPEAR	TASSE	TUCHUN	WARHEAD	WINGOVER
SCUTAGE	SPEARER	TASSET	TWIBIL	WARISON	WOMERA
SERGEANT	SPEARMAN	TEARGAS	TWIBILL	WARLESS	WOMMERA
SERJEANT	SPONTOON	TELEMAN		WARLIKE	WOOMERA
SHAKO	SQUAD	TENAIL	UHLAN	WARLORD	
SHOGUN	SQUADRON	TENAILLE		WARMAKER	YARDBIRD
SHOOTOUT	STALAG	TESTUDO	VAMBRACE	WARPLANE	YATAGAN
SHOTGUN	STINKPOT	THANE	VANQUISH	WARPOWER	YATAGHAN
SHRAPNEL	STRAFE	TOLEDO	VEDETTE	WARRED	
SKIRMISH	STRAFER	TOMPION	VELITES	WARRING	ZOUAVE
SNIPE	SUBDEPOT	TONLET	VENTAIL	WARRIOR	
SNIPER	SUTLER	TOPEE	VESICANT	WARSHIP	
SOLDIER	SWABBIE	TOPI	VETERAN	WARWORK	

NAUTICAL

ABAFT	BARGEMAN	BODKIN	CAIQUE	CLEW	DAHABEAH
ABEAM	BARQUE	BOGAN	CAISSON	CLUBHAUL	DAHABIAH
ABOARD	BARRATER	BOLLARD	CANAL	COASTING	DAHABIEH
AFT	BARRATOR	BOLTROPE	CANALLER	COBLE	DAHABIYA
AFTMOST	BARRATRY	BOSUN	CANOE	COCKBILL	DAVIT
AHOY	BARRETOR	BOTEL	CANOEIST	COCKBOAT	DEADWOOD
AHULL	BARRETRY	BOTTOMRY	CAPTAIN	COCKPIT	DEBARK
AIRBOAT	BATEAU	BOUSE	CARACK	COIL	DECKHAND
ALEE	BATTEAU	BOWSPRIT	CARAVEL	COMPASS	DECKING
AMIDSHIP	BEACH	BOXHAUL	CARINATE	CONN	DEMERSAL
ANCHOR	BEAM	BRAIL	CARLINE	CORACLE	DHOW
APORT	BECKET	BREAM	CARLING	CORDELLE	DIAPHONE
ARGOSY	BELAY	BRIG	CARRACK	CORSAIR	DINGEY
ARK	BENTHAL	BRINY	CARVEL	CORVET	DINGHY
ARMADA	BENTHIC	BROACH	CASSETTE	CORVETTE	DINGY
ASDIC	BENTHOS	BUGEYE	CAT	COX	DINK
ASEA	BERTH	BULKHEAD	CATBOAT	COXSWAIN	DISMAST
ASHORE	BIBB	BUMBOAT	CATFALL	CREW	DOCK
ASTERN	BIDARKA	BUMKIN	CATHEAD	CREWLESS	DOCKAGE
AWASH	BIDARKEE	BUNTLINE	CATSPAW	CREWMAN	DOCKER
AWEATHER	BILANDER	BUOY	CATTED	CREWMATE	DOCKHAND
AWEIGH	BILGE	BUOYAGE	CAULK	CROJIK	DOCKLAND
	BIREME	BUOYANCE	CAULKER	CRUISE	DOCKSIDE
BACKOUT	BOATEL	BUOYANCY	CAULKING	CRUISER	DOCKYARD
BACKSTAY	BOATHOOK	BUOYANT	CHANDLER	CURAGH	DOGGER
BAIDARKA	BOATMAN	BURGEE	CHANTEY	CURRACH	DOGWATCH
BAREBOAT	BOATSMAN	BURTON	CHANTIES	CURRAGH	DORIES
BARGE	BOATYARD		CHINE	CURRENT	DORY
BARGEE	BOBSTAY		CHOPPY	CUTWATER	DOWNHAUL

DOWNWIND
DRAGLINE
DRAGNET
DRAIL
DRIFT
DRIFTAGE
DROGUE
DROMON
DROMOND
DUGOUT
DUNNAGE

EARING
EASTER
EASTERLY
EASTING
EASTWARD
EDDY
EUPHROE
EURIPUS
EXEC

FAIRLEAD
FALTBOAT
FELUCCA
FERRIAGE
FERRY
FERRYMAN
FID
FIREBOAT
FIREROOM
FLAGSHIP
FLATBOAT
FLEMISH
FLOATAGE
FLOATEL
FLOTA
FLOTAGE
FLOTILLA
FLOTSAM
FLUYT
FLYBOAT
FOGHORN
FOLDBOAT
FOOTROPE
FOREBODY
FOREBOOM
FOREDECK
FOREMAST
FOREPEAK
FORESAIL
FORESTAY
FOREYARD
FRIGATE
FUTTOCK

GABBARD
GABBART
GALE
GALIOT
GALLEASS
GALLEON
GALLEY
GALLIASS
GALLIES
GALLIOT
GANGWAY
GANTLINE
GARBOARD
GARVEY
GENOA
GONDOLA
GRAPLIN
GRAPLINE
GRAPNEL
GUNKHOLE
GUNROOM
GUNWALE
GUYOT
GYBE
GYROSTAT

HAAF
HADAL
HALLIARD
HALYARD
HANK
HARPING
HATCHWAY
HAULYARD
HAWSE
HAWSER
HEADRACE
HEADSAIL
HEADSTAY
HEADWAY
HEADWIND
HELM
HELMLESS
HELMSMAN
HOMEPORT
HOY

ICEBOAT
INBOARD
INHAUL
INHAULER
IRONCLAD
ISOBATH
ISOTACH

JACKSTAY
JACKY
JAYGEE
JETSAM
JETSOM
JETTISON
JIBB
JIBBOOM
JIBE
JIBER
JOHNBOAT

KAIAK
KAYAK
KAYAKER
KAYAKING
KEDGE
KEEL
KEELAGE
KEELBOAT
KEELHALE
KEELHAUL
KEELLESS
KEELSON
KELSON
KETCH
KEVEL
KEVIL
KILLICK
KILLOCK
KYAK

LAGAN
LAGEND
LANDFALL
LANDING
LANIARD
LANYARD
LARBOARD
LASCAR
LATEEN
LATEENER
LAVEER
LEADSMAN
LEE
LEEBOARD
LEEWARD
LEEWAY
LIFEBOAT
LIFELINE
LIGAN
LIGHTER
LIMEY
LINER
LOCKAGE

LOGBOOK
LONGBOAT
LONGSHIP
LORAN
LUFF
LUGGER
LUGSAIL
LUMPER
LUNAR

MAINMAST
MAINSAIL
MAINSTAY
MAINTOP
MAKEFAST
MANROPE
MARINA
MARINER
MARITIME
MARLINE
MARLING
MAST
MASTHEAD
MASTLESS
MATELOT
MAYDAY
MIDSHIP
MIDSHIPS
MIDWATCH
MIZEN
MIZZEN
MONOHULL
MOONSAIL
MOOR
MOORAGE
MOORING
MUTINEER
MUTINOUS
MUTINY

NAUMACHY
NAUTICAL
NAVAID
NAVAL
NAVICERT
NAVIES
NAVY
NEAP
NERITIC
NORTHING

OAR
OARLOCK
OARSMAN
OFFSHORE

ONSHORE
OOMIAC
OOMIACK
OOMIAK
ORLOP
OROMETER
OUTBOARD
OUTHAUL
OUTPORT
OUTSAIL

PARRAL
PARREL
PATAMAR
PATTAMAR
PEDALO
PELAGIC
PELORUS
PHAROS
PIGBOAT
PILOTAGE
PILOTING
PINKEY
PINNACE
PIRACY
PIRAGUA
PIRATE
PIRATIC
PIROGUE
PIROQUE
POLE
POLYNYA
PONTON
PONTOON
PORT
PORTAGE
PORTHOLE
PORTLESS
PRAM
PRATIQUE
PRAU
PROW
PUNT
PUNTER
PURSER

QUANT
QUAY
QUAYAGE
QUAYSIDE

RACEWAY
RAFT
RAFTSMAN
RANDAN

RATLIN
RATLINE
RATTLING
RAZEE
RECHART
REDOCK
REEF
REEFER
REGATTA
RESAIL
RESHIP
RHUMB
RIBBAND
RIGGING
RIPTIDE
RIVAGE
ROBAND
ROBBIN
ROGER
ROW
ROWBOAT
ROWLOCK
RUDDER

SAILBOAT
SAILER
SAILOR
SALTIE
SALVOR
SAMPAN
SANDBAR
SCEND
SCHOONER
SCHUIT
SCOW
SCUBA
SCULL
SCULLER
SEABAG
SEABEACH
SEABED
SEABOOT
SEABORNE
SEACOCK
SEACRAFT
SEADOG
SEADROME
SEAFARER
SEAFLOOR
SEAFRONT
SEAGIRT
SEAGOING
SEAMAN
SEAMARK
SEAMOUNT

SEAPORT	SOFAR	STUNSAIL	TIDEWAY	UNDERTOW	WHERVE
SEASICK	SONAR	SURFBOAT	TOMBOLO	UNDERWAY	WHITECAP
SEATRAIN	SONARMAN	SURFY	TOPMAST	UNDOCK	WINDAGE
SEAWARD	SONDER	SURGE	TOPSAIL	UNMOOR	WINDWARD
SEAWAY	SONOBUOY	SURGING	TOPSIDE	UNSHIP	WORKBOAT
SEXTANT	SPAR	SURGY	TORPID	UPHROE	
SHALLOP	SPARLIKE	SWABBIE	TOWBOAT	UPWIND	XEBEC
SHANGHAI	SPARRED	SWIFTER	TOWLINE		
SHANTEY	SPARRING		TOWPATH	VANE	YACHT
SHIPLOAD	SPENCER	TAFFAREL	TRAWLER	VANG	YACHTER
SHIPMAN	SPILING	TAFFEREL	TRIMARAN	VEDETTE	YACHTING
SHIPMATE	SPONSON	TAFFRAIL	TRIREME	VESSEL	YACHTMAN
SHIPSIDE	SPRIT	TANKER	TRYSAIL	VIDETTE	YARDARM
SHIPWAY	STAITHE	TANKSHIP	TSUNAMI	VIKING	YAW
SHIPYARD	STAYSAIL	TARTANA	TUGBOAT		YAWL
SHORAN	STEAMER	TELEMAN	TYE	WAISTER	
SICKBAY	STEEVE	TEXAS		WARDROOM	ZEBEC
SKEG	STEEVING	THOLEPIN	UMIAC	WATERAGE	ZEBECK
SKIFF	STEMSON	TIDAL	UMIACK	WATERMAN	ZONETIME
SKIPPER	STERN	TIDELAND	UMIAK	WATERWAY	
SKYSAIL	STERNSON	TIDELESS	UMIAQ	WHARF	
SLATCH	STERNWAY	TIDELIKE	UNANCHOR	WHARFAGE	
SLIPWAY	STOWAWAY	TIDEMARK	UNDERSEA	WHEELMAN	
SLOOP	STRAKE	TIDERIP	UNDERSET	WHERRY	

PERFORMING ARTS

ACCENT	ANGEL	AUBADE	BAROQUE	BONGOIST	CADENCY
ACROBAT	ANIMATO	AUDITION	BARRE	BOUFFE	CADENT
ACTABLE	ANTHEM	AUTEUR	BARYTONE	BOURDON	CADENZA
ACTOR	ANTIMASK		BASS	BOURREE	CAKEWALK
ACTRESS	APPLAUD	BACKBEAT	BASSI	BOUSOUKI	CALLBACK
ADAGIO	APPLAUSE	BACKDROP	BASSIST	BOUZOUKI	CALLIOPE
AGITATO	APRON	BACKER	BASSO	BOW	CALYPSO
AGON	ARCO	BAGPIPE	BASSOON	BOWING	CAMEO
AGONES	ARIA	BAGPIPER	BATON	BRASS	CANCAN
AIR	ARIETTA	BALLAD	BATTERIE	BRAVA	CANSO
ALASTOR	ARIETTE	BALLADE	BATTU	BRAVO	CANTATA
ALLEGRO	ARIOSE	BALLADRY	BAYADEER	BRAVURA	CANTICLE
ALLONGE	ARIOSO	BALLET	BAYADERE	BUFFO	CANTO
ALMA	ARMONICA	BALLON	BEAT	BUFFOON	CANTOR
ALMAH	ARPEGGIO	BALLONNE	BEBOP	BUGLE	CANTUS
ALME	ARSES	BANDORA	BEGUINE	BUGLER	CANZONET
ALMEH	ARSIS	BANDORE	BELL	BUNRAKU	CAPO
ALPHORN	ARTIST	BANDSMAN	BERCEUSE	BURLESK	CARILLON
ALT	ARTISTE	BANJO	BLUESMAN	BUSKER	CARIOCA
ALTHORN	ARTISTRY	BANJOIST	BLUESY	BUZUKI	CARNEY
ALTO	ASIDE	BARD	BODHRAN		CARNIE
ALTOIST	ASSAI	BARDIC	BOLERO	CABARET	CARNIVAL
AMOROSO	ATABAL	BARITONE	BOMB	CACHUCA	CARNY
ANDANTE	ATONAL	BARKER	BONGO	CADENCE	CAROL

CAROLER	CLARINET	DEEJAY	FIFER	GRACIOSO	JUGGLER
CAROLLER	CLARION	DERRY	FIFTH	GRAND	JUGGLERY
CAROLLING	CLAVE	DESCANT	FIGURANT	GRAVE	
CAST	CLAVIER	DIAPASON	FIGURE	GRAZIOSO	KABUKI
CASTANET	CLEF	DIATONIC	FILM	GRIOT	KALIMBA
CASTRATO	CLOG	DIRGE	FILMABLE	GUIRO	KANTELE
CAVATINA	CLOWN	DISCANT	FILMDOM	GUITAR	KARAOKE
CELEB	CLOWNERY	DISEUSE	FILMER		KAZACHOK
CELESTA	CLOWNISH	DITTY	FILMGOER	HABANERA	KAZATSKI
CELESTE	COACTOR	DIVA	FILMIC	HAM	KAZATSKY
CELLIST	COAUTHOR	DOLCE	FILMLAND	HAMARTIA	KAZOO
CELLO	CODA	DOLOROSO	FINALE	HAMMY	KEY
CEMBALO	COLORIZE	DOWNBEAT	FINALIS	HARMONIC	KEYBOARD
CHACONNE	COMBO	DRAMA	FIPPLE	HARMONY	KITHARA
CHAINE	COMEDIAN	DRAMATIC	FLAMENCO	HARP	KLEZMER
CHAMADE	COMEDY	DRAMEDY	FLAT	HARPER	KOLO
CHANSON	COMIC	DRESSER	FLAUTIST	HARPIST	KOTO
CHANT	COMICAL	DRUM	FLOP	HAUTBOIS	KRUMHORN
CHANTER	COMP	DRUMBEAT	FLUTE	HAUTBOY	
CHANTEY	COMPERE	DRUMHEAD	FLUTER	HEAVY	LANCIERS
CHANTOR	COMPOSER	DRUMMER	FLUTIST	HELICON	LANDLER
CHASSE	CONCERT	DRUMROLL	FLYMAN	HEMIOLA	LARGANDO
CHEVALET	CONCERTO	DUET	FOIL	HEMIOLIA	LARGO
CHIMES	CONGA	DUETTIST	FOLKIE	HEPCAT	LEGATO
CHIVAREE	CONTINUO	DUI	FOLKY	HERO	LEGGIERO
CHIVARI	CORANTO	DULCET	FORTE	HEROINE	LEGIT
CHOIR	CORNET	DULCETLY	FORZANDO	HIT	LEGONG
CHOIRBOY	CORYPHEE	DULCIANA	FOUETTE	HOOF	LENTANDO
CHORAGUS	COSTUME	DULCIMER	FRET	HOOFER	LENTO
CHORAL	COTHURN	DUMKA	FUGAL	HORN	LIBRETTO
CHORALE	COTHURNI	DUO	FUGATO	HORNIST	LIED
CHORALLY	COULISSE		FUGUE	HORNPIPE	LIGATURE
CHORD	COUPE	EMCEE	FUGUIST	HULA	LOGE
CHORDAL	COURANT	ENCORE	FURIOSO	HUMORIST	LULLABY
CHOREGUS	COURANTE	ENSEMBLE		HYMENEAL	LUTANIST
CHORIC	COURANTO	EPILOG	GAGAKU	HYMN	LUTE
CHORINE	COURU	EPILOGUE	GALLIARD	HYMNIST	LUTENIST
CHORUS	COWBELL	EPITASIS	GALOP	HYMNODY	LUTHIER
CIMBALOM	CROON	ETUDE	GALOPADE		LUTIST
CINEAST	CROONER	EXEUNT	GAMBA	ICTUS	LYRE
CINEATE	CROTCHET	EXODOS	GAMELAN	IMPROV	LYRICISE
CINEMA	CRUMHORN	EXTRA	GAVOT	INGENUE	LYRICIZE
CIRCUS	CRWTH		GAVOTTE	INTERVAL	LYRICIST
CITHARA	CUE	FADING	GEEK		LYRIST
CITHER	CYMBAL	FADO	GEISHA	JAZZ	
CITHERN	CYMBALER	FALSETTO	GERMAN	JAZZLIKE	MADRIGAL
CITHREN	CYMBALOM	FANDANGO	GIGA	JAZZMAN	MAESTOSO
CITOLA	CZARDAS	FANFARE	GIGUE	JESTER	MAESTRO
CITOLE		FANTASIA	GITTERN	JETE	MAGE
CITTERN	DANCE	FANTASIE	GLEE	JINGLE	MAGI
CLAP	DANCER	FARCE	GLEEMAN	JIVE	MAGIAN
CLAPPER	DANSEUR	FERMATA	GLISSADE	JONGLEUR	MAGICIAN
CLAQUE	DANSEUSE	FIDDLE	GOBO	JOTA	MAGUS
CLAQUER	DEADPAN	FIDDLER	GONG	JUBA	MALLET
CLAQUEUR	DEBUT	FIFE	GOOMBAY	JUG	MANDOLA

MANDOLIN	MOVIEOLA	OVERACT	PRELUDE	ROOT	SHOWMAN
MARACA	MOVIOLA	OVERTONE	PRESA	ROSIN	SHTICK
MARCATO	MRIDANGA	OVERTURE	PRESCORE	ROTTE	SHTIK
MARCH	MUDRA	OVERWORD	PRESTO	ROULADE	SIDEMAN
MARIACHI	MUM		PRIMO	RUBATO	SIDESHOW
MARIMBA	MUMMER	PAINISM	PRODUCER		SINFONIA
MARQUEE	MUMMERY	PANDORA	PROGRAM	SACBUT	SING
MASKING	MUSE	PANDORE	PROMPTER	SACKBUT	SINGER
MASQUE	MUSETTE	PANDURA	PROPMAN	SAGBUT	SINGSONG
MATINEE	MUSIC	PANPIPE	PROTASIS	SALPINX	SIRVENTE
MAXIXE	MUSICAL	PANTO	PSALTERY	SALSA	SISTRUM
MAZOURKA	MUSICALE	PARLANDO	PSALTRY	SAMBAR	SITAR
MAZURKA	MUSICIAN	PARLANTE	PUNKER	SAMBUCA	SITARIST
MBIRA	MUTE	PARODOS	PUPPET	SAMBUKE	SITCOM
MEASURE		PARTERRE	PUPPETRY	SAMISEN	SKA
MEDIANT	NABE	PARTITA		SANTIR	SKETCH
MEGASTAR	NATURAL	PAS	QUARTET	SANTOUR	SKIFFLE
MELISMA	NAUTCH	PASSAGE	QUAVER	SANTUR	SKIP
MELODEON	NEUM	PASSE		SARABAND	SKIT
MELODIA	NEUME	PATRON	RAGA	SARDANA	SLUR
MELODIC	NOCTURNE	PAVAN	RAGTIME	SAROD	SMASH
MELODICA	NOH	PAVANE	RAP	SARODE	SOAPER
MELODISE	NONET	PAVILLON	RASE	SARODIST	SOL
MELODIST	NOODLE	PAVIN	RATTLE	SAX	SOLFEGE
MELODIZE	NOTATION	PEDAL	RAVE	SAXHORN	SOLFEGGI
MELODY	NOTTURNO	PEDALIER	REBEC	SAXTUBA	SOLO
MENO	NUDIE	PEGBOX	REBECK	SCALE	SOLOIST
METER		PIANIST	RECITAL	SCAT	SONATA
MEZZO	OATER	PIANO	RECORDER	SCENA	SONATINA
MIME	OBLIGATO	PIANOLA	REED	SCENARIO	SONG
MIMESIS	OBOE	PIASABA	REEDMAN	SCHERZO	SONGBIRD
MIMIC	OBOIST	PIBROCH	REFRAIN	SCORE	SONGBOOK
MIMICKER	OCARINA	PICCOLO	REGAL	SCRIM	SOPRANO
MIMICKING	OCTAVE	PIERROT	REGGAE	SECONDO	SORDINE
MIMICRY	OCTET	PIPE	REGISTER	SEGNO	SORDINO
MINSTREL	OCTETTE	PIPER	RELEVE	SEGUE	SOUL
MINUET	ODEON	PIQUE	REPRISE	SEMITONE	SOUNDBOX
MIRLITON	ODEUM	PIT	REQUIEM	SEMPLICE	SOUNDMAN
MODAL	OFFBEAT	PITCH	REST	SEMPRE	SOURDINE
MODALITY	OFFKEY	PIU	REVERB	SENNET	SPICCATO
MODE	OFFSTAGE	PLAGAL	REVUE	SEPTET	SPINET
MODERATO	OLIO	PLAYACT	REVUIST	SERENADE	SPINTO
MOLTO	ONSTAGE	PLAYBILL	RHAPSODY	SERENATA	STACCATO
MONODY	OOMPAH	PLAYBOOK	RHYTHM	SERPENT	STAFF
MORCEAU	OPERA	PLAYDATE	RHYTHMIC	SEXTET	STANZA
MORCEAUX	OPERATIC	PLAYER	RICERCAR	SFORZANDO	STARDOM
MORDENT	OPERETTA	PLAYLET	RIDOTTO	SFORZATO	STASIMON
MORRIS	OPUS	PLECTRUM	RISER	SHANTEY	STAVE
MOSSO	ORATORIO	PLIE	RITARD	SHARP	STEP
MOTET	ORGAN	PLOT	ROADIE	SHAWM	STOOGE
MOTIF	ORGANIST	POCO	ROADSHOW	SHOFAR	STRAIN
MOTIVE	OSSIA	POINTE	ROCK	SHOWBIZ	STRAWHAT
MOTIVIC	OSTINATO	POLKA	ROLE	SHOWBOAT	STRETTO
MOVEMENT	OTTAVA	POSTLUDE	ROMANTIC	SHOWCASE	STRING
MOVIEDOM	OUD	POSTSYNC	RONDO	SHOWGIRL	STRIPPER

STROPHE	TALKIE	TIMBAL	TROUPING	UPBOW	VIVACE
STROPHIC	TAMASHA	TIMBALE	TRUMPET	UPRIGHT	VOCAL
STRUM	TAMBOUR	TIMBRE	TRYOUT	UPSTAGE	VOCALIST
STRUMMER	TAMBOURA	TIMBREL	TUBA	USHER	VOCODER
STUNTMAN	TAMBUR	TIME	TUBAIST	UT	VOICING
SUBBASS	TAMBURA	TIMPANO	TUBIST		VOLANTE
SUBITO	TANTARA	TOCCATA	TUCKET	VALSE	VOLE
SUBTONIC	TANTO	TOESHOE	TUMMLER	VEEJAY	VOLTI
SUITE	TARDO	TONETTE	TUNE	VEENA	
SUPE	TELEFILM	TONGUING	TUNING	VEHICLE	WALTZ
SWELL	TELEPLAY	TONIC	TURKEY	VELARIUM	WARBLE
SWING	TEMPI	TOUCH	TURN	VELOCE	WARHORSE
SYMPHONY	TEMPO	TOUR	TURNOUT	VENUE	WEEPIE
SYNTH	TENOR	TRAGEDY	TUTTI	VERITE	WIND
SYRINX	TENORIST	TRAGIC	TUTU	VIBIST	WOODWIND
	TENOUR	TRAGICAL	TWEEDLE	VIBRATO	WOOFER
TABLA	TENUTO	TREBLE	TWEETER	VIGOROSO	
TABLEAU	THEATER	TREMOLO	TWOFER	VILLAIN	ZANZA
TABOR	THEATRE	TRIAD	TYMBAL	VILLAINY	ZAPATEO
TABORER	THEME	TRIANGLE	TYMPAN	VINA	ZARZUELA
TABORET	THEORBO	TRIGON	TYMPANO	VIOL	ZILL
TABORIN	THEREMIN	TRILL	TYPECAST	VIOLA	ZITHER
TABORINE	THESPIAN	TRIO		VIOLIN	ZITHERN
TABOUR	THRENODE	TRIPLET	UKE	VIOLIST	ZYDECO
TABOURER	THRENODY	TRITONE	UKELELE	VIOLONE	
TABOURET	THRUM	TROMBONE	UKULELE	VIRGINAL	
TACET	THRUMMER	TROUPE	UNISON	VIRTUOSA	
TALA	TI	TROUPER	UPBEAT	VIRTUOSO	

SPORTS

ABSEIL	ATHLETE	BAREBACK	BLOOPER	BRACER	CABER
ACE	AUDIBLE	BASEBALL	BLUELINE	BRASSIE	CABESTRO
ACROBAT	AXEL	BASELINE	BOARD	BREAK	CABRESTA
AEROBICS		BASEMAN	BOBBLE	BRIDLE	CABRESTO
AGGRO	BACKBEND	BAT	BOBSLED	BRIDLER	CADDIE
ALPINISM	BACKCAST	BATBOY	BOCCE	BRIDOON	CADDY
ALPINIST	BACKHAND	BATSMAN	BOCCI	BUCKAROO	CAESTUS
ANGLE	BACKLASH	BEANBALL	BOCCIA	BUCKAYRO	CAGER
ANGLER	BACKSPIN	BENCH	BOCCIE	BUCKER	CAMEL
ANGLING	BACKSTOP	BIATHLON	BODYSURF	BUCKEROO	CANCHA
APAREJO	BACKUP	BIKEWAY	BOGEY	BUCKTAIL	CANOE
APPEL	BAFF	BIKINI	BONSPELL	BULGER	CANOEIST
AQUACADE	BAFFIES	BIRDER	BONSPIEL	BULLDOG	CANTER
ARBALEST	BAFFY	BIRDIE	BOOGIE	BULLPEN	CANTLE
ARBALIST	BALKLINE	BIRDING	BOWL	BULLRING	CAPEWORK
ARBELEST	BALL	BIRL	BOWLER	BUNKER	CAPIOLE
ARCHER	BALLGAME	BIRLER	BOWLING	BUNNY	CARACOL
ARCHERY	BALLHAWK	BIRLING	BOWMAN	BUNT	CARACOLE
ARENA	BALLPARK	BLACKOUT	BOWSHOT	BUSHER	CAROM
ARMLOCK	BARBELL	BLOOP	BOWYER		CARROM

NOBBLER	POSTGAME	RIPOSTE	SITUP	SPURGALL	TRACK
NOCK	POSTRACE	ROADWORK	SITZMARK	SQUAD	TRAINER
NONTITLE	POWDER	RODEO	SIXTE	SQUASH	TRAPBALL
NORDIC	PREGAME	ROLLOUT	SKATE	SQUID	TRAPEZE
NOSEBAG	PRELIM	ROOKIE	SKEET	STADIUM	TRAPPING
NOSEBAND	PREMEET	ROSIN	SKEETER	STANDOFF	TRAVERSE
	PRERACE	ROSTER	SKEIN	STEM	TRAWL
	PROETTE	ROUGH	SKI	STIRRUP	TREBLE
OFFSIDE	PROMOTE	ROVER	SKIABLE	STOCCADO	TRIFECTA
OFFTRACK	PROMOTER	ROWER	SKIBOB	STOCCATA	TROLL
OLYMPIAD	PSYCH	ROWING	SKIING	STRIKE	TROTLINE
ON	PUCK	RUGBY	SKIJORER	STROKE	TROUNCE
ONSIDE	PUGILISM	RUGGER	SKIORING	SULKY	TRUDGEN
OUTCURVE	PUGILIST	RUNBACK	SKITTLE	SUMO	TRUDGEON
OUTFIELD	PUNTO	RUNLESS	SKIWEAR	SUPERFAN	TRYOUT
OVERHAND	PUSHBALL	RUSHING	SKYBOX	SURF	TUBE
OVERSPIN	PUSHUP		SKYDIVE	SURFER	TUCK
OVERTIME	PUTOUT	SABER	SKYDIVER	SURFING	TUMBLING
	PUTT	SABRE	SLALOM	SWAM	TURFMAN
PADDLE	PUTTER	SACK	SLAM	SWEEP	TURFSKI
PADDOCK		SADDLE	SLED	SWIM	TURNHALL
PALESTRA		SADDLER	SLEDDER	SWIMSUIT	TWINIGHT
PALFREY	QUARTE	SADDLERY	SLEDGE	SWIMWEAR	
PALOOKA	QUARTER	SALCHOW	SLEEPER	SWINGMAN	UMP
PAR	QUINELA	SANDLOT	SLEIGH	SWUM	UMPIRAGE
PARAKITE	QUINELLA	SAVATE	SLEIGHER		UMPIRE
PARRY	QUINIELA	SCATBACK	SLICE		UNDERCUT
PASE	QUINTAIN	SCHUSS	SLOTBACK	TAILBACK	UNDERDOG
PASS	QUINTE	SCHUSSER	SLUG	TANDEM	UNITARD
PASSADE	QUIRT	SCLAFF	SLUGFEST	TAPADERA	UPFIELD
PASSADO	QUIVER	SCLAFFER	SLUMP	TAPADERO	UPSET
PELOTA		SCORE	SNAPBACK	TEAM	
PENALTY	RACE	SCOREPAD	SNATCH	TEAMMATE	VARSITY
PENNANT	RACING	SCORER	SNELL	TEAMWORK	VAULT
PESADE	RACKET	SCRUB	SNIGGLE	TEE	VAULTER
PIAFFER	RACQUET	SCRUM	SNORKEL	TELEMARK	VIGORISH
PICADOR	RAH	SCUBA	SNOWPLOW	TENNIS	VOLLEY
PICKOFF	RAILBIRD	SCULL	SNOWSHOE	TENNIST	VOLLEYER
PIKE	RALLY	SCULLER	SOARING	TENPIN	VOLTE
PIOLET	RALLYE	SECONDE	SOCCER	THINCLAD	VORLAGE
PISCARY	RAPPEL	SEED	SOFTBALL	THIRTY	
PISCATOR	RASSLE	SELLE	SOKOL	THRUST	WAGER
PISTE	REDSHIRT	SEMIPRO	SOMERSET	THRUSTER	WAHINE
PITCH	REF	SEPTIME	SORING	TIE	WAIVER
PITCHER	REFEREE	SERVE	SOUTHPAW	TILTYARD	WARMUP
PITCHOUT	REGATTA	SERVER	SPELUNK	TIPCAT	WARSLE
PITON	REIN	SERVICE	SPIRAL	TITLIST	WARSLER
PIVOTMAN	REINSMAN	SET	SPITBALL	TOEHOLD	WARSTLER
PLATOON	REMATCH	SETLINE	SPITTER	TOPSPIN	WEAKSIDE
PLAYDOWN	REPLAY	SHAG	SPORT	TOREADOR	WEBBING
PLAYER	RESERVE	SHANK	SPOTTER	TORERO	WEDEL
PLAYOFF	RETURN	SHINNEY	SPREAD	TORO	WEDELN
POINTMAN	RIATA	SHUTOUT	SPRINT	TOSSUP	WEDGE
POLO	RINGER	SIDELINE	SPRINTER	TOUCHE	WICKET
POLOIST	RINGSIDE	SIDESPIN	SPUR	TOURING	WIDE
POMMEL	RINK			TOURNEY	

WIDEOUT	WINGER	WOODY	WRESTLE	XYST	YOKOZUNA
WINDSURF	WIPEOUT	WORKOUT	WRESTLER	XYSTOS	
WINDUP	WOOD	WRASSLE		XYSTUS	ZONE
WINGBACK	WOODIES	WRASTLE